DAILY DEVOTIONAL SERIES

WISDOM
HUNTERS

SEEKING
DAILY
THE
HEART
OF
GOD

BOYD BAILEY

DEDICATION

TO MY GRANDMOTHER,
KASTELL GOSS
&
RITA'S LATE GANDI MAMA,
LUCILLE ISBILL

Thank you both for romancing God's word
with passion, persistence and prayer.

Published by Wisdom Hunters, LLC.
Distributed by Family Christian Stores

Scripture taken from the Holy Bible, New International Version®, NIV®
Copyright © 1973, 1978, 1984 by International Bible Society.
Used by permission of Zondervan. All rights reserved.

Cover design by truthinadvertising; atlanta GA (www.truthinadvertising.net)

Wisdom Hunters, LLC.
1080 Holcomb Bridge Road
Building 200, Suite 140
Roswell, GA 30076
Visit us at www.WisdomHunters.com

The Wisdom Hunters name and logo are trademarks of Wisdom Hunters, LLC.

ISBN: 978-1-59391-148-5

TABLE OF MONTHS

FORWARD 4

ACKNOWLEDGEMENTS 5

INTRODUCTION 6

JANUARY 7-38

FEBRUARY 39-68

MARCH 69-100

APRIL 101-130

MAY 131-162

JUNE 163-192

JULY 193-224

AUGUST 225-256

SEPTEMBER 257-286

OCTOBER 287-318

NOVEMBER 319-348

DECEMBER 349-380

ABOUT THE AUTHOR 381

SCRIPTURE INDEX 382-383

IN KENYA WITH 410 BRIDGE 384

FORWARD

"Not another devotional book!"

Do you find yourself saying this? With all the devotionals available today, perhaps it is a valid reaction to this new book. Yet as someone who has spent much of my life reading devotionals, and updating several of the classic ones, allow me to share my response.

We should remember the primary purpose behind devotionals. The good ones were not written as a replacement to spending time in the Word of God, or in order to salve our conscience that we are having our daily "time alone with the Lord." To the contrary!

A good devotional is designed to be a tool to help us dig more deeply into God's Word, in order to know Him better. A two-minute devotion should only whet our appetite for more time with our Lord, learning of His character and His ways.

To that end, Boyd Bailey, my friend of many years, has written this series of devotions. Knowing his heart is to help people take the truths of the Lord and apply them to their everyday lives, puts the ball squarely in your court as the reader.

What will you do with the truths presented here? Will you simply read them for your daily "fix" with God? Or will you truly submit yourself to the truths Boyd shares from God's Word, reading the Scripture quotes in their context, and endeavoring to know more?

My prayer, of course, is that you would do the latter, and that your life and walk with the Lord would thereby bring Him greater glory, and "that you may know him better" (Ephesians 1:17, NIV).

Jim Reimann,
Best-selling author, and editor of the updated editions of:

- MY UTMOST FOR HIS HIGHEST
- STREAMS IN THE DESERT
- LOOK UNTO ME, the Devotions of Charles Spurgeon
- HEAR MY VOICE, the Devotions of Charles Spurgeon - *coming Fall 2010*

ACKNOWLEDGEMENTS

*Thanks to my wife **Rita** and the girls: **Rebekah**, **Rachel**, **Bethany** and **Anna**, and our two sons-in-law **Todd** and **Tripp** for letting me do life with you.*

*Thanks to **Brittany Thoms** for encouraging me, reminding me and editing for me. Your boundless energy around this book kept me focused on finishing well.*

*Thanks to **Andy Thoms** for giving his pregnant wife permission to quarterback this project, and for his informal marketing and sales of the book.*

*Thanks to **Cliff Bartow** who asked me to stretch myself and compile 366 daily devotionals that could encourage people from all walks of life, especially business leaders.*

*Thanks to **Jim Reimann** for meeting with me monthly and coaching me to become a writer to the heart and head who is concise, clear, compelling and Christ-centered.*

*Thanks to **Bob Lewis,** my business coach the past four years, who suggested the "Seeking Daily" title, and whose wisdom and counsel gets me out of trouble and keeps me out of trouble.*

*Thanks to the **Ministry Ventures** staff that stays focused on Christ and serving people like no team I know of, I so am proud to serve the Lord with you.*

*Thanks to **Lee McCutchan,** my original editor of the daily devotional, "Wisdom Hunters...Right Thinking." Lee your faithfulness fires me up everyday!*

*Thanks to **Don Kooima** who was precise in every detail required to print and publish this project with excellence.*

*Thanks to the creative genius of **Michael** and **Sheila Dolinger** who captured the heart of "Seeking God" in the look and the feel of the book.*

Thanks to the encouraging many who regularly write to tell me how the Lord has led you into a deeper walk with Him, as a result of regular time in His Word.

Thanks to my heavenly Father for loving me, and extending His grace and blessing through the power of the Holy Spirit, and His inspired written word, the Bible.

Boyd

INTRODUCTION

Seeking daily the heart of GOD is a goal I don't always accomplish, but it is where I want my heart to wander, as I wake up to start each day. Like the Psalmist who says, "Let the morning bring me word of your unfailing love, for I have put my trust in you. Show me the way I should go, for to you I lift up my soul" (Psalm 143:8). Character calibration by Christ in the morning makes my heart align with heaven's agenda, and gets me off on the right foot of faith. Time with GOD is a time saver that I am learning I can't live without.

But I still struggle to stay consistent and true to trust Him. Life is messy and it tends to mess up my regimen of praise and prayer, but I persist because I know He knows I have to live life through the ups of answered prayer, and the downs of discouragement from unmet expectations. These writings are not from a monk who has mastered piety, asceticism or holiness. The words you are about to engage are written from a fellow struggler seeking to know and understand his Creator. Like Peter some days I want to stay with Jesus on the mountaintop of worship, and other days I trudge through the valley of despair. But my overarching desire is to be loved by my heavenly Father, so I can in turn learn to love others and myself from the overflow of His tender mercy and grace.

It is regular visits back to the cross of Christ that remind me of GOD's great love. The Lord's transaction of grace covered my sin, and freed me into a relationship of intimacy with the Almighty. It is in the shadow of my Savior's suffering that I am able to deal with suffering. When I recall His unjust rejection, I am then able to handle rejection. His love for those who did not deserve love compels me to love without expecting anything in return. His unselfish service motivates me to not only serve, but also invite being treated as a servant. His trust in the face of fierce trials fashions my faith to focus on Him.

David was a man who sought the heart of GOD (Acts 13:22). He was not a sinless seeker, but one who needed a Savior. He sought the Lord in spite of his lies, his lust, his adultery, and his murder. Satan's scheme is to get us to give up, or not feel worthy of worship or the wonder of His great grace. So we seek Jesus because we need Jesus, not just for our salvation but also for our sanctification. Because we are a work in progress, we stay in a prayerful process. Only when we quit showing up do we fail to see security in our Savior.

Lastly, these writings are somewhat autobiographical as they reflect the place I currently find myself – at work and home, failures and successes, fatigue and rest, fear and faith, uncertainty and hope, hurt and healing, anger and forgiveness, rejection and acceptance, apathy and love, and gloom and gladness. I write out of real life to real people about a real GOD. I pray the Lord will love on you, as you linger before Him in meditation.

Seek Him even when you don't feel like it, or when you are too busy, and He will reward your faithfulness. The Bible says, "And without faith it is impossible to please GOD, because anyone who comes to him must believe that he exists and that he rewards those who earnestly seek him" (Hebrews 11:6). I am still learning and I have a lot to learn, but I know this one thing: like a farmer who day in and day out plows, plants and cultivates will one day by GOD's grace be blessed with a harvest, so will you. The Bible says, "Blessed are they who keep his statutes and seek him with all their heart" (Psalm 119:2).

Boyd Bailey

WISDOM SEEKERS

> "The whole world sought audience with Solomon to hear the wisdom
> God had put in his heart."   1 KINGS 10:24

Wisdom is a cherished commodity by most. People are drawn to wisdom. It is attractive and winsome. Wisdom represents a word from the Lord. Therefore, its value is enormous. Wisdom is one reason we attend church, listen to good Bible teaching and engage with older mentors. Wisdom has to be sought out and asked for. It does not come naturally. It is a gift from God (Proverbs 2:6). It is precious and extremely valuable. It is a gift that protects you from decisions that could haunt you for a lifetime. It is a gift that gives you the confidence to carry on or stop. Wisdom is a weapon God wields on behalf of His warriors. Wisdom cuts through confusion and replaces it with clarity. It distills decisions into a sequence of small successes. It warns of impending danger.

However, wisdom is not immune to sin. A wise man or woman still needs accountability, maybe more so. Indeed, wisdom is susceptible to pride (Jeremiah 9:23). A wise heart intermingled with pride thinks it can rise above the rules. It can be so subtle in the beginning, but its inner convictions begin to rot, like a termite-infested foundation. If pride is not kept in check, it will convert wisdom into cockiness. Sad is the state of a once-wise leader, who allowed pride to water down his fear of God. Wisdom is God's gift to carry out his Kingdom-initiatives. If spent on self, it becomes a cheap imitation.

So seek out the truly wise, those who have God as their top priority. A mutated wisdom suffers from spiritual malpractice, but a pure strain of wisdom gives spiritual life. It is wisdom coupled with humility, and obedience to God, that finishes well. Authentic wisdom is appropriate to apply in all situations. Search for it in the Bible, books, people, circumstances, film, life experiences, and creation. Once you find it, don't take it for granted. Thank God for wise outcomes. Use it for His glory and for His purposes. Allow wisdom to humble you, rather than give you a sense of superiority. We are all seekers of God's wisdom. We will seek it until we get to heaven.

Wisdom is active and alive, and always in need of a fresh infusion from God. Use prayer as a bridge to the wisdom of God. Ask Him often for His perspective and His heart on the matter (James 1:5). Allow wisdom to draw you closer to your heavenly Father in worship and dependence on Him. Dedicate often your wise intentions to Him. Keep your heavenly Father as your filter for wise decision-making.

Be a generous dispenser of wisdom to others. Make time for people to get to know your heart, and understand the life-lessons God has forged into your faith (I Kings 4:34). We all have wisdom we can offer to others. Carve out time just to listen to another's travails. Their "top of mind" issues need attention. Be available to listen patiently with understanding, and then in humility offer options for their consideration. Wisdom is polite. It gives answers when asked all in a spirit of grace, as a fellow wisdom-seeker.

Seek wisdom and give wisdom; wisdom motivated by humble submission to God!

J2 RIGHT THINKING

"For my thoughts are not your thoughts, neither are your ways my ways,' declares the Lord. As the heavens are higher than the earth, so are my ways are higher than your ways and my thoughts than your thoughts." ISAIAH 55:8

God's will does not always make sense. It may not make sense because we factor in our own understanding. If left to our understanding, we would be miserable. There is a greater pool of knowledge reserved for us in Christ. Do not underestimate its value and availability. It is valuable because of the divine direction that can save us from running down paths that waste our time and the time of others. God's way may not make sense now, but it will later. His thoughts and ways are easily accessible by faith. Faith is our constant connection to God-thinking, but we struggle with this because we have been programmed differently. Some of us wrongly think we don't deserve God's grace; therefore we need not receive God's grace. We cannot live the Christian life without the grace of God. God's way is the grace way. We give Him glory and He gives us grace. We give Him praise and He gives us peace. We give Him worship and He gives us con-fidence. This is the way of God. He created the original "road less traveled." Avoid the mindless masses and follow God. His ways may not be the most popular, but they are the most produc-tive. His thoughts transcend our thoughts.

God-thinking takes discipline. This temporal world does not necessarily reward eternal think-ing. In fact, it may punish you to think God-thoughts. You think people outside of Christ are lost in their sins and hell-bound. The world thinks you are narrow in your thinking. Yet these are Jesus' thoughts. This is not popular thinking; and may be not practical, but it is true. As a follower of Christ, you can think God-thoughts. You can think like God because you have the mind of Christ (I Corinthians 2:16). Your conversion experience infused you with a new worldview. No longer are you limited by what you can do, but by faith you anticipate what God can do. Instead of thinking self-centered thoughts, you focus on God-centric thinking. When you think like Jesus you do not have to be in control. You trust Him to handle people and circumstances in His timing. This is tapping into the mind of Christ that exists to renew your thinking on a moment-by-moment basis. God-thinking is only a faith-step away.

The mind of Christ gives you an advantage. You do not have to think inaccurate thoughts. Zealous ignorance tears down, while passionate truth-thinking builds up. Test what you believe and see if it withstands the scrutiny of critical-thinking (Acts 17:11). Critical-thinking based on the Word of God. You may currently believe something that is untrue. You may believe God does not love you, and He will not forgive you. This is not true. He loves you right where you are and wants His very best for you. God's best is *best*. Why settle for anything less?

Think God-sized thoughts and expect God-sized results. Make His ways your ways, and incorporate His thinking into your thinking. It may seem peculiar at first, and others may label you as strange, but you know better. This is right-thinking. You can't go wrong with right-thinking!

CALL FOR WISDOM

"This calls for wisdom." REVELATION 13:18A

Wisdom is required more often than we realize. It is wisdom that cuts through emotion and gets to the reality of the situation. "What is the wise thing to do?" is an effective question in decision-making. "What is best for the enterprise?" is a wise question to ask as it relates to business and ministry. Many times God speaks through money, or the lack thereof. So, if money is tight, then we need to be extremely wise with expenditures. Wisdom says cut back on expenses, and do not add additional costs. At this point it is not about lack of faith, it is about being a wise steward with what you have, so you can be trusted with more. Wise stewardship attracts generous givers.

Another characteristic of wisdom is not to be impatient or desperate. Wisdom takes a step back, and thoroughly evaluates a situation before charging ahead. So, do you solicit wisdom on a consistent basis? Knowledge and experience mixed with common sense and discernment is a great recipe for wisdom. Wisdom is seeking to understand God's perspective on matters. This is why the wisdom found in God's Word is so relevant for living.

The Bible is a treasure-trove of wisdom waiting to be discovered by the wise wisdom hunter. Therefore, not only pray, read, and meditate on the Bible, but also seek out the wise (Matthew 12:42). Look for people with gray in their hair who exhibit wise behavior. The wise will help you validate the inklings of wisdom you are beginning to grasp from your study of Scripture. Read books and listen to messages of wise men and women. If you hang-out long enough with wisdom, it will rub off on you. Take every opportunity to call on wisdom. Be wise in your relationships. Be wise with your money. Be wise with your time. Before you realize it, your wisdom will attract others who are hungry for the same.

Moreover, the crown jewel of wisdom's accumulation is the fear of the Lord. "The fear of the Lord is the beginning of knowledge, but fools despise wisdom and discipline." (Proverbs 1:7) The fear of God positions you to receive wisdom. Having no fear of God means you lack wisdom. No wonder our world is filled with fools. We have lost our fear of God, and wisdom has eluded us. The fear of the Lord is an incubator for wisdom. God dispenses wisdom to those who fear Him.

Love God, but fear Him. Worship God, but fear Him. Learn of God, but fear Him. Serve God, but fear Him.

Your fear of God qualifies you for wisdom. Do not become so familiar with God that you lose your fear of God. This is unwise, and leads to foolishness. Wisdom awaits your harvest call. Pluck it and enjoy, like plump, luscious fruit on a hot summer day. Taste and see that wisdom is good. No one has ever complained of attaining too much wisdom. Call on wisdom often. Seek out the wise, and ask them and God for wisdom.

This is the wise thing to do!

J4   WISDOM FROM HUMILITY

"When pride comes, then comes disgrace, but with humility comes wisdom."
PROVERBS 11:2

Wisdom is packaged with humility. It is an intricate part of humility. Humility contains an enormous amount of valued content. Indeed, wisdom is one of its highly revered resources. If you want wisdom, you will appropriate humility into your heart. Humility delivers wisdom, like a chauffeur delivers his client. Wisdom travels with humility. In some ways wisdom takes a back seat to humility. The humble understand their need for the wisdom of God. There is not the pretense of a self-appointed guru, who thinks he already knows everything. Humility is crystal clear in its need for Christ's thoughts to intersect its intelligence. Humility is smart enough to confess what it does not know.

Too much of life is beyond the reach of human reason. There has to be more than man's comprehension. We are not objective enough to figure out the best choice with our own limited understanding. We need the wisdom of God to wash our thinking and leave His righteous residue. Humility positions us to receive wisdom from God and others. It is a growth process. Jesus grew in wisdom (Luke 2:52).

Pride pushes you out of position to receive wisdom. It is like a first baseman in baseball lining up in left field. He is out of position once the ball is hit. No one is on first base to receive the ball. Without humility you are out of position to receive wisdom. You may even desire wisdom, but without humility you will be hollow in heavenly instruction. God rarely imparts His wisdom to a proud person, because He knows he cannot be trusted. Why entrust such valuable information to one who will squander it, or spend it all on himself? God knows the humble in heart will be a good steward of wisdom. Indeed, humility places in the heart a hunger for wisdom. It gives you an appetite for wisdom's morsels.

Once you adjust your spiritual diet to consume wisdom, you will never go back to the junk food of worldly wisdom (I Corinthians 1:20-30). The world's wisdom is positioned in pride. It is a power struggle over who can be the shrewdest and the quickest to out-smart their opponent. Everything is competition to the proud. It foolishly jockeys for position in its own power. Humility, on the other hand, is patient to wait on God. There is a depth of due diligence and determination that accompanies wisdom, born out of humble trust in God. Disgrace is the traveling partner of pride. Pride may get you what you want, but only with a wake of disgrace in its rearview mirror.

Better to be humble and follow the ways of wisdom. Wisdom rests well. Wisdom gives grace. Wisdom gets results with no regrets. So, humbly invite in the gracious wisdom of God!

WISDOM'S WEALTH

> "But where can wisdom be found? Where does understanding dwell?
> Man does not comprehend its worth... And he said to man, 'The fear of the Lord—
> that is wisdom, and to shun evil is understanding'." JOB 28:12-13A, 28

Wisdom is like money. Its value compounds over time. If you regularly add wisdom to your life, you become wealthy in the ways of God. This is why it is imperative that you get wisdom above most everything else in your life. Wisdom is the ability to discern right from wrong and to understand what is true and lasting. It is your ally that will assist you in defeating the enemy. Satan is toothless in the presence of the wisdom of God. Do not attempt to defeat the devil with your own limited understanding. Rather, crush him with the weapon of wisdom. A life built on the foundation of wisdom can withstand the winds of change and the waves of adversity (Proverbs 28:26). Wisdom keeps you engaged with God's perspective. It is a life preserver for the drowning, a compass for the lost explorer, and a light on a dark and perplexed situation.

Wisdom is like gold, and gold is not always easy to find. There is a price to pay. There is a price to pay in the process of its discovery, and in its acquisition (Proverbs 16:16).

Gray hair does not guarantee wisdom, but examined experience does position you to obtain wisdom. It is possible to be an old fool, or to be wise beyond your years. Youth or aged, smart or average IQ, with either you can gain wisdom.

Wisdom begins and ends with the fear of God. The fear of God means you engage His teaching with your heart and mind (Proverbs 15:33). Wisdom precludes a passive relationship with God. Wisdom means you meditate on His ways and truths. You prayerfully and respectfully ask Him why, what, and how as it relates to his way of doing things. As followers of God we have the mind of Christ. Through contemplation on His word and understanding of his truth, wisdom will begin to reign in our everyday life. By God's grace, wisdom will allow you to synthesize multiple options into the best course of action.

Wisdom can take a complex situation and offer simple solutions. Wisdom has the uncanny ability of cutting through the layers of agendas and motives, to the real issues. Wisdom is a no-nonsense defender of common sense and truth. It is very practical.

Wisdom originates from God, and resides with Him. He has the trademark and the patent. Anyone who attempts to take credit for its effectiveness may risk losing the rights of its use. Humility tempered with wisdom leads to wise decision-making. Take time to listen and learn from wise people. This could save you heartache from a relational train wreck or the loss of money from a bad financial decision. Be wise; listen to both God and His wise mentors.

You get wisdom to give wisdom, sharing wisdom's wealth with those who steward it well!

J6 TEACH CHILDREN WISDOM

"Pains as of a woman in childbirth come to him, but he is a child without wisdom; when the time arrives, he does not come to the opening of the womb." HOSEA 13:13

Children need to be taught wisdom. Yes, sometimes it's hard for them to grasp its meaning because of their age and stage in life. Wisdom comes through understanding, and applying God's Word to life experience. Many individuals are limited in their perspective of both, so it's wisdom that guides them from unwise decision-making. Wisdom is one of the wonderful gifts you can give your child. Therefore, make its knowledge inviting and practical.

Tell stories of individuals who made wise decisions, and the positive effects that followed. Then contrast these uplifting illustrations with those who chose an unwise path, and suffered harm as a result. Stories arrest the heart and illuminate the mind. We owe it to our offspring to engage them in conversations about real-life people. Otherwise, they stay oblivious in a "bubble" of unrealistic living. Indeed, wisdom comes by allowing them to spread their wings, and begin decision-making while they still live under your roof.

Start them out young by helping them make money decisions. Show them the pattern of "share, save and spend" from your own financial management. Then lead them to do the same. Watch them smile as they experience the joy of generosity. Be proud as their discipline and patience grows; they will be able to save for something they want, and then purchase their prize with cash. Be an example of smart spending and you may become a recipient of its fruit as your child learns how to be a savvy shopper. Financial wisdom is a practical gift whose principals you can use to train your child (Ephesians 6:4).

Good judgement in choosing friends is another facet of teaching your child the ways of wisdom. Make sure children understand the propensity to be like the people they hang out with (Proverbs 13:20). It's wise to choose friends whose faith is growing and robust. Go with friends who lift up, instead of those who pull down. It is unwise to flirt with friendships that dilute growth with God. Discuss why they need to avoid friendships that become a wedge between child and parent. Wisdom does not settle for the shallow acceptance of just any friend. Wisdom has a high standard for friendship. Challenge your children to pray for friends who compliment their faith, who move them closer to their heavenly Father. Wise friends rub-off on your children in wise ways.

Lastly, discuss with your child regularly the wisdom of God. He gives wisdom (Proverbs 2:6). Read with them from the Bible, and discuss the meanings of particular verses. Make the discussion of Scripture a part of your everyday life. Take your Bible to church. Underline the phrases that leap from the page into your heart and mind. Then discuss its application to your life over lunch. Ask your child to hold you accountable to the truth God is teaching you.

You cannot improve on the wisdom of the Lord. God's wisdom will follow them the rest of their lives. It will be with them when you are absent. You can be at peace when you have a child who is wise in the ways of God.

You are wise when your goal is to grow up a wise child.

Wise children become wise adults!

WISE FEAR

"The fear of the Lord is the beginning of knowledge, but fools despise wisdom and discipline." PROVERBS 1:7

There are good fears. The fear of God is one of them. It is foundational. It feeds all other good fears. Wise is the man or woman who first fears God. Fear of God is fervent at the beginning of your faith walk. It is the honeymoon stage of your marriage with Christ. You don't know any better than to do what is expected. But, if the fear of God is neglected, you drift into disobedience (Psalm 36:1). Like any other belief or discipline, the fear of God needs to be fostered by faith and obedience. Fear of God keeps you honest with Him and with yourself. It is the beginning of accountability. The grace of God, without the fear of God, is an illusion. There can be no grace without fear, just as there is no fear without grace. Foolish is the one who does not fear God. The fruits of not fearing God are foolish choices and undisciplined living.

Furthermore, success is an enemy to fearing the Lord. The more you experience success, the more you are prone not to fear. However, the opposite needs to be true. The more successes you enjoy, the more you need the fear of God and the fear of sin's consequences. Success many times grants you autonomy. It is here that you are wise to increase your level of accountability. Be brutally honest with yourself. You can't handle autonomy without accountability. David couldn't and he was a man after God's heart (Acts 13:22). Autonomy without accountability leads to a series of bad decisions, and left unchecked, to immoral behavior. No one is above the law, and no one is above accountability.

Wise is the leader who builds accountability into his faith, finances, family, work, and leisure. Those who don't think they need it; need it the most. Maybe you start by hiring a personal assistant of the same gender who is with you at work and on business trips. This is your opportunity to mentor a young, up-and-coming leader, and it is his/her opportunity to hold you accountable. We all do better when others are watching. Fear of the Lord keeps you from sinning (Exodus 20:20). Invite accountability from your spouse, board, boss, and accountability group. Be transparent with your professional and personal finances. Tell your spouse when you become emotionally attached to someone else. Be very discreet about your alone time. Idleness leads to indiscretion. You are wise to reserve solitude for your Savior, your spouse, and special friends.

Fear of God is your friend. Fear of the consequences of sin is smart. Fear of being unaccountable is wise. Fear of God is freeing. Therefore, fear God, hate sin, and trust Him!

J8   WISE WEALTH

"A man who has riches without understanding is like the beasts that perish."
PSALM 49:20

Wise wealth sees the small value of riches without God's redemption. It is otherworldly in its view of wealth. The creation of wealth is for Christ's purposes, and not the world's ways. This is why the wealthy, who are wise, seek to understand God's game plan for their gold. They prayerfully come up with a plan, and then they commit their actions to the Almighty. Then He brings success to their financial plan (Proverbs 16:3, NLT).

This is the process in which the Spirit leads and brings about success. Plans without prayer are perturbing and miss God's best. Actions committed to Christ carry-out God's game plan. To gain understanding is to frame your financial discussions with an eternal backdrop of motivation. Wealth is a stewardship not to be taken lightly. It is a belief that the Lord's blessing is much larger than life, and a lever for the Lord today.

Indeed, understand that finances are finite. You have a window of generosity that will close one day. Don't wait until riches grow wings and fly away (Proverbs 23:5) to some faithful soul who understands the significance of "stuff" to your Savior. Riches are like hailstones; they fall from Heaven in different sizes, garnering our attention while rattling on the tin roof of our trust.

But after a while, after it draws attention to itself, it melts away into the silent ground, gone. So it is with "stuff". It can be "here today and gone tomorrow". It is wise to give aggressively what you have today; instead of hoping to give what you may not have tomorrow.

Missionaries need malaria medicine now. Orphans need homes today. Growling stomachs need more than gruel...immediately. Churches are waiting to be built, once they receive their necessary start-up capital. Humanitarian work and the spreading of the Gospel will happen exponentially, as the wealthy collaborate with Christ, and obey. Run the risk of liberating your wealth for the Lord. It is His to give.

God has made us to be kind, and not beastly, in our view of wealth. Animals are driven by self-preservation, and by instinct. But we are children of our heavenly Father. He is gracious and generous in bestowing His good gifts (Matthew 7:9-11). He uses wealth for His ways, so wise are you to do the same. Sanctify your "stuff" for your Savior: look to the Lord on where and how to save, invest, spend, and give.

Beasts perish with a peon of purpose. You graduate to be with God. At your commencement with Christ you want to be found financially faithful. The wise use of wealth supports eternal initiatives. Wise wealth does not intimidate, nor is it intimidated. It prayerfully releases riches for God's Kingdom. It is all about investing in and executing the Almighty's agenda.

Wise wealth wraps itself around God's redemptive plan through faith. It understands and applies God's generous game plan!

WISE SAVER

"Joseph stored up huge quantities of grain, like the sand of the sea; it was so much that he stopped keeping records because it was beyond measure."
GENESIS 41:49

There are wise savers and there are greedy savers. People are attracted to wise savers. Wise savers are responsible and trust God to provide through a plan. God expects us to save, and He blesses our efforts. A "Joseph Fund" is foresight to prepare for hard times. There is great wisdom in realizing good times will not roll on forever, and will one day come to a screeching halt. It may come in the form of healthcare needs, a collapsing career, or a depressed economy. Financial fatigue, even famine, may not be far off in our future. Therefore, it is imperative to store up for the lean times. This does not mean hoarding to the extent of not helping those in need. But it does mean to spend less than your make, give generously, and save the rest. It is much better to be on the making-interest side of the ledger than the paying-interest side.

We save, so we can better serve. Faith and savings are not opposite ideas. They actually compliment each other. Because we have faith in our heavenly Father, we prepare for the worst and hope for the best. Do not spiritualize away saving. Be cautious of not blaming Christ for your lack of preparation. He gives us faith and good fortune to further His Kingdom. Start today by diligently saving (Proverbs 21:5). Use debt wisely, or even avoid it completely. What is the worst thing that can happen to you if you are completely debt-free? You may postpone some of your purchases, but there is no real downside.

Now ask yourself: what is the worst thing that can happen if you are left holding a balance sheet full of debt with little savings? You could lose everything, go bankrupt, and have to depend on family or friends. Debt can be devastating; savings can be your salvation.

Therefore, seek to be a saver and not an impulsive spender. Plan to save little-by-little (Proverbs 13:11). Faith and presumption are two opposite strategies. One trusts God with a plan, and the other lives life without a plan, blindly hoping things work out. Systematically save with both a short-term emergency fund and a long-term contingency fund. An emergency fund is there to keep you from going into debt when cars break down, appliances need to be replaced, or the house needs painting. A long-term contingency fund helps you finance college costs for your children, or supplements your income when you are unable to work as much. Saving is sensible and spiritual. Start with an automatic draft in a mutual fund that is hard to access. Have a goal to pay your house off when your children graduate from high school. Then you have the option of using your mortgage payment to offset college expenses.

Consistent savings may mean a lifestyle change. Pull the plug on presumptive living. Cut-up credit cards that prop-up an unrealistic lifestyle. Credit card living will eventually collapse like a house of cards. By God's grace save more and spend less. Hire a financial planner or coach to hold you accountable. Your systematic savings will position you to serve others.

You save, so you can give. Savers are wise!

J10 WISE WARNINGS

"They serve at a sanctuary that is a copy and shadow of what is in heaven. This is why Moses was warned when he was about to build the tabernacle: 'See to it that you make everything according to the pattern shown you on the mountain.'" HEBREWS 8:5

Wise warnings come from wise people. They are wise because they speak from experience, with pure motive, and a reliance on God and the understanding of His word. Do not dismiss lightly those whom the Lord brings into your life. They remind you of right and warn you of wrong.

You are wise to frequent this quality of friendship, with a pattern of living that is inviting. Their life has not always been "a bed of roses," but they have persevered through their problems by the grace of God. They overcome because they regularly obtain grace and mercy from their heavenly Father (Hebrews 4:16).

Listen to couples with imperfect, but growing marriages. Learn from them from their past mistakes. Take to heart their warnings of neglect and indifference in marriage. Good and maturing marriages take time and intentionality. Your marriage is destined for a train wreck if you do not heed the warning signals of apathy and anger. God has designed your lives to receive encouragement and instruction from wise mentors; listen intently and learn from them (Proverbs 12:15). Submit to relationships of accountability, and witness the trust of your spouse flourish as a result.

Always watch for warning signs at work. Before you engage a new employee, call his last employer; validate his creditability and competence. Honest past employers will give you a fair warning about a flaky engagement with an ex-employee. People may interview well, but fit in poorly after they are employed. Let the wisdom of your interviewing team protect you from professional relationships that are not a cultural fit.

Wise warnings work. Wise warnings work on behalf of God. He speaks through those who are submitted and obedient to Him. Wise warnings will win-out if applied personally and prayerfully. If you ignore them, you expose yourself unnecessarily to unjust people and unfair circumstances (Proverbs 14:16). God's protection thrives in the heeding of wise warnings. If several people you respect tell you to slow down, then you need to slow down. If more than one person questions your attitude, then ask them to hold you accountable for an attitude adjustment. If others notice patterns of anger, then search your heart for healing. Use the rule of three. If you hear the same thing three times in godly counsel, God is speaking loud and clear.

Watch for wise warnings and process them. This is God speaking. Wise people apply wise warnings!

WISE CHILDREN

"Listen, my son, to your father's instruction and do not forsake your mother's teaching. They will be a garland to grace your head and a chain to adorn your neck."
PROVERBS 1:8-9

Wise children listen to their parents. They listen to their mom or dad, whether their parents love God or not. God has placed parents over their children for protection and teaching. Some parents may not provide either of these, but they can still be used by God, to deliver His instruction. Therefore, listen to your parents. Listen when it hurts and listen when you don't completely understand. If they intimidate you, talk with them about it. Let them know that you want to honor them by listening to their advice and commands. It pleases the Lord when you obey your parents (Colossians 3:20).The older you get as a child, the harder it becomes to listen to your parents. It becomes harder because you want to become your own person. It becomes harder because you begin to discover that your parents are fallible, and sometimes even fragile in their faith. They are moody and have misguided motives. They can be overprotective, insensitive, and angry. Yet they still love you with their whole heart. They want God's very best for you, and sometimes struggle with how to relate and care for you.

Be patient with your parents. Do not dismiss them as irrelevant and weird (though sometimes we certainly are!). Only a foolish child focuses on his/her friends to the neglect of the parents. Learn how to lovingly listen to your dad and mom. Learn how to patiently process their instruction and teaching. They sometimes seem redundant, condescending, and patronizing. Remember, they love you. Be patient with your parental unit. They want you to experience God's will to its fullest. Trust them to trust Him. Moses' parents protected him by their faith in God (Hebrews 11:23).

You listen to your parents because you care. They stick their nose into your business because they care. Indeed, an unengaged and apathetic parent communicates a careless concern. This is malpractice mothering and fatalistic fathering. But a wise child still cares for his careless parents, because he/she knows it is the right thing to do. Unselfish service to selfish people will build a bridge to the Savior. Your life may be the only book about Jesus your unrepentant parents are willing to read.

Therefore, listen and learn from your parents, even if they are lazy in their faith. You honor them when you learn from them (Ephesians 6:1-3). Your interest in them may very well ignite their interest in Him!

J12   WISE LEADERSHIP

> "Choose some wise, understanding, and respected men from each of your tribes, and I will set them over you."   DEUTERONOMY 1:13

The selection process of wise leadership can make or break an organization. And we are constantly faced with this in our families, church, work, schools, civic groups, and professional associations. Wise leadership does not come about as a result of pride's persuasion. It is not found in the "tit for tat" of petty politics. So where do you look for wise leaders? A good place to begin is within the ranks of those who already exhibit wise leadership (Acts 15:22). You see it in the open and authentic environment they create in their work and home, by their own honesty around personal weaknesses and strengths. Indeed, wise leaders are excellent listeners. They listen with the intent to understand. Wisdom desires understanding of what you are thinking and what you are feeling. You observe their wisdom in one-on-one conversation, as they know what questions to ask. They challenge you to think, and offer counsel as is appropriate.

Wise leaders are not gurus, or know-it-alls. They instead are smart enough to understand the vastness of what they don't know. Moreover, a wise leader is respected (I Timothy 3:8). Those who know them the best respect them the most. If those in someone's inner circle lacks respect for the person in leadership, so will those outside their circle of influence. Indeed, respect comes over time. It is the result of doing what you say. It is integrity in living out what you say you believe. Consistent Christ-like behavior invites raving reviews of respect. Wisdom and respect go hand-in-hand. They promote each another.

Last of all, wise leadership points toward God. (Any infatuation with them as an individual is directed to their heavenly Father). Wisdom can only remain in a humble heart. It is within the incubator of humility that wisdom germinates and flourishes. Therefore (aptly so) a wise leader shows humility in their heart for God.

God entrusts wisdom to the humble of heart. He is stingy in giving wisdom to the proud. Pride cannot be trusted to use for His glory. God-given wisdom is priceless. Even religious leaders can forget the Lord's wisdom (Jeremiah 2:8). It is the application of wisdom that matures relationships, facilitates faith, and grows business and ministry. Wise leaders do not always tell you what you want to hear, but listen to them. Their words are sometimes hard, and seem at the moment as intolerant and insensitive. But this is the maturing process. Wisdom makes foolishness uncomfortable. It is wise leadership that leads you beyond mediocrity and immaturity. Wise leaders lead you to grow in your relationship with Christ. They promote God's agenda.

Follow wise leaders and be a wise leader. Patiently and prayerfully select and appoint wise leadership!

> "Who is wise? He will realize these things. Who is discerning?
> He will understand them. The ways of the Lord are right; the righteous walk in them,
> but the rebellious stumble in them." HOSEA 14:9

Wise living keeps the realization and understanding of God in the vortex of your thinking. God awareness is center piece. "What would Jesus do?" becomes a way of life. His desires, His motivations, His thoughts, and His character become paramount in your thinking. This leads to wise living because it is based on Christ-like living. God's ways are the path to wisdom. The wisdom of God is unfathomable. But He is willing to share it. In fact, His preference is to shower His children with raindrops of wisdom. He delights in imparting His game plan for living.

However, it takes a regular realization on our part for the wisdom of God to penetrate our thinking. We become people of the book. Joshua said it best, "Do not let this Book of the Law depart from your mouth; meditate on it day and night, so that you may be careful to do everything written in it. Then you will be prosperous and successful" (Joshua 1:8).

Wise living includes the ability to discern right from wrong and good from best. Use the Bible as your guide for wise recommendations. Your ability to discern will grow as you mature in the faith. You may be a pretty good judge of character, but God wants to grow you in this area. Your discernment is a gift to your husband for protection against unwise decision-making (I Corinthians 2:14). He may not appreciate this yet, but he will if he is wise. Therefore, present your insights with grace and humility. By faith extract your overly aggressive emotion and replace it with a prayerful appeal. Hold your suggestions with an open hand and trust God to work on your husband in His timing. He is accountable to God. Sweet relief. You do not have to change him, but God can.

What God changes stays changed. What you change has a tendency to revert back to its old way of doing things. Indeed, you see what needs to be done like the nose on your face. Be patient. Let your husband fail. Plant seeds, pray, and watch the Holy Spirit turn the heart of your husband in the right direction. It is not about you convincing him; rather it is all about the Spirit of God convicting him. If he is wise, he will heed your discernment (Proverbs 18:15). He may have to fall on his face first. Use your discernment like the steady hand of a skilled surgeon with a sharp scalpel. Avoid bludgeoning him with your accurate insights. The right timing, tone, and transparency are terrifically effective.

Wise is the husband or wife who listens to their spouse. Therefore, be humble and teachable. Understanding and discernment will follow. This is wise living!

J14   WISE LISTENER

"Listen now to me and I will give you some advice, and may God be with you…
Moses listened to his father-in-law and did everything he said."
Exodus 18:19a, 24

God sends people your way who offer great advice. Therefore, listen intently…you never know who may be speaking on behalf of God. These may be people you trust or distrust. But either way, do not allow pride to stand in your way of listening to what they say. Wisdom can come from the most unlikely sources. Therefore listen with discernment. Job learned that not listening could lead to loss (Job 36:12).

Do not be a non-thinking listener. Wise listening involves a functioning brain. The intent of wise listening is to separate the wheat from the chaff. For example, you may be laboring away unnecessarily in stress and anxiety. Your stress may be self-inflicted. You may need a better system for processing the needs of people. You may also be trapped in the never-ending cycle of busyness. Your life and organization are more complex than even six months ago. You need a better process for handling issues and complaints. People are starting to grumble. You are weary, and they are frustrated.

The most obvious adjustment may be to involve others in helping you serve the people or the enterprise more effectively. Take the time to recruit and train others. This takes time and trust. But, if you do not start today preparing for tomorrow, you will wear out or even burn out. If this 'choking point' is not remedied you could lose your credibility. People will choose to go somewhere else, and you will lose your influence. Do not try to talk your way out of your responsibilities, but rather listen to those who are offering you advice, and prayerfully consider their counsel. This may be the optimum time for you to let go and trust others. Listen to what other proven leaders have to say, and obey.

So who in your life is currently offering you advice and counsel? Is it your wife? Is it your father or father-in-law? Is it your mother or mother-in-law? Is it your boss? Is it your employee? Is it your friend? And are you truly listening? Or are you just going through the motions and not really adjusting or modifying your behavior? There is a very good chance that the methods you have employed up to now will not propel you into the future.

This time of uncertainty may be a good time to evaluate the basics of life and work. What is the purpose? What do you do best? What is your capacity? Do you value quality over quantity? Do relationships have priority over tasks? What is your motive? This honest self-evaluation, coupled with the counsel of others, will help take you to the next level of living. Proverbs 1:5 states it well, "let the wise listen and add to their learning, and let the discerning get guidance."

Above all else, listen for the Lord's voice among the various voices that vie for your attention. Obey the voice of God!

> "Then the king said, 'Bring me a sword.' So they brought a sword for the king.
> He gave an order: 'Cut the living child in two and give half to one and half to the other.' "
> 1 KINGS 3:24-25

A wise process protects. It protects life. It protects relationships. It protects resources. It protects commitments. The process on the surface may not seem smart, but time wins you over with its wisdom. It is tempting to bypass the process. After all, you know what needs to be done, or so you think. It is tempting to barrel ahead into activity because the need is so great, and the time seems so short. But even if you are confident of the needed outcome, still trust the process. At the very least it will involve others, who need the process for understanding around requirements and support of a new role. For example, your work may require a new position to be filled. Will you fill this role with the first interested warm body, or will there be a defined process for the protection of the company, and the protection of the one being interviewed? The rule of three is normally a wise process to employ. Interview three legitimate and good candidates with the purpose of selecting one.

During the process of interviewing you may discover new issues related to what the job really requires. You may even rewrite the job description. Perhaps this process of employee selection needs to include four or five other interviewers. Their perspective and wisdom is invaluable, as you seek to discern the best qualified person for the position. These "people" processes need not be rushed, so everyone is protected from unwise decision-making. Opportunity evokes emotion. Process channels positive energy into better options.

Jesus understood this. He spent a 30-year process of preparation before he embarked on a relatively short three years of ministry. In addition, he took his followers through a process of discipleship, teaching, and on-the-job training. His process with people was pregnant with questions, discovery, and hands-on experience. Ultimately, his process culminated with the cross and the resurrection.

Therefore, some processes require death before there can be life. The death of a vision may be needed, before it can be realized. Hence we are all in a process. We are all learning along the way, in preparation for God's next assignment. Process grooms you for greatness. If you run ahead of the process, you may very well disqualify yourself from greatness. Therefore, it is wise to be patient in the process and enjoy its excursions. Your vision may be dormant at best, or even dead for now. Do not give up on its feasibility. This may be part of God's bigger process. Process is His protection for your family. Without a prayerful process you might over-commit; to the neglect of those who need you the most.

Indeed, you can implement prayer immediately as your number one process component. Make Christ your process consultant. Default to "what does Jesus think?" before you ask Him to bless your "seat-of-the-pants" process. Prayer is your best process. Employ it well and employ it often. Allow prayer to define the process, initiate the process, and conclude the process. Prayer that seeks the wisdom of God and the wisdom of godly counselors is almost guaranteed a great process. Therefore, weave prayer throughout the process, and watch God work. Allow the Holy Spirit to drive the process.

Hearts, minds, and spirits align around a prayerful process. You can't beat a process interwoven with intercession and punctuated by prayer!

J16 GOD'S WISDOM

"I will give you what you asked, I will give you a wise and discerning heart..."
1 KINGS 3: 12A

The wisdom of God goes beyond your ability to understand right and wrong. It gets to the heart of the matter. Wisdom asks, why do you want to do what you want to do? What is your motive? Are your third? Is your priority: God first, others second and you third?

Opportunities should become options to further God's Kingdom, rather than a way to exploit your power and status. This is the motive God looks for to pour out his blessing of wisdom (Ecclesiastes 2:26). He is looking for centered people whose heart's desire is to obey God and follow His ways. Yes, books can increase your knowledge, but only God can bestow wisdom upon you. In fact, knowledge can work against you, if it just feeds your ego and pride. Knowledge can even be a turn-off. People are attracted to what you do ,with what you know. They want to see you apply the truth you have acquired. This is wisdom.

Wisdom is taking the perspective of God and transforming the human world-view.

So you decide not to marry someone, because it is not the wise thing to do. They are a nice person, intelligent, financially secure, and even religious; but they lack an unselfishness and commitment to you and God. Wisdom is a God-thing that only comes from Him.

God's wisdom comes from God, and is received through a heart of character. God does not entrust His thoughts with someone who will prostitute his wisdom for wrong purposes. He is looking for a heart of humility and honesty. Someone who, like a child, says, "I need you and I need your direction." And without the wisdom God, says, "I am lost and unclear on God's ways." Humility is the gateway to wisdom (Proverbs 11:2). It is what sustains it.

Your humility means you are teachable to learn from God. Your honesty means you will use God's wisdom in an honorable way. Wisdom can be used to settle disputes between individuals or organizations. It can assist you in becoming an expert in your career. Wisdom extracts nuggets of knowledge, and becomes a paint brush in the hands of a skilled artist who can translate information into a beautiful portrait. Wisdom can lead you in your decision-making, so you are consistent to ask, "What is the wise thing to do?" You search the Scriptures daily and God fills your wisdom basket. You hang out with wise people and learn from their mistakes and from their wise decisions. Wisdom is not microwavable; it marinates in your mind. It becomes digestible over time.

Therefore, be patient; talk to God about your need for wisdom and seek godly counsel. He will answer your prayer. The other things consume your thinking will take care of themselves. Wisdom eventually wins. It is a steady and sure road. Because of your responsible pace, you can avoid some of the potholes of life instead of racing through life, swerving in and out of bad decisions and eventually crashing.

Ask God for wisdom. It is His reward (Proverbs 9:12). Wisdom is a wise request!

> "In the beginning God created the heavens and earth.
> GENESIS 1:1

God has big vision. His vision is enormous. He wrote the book on vision. He is the original visionary. His vision is so large, we are unable to wrap our minds around its implications. Even if we had infinite lifetimes to live, we couldn't completely comprehend God's vision. He launched His initial vision with creation. Creation was His baby. This was God's opportunity to express Himself through the creation of the earth, the sun, the moon, the stars, plants, animals, sky, water, and most importantly man. Man was the crown jewel of God's creation, because he was created in the likeness of God (Genesis 1:27). Man was the image of God. Man is a mirror of his Maker. Our Lord is an extraordinary visionary. He takes nothing and makes something. He lifts up what seems to be insignificant dirty-dirt, and breathes life into it so it becomes a beautiful human being.

God is the expert at taking colorless capability and crafting it into a technicolor transformation. His vision is macro: He illustrates His creativity and complexity through the creation of earth and all it contains. His vision is also micro, because He has created no two people the same. Each plant and animal is unique in their own special way. Above all else, His vision is personal for every single individual. God has a vision for your life that is larger than you think. We tend to limit the Lord's vision with our unbelief and fears. We get so caught up in our day-to-day responsibilities that we forget to focus on the father of vision, Jesus Christ.

Therefore, lift your heart and mind to the Lord, and ask Him what His vision is for your life. By faith, do not be afraid to stretch yourself into seeing things like He sees things.

What we see as obstacles, He sees as stepping stones. What we see as limitations, He sees as His provision. What we see as fear, He replaces with faith.

Do not grow tired of doing well. Tackle life with the energy and excitement of someone consumed with a fresh vision from heaven. Ask the Lord to baptize your vision under the water of His wonder. Ask Him to take your old and stale vision, and bring it alive with faith and hope. Raise the bar of your belief, so you are bold to ask things of God you have never asked, to believe things from the Lord you have never believed, and to do things by faith that you have never done. Go to the one who is Lord over all visions, and ask Him to infuse yours with life and largeness. Do let your education, income, relationships, or past failures limit you in your pursuit of His vision for your life. Indeed, your failures are His opportunities to flourish with a fresh vision for you and your family.

Lift up your eyes from the obvious, and look for the opportunity that stands next to you. Give yourself permission to "think outside the box" of the ordinary, and trust God with the extraordinary. Vision is most effective when updated and stretched. Do more than dust off an old vision. Pray for the Holy Spirit to birth a God-sized vision in your soul. It may mean moving. It may mean changing careers. It may mean more education. It may mean admitting failure and starting over. Whatever it means for you, focus on God and His vision for your life. He knows how to create a life-changing vision. By faith, ratchet up a more robust vision.

Look to the Lord of vision and craft your vision around His. He has big vision!

J18 DOUBT GOD

"Now the serpent was more crafty than any of the wild animals the Lord God had made. He said to the woman, 'Did God really say, 'You must not eat from any tree in the garden?' "
GENESIS 3:1

Satan's first goal is to get you. If he is unable to get you, his next step is to get you to doubt God. After all, what good is faith that is watered down by doubt? This is not to say we may go through seasons of doubt as disciples of Christ. But doubt is not the ongoing pattern of a serious and faithful follower of Jesus. Thomas was a doubter for a time, but when he came face-to-face with his resurrected Savior and Lord his doubts fled like an exposed bandit. Do not underestimate the enemy's endeavors to get you to doubt God. If he is successful in planting and growing seeds of doubt, your faith will be stunted. Your faith will be choked to death by these weeds of worry, by the crab grass of the cares in this world.

In some ways, when you first believed it was easier to trust God. Now that you have aged in years as a Christian, you may have formalized your faith, to the point the miraculous has been replaced by the mundane. Questions of doubt have replaced God's promises of assurance.

Did God really say my relationship with Him is based on my belief in Jesus Christ as His son, and the only way to heaven (John 14:6)? Did God really say that those who believe in Jesus go to heaven, and those who reject him are separated from God eternally in hell (Revelation 20:15)? Did God really say that I am to pay my taxes that are due the government as an example of a good citizen (Mark 12:17)? Did God really say I am to honor my parents even if they are undeserving of honor (Ephesians 6:1-3)? Satan may be seducing you with these subtle messages of doubt. Did God really say to volunteer in the church, start tithing, stay in this marriage, forgive my friend, invest in my family, and help my neighbor? Did He really say to trust Him even when I don't feel Him? Am I to obey Him when I don't understand why or how? The answer, no doubt, is yes.

Just say yes to God's Word, in opposition to the enemy's subtle and sometimes not so subtle questions of doubt. Answer the devil's leading questions of doubt with a resounding vote of confidence of what God has told you to be true. Satan will try to convince you that God is somehow holding back on what's best for you. He may be holding back, but only for your good; not for your detriment or frustration. Be aware of Satan's schemes. He is determined for you to doubt God and thus doubt yourself and others. But you know better. Replace his temptations to doubt God with God's assurance of faith.

God has given you eyes of trust to see the unseen (2 Corinthians 4:18). Your Lord has proven Himself time and time again as faithful and dependable. Even when we have strayed, our Savior has been there for us when we made the turn back to truth. Christ is totally trustworthy. There is no need for any inkling of doubt in Him, or His word. Believe His warnings as His protection. Believe His promises as His assurance. Believe His principles as His rules for living. Believe in His track record as His promise of provision. Believe His truth that sets you free from the dregs of doubt. Doubt the doubter. Remind him of what God really said. Faith flourishes in a doubt-free environment. God can be trusted without a shadow of doubt.

Doubt the devil, yes. Doubt God, no!

GOD BACKFILLS

"I will repay you for the years the locusts have eaten—the great locusts and the young locust, the other locusts and the locust swarm—my great army that I sent among you."
JOEL 2:25

God can make up for wasted time. He specializes in redeeming rough seasons in our life. What has become a torturous transition, He can use to love you into a closer relationship with Him. Where else can you go for eternal life than to the one who is eternal (John 6:68)? Allow God to backfill this blot on your past. He can rebuild what has been broken, and even destroyed.

You may have been embarrassed and humiliated, but this is not beyond God's long arm of restoration. Injustice may have invaded your unsuspecting life. Unaware and unexpected, you lost everything you had spent a lifetime building. Poof, in a twinkle of an eye, it was gone. Your career was gone. Your family teetered on division. Your reputation was tattered and all but obliterated. Your joy was gone. Your finances were depleted. Your energy was sapped. And your faith was shot full of holes. Your desire to move forward in life was severely stalled. Worst of all you wondered where the Lord was in all of this reversal of fortune. You were on the fast track to bitterness, because of your feelings of betrayal. You may have hit rock bottom, and now there is no where to look but up, look up to Jesus. He is your hope, your rock, and your refuge. Look up to the Lord even though He may seem a million miles away. Now is the time to practice what you told others all those years. Trust God during this time of turmoil. God wants to backfill your loss. Your pit of pity He can fill with hope (Psalm 40:2). Your broken relationships that are buried in a cistern of hurt, He can retrieve with forgiveness. Your financial black hole, He can shine the light of His provision and opportunity.

In Christ, your best days lie ahead. Submit to His healing. Let go of your hurt and pride, and hang on to Him. He is the best thing you have going for you. Let these failures forge a stronger faith in you and in your family. Face the fact that you are forgiven, and move forward in the power of the Holy Spirit. Lean on the Lord. He can handle it. He is your stability in this storm of insanity. God is there for you to rebuild your reputation, and to give you daily doses of hope and encouragement. Your eruption of raw emotion will grow you into a more sensitive and compassionate follower of Christ. He has brought you through this crisis of faith to allow you to coach others through the same. You are a living and breathing testimony of the grace and love of God. Project His faithfulness on other fledgling followers of Jesus. Let the Lord backfill the hole in your heart and life with His love and faithfulness. His filling of right attitudes and actions will bar the door of your mind from bitterness and backstabbing. Invite the Holy Spirit to backfill your soul with His fruit of love, joy, peace, self-control, purity, forgiveness, and humility. What God fills proves faithful. What God fills He controls and comforts.

Use the lessons of the past as a reminder for the Holy Spirit's filling in the present. His backfilling results in faithfulness going forward!

J20 LIVE IN HIS PRESENCE

"After two days he will revive us; and on the third day he will restore us; that we may live in his presence." HOSEA 6:2

Live in His presence, so you can better live in the present. His presence is a reality check. His presence is pure and is purifying. You cannot live in the presence of the Lord and not be changed.

Christ is combustible. His expectation is Lordship over His followers. This is why we submit to Him each time we enter into His presence. His looming presence means He is Lord of our life. We could say that He is ever-present; therefore we are perpetually in His presence. So whether we acknowledge His presence or ignore it, He is still there. It is, of course, to our advantage to acknowledge the Almighty all the time, and this can become the habit of our heart.

Always look for ways to continually and quietly crown Christ as the Lord over our life. It is in His presence that this comes to light. This is why you intentionally enter into His presence. You need the reminder more than He needs the recognition. Although it is a form of respect to regularly recognize the one you love most; come into His presence out of sheer love and respect, with no agenda but worship. The goal is to live in His presence, so you can live in the present. His presence arrests your worries, and locks them away, so you can live in today. His presence purifies your heart and mind (I Thessalonians 3:13). His presence comforts and encourages like none other. It is living in His presence that provides strength for your life-long journey. His presence is where love lingers and holiness hovers.

It is in the presence of Jesus that your perspective is aligned with the Almighty's. God is great at giving a gut check. Take the time to tarry with the Lord. Christ can keep you from insignificant commitments. His presence points to your spot in His will.

The presence of God is experienced positional and volitional. You know in your head that He is always present. But your heart must volitionally engage with Him, for you to experience Him practically. Learn to practice His presence. Think about Him often. If men can think about sex every seven seconds, surely thoughts about their Savior can exceed this. Women tend to worry regularly. So a healthy habit is to send worry out the back door of your mind's control, and invite the Lord in through the front door of your heart's faith. He does "stand at the door and knock" (Revelation 3:20).

Moreover, live in His presence, so you can live in the present. You stay tethered to eternity, but experience the moment. Live in the present, because this is where people live. You can help people live through another day, when you lead them into His presence. Living in His presence is as much human as it is divine. It is as much vertical with heaven, as it is horizontal with people. Live in His presence. After all, He is already there. So above all else, stay aware and alert of the Almighty's precious and purifying presence.

Practicing His presence produces lasting relationships and right results. It revives and restores!

"I know, O Lord, that a man's life is not his own; it is not for man to direct his steps."
JEREMIAH 10:23

We do not own our lives. We have been bought with a price (I Corinthians 6:20). As followers of Jesus, His sacrificial blood purchased our freedom from the fire of hell, sin, and death. By faith, we are owned by him. A great exchange took place when you believed in Jesus. What's yours became His, and what's His became yours. The life of Christ became your life. It is not your life to define, but His. He has wrapped a wonderful definition around who you are in Him. You are a child of God. You are secure, because your Savior keeps you. You are valuable, because the Lord values you. You are protected, because the Almighty owns you. The Bible is God's glossary of how to define oneself. Scripture gives you a family tree of faith for you to trace back your religious roots. It is a mirror of how God sees you. He sees you as accepted in His son, though you suffer rejection from others. Cherish and enjoy daily the acceptance of Jesus. Your mistakes are His opportunity to affirm His acceptance. There are still consequences to your sin, but He is always available to receive you back, because you are His. He accepts and receives back His own.

Furthermore, He directs His own (Isaiah 48:17). His desire is for you to understand and follow His plan for your life. Praise God, it is a step-by-step process, and He directs your steps! Some days you may feel like it is three steps forward and two steps back, but do not be discouraged or dismayed. God is still directing your steps. Though tedious and laborious at times, the Lord leads you in lock, step with His steps. In His steps is the wise way to walk. Do not run ahead thinking you have to set a record for speed or quickness. In fact, fast steps may cause you to backtrack and have to learn all over again what God was trying to teach you. Walk patiently with Him and watch Him at work. The Holy Spirit is your step director. You are in His step class for instruction in His word and exercise in faith. Learn how to let the Lord direct your steps. Prayerfully listen to the quiet prompting from His spirit. Stop when you need to stop. Speed up when you need to speed up. Slow down when you need to slow down. God directs the steps of a submitted and surrendered man or woman.

Stubbornness is hard to direct (Psalm 81:12). Pride resists direction. Independence attempts to self-direct. Listen to your spouse or close friend. He may speak His next steps through them. Self-direction is like traveling alone to a new destination without a map, or an orientation to your surroundings. It is futile and frustrating. It leads to fatalistic thinking. God-directed steps, on the contrary, are a paragon for peace. You can rest in His far-reaching perspective and other worldly wisdom. He gives divine directions that determine His will for your life. Step by step He leads you. You can trust that His way is the best way. Be patient. Watch Him work in spite of adversity and a lack of resources. Avoid a two-step with yourself. Stay in step with your Savior. Allow your Maker to define your moves. Lock step with the Lord is the wisest way to walk. Resist directing your own steps.

Trust in your walk with Him. Allow His direction to define your steps!

J22 FIERY HEART

"But if I say, 'I will not mention him or speak any more in his name,' his word is in my heart like a fire, a fire shut up in my bones. I am weary of holding it in; indeed, I cannot."
JEREMIAH 20:9

The word of God flows through the human heart like orange hot lava out of an erupting volcano. Nothing can hold back the effects of God's word. It penetrates the hardest of hearts and disturbs its apathy. It ignites a tender and teachable heart with confidence and gratitude. The heart cannot contain the word of God anymore than a mother can hold back her joy after the birth of her baby. There is an explosion of endurance and excitement that happens when Scripture seeps into the soul. It cuts into your being (Hebrews 4:12). You cannot remain unchanged by the living word of God. It arrests your thinking. Scripture engages you with eternity; its eternal truths demand a response.

Any open-minded person who seeks to understand the Scripture will benefit now and for eternity, if he embraces its claims. You cannot shut a person up who has been spoken to by the Lord, via His word. The Bible is a conduit for knowing Christ. It facilitates faith like nothing else. As a follower of Jesus you engage with eternal purposes when you hide God's word in your heart. You hide it within, but it explodes without. Truth in is truth out. Moreover, Jesus was a man of the Word (Matthew 13:14). The Scripture was fire in His bones. He spoke like no one else because His authority was not in His words, but in the words of His heavenly Father.

You can stand confident in Christ when your decisions and rationale are based on the Bible. The Word of God perseveres. It is your teacher. The Bible defines your belief system.

Lastly, learning and obeying the Bible frees you from the excuse of not knowing; understanding and applying the truth makes you accountable. If you really want to comprehend and increase your accountability, then teach the Scripture. Teachers adhere to a higher standard (James 3:1). A teacher who does not teach is frustrated and worn out. It has to come out, or you are hard to live with. Don't hold back any longer what the Lord is teaching you. A teacher must tell, or they will not feel well. The Bible begins to boil in a heart full of truth. Sin surfaces to the top; and the Lord skims it away by His grace and forgiveness. The fruit of the Spirit has the potential to flourish in a heart flush with the Word. Faith and hope hang-out in a heart recalibrated by Christ's words.

The Bible is your reality check. Though Holy Scripture is up to 3,000 years old, it keeps you relevant today. Carry Scripture with you. Read and study it with others. It is a fire that melts fear and burns away bad attitudes. Scripture leads you to your Savior. Stoke the fires of your faith with God's word.

Watch it burn brightly. You will see Him!

"Woe to him who builds his palace by unrighteousness, his upper room by injustice, making his countrymen work for nothing, not paying them for their labor."
JEREMIAH 22:13

Anything worthwhile is worth doing well. If you are building a family, frame it well. Furnish it with faith, love, hope, and the fear of God. If you are building a business or ministry, grow it relationally and systematically. Pour its foundation with honesty, trust, and excellent work. If you are building a life, develop it with discipline, forgiveness, humility, grace, service, and obedience to God. Spend your time building people, processes, projects, and enterprises that are sustainable and eternal. Seek to focus on endeavors, which contribute to and facilitate faith-based initiatives. Indeed, build people who will improve on your accomplishments. Above all else, dedicate your building to God (Nehemiah 3:1).

You are now positioned as a leader of leaders, so lead leaders well. At this stage of life you have the stewardship to mentor mentors, so pour yourself into those who will mentor others. Build spiritual disciplines into faithful followers of Christ.

Do not neglect developing disciples. Disciples of Jesus need a firm foundation of faith. It is imperative to model for them mastery of the Master's words. Let the Word of God flow freely from your speech. Speak it and live it on behalf of your Savior. You build lives that last when you ground them in the Good Book. The legacy you leave is predicated on the people with whom you invest. Therefore, keep your children "top of mind." Make them your number one building project. Begin when they are tiny telling them about Jesus. As they grow, instill the principles of Scripture into their hearts and minds. Relate to them stories of God's faithfulness in your life all these years. Confess how your heavenly Father forgave you at your points of failure. This authentic home environment grows small children into giants of the faith. Build into your children now, and they will leave a legacy of faith. Build for generations to come (Psalm 48:13).

Moreover, build your ministry or business into one that lasts. This is assuming it is the Lord's will for it to last. If not, at least you have exercised stewardship well. A business or a ministry that is built to last is carefully constructed with the bricks of vision, mission, and values. Vision, mission, and values are embedded in the DNA of the enterprise. Strategy, objectives, goals, and metrics all flow from this synergistic source. There is a compelling cause that everyone is motivated around. This is vision. There is clarity of purpose of what needs to get done. This is mission.

And there is agreed-upon behavior that defines the culture. These are values. If your vision it too small, only little people will venture forth. If your vision is so massive that it becomes unrealistic, then no one will take you seriously. However, if your vision is prayerfully aligned with God's will, He will accomplish great things through you and others. Cast a God-sized vision that can last beyond your lifetime. Indeed, keep your team on mission-critical initiatives. These are building blocks for the business. Wise leaders learn to run with what works, and dismiss what doesn't. Tell stories that illustrate your mission. This keeps everyone focused on the reality of why they show up every day. Do not get so busy you forget to review His building plans.

What He builds lasts, as long as He wills!

J24   INFLUENTIAL ADVOCATE

> "Furthermore, Ahikam son of Shaphan supported Jeremiah, and so he was not handed over to the people to be put to death." JEREMIAH 26:24

We all need influential advocates. We need people who can plead our case with authenticity and authority. We are all limited in our ability to influence our own outcomes. This is why God uses influential advocates to further His purposes on our behalf. It may be at work that you need another to introduce you to someone significant within a particular department. Without his support you will be severely limited in your progress and productivity. This may require a form of politics, but do not allow your pride to keep you from gaining an endorsement from key players. Make sure you have an influencer go ahead of you who can create a safe environment of acceptability. If you run ahead with unbridled zeal, you may run into a brick wall and then wonder why you have stalled. It may be because you are new to the organization that you need to 'ride the coat tails' of someone else's character.

Later, after you have proven yourself, you will be able to navigate further along, without waiting on an influential advocate. It is much better for another to praise you than for you to "toot your own horn" (Proverbs 27:2). If you are perceived as a self-promoter, then you will be placed in the penalty box of opinion by your peers. People shun self-promoters. But let another influencer pave the way for your project, and all will be pleased. Be patient and pray for this. Stay prepared where you are, and pray for God to use another influential advocate to convince others of your creditability and stellar performance. You need the support of other influencers to succeed.

The flip side of this equation is your opportunity to be an influencer, on behalf of others who are pregnant with potential. Prayerfully consider this, but be very careful to whom you lend your endorsement. Your influence is extremely valuable, and needs to be stewarded wisely. People will not seek out your recommendations if you continually send them crummy characters. Be responsible, do due diligence to those desiring your introduction. Normally you can feel good about 'going to bat' for another if you, or someone you trust, have known them for a long period of time. You have witnessed their interactions with their family, their friends, and their faith. There is a consistency in their character. They are honest. They are teachable. They are humble. They submit to authority. They are grateful and content. They manage their home and their finances responsibly. They are competent. You can be an aggressive advocate of influence for this quality of person.

Above all else, appeal to your most influential advocate, Jesus Christ, for yourself and others (I Timothy 2:5). His influence is persuasive, and it never wanes!

PRAYER REVEALS

> "Call to me and I will answer you and tell you great and unsearchable things you do not know." JEREMIAH 33:3

Prayer reveals the heart of God. His heart is full of loving-kindness. He has loved you with an everlasting love (Jeremiah 31:3). He has drawn you to Himself with His unrelenting loving-kindness. This is attractive and compelling. This is what prayer reveals. Prayer becomes a revelation of what's true about God. His heart is hungry for your heart. Prayer is designed to align the Almighty's heart with yours. Relish the revealed heart of God. Indeed, it is in this quiet place that you see His face. Prayer reveals the face of your Maker. It is in a posture of worshipful prayer that you see something like a veil covering Christ's face, but prayer pulls it back to display the glory of God. The friendly face of your heavenly Father is waiting to welcome you into an understanding of Him and His will for your life. His face is inviting and confident. Rejection is not part of His repertoire. Intimacy is His intention.

Prayer places you up close and personal with your Lord and Savior, Jesus. It is a safe place when you see His face (Genesis 33:10). It is a place of comfort and calm. Moreover, prayer offers the reassuring tone of His voice. His voice is unique. We are His sheep. As His sheep, we recognize and respond to His voice (John 10:26). His tender call has the rhythm and rhyme of compassion and hope. Yes, there are times we detect firmness in His words. This is for our protection. He is not a kill-joy, but rather a joy-giver.

There is no other voice like His. The Lord's voice is intimate like the rustle of sheets. Listen to His voice, and you will learn to be content. Listen to His voice, and you will understand how He communicates with clarity and conciseness. Prayer is the place His voice is best understood. Prayer unlocks the language of the Lord.

Prayer also extends the eternal hand of God. He reaches down to deliver you through dreaded decisions. His hand is ever-extended to lead you into eternal purpose, and not leave you caught-up with inconsequential activities. The hand of your heavenly Father caresses your worried soul with comfort and calmness. His arms embrace you with the hug of a loving parent, locked around a fearful child. Prayer reveals the holy hands of God, hands that reach out to hold your hand, and lead you into righteousness.

The arms of your Maker are never so short that they cannot meet your point of need (Numbers 11:23). We all need a hand from time to time, especially a hand from our heavenly Father. Bow in prayer, and allow God to place His hand of blessing on your head. His commissioning is your confidence and hope. Prayer is the air of eternity. Inhale and exhale it often. Do not smother your soul with prayerlessness. An asphyxiated soul is dead to the ways of God. Keep it robust with prayer's revelations.

Call, and He will answer you!

J26 PUT INTO PRACTICE

"Therefore everyone who hears these words of mine and puts them into practice is like a wise man who built his house on the rock."   MATTHEW 7:21

The purpose of learning truth is its use. Unused, truth expires and becomes stale. When you hear truth and put it into practice, you are wise. When you hear truth and ignore its application, you are foolish. Foolish is the man who acknowledges truth outwardly, but never applies it inwardly. His foundation for faithfulness is fragile, so when the winds of adversity strike, his character collapses under its crushing blow.

Someone may show-up for the Bible study or attend a soul-stirring retreat, hear truth, but never change for the better.

How can this be? This happens when people do not follow through with what they know to be right and true. There is a 'disconnect' between their head and their heart. The discipline to stop bad habits and start new ones is rationalized away with convincing excuses. We deceive ourselves by saying, "I don't have enough time," "I am not spiritual enough," "I will get around to this one day," or "God will understand if I wait." John described self-deception's affect on truth, "we deceive ourselves and the truth is not in us" (I John 1:8b). Truth cannot co-exist with deception, so jettison deception and apply truth now. If you wait, you will wander from its application. The present is the wisest occasion to receive His gift of grace, and to engraft it into your life. You are responsible for the truth you have received. Therefore, steward it wisely. Use it before you lose it, by being a practitioner of truth.

Lastly, apply truth in doses that can be digested into your character. Do not be overwhelmed by multiple things in your life that need to change. Choose one thing, like loving your spouse with abandonment and sensitivity. Paul said in Ephesians 5:25 for the husband to 'give himself up' for his wife. Without saying a word, serve in secret, so your spouse can experience your unselfish care and concern. Get into their world by loving them at their point of interest. It may relate to entertainment, cooking, or yard work; but serve them in ways that will say to them, you care.

At work, you have the opportunity to put into practice the radical teaching of Jesus, to treat others like you want to be treated, "Therefore, however you want people to treat you, so treat them, for this is the Law of the Prophets" (Matthew 7:12 NASB). Think of a colleague you need to forgive for they let down the team. If you were in their shoes, you would appreciate this gift of mercy. You can put into practice the 'golden rule' because you are golden now that God has graced your life. God has filled you with His grace, so you can live a gracious life. Focus on building the foundation of your life and character with one brick of truth at a time. This architecture designed by the Almighty will endure. Leave a lasting legacy in your children by putting into practice what you know to be truth. The teachings of Jesus are truth. Therefore, believe and apply.

Put into practice His principles, and persevere!

COME TO ME

"Come to me; all you who are weary and burdened, and I will give you rest. Take my yoke upon you and learn from me, for I am gentle and humble in heart, and you will find rest for your souls. For my yoke is easy and my burden is light."   MATTHEW 11:28-30

Sometimes your soul needs to catch up with your body. There is a disconnection created by distraction and busyness. You are weary of life and work. This soul-fatigue will follow you until it finds rest. It is relentless in reminding you of what is important and necessary. The warning lights of weariness flash in the face of your faith. You are tired and troubled with nowhere to turn. This is when you can turn your eyes upon Jesus. He offers a constant invitation to come to Him. Burdens bear down on your back of responsibility like a ton of bricks, but Jesus is there to ease the pressure. Health issues assault your body like unceasing fire-fighting from the enemy, but Jesus is there to soothe the pain through prayer. Marriage confusion has the best of you, and you are ready to give up, but Jesus has the answers as the supreme counselor. Work expectations have overwhelmed your ability to execute the right results, but Jesus is there to impart His wisdom and discernment. Do not let failure talk you into giving up. You can carry on with Christ. Submit to His restful invitation. Take Him at His word, and yoke-up with His humility and gentleness. His extension of rest is received by faith. The yoke of Jesus gives hope and encouragement to the soul.

Start by aligning your calendar with Jesus time. A partnership with Christ requires time and attention. You cannot maintain a relationship with Him without investing in Him. Jesus went to the mountain to commune with His heavenly Father, and when He came down, large crowds followed Him. Why? People follow leaders they know they can trust. When you spend time with Jesu,s you build trustworthiness. You go to the mountains alone to pray, and you come back surrounded by followers. They know you have been with Jesus (Acts 4:13). When they know you have been with Jesus, they are reassured that you are depending on Him for wisdom and direction. Your motives are pure. This business or ministry is not your deal; it is His deal. You gain instructions from Him on how to execute His plan. Followers take great comfort when their leader pauses to pray, and takes time to receive the Holy Spirit's discernment over issues of vision and strategy.

Therefore, slow down each day, and listen to the voice of the One who created the world with a word. His words are powerful and freeing. They are comforting and convicting. The word of God will save you from unwise decisions, and free you to make wise ones (Proverbs 30:5). Take your life and organize it around the priorities of Christ. Get away, and get with Him. Give your soul a break. It is strained under the barrage of activity. Take a step back and reevaluate. This requires faith. Let others into your confidence. Trust in them that they are agents of the Almighty. His angels surround those who fear Him. Be accountable to be alone with Almighty God. This sensitive soul-care reaps temporal and eternal rewards. A well kept soul results in robust living. Go to Jesus. He is asking you to come.

Come quickly to Christ. Your soul deserves to catch up!

J28 DIVIDED AGAINST ITSELF

> "Jesus knew their thoughts and said to them, 'Every kingdom divided against itself will be ruined, and every city or household divided against itself will not stand.' "
> MATTHEW 12:25

Humility unites; pride divides. Patience pauses; anger accelerates. Indeed the nature of division is to reduce someone or something into a lesser status or significance. This is what division does. It divides. It divides families, nations, and cities. There is an implosion that takes place under the watch of divisive behavior. If you continue to battle in the home, walls will build up to the point of total division, because it ruins. It ruins communication and intimacy. It ruins teamwork and trust. It ruins peace and contentment. Indeed, the devil uses division as one of his primary weapons for worry and fear. If he can divide husbands and wives, he has conquered husbands and wives. Division defeats marital maturity, and replaces it with childish tirades. The enemy has won when husbands and wives think the other has become the enemy. Division deceives both parties into thinking that they cannot work together, so they fight it out. It is irrational and irresponsible. Indeed, anger drives division. There is an obsession to have one's way regardless of the shattered outcome. Things are done just to spite the other. Patience is thrown to the wind, and replaced with accusations and insults.

Division is the fruit of pride. There is no room for compromise; much less death to self. It drives couples to unreasonable demands and proud pontifications. Division creates losers and lasting regrets. It is a road that leads into a downward spiral of ineffective living.

Therefore, unite around humility. Humility relates from a position of brokenness. There is an appeal to the common sense of Christ and the wisdom of God. Mutual submission to your Savior Jesus becomes the starting point of discussion. Divorce is off the table, and no possession or position comes between either party. This is how division is defeated. There is a determination by everyone involved to depend on God and godly counselors for instruction and accountability. Emotional hostage-taking is prohibited, and manipulative moves are unacceptable. Instead, the fruit of the Spirit (Galatians 5:22) is the baseline for discussions. Unity is fostered around respectful and responsible discussions. This is the place where patient and cool heads prevail.

Lastly, identify the true enemies as pride, fear, selfishness, and the demons of hell. Take a frontal assault of faith on the adversary, instead of backstabbing each other with betrayal. Unity flourishes in a foray of forgiveness. "Forgive first and discuss second" is a good rule of thumb. Unity requires thinking the best of each other. Past failures are not held over the other as a hammer of guilt, and current hurts are not glibly dismissed. There is a healing that takes place around unity. People who pray together unify over time. Unity is a beautiful outcome for couples who pray together. As your heads hit the pillow each night, pray for one another before you slip into sleep. Let nighttime prayers romance you before you dose off and dream. Unified, your marriage and ministry will stand; divided it will fall. Therefore, unify around God and His word. In Christ you will stand (Romans 12:5).

Stand strong with your Savior. He forgives. He saves. He unifies!

LACK OF FAITH

"And he did not do many miracles there because of their lack of faith."
MATTHEW 13:58

Jesus blesses faith. There is no doubt about it; faith matters. There is a direct correlation to our faith in God and His responsiveness. He, of course, can do anything, and He is willing to do big things on your behalf, but He is looking for faith. He is searching for men and women with big vision; because big vision reflects a big God. We serve a large Lord who deserves a giant vision, fueled by great faith. Sometimes we mope around like God has lost control, and Christianity is hurling into irrelevance. Granted, the church has become sterile in some sectors of the world, but where faith is alive the church is on fire. Christ will not contain His blessings where He discovers followers who live by faith. There is a tipping point of truth in their community of faith. Indeed, prayer is prevalent when the faith community believes God for big things (Acts 4:24). God blesses belief.

Your faith expands as it remains on the Faithful One. Your focus on Jesus is what enlarges your eye into eternity. Like the disciples, He is your rabbi (John 1:38). It is the dust from His feet that flies back in your face as you follow Him. It marks you with His character and confidence. You are a Jesus–follower, by faith. Therefore, be bold in your belief. He is the one who has called you to this eternal endeavor, and He is the one who will pull it off. Keep your motive pure by glorifying Him. Enlarge your vision of what He wants you to do by ten fold, maybe a hundred fold. Do not sell short your Savior. Why settle for a few who might find Christ, when you can trust God for hundreds, even thousands who will grace the gates of glory, because you believed big. Your huge faith in your heavenly Father is what matters most. Moreover, He will move on to someone else, if you are not available to be used unconditionally.

So don't let the eternal leverage of the Lord pass you by. Flush your faith from motives of control, and with an open hand, trust God to take His vision wherever He likes. An unleashed vision has limitless possibilities. Fuel your God-goal with big belief. Give Him your five loaves and two fish of ability (Mark 6:38-44). Watch Him pray over it, and bless it bountifully and beautifully. Christ is not challenged by circumstances, and your Savior may be just getting started with you. Furthermore, don't leave any faith on the table of distrust. He will accomplish a greater vision through a humble, broken, and believing vessel. Eternity accepts no excuses. So, trust and be amazed at what the Almighty accomplishes through you. You lose only if you lack faith. Therefore, be one who believes big in Him. Miracles matter to your Master, because He manufactures them by faith.

God's industry is all about doing the impossible. Faith facilitates the miraculous!

J30 GRATITUDE FOLLOWS GENEROSITY

> "You will be made rich in every way so that you can be generous on every occasion, and through us your generosity will result in thanksgiving to God."
> 2 CORINTHIANS 9:11

Gratitude to God follows generosity for God. Therefore, thank God for the generous people He has placed in your life. People with the gift of giving have an uncanny ability to match resources and relationships with compelling needs. Paul described these dear people, "We have different gifts, according to the grace given us...if it is contributing to the needs of others, let him give generously..." (Romans 12:6a, 8a). It brings them great joy when they are able to give to a humble heart with a huge vision. Nothing satisfies a godly generous giver more than to significantly leverage their stuff for Kingdom outcomes. It is not a matter of if they are going to give, but where they are going to give. Generous givers prayerfully scan their surroundings to discern where God is working and where they can invest around their passions. The passion of some generous givers revolves around the poor, for others it may be building buildings. Evangelism, discipleship, and church planting grip the hearts of many visionary givers. It is a compelling vision that causes them to give themselves into greater participation.

Furthermore, it is in the middle of generosity that God can be found. God is a giver (Deuteronomy 26:1). He gave His only son (John 3:16). He gives daily bread (Proverbs 30:8). He gives eternal life (John 10:28). Indeed, generous givers grow in their faith because God is in close proximity. There is a very good possibility that a generous giver is growing closer to God rather than away from God. It makes sense that godly generous givers give to causes where God is at work, because it is thanksgiving to God that motivates their giving. The optimal opportunity for the godly generous giver has Christ at the core, because they understand the long-term solution to life is the Lord. Money can muster short-term results, but the ongoing life change will only happen when Jesus is at the heart. Thank God that generous givers give others the opportunity to know the Lord, and follow Him in discipleship and maturity.

Lastly, finances without faith in Christ provide a temporary solution at best. Therefore, godly generous givers understand the strategy of giving to causes that lead to their Savior. Where He is preeminent, He sustains the work. Indeed, the fruit of your thanksgiving to God tells the generous giver they are investing in the right environment. So remember, gratitude to God follows generosity. Moreover, if you are a gifted giver then exercise your gift to the glory of God. Pray for the right giving plan for you, and then give hilariously to heavenly causes. Keep Christ in the center of your giving. He is the exit strategy into eternal life in heaven.

You cannot out-give God, but you can partner with Him on opportunities both of you are passionate about. Above all else, be extremely grateful to God for the generous givers in your life. Emulate them and thank them!

"When they received it, they began to grumble against the landowner. These men who were hired last worked only one hour,' and you have made them equal to us who have borne the burden of the work and the heat of the day." MATTHEW 20:11-12

Grumbling is not fun to be around. It grates on both the giver and the receiver. Indeed, certain attitudes and environments increase the probabilities of grumbling. Injustice, misplaced expectations, ingratitude, discontentment, greed, misunderstanding, and comparison all accelerate the reaction of grumbling. Grumbling loves to draw a crowd that is sympathetic to its mistreatment, and many times does not disclose all the facts, and there is a skewed understanding of the situation. Instead of taking the high road of humility and acceptance, grumbling attacks authority, and acts like it is the center of the universe. Grumbling lacks integrity around commitments, and makes excuses based on perceived injustice. But Jesus was clear; he said to "stop grumbling" (John 6:43).

Grumbling is not good. It gets everyone lathered-up in distracting and detrimental behavior. Indeed, it is easy to constantly compare yourself to others, and grumble under your breath that you are better, and somehow deserve more than your menace. You complain because they receive more pay, even though you forget that when you started the job, you were the highest paid. Greed can fuel grumbling as much as anything; and grumbling is relational suicide, because it feeds on gossip and ingratitude. The tongues of perfectly good people become tainted under the influence of grumbling. It is a sad sight to watch. Grumbling converts good people into grumpy grown-ups. However, grumblers can get a life. Grumbling can easily be escorted out the back door of your life through maturity, trust, acceptance, and responsibility. Grumbling is for small people, and contentment is for big people. Furthermore, grumbling ceases in the face of fulfillment from your heavenly Father. Israel experienced this in their wilderness (Exodus 16:12).

Lastly, God-grumbling is the worst kind of grumbling. Anytime you murmur against your Master, you are setting yourself up for disappointment. Yes, you can complain to Christ, but do not obsessively worry over matters out of your control. Express your disappointments and fears to your heavenly Father, and then trust Him with the outcome. There is no need to go on an extended tirade against God and others. He knows and understands you and your situation. He is more concerned about changing you than in changing your circumstances. He is interested in you becoming more like the character of His son Jesus. It is the character of Christ that matters most in the middle of unfair or unjust situations. A heavenly focus puts into perspective earthly expectations.

Free yourself from grumbling by giving it over to God. Trust Him that His plan and process are perfect for you, and what is best for others. Congratulate your peers on their good fortune, and be grateful for all that God has given you. Salvation in Christ and having a relationship with Him is enough for a lifetime of contentment and gratitude. Therefore, replace grumbling with gratitude, and applaud those ahead of you.

Grumbling gets you nowhere, but gratefulness gets you all you need. Reject the rumblings of grumbling!

SURVIVAL MODE

"All her people groan as they search for bread; they barter their treasures for food to keep themselves alive. 'Look O Lord, and consider, for I am despised.'" LAMENTATIONS 1:11

Survival mode is relative. For some it is searching for the next meal, or nutritional survival. For some it is tangling with a teenager, or parental survival. For some it is the struggle to define themselves, or survival of purpose. For some it is desperately seeking to make ends meet, or financial survival. For some it is the healing of a broken and wounded heart, or emotional survival. For some it is the ability to withstand conflict at home and work, or relational survival. For some it is the unending and confining responsibility as a caregiver, or physical, emotional and financial survival. And most importantly, for some is the inner struggle with God and the meaning of life, or spiritual survival. Indeed, it is not all bad to experience a sense of desperation. It is when we are at the end of ourselves that we are the most in need of the Almighty.

Sometimes our circumstances strip us naked before our Creator. We feel exposed, vulnerable, embarrassed and exhausted. It is an uncomfortable position. Life seems to be swirling out of control, because we are in survival mode. We feel like we are two steps away from total despair and depression, even to the point of contemplating suicide. Survival mode means we are on the verge of giving up. We are not sure the marriage is worth it anymore. We are not convinced that Christ is all that He is cracked up to be. Life stinks and we are just trying to get through another day. Our goal is to seek out a living and get by the best we can. Indeed, survival mode can become a way of life, if there is not an intervention of eternal consequences. Therefore, do not become satisfied with survival mode; instead let the Lord love you through this. Scripture teaches, "No, in all these things we are more than conquerors through him who loved us" (Romans 8:37).

The abundant life (John 10:10) in Christ is much more than survival mode. So, use survival mode to lead you to revival mode. Ask God to use this time of desperation to revive your relationship with Him (Psalm 85:6). Pray for the Holy Spirit to ignite your soul and revive your heart of intimacy with your Savior Jesus. Repent from watering down the Word of God, and revive its application to your everyday life. Ask Jesus to transform your life into a robust revival rather than sedentary survival. Survival may be for the fittest, but revival is for the faithful. It is not those who 'gut it out' alone who experience God, but those who invite the Lord and others into their inner circle of influence. Break the cycle of cynicism, by turning your hurts over to Christ your caregiver. Allow the gentle Spirit of God to lead you through survival to revival. Pray for a revival of relationships, finances, health, work, parenting, and emotional energy, and then trust God with the results. Do not continually strive to survive. Instead, rest in Him to revive. A revived soul does more than survive. It flourishes by faith in God.

Live through survival mode into revival mode. But do it all by the grace of God!

F2   JOY IS GONE

"Joy has gone from our hearts; our dancing has turned to mourning."
LAMENTATIONS 5:15

What happens when the joy is gone? It is not fun anymore. What we are experiencing is not what we signed up for. Indeed, a joyless state is not a good place to stay over a prolonged period of time. It may be you just lost a loved one suddenly, and without warning. You grieve because of your tremendous loss, but their great gain is they knew Jesus. It is not unusual for joy to rise from the ashes of our grief. Joy does come at dawn after the dark night of the soul (Psalm 30:5). Your heart laments and longs for one more conversation and warm embrace from the dear one departed to heaven. But joy comes when you know they are with Jesus.

Jesus and joy go hand in hand. He understands that joy comes from obedience and faithfulness to God's call. It was for the joy that was set before Him, that He endured the cross and despised its shame (Hebrews 12:2). Consider Christ, along with His model of endurance and obedience, in the middle of opposition and persecution. Do not grow weary and lose heart. The Lord is your lesson in joyfulness. Jesus never forgot the bigger picture of hope for a better tomorrow. Hope ultimately leads to heaven. Just the thought of heaven's hallelujahs brings a smile to the face of faith. Joy is set before us in the person of Jesus Christ, reigning on His throne of grace. It is imperative that we stay fixed on Him. Our faith flees when it loses perspective from the Prince of Peace. Joy is found in Jesus. He wrote the book on experiencing joy in the midst of misery.

Joy, at the very least, lies dormant within every disciple of Jesus Christ. Therefore, awaken it from its slumber if you have slid into a joyless state. Look to the Lord for an infusion of His eternal joyfulness. Joyfulness is found in His hopefulness. Do not allow joy killers to rob you of hope and peace. A naysayer will always be around to remind you of his reality. But a definition of reality without hope is wrong for the follower of Jesus Christ. Therefore, reject joyless jabs from revisionists of a hopeless reality. Instead, seek out companions of Christ set on seeing Him as the joy giver. Jesus is a dispenser of joy. Navigate toward His lighthouse of love and enjoy Jesus. You know His love; this is joy. You know His forgiveness; this is joy. You know His faithfulness; this is joy. You know His mercy; this is joy. Joy is not based on changing circumstances, but on knowing an unchanging Christ. Seek Him in your sad state and you will not have to search far for joy. When you find Jesus, you have found joy. Confusion will try to keep you from Christ, but want of joy motivates you to your Master. Make joy a juggernaut of obedience in your ruthless pursuit of Him. Give joy to the world. Giving joy brings joy.

Therefore, receive Jesus and give Jesus, because He is joy!

SHATTERED PLANS

> "My days have passed, my plans are shattered, and so are the desires of my heart."
> JOB 17:11

Sometimes our plans do not go as we had hoped. In fact they were shattered. They were obliterated in front of your very eyes. You were almost breathless when the fact of your dismissal finally set in. In your shock you could have been pushed over with a feather. Certainly plans are made to be adjusted, but this one blew up in your face. It was devastating, to say the least. In some ways you had positioned your career for this one opportunity and it failed to materialize. Your emotions vacillate between bewilderment and anger toward God. Your desires feel snarled and disjointed. You are not a happy camper. This may be your dark night of the soul, because your proud plan has been emasculated. It doesn't make sense. The money was there, along with the relationships and resources that were poised for deployment. It was as if the stars were aligned. And then, in what seemed like an instant, your plan became irrelevant. Its course was altered into ambiguity, like it vanquished over night.

Now you are positioned to start over. It is hard to assemble the energy for another assault on your vision. It is time to give up and give in to defeat, because God is still in control. He controls your plans and their successful launch. He can still be trusted going forward. Just because things have not worked out according to your timetable is no reason to quit trusting Him. Trust the Lord with a reengineered plan that will be better than the former. His ways are much better than your ways (Isaiah 55:8-9). There is no human comprehension to what God has in store, if you remain faithful to Him. Indeed, His ways (Isaiah 2:3) can be hard to understand. The cycle of digesting His will into your mind and soul is like 'chewing cud'. This is a repetitive process that requires time and patience. The desires of your heart need validation. This is part of His plan, and this is where prayer plays a vital role. Take the broken pieces of your plan and place them at the feet of Jesus. He will take your shattered plan and piece it back together with His enhancements. A crushed plan in the hand of Christ has much more potential than your perfect plan buried in your grasp. You limit the Lord by holding on in distrust or fear.

Lastly, like the expressed genius of an artist, the newly formed plan has the depth and breadth of a masterpiece. It is an original crafted by the hand of God. Therefore, do not settle for anything less than your Master's plan. His master plan is monumental and can move mountains. Your desires may be dead, but now is the time to submit to God in a fresh and humble way. Watch in delight as He resurrects your desires to align and connect with His. He has slowed you down so your plans partner with His. See your shattered plan as a blessing not a curse. God loves to take what is broken, lift it up, and make it whole again. Place your plans and your heart in His hands.

He is the author and the finisher of your faith (Hebrews 12:2). He is the plan provider and He makes shattered plans better!

F4   TIMES OF TROUBLE

"But I will sing of your strength in the morning I will sing of your love;
for you are my fortress, my refugee in times of trouble." PSALMS 59:16

Times of trouble are ever looming in our life. It is either approaching us, surrounding us, or engulfing us. Times of trouble are never too far off, so we should not be surprised when they arrive. It may be relational trouble born from a marriage gone badly. It may be you are in trouble at work, because of someone else's choices. You trusted a peer to perform with excellence, but they let you and the company down with a sub-par performance. Now some hard decisions have to be made, perhaps financial cuts and layoffs are the reality of the situation. The business has gone from times of abundance to times of trouble. Indeed, the naive act like things will always be alright, while the prudent plan ahead (Proverbs 22:3). Wise is a leader and his team who plan for lean times, with prayerful and financial forethought.

Times of trouble can take us down, if we are not rooted in the Word of God. God's Word is our anchor in adversity. It reminds us to place our hope in heaven and not on earth. The principles of Scripture teach us how we need to act and what we need to do while we wait on God. The Bible is our blanket of comfort and security. We gain our strength from our Savior Jesus, as He is defined and described in Holy Writ. We trust Him when we know Him, and we come to know Him through His word. Times of trouble tempt us to not trust God. However, trust looks trouble in the eye and is not terrified. Trust trumps trouble. This was Daniel's demeanor in the lion's den (Daniel 6:22).

Furthermore, there is an urge to overreact during times of trouble. Instead of giving God control, we seize control and won't let go. A closed hand cannot trust, while an open hand releases control to Christ. Let go, and let the Lord lead you through this time of trouble. We think we are in control, but in reality we never have been and never will be. Christ is in control. You can sing to heaven and not murmur to man, because God is omnipotent. The Almighty is all-powerful. The Lord is large and in charge. Therefore, you can exclaim in praise over His all-encompassing power (2 Chronicles 20:22). Your song of satisfaction is for God alone, because you have experienced His loving kindness in the middle of your times of trouble. Your refuge is His righteousness, not your riches. You came into this world without, and you will leave this world without (Job 1:21). So, in between your first and last breath take your refuge in the One who introduces you to life and death. Use times of trouble to trust Him deeply, and love Him sweetly. Times of trouble lead to opportunity so seize this moment for your Savior.

Above all else, praise God for His provision of peace during times of trouble. Trouble is your ticket for trust!

FAITH VERSES FEAR

"When I am afraid, I will trust in you. In God, whose word I praise, in God I trust; I will not be afraid. What can mortal man do to me?"   PSALM 56:3-4

Fear is a formable foe of faith. It lurks around our life in search of leading us to distrust our Lord. Fear is subtle with its sneak attacks on our attitudes and its bold frontal barrage on our beliefs. It does not disappear until we get to heaven, and it always fights back, even after we extinguish it with our total trust in God. Fear is like a bed of fire ants, you eliminate their unholy mound with a baby-powder-like deterrent, but they regroup and rebuild not too far away. Indeed, trusting in the Lord is the terminator of fear. However, fear seems to recreate itself with whatever appendage of doubt is left. It grows within the next uncertain circumstance that comes our way. Fear thinks it has us in check on the chessboard of our life, but the truth is... Jesus checkmated fear on the cross. Now it is up to us to appropriate His triumph by our trust in God.

Furthermore, there are many times when we are in transition from fear to faith. It is a transition of trust in God that our cares co-mingle with Christ's care. There is a holy tension that transpires in our transition into trust. It is in this twilight of trust that light gradually overcomes darkness. Faith dissolves doubts as the sun drives away the mists. Your mind may be a little murky, but you renew your thinking (Romans 12:2) with the truth that God is very present. Your confidence may be crumbling, but you keep your eyes on your Savior. Your prayers may be clumsy, but you still cling to Christ. Your relationships may be reluctant, but you rely on the Lord. Use this transition from fear to faith to grow your mercy and compassion. Indeed, doubting can drive us to God, and it grows us into a more patient and humble human beings. It strengthens our trust and makes us hold faster to heaven. Hope trusts in this transition from fear to faith.

Moreover, mortal man has not made a permanent impression on the saints of God. Immortal and Almighty God is your new insignia. Embedded on the coins of your character is the faith-filled inscription, "In God I Trust." Followers of Jesus have the eternal seal of their Savior as their newfound identity (Ephesians 4:30). Do not allow the patterns of your old life to feed any fading fears in your new one (Romans 6:6). The former fears of your proud past have been replaced with faith, love, and hope in your humble here and now. Faith has banished fear; therefore you can continually celebrate. Praise points you to Providence; after all it is all about Him. This is why faith brings forth praise. When you trust, you can't help but sing from your soul. Indeed, faith in the Lord facilitates praise and is a product of praise. It is in our praise of God that our fears fade, and our faith flourishes. Therefore praise Him, trust Him, and fear no one.

No one can take from you what you have already given to Him. Faith is a fear killer, it overcomes!

F6   HOW LONG?

"My soul is in anguish. How long, O Lord, how long?"
PSALM 6:3

"How long?" is a fair question to ask of the Lord. He does not expect us to suffer in silence. In fact, it is okay and desirable to pour out our petitions to Him. We need heaven's healing. It is when we verbalize our vexing to our loving heavenly Father that we feel relief. Just to know that the Lord listens to our heartfelt cries, no matter how petty or profound, is reassuring. Sometimes we can't sleep well at night. We wake up in anguish with our mind racing. Our heart needs a touch of grace and peace from Jesus. A troubled heart has a hard time with sweet dreams, because there is a dread or disappointment that dogs its quality of rest. However, deep sleep accompanies those who are able rest in Him. Rest is a result of resting in the Lord's presence (Exodus 33:14).

The pain will linger until you see Jesus face-to-face, because it is a touch from the Lord that will get you through this difficulty. Therefore, do not let this momentary affliction keep you from experiencing God. Adversity is meant to engage us with eternity (2 Corinthians 4:17). If everything were easy, we would be prone to forget our heavenly Father. So in the interim on earth, it is okay to ask, "How long?" Questions keep us from being clueless with Christ, by driving us to our knees in dependency on Him. How long before you can be married? How long before your parents will be more understanding? How long before your teenager will mature? How long before the doctors can diagnose your ailment? How long before you can change career, or get a promotion? How long before finances are not such big issues?

All of these are fair questions and need to be asked. It is wise, healing, and hopeful to lift our concerns to Christ. But once we go to God with our questions, then it is imperative that we listen to His answers. It is not enough just to question. We must be willing to listen to the Lord. His answer is simple yet profound. "As long as it takes" is His compassionate reply. As long as it takes to accomplish His will. As long as it takes to mold us into the image of His son Jesus. As long as it takes for us to learn the lessons of faith, patience, love, and forgiveness. As long as it takes to break our stubborn pride and replace it with gracious humility. As long as it takes to die to ourselves. As long as it takes for God to glorify Himself through our lives. Questions keep you coming back to Christ for His love and direction. His unfailing love is a warm blanket that comforts a cold heart. It is a cup of fresh, filtered water for a thirsty soul. His unfailing love embraces, sometimes physically heals, giving relief to your broken body. His unfailing love wipes the tears from your eyes and holds you close where you are secure in Him. So above all else, in your state of questioning and confusion, receive God's unfailing love. How long before you can be loved by the Lord? Right now.

His love will see you through, so invite Him to love on you as only the Lord can!

WAIT IN EXPECTATION

"In the morning, O Lord you hear my voice; In the morning
I lay my requests before you and wait in expectation." PSALM 5:3

After we pray we wait in expectation, which means we don't fret or wait fearfully. We wait expecting God to engage in our world, while faith fills our soul with expectation. However, be careful with flippant prayers that are shot off randomly with no recognition of royalty in the room. Christ's kingship is marginalized when men or women pray aimlessly, void of expectations. Prayer becomes a commodity when its compelling nature ceases to exist, so make sure to pray in the Spirit (Ephesians 6:18). Therefore, do not grow weary in awaking each day in prayer, like the priority of your daily bath. You need not neglect the cleansing of your soul anymore than you would the bathing of your body. It is when you are the freshest, and fatigue is the weakest that you engage best in prayer. One hour of prayer in the morning is worth two hours at night, because your mind has yet to be soiled with the complexities of the day (people have not yet become a problem). When you send up your prayers at sunrise, you can expect peace of mind at sunset, and avoid giving your piece of mind in between. Morning prayers sow seeds of self-lessness that bear fruit during the day in patience, peace and productivity.

Indeed you wait, expecting God to answer in His timing and in His way. But your waiting is not without doing. As you pray and wait for the Lord to send out workers into His ripe harvest (Matthew 9:37-38), you venture into the world and learn to love people. As you pray and wait to be healed from a dreaded disease or aggravating ailment, you go to a well-trained doctor to administer the latest medicines and treatments to help remedy your illness. As you pray and wait for a job, you go out and enlist in projects or labor that expose you to new opportunities, and provides for your family in the interim. As you pray and wait for a relationship to be repaired, you reach out and seek to love them along the way with encouraging words and acts of kindness. You do your part as you wait expectantly on God to do His part. Waiting listens to the Almighty and then acts.

Expectations of God are good. Just make sure you align your expectations with His in prayer. Prayer without expectations would be cruel and unusual punishment. Yes, no expectations may mean no disappointments, but this is where prayer and faith fill in the gaps. It may mean no hope, no motivation to move forward, and no opportunity to trust God with outrageous possibilities. You can expect good things from God, "Now to him who is able to do immeasurably more than all we ask or imagine, according to his power that is at work within us..."(Ephesians 3:20). Therefore, do not confuse having no expectations of God, with having no expectations of people. God is trustworthy 100% of the time. He can be trusted regardless, so expect this of Him. He loves to see His children wait expectantly on Him. This trusting posture invites Him to answer prayers you never dreamed possible. You trust Him exclusively, as you wait expectantly.

And oh, He knows how to exceed your expectations. Wait and see!

F8 LOVE IS PATIENT

"Love is patient…"   I CORINTHIANS 13:4

Love is patient. It is patient because it is more concerned with the welfare of another than its own needs. It is patient because it is motivated to make the relationship right, over being right. Patience is the prerogative of the person who loves, so love can't help but be patient. It is the job description of everyone who loves, because patience is the outcome of people filled with the Holy Spirit. Patience comes out of your heart when love dominates your heart (Ephesians 4:2). Therefore, when the pressure of life squeezes you, patience comes out. Like a chocolate covered cherry, there is something delicious on the inside.

Furthermore, patience stunts anger by not feeding its appetite. It lovingly out sources anger to grace and forgiveness. Patience understands that most anger is destructive and self-centered, so it deflects anger by being other-centered. It looks out for the welfare of other human beings for their sake and for the purpose of being an image bearer of Christ. When people see patience they see the example of Jesus in His attitude and behavior. He was more patient with sinners who didn't know any better than He was with religious leaders who should have known better (John 8:7). Patience oozed out of the pores of Christ's character like a perspiring body on a hot and sultry summer day at the beach. Patience is priority for people who seek to love like their Savior loves. Indeed, patience is not reserved for the radically righteous, but is accessible for all who desire to love.

So, learn to love in a patient manner. The reason you are patient with your spouse is because you love him or her. The reason you are patient with people who make you uncomfortable is because you love them. There is a difference between being reluctantly tolerant and lovingly patient. Patience begins with loving oneself, so do not despise or look down on how God has made you. If you don't love and respect yourself, you will be impatient with your love and respect of others, so relax. The second greatest command is to love others as you love yourself (Matthew 22:37-39). Jesus patiently loves you just like you are, therefore you can love others, and exercise patience in the same unconditional way Christ loves you. Patient people actively and meaningfully plan to love, so be patient with the incompetent customer representative that barely speaks English. Be patient with your single parent restaurant server who is tired, afraid and anxious. Be patient with your family member who is outside of the faith and uncomfortable with your character. You love when you are patient, therefore pray for patience and you will increase your capacity to love.

Be like Jesus and be a patient lover of people!

LOVE IS KIND

"Love is kind…"   I CORINTHIANS 13:4

Love is a "killer application" for Christians, thus we "kill them" with kindness. Kindness means you are pleasant to be around, because your countenance is inviting and interested. It is as much an attitude as anything, and it is the ability to see beyond the immediate to the potential. Kindness means you go out of your way to love on someone. For instance people who are unlovable become prime candidates for your kindness, an example is a family member who is far from God, deep down they desire unconditional love and kindness. Indeed, kindness is a natural application of love, because it makes one feel loved. It is the ability to be accepting when everything within you is screaming rejection. It is a strategy for forgiveness when you are wronged or when someone takes advantage of you. When your trusting spirit has been violated, you still love by being kind, you stop fighting and you start forgiving.

Love keeps you kind, especially toward those who are closest to you. They do not deserve you dredging up hurtful, bitter and unforgiving words from the past. For instance, love is kind in its conversations. Harsh and abrasive speech is absent from kind conversation. Love produces words that are "kind and tenderhearted" (Ephesians 4:32). Love is able to extend kind words that cheer up heavy hearts (Proverbs 12:22). Moreover, pray to God for kindness to reign in your relationships with kids and teenagers. Children translate kindness into love, for it is their language of love. We all have blown up and lost our temper over disrespectful attitudes and actions from our offspring. The temptation is to disrespect when we have been disrespected, and the natural response is to become angry when someone else spews out his or her frustrations on us. But God has not called us to natural responses, but supernatural ones. Kindness in the face of frustration is a fruit of the Spirit, and only through submission to your Savior will kindness become front and center. The fullness of the Holy Spirit in your life is what causes kindness to come forth.

Lastly, loving others with kindness does not preclude difficult decisions. Kindness is not patronizing, but it is authentic care and concern and it is able to deliver hard truth that softens hard hearts. You can dismiss an employee with kindness; likewise you can disagree in a heated debate with kindness. Harshness has no hold on those who are controlled by Christ. Therefore, kindly love people through difficult situations, like serving those who are experiencing financial difficulties. Kindness is king for followers of King Jesus, so love with kindness and watch them come around and embrace Christ. Kindness kills sin and sadness, and it brings to life love, forgiveness, and hope. Allow Jesus' loving kindness to flow through you, for kindness toward the needy honors God (Proverbs 14:31).

Kindness resides where love is applied, because love is kind!

F10   LOVE IS NOT ENVIOUS

"It does not envy…" I Corinthians 13:4

Love is not envious. It celebrates the good fortune of others, and it smiles when someone succeeds, because love is an envy eraser. It can't wait for someone else to reach their goals and get the attention and accolades, for it is emotionally secure and mature. Love does not depend on the "desire to get" for contentment, because its contentment rests with Christ. It is content knowing that God "rains on the just and on the unjust" (Matthew 5:45). God's grace and blessing cannot be figured out or bottled in a formula, for He withholds or gives His blessing at His discretion. Love understands this and is not envious of those who are lavishly blessed by the Lord. Christ of course, has established principles that if obeyed, lead to blessing (Psalm 119:1-2). If you obey your parents you will be blessed by their wisdom, experience, and love. If you follow the laws of the land you will be free from serving a prison term or paying fines. God's truth can be applied and benefited by both believers and unbelievers. His ways work; so do not get worked up over the wicked succeeding. Success in life is an option for anyone who implements the principles embedded in God's Word. Therefore, choose to ignore envy and its dead-end road that results to comparison and disappointment. Envy attracts the immature, the insecure, the greedy, and the faithless. Comparison with people is an incubator for envy. Instead, reserve your comparisons to the character of Christ and be comfortable with yourself. Your personality, your looks and your gifts are from God, so be whom God created. Love is content to be God's unique creation. Envy looks at the stuff of others and salivates for the same. Envy wants to get, while love wants to give. It wants a woman's smooth skin, a man's car or wealth's options. Love overcomes these sometimes surreal and selfish desires by finding contentment in Christ. Therefore, go to Jesus your Savior for security, love and affection. Seek the affirmation of Almighty God in place of the acquisition of stuff.

Moreover, love is well versed in congratulating, by making milestones out to be a big deal. Love takes time to revel in the moment of accomplishment and looks for reasons to recognize the good in others. For example completed projects, anniversaries, and birthdays are celebrated as a team. Furthermore, a sure remedy for envy is giving. Love gives sincere compliments, money, credit, time, and it gives the benefit of the doubt. Love's generosity deflates envy's influence. Lastly, wish well those who have done well and be grateful to God for their good fortune. A mature man or woman is motivated to excellence by those who have achieved. Love those who succeed and recognize their achievements. Promote your protégé, or be glad for the success of your ex-spouse. Learn from, instead of loathing your competition. Love your enemies (Luke 6:35) and pray for them, and love those who forgot you after you helped them succeed. Envy leads to a life of discontentment and sorrow, but love is Christ-centered, content and joyful.

Envy has no place for a person who lavishly loves God and people!

LOVE DOES NOT BRAG

"It does not boast…"   I CORINTHIANS 13:4

Love does not need to brag, because those who boast seek security within themselves. Boasting is for those who need something more than eternity's endorsement. It is bad because it brings the attention down to one person instead of the team. This is a struggle for all of us, because we want our peers to admire our abilities, our accomplishments, and we want them to see us as intelligent and capable. We want to be perceived as spiritually mature, and we want to have a reputation as a man or woman who loves and respects our spouse, children, and family. We want to reveal our résumé and the reason for our current position is because of our hard work and perseverance. Our flesh lobbies for recognition, and even the most committed disciples struggled with taming their egos. James and John wanted to know which side of the throne they would sit when Christ entered into His kingdom (Mark 10:40-42). However, love learns to leave these matters in the Lord's hands by reflecting attention away from itself. It is the ability to tell a story without having to be the lead actor in the plot. Love lifts up others and lowers itself. You are able to bring out the best in people, because you extend to them sincere compliments and affirmation. Love is not all about you, but all about others.

Love seeks ways to give its Savior credit for accomplishments. It is not a flippant, "Praise the Lord," rather it is heartfelt humility and thankfulness. There is communication with body language and words that says without God we would have failed. He answered prayer by giving us wisdom. He opened and closed doors, and transformed hearts. He grew our character, provided and forgave our sin. He blessed us with family and friends who love Him. Love looks long and hard to the Lord and any boasting is limited to Him and to heaven's benefits. James framed well the evil intent of boasting in ourselves; "As it is, you boast and brag. All such boasting is evil" (James 4:16).

Boasting takes what is not deserved, however love gives what is not deserved, grace. Love serves in sincere silence, while its goal is not selfish ambition or self-preservation (Philippians 2:3-4). Its mode of operation is serving, not demanding. Love smothers the need to brag, and it is so caught up with the purpose of reaching out to others that it forgets to "feather its own cap." Love wants to know what you know, by understanding your passions, fears, and dreams. Bragging is all about self; love is all about others. Ironically, boasting is totally unnecessary, because the truth will eventually triumph. You do not have to tell others what they already know or will discover. Love understands this and rests in the revelation of 'who you are' will come out overtime, good or bad. Love trusts God to elevate its standing in His timing. Boasting repels people, but love draws them inward. Therefore, invite people in with your love and lead them to the Lord. He gets the glory and you get the incredible satisfaction of following Him. Above all else, let your love brag on Jesus.

Give God glory and people credit for your success. This is love, to brag on others and to lift up Christ!

F12 LOVE IS NOT PROUD

"...it is not proud."   I Corinthians 13:4

Love is not proud. Indeed, there is no room for pride in a heart of love. Pride is an anchor to love that restrains its rich offering. It prolongs the inability to love by short-circuiting agape's effect. Pride is a precursor to loveless living; it struggles with love because it requires a focus off itself and onto others. Pride is deceptive as it always negotiates for its own benefit. There is a driving force behind pride that is unhealthy and unnecessary. Moreover, it is indiscriminate in its seduction of either gender. Men may be the most susceptible to pride's illusion, but women can be deceived just as well. Eve fell into this trap in her debut with the devil (I Timothy 2:14).

Pride's feeling of superiority slices into the soul like a sharp surgeon's scalpel. It inserts its influence deep and wide. You can be controlled and wired by pride and not even know it. Love longs to have the same status as power-thirsty pride. Love seeks to diffuse pride's time bomb of terror and intimidation. Love outlasts pride if applied humbly and heavily. Love drives pride from a controlling heart and frees it to become trusting. Instead of demanding its own way, love seeks to make those around it successful. Love listens, pride talks. Love forgives, pride resents. Love gives, pride takes. Love apologizes, pride blames. Love understands, pride assumes. Love accepts, pride rejects. Love trusts, pride doubts. Love asks, pride tells. Love leads, pride drives. Love frees up, pride binds up. Love builds up, pride tears down. Love encourages, pride discourages. Love confronts, pride is passive-aggressive. Love is peaceful, pride is fearful. Love clarifies with truth, pride confuses with lies. Love and pride are mutually exclusive. Love dies with pride, but comes alive with humility.

Most importantly, humility is a hot bed of love. It has the opposite effect on love than pride. Humility invites love to take up permanent residence in the human heart. Love covers a multitude of sins (I Peter 4:8), and humility understands love is reserved for everyone. Love forgives even the worst of sinners, as pride struggles in a life of bitterness and resentment, thinking somehow it is paying back the offender. This state of unresolved anger only eats up the one unable to love and forgive. Furthermore, humility positions you to love and to be loved. Humility knows it needs help in the arena of receiving agape. Your humble heart yearns for love from your Lord Jesus Christ. Once you receive the love of your heavenly Father, you can't help but dispense it to others hungry for a hug. As you receive love, you are capable to give love. Therefore, let the Lord love on you and allow others to love you, so you can in turn love. Proud hearts melt under the influence of intense and unconditional love. The calling of Christians is perpetual love, so be guilty of love.

Your love is healing and inviting. Pride exits when humility enters, and then you are in a position to love!

LOVE IS NOT RUDE

"…it is not rude." I CORINTHIANS 13:5

Love rejects rudeness, because it is reserved for the insensitive and the insecure. Rudeness is impolite and disrespectful. Indeed, a rude reply stands ready on the lips of an unlovely life. A rude person uses coarse words that rub you the wrong way. They pride themselves in 'being without airs', but they are insensitive in the timing and the tone of their conversations. They hurt feelings 'at the drop of a hat' and seem to alienate people on purpose. However, love is the light that leads rudeness out of darkness (Romans 2:19).

A rude person is a rascal to work alongside, because you never know when they are going to offend you, or someone else. You lose confidence in rude people because of their volatile nature. You don't want to be embarrassed around one of their outbursts, or social indiscretions, thus you shun their presence. Rude people become loners by default. Over time, no one can tolerate a barrage of irreverence and sarcasm. Even the most accepting and forgiving saints grow weary of rudeness. Indeed, rudeness has no place in a caring culture. Love expunges rudeness like a healthy body does a virus, it uses tough love to escort rudeness out the door of friendship. Because you love them and those they influence, you need to be very direct and matter-of-fact in your communication with a rude person. Direct conversation is the only way they begin to 'get it'. Love takes the time to be very candid and clear with rude people who run rough shod over others. However, be careful not to be rude in dealing with the rude. Do not lower your standards to theirs. Be prayed up and filled up with the Spirit before you encounter the rude with truth (Romans 9:1).

Furthermore without patronizing, love is able to find at least one thing they admire in someone else. Even if a person is full of himself, there lies dormant within him or her some redeeming quality. Love is able to pull out the potential for good that lies deep within a selfish soul, like Barnabas who saw possibilities in Saul (Acts 9:27). Love looks beyond the hard crusty exterior of someone's character, and understands fear may have locked his or her love into solitary confinement. They feel lost, lonely and afraid. Nonetheless, love is able to get past this rude roadblock and inject faith. Faith in God, faith in oneself, and faith in others frees one from rudeness. The Almighty's rude awakening transforms an impolite heart into kindness and grace. When love has its way, rudeness will run away. Love the rude and watch what God can do. Their sarcasm is a smoke screen that hides a lonely, loveless and hurt heart. Rude people are reaching out, but they don't know how. Stay committed to your rude roommate, relative, parent, child, or colleague. Love them to Jesus, and your unconditional love will melt away their iceberg-like insecurities. Pray they will see themselves as Christ sees them, and pray they will love and be loved. Love loves the rude and is not rude.

Therefore, be persistent by staying engaged in unconditional love. Watch the rude walls come down as you bombard them with consistent acts of love.

F14 LOVE IS NOT SELF SEEKING

"…it is not self seeking." I CORINTHIANS 13:5

Love is not self-seeking. It seeks instead the Kingdom of God and His righteousness (Matthew 6:33). Like a heat-seeking missile love is locked onto the warm heart of God. Self is lowered to the bottom shelf and God is elevated to the top shelf. Love understands that it is all about Him; its top priority is not to look out for number one, but to look to the One. Love seeks its Savior Jesus moment by moment for wisdom and direction. Self seeks its own way; love seeks God's way. Self seeks praise; love seeks to praise. Self is fearful of being found out; love is an open book. Self is self absorbed; love is saturated in the Spirit. Self is preoccupied with pleasing people; love is compelled to follow the commands of Christ. The goal of love is self-denial, and to others on behalf of Jesus. Love dies daily to self and comes alive for Christ.

Moreover, the motive to love is not easily managed. There are competing forces that vie for your attention. Therefore default often to prayer. Prayer may be your most potent precluding power against a self-seeking mindset. The very nature of prayer assumes seeking God and not seeking self. Prayer aligns with the Almighty's agenda and is a confession that self is submitting to God's will. Indeed, prayer is your expression of love for the Lord. It is places your affections above self-satisfaction toward what pleases God. It is very difficult, if not impossible, to remain self-seeking when seeking the Lord in prayer, confession, and repentance (Hosea 10:12).

Furthermore, this self-seeking scenario also applies to our horizontal relationships with people. Love seeks to meet the needs of people first, even above their own. Love understands and is not afraid to deny self for the sake of a spouse or friend. Families provide a daily opportunity for selfless living, for example you can selfishly demand your way, or you can lovingly serve others. For instance, it is more fulfilling to seek the welfare of widows and orphans over a self-seeking life of leisure. Use your position and influence for the good of the people, by giving up and/or giving away self-seeking inurnments. This is counter-intuitive and counter-cultural. Someone will probably take advantage of your good will; as a consequence your unselfishness may become a chronic cross you bear. But any cross you bear is a reflection of the cross Christ bore. If it had been about His physical and emotional needs, He would not have been obedient to the cross (Hebrews 12:2-3). The goal of Jesus was to do the will of His heavenly Father (John 17:4). Jesus loved by doing God's will over His will. He subjugated His selfish desires to eternal interests. Since Jesus trusted His heavenly Father, so can you. Your choice to love others may mean death to your own desires, but it will provide life in your relationships. As Jesus said, "The first shall be last, and the last shall be first" (Matthew 19:30, KJV). Love may finish last in man's eyes, but win the gold in God's eyes.

Love seeks its Savior first, and it serves others. Love is a Savior-seeker, not a self-seeker!

LOVE IS SLOW TO ANGER

"...it is not easily angered."   I CORINTHIANS 13:5

Love is slow to anger and it is not easily angered. It is not in a hurry to get angry, because it knows God is at work. Love knows God can handle the irregular person and/or the stressful situation. Most of the time, the best thing love can do is refrain from anger. A calm response does diffuse an angry outburst (Proverbs 15:1). Poverty, AIDS, and terrorism should work us up much more than traffic, forgetful servers, and not getting our way. Indeed, apply anger appropriately and proportionately to the degree of injustice to the underdog. But, love overlooks the silly things that really don't matter that much in the big scheme of things. A friend or family member who is rarely on time is no reason to get angry. Instead, adjust your expectations and build a time buffer into your schedule. Why get angry when a little bit of adjustment remedies the situation? Love adjusts rather than stews in anger; it calms the nerves, while anger boils over your blood pressure. Love filled living is by far a healthier way to live physically and emotionally.

Furthermore, love is able to keep the big picture in mind. It understands that tomorrow is another day and there is no need to stress over this temporary set back. God will work things out in His timing, for He can be trusted. It is much wiser to trust God with your spouse, instead of attempting to whip him or her into shape with your anger. God's discipline is much more thorough and precise. He puts His finger on an attitude or action and won't let up until He is satisfied with the resulting change. Love knows how to trust God. Therefore, pray to God before you get angry. Ask the Lord to increase your love quotient before you lash out in anger. Love understands there are better ways and a better day ahead. However, there are times love sees the need for anger. Your love needs to rise up in anger over the abuses of drugs and alcohol. These are enemies of the state and deceivers of unsuspecting souls that wreck relationships and take lives. Your love can confidently invite anger to rise up and rebuke these artificial enhancers of hope that logically lead to death. Love doesn't stick its head in the sand of isolation and detachment, but engages by offering wise choices and compassionate counseling.

Love is all about solutions to the seduction of sin. Love is angered by sin's control on the soul of a loved one. It drives us to our knees in our own confession of sin, and to our feet to be a part of the solution. Love gets angry at times, but it is anger that is reserved for right occasions. Jesus administered anger at the appropriate time (Mark 3:5, John 2:15). Love understands that anger used selectively and prayerfully has the greatest effect. The passion around love means you are concerned and invested. So aggressively love without "flying off the handle" just to make a statement. Love unconditionally instead of attempting to intimidate through anger. Love for the long haul gets healthy and happy results. Love will anger at times, but only after much prayer and patience. Love more and be angry less.

Above all else, be rich in love and slow to anger (Psalm 145:8). This high road to heaven illustrates the long-suffering love of the Lord!

F16 LOVE FORGIVES

"…it keeps no record of wrongs." I CORINTHIANS 13:5

Love forgives continually and it forgives comprehensively. Forgiveness wipes clean the slate of offense, hence it is freeing for everyone. Indeed, forgiveness was the heartbeat of Jesus. Some of His last words requested forgiveness from God for the ignorant acts of His offenders (Luke 23:34). Christ's greatest act of love was the forgiveness He extended by His voluntary death on the cross (Colossians 2:13-15). Jesus described His own act of love when He said, "Greater love has no one than this, that he lay down his life for his friends" (John 15:14). Jesus was the epitome of love and forgiveness; He owns the trademark.

Furthermore, forgiveness is the fuel for living a life free from the clutter of cutting words or unjust acts. A life without forgiveness is a lonely life locked up in a solitary confinement of sin. Forgiveness flows when you have been authentically and thoroughly forgiven. Half-hearted forgiveness is the destiny of those who have not tasted the tender touch of forgiveness from their heavenly Father. Unless the forgiveness of God has graced your heart and soul, your capacity for forgiveness will be foreign and futile. It is the grace of God and faith in Him that fuels forgiveness in followers of Christ. The job description of Christians is to love with forgiveness because we have been forgiven (Colossians 3:13). Think about the depth and breadth of your forgiveness. Ignorant acts, they are forgiven. Drunkenness, it's forgiven. Lust, it's forgiven. Immorality, it's forgiven. Hate, it's forgiven. Ignoring God, it's forgiven. Unbelief, it's forgiven. Love forgives because it has been forgiven.

Remember where you were BC (before Christ) and reflect on where you would be today without His love and forgiveness. Recall what it was like to be lost and bound up in your sin and celebrate how far God has brought you. Love is extremely grateful for God's goodness and redeeming power. Forgiveness is second nature and somewhat automatic for followers of Jesus who are consumed with Christ's love. They are enamored with God's love for them and others. When you have been forgiven much, you love much (Luke 7:47). Your capacity to love is directly tied to your willingness to receive Christ's forgiveness. Accept the Almighty's forgiveness so you can extend forgiveness. Let go of unforgiveness and replace it with His unconditional love. Love looks for excuses to eliminate hard feelings, as it replaces resentment and bitterness with love and forgiveness. Love by forgiving your family member who may not even know they hurt your heart. Love by forgiving your friend who volitionally violated your confidence. Love by forgiving your father and mother who are preoccupied parents. Love by forgiving your child who is ungrateful and selfish. Love by forgiving yourself for your stupid decisions. Forgiveness forgets the past, engages in the present, and hopes in the future. Extend forgiveness indiscriminately and receive it graciously. Delete any record of wrongs from the hard drive of your heart. Call, write, or initiate a freeing conversation of forgiveness.

Reject the temptation for indignation and humbly receive God's grace instead. Love liberally, by regularly relying on forgiveness. Love forgives!

LOVE AVOIDS EVIL

"Love does not delight in evil…"   I CORINTHIANS 13:6

Love avoids evil, by not delighting in its alluring temptations. Evil is an outcast of love, and it has no room for sin in its circle of wise influences. Evil seeks to destroy love; indeed sin is the 'hatchet man' for hell and it lures in both the rich and the poor. It is relentless in its pursuit to replace love with lust. Sin takes well-meaning workers and grinds them into workaholics. It takes people under extreme pressure and turns them into alcoholics. It portrays drugs as cool, euphoric, and romantic. But love sees beyond the momentary escape, the temporary release, and the artificial high. Love longs for the authentic and the real. Love does not cohabitate with sin because it is counter to the cause of Christ.

Sin is the enemy and love does not sleep with the enemy. Love does not flirt with sinful people or experiment with sin. It is not worth it, not to mention that sin and evil breaks the heart of God. Sin may lure you in with good looks and false promises, but its outcomes are outrageously bad. There is no good that comes from a force that is the antithesis to the Almighty. Satan will continue to unleash his evil strategies until our Savior returns the second time. Then after a period of time, the devil and his evil endeavors will be cast into the lake of fire forever (Revelation 20:10). But for now the role of love is to reject any demonic evil advances.

Jesus Christ is the focus and attraction for those motivated by love. Faith is not lukewarm for men or women who love God, for they fear becoming the saliva of their Savior (Revelation 3:16). Without hot and committed love you are disqualified to engage in Kingdom initiatives. Furthermore, love does not perceive church attendance as a perfunctory exercise out of obligation or guilt. Love sees the church as the Bride of Christ, so it is not cold or dispassionate toward Christ or His church. Committed disciples of Christ can not straddle the fence with one foot flirting with sin and evil. Love is an either/or proposition not a both/and one. You are either for Him or against Him (Luke 11:23). The passion of Jesus followers is to love and obey God and when your focus is full of Him there is no room for evil. The agenda of love is to delight in the Lord, as it is preoccupied and pulsates in pleasing God. Love can't wait to commune with Christ, because its desire is intimacy with Almighty God. Love flushes out evil desires and sinful thoughts as it loves and obeys God. Love has no time for sin because it is caught up with Christ. Therefore, stay away from sin, run from evil, and run toward God. Disengage from people who lean toward evil. Be true to the One who loves you most. Love Him back and watch Him cover your back.

The cross of Christ (His love) overcame evil. So above all else, express your love by delighting in Jesus!

F18 LOVE ENJOYS TRUTH

"...rejoices with the truth."   I Corinthians 13:6

Since love enjoys truth, it seeks it out and rejoices in the ramifications of its application. Love knows truth comes from the Father, and it is His way to lead and direct you in His will. Truth is a tremendous asset to love because it illuminates the way. Truth teaches love where to apply itself, and love teaches truth how to apply itself. Truth delivered in love brings joy; indeed it brings a smile to the face of love. Love is pleased to give and receive the truth. However, love without truth is shallow and sentimental, because it has no lasting affect. Truth without love is harsh and abrasive and is rarely received well. Love and truth need each other. Together they make a dynamite duo.

Jesus modeled this with people, when He lovingly spoke to the woman caught in adultery and her accusers. He confronted the sin of both parties with a spirit of redemption and love (John 8:3-11). Indeed, love uses the truth as a facilitator of faith and obedience to God. It can't wait to understand and apply truth because it knows its positive outcomes. Love knows that truth is a tool of the Lord to grow you up in Him and it gets excited over the possibilities of becoming more like Jesus. Truth has this affect on the character of Christ's followers and is the remedy for ignorance. It is no excuse to remain obliviously to bad habits. For example, truth reveals disrespectful attitudes in wives and replaces them with ones of respect. Truth exposes husbands who lack love and invites them to confession and repentance. Moreover, love takes the time to speak the truth in love (Ephesians 4:15). Many times you can most effectively deliver truth with questions. Help people discover truth without telling them what to do. Love understands this process of honoring others by facilitating the understanding and the application of truth. Questions like, "What do you think you need to do? Do you really want to do this? Why do you want to do this? Have you prayed through this? What does God think? What do your spouse and friends think?" Love loves questions; because they help sincere seekers get to the essence of truth through their own self-discovery.

God used a question from the very beginning when He inquired of Adam where he was in the garden (Genesis 3:9). God knew the answer, but He wanted Adam to think through his curious condition. God loved and respected Adam so much that He gave him the opportunity to reason and reflect on truth. Socrates may have branded the method of question asking, but God invented it. Nonetheless, love leads others into truth because it is a patient lover of truth. Love longs for truth to be exposed and embraced. This is what it means to love God with your mind (Matthew 22:37-39). The wisdom of this world lacks authentic love, but the wisdom of the Lord is pregnant with real life love. Be glad that your parents, friends, and teachers lead you into the discovery of the truth. It is because they love you that they speak the truth. Therefore, love truth and lovingly speak the truth. Love knows Jesus intimately, for He is Truth (John 14:6). Love is a cheerleader for truth, so as a Christ follower cheer on truth.

Romance truth and allow it to court you. Above all else, express your love by embracing truth and rejoicing in its outcomes!

LOVE ALWAYS PROTECTS

"It always protects..."   I CORINTHIANS 13:7

Love always protects. It protects because it loves, and it loves because it protects. Love protects physically, if you love someone you do not want them to suffer bodily harm. You provide for them an environment that protects them from the elements. You shield them from harmful substances that might damage their bodies. You keep them safe by obeying the speed limit and not driving recklessly. You protect them by not endangering their lives with unnecessary risks, if you love someone you protect them.

Wives love to be protected; it makes them feel valued and cherished. They yearn for physical, financial, and emotional protection. Husbands, when you keep your wife safe and sound you speak their love language. Your provision of a dependable automobile and a secure home screams love, moreover because you love your family you protect them from unwise financial exposure. For example, you don't "bet the farm" and place your house at risk. Your temperament might be able to handle high risk, and even thrive on it, but because you love your family you do not personally expose them to "on the edge" endeavors. You do not want them to fear being unprotected within an unstable home environment. Indeed, love protects emotionally because it understands the sensitive nature of others. Emotional protection allows children to grow up well adjusted and loved. Adolescents are vulnerable and tender; they need the loving protection of their parents. Moreover, love prays for the protection of the ones it loves. Pray for their hearts to be protected from the evil one (2 Timothy 3:3) and from unwise influences. Pray for the testimony of those you love to remain unsoiled and fresh in their walk with Christ. Pray for the Holy Spirit to protect well-meaning loved ones from straying away from God's best in relationships. Furthermore, pray for protection from yourself. If not careful you can talk yourself into almost anything. Sometimes you can become your own worst enemy, so pray for protection from yourself and be accountable.

Lastly, think of ways to protect your friends and work associates. Your wisdom and counsel provide loving protection (Proverbs 4:6). A small encouraging word may protect peers from over-commitment. Your colleagues may need your permission to say no, just so they can let go. Do not underestimate your actions for what you do provides protection. Your model of appropriate behavior with the opposite sex protects you, and provides an example of discretion for those you influence (Proverbs 2:11). You love others by creating an environment of protection.

Therefore, pray for God's protection and provide protection. Love always, always protects!

F20 LOVE ALWAYS TRUSTS

"It always trusts..."   I CORINTHIANS 13:7

Love always trusts for it is a staple of love. If you are always suspicious and uncertain, then love is lacking. Love thrives in an environment of trust, but shrivels away in a spirit of distrust. It is very difficult to love without trust for it is a lubricant for love. It calls out love like an engagement invitation. Trust is what it takes for a love relationship to flourish and take root. Therefore, look for the best in someone else and trust them even though they may not have been trustworthy in the past. Love is all about second chances. Of course you must be responsible as a good steward of money and time. Don't blindly believe everything everyone tells you, have instead a process of 'trust and verify'. But on the other hand, love does not 'write someone off' when they fail to meet expectations, or when they blatantly experience failure. Love picks them up and says, 'I will trust you again.' 'I have not given up on you.' 'You are on the team.' 'You are a child of God; therefore you deserve another opportunity to succeed.'

Love is all about making people successful. It trusts others in their success; for example when you love someone you trust them to carry out the plan. Love sees trust when others see distrust. Love sees potential when others see disqualification. Love sees success when others see failure. Love sees a hurting human being when others see someone who is just angry. Love thinks the best, but distrust thinks the worst. Love and trust feed off each other. They propel one another to greater heights. Love always trusts. This is especially true with Almighty God; love trusts God for He is trustworthy. His track record of trustworthiness is without blemish. He can be trusted. If you love Him, you will trust Him. Your affection and love are meant to originate in heaven not on earth. Love leans on and listens to the Lord because it trusts the Lord (Deuteronomy 30:25).

So the goal is to fall more deeply in love with God. Go deeper with God, and you will become more and more infatuated with Him and His ways. John explains it well, "And so we know and rely on the love God has for us. God is love. Whoever lives in love lives in God, and God in him" (I John 4:16). Indeed, His love relationship is based on trust. God is your lover. He is a lover of your mind, soul, body, and emotions. You can trust Him to love you authentically and unconditionally. He has no inhibitions in His love toward you, for His intimacy is uninhibited. Therefore, you love better when you regularly receive the love of God, because He loves you, you love better and because you love, you trust. Sad is the soul that has not learned the secret of loving by trusting. The conditional lover is always looking over their shoulder in distrust. Cynicism creates a cold heart. However, your heavenly Father wants to flood your heart with love. Trust Him with this. Weak is the man or woman who does not love and trust God. Your trust in God accelerates in direct proportion to your intimacy with Jesus. Therefore, love the Lord long and hard. Hug heaven often and watch your trust increase.

People come back to where they know they are loved. Love always trusts!

LOVE ALWAYS HOPES

"It always hopes..."   I CORINTHIANS 13:7

Love always hopes; it hopes for the best and is prepared for the worst. It is hopeful because its hope is in the Lord. As the old hymn proclaims, 'Our hope is built on nothing less than Jesus Christ and His righteousness'. When we love God we also hope in Him, because we are sure of His promises that transcend hope to provide assurance, like 'I will never leave you or forsake you' (Hebrews 13:5b, KJV). Moreover, faith helps us be sure of what we hope for, He says in Hebrews 1:1, 'Now faith is being sure of what we hope for and certain of what we do not see.' Faith, hope and love are all first cousins; they compliment each other and support one another.

Love hopes because it knows the end of the story, for heaven is its destiny. It bridles its emotions to not fear, because love casts out fear (I John 4:18, KJV). Hope conquers death and fear, because Jesus has gone before us and done the same (Acts 2:23-24). Therefore, you can be hopeful because you get to hang out in heaven with your Lord and Savior Jesus. But there is something just as big that you can hope for in real time. You can hope that others you love will place their faith in Jesus Christ. You know it is God's will for them to be saved from their sin (2Peter 3:9), but your part is not to get them saved, but to love them to the Lord. Some plant and some water, but it is God that makes faith grow (I Corinthians 3:6). It is the Lord that convicts and draws people unto Himself. But be hopeful, if God can save us, He can save anybody. Do not give up on praying for and loving on your family and friends, because love always hopes.

Love always hopes, especially when you are drowning in adversity. You may feel like you can only come up for air one more time. The undertow of your circumstances may be sucking you out into the sea of despair. Your emotional energy may be over-spent and close to bankruptcy. Your marriage seems hopeless, but you are still called to love. Your health has ravaged hope, but you are still called to love. A relationship may be hopeless, but you are still called to love. Your finances are struggling to be hopeful, but you are still called to love. Hopelessness has high jacked your work, but He still calls you to love. Love in spite of your sorry situation and the feelings of hope will catch. You do not have to love the situation, but you can still love those around you. You can love the Lord and you can love yourself. It is okay to not like what you are going through right now, but still love. Love, because love leads to hope and drops despair. Hope follows love, like ducklings follow their mother. Love is a creator of hope. Therefore, anticipate the outcomes of aligning with Almighty God's agenda.

Love Him and love others, especially love when you don't feel like loving. Be hopeful, for love always hopes!

F22 LOVE ALWAYS PERSEVERES

"It always perseveres…"   I CORINTHIANS 13:7

Love always perseveres. It does not give up. This is why the love commitment of husbands and wives is 'till death do we part. This is the assurance that accompanies love, for it is loyal in the face of hard times. "I don't love you anymore" is not an option for couples committed to Christ. Love always perseveres. It perseveres through problems. It perseveres through misunderstandings. It perseveres though uncertainty. It perseveres through 'knock down, drag out' arguments. It perseveres through persecution. It perseveres through divorce. It perseveres through abandonment. It perseveres through a lawsuit. It perseveres through being fired. Love becomes better instead of bitter when experiencing a raw deal, but God's grace and love provides you the lasting ability for extraordinary love. Indeed, love is lethargic if your heavenly Father does not personally love you. It is sluggish in its application to others, if you are not daily loved by the Lord. You can't be an unconditional lover, if you don't receive the unconditional love of Jesus. Therefore, love always perseveres in the process of being loved and extending love.

This is why a parent perseveres in their love for their child. They can only give up on loving their loved one when their heavenly Father gives up on loving them. Parents persevere with their children, because they love their children. Even through the hurt, rejection, selfishness, financial irresponsibility, and anger, love still stands. Love will not stand down to the devil's strongholds in a young person's mind and heart. Moreover, love perseveres in reminding them of the truth. Remind your children that their identity is in Christ. Your child is accepted in the beloved (Ephesians 1:6); remind them of this. Your child is forgiven by you and God; remind them of this. Your child is uniquely gifted by God; remind them of this. Love perseveres in reminding and revealing truth to those it loves. Pray the eyes of your child's heart will see and understand the truth of who they are from God's perspective. They are longing for love, so be the lead lover in their life.

Lastly, persevere in your love for your parents. Parents can be distant and disinterested, but still love them. To some degree they may still be licking the wounds of their past hurts and disappointments. They need love as much or more as anyone else. Love your mom and dad while they are still alive. One day they will not be around to love, so leave all your love for your parents in this life. You plan for no regrets when you aggressively love them now. They may have chronically hurt you, but still love them. They may not love back, but still love them. They may be caught up in their own cares, but still love them. Love knows better, so it perseveres beyond bitterness and betrayal. Lastly, you lose when the flames of love are extinguished by sheer exhaustion. You may need to rest, receive, and be rejuvenated by the loving relationship of your friend Jesus. Slow down and be loved; persevere in your love and one day you will be proud you did.

It is an invaluable investment, because love leaves no regrets. It always perseveres!

LOVE NEVER FAILS

"Love never fails…"   I CORINTHIANS 13:8

Love never fails, because you are successful when you love. Failure is not an option for love; because you cannot not succeed. Success is guaranteed with love, though it may seem like you are losing when love is not getting the desired results. You could have labored in love with someone for a long period of time, and they still seem unfazed by your unconditional agape. However, you are still successful; you get an "A" for your consistent efforts to love. Some may describe your scenario as unsuccessful, but you know better. You know if you have been obedient to love, the results are in God's hands (Deuteronomy 30:16). He is the one who can soften a hardened heart, and He is the one who can change a person's mind. Love never fails because Almighty God is its author.

Your part is to love and His part is to draw people to Himself (Jeremiah 31:3). Indeed, love in your leadership and you are successful. Love in your marriage and you are successful. Love in your friendships and you are successful. Love in your speech and behavior, and you are a roaring success. Unfortunately, a person can have a rich net worth, but a character that lacks love. If they fail to love, they fail. Furthermore, your increase in resources provides a variety of options to express your love. Make it a goal to be as successful in your loving, as you are in your business or career. Long to out love your peers and you will experience extraordinary outcomes. The Bible paints a beautiful picture of love as a matter of obedience, "Now that you have purified yourselves by obeying the truth so that you have sincere love for your brothers, love one another deeply, from the heart" (I Peter 1:22). This is why moms are celebrities of love; they love long and they love hard. Moms are unselfish lovers, because they love when no one is looking… in the middle of the night they minister to their little ones. Your motherly love is a badge of honor. Moms are the unsung heroes of unselfish love.

You may feel like a failure with your children, because parenting is hard. It is hard to teach, train, and lead your children to obey God, and sometimes it is hard to love them. You want to pull out the hair from their sweet little scalps, instead of planting a loving kiss on their fragile forehead. Indeed, love can be illusive during the pains of parenting. Furthermore, in parenting, it is hard to measure your effectiveness. It may be that your child is well into adulthood, before you really know their commitment to God. But even in your parental frustrations, you still love your child. You never stop loving them, and because you never stop loving them you do not fail. You are successful when you love by imparting wisdom (Proverbs 4:6). Indeed, there are lots of ways you can fail. You can fail in your job. You can fail in your finances. You can fail in school. You can fail to follow up. But, you can never fail when you love. It may mean resigning from a responsibility so that you have more margin for love. By faith, place yourself in a better position to love more robustly. Be motivated to love with an eternal motivation.

● Heaven gives you high marks for your unconditional love, so stay enrolled in the school of love and graduate when you get to glory. Lovers succeed for love never fails! ●

F24 LOVE IS THE GREATEST

"And now these three remain: faith, hope and love. But the greatest of these is love."
I CORINTHIANS 13:13

Why is love the greatest out of three worthy contenders? It is the greatest because it is God, for He is love (I John 4:8). The apex of God's attributes is love; this is why you go to God first for love. He is the lover of your soul, and the love of God way exceeds earth's limited love. This is the reason you look to Jesus as the supreme example of how to love. He says the two greatest commands hinge on love (Matthew 22:37-39). Love is God's 'gold standard', as it rises above other compelling character traits like faith and hope. Love is a theme that covers your character, seasons your service for Christ and flavors your faith. It gives off a sweet aroma through trust and gives gusto to grace. Love adds hotness to hope, pungency to patience, and spice to selflessness. It portrays brilliant Technicolor to life, in contrast to our otherwise bland black-and-white loveless living. You can serve, provide for your families, cook a meal, feed the poor, attend church and even worship, but if these lack love, you lose. You lose the blessing of God, and lose heaven's reward because your motivation was not for your Master Jesus Christ. Love is the greatest because it aligns your heart with Almighty God and is not lacking.

• You are the greatest when you love, because it draws attention to Jesus. Hands down, heaven is the happiest over your unconditional and relentless love. Furthermore, meditate on love, as you rise in the morning, work during the day and eat dinner at night with your family. Your spouse longs to be loved, this is their greatest need from you. So, love them lavishly in how they want to be loved. Think often on love and your actions will begin to follow your thoughts. What drives you? Is it love? Make love your motivation and your happiness will spill over on to others. Love jump-starts joy, it prolongs peace; it decreases pride and increases humility. Therefore, love long and hard, love unbiased and unencumbered, love early and love late. Love the rich, the poor and everyone in between. Love during the good times and the bad. Love the deserving and undeserving. Linger long in your love and you will be a lasting influence for the Lord. •

Lastly, great love takes on different forms. Your situation may require tough love, full of accountability and action. Or, your friend may be crying out for tender love that reeks with encouragement and lots of listening. Pray for God's wisdom and discernment on how to love and then trust Him with its application. Your greatest contribution to mankind is love on behalf of the Lord Jesus Christ. Your greatest gift to God and others is love. Because He loved you first, you can love (I John 4:19). God is great and He makes you great with love. You are your greatest when you get and give love.

Therefore, by the grace of God seek to be a great lover. Love is the greatest in God's eyes!

HONOR MARRIAGE

"Marriage should be honored by all, and the marriage bed kept pure,
for God will judge the adulterer and all the sexual immoral." HEBREWS 13:4

Marriage is a sacred institution of God, and it is not to be taken lightly or treated with disrespect. It is easier in most cases to get a marriage license than a driver's license, but this does not give you a license to live a reckless marriage. To honor marriage means there is an understanding of commitment and a preparation for its success. Marriage requires much more than love. It is not a convenient way to guarantee sex or risks divorce when you get tired of one another, or don't love one another. To honor marriage is to make a lifetime dedication to one person. Just as Jesus is committed and faithful to his bride the church for eternity (Revelation 19:7), so is your marriage commitment.

Moreover, keep your marriage bed pure. You honor marriage when you keep the Lord's definition of a man and a woman exclusively devoted and in love with each other, under the submission of Almighty God. Do not chase after a fantasy of sexual perfection with someone other than your spouse. Sex outside of marriage is wrong and breaks the heart of God, and it crushes the spirit of your spouse. It is not a casual infraction for its effects are for a lifetime. However, leave it to God and a scriptural process on how and when to judge the adulterer. Hold back your rocks of verbal assault and forgive (John 8:3-11). Most importantly, prevent unfaithfulness by keeping your marriage bed pure and honorable by falling deeper and deeper in love with the man or woman God has given you.

Lastly create boundaries together, for example commit to one another that divorce is not an option. This fidelity to your mate starves fear, intimidation and manipulation. Furthermore, agree to never be alone with someone of the opposite sex. This is a way to honor each other and find yourselves in a compromising situation, or at the very least avoid the appearance of evil. A marriage discipline of fidelity takes effort, definition, and accountability. Yes, you trust your wife or husband, but do not be naive to think that temptation, Satan and other lonely souls are not out to snare your spouse (Proverbs 7:10-23). Be on the offensive by planning purity. One way to plan purity is to honor your spouse with your words. Disappointing and dissatisfying words about your husband or wife, which are shared indiscreetly with the opposite sex, will fuel the fires of unfaithfulness. Unfaithfulness starts with words, is furthered by a disrespectful attitude, and is executed by actions facilitated over a meal or a walk with a "friend." Therefore, remain true to your marriage vows and your marriage mate by exercising patience and understanding.

Be smart and create a robust love life, for a satisfying sex life at home is a strong preventative to adultery outside the home. Above all else, honor your marriage by first honoring God!

F26 SUCCESSFUL MARRIAGES

"For this reason a man will leave his father and mother and be united to his wife, and the two will become one flesh." EPHESIANS 5:31

Successful marriages are a result of a series of mistakes, and many times marriage lessons are learned by trial and error, or "trial and terror" as some husbands and wives have experienced. Indeed, successful marriages just don't happen by chance, they are not created like a clock, to be wound up and never given attention. You become one flesh in marriage, but practically it takes a lifetime of hard work, forgiveness, love and respect to enjoy oneness. One flesh implies unity of purpose. It is alignment around beliefs and behavior, and if this is void in marriage you become vulnerable to misplaced expectations and perpetual misery. Marriage requires at least as much work as work.

Hard work is a necessity for successful marriages. This seems obvious, but we tend to drift toward being spousal sluggards when we become intoxicated by apathy. However, hard work is the fuel that keeps a marriage going forward. We see the fruit of hard work in our career and raising children, as it produces satisfaction and significance. But these results come from many hours of planning, communicating, training and teaching. Indeed, your marriage is a direct result of the amount of effort you have expended. Don't expect a harvest of marriage success if the seeds of forgiveness, love and respect have not been planted in the soil of humility and trust. Furthermore, the weeds of busyness have to be intentionally pulled out, before they choke out your love and friendship with your spouse. Busyness is the enemy of best marriages, so labor toward a marriage with much margin. Robust marriages take time and trust.

Lastly, successful marriage is laced with forgiveness, love and respect. Forgiveness in marriage means you take the time to say, "I was wrong" and "I am sorry," and it means you take responsibility to confess your anger and selfishness. Moreover, it is the ability to not hold a grudge. God like forgiveness forgives even before the offense has been committed (Colossians 3:13). It accepts apologies and does not bring up past hurts as a club of resentment. Forgiveness is the 'footers' in the foundation of a successful marriage. Above all else, successful marriages are made up of unconditional love and radical respect. No wife has ever complained of too much love, or a husband of an over-abundance of respect. Love is emotional, physical and volitional. Husbands, you are to love sensitively, intimately and willfully (Ephesians 5:25). Wives respect your husband out of love and loyalty. Make sure he knows you are with him and for him no matter what. Respect is void of fear, so you trust your husband because he is accountable to God. Furthermore, marriage is your laboratory for Christianity, because you learn to live for the Lord, by learning to live for each other. You die to yourselves and come alive to each other. Marriage is your mirror of obedience to Jesus.

Successful marriages reflect your oneness with your Savior. Be a marriage success as God defines success!

PRAYING HUSBAND

"Isaac prayed to the Lord on behalf of his wife, because she was barren.
The Lord answered his prayer, and his wife Rebekah became pregnant." GENESIS 25:21

A praying husband appeals to the Lord for the sake of his wife. He bombards heaven on behalf of his bride with big things like having babies, and he is consistent in praying for his wife everyday for important matters like peace and security. Prayer is one of God's select weapons, which a husband can wield in defense of his woman. God has called you to be the spiritual warrior of your home and prayer is your first line of defense. If prayer is compromised then you have no air support from your heavenly Father. Without prayer covering your home and wife, you and your family are open to blistering assaults from the devil and his demons, so pray for God's hedge of protection (Job 1:10). The strategy of the stealth enemy is to keep you busy with only a token of prayer on your breath. An overly active man is probably a prayerless man. A man consumed in his own deal is probably a prayerless man. A man absorbed in pride is probably a prayerless man. A man who serves a small God is probably a prayerless man. A man angry at his wife is probably a prayerless man. A husband whose prayers are hindered, knows he needs to pray for his wife, but doesn't is a man powerless as spiritual leader (I Peter 3:7).

Prayer for your wife leads you to forgive your wife, prayer for your wife leads you to love your wife, and prayer for your wife leads to the abundant life. You cannot pray for your wife and stay mad at your wife. You cannot pray for your wife and not want to hang out with your wife, for prayer facilitates intimacy. Prayer changes your heart and hers. Therefore, agree together for a time apart just to pray (I Corinthians 7:5), for prayer unleashes the resources and the blessings of God. Satan shutters at the thought of a praying husband. A husband will win the battle of leading his family if he fights the enemy on his knees. It is a posture of desperation for God that brings victory and reconciliation. Husbands, prayer is your most potent marriage resource.

Therefore, get on your knees and do not get up until you have persevered in prayer for your helpmate, courageously cry out to God on her behalf. Pray for her inner beauty to be reflected in her gorgeous countenance. Pray for her to feel God's love and security. Pray for her to feel your love, support, and respect. Pray for her to be at peace with God, herself, and you. Pray for her to forgive herself and to love herself. Pray for her to have wisdom and discernment as a wife and a mom. Pray for her to love God and hate sin. As you pray, see her as God sees her. She is a child of God and in Christ she is holy and acceptable. Thank God for your wife and thank Him for her love for you. Thank Him for her unselfish service. Thank Him that she puts up with your idiosyncrasies. Pray for your wife that she will receive spiritual nourishment from God's Word, and spiritual leadership from you. Pray for her daily and deliberately. Pray for her when you are happy and pray for her when you are sad.

However hang on, because as you pray neither of you will ever be the same. Prayer for your wife is profitable; it solicits heaven on her behalf!

F28 RISK AND REWARD

"And Caleb said, 'I will give my daughter Acsah in marriage to the man who attacks and captures Kiriath Sepher.' Othniel son of Kenaz, Caleb's younger brother, took it; so Caleb gave his daughter Acsah to him in marriage." JUDGES 1:12-13

Risk many times precedes reward and reward may follow risk. Indeed, war is risky, because you endanger your life and limb. The stakes are high. However, the reward of war is life, liberty, and the pursuit of happiness. The victor enjoys the spoils of war, while those humiliated in defeat suffer loss. Indeed, marriage is risky, because it entails the co-mingling of money, time, trust and loyalty. What's yours becomes hers and what's hers becomes yours. You become one flesh, for it is a relationship of oneness (Genesis 2:24). But the rewards of marriage are love, joy, peace, companionship, sex, children, and spiritual/emotional maturity to name a few. The many risks of marriage are overshadowed by the mammoth rewards it hands out to the husband and to the wife.

Business and ministry are risky undertakings. You have prayed about an idea and now you are on the precipice of launching your start-up enterprise. You have invested a tremendous amount of sweat equity and financial resources. Your spouse has been extremely patient, but now you are at the point of no return. The stakes are high; you may lose a ton, or you may gain a lot. There is a risk of failure, which means your confidence may crater and your reputation may reel from your inability to deliver. But, the rewards are the sense of accomplishment and the ability to build an enterprise defined by a Christ-centered culture. Like David, your model of risk-taking may inspire others to greater vision (I Chronicles 11:19). You have the reward of positioning yourself to invest in and influence Kingdom endeavors. Keep this your goal, regardless of whether you fail or succeed. Success will always be accompanied by mini failures. So, stay focused on God and obedient to His calling. Risk and reward are kept in a right perspective through prayer. God will lead you by His Holy Spirit, because these initiatives come from a divine directive. Therefore, there is no need to take unnecessary risks. Be patient and God will lead you to just the right opportunities, at just the right time.

Over a lifetime there are limited God-ordained opportunities that require risk. Therefore, allow the Almighty to guide you through the risky terrain of life, and make sure you avoid shortcuts by waiting on Him. Pay the price of patience, and seize the moment only when your faith, His Word, and godly counsel validate your direction. Persevere in the process, because God may ask you to do things that seem larger than life. He has prepared your way with people and resources, so follow hard after Him, and what may seem risky to others will be peaceful to you. When you draft off the wake of Holy Spirit directives, you are positioned for rewards. However, for some the rewards remain dormant until death. Your risk may be living an obscure and obedient life to Christ, with only the joy of remaining faithful. Indeed, the reward of knowing and obeying Him is eternal and enough. The risk is rejection from people, but the reward is acceptance in Him.

What a privilege to honor, serve, love, and worship Jesus. And then your greatest reward is when you see Him face-to-face and hear, "Well done" (Matthew 25:23)!

PARENTAL GIFT

"Marry and have sons and daughters; find wives for your sons and give your daughters in marriage, so that they too may have sons and daughters. Increase in number there; do not decrease." JEREMIAH 29:6

For a parent it is hard to give away a child in marriage. In marriage you do gain a son or daughter, but you still feel like you are losing something. For some parents it is much easier to give away time and money than to give away a child in marriage. Even when you know in your heart it is absolutely God's will, it is still difficult. However, this is another opportunity to point you back to God, for His timing is impeccable. Yet it still may be hard to accept that marriage for your child is imminent. You may reflect, "This soon-to-be married adult child can't already be ready for marriage." It seems like yesterday when he or she was still in diapers, puttering around and bumping into things as they learned to walk. Walking led to talking; talking led to reading; reading led to writing; and writing led to graduation. She or he graduated from kindergarten, middle school, high school, and college. You were there for their first step, their first day of school, their first sleep-over, their first sickness, their first school play, their first athletic event, their first date, and hopefully, by God's grace, their first and only marriage.

It is hard to entrust your baby with someone whom you have known for only a minimal amount of time. Even if this new in-law loves God, it is still difficult. You know in your heart this person is the one, and you know they are meant for each other. You know their character and maturity is robust and real. This is the right relationship, in the right way, for the right time. It is right. Now as the parent, you have to loosen your grip and let go. This is similar to the process you have gone through in each of your child's transitions through life. During the good or bad stages, you hold them with an open hand and trust God with their life. This is a transition of trust for you, as you "let them leave so they can cleave" (Mark 10:7).

God can be trusted with your adult child; like you have trusted Him in all other areas of your life. Your child is not exempted from this total trust. He will do a much better job of watching over them than you ever could with your limited time and wisdom. His influence is far-reaching, and its expanse is much broader and deeper than a parent ripe with the truest of character. This is the role of our heavenly Father, as He takes care of your children, because they are His children. It is reassuring to know you co-parent with God to pull off this impossible task of parenting. You cannot do it by yourself, but with your heavenly Father all things are possible. He is an expert in managing the process of your children "leaving and cleaving." Your part is to pray and be a good parent. Indeed it is time for celebration. God's will is on display through this Christ-ordained marriage for He has orchestrated a beautiful symphony of lives. Their harmony of love is uplifting and inspiring. Listen to the applause of heaven. As parents, you have done well and you can be proud.

You have gained a son or daughter. Above all else, your heavenly Father is smiling and well-pleased (Matthew 3:17)!

CHANGE MANAGEMENT

> "Therefore, this is what the Lord says: 'I will return to Jerusalem with mercy, and there my house will be rebuilt. And the measuring line will be stretched out over Jerusalem,' declares the Lord Almighty." ZECHARIAH 1:16

Change will manage you or you will manage change, and sometimes a little of both takes place. Change is inevitable. It may come from external forces out of your control, or internal initiatives under your leadership. So, be careful not to fight change for it will bloody your stubborn nose of resistance. Like the flow of a river, enjoy following the current and do not exhaust yourself by fighting to go upstream. Embrace change and enjoy its benefits, for it comes sooner or later. Those who accept change use it wisely and esteem its value. Those who reject change die a slow death of denial. Moreover, team members need a wise manager who can frame change as a positive reality and not a negative nuisance. Leaders need to take responsibility during change to negotiate its transitional turns. Like hugging a steep and curvy road without the benefit of guardrails, the leader needs to drive change carefully and prayerfully. The same can be said about the change your home life can expect. Prepare your family for change, for it is coming, so enjoy today in anticipation of tomorrow. Prepare them for the change from home to school, and train them in how to transition from a single adult into a married adult. Be patient when your husband goes through a change in careers and when your wife goes through the 'change'. Your home is a hot bed of change, so be aware and prepare.

Keep "top of mind" that God is Lord over change, as the sands of time flow through His fingers. Unwillingness to change may mean the fear of God is absent (Psalm 55:19). Christ is the ultimate change agent, and you can trust that He manages change for His purposes (Proverbs 21:1), so don't lose sight of the Lord's leading. Lean heavily on the Lord during these changing times. Furthermore, there is a process that facilitates an understanding of change. Individuals and organizations digest change better when educated around the sequence of events that occur during the change cycle. Many times something has to die. An old way of doing things may need to be put to rest. At the beginning of change there is an invitation to bury 'out of date' expectations and methods. Also, fears need to be addressed at the outset of change. People are afraid of what they might lose: jobs, status, pay or influence to name a few.

The next stage of change is a process of gathering new information, while defining a structure that facilitates clear communication and effective implementation. This is where managers of change need a ton of patience and empowerment. This time of preparation for change needs to be driven by the team, not controlled by the leader. The leader needs to participate in collaboration with the various teams, but trust them with the crafting and execution of the plan. Change will be remiss of effective results if the manager tries to manipulate all the outcomes. However, if managed well everyone celebrates over the fruit of successful change. Above all else, never lose the spirit and wisdom of Christ during the shifting courses of change. His values, principles, and purposes never change, so embrace the never-changing Christ throughout the process of change (Colossians 2:8). Laugh a lot at yourself and with others, because humor lubricates the hinges of change.

Change is inevitable and Christ creates change. Therefore, walk with Christ through transitions and you will be changed all for the better!

M2 SEDUCTIVE SHORTCUTS

"When Pharaoh let the people go, God did not lead them on the road through the Philistine country, though that was shorter. For God said, 'If they face war, they might change their minds and return to Egypt.' So God led the people around the desert road toward the Red Sea. The Israelites went up out of Egypt armed for battle."   EXODUS 13:17-18

Shortcuts are seductive, because they are appealing and inviting. Shortcuts caress our pride, stroke our ego and garner immediate gratification. We sometimes seek short cuts while driving, in preparation for school exams, career advancement, marriage maturity, parenting skills, financial success, and spiritual development. Shortcuts are attractive to your clever side, because you think that with enough ingenuity and smarts you can bypass the normal rite of passage. However, the downside of shortcuts is their deception for a faster way may be short circuiting God's best. Just because it is easier does not qualify it as the will of God. In fact, ease of execution may be evidence against God's will; instead a season of suffering may be His plan (1 Peter 4:19).

So do not depend on circumstances alone as your barometer of where God is leading you. You may feel pressure from people, pride, politics or finances to take the most expedient route. But be careful because expedience can be an excuse for the impatient and the distrusting. If you miss this opportunity, there will be others for God is much bigger than this one deal. Do not underestimate His wisdom in taking you through this laborious and sometimes painful process. It will be worth the wait, because it is the process that is preparing you for His next steps. If you rush through the process, you may miss God's best.

Many times He is unconventional in His approach. This is the nature of God for He will not be hemmed in or backed into a corner. Cut God some slack by giving Him the latitude to lead you however and wherever He desires. Just because a friend of yours went down a similar road does not mean you should follow. God's will for you may be just the opposite. One thing is for sure; He will get the glory when you are patient to follow Him in trust and obedience. God's glory is your goal (1 Corinthians 10:31).

The glory of God is your objective, so keep God's glory as your litmus test and your other initiatives will take care of themselves. The short cut is tempting, but it may be more complicated than you can comprehend for now. Its complexity will certainly compound if you have to back track from the short cut and start all over again. It is much better to wait and do this once and for all. There will certainly be adjustments along the way, but have faith in God that He is facilitating His will, even if some of your questions still remain unanswered. He has got your back, even though the enemy may be breathing down your neck and whispering words of doubt. God is in control. It is much better to take the longer route with God, than the shorter one without Him.

Travel instead on the proven path of Providence. Indeed, faith in Christ rejects seductive shortcuts!

TIES THAT BIND

"I led them with cords of human kindness, with ties of love;
I lifted the yoke from their neck and bent down to feed them."
HOSEA 11:4

You were not created to bear your burdens alone. God is there to come alongside you and lift your burdens with His love and kindness. Burdens borne alone will break your spirit and crush your confidence. It is the compassion of Christ that lifts you to new levels of love and assurance. Do not hide your burdens in the depths of your dark side, for if you stuff hurt into the back of your mind it will slowly seep back out in unhealthy behaviors. Praise your Savior for He daily bears your burdens (Psalm 68:19).

Someone may have let you down in a big way, because you loved them much, they have disappointed you greatly. You love large, but they rarely reciprocate back the same degree of love and kindness. This subtle, and sometimes not so subtle, rejection has grown into a big time burden. You tried to ignore its effect on your heart, but overtime your heart has become calloused. Ironically, you are becoming like the one who has inflicted the harm. This burden of hurt will crush you if you do not come to terms with its raw reality. Service for your Savior and busyness in Kingdom activities will not erase its effect. This is first and foremost between you and your heavenly Father. Go to Him and lay your burdens at His feet. Allow Him to tie up and bind your broken heart with His kindness, love, and forgiveness. He alone can bear this burden. No need to patronize the provider of this pain, or reject the one who has resisted your love. Instead, take it to the Lord and trust Him to bear this burden on your behalf. His love and kindness ablate attitudes birthed out of dire dysfunction, so focus on your heavenly Father's soul food.

Manna from heaven is full of nourishment for your soul. His Word is warm and moist bread for your life. His answered prayers are cool, refreshing living water that results in mature faith and garners hope for your heart. Let the Lord nourish your needy self with eternal nutrients. He will nurse your hurt heart back to health (Matthew 13:15). A healthy heart, made whole by its Maker, is in a position of strength to do the same for friends. He bears your burden, so you can be a burden bearer for another (Galatians 6:2).

Make it a point to ask others about their tears and trials. Your kindness and love can be the tie that binds someone's sick condition of despair into one of hope and encouragement. Look for a way to bear a brother or sisters burden in prayer, for it positions you to leverage kindness and love on behalf of the Lord. Prayer is extremely efficient and effective, so be a channel of Christ's love and kindness by saying a simple prayer. The Holy Spirit is the glue of grace, so pray for His regular and robust filling. Love and kindness are evidence that you are overflowing with the Spirit's influence. So, share your burdens with your heavenly Father, and those you can trust.

Then bear the burdens of other people in the faith. These are the ties that bind and lift you to live!

M4 BE GLAD

"Be glad, O people of Zion, rejoice in the Lord your God, for he has given you the autumn rains in righteousness. He sends you abundant showers, both autumn and spring rains, as before." JOEL 2:23

The follower of Jesus cannot remain sad. Yes, there are seasons of sadness, but you are not meant to stay there, as you walk with your Savior through gloomy times. Indeed, be grateful to God for little things like rain, the warmth of the sun, and the cool of the night. God Almighty is the author of all of these and He is forever creating good things for His children: relationships, laughter, a full stomach, a good night's rest, healthy children, a free nation, and the opportunity to share all of our gifts from God. His blessings solicit smiles on the face of His children. Giving gladness is a vital role of your heavenly Father; even in the middle of severe sadness, He dispenses gladness.

The gladness of God is uncanny in its ability to keep you poised with a peaceful perspective. People and circumstances can shell out sadness, while Christ's compassion brings gladness. Therefore, go to God often for the gift of gladness. Receive His roaring laughter (Job 8:21), as a reminder not to take ourselves, others, or situations too seriously. Fight sadness with gladness, so when you are tempted to torture your mind with sad thoughts, choose instead to fill it with glad memories of good things. Yes, pain is ever-present; emotional pain may emerge often, your physical pain may be perpetual and financial pain could be flirting with your peace of mind, or relational pain may be assaulting you with rejection. Pain is a part of life, but do not allow pain to pin you to the mat of victimized living. Pain will try to steal your gladness and replace it with sadness. It will show up on your face in a scowl and/or a jaw that juts out. Be glad instead and allow the calm of Christ to caress your countenance. Slow down and let your trust in the Lord massage your mind. Trust in Christ brings you glad tidings.

This is why we worship God in place of the things of this world. Anything outside of the Lord has the potential to let you down. Money will fall short and even contribute to sadness. Children can break your heart and your spouse will make you sad. Friends will fail you and circumstances can crush your motivation to care. But Christ followers have a heavenly Father that gives gladness in the middle of sadness. Abandonment to the Almighty is fertile ground for a growing faith and a glad face. You cannot remain sad if you are fully abandoned. Unconditional surrender to your Savior solicits gladness and a triumphal spirit comes from being in Christ (2 Corinthians 2:14). Peace and contentment are first cousins and the fruit of a glad attitude. Anybody can live a chronically sad life, but those who look to their Savior Jesus cannot help but be glad. He is the giver of all good things that satisfy (Psalm 103:5). Therefore, be glad for the grace of God that gushes from heaven like a generous geyser. See gladness as a result of you resting in the presence of God and engaging with a community of Christ followers.

Allow grace to govern your thinking, because gladness grows in a heart overflowing with gratitude for God's grace and all His good gifts!

BAD TO WORSE

"It will be as though a man fled from a lion only to meet a bear, as though
he entered his house and rested his hand on the wall only to have a snake bite him."
AMOS 5:19

Sometimes things have to get worse before they get better. Your finances, relationships, job and health may all have to get worse before they get better. This is not fun, but it is reality. The wheels of God's will are in motion and this is part of the process, but a better day is coming. Adversity can be agonizing, but it does not have to be forever. Indeed, it is hard to follow hard after God when times are hard. You want to take matters into your own hands and fix them, but you can't do it alone. You need God and you need others. Use this time of downward spiral and look up to your Savior Jesus, let go and allow Him to love on you. Search your character and see what needs to change for the better. It is during this time of crumbling circumstances that dependence on Christ needs to be front and center. Yes, fear may be pursuing you like an uncaged lion. In your mind, there is a lion behind you and a bear in front of you. There is nowhere to turn; it seems you have used up all of your options. Your home was a sanctuary of peace, but now its serpents of insecurity attack you. People are more patient when things are going well, for they overlook indiscretions or idiosyncrasies during the good times. But now things are in the process of going from bad to worse. People's patience is wearing thin, and they are looking for a scapegoat, so surrender to your Savior during this surreal time.

Trust God and take responsibility, by not running from your role as leader. Get down on your knees in prayer and then get up and lead on in the power of the Holy Spirit. Confess and repent of your sin and then rise with a radical faith that will see you through. Now is the time to increase your dependence on God and decrease your need for clever tactics. Use this transition from bad to worse as an excuse for self-denial. Come alive in Christ and conform to His image. Do not complicate the fact that faith in Him is your greatest asset. Reject fear and replace it with raw reliance on the Lord. Paul experienced survival with his Savior, "I have worked much harder, been in prison more frequently, been flogged more severely, and been exposed to death again and again. Five times I received from the Jews the forty lashes minus one. Three times I was beaten with rods, once I was stoned, three times I was shipwrecked, I spent a night and a day in the open sea, I have been constantly on the move." (2 Corinthians 11:23b-26a).

People are watching for you to waver in your commitment to God's call, so stay where He has called you and watch Him work wonders. Faithful is He who has called you for He will do it (I Thessalonians 5:24) Face your fears in faith, for you are kept and protected by the grace of God. The Lord is good and things may get worse, but His will undoubtedly will prevail. You can look forward to "better," knowing you did not compromise your convictions. You stayed true to your calling because you knew Christ was in control. He will see you through this, so follow Jesus by faith. Through the thick and thin be true to Him. His work will not be stopped and what He initiates He completes. Let go of hell's harassment and hold on to the hope of heaven.

Allow your character to become better during this bad time. Christ is your Master not circumstances; therefore walk with the Lord from bad to worse to better!

M6 COMPLACENT SECURITY

"Woe to you who are complacent in Zion, and to you who feel secure on Mount Samaria, you notable men of the foremost nation, to whom the people of Israel come!"
AMOS 6:1

Complacent security believes an illusion, for it acts like everything is okay when things are not okay. It is just a matter of time before the walls of deception come tumbling down. Passivity is subtle and subversive; it is a house of cards waiting to fall as the winds of adversity begin to blow. Pride and hyperactivity can lull you into thinking things are all right when they have in reality gone wrong. You think you are safe, but you are in real danger (Deuteronomy 29:19). It is unwise to make assumptions about God or others by remaining in a state of complacent security. You cannot act like it is business as usual if the financial foundations of your business or home are crumbling.

Your spouse will not survive if you continue to plow ahead in your naïve pride, as if everything were fine. He or she may be forcing a smile on the outside, but dying a slow death on the inside. Money can mask many things, but eventually anger and/or injustice will burst forth from complacent security. You can deal with the passive decision-making that created chaos, or it will deal with you. Yes, it is humbling and sometimes humiliating, but you can thank God for this second-chance opportunity, so change before it is too late. Indeed, pride may have delayed the inevitable by isolating you from people who know better, so invite them back into your life. Ask them for their advice and then follow their wise counsel. Sincerely apologize and remain accountable, for your confession is healing for everyone (James 5:16).

You can break out of your complacent security with the help of your Savior for Christ is not complacent. His security is based on the Word of God and not on the ways of the world. Stay engaged with the agenda of eternity and it will puncture the protective bubble that shields you from life's inevitabilities. Indeed, the opposite of complacent security is concerned security. It depends on Christ and His definition of reality. Concerned security initiates and gives full disclosure of the facts to preclude any misunderstandings. Information is given freely, instead of fearfully withheld. Concerned security collaborates with others in carrying out the plan. So, take the time to survey your peers, your clients, or your family. Ask them for their perspective and how they define the problem. If you ignore the obvious and plow ahead instead, it will be to your downfall. Therefore, ask God and others often for a reality check. Be secure in Christ and concerned about connecting His character and will to your behavior and actions. Pack up and leave your little insecure world, and experience God's abundant life. Live large for the Lord and stay connected and secure in Him.

It is a mature faith that stands the test of time. Your concerned security replaces complacency!

THE VISION

"The vision of Obadiah, this is what the Sovereign Lord says about Edom—
We have heard a message from the Lord: an envoy was sent to the nation to say,
"Rise up and let us go against her for battle."   OBADIAH 1:1

The vision God has placed in your heart cannot be ignored, because it is His vision for you. Indeed, your God-given vision can be daunting for it requires extraordinary faith that feels uncomfortable and overwhelming at times. Your leadership is challenged and stretched. You become assertive in ways that seem unnatural for your personality and temperament, but this is God's way of growing you and implementing His vision simultaneously. A big vision accompanied by a large Lord, led by a leader of humble faith is fun to watch. Some days you pinch yourself, wondering why God chose you to carry out this creative assignment on His behalf. Other days you tremble with feelings of anxiety, in awe of how the next few phases of the vision can become a reality. Money and time are both short, but your provision flows from the Lord (1 Timothy 6:17).

Yes, God is at His best when you feel overwhelmed with responsibilities and worry. He has prepared you and others for this vision of Kingdom significance. Moreover, do not oversell or understate the vision He has placed in your heart. Trust that the Holy Spirit will reveal its significance over time. A vision starts with an 'acorn' of an idea, but then grows into an 'oak tree' of influence. This takes time and outside resources that you cannot control. The more patient you are, the more vital the vision becomes, so do not present a 'half-baked' vision. You know you want to be a mom, build a business, or serve overseas. This is good, but let your concept for Christ mature. Like an infant in the womb, give the vision time to grow so it can be birthed in good health.

Lastly, the vision God has lodged in your life requires all of you to be fully focused. There are two focuses: the focus of the vision and your focus on the vision. Therefore, you cannot flirt with focus for it must become your focus. Start by crystallizing the idea Christ has placed on your heart. If you cannot clearly articulate the vision in a sentence, it is not focused. Clear communication of the vision is concise and compelling. If others see it, they can conceive it. Secondly, focus on the vision in prayer and do not be distracted by other good opportunities. Furthermore, the vision is "top of mind" for you, but it takes time to register into the heart and mind of others. Your part is to cast the vision; their part is to catch the vision. So, present the vision in a relevant way to your audience, and seek to align like-minded passions. Communication of vision takes repetition. What is familiar to you may be foreign to your followers. However, in the process the vision becomes better focused; you are more focused and it comes into focus for others. This is the vision God has given you, so be true to the Almighty the author of the vision.

Your vision of God determines the quality and quantity of your vision. So, stay fixated by faith on your heavenly Father for the vision flows from Him!

M8 GOD INTERRUPTION

"The word of the Lord came to Jonah son of Amittai: Go to the great city of Nineveh and preach against it, because its wickedness has come up before me." JONAH 1:1-2

God may be interrupting your plans. He does this from time to time according to His will. You were going in one direction, and He stopped you in your tracks and led you in an about-face. It can be disconcerting and more than a little scary. But do not be surprised if this happens to you. Your current path may be the opposite of what He intended. Maybe you got in a hurry and ran ahead without Him, or maybe you have been reluctant to move forward and missed Him. Either way the Holy Spirit has now arrested your attention and is leading you into uncharted waters, like Phillip you are an agent of God (Acts 8:29). You may be uncomfortable with the assignment because of the novelty in its nuances. God is moving you out of your comfort zone into His arena of obedience. If you disobey and stay put, you jeopardize proclaiming Jesus to the fullest.

The consequences of disobedience are not isolated to you alone. They ripple throughout your relationships. Don't wait for people to be hurt, before you say "yes" to heaven's directive. God interrupts for a reason and for a season. The reason may be to protect you from a convergence of bad decision making. You don't know what's around the corner of your life, but He does. He is watching out for you, so this severe turn in His will may be to protect you from a pattern of bad behavior. Do not allow pride to keep you from changing your mind. Promptings from the Holy Spirit make pride uncomfortable, because it means giving up control and submission to humility. If you continue to drive forward in pride, you are destined for unnecessary pain (Ecclesiastes 2:23). Take this interruption as a sign from God to slow down, reevaluate and recalibrate.

Interruptions from the Lord are not to be ignored. He has something better if you are willing to be bold in your obedience. He will prepare you and provide for you, as you move in this new direction. Some people will resist, but others will be relieved that you are leading them in a different direction. They felt a hesitation in their heart to move forward, but did not want their disagreement to be perceived as disloyal. So, your honesty about the reality of the situation has given them permission to be open about their reservations. This can happen at home or at work. You may have agreed as a team to spend money on a project or a person, but now the funds are not available and wisdom does not spend what it does not have. God many times interrupts your plans through a decrease in cash. His interruptions are intended to get you into environments where you can be blessed. So see His interruptions as a step up, not a step down. Thank Him that He cared enough to stop you in your tracks and redirect you down a better path.

Indeed, invite divine diversions. You are wise when you follow the Lord's interruptions!

TAKE RESPONSIBILITY

"Pick me up and throw me into the sea,' he replied, 'and it will become calm.
I know that it is my fault that this great storm has come upon you."   JONAH 1:12

Mature leaders take the blame and they do not make excuses, instead they take responsibility. Leaders take responsibility for their own actions and for the actions of their team. There is no "he said/she said." A leader knows when he could have done a better job of planning, collaborating, and communicating. So, when the expected results do not materialize, the responsible leader takes a step back, and asks the question, "why?" This pause for retrospection is healthy for him or her, and it is healthy for the organization. If blame is shifted or ignored, then an opportunity is lost for everyone to grow. It is interesting why some leaders do not want to take responsibility for negative outcomes. Many times there is the fear of losing something. There may be a fear of a loss of respect, loss of reputation, loss of control, loss of leadership, loss of effectiveness, loss of momentum, or even to the extreme, loss of a job.

However, you want a leader with a sense of urgency around realistic concerns, but not one who panics because he is engulfed by fear. Ironically, a leader who comes clean with his failures and takes responsibility, gains instead of loses. He gains perspective, respect, and another opportunity to succeed. He gains resources and more committed followers. Fear is a lousy long-term motivator. It can jump start apathy, but overtime it erodes a leader's confidence and leadership. Fear assumes the worst, jumps to the wrong conclusions and like Jacob makes unnecessary drastic changes (Genesis 32:7).

Moreover, prayerful change is a logical context for growth. For example it is a good opportunity to deal with passive aggressiveness. Christians can be the world's worst at smiling on the outside, but disagreeing on the inside. It is the sin of silence that comes back to roost in relational confusion and hurt. On the contrary, the leader and his team can use transitions to better communicate and understand each other. Over communication is a required course, not an elective during the dynamics of change.

It is in the climate of change that a leader has a greater responsibility to lead. Without intentional and prayerful leadership, everyone will default to "what is right in his own eyes" (Judges 21:25 KJV). The responsible leader loves and leads the team beyond low levels of performance to new levels of efficiency and effectiveness. The overriding goal of change management is to establish new and improved processes and people. Change can be a catalyst for a more excellent way. Responsible leaders understand God's goal of transformation for themselves and for the team. So, be a responsible leader who takes the blame for failure, and who shares the credit for success.

Trust the Lord and lead others to do the same. In Christ there is calm, therefore take responsibility and trust Him!

M10 ASK FOR RELIEF

"My son, if you have put up security for your neighbor... if you have been trapped by what you said... then do this my son, to free yourself, since you have fallen into your neighbor's hands: Go and humble yourself; press your plea with your neighbor." PROVERBS 6:1A, 2A, 3

Sometimes you need relief. You need relief from pain, from work, from an obligation, from a relationship, from a financial commitment, or from over commitment. The discomfort has become distracting, as you have become ensnared by an unwise decision. You need some radical relief, however relief is not a pass to be irresponsible. It is an opportunity for you to humble yourself and to ask for a change in something that is out of your control. You may or may not receive the needed relief, but at least you have positioned yourself for the possibility. Relief many times results from a humble request.

Anytime you feel trapped, it is natural to request some level of relief. Maybe you are entangled in a business deal that does not reflect your values. The upside financial potential is very positive, but it is not worth compromising your convictions. Now may be the time to exercise your escape clause. Leave some cash on the table, because no amount of money is worth this conflict of interest (Proverbs 13:11). Lay your pride aside and ask for a reprieve. You may be labeled a loser or strange, but this is okay if you know the Lord is leading you in this direction. Maybe you are engaged to be married, but something is not right. You do not have a peace; therefore move quickly to disengage and delay disaster. It is better to suffer a broken engagement, than to see divorce sever a messy marriage. You may need relief in the area of time, for your margin account is overdrawn and you are suffering from daily relational fees of frustration. Ask for relief from some whom you dearly respect, more than likely they will understand and be relieved; indeed relief relieves everyone.

Moreover, relief comes through the channel of humility and action. Pray for an attitude of humility and respect before you request relief. Don't wait so long that the pressure you are feeling crushes your spirit and produces panic. Humility is willing early on to get everything out in the open for discussion and discernment. When you stifle your fears, you set yourself up for a resentful attitude. People under severe pressure suffer resentment under the burden of unprocessed feelings. So in humility, go and share your heart. Take a chance and process your fears and worries with the authorities God has placed in your life. Humility goes a long way toward disarming the one to whom you are appealing for relief. Agree with their concerns, and at the same time offer them creative solutions. Humility is not irresponsible, so it doesn't walk away and leave the other party in the lurch. But, humility does come in the form of a prayerful and action-oriented appeal. Seek out and sit down with the decision maker, since written correspondence is limited to cold facts and not warm hearts. Hearts engage hearts with eye-to-eye contact, so go in person, share your heart, be respectful, ask for relief, and hope for the best. God will bless your honest and humble efforts. You never know who may take a stand on your behalf for His disciples abound (Acts 11:29).

Above all else, seek the Lord first for relief for He is your most dependable reliever. Ask for relief and watch God work!

INTEGRITY LOST

> "Her leaders judge for a bribe, her priests teach for a price,
> and her prophets tell fortunes for money."   MICAH 3:11

Integrity is not for sale to those who love their Savior Jesus. There is no amount of money or status that can lure integrity away from someone who values its influence, accountability, and positive outcomes. Integrity is your "union card" for leadership and it is evidence of your faith in Christ. Integrity may be your greatest value that is not itemized on your balance sheet, and it is not for sale with serious followers of the Lord. Like Esau selling out his birthright (Genesis 25:25-34), your appetites can exchange your integrity for instant gratification. Indeed, it is a lopsided loss to let go of a lifetime of faithfulness for a moment of problematic pleasure.

Moreover, the love of money makes one vulnerable to losing their integrity (I Timothy 6:10). Money can maneuver your motives into a less than desirable condition; so make sure not to masquerade your good works around a drive for wealth. You cannot reason your way around wrong methods of obtaining money, even for the sake of worthy outcomes. You do not have to compromise your God-given convictions to grow your net worth. Effective leaders in the long run are given respect, trust, and goodwill because of their position, authority, and track record of integrity. How much is your creditability worth? Certainly it is more valuable than anything money can buy (Proverbs 22:1). Indeed, integrity is being true to yourself and God's calling on your life, so be who you are in Him. It does not have to prove itself; rather it rests in being itself. Align your doing around your being, for this integration is the essence of integrity. Furthermore, if you have lost your integrity, it can be found in Christ, so go to Him in honesty and humility. Be forthright with your heavenly Father about your failures, and blown opportunities. Let Him love you through this time of transition and rebuilding of trust.

It will take time for those who have been hurt to begin healing and reconcile. But, the longer you prove to yourself and others that you are the real deal, the more your integrity will blossom. A track record of faithfulness fertilizes the roots of integrity and produces lasting fruit. Cultivate integrity through prayer and service, then watch it grow. Take the time to do what you say, because follow-through and consistency create credibility. Invest in others, so they don't feel you have used them just to accomplish your agenda. Integrity insists on doing what's right, in the right way, and at the right time. Integrity does not belittle others, or get caught up in the seduction of stuff. It gains traction through gratitude for God's grace, instead of losing its footing on money's blind ledge of allegiance. Integrity provides peace and stability, and it is found by walking with your Lord.

"The man of integrity walks securely, but he who takes crooked paths will be found out" (Proverbs 10:9). Therefore gain it, retain it, and do not sell it out at any price!

M12   HOPEFUL WAITING

"But as for me, I watch in hope for the Lord, I wait for my Savior; and God will hear me."
MICAH 7:7

Hope allows you to wait patiently on the Lord. It is hope in Him that is heaven's guarantee of grace. Because of the things that are out of your control, it is wise to practice hopeful waiting. Otherwise, you will live in frustration and fear over matters you can not mandate or manipulate. This is where hopeful waiting pays great dividends. You choose to hope in Christ rather than placing your trust in ever-changing circumstances. This is a wise bet. If however your hope is embedded in an organization or institution, all bets are off. Both can and will fail to meet your expectations, but hopeful waiting trumps broken promises of the company. You place your trust and hope in God's provision rather than the ever-changing commitments of corporate.

The same can be said of what should expect from people. They can be fickle at and undependable, indeed some people hurry away when things get tough. They make excuses or excuse themselves from responsibilities. Difficult times raise up heroes and bring down imposters. Therefore, patient people learn hopeful waiting in their dealings with others. You wait on people, not in a naïve and irresponsible way, but in a way that honors them and Christ. You are hopeful while waiting for him or her to follow through with their original commitment. If there is no progress on their part, then there are consequences to their concessions. If there is a pattern of non-productive living and working, then hopeful waiting is trumped by wise stewardship. You always wait on the Lord, but as you wait be an excellent steward of His resources, for waiting does not mean wasting. Like the faithful manager you work wisely while you wait on your Master (Matthew 25:15-28).

Wait on Him and hope in Him for this is a wise sequence of activity and thinking. God is not going anywhere without you (Deuteronomy 31:6). Circumstances change and people leave, but He is still there for you to trust and obey. There is no need to run away and hide for God has revealed Himself just for you. His wisdom is there for the asking. Your Savior gives you stability, because a firm footing is found by faithfully waiting on Him in hope. Do not be shaken and stay put until He tells you differently. All hell may break loose around you, but heaven is still in control within you. Allow the Holy Spirit to lead you, even while people swirl out of control. God is listening, so speak to Him often in prayer. It may be difficult to get an audience with your adversary, so go quickly to your Savior. This is what hope does; it depends on Christ. He will come through, as He has in the past. You can wait hopefully in Him, because He fulfills His promises with pleasure. Be patient and hopeful as you wait on Him. He will do what He originally set out to accomplish. Trust Him with this and do not be overwhelmed by inactivity. His hope is certain and true. Therefore, remain faithful to the most trustworthy One.

Wait on Him and hope in Him for this prayerful sequence with your Savior is security indeed. Watch, wait and hope for He hears your heart and feels your pain!

GOD ENABLES

"The Sovereign Lord is my strength; he makes my feet like the feet of a deer, he enables me to go on the heights." HABAKKUK 3:19A

God is your enabler for there is nothing you cannot do that He has destined you to accomplish. It is His eternal enablement that carries you forward. Indeed, the next phase of your character growth may be painful. The development of your business or ministry to the next level could be daunting. The skills you need as a parent are scary, and it seems impossible to balance work, home, and hobbies. But God is bigger than your frailties, fears, and family. He will enable you if you let Him, so do not carry alone this burden of becoming better. Your Savior is your enabler of bigger and better things. Yes, in your own strength you will remain frustrated, frazzled, and stuck. There is no amount of self-discipline that can accomplish by itself God's results.

It is through the empowering of the Holy Spirit that you are able to endure and execute the will of the Lord (Isaiah 63:11). As a child of God you can off-load your fatigue to your heavenly Father and rest in Him. You can outsource your anxieties to the One who can enable you to execute eternity's agenda. His grace qualifies you to carry out this life's assignment. You have been crucified with Christ (Galatians 2:20) and sealed by His spirit (Ephesians 4:30). You are a valued member of Christ's community. Others have traveled this road of trust and did much more than survive. They thrived because the Lord enabled them with His wisdom and grace. This season of life may be hard for now. It is difficult because you are not sure how to navigate everything that needs to be done, and some things need to be left undone. Allow the Sovereign Lord to enable your actions or inactions. Seek out His power before you traverse up this next path of trust. Pray for His eternal enablement, for He is your strength as you embark on the next steps.

Part of accepting God's enablement is admitting areas of weakness. No amount of prayer can transform you into something God never intended. This is important to accept. He cannot enable what doesn't contain the raw skills or gifts to develop. If you are good with numbers, then allow Him to grow you in this area of data analysis. If not, then free yourself by allowing another to enjoy the responsibility of drawing financial conclusions and estimates. Stop striving to be someone you are not. Know your limitations and humble yourself by confessing them to others. To get to the next level, both professionally and personally, it probably means giving up some responsibility for the sake of progress. You could handle this role up till now, but others more skilled are available to step in and do a better job. Successful people understand this natural transition of responsibilities. Allow Him to enable you with this different level of leadership. Change and transition expose weaknesses and strengths. Use this time of vulnerability and enable your leadership development. Like photo development in a dark room, He is exposing your professional profile in a fresh way. This dark time is illuminating the Lord's best for you. God's enablement may mean letting go of the good, and focus on what you do best. Cooperate with the Holy Spirit; He strengthens what He enables. God's enablement gives you the resources and the wisdom to carry out His plan.

Look to the Lord often for His eternal enablement. His enablement strengthens and lasts forever!

M14 QUIET LOVE

"The Lord your God is with you, he is mighty to save. He will take great delight in you, he will quiet you with his love, he will rejoice over you with singing." ZEPHANIAH 3:17

The love of God quiets the soul. There is nothing more soothing to the soul of man or woman than the love of their Savior. His love transcends the "trash talk" of troubled people. The world's remedies can be loud and obnoxious, but not the Lord's love. His love penetrates the proudest of hearts with gentle promptings of care and concern. Pride likes to figure things out without assistance from the love of the Lord for it sees the receiving of love as a sign of weakness. To be loved means you are dependent on something other than yourself for significance. But, the love of God provides purpose for every recipient; quietly and effectively God's love calms your nerves and reminds you of whose you are. You are important because you are His. You are the objects of God's quiet and lavish love, for He only loves whom He values. Love covers a multitude of sin and sorrow. Above all, love each other deeply, because love covers over a multitude of sins" (I Peter 4:8).

If you are stressed, let Him quiet you with His love. If you are fearful, let Him quiet you with His love. If you are angry, let Him quiet you with His love. If you are rejected, let Him quiet you with His love. If you are confused, let Him quiet you with His love. If you are desperate, let Him quiet you with His love. His love is active and effective. It is not a lost love waiting to be found. His love initiates, and it is seeking to find you and love you at your point of need. The love of the Lord is calling out for you, like a mom who stands at her front door calling her children to come in from play. Don't get so busy playing and/or working that you miss God's invitation to love. Don't be so worried about work that you ignore the Lover of your soul. His love lingers over your life waiting to invade, so invite His intimacy. God is with you and He is mighty to save. He delights in you and desires His very best on your behalf, so be quiet and listen. Do you hear His compassionate voice? Do you feel His calming presence? His warm embrace may squeeze a tear from your eye; for this is what His love does, it moves your emotions. He loves you simply because you are His. He cannot 'not' love you, so be still and be loved by the Lord.

Your Savior's love is safe within unsafe surroundings. When all hell breaks loose, you can be comforted by heaven's love. You are your Father's child, and you are very, very precious to the One who has saved you from loveless living. Act like you are loved, as a loved one of Jesus. Let Him love you often and allow Him to love you completely. His love pursues you with a calm and quiet persistence. Give in to your greatest lover for He romances your soul with pure intentions. Rest and trust in your Savior's love for it never fails to quiet your nerves. His love rejoices when you rejoice and cries when you cry. His love understands, and the Lord's love never lets up. He is relentless in His concern, care and compassion. Therefore, accept your date with destiny.

Enjoy your divine romance. Above all else, allow Almighty God to embrace you with His radical love!

"The sorrows for the appointed feasts I will remove from you;
they are a burden and a reproach to you."   ZEPHANIAH 3:18

Sorrow can be like a stab in the back, painful and alarming. Sorrow is not easy to swallow when it is sudden like an unsuspecting car accident, or it can tarry like a terminal disease. Sorrow saps hope from your heart and courage from your countenance. It is a drain on the disposition in the mightiest of men. You cannot hide sorrow, for it shows in your face and flows through your words. Like an uninvited guest, sorrow may stay longer than you intended and become a nuisance that never seems to go away. Sorrow makes a heart sad, it weighs on the mind, and it steals away the majority of your motivation.

Sorrow is delivered by death. When you lose someone you love dearly, sorrow is a natural and healing outcome. In most cases you must first trod through the sand of sorrow before you can arrive at the sea of gladness. It is a process where your Savior accompanies you for He understands. He was a man of sorrow who was acquainted with grief (Isaiah 53:3). Sorrow for your Savior is not a foreign language, He is fluent and has more than survived its purging process. Sorrow is not static for it moves you to seek out what matters most. When sorrow arrives at the doorstep of your life, your Savior's presence becomes more precious than ever before. It may come in the form of a teenager who chooses not to talk anymore. This breaks your heart, however this too shall pass. A teen's transition into young adulthood is hardest for them. Their internal conflict of confidence and emerging emotions is enough to cause one to clam up. They want to be on their own, so they think they don't need their parents anymore. This semi-rebellious rejection is a magnet for sorrow, because it hurts to not be needed anymore.

But Jesus is the Savior of your sorrows. His grace is like a miracle-working detergent that removes the deepest stains of sorrow. He can erase sorrows that have etched themselves into your emotions. He can extract sorrows that have embedded themselves into the archives of your attitude. He can lift sorrows that have burdened your heart and have weighed down your actions to the point of inertia. Therefore, allow His love to squeeze the sorrow from your weeping heart. Like a towel drenched in water, He can wring your eyes from the flood of tears that have disabled your discipleship. It is okay to be sorrowful, but it is not okay to remain sorrowful. Jesus can remove your sorrow by His comfort, or His cleansing. Your removal of sorrow may be contingent on your confession and repentance of sin. Whatever the source of your transgression, give it over to the Lord. Sorrow seeps out of a heart that often does business with the Almighty. Your sorrow may be the natural outcome of grief and/or regret. But now is the time for Christ to bring closure and heal your heart. Sorrow need not keep you sad indefinitely for it is a pass through to His peace. Furthermore, do not bear your burden alone. Allow your community of Christians to love you through this time of trial. Joy is with you in Jesus and His followers.

Sorrow is for a season, but joy and peace are for an eternity. Tomorrow's hope dissuades today's sorrow!

M16 CONFRONT TO CONNECT

"Faithful are the wounds of a friend, but the kisses of an enemy are deceitful."
PROVERBS 27:6 (NKJ)

Confrontation means there has been a disconnection, something has severed trust. It may be relational, emotional or financial, or not feeling love and respect. Whatever the reason for the disconnection, confrontation needs to seek out a reconnection. This is what a faithful friend does who cares, they seek to reconnect where there has been a "disconnect." Your salvation in Jesus brought into relational wholeness with heaven, so you could model the same on earth. Scripture teaches, "All this is from God, who reconciled us to himself through Christ and gave us the ministry of reconciliation" (2 Corinthians 5:18). However, if ignored delayed confrontation deteriorates into disconnection. It dilutes understanding, trust, and intimacy. This is why wise leaders keep short accounts; indeed they speak freely about their concerns early. If a leader ignores his or her obvious feelings of frustration, they will naturally distance themselves from the team and the organization. But if they confront early on in a spirit of respect and understanding, they stay engaged with the enterprise and the individuals, and therefore avoid creating a culture of control and distrust.

This is true in marriage; a wife may confront her husband when she does not feel loved. This is a natural response when she feels distant from her spouse. Depending on the context of the confrontation, the husband may respond positively (if he is smart!), or he may push back defensively, if he senses a combative or controlling spirit. It is normal and healthy to desire and seek out relational connection. This is how God has wired people; just make sure you set yourself up for a successful connection and not an aborted one. Your husband is much more receptive to receiving your emotional advances in a spirit of respect. Use questions like, "Sweetheart, can we sit down sometime today to discuss the children's schedule for the upcoming week?" This gives him time to process and prepare, if he feels pounced upon or backed into a corner, he will react defensively. Indeed, in this situation healthy confrontation gives a couple the organizational connections they need to be more effective in managing their family responsibilities.

Furthermore, caring confrontation creates a culture of teamwork and trust. A connected culture creates communication channels that build great organizations. Sadly though, a disconnected leader encourages disconnected individuals, which feed disconnected departments, which facilitate disconnected divisions, which ultimately leads to a disconnected and dysfunctional organization. So, most importantly start by connecting with Christ, vertical relational reconnection facilitates horizontal relational reconnection. Sin subtly or not so subtly severs relationships, but confession leads to connection. David a most effective leader said it well, "Then I acknowledged my sin to you and did not cover up my iniquity. I said, 'I will confess my transgressions to the LORD' – and you forgave the guilt of my sin" (Psalm 32:5).

Therefore, make your motives and methods of confrontation for the purpose of reconnection. Indeed, friends who care, confront to connect!

"Ask all the people of the land and the priests, 'When you fasted and mourned in the fifth and seventh months for the past seventy years, was it really for me that you fasted? And when you were eating and drinking, were you not just feasting for yourselves?" ZECHARIAH 7:5

Right motives can be illusive. One minute you can be as pure as the driven snow in why you do what you do, but subtly you can slip into suspect behavior. Therefore, you need to be relentless and honest in reviewing your motives. Sure you can never shake self-preservation and some level of pride, but you can ask the Lord to cleanse your motives and mark them with His purposes. You can make faith in Jesus a filter for right motives. "Why would Jesus do this?" is a wise question that helps you get to the heart of the matter. The "why" question reveals intent and encourages honesty.

Regularly asking why addresses your motives. You may want to give to someone, but why? You may want to serve someone, but why? You may want to sacrifice an opportunity, but why? You may want to perform a religious duty, but why? Where does your devotion reside? What drives you to do good things? If your reasons are self-serving, then you have missed managing your motives for eternal purposes. Your motive may be to use religion and the church to promote your profession. God does not like to be used for anything other than His glory. If you serve because it makes you feel better or to feed your ego, your motives are dysfunctional. If you are trying to make up for your shady past or you are driven by guilt, then you are operating out of bounds. As a consequence, your misguided motives will cause others to feel or act strange. Wrong motives have a ripple effect on relationships and organizational dynamics. Unhealthy motivation that seeks attention and credit will compromise principles and values in an effort to reach its desired results. Misguided motives are driven by whatever means it takes to justify worthy results, but lasting fruit results from the seeds of pure motives.

Moreover, dishonest motives are a recipe for rejection. Neither people nor God accept those with sinful motives. Spiritual people can discern inauthentic living a mile away. Therefore, do an audit of authenticity, and stop doing acts of righteousness that draw people to yourself instead of to your Savior. For example fast and pray with discretion and give anonymously (Matthew 6:5-6). Serve when no one else is watching and you are guaranteed not to get the credit. Ask about others instead of talking about yourself. Help make other people successful instead of using them for your success. Focus on the Almighty's accomplishments and not your own. Furthermore, do not default to fear as the driving force of your life. Fear may be the worst motive of all for it causes you to believe lies and to act on them. Fear leads you into out-of-balance living as it races to be right, so substitute fear with faith. Faith keeps you focused on your heavenly Father and He replaces your fears with peace and contentment. He can be trusted; so do not force things to happen in your own strength. Instead, do all for the glory of God. Let your love of Lord and people lift your motives to a more noble level. Continually allow the Holy Spirit to scrub your motivations.

Ask often, "Why would Jesus do this?" Indeed, mimic your Master's motives, for right motives reap God's rewards!

M18 GENTLE AND HUMBLE

> "Rejoice greatly, O Daughter of Zion! Shout, Daughter of Jerusalem!
> See, your king come to you, righteous and having salvation, gentle and
> riding on a donkey, on a colt, the foal of a donkey."   ZECHARIAH 9:9

Jesus is gentle and humble, and He is aggressive and brave. Gentleness does not exclude aggression, nor does humility cross out courage. Jesus is King of creation and ruler over the world, but He rules and leads with gentleness and humility. He describes Himself this way, "Take my yoke upon you and learn from me, for I am gentle and humble in heart, and you will find rest for your souls" (Matthew 11:29). Power is not a rod of rejection for the gentle and humble leader. A gentle and humble leader uses his position of influence to serve others to be their best. He brings to bear resources and relationships that facilitate the unity of the team. His gentle and humble approach to people increases their probability for success. There is no need to inflict fear as your mode of operation. Why cause people to cower in contempt because they are afraid?

Fear is a leadership technique of the insecure and incompetent leader. It is no excuse to use intimidation as a tool for obtaining results. Certainly there are seasons of intensity that call for elevated effort and focused attention above the norm. But these windows of change are an opportunity for the leader to provide stability and calm, it is a demeanor dependent on the Lord. Gentleness and humility lubricate the relational machinery of a home or enterprise. Gentleness is aggression under the control of the Holy Spirit and humility is courage that is first committed to Christ. Yes, some will take advantage of you and the situation, but over the long haul humility wins. You win over people and you win over accounts. You win over adversity and you win over the team's loyalty. You win the respect of your family and friends, most importantly you win God's blessing. Yes, gentleness and humility risk rejection and risk being trampled upon, but you cannot go wrong emulating the character of Christ. Your position of influence as a parent, pastor, executive, volunteer, sole proprietor, or teacher is not a place for pleading and/or passive aggression. Instead, use your influence to gently lead by example and to humbly confront those who are stuck on their agenda.

Gentleness and humility are children of great faith. This pride-less posture seeks daily filling from the Holy Spirit and wisdom from God (Ephesians 3:14-19). A gentle follower of Christ has been broken before God. Like a wild and robust stallion your will must be broken and aligned with the Almighty's purposes. Indeed, use this time of resistance to graft the gentleness of Jesus into your soul, and to embed the humility of your heavenly Father into your heart. Stay true to your personality and temperament, so be loud and bold if this is your wiring. But whoever you are, do everything in a spirit of gentleness and with a humble heart. Deflect attention from you, and trust Him for the proper recognition in His timing.

Turn away from arrogance and pride. Embrace gentleness and humility, for they are twins birthed from transformation in Jesus!

LEADERSHIP VOID

"The idols speak deceit, diviners see visions that lie; they tell dreams that are false, they give comfort in vain. Therefore the people wander like sheep oppressed for lack of a shepherd."   ZECHARIAH 10:2

People wander aimlessly due to lack of leadership, but they want to be led. They want to be led by loving leaders who listen to the Lord and who listen to them. Look for leaders like Solomon who petition the Lord on how to lead, "Give me wisdom and knowledge, that I may lead this people, for who is able to govern this great people of yours?" (2 Chronicles 1:10). This is God's design, for He has wired people to resist wandering and to want leadership. You are followers of Jesus Christ and followers of those He has placed in authority over your life. Yet, if someone who is in a position of leadership does not lead, there is doubt and confusion. People wander around disconnected and disinterested because they are unsure where to turn, but eventually someone will fill the leadership void by default.

Some ambitious soul will fill the empty shoes of leadership, even if he or she is unable to lead effectively. A silent coup takes place when the responsible leader abdicates their leadership. An uncalled character backing into leadership by default is worse than having no leadership. But the followers can easily lose perspective and settle for less, because their hunger pains for a leader can cause them to use poor judgment. Just like the people begged Samuel for a King, and later regretted their request (1 Samuel 8:4-21). Therefore, do not settle for anything less than God's choicest servant as shepherd over His flock. Be prayerful and patient; God will send His called leader in His timing. It is better to have an open position of leadership than to fill it with the wrong person. It is expensive and emotional to extract a lackluster leader. Wait and work toward God's best.

It may be a Pastor, CEO, Headmaster, Administrative Assistant, COO, or husband that you need, so continue to trust God for His choice. Don't just fill a slot for expedience. Make vitally sure their chemistry, character, and competence align with your culture. On the other hand, if you are in a position of leadership, lead. A good motto is to "lead, follow, or get out of the way." People expect you to lead and they are confused if you don't. What are you waiting for? You will not lead perfectly, so press on. Faithful followers are not looking for perfect leaders, they are praying for honest leaders with passion and Holy Spirit led persuasion. Indeed, leaders who love God and people will never lack a following. Let go of your fear of leading, release control and have faith that God has placed you in this position of leadership. He equips those He calls to carry out His assignment. You may just lead here for a season, therefore lead with abandonment on behalf of the Almighty. Seek the Lord as the leader of your life, work, family, and ministry. Follow hard after God, so you can effectively lead people. Ask Him for wisdom and stay focused on the mission. Get your marching orders from on high and then execute them down low. Effective leaders love to lead and their Holy Spirit infused energy engages others in shared goals. Perhaps the people are looking to you for leadership.

Therefore, on behalf of your Lord and by His grace; lead. Follow Him and lead them!

M20 EXPECTS RESPECT

"A son honors his father, and a servant his master. If I am a father where is the honor due me? If I am a master, where is the respect due me? Says the Lord Almighty..." MALACHI 1:6

Almighty God anticipates respect due His name, for He is your heavenly Father, your Lord and Master. The quantity of respect due Him makes respect to the monarchs of this world look miniscule. This is one reason followers of Jesus attend church; it honors Him. Worship, teaching the Bible, and fellowship with other followers of Christ respects the Lord. It may be subtle but people slip into a role reversal when they expect respect from people on earth, while they extend little or no respect toward heaven. It is because of your honor and admiration of Him, you can't help but exclaim His goodness and glory.

Therefore, respectful people are quick to extend respect. They do not sit back and wait to be respected, but take the time to offer respect. So, love God as your heavenly father and submit to Him like your master. It is disrespectful to disregard the things of God and drive ahead in your own strength. However, respect slows down, listens to the Lord, and connects with Christ's wisdom. You show respect by relishing your role as follower and God's role as leader. Be respectful with regular prayers and by following His voice of reason. Moreover, respect for the Lord leads to respect for others. This is a natural place to grow in your respect for people. People are all made in the image of their Maker and they long for respect. The DNA of your soul regularly requests respect. So, start by receiving respect from the One who is entitled to all respect. God honors His children, and He respects you as the apex of His creation. He does not disrespect His own, you are a work of His grace and a reflection of His glory. Once you receive God's respect give it to others, even when they are disrespectful. Your loving kindness leads to respect. Wisdom says, "A kindhearted woman gains respect..." (Proverbs 11:16).

Respect does not mean you mutter disagreement on the inside and smile on the outside. It means you voice your concerns and conflicting ideas clearly, concisely, and with a spirit of humility and calmness. Respect resists attacking people and instead challenges assumptions and processes, so it goes a long way in relational growth. There is a good chance a wife will experience deeper love at a more consistent level when she respects her husband. The Bible teaches the husband is to love his wife and, "...the wife must respect her husband" (Ephesians 5:33b). Therefore, figure out what makes your husband feel respected. It may be bragging on him in front of friends, or pulling back your spending. Respect wells up in his heart when you want to spend time with him and learn about his work. It sets the table for love, as it is an invitation to be loved. Respect is foundational for relational intimacy, so use it well and extend it often.

No one has ever complained about too much respect. Therefore, pay your respects often to God and man!

THE "D" WORD

"What therefore God has joined together, let no man separate."
MARK 10:9

Divorce is not an option for committed followers of Christ, as it is omitted from their vocabulary. Yes human frailty wants an out, it doesn't want to be uncomfortable or inconvenienced, but marital challenges are God's process of purging. Relational reconciliation within the bonds of marriage is proving ground for all other relationships. Marriage mandates focused fidelity and faith in God, for it is not a relationship of convenience, rather one of conviction. You cannot give up on your spouse, except in the case of adultery, but even in unfaithfulness their repentance and your forgiveness can heal the severance of trust and intimacy. Moreover, marriage is a reflection of your Master. Whatever God does is not to be taken lightly, for the Lord is in the marriage-making business. He joins a man and a woman together in marriage, as a mirror of your relationship with Him; it is final and forever (I John 5:11-20).

Furthermore, there is no need to run and hide when you let down your spouse. When the bubble of marital bliss bursts; be kind, patient, and forgiving. It starts by allowing Christ to cleanse your heart, because left on its own the heart becomes selfish, proud, immature and demanding (Matthew 15:19-20). Therefore, put self into a deep sleep and hypnotize it with heaven's expectations. Jesus came into your life so you could be a servant to all, especially to your spouse. He gives you peace so you can be a peacemaker in your home, so be a justice of the peace in your home under the power of the Holy Spirit. Christ-centered marriages create peace and quiet, so submit to the Lord together and experience Him, who produces a peace that passes all understanding (Philippians 4:7-9).

Lastly, God's marriage design overcomes divorce's destruction, by creating environments of encouragement and the building up of one another. Children feel the safest in a family where divorce is not an option. The Lord hates divorce (Malachi 2:16), because He knows it results in a lifetime of disappointment and disillusionment. Indeed, one way to dumb down divorce is to exalt marriage. Make marriage mean something, by seeing marriage as a mandate from your Master. Accept marriage as a privilege and a responsibility. Marriage is a not a man's pass for sex, or a woman's gateway for security. Marriage is a divine appointment for a lifetime; it is not a temporary assignment until things get difficult. Marriage is an enlistment of service for your spouse on behalf of your Savior. It is designed to draw you closer to God in dependency and trust; it is a facilitator of faith. God uses marriage for His glory, as a reflection of His unconditional love and forgiveness. If divorce is your secret trump card when things get rough, then you are destined to ruin your marriage with a self-fulfilling strategy. Therefore, agree together to put to death divorce talk and instead become broken before the Lord. See your marriage sealed by the Holy Spirit never to be separated by man. Your marriage is not a mistake, so be hopeful by persevering.

You were joined together in marriage by Jesus, for Jesus; not to be destroyed by man's decree of divorce!

M22 MONEY MOTIVATED

> "... Jesus entered the temple area and began driving out those who were buying and selling there. He overturned the tables of the money changers and the benches of those selling doves, and would not allow anyone to carry merchandise through the temple courts." Mark 11:15-16

Money motivation is not the best motivation; in fact it can make you down right miserable. It makes you and those around you frustrated, because money-motivated people are never content. They have an insatiable desire for the next deal, or the next opportunity to make more. An all-consuming desire for money leads you to compromise common sense and character. Ironically, your family suffers the most even when your desire is for them to enjoy the benefits money may produce. Moreover, money-motivated individuals stoop as low as using the Lord to line their pockets. Religion and church become a means for more creating cash. This angers God for He is moved by righteous indignation when His bride is prostituted for worldly purposes. The church is a conduit for Christ, not a clearing house for economic gain. It is a house of prayer (Isaiah 56:7).

He is greatly grieved when money becomes the driving force of any institution or individual. A church bound up in debt is destined to ineffectiveness. If the Bride of Christ is preoccupied with paying the bills, then the mission will be watered down and even ignored. Money-driven ministries miss the opportunity to trust God and wait on Him to provide in ways that exceed human capability. Businesses that are driven by bottom line performance alone contribute to an unhealthy company culture. People are willing to work somewhere, for less money, if they know the culture has a much bigger vision than just making money. There is so much more to life and work than money (Matthew 6:25).

Contrast money motivation with mission motivation, which is the antithesis for it has a greater purpose in mind. The focus is on excellent work accompanied by eternal expectations. The mission is what drives you to do more because a transcendent spark ignites within your soul. Money becomes a result not a reason when the mission creates a culture of care and collaboration. The mission gives you permission to say no. Enterprises and individuals are defined more by what they say, "no" to than "yes." A well-focused team makes it a habit to defend the mission. There is a discipline in decision-making that characterizes mission-driven people and organizations. Paul said "But one thing I do: Forgetting what is behind and straining toward what is ahead..." (Philippians 3:13).

Mission is the master of money, so focus on the mission of your Master Jesus and you will be much more productive in the long run. Mission motivation keeps you trustworthy, effective and blessed by God!

WHY ME?

"But why am I so favored, that the mother of my Lord should come to me?"
LUKE 1:42

Sometimes you wonder why God has blessed you so much. You pinch yourself because of the overwhelming blessing of God. It may be gratitude for life itself, or it may be a new baby. It may be the blessing of God a good friend is experiencing, or your joy may be because your children married people who place God at the top of their priority list. Your career has taken off to a level of success you never imagined and your financial abundance exceeds your expectations many times over. You often question why you are the recipient of God's magnificent grace. The magnitude of His blessing seems to be greater than normal, because you are the object of Almighty God's sovereign selection of unmerited favor. It is good you have not gotten over your gratitude to God. Your faith would be suspect if you routinely expected God to go over the top on your behalf. This type of presumption regarding God's favor is influenced by pride, because it not only expects, but also demands the blessing of God. However, joyful obedience is God's expectation of you; He expects your surrender and submission. Doing His will is the least you can do, for He has chosen you for this opportunity to exalt Him. Never get over the fact that faith in God and obedience to His commands positions you to be blessed at His discretion men are man great and given strength (I Chronicles 29:12, LB).

Furthermore, embrace those who have been graced with God's blessing. Wish only His very best for them. Do not be jealous because you did not receive what they received. The Lord made us all uniquely, the Bible says, "And since we have gifts that differ according to the grace given to us, let each exercise them accordingly..." (Romans 12:6a). Be grateful instead that you can hang out with those on whom God's hand rests. He will choose to bless others differently from you, but blessing differentiators are meant to promote celebration not division. This is how God expresses His sovereign control. He even blesses those outside the faith to promote His kingdom. He uses His indiscriminate blessings to draw good, but unredeemed people to Himself.

Blessing is the Lord's lightening rod for remembrance of a righteous God. The next time a friend is blessed by God turn your inner snarl into an authentic smile. Be extremely grateful that He allows you to live or work with someone who is blessed to have the hand of God on his or her life, "Rejoice with those who rejoice..." (Romans 12:15). These special chosen servants are rare indeed. They are energizing to be around because they encourage you to be better. You do not feel patronized, but privileged to be in their presence. Trustworthy followers of Jesus are rare, so seek to learn from them and model their wise and humble ways. Watch how God works in their life, while emulating their pure heart for the Lord. God has you where you are for a season. Seize this time to learn from those that know how to lean on the Lord. Be thrilled that He has trusted you with this relational stewardship. God's blessing is bountiful, so be aggressively appreciative that you and others are so blessed. Gratefully accept His blessing on your life and the life of others.

When you ask, "Why me?" remember it is because He wants you to be blessed on His behalf. Therefore ask, "Why not me?"

M24 FEELING EXCLUDED

> "Blessed are you when men hate you, when they exclude you and insult you and reject your name as evil, because of the Son of Man." LUKE 6:22

No one likes to feel excluded for it is disrespectful and distasteful. Exclusion may come in the form of blatant rejection or ignorant ignoring. In either the case, the results are feeling left out of the loop. You were not included in the decision making process, or you were not invited to the event. Your opinion was not valued or appreciated. You may have been excluded volitionally or by accident. If your exclusion was an oversight this helps sooth your sensitivity, but if you were left out on purpose then you have to wonder if you are really needed. People can exclude others passively or proactively. Either result is ugly. Exclusion communicates 'I don't care what you think' or 'I don't need you'.

Exclusion is the opposite of team development and a sense of family. It is counter-productive to building a culture of care. Wise and teachable leaders will extract exclusion from the enterprise by identifying its source and addressing the issue. Exclusion is an enemy to high morale and quiet confidence. When excluded people tend to believe the worst, then mistrust and miscommunication gain ground and undermine the personal development of people. Healthy organizations, on the other hand, exclude exclusion. There is a conscious attempt to include the team in strategic decision making. This takes time, especially in an environment of rapid change. There needs to be enough lead time to process information. Make sure to build buffer time into your corporate calendar to allow for clear communication. This will save you time in the long run. Therefore, eagerly exclude exclusion by building a culture of collaboration.

Fortunately our Lord and Savior, Jesus Christ is all-inclusive. He accepts sinners and saints alike. He includes rich and poor, educated and uneducated, nationals and foreigners, new and old. The Cross of Christ invites all who believe to belong to His family. "And the Spirit and the bride say, 'Come.' And let him that heareth say, 'Come.' And let him that is thirsty come. And whosoever will, let him take the water of life freely" (Revelation 22:17, KJV). In the Body of Christ everyone is affirmed for his or her unique role and responsibility. So at home, work, or church don't forget the ones who have been around the longest or the silent ones. Inclusion means you collaborate on defining the meeting agenda. You trust others to craft their own procedures, objectives, and goals, but you verify with an efficient process. You learn to manage the process and lead people. Inclusion requires servant leadership and prayerful attention to detail. If you run too fast, you will rush right past the opportunity to include others in a better decision. The wisdom of the whole way exceeds the insight of one, so slow down, include others, pray, and plan.

Most importantly you are integrated into God's will, and you are a significant part of Providence's plan. Even when excluded by men He includes you!

OVERCOME BY FEAR

"Then all the people of the region of the Gerasenes asked Jesus to leave them, because they were overcome with fear. So he got into the boat and left." LUKE 8:37

Fear drives out faith and overwhelming fear withdraws its invitation to Jesus. Indeed, Jesus is a gentleman, so He does not tarry where He is not trusted. He will not remain where He is not wanted, and He does not negotiate to be needed. Indeed, faith reaches exhaustion in the face of overwhelming fear. This is especially true when your chronic fear relates to money. Money, more than anything can make you myopic to faith in God. You get so consumed in the crisis of current affairs that you forget your anchor in Almighty God. Money, or the lack of it may be what's killing you. However, money is a symptom to something else below the surface of your fears. Money is not the answer; Jesus is the dependable security you desire.

Do not dismiss prayer and patience, just because you feel out of control. This is where you are tempted to behave like an atheist. You say you believe in God, He is in control and you trust Him, but then your behavior betrays your beliefs. You act like an unbeliever when your actions marginalize your Master. Indeed, it is when the bottom falls out that faith in the Lord needs to be your mainstay. "Be still and know that I am God" (Psalm 46:10). This is when you need Him the most, so be wise and ask Jesus the gentleman to remain with you when "all hell breaks loose". Satan loves to see you alone. He wants you to battle Him in your own strength. He wins when Jesus is run off and fear drives you into irrational actions. Fear keeps you under the curse of always looking over your shoulder in doubt. And all the while your Savior is right beside you, waiting to be your calming force. Take the time to tarry in trust with the One who is totally trustworthy. Do not drive Him away in denial. Rise up from under the load of your languishing condition and come to Christ. Look to Christ for perspective and patience. Don't panic. Ostracize your overwhelming fear by faith. Place it on the stubborn shelf of self-denial and surrender to your Savior.

Now is your opportunity to stand firm and courageous in Christ. Do not run Him off, for He will only stay where He is wanted. Talk is easy, but your walk with Him is what matters most. He desires an authentic and teachable heart. He can do this for you by faith; so let these uncertain times embolden your beliefs. Go deeper with Jesus during desperate days. He is a gentleman waiting for your invitation to stay and not go away. When fear attacks, be overcome by Christ's confidence and warm embrace. Say with David, "The LORD is my light and my salvation— whom shall I fear?" (Psalm 27: 1). Furthermore, be real with those around you. Some of them have gone before you; learn from them. Trust them as a resource, for fear is flattened by the faith of friends. Trust them and Him.

Fear flees in the face of faithfulness, so escort out the fear of failure. Above all else, be overcome by faith's reassurance and not fear of financial loss!

M26 SELF JUSTIFICATION

" 'You have answered correctly,' Jesus replied. 'Do this and you will live.' But he wanted to justify himself, so he asked Jesus, 'And who is my neighbor?'" LUKE 10:28-29

Christians are justified by faith not by self, for self-justification always has an excuse. There is no taking responsibility, but instead looking for a loophole in obedience. Contrary to one committed to Christ, those who seek self-justification are moving away from the Lord. They live on the edge of self-reliance instead of the center of submission to their Savior. People seeking self-justification avoid being held accountable for their actions. There is always a reason why something didn't get done or can't be done. They may have even delegated a responsibility, but have not maintained accountability. Accountability is not a friend of those seeking to justify themselves. Self-justification remains silent when it needs to speak up for clarification. It complicates matters by avoiding simple solutions that could be obtained through teachability and truth seeking. Self-justification has an aversion to trust and a resistance to reality. It may smile in agreement, but still not change. Self-justification is for those who want to make the rules and decide which apply to them. This lifestyle choice is a house of cards that overtime tumbles down under the caricature of obedience. Eventually these types of people will implode. Their relationships unravel and their status becomes suspect. Their influence remains inward and they become victims of the small world of self-justification.

However, those justified by faith have an entirely different take on life. You understand the need to listen to understand and follow the ways of Jesus. You are compelled to mature your faith in Christ. There are no excuses on your lips, only questions from their heart on how to be transformed by the Holy Spirit. You eagerly submit to authority and are looking for ways to better communicate and be held accountable. You are set free from your little world and are thoroughly engaged with eternity and the team around you. Your goal is to integrate your faith into every aspect of your life. Christ is the focus when you are justified by faith. The Bible says, "So the law was put in charge to lead us to Christ that we might be justified by faith" (Galatians 3:24).

You know you are justified by faith when you are 100% surrendered to your Savior Jesus. You are attracted to His and other individuals' questioning of your actions. You invite accountability and your goal is to engage in a higher quality of living by becoming more like Christ in your motives. Justification by faith means you are made right by God. There is no need to hide anything for authenticity is the fruit of faith and pretense is the fruit of fear. So trust God and others with your strengths and struggles. Be a good neighbor by getting beyond yourself. Faith-filled living focuses on the needs of others and it takes responsibility.

It trusts Christ instead of testing Christ. By faith, Jesus has already justified you now and forever more!

CONNECTION AND TRUST

> "So he got up and went to his father. But while he was still a long way off,
> his father saw him and was filled with compassion for him; he ran to his son,
> threw his arms around him and kissed him." LUKE 15:20

Connection is a common craving for those created in the image of God. You were made to connect with Christ, your spouse, your parents and children, friends and those with whom you have daily contact. You want connection with the Body of Christ and with your community. Connection is critical to relational health, without it you feel alone and fearful. There is a much higher probability for mistrust and misunderstanding when connection is void. Indeed, you can be disconnected from someone and not realize what's happened. You may feel like everything is just fine because on the surface things are running smoothly. But when you take the time to do a relational audit, you may discover some degree of unintentional disconnection has transpired. Take the time to build back this trust. Do not blame others or ignore its reality. Instead with a posture of humility and a position of brokenness, extend an apology and accept the love and forgiveness of the offended party. This is the spirit of mature men and women. Relational restoration is the goal of all who are seeking to follow Jesus Christ. You have a ministry of reconciliation (2 Corinthians 5:18).

Moreover, connection with Christ is the noblest need. Trust in Him penetrates your being when you experience a high degree of connectivity to Christ. However, when you experience a divine disconnect, you become prey to Satan's fearful lies. He seeks to make you a victim of his vicious cycle of cynicism and thinking the worst. The enemy exploits relational disconnect with fear, anger, and suspicion. He does this in your marriage and in your working relationships. However there is conduit for connection, sincere surrender to God Almighty links you with the Lord. He lifts up those bowed in submission to Him and loves them to Himself. The love of God dissolves disconnection and replaces it with connection. When you humbly receive the love of Christ, you connect. When you humbly receive the love of people, you connect. Love leads to connection, because love covers a multitude of sins (I Peter 4:8).

Furthermore, connection travels on the road of clear communication and care. Communication and care connect by understanding. This takes time, unselfishness, and discipline, but this is the high road of extending honor to others. Pray about how to best connect with your spouse, child, or friend. Commit to this over the long haul, and assure them that disconnection is not an option. Give and receive love and respect, then watch connection progress aggressively. Go often for hugs from your heavenly Father and linger long in the love of the Lord. Connection with Christ sets the table for connection with people. The fruits of connection are peace, assurance, and trust.

Stay connected for Christ's sake. Stay joined to Jehovah and feast on its fruit of faith!

M28 EXHAUSTED FROM SORROW

"When he arose from prayer and went back to the disciples,
he found them asleep, exhausted from sorrow." Luke 22:45

Sorrow is exhausting for it saps your energy deep down into the depths of your soul. It is fatiguing to experience and to watch, as sadness slits open a hurting heart. It is the fruit of anticipated or actual loss and it seems to linger longer than is needed. It is a hard place to live, because it is emotionally exhausting. Patience runs thin when sorrow relentlessly rocks your world, and anger seems to have the upper hand. Sorrow is a natural outcome from a broken heart, a diseased body, or a depressed mind. However, there is no getting around sorrow in this lifetime, since it is a consequence of original sin (Genesis 3:16-17). Many times sorrow seems unfair and unnecessary for it causes you to pause when you are ready to move on. But it is during times of sorrow that you can connect with God and people in authenticity and intimacy. Indeed, sorrow is a reminder of your limitations, and it leads you into an uncertain fog of emotion. It is very difficult to make wise decisions during a rainstorm of sorrow. You become flooded with fear and are pelted with large drops of dread. Sorrow is a struggle for survival and it desperately desires security. The need for peace and comfort screams for attention. If this legitimate need is left unmet, then fear fills the void. Indeed, sorrow can be a facilitator of faith, or an exercise in futility. It is meant to draw us close to Christ. Sorrow is a path to prayer and prayer brings vitality and focus.

It is through prayer that you are reminded of the awesome God you love, serve, and worship. He reigns over heaven and earth, and He is Lord over life and death. Prayer protects you during sorrow's times of vulnerability. Sorrow creates emotionally frazzled feelings, and thus openness to indiscretion. It is during seasons of sorrow that Satan's deceptions are alive and well. He will try to convince you that you are not loved or appreciated. He will try to lead you to look for love in all the wrong places. Temptation is untamed during times of sorrow. You are exposed to emotionally charged and unwise decision making. Do not allow fear to be the foundation of your relational and financial transactions. Furthermore, the devil wants you to stay mad at God and His people. He knows anger exhausts you. He wants to keep you fatigued in your faith and immobile in your engagement with eternity. However, it is through prayer and meditation on the Word that your Maker will comfort and heal your hurting heart (Psalm 119:28).

Prayer pries open the prison doors of pride and fear; and it gets the attention off you and onto others. Prayer flushes your mind with forgiveness and feelings of faithfulness. It is in prayer that sorrow is laid at the feet of the Man of Sorrows, Jesus (Isaiah 53:3). He sincerely understands your severe sorrow. He knows you hurt. He knows you are afraid. He knows you need Him and He wants you to awaken to His assurance. Do not let the circumstances crush your faith into a coma of inactivity. Use your sorrows are an excuse to hang out with your Savior. Have a little talk with Jesus. Tell Him all about your troubles. He will answer by and by. Your sorrow becomes His security. Jesus transforms your sorrow into His Kingdom outcomes, so follow sorrow to your sympathizing Savior. Share your sorrows with Him and watch Him create memories of His comfort and care.

Pray for a resurrection of joy to follow the death of sorrow. Ask Jesus to strengthen your exhausted soul!

BEST FOR LAST

"Everyone brings out the choice wine first and then the cheaper wine after the guests have had too much to drink; but you have saved the best till now." JOHN 2:10

Jesus sometimes saves the best for last. He delights in delivering the unexpected to the unsuspecting. He waits until there is opportunity to show up where the needs are rampant, but the solutions are few. Then He meets the need unconventionally and boldly. Many times this is His method, because Christ is counter-intuitive. He wants others to ask, "why?" Why did Jesus save the best for last? One reason the Lord saves the best for last is to honor the recipients. Those who persevere deserve the best. For example, in relationships the fruit of long-term commitment produces the best experiences. Trust, contentment, and fulfillment all earn their right in relationships that resolve to remain true. God blesses those who wait, "Wait for the LORD and keep his way. He will exalt you to inherit the land..." (Psalm 37:34). You experience the best God has to offer when you save yourself for marriage. Sex within the bonds of marriage exceeds exponentially the settlement of premarital capitulation to hormonal-driven sex. Otherwise, you risk disease and a lifetime of disrespect and regret. Waiting on the best brings out the best, for trust in God fosters hope that there must be something better to look forward to in the future. It protects you from impatient impulses that can instantly implode.

Waiting for the best is difficult at times, because it means depending on others to accomplish the goal. The outcome is out of your direct control. You have to trust that others can execute the project better than you can by yourself. Your sphere of influence will remain stunted if you try to do everything yourself. You will be limited by your time, energy, and intellect. Your capacity is a drop in the bucket compared to the resources of an aligned team; you need each other's gifts and skills (Romans 12:4-5). It is your best that brings out the best in others. Therefore, be the best at what you do and expect others to do their very best. Excellence attracts excellence, as mediocrity attracts mediocrity. Be the best that you can be and see to it that others do the same. Best breeds best.

Lastly, trust Jesus to take people and circumstances under your influence and bring out His best. Let go and let the Lord run with the opportunity, and He may surprise you with joy. The best is yet to come if you look to the Lord for His best outcomes. Your humble request of God will result in much more than your capabilities, for Christ has no capacity issues. He is looking for those for whom He can trust with His best. He wants those whose faithfulness to Him far exceeds their earthly ambitions. Do whatever He says and watch Him carry out His very best, because obedience leads to His best. Believe the best is yet to come. Don't settle for less than best. Believe the best in others. Trust Him for the very best. Expect the best. Be your best.

Pray and ask God for His best. Be patient, wait on Him, and remind yourself often... He saves the best for last!

M30 REAP THE BENEFITS

"I sent you to reap what you have not worked for. Others have done the hard work, and you have reaped the benefits of their labor." JOHN 4:38

It is okay to reap the benefits from the work of others, for this is the Lord's law of the harvest. You cannot do everything yourself, but you can build on the efforts of others. Your skill set is needed for this season of work. You can develop the enterprise and relationships further because someone else was faithful to pay a steep price in the beginning. Work and ministry are not done in a vacuum, as they are the result of the prayers and perseverance of other people's faithfulness. Moreover, there is a harvest of character. You reap today what was previously placed in your heart. If the Scriptures were sown into your mind and heart by your parents and/or teachers, then you will experience a harvest of character by the power of the Holy Spirit. You are a product of faithfulness: God's, yours and others. You reap the good and the bad, depending on what was sown into your life all these years. Your harvest may haunt you, or it may help you. If a corrupt seed has rooted itself into your thinking, then God can renew your mind by extracting lies that have grown up and choked out truth. If however, truth has been sprinkled over your soul by good teaching and personal study of God's Word, then you are ripe for a harvest of righteousness. Indeed, be grateful for the positive examples God has placed in your life. Parents, teachers, mentors, leaders, and friends have all sown good seeds into your life all these years. Many faithful men and women have unashamedly labored for the Lord, so you imitate them and Him (I Thessalonians 1:6). You can see heaven more clearly because you stand on the obedient shoulders of past preservers. Opportunities have been created and await your engagement because of the faithful followers of Christ who went ahead.

Therefore, do not miss this unprecedented time of harvest. The fields are white; so do not be yellow with fear, unwilling to trust God. Resist western conveniences that may dilute your courage in Christ. Forgo the fear to move out of our comfort zone into a different time zone. Now is the time to enter into the harvest of souls for your Savior with abandonment and anticipation. He is calling is clear for He has freed you from finances and from self, for the sake of the call. Just as a field not harvested rots for lack of attention, so does the human heart. Follow your heart and you will follow Him. Two thousand years of sowing has produced a ripe harvest never before seen in human history. This is His story that needs to be told. Malaria-stricken missionaries have not labored in vain. It is no accident technological advancements have flattened our world by the exposing and expanding of our faith. Economic and evangelistic opportunities are begging for attention. The time is now. The fields of faith are ripe and waiting for obedient individuals to go where God is already working. Yes, there are plenty of people at home who need Him, but why should someone hear the good news twice when many in the world have not heard it once? Harvest requires work, but its labor is full of joy and fulfillment, so venture out and experience the bountiful benefits of experiencing heaven in the harvest. Be grateful for those who have gone on before and steward the fruit of their faithfulness. Be radically obedient. Weep over the need for reapers.

Pray to the Lord of the harvest to send forth laborers. Say yes to your prayer for laborers until He says no!

SMALL GROUP

"Then Jesus went up on a mountainside and sat down with his disciples."
JOHN 6:3

A small group is necessary for sincere disciples of Christ to thrive in an environment of encouragement and accountability. It is in the confidentiality of a small group that you really begin to understand yourself, others, and God. Without the reality check of the group, your perspective drifts into detrimental living. Jesus structured a small group prayerfully by inviting those who were teachable and available. He knew small groups were wise wards of the soul. It is within the care and concern of a small group that special things take place. Prayers are answered. Tears are shed. Joy erupts. Frustrations are vented. Teaching occurs. Truth is unleashed. Dumb decisions are averted. Wise actions are initiated. Work is found. Families are freed up. Accountability is invited. Love is applied. Character is cultivated. Fun flows.

It is in the confines of a Christ-centered small group that the Holy Spirit woos each heart. He is free to roam and romance each soul to Himself. No wonder the work of the enemy seeks to lure you away from the safety of a small group. Outside of the security of the group you are fair game for his demons of destruction. Wavering disciples become sitting ducks when they struggle alone; dying in desperate silence. You give up the good and give in to the bad without the guardrails of the group. This community of home care was the model of the early church (Acts 2:46).

So, engage with those you would like to get to know better. Seek out spiritually mature followers of Jesus. You are secure in Christ and your small group feeds these feelings of security. A healthy small group is not co-dependent, rather interdependent and Christ-dependent. The group rises to the occasion when a crisis occurs. They minister hope to each other. It is a microcosm of the Body of Christ. Large groups leverage wonderful corporate worship and praise. Gifted teachers thrive in the throngs of bigger is better. However, accountability and care get lost in largeness. It is in the small group that the teaching is synthesized down for personal and practical application. Questions and answers flow unguarded under the influence of the small group. Furthermore, prayer proceeds specifically and supportively within a community of trust. Your prayer life goes to a whole new level because the Lord becomes more intimate through specific supplications. Indeed, the transitions of life are lubricated through the love and acceptance of the group. Christ-centered groups develop Christian communities who reach into the community.

So, be a small group that submits to the authority of the Lord and His church. A small group led by the Spirit encounters Christ!

COMPELLING CROSS

A1

"When you were dead in your sins and in the uncircumcision of your sinful nature, God made you alive with Christ. He forgave us all our sins, having canceled the written code, with its regulations, that was against us and that stood opposed to us; he took it away, nailing it to the cross. And having disarmed the powers and authorities, he made a public spectacle of them, triumphing over them by the cross." COLOSSIANS 2:13-15

The cross is compelling because Christ is compelling. His character is compelling by the depth of its delivery. His love is compelling by the extent of its capacity. His holiness is compelling by the respect it demands. His forgiveness is compelling by the thoroughness of its cleansing. His power is compelling by its ability to disarm the enemy and deem him powerless. Therefore, the cross compels Christ's followers to be like Him. There is nothing neutral about the cross. Either it compels you, or it repels you. The cross either frees you to forgive, or it drives you away stuck in a cycle of cynicism. The cross either leads you into a life of hope, or it discourages you to remain in a state of fear and uncertainty. You cannot embrace the cross and self at the same time. It is not possible. If it were possible, it would not be advisable. A house divided will not stand (Luke 11:17). A heart divided will collapse under the weight of diluted loyalties. Therefore, the cross compels you to make a radical commitment to Christ. The cross looked for a moment like man's torture chamber, but instead it turned into God's remedy for redemption. The cross is not a caricature of compassion; it is compassion. It is God's love personified. Man won the physical battle that day, but God won the spiritual one. It took physical death to triumph over the enemy in the spiritual realm. Thus, the cross compels you to overcome.

Go back to the foot of the cross. This is where the love and the blood of Christ flowed down together for you. This is a rare combination that has compelled millions for generations, to extend the love of God to the lost and the least. The foot of the cross is compelling because it is the location for the most leverage, "For the message of the cross is foolishness to those who are perishing, but to us who are being saved it is the power of God" (I Corinthians 1:18). When you and I kneel at the cross, our life has exponential upside in the hand of God. Your outrageous obedience ripples across race, generations, and even the globe. The cross launches you to live for the Lord.

Indeed, the cross you bear is compelling (Luke 14:27). It is compelling because it reflects the sacrifice and salvation of the cross of Christ. Moreover, the cross you hold high in word and deeds draws all men to Jesus (John 12:32). All cultures, denominations, races, and socioeconomic classes are compelled by Christ. His cross invites, and even demands, a response. To remain neutral is not an option. The cross either compels you to repent, or it repels you to perpetuate in your sin. You can choose a divine destiny, or one of your own making. The cross means death to self and sin, but life in Christ. "If anyone would come after me, he must deny himself and take up his cross and follow me" (Mark 8:34). On the surface the cross seems only to represent death, but underneath it is life. Jesus died to give you life.

Indeed, Christ and the cross are compelling to the upmost degree. Therefore, be captivated by the cross and you will become fully alive in and for Him!

A2   FOLLOW HIM

> "And anyone who does not carry his cross and follow me cannot be my disciple…"
> LUKE 14:27

You follow Jesus because of His invitation and His worthiness. You follow Jesus because His way is the best way and because you are His disciples. You follow Jesus because there is none other that offers an abundant life on earth and eternal life in heaven. You follow the Lord because He is your leader into His will. He is worth following because He can be trusted; He will not lead you astray. The Lord's leadership is pristine, potent and practical. Therefore, pursue Him as a faithful follower. Do not hold back one ounce of obedience and loyalty to your leader Jesus Christ. Where He leads, follow. Where He leads, go. His path will be painful at times, but it is in your pain that He purifies. Follow Him and you will be forever grateful for He does not disappoint.

Indeed, follow Him through your difficult days. Do not give in to the temptation to quit. Where else is there to go? This is the insightful question Peter posed out of frustration (John 6:68). It is in your adversity that you desire the Almighty. He is not occupied with a celestial distraction somewhere far away. He is still leading you through this valley of despair. Do not give up on Him for He has not given up on you. He still lovingly leads even though the resistance you feel may be rubbing your soul. He will pull you through this present predicament. Use this time of challenge to strengthen your faith in Him. Stay behind Jesus and depend on His wisdom and care. He can handle the forces of hell, much less any other circumstance that is crushing your confidence. Follow Him through this fog of fear. He is just ahead and can be trusted without reservation.

Moreover, follow Him in your success. These good days may be for a season, so shower all the glory of God over your accomplishments. Progress and positive results are cause for celebration and praise to the Lord. Make sure everyone knows that you answer to a higher accountability in Almighty God. He is the reason for your financial rewards and your accolades from impressed onlookers. Success is meant to inspire us to follow Him with even more intense abandonment and humility. The momentum your Maker has given you is to propel you ahead in faithfulness. Follow Him through this season of success so you will not be swayed to depend on self. Self followers self-destruct. Jesus followers, on the other hand handle success with humility. Give God the glory during these good times. Leverage the Lord's blessing for His Kingdom. Follow Him.

Lastly, follow Him and become fishers of men (Mark 1:17). Jesus is in the soul-saving business. So as you follow the Lord, you become very interested in His business. You take stock in saving souls, because this is the industry of His Kingdom. His investments provide the greatest long-term return. You fish for men and women because your heavenly Father longs for their love and loyalty. You follow Him so others may follow Him. Follow Him so your family may follow Him. Follow Him so your friends may follow Him. Follow Him so your foes may follow Him. Faithfully follow

God, and you, will inspire others to follow God. Disciples follow their wise and loving leader Jesus!

AVOID EXTREMES

"The man who fears God will avoid all extremes."
ECCLESIASTES 7:18B

Extremes tend to get you into trouble. They put relationships on edge and require an exorbitant amount of energy to maintain. Extreme love seems okay, but not to the extent of neglecting responsibilities or feeding ego. You can have too much of a good thing, such as too much humility or excessive exercise. Anything taken to the extreme causes damage somewhere. It may be emotional neglect of your family, or the lack of time to maintain your home. You say, "But I need extra time at work to get my business (or ministry) off the ground." This may be true, but if you launched your business two years ago and you are still working overtime, something needs adjustment. What was meant to be extreme for a season can become a habit for a lifetime. Left unchecked, extreme behavior is destructive. Ironically, you start out with a goal of productivity, but the result can become counter-productive. Maybe for a season you need to reverse these adverse trends with extreme actions in the opposite direction. Your physical, spiritual and emotional well being may be craving a sabbatical to recover from years of over-commitment and/or abuse. You may need to totally abstain from alcohol, because its abuse has begun to control you. Extremes, often times need to be battled by extremes. But be careful, because extremes can be a vicious cycle that never ceases.

Furthermore, the fear of God is your lasting remedy for extinguishing extremes. Embrace the eternal and you will encounter extremes with balance and brevity. Because you fear God, you will trust Him to live out a balanced life. Fear of God keeps top of mind your passion to love and obey Him. Christ becomes your mode of operation. Look to Jesus, and admire how He aligned His heart and schedule each day to follow the will of His heavenly Father. He prayed 'not my will, but your will be done' (Luke 22:42). This is the pattern for people who want to exhibit abundant living. He said yes to what most people would say no to. And He said no to what most would say yes to. He was counter-cultural and counter-intuitive with His choices. His focus on the eternal made time with a Samaritan woman seem extreme, but it was normal to Jesus (John 4:4-6).

Jesus redefined extreme. His life is the normal Christian life. So make sure your definitions of extreme are accurate according to the Lord's. Indeed, extreme sports may be entertaining to watch, but they are no way to live an ongoing life. God desires men and women who fear Him and who are consistent to walk in His ways (Psalm 128:1). He is looking for steady obedience over the long haul. People who have extreme fluctuations of "everything is great" to "everything is terrible" are undependable. Their availability is based on wavering circumstances, instead of their unwavering Lord. Your rock and refuge is Jesus. He gives you the foundation for stable living, so fear God and you will be free from extreme measures. It may take longer than you like, but be consumed by Him and you will marginalize extremes. This can be extremely difficult, but with the Lord all things are possible. Trust Him and reject earthly extremes.

Your family and friends will be extremely grateful you did. Fear God and avoid all extremes!

A4 FAINT-HEARTED FAITH

"From the ends of the earth I call to you, I call as my heart grows faint; lead me to the rock that is higher than I. For you have been my refuge, a strong tower against the foe."
PSALM 61:2

Sometimes it seems like you are a million miles away from your Master Jesus. It's like He is doing big business on the other side of the world in Africa, India and China. Your small concerns seem trivial in the big scheme of our Savior's strategy. Like in the Parable of the Talents (Matthew 25), your Master has left you to faithfully manage His stuff while He has gone away. However you grow impatient, bored and even faint-hearted from fear and/or fatigue. You wonder if faithfulness to your heavenly Father is really worth the effort, and you question the cause and your calling. It was exciting when you first started on this journey of faith, but now it is unfocused and uncertain. Your mind may have migrated to a melancholy and depressed state. Your heart grows faint without the fire of fresh faith. Left unchecked, a crevice of concern can become a canyon-like crisis between you and Christ. Life may have brought you onto a fearful ledge and you are paralyzed for fear of falling. The distance makes you dizzy in the faith, while you look down at the landscape of life. You experience an acrophobia of unbelief without the intimacy of Almighty God. However, now is the time to grab hold of the Lord's arm for stability. Even when you are on the verge of despair, God is there. No spot is too dreary and no condition is too deplorable. Whether life or death, prayer is available.

Prayer is there for you to puncture heaven's portal in the middle of your trials. You may be experiencing provocation from insensitive souls. An undiagnosed illness that saps your energy may be gnawing on your nerves. Your faithfulness goes unnoticed and unrewarded, and that perplexes you. You may be overwhelmed because of your total lack of control over the cruel circumstance you wake up to every morning. One or all of these trials may be smothering your heart. Because your heart is faint, it is unable to pump the blood of belief to the extremities of your faith. Your eyes are moist with tears. It is okay to cry. Cry out to Christ for it is heaven's substitute for spiritual speech. God is the center of life, hope, love and joy. Christ is the spiritual cardiologist for your suffering heart. Look to the Lord to lead you into His next steps, as He guides you to higher ground.

Furthermore, He wants to lead you from survival to revival. A Holy Spirit initiated revival brings new life to lethargic faith. Lean into the Lord, and lean on the Lord during these lean times. It is legitimate for a man or woman to be led by the Lord to His rock of refuge for rest and recovery. Christ carries you to His tower of truth to renew your mind and revive your heart. Move away from the ledge of illegitimate longings, and move toward your trustworthy Lord. You lean into Him for grace upon grace. You ask Him to embolden your beliefs. Climb up with Christ while your heart pumps the blood of bold belief.

Above all else, you are faith-hearted and not faint-hearted when you journey with Jesus. Trust in Him is a strong tower against your foes!

FAINTING FAITH

"As the deer pants for streams of water, so my soul pants for you, O God. My soul thirsts for God, for the living God. When can I go and meet with God?" PSALM 42:1-2

A fainting faith is forever in search of its heavenly Father. There is a building intensity for intimacy with the Almighty. Sometimes your faith faints from sheer exhaustion. It passes out for lack of prayer or even during prayer. Indeed do not allow divine duty to drive you for very long. This is not a sustainable pace or prayer-friendly posture. Rest instead in the continual call of Christ. Service to God, without communion with Christ, leads to spiritual fatigue. Your soul's life is sucked out, because fainting faith leaves you in a state spiritual fatigue. The scary thing is, your faith can be on the brink of fainting and you are unaware, therefore keep your life pace governed by grace or you will out-run your soul. Time with your Master requires margin. In fact, any significant relational investments take place in the margin of your life. Margin is like the white space on a page of paper. It makes reading enjoyable, digestible, and inviting to the eye. In the same way lives with margin are inviting. You do not interrupt people with margin, because they know how to make time for those who matter. So it is in your time with Jesus, carve out space on your calendar to be with your Savior. You do this by faith, trusting the Lord will make up for any lost time. Christ can get things done without you. "With man this is impossible, but with God all things are possible" (Matthew 19:26).

Even elegant animals like deer understand the need to stop and drink water. The instinctive animal has no other thought than to slow down and drink as often as is needed. So it is when you wish to hydrate your heart. Your soul cannot stand sustained times without its Savior. Jeremiah reprimanded the people for ignoring their need for the Lord, "...they have forsaken the LORD, the spring of living water" (Jeremiah 17:13b). Just as water is necessary for the body to function, so drinking from divine resources is required for our soul to sustain itself. Otherwise your faith faints for lack of the Lord. Your soul's thirst is a perpetual appetite that can only be quenched by Christ. Drunkards try to replace their soul's longing with liquor. It doesn't work, for it makes matters worse by seeking a substitute for their Savior. Drink is a synthetic savior for a thirsty soul.

Lastly, you can go and meet with the Lord immediately. He is always accessible. Get on your knees and pour out your soul in prayer. Drink in the love of the Lord. Guzzle down the grace of God. Sip on the joy of Jesus. Furthermore, go to church and lift up your soul in worship to your great and mighty God. Drink in the praise and adoration of God's glory with other sincere believers in Jesus. Your soul is satisfied in environments that engage you with eternity. Worship, Bible study, prayer, and community with Christ followers quench our thirsty souls. The world parches your soul, but heaven hydrates your heart. Your faith will flourish and not faint as you take the time to quench your thirsty soul.

Drink often with Jesus. "For the Lamb at the center of the throne will be their shepherd; he will lead them to springs of living water" (Revelation 7:17). He refreshes!

A6 FRIENDS COMMUNICATE

"Tychicus will tell you all the news about me. He is a dear brother, a faithful minister and a fellow servant in the Lord. I am sending him to you for the express purpose that you may know about our circumstances and that he may encourage your hearts." COLOSSIANS 4:7-8

Friends communicate, for this is at the heart of friendship. If a friendship is denied communication, it will begin to wilt. Like a plant without water, friendship without communication dries up. Yes, friends can go for years without seeing each other and still connect. However, a vibrant and growing friendship needs communication. There is an intentional effort to understand how each other are doing. You pick up the phone, write a letter or e-mail, or make a personal visit. It may be sending a message through a friend. This is effective, though not quite the same as showing up in person yourself. New friends are a blessing, but what about the friends who have been with you over all these years? They have been faithful, and have not discarded or ignored you like an old pair of shoes. It is easy to fall into the trap of only being with friends who can do something for you, but friendship is a two-way street. Sometimes friendship requires you to be the initiator. Your friend may find himself in a high-maintenance stage of life. Do not let his or her one-way communication discourage you. You are a friend indeed when you communicate regularly with someone preoccupied with life issues.

Most importantly make Jesus your best friend, and communicate with Him often. It may require real-time communication, but He is ever-present to be your friend. Your Christian maturity naturally leads to friendship with Jesus (John 15:14-15). What a friend you have in Jesus, so communicate with Him regularly. He is a friend who is always available and who always cares, as He listens attentively and cares compassionately. He listens with an ear of understanding, and He comprehends your circumstances. He cares and He invites your communication, because faith in Christ means you are a friend of Christ. Like Abraham you are God's friend (James 2:23). You are friends, so you can talk with Him directly and openly about your feelings and fears. However, you cannot be a friend of the world and of God's at the same time, "Anyone who chooses to be a friend of the world becomes an enemy of God" (James 4:4).

So talk to the Lord in prayer, and ask others to talk with Him on your behalf. Allow them the joy of praying to their best friend for another friend. This builds friendships in both directions, as friendship with God and people can feed off each other. If you want to feel close to God, talk with Him like a friend. "The LORD would speak to Moses face to face, as a man speaks with his friend" (Exodus 33:11). He is still Lord and holy, but He is also a friend. Friends are friends forever, and friendship with Jesus is for eternity. Communication is a great friend of friendship, so reach out with the goal of their encouragement and watch your friendships flourish.

Paul modeled this in his love for people, "But we ought always to thank God for you, brothers loved by the Lord, because from the beginning God chose you to be saved through the sanctifying work of the Spirit and through belief in the truth" (2 Thessalonians 2:13).

HONOR FAITHFULNESS

"..but honors those who fear the Lord, who keeps his oath even when it hurts."
PSALM 15:4

Faithfulness naturally flows from your fear of the Lord and both are honorable. These attributes are honorable because their focus is reverence, respect and fear of God. Fear of God is honorable, as it esteems value at its highest level, and there is no one or nothing more valuable than the Lord. You stand in awe of the Almighty because you fear Him, and you obey Him because you fear Him. You worship Him because you fear Him, and you remain faithful even when it is costly. The fear of the Lord facilitates faithfulness.

Furthermore, you are to honor those who fear the Lord. You may have a parent or grandparent who has remained faithful all these years in their love for Jesus. Their life is a resume of repentance and obedience to God. Honor them for they have prayed with you and for you. Make a big deal out of their faithfulness to do the right thing, even when it required sacrifice. Honor elderly saints in front of your children, so these young ones can appreciate a life that invested wisely in what matters to God. Hopefully, they will emulate the admirable traits of those you honor. Moreover, honor the faithful Christian workers in your life. It may be a pastor, missionary, evangelist, teacher, or spiritual entrepreneur. Honor them for the sake of the next generation.

How do you honor those who fear the Lord and are faithful to do the right things? You honor them by listening to their wisdom and applying it to your life. You compliment the faithful when you receive truth from them and integrate it into your behavior. God designed your heart to be a sanctuary and refuge for truth. Wisdom is God's daughter who is not shy about going public (Proverbs 1:20). When you learn and apply the principles of the faithful, you become people of principle. Your obedience to God honors those who obey God. Honor takes on the characteristics of Christ and His followers. Your obedience under fire will not go unnoticed in heaven or on earth. Your heavenly Father honors your faithfulness. Those who love you the most honor your faithfulness. Therefore, remain honorable and honor faithfulness for this honors God.

Jesus said, "...all may honor the Son just as they honor the Father. He who does not honor the Son does not honor the Father, who sent him" (John 5:23).

A8 LEADERSHIP AND FRIENDSHIP

"Faithful are the wounds of a friend, But the kisses of an enemy are deceitful."
PROVERBS 27:6

Lead first and be a friend second, for an effective and efficient enterprise understands that leadership trumps friendship. Just as the old saying goes, "Lead, follow, or get out of the way." Wise and intentional leadership is necessary for the health of the organization, and leadership is watered down when friendships dictate strategic direction. Friendships should forge the team, but not unduly dilute excellent outcomes based on courageous leadership decisions. If a leader is preoccupied with what a friend may think or do, then he risks diminishing his decision for the sake of sparing someone's feelings. Politics are not the plumb-line. The standard for leadership decisions are the values and principles of the organization.

Friendship can become a fruit of wise leadership, but it is not meant to drive wise leadership. Indeed, loyalty to friends is an important and valued attribute of an effective leader. But do not allow loyalty to cloud your rationale of what's best for the team. Sometimes the best thing you can do for the team and your friend is to either fire him, or reassign him. Make sure your leadership is grounded in principle so your friendships will not be a threat to doing what's right. Let a friend know up front how much you value him, but not to the detriment of what's best for the business or ministry.

Furthermore, friends can be the hardest or the easiest to lead. It all depends on yours and their expectations. Does your friend perceive you as a partner or a boss? Is your perception of your friend one of high value or just one of expedience that gets results? Therefore, lead first in humility, courage and clarity. Let your friends know up front what you value as a leader and how they fit into the big picture of organizational success. Constantly ask, "What's best for the team?" instead of "What does my friend want?" You lead first by defining the role of friendship on the team, and you keep leadership a priority by not playing favorites. This promotes teamwork and diffuses jealousy.

Lastly, wise leaders make hard decisions, even when it adversely affects a friend. This protects the integrity of the organization. Paul felt this tension when he decided that his friend John Mark was not mature enough for the responsibility of a mission trip, "Barnabas wanted to take John, also called Mark, with them, but Paul did not think it wise to take him, because he had deserted them in Pamphylia and had not continued with them in the work" (Acts 15:37-38).

SHARE CREDIT, TAKE BLAME

"For by the grace given me I say to every one of you: Do not think of yourself more highly than you ought, but rather think of yourself with sober judgment, in accordance with the measure of faith God has given you. Just as each of us has one body with many members, and these members do not all have the same function..." ROMANS 12:3-4

Credit is not created for one person, because if any one person holds onto it; it corrupts. It corrupts his judgment by causing him to think more highly of himself. Confiscated credit gives you a false confidence. It is a confidence based on the illusion of invincibility instead of the reality of culpability. Credit is a pearl of great price that needs to be shared, so share it often and share it liberally. Wise leaders quickly give away credit to individual team members and to the team as a whole. Credit given is recognition of the contribution, skill, and smarts of the staff. A leader who dispenses credit knows he or she has severe limitations. Very little excellent execution and follow up would occur outside of the people who give tedious attention to the details of implementation. You give credit where credit is due because the team represents the eyes and ears of your leadership. Secure leaders can't wait to give away the credit. It burns a hole in the pocket of their ego.

Strong leaders understand how to value others and their unique contribution to the culture of the organization. Therefore, share the credit by praising people publicly and privately for their character and values. This affirms them before their peers and puts the emphasis on what's really important. Provide financial rewards for this spreads the wealth around and communicates care and generosity. Recognize specific achievements, like a project completion or graduation from a professional training program. This encourages their growth and development.

Moreover, a leader takes the blame for this model's responsibility for actions. A leader "keeps the buck" of blame instead of passing it on. He is as quick to take the blame as he is to share the credit. When there is a break down in process or a 'dropped ball' of responsibility, the only name he mentions is his own. He is the culprit in crisis. Like a surge protector, he buffers the blame from the team by standing in the gap with mature leadership. He has no claim to fame, but he does take the blame when things go south. A leader's example of blame-taking is infectious to followers. Followers unconsciously find themselves emulating the same blame ownership in their spheres of influence. "I am responsible," and "I missed the deadline" are common statements of blame-takers. When you learn how to effectively take blame and give credit, you are on your way to mature leadership.

Mature leadership trusts the Lord, who blesses trusting leaders. He empowers people through leaders who share the credit and take the blame!

A10 GREAT FAITH

"When Jesus heard this, he was amazed at him, and turning to the crowd following him,
he said, 'I tell you, I have not found such great faith even in Israel.' "
LUKE 7:9

Great faith comes from believing in your great God. There is awe with the Almighty for it is enamored with eternal matters. What matters to your Master, matters to you. Great faith in our heavenly Father is produced in a heart of humility, contentment, gratitude and dependence. You see yourself as ordinary person blessed by an extraordinary Savior. You have been rescued from the snares of sin and placed in a position of being God's child. Your old life of self-focus, contrasts with your new life of focus on others. You are free from fraternizing in trivial pursuits and are compelled to follow Christ's commands. Great faith grows you more like Jesus.

Just as Jesus was under the authority of His heavenly Father (John 10:17), so you are expected to be under Christ's authority. God's Kingdom requires surrender and submission to His authority, not asking God to bless your efforts after the fact. You prayerfully and humbly submit your plans to the cleansing power of the Holy Spirit. Once the Spirit has scrubbed your intentions, then you are free to move forward. When you remain under His authority, you are able to hear His commands clearly. Great faith acts on what it hears from the Lord, for instant obedience is evidence of great faith.

Great faith is not afraid to obey Jesus. It may seem overwhelming at the time, but when God says so, it is done. So you are wise to instantly obey what He says. Do not hesitate when you hear from heaven. He has His reasons for wanting obedience from you now. For one thing, He knows you might forget if you fail to obey now. He knows your fragile memory can miss Him. So when you instantly obey, you don't run the risk of forgetting your heavenly Father's instructions. Instant obedience feeds great faith in God.

Moreover our great faith grows others. Your children see your great faith and are challenged to do the same. It serves them well when you are not around. Your friends and acquaintances see your great faith and they have hope. Your unbelieving relatives see your great faith and come to believe there has to be a God behind such bold belief. Above all else your heavenly Father sees your great faith and sees someone He can trust. He can trust you with His blessing, His healing, His wisdom, and His resources. Great faith is trustworthy because it is grounded in God. It is not blind and irresponsible, rather it sees the unseen and stewards it well. Great faith is found among the ordinary. It is engagement in everyday life that invites great faith.

Your role as a regular Christian makes you a compelling candidate for great faith. Indeed great faith promotes God's greatness!

"These [trials] have come so that your faith—of greater worth than gold, which perishes even though refined by fire—may be proved genuine and may result in praise, glory and honor when Jesus Christ is revealed."   I PETER 1:7

Genuine faith is by the grace of God, and trials prove its authenticity. Fire exposes faith forgeries; so is your current challenge a test in faithfulness? It may be hard to hold up your head of faith because of the difficulties you are experiencing. Your Savior seems to be on Sabbatical, but you still seek Him. You fill in the blanks by faith and you love Him even though you cannot feel Him. Your faith facilitates fervent love for your Lord, so you believe in Him even though you are unable to see Him. Furthermore, your faith under fire inherits inexpressible joy through prayer, which seems strange to the uninformed. People may become curious about or a little perturbed by the persistent peace and assurance that travels within the depths of your soul. You know you are saved by the grace of God, for this is your baseline. Salvation by faith in Jesus Christ is your foundation and this was your launching pad for a life consecrated to Christ.

Because you have entrusted Him with eternity, you can trust Him with this temporary trial. Because you trust Him with your soul, you can trust Him with this sorry situation. Do not fret that your faith is under fire, for this unreasonable affliction is meant to stoke the fires of your affections for Christ. Turn the tables on trouble by traversing deeper into your devotion to Jesus. It takes troubles to tear off encumbrances to your eternal perspective. Lukewarm living tends to create cataracts around your spiritual eyes. When you start out as a new Christian your faith is fresh, but you have infantile intimacy. You discovered that growth in your faith (like all relationships) comes from resistance. Sometimes life pushes back with pressure and prickly circumstances, and it is when Christ comes into your conflict that your faith increases. Your faith is the most valuable asset you own. Your money may move you closer or further away from faith, but it cannot acquire faith. Salvation was purchased by Jesus on the cross. Therefore, the currency that Christ receives is faith. Yes, give generously to good works, but do not depend on your benevolent acts as a surrogate for belief.

Moreover, allow your current crisis of belief to increase your faith, as it grows in your mind and heart its value increases. Your faith either diminishes or compounds in worth. If your only faith experience is your salvation, then your faith is stunted. Stunted and immature faith is no match for the inconvenience and injustice of this world. God wants to grow your faith into robust authenticity. Indeed His revelation is the most compelling under pressure. Therefore, see these tough times as a transition from your "teen" years of faith into your "adult" years of faith. Genuine and growing faith can be the fruit of fiery trials. The Lord's love will lead you through this tough time, as you learn lessons in faith from teachers of trials. Moreover, your strong and authentic faith will be a springboard of comfort to others. Effective ministry is one incredible outcome of adversity. Nonetheless, genuine faith is God's ultimate goal.

Genuineness is like gold. It's valuable, compelling, inviting, and everlasting. Above all else, it glorifies God!

A12 LOVE HIM

"Love the LORD, all his saints! The LORD preserves the faithful,
but the proud he pays back in full."   PSALM 31:23

God commands His saints to love Him, and He loves you so you can love Him. Love and the Lord go hand-in-hand, for you are locked into a love relationship with your Savior. The question is not if you love the Lord, but how you love the Lord. Yes, your love for Christ pales in comparison to His love for you. However, you love because the Lord is worthy of your love. He longs for your love, and He invites and desires your love. Indeed, God is honored and worshiped when His saints love him. Your love holds Him in eternal esteem, what joy, for you can love the Lover of your soul. Unredeemed sinners cannot love the Lord because they are incapable of loving Him. This is a perk that only disciples of Christ can enjoy. Unless you have been converted by the free grace of God, you cannot love Him. Love for the Lord is not unlocked until you turn the key of faith. It affords you the opportunity to love the Lord, and you will remain unfulfilled, lost and confused until you are able to love Him.

Loving your Creator completes you, His creation. Your relationship with the Lord is tolerable at best without an engaging and loving relationship. Loving the Lord moves you out of the basement of embarrassment to the balcony of basking in His presence. Love lifts you to the Lord and He is drawn to your love. He loves to be loved by His children. It is love of the Lord that starts you out in faith and sustains your faith. Loving the Lord fuels your faith, energizes your soul and galvanizes your beliefs. It inflames hope and feeds forgiveness. Furthermore, loving the Lord is a catalyst for becoming more like Him. You take on the traits of whom and what you love. You are a reflection of the objects of your affections. Therefore, love Him because you want to be like Him. Love is a magnet that draws you toward your model for living. Transformation into the character of Christ is the goal for those who love Him.

Indeed, your love for Him transforms your behavior. So, love the Lord with your whole being. Love Him with your body, soul and spirit. Love Him physically by taking care of the body He created. Keep it pure and healthy. Love Him emotionally by processing and expressing your feelings. Allow Him to convert your anger into holy passion. Allow your love for Him to explode in the emotion of thanksgiving, praise and celebration. Moreover, love Him with your spirit. Connect with Christ in prayer and meditation on His Word. He reveals His will for seeking souls, so love Him in the morning, in the noontime, and love Him when the sun goes down. Since loving Him is right, you don't want to be wrong.

Therefore, love the Lord without ceasing. Execute His greatest commandment by loving your Lover!

LOVE THE LORD 13

"Love the Lord, all his saints! The Lord preserves all the faithful,
but the proud he pays back in full."   PSALM 31:23

Some things are hard to love, but God is not one of them. He is easy to love, because He is love (I John 4:16). However, you can be so busy getting your own needs met you forget to love the Lover of your soul. You can love Him, because He first loved you (I John 4:19). It is a reciprocal love relationship in which you are privileged to participate. If you receive His love without loving Him back you miss the full-orbed affect of love's design. A one-way love is not God's best. His best is to be loved by Him, and then to regularly and relentlessly love Him as your heavenly Father. He desires and can't wait to be loved by one of His children. Any lover loves to be loved, and God is no exception. His love is an invitation for you to love Him back. Do not be shy about loving God, for you can love Him even if you don't know exactly how. After all, how do you love someone who has everything?

One way is to love Him with your time. You do spell love, T-I-M-E, so it is impossible to love without investing time. Time may be the most valuable asset you have to give. Your investment of time is an expression of your love. If you say you love Him but fail to spend time with Him then your love is shallow, sentimental and expedient. A confessed love without commitment is a caricature of love. His unconditional love is your baseline for loving Him for it is radical and redeeming. The love of God has no beginning or end, and it is boundless in its intensity and borderless in its expression. Your capacity to love is directly proportional to how much you allow Him to love you. If you are closed and conservative in your acceptance of His love, you will lack liberality in your love for Him.

Another way you love Him is by loving others. John's teaching is clear, "Dear friends, since God so loved us, we also ought to love one another. No one has ever seen God; but if we love one another, God lives in us and his love is made complete in us" (I John 4:11-12). You love Him when you feed, clothe, educate, and create jobs on behalf of Christ. You love Him when you season your actions with words of grace and hope. You love Him when you forgive a parent or a child who has disrespected and hurt you profoundly. You love Him when you do your work well unto the Lord. You love Him when you remain faithful in your marriage, even when your spouse has not. You love Him when you confess and repent of your sin, because you know He hates and despises concealed sin. You love Him when you love the unlovely. Humility finds reasons to love, while pride tends to procrastinate from a love affair with the Lord. Love Him with all your heart and watch Him heal your heart.

The consequences of loving God are without total comprehension. He desires and invites your love; therefore love the Lord!

"And the leaders and the officials have led the way in this unfaithfulness.
When I heard this, I tore my tunic and cloak, and pulled hair from my head
and beard and sat down appalled."   EZRA 9:2B-3

Be careful not to get comfortable with sin, especially the sin of leaders. It has a way of gaining respectability and acceptance. What used to be appalling a generation ago has become standard every day affair. Culture can become all-inclusive to the point of ethical anarchy and moral disillusionment. There is a movement afoot to legitimize and legalize sin. Its victims will be you, your children, the church, and society. This threat to common sense and authentic moral living is not going away. If anything it is gaining steam, and even more appalling is the unfaithfulness of those in leadership. So be careful for you become like those who lead you. If Christ and His Word are accepted as the ultimate standard of leadership, then faithfulness to God can be expected. On the other hand, if unfaithful leaders are compromising long-held Christian beliefs and traditions, then unfaithfulness to God can be expected.

So, how will you respond to the desecration of divine direction? If you hope it will go away by ignoring it, you will wake up one day under the total dominant influence of unfaithfulness to God. If you accept it incrementally, it will slowly eat away at the moral fabric of culture until you are left barren and broken with the next generation exposed. The unfaithfulness of a leader's behavior must become a "line in the sand" of intolerance. It is at this point of unfaithfulness that changes in leadership are required. Tolerance of unfaithful leaders is irresponsible and un-Christian. There is a time for the silent moral majority to become appalled by the unfaithfulness of leaders. It is responsible and right to be outraged by people who take advantage of public trust for their private pleasure. There are consequences for leaders who dismiss the Bible as irrelevant, or at the best pick and chose the commands that are expedient for their maligned motives. The Bible is not a menu for unfaithful leaders to manipulate for their purposes. Nonetheless, this is where God-fearing people take responsibility.

It begins by confessing and repenting of acceptance of sin. The sin of silent acceptance needs to be awakened and banished from your behavior. Jesus was the hardest on the hypocrisy and unfaithfulness of religious leaders (Matthew 23:13-51). Therefore, judgment does start in the house of God (I Peter 4:17, KJV), for His people are the ones who need to be so appalled by sin that they fall broken before the Lord. You cannot address unfaithfulness in your leaders until it is addressed in your own hearts. But once you have come clean with God, then you have the moral authority and responsibility to confront unfaithful leaders. Unfaithfulness to God is a federal offense in heaven, and so should it be on earth. It is time for God's people to awake from their apathetic slumber over sin, and sound an appalling alarm.

Unfaithfulness is a hideous hypnosis that must be broken by brokenness. You can start with your own confession and repentance, and trust God with the sweeping effect of His Spirit across the land. Be appalled. He is!

The people, however, were still sacrificing at the high places, because a temple had not yet been built for the Name of the LORD. Solomon showed his love for the LORD by walking according to the statutes of his father David, except that he offered sacrifices and burned incense on the high places.   I KINGS 3:2-3

High places haunt, hurt, and hinder your relationship with God, because they are direct competitors with Jesus. They are altars of worship from your past that you never completely destroyed, or removed from your life. You are deceived when we think they can co-exist with Christ and not bring you harm. You tolerate them; even thinking your love for the Lord allows you to have this mistress who in fact derails you into not finishing well. The wisest man in the world next to Jesus learned this the hard way. Solomon thought he was smarter than God (not so wise), and went to the high place of degrading marriage, but it blew up in his face by debilitating his family. His high place of pride kept him from experiencing God's best and from finishing well. No one is immune from its insidious outcomes.

Your high place may be the propensity to drink too much; indeed, alcohol has become your altar of escape. Or, you may be secretly serving the god of sex. The Internet with its streaming video, or publications with their glossy photos, have captured your affections in direct opposition to your devotion to Christ. Your high place may be the residue of salty language, eating too much, or exercise (the lack of, or obsession with). High places are indiscriminate; they bring down celebrity Christians and everyday followers of Jesus. Therefore, God's remedy is to rid them from your life, destroy them before they destroy you. Paul described your need for and the ability to discard your old habits, and put on new spiritual disciplines in Christ, "You were taught, with regard to your former way of life, to put off your old self, which is being corrupted by its deceitful desires; to be made new in the attitude of your minds; and to put on the new self, created to be like God in true righteousness and holiness" (Ephesians 4:22-24).

Lastly, hunker down in your faith and ask heaven to help you obliterate the high places in your heart. Ask your spouse, or a trusted friend to help you identify and define them. Then invite them to hold you accountable to a process of removing high places from your home and work. It may be as obvious as anger, or as discreet as undisciplined thinking. It may be necessary for you to add, or uninstall software on your computer. The seriousness of its influence on your life may require a drastic step like dumping your boyfriend or girlfriend, or changing jobs. If it is the high place of money, ignore its allure by giving more away. Develop friendships that have nothing to do with finances, only an opportunity to grow a relationship without getting something in return. Above all else, go to the low place of increasing your dependency on God, and decreasing your dependency on yourself. He must increase and you must decrease (John 3:30 KJV). Your path to heaven, absent of high places, leads you into a life that finishes well.

Your worship is much higher than high places; it is Jesus and Jesus alone!

A16 POWER'S PRIDE

> "... His fame spread far and wide, for he was greatly helped until he became powerful. But after Uzziah became powerful, his pride led to his downfall. He was unfaithful to the Lord his God..." 2 CHRONICLES 26:15B-16A

Pride is a natural result of power, and left unchecked pride will cause you to do regretful things. It is what keeps couples from communicating, and strains relationships by leaving them in a rut. It confines Christ to Sunday's ritual and the routine of worship. Pride feeds a sense of superiority, so when you reach a certain status in life or work you become a candidate for power's pride. Therefore, be aware of surroundings that bestow power and invite pride. Success invites praise of your skills, gifts, and abilities. You are trusted because of your character and track record. As a consequence, you will gain more and more autonomy, while solidifying a powerful position. This is the time to install boundaries in your life, which help avoid the slippery slide to your downfall.

Indeed, one wise behavior is to share your power. Trust others with their area of expertise, because you do not have the time or the know-how to do their job. Not only is it smart to delegate and trust; it is extremely practical. If you attempt to control everything and everyone, you will squelch creativity and quickly run out of capacity. Your most capable people will feel smothered and resentful. Power's pride makes you feel like you have to be in control. This false sense of superiority has its roots ensnared around insecurity. You will drive people away and drive them crazy with your desire for control, so give it up before people give up on you. Indeed the Lord sees through prideful tactics. The Bible says, "God will bring down their pride despite the cleverness of their hands" (Isaiah 25:11b). Instead, replace your sense of power with service. Seek out another's felt need and serve them. Try to understand where others are coming from, and then release resources around their goals. Become a facilitator of another's agenda, and before you know it power will lose its grip on your psyche.

Above all else, fight power's pride with prayer's humility. Your posture of prayer and humility will foster a spirit of security and trust in God. Prayer pries open a clinched fist of control. Prayer and humility will free you to trust your team with their bigger and better ideas. Dependence of God frees you from depending on intimidation and fear. Fear of God unshackles you from fearing people. Stay on your knees in gratitude to God for your position of influence. Daniel prayed, "I thank and praise you, O God of my fathers: You have given me wisdom and power..."(Daniel 2:23a). Seek Him for wisdom on how to serve, love and lead your family and team. Power is not an opportunity to be served, but rather to serve. Servant leadership deflates power's pride.

Serve God and people with humility and patience. Then watch pride fade into the sunset. Instead of a downfall from power's pride, you will witness a windfall from prayer's humility!

GOD'S PASSOVER

"The blood will be a sign for you on the houses where you are; and where I see the blood,
I will pass over you. No destructive plague will touch you when I strike Egypt."
EXODUS 12:13

God's Passover for the Christian is the blood of Jesus Christ. The cross of Christ is the reason God's judgment of hell is withdrawn from believers. The blood of Christ brings you to God and repels you from sin. It is the process of blood sacrifice that God has prepared for those who desire to follow Him. His only son's shedding of blood proved to be the final sacrifice for the sin of mankind. Yes, it was a gory event tied to a grace-filled consequence. Jesus went through the muck and the mire of man's sin to lead you to salvation. It was not a pretty process, but it was a radically redeeming one.

Christ's unconditional love on the cross has empowered you to love indiscriminately. His torturous death on the cross has equipped you to die daily to our worldly whims. Christ's focus on the will of His heavenly Father as He faced the cross compels you to pray, "Your will be done" (Matthew 26:42). It is the cross of Jesus that gives individual believers God's Passover. God gives you a pass from His judgment, and it is a pass stamped with the blood of His son Jesus. Once you believe in Jesus as the Lamb of God who was slain for your sins, your past, current and future sins are covered. God's Passover is thorough and complete. Therefore, celebrate religiously the radical love and grace of God's Passover. Do not take for granted this emancipation from sin, sorrow, and death. It is cause for solemn and joyful celebration.

His Passover is meant to be celebrated corporately and individually. This is one reason to stay engaged with Christ's bride, the church. The church of Jesus Christ is designed to raise the roof in worship and celebration for God's Passover through His son, Jesus. This weekly celebration is not meant to settle into a take-for-granted posture that is expedient for the moment. Rather this first day of the week is set aside to celebrate God's Passover. Believers remember, so they don't forget. It breaks the heart of God when a church with a steeple outside, forgets the cross inside. Therefore, celebrate corporately and in community with energy and thanksgiving, because of God's Passover through the Cross of Christ. Lastly, celebrate God's Passover individually. Consider making a big deal out of the anniversary of your spiritual birthday; perhaps as part of your physical birthday celebration tell the story of your spiritual birth. God's Passover in Christ is to be remembered and celebrated, both in community and individually.

Enjoy and be grateful, for what great things He has done. God's Passover in Christ is pre-eminent!

A18 DEATH'S FRUIT

"And Jesus answered them, saying, "The hour has come for the Son of Man to be glorified. Truly, truly, I say to you, unless a grain of wheat falls into the earth and dies, it remains alone; but if it dies, it bears much fruit." JOHN 12:23-24 (NASB)

There must be a death before there can be fruit. This is why Jesus Christ is still fruitful after nearly 2,000 years. His death was meant to bear fruit and it has. The fruit of His life, change is represented in billions of lives that have been altered for eternity. Transformation took place because of death for it is the soil for life. The death of Jesus Christ catapulted the plan of God heavenward. No one close to Him wanted Him to leave. How could anything come from losing the One who had given life, healed the sick, and taught with riveting truth? It didn't make sense that He had to die. He was just getting started, why put the breaks on the gigantic momentum, which was occurring in that part of the world? Yet, still today there are those who mock the death of Jesus, as just another prophet who was martyred for His faith. However, death was God's plan to give life.

But Jesus was much, much more than a martyr. He was the son of man, but He was also the Son of God. He was God's Son who died as the payment for all past, present, and future sins of mankind. This is where the fruit of faith begins. When you believe the death of Jesus was predestined by God as a good thing, then you have a foundation for fruit bearing. Yes, all things do work together for good (Romans 8:28). The cross of Christ is one of God's good things, so make sure you thank Him for the sacrifice of His only son. He gave life so we could receive life. When you believe in His death for your sins, you receive His life. Christ in you has put to death your old life, so now that you have been crucified with Him, you are positioned to bear much fruit.

This is why you die daily. You die to yourself, so you and others can live for God. Fruit results when you deny self and remain in Him. Jesus said, "Remain in me, and I will remain in you. No branch can bear fruit by itself; it must remain in the vine. Neither can you bear fruit unless you remain in me" (John 15:4). Therefore, what is something to which you have not died that may be holding back your fruitful living? If you do not die, you remain alone. To not die to self and sin is to separate you from fruit, friends, and faith. But you do not have to remain alone. On the contrary, daily death by faith frees you to experience fruitful living. The fruit of your other-centered living becomes abundant and pervasive. You pollinate other lives that, in turn, bear fruit. However, death is not always easy. The road to crucifixion with Christ may be wrought with criticism from those who think you are too religious, or a little weird. However, the fruit from your life will speak for itself. Your children's love for God will resonate for eternity. Your generosity will silence even the most outspoken critics. Your teaching will transform lives in the here and now. Fruit is God's eternal evidence that motivates you to remain faithful with Christ.

Therefore, stay dead to yourself, and watch Him live through your bearing much fruit. Indeed, death's fruit is rooted in the cross!

REMAIN FAITHFUL

> ... "This calls for patient endurance on the part of the saints who obey God's commandments and remain faithful to Jesus." REVELATION 14:12

Faithfulness tends to be relegated to the few. However, for the committed follower of Christ, the clarion call is to remain faithful. He is the object of your adoration and your obedience, and He deserves and desires your faithfulness. It is easier to remain faithful when the object of your faithfulness is as pure as the driven snow. There is nothing about Jesus that doesn't solicit faithfulness. His fairness invites faithfulness. His grace and generosity generate faithfulness. His love longs for faithfulness. His anger admonishes faithfulness. His holiness inspires faithfulness. His compassion creates faithfulness. His forgiveness foretells faithfulness. His judgment motivates faithfulness. His life models faithfulness. Jesus remained faithful to the very end, so can you in Him.

Is there anything about Jesus that is repulsive to remaining faithful? Who else can you go to for eternal life (John 6:68)? Faithfulness to Jesus is par for the Christian life. He is the standard by which you live. Even under the onslaught of illness, you remain faithful. As circumstances around you crumble, you remain faithful. When people mistreat you and misunderstand you, you remain faithful. If you lose your job, you remain faithful. When a close friend lets you down and rejects you; you still remain faithful to Jesus. Faithfulness to Jesus is the repetitive chorus for Christian living. Moreover, His faithfulness to you is the measure of your capacity to remain faithful. The indwelling of the Holy Spirit's power in your life provides the capability to remain faithful. Indeed, remaining faithful to Jesus leads to remaining faithful to others.

Remaining faithful to people is a natural by-product of remaining faithful to Jesus. People can be disappointing and down-right disturbing. But, your faithfulness may be the very thing that draws them to Jesus. Certainly, your remaining faithful will give them pause to reflect on your radical love and forgiveness. Faithfulness reminds people of truth. Paul said, "I am sending to you Timothy, my son whom I love, who is faithful in the Lord. He will remind you of my way of life in Christ Jesus..."(I Corinthians 4:17). Therefore, make it a goal to remain faithful to an undeserving relative or friend. This becomes a magnet toward God and not a detour to the devil. You may need to dissolve a working agreement, but you can still salvage the relationship. You can remain faithful even when the other party doesn't. Let your faithfulness, not your feelings, be the gage for your giving, your service, your forgiveness, and your love.

Above all else, remain faithful to Jesus for He is the Faithful One!

A20 PURE JOY

> "Consider it pure joy, my brothers, whenever you face trials of many kinds, because you know that the testing of your faith develops perseverance." JAMES 1:2-3

Pure joy is the position and privilege of the person who follows Jesus Christ. And ironically, Jesus-generated joy is discovered and developed in the face of trials. Trials are designed to bring out God's best and consequently, your best as well. Your current trial by fire is so your faith can become more sincere and real during the affliction of adversity. This is your time to experience God's faithfulness, for His joy and contentment are calming. The presence of Christ gives you reassurance and peace. He is the joy giver, while Satan is the joy killer. Therefore you can smile, because your smile under trial is the result of pure joy. Pure joy because God can be trusted. Pure joy because your faith is real and robust. Pure joy because Christ is faithful. Pure joy because you will persevere by faith. Indeed, untested faith is a naïve faith. Your faith is immature and judgmental until it has been refined through various trials. You can understand others' perspectives and respect them more when you have been broken over your own inadequacies and sins. Trials slow you down to look into the mirror and ask what needs to change. How can you lead and serve your family and friends during this time of unprecedented turmoil and tentativeness? Pure joy comes as a result of your faith changing and growing.

God is your change agent. The work of God in and through your life produces pure joy. Change can be painful, but God administers pure joy at the point of your pain. It is the result of the Holy Spirits fullness, "And the disciples were filled with joy and with the Holy Spirit" (Acts 13:52). Therefore, learn how to accept the pure joy of the Lord, for it is available for you to receive. Do not see your present predicament as a set back. Instead, see you current condition as an opportunity to engage more deeply and more fully with your heavenly Father. Sometimes it takes trials and tests to slow you down, so you will look into the joyful face of Jesus. He is the embodiment of pure joy.

Jesus understood pure joy, because He was focused on following the will of His father (John 17:4). His heart was full of joy because He knew He was about His Father's business. Yes, His heart broke at times, but it was out of joyful obedience that He suffered (Hebrews 12:2). In the middle of His most adverse circumstances, He still cried out to His heavenly Father. His intimacy with the Father compounded during difficulty. No person, circumstance or the devil kept Him from pure joy. Therefore, invite the pure joy of God to reign over your anxious heart. It is okay to smile and place your refined faith in Him. He is building your faith capacity for the long run. The Bible says, "May the God of hope fill you with all joy and peace as you trust in him, so that you may overflow with hope by the power of the Holy Spirit" (Romans 15:13). Pure joy does not depend on good circumstances, instead it thrives during trials and tribulations.

Unleash the pure joy that already lives within, for He is faithful. Above all, promote pure joy and persevere in its promise!

PARENTAL FAITH

"I am reminded of your sincere faith, which first lived in your grandmother Lois and in your mother Eunice and, I am persuaded now lives in you also." 2 TIMOTHY 1:5

Your parents' faith is a gift from God and is not to be taken for granted. What a rock of reassurance you have in a legacy that loves the Lord. They stand for the truth of God and they live it with humility and grace. It is because of their faith that you have faith. They instilled in you early on the fear of God and the love of God. Their awe and respect of God inspired your soul to do the same. Your parents' faith has been a flame of passion for your own walk with Christ. You watched them pray, and so you pray. You watched them trust God, and so you trust God. You watched them love people, and so you love people. You watched them forgive, and so you forgive. You watched them do the right things, and so you do the right things. You watched them be generous, and so you are generous. Your parents are a model of faithfulness in the ways of God. What a gift! What a reason for joy, thanksgiving and celebration.

Have you loved on your parents and thanked them lately for their gift of sincere faith? Take the time to tell them how grateful you are for your faith upbringing. Thank them and God for your training and teaching all these years in the great truths of the Bible. Their faithful teaching of truth and modeling of truth made it easy for you to embrace truth. Now you have the opportunity to do the same for your children. The Bible says, "For you know that we dealt with each of you as a father deals with his own children, encouraging, comforting and urging you to live lives worthy of God, who calls you into his kingdom and glory" (1 Thessalonians 2:11-12). Model for your children what has been modeled for you; service, selflessness, confession and repentance of sin, faithfulness, and forgiveness. Keep the faith alive by putting to death the devil's attempts to derail your legacy of love for the Lord. Be a legacy builder not a legacy killer.

If you have failed your faith role as a parent, now is the time to come back to your roots. It is never too late to pick up your parental baton of faith. You know in your heart it is the right thing to do. You have explored the other road most traveled. This faithless road is full of sin and deception, hurt and harm. It is a process full of pride and ego. This unrighteous road is so crowded that you learned quickly that it was filled with peril and life accidents. Now you are back on a search for the faith of your fathers. Your mother's prayers have wooed you back to do the same for your children. It is time to put away foolish and immature ways. Your deep desire is to imitate the sincere faith of your parents. They were smarter than you realized, so unleash the faith of your childhood that was endowed by your parents. Appreciate and accept their indoctrination of God's wisdom and allow it to serve you well in your adult responsibilities. However, do not lament your life if your parents lacked faith. Instead, apply the faith of surrogate spiritual parents. You are positioned on a faith walk for your kids, so walk wisely. Keep giving the gift of faith to your family.

Sincere faith can be passed on from one generation to another. So by God's grace, be relentless, passionate and disciplined to keep the faith alive!

A22 FAITH LIVING

"...but the righteous will live by his faith..."   HABAKKUK 2:4B

Faith living is focused on God living. It is the road less traveled. Even for believers in Jesus Christ, faith living is not always predominant. But it really is the only way to live. Why settle for anything less? If you limit yourself to your efforts and your logic, then you only tip God with your faith. He is calling you beyond the honeymoon stage of faith to mature faith. The Bible teaches, "Anyone who lives on milk, being still an infant, is not acquainted with the teaching about righteousness. But solid food is for the mature, who by constant use have trained themselves to distinguish good from evil" (Hebrews 5:13-14). His desire is for you to come alive with a faith that is active and growing. A faith that only thinks of the past is anemic and stunted. Faith alive is passionate about God's vision for the future, and it is focused the possibilities of today.

It is His creative genius that infatuates the follower of Christ. His ability to create relational opportunities is staggering. He is the network weaver par excellence. By faith He can be trusted to lead you to just the right people. People whom you can serve and people who can join you to accomplish God's will. This is faith living. It is looking beyond the new relationship of today and sensing where God wants to take it tomorrow. Determine ways to bring value to another person. It is not about what you can get from them, but it is all about how you can serve them. This is faith living. It is placing the needs of others before your own, and trusting God to meet your needs. The Bible says, "This service that you perform is not only supplying the needs of God's people but is also overflowing in many expressions of thanks to God" (2 Corinthians 9:12). He releases you to serve others with His freedom in Christ. This is normal Christian faith living.

However, faith living is not irresponsible living. This is not some blind excursion that ignores the needs of your family. It is wrought with prayer and godly advice. This implies that faith living is not lived in a vacuum, but lived in concert with those around you. Abraham went by faith to a new country (Genesis 12:4-5), but he exercised this transition while taking care of the needs of his family. Yes, faith many times requires sacrifice and service, but not in the guise of unwise decision-making. Faith living trusts God's timing and does not rush into battle without a plan or weapons. You trust God to prepare you and provide the needed resources to carry out His will. You are no match for Satan without the weapons of spiritual warfare. Faith living recognizes our battle is not with flesh and blood, but that our battle is waged in the spiritual arena (Ephesians 6:12). Therefore, do not see people as obstacles, but as part of God's plan to teach you His ways and to grow you in faith. Allow God and others to exploit your strengths and shore up your weaknesses. Be who God created you to be.

Therefore, live by faith and not by sight. You are truly alive when you live by faith in God alone!

"Because of the Lord's great love we are not consumed, for his compassions never fail.
They are new every morning; great is your faithfulness. I say to myself,
'The Lord is my portion; therefore I will wait for him.'" JEREMIAH 3:22-24

The love of God keeps you from being consumed by the fiery flames of grief. Your sorrows can overwhelm you, but He is there as your loving heavenly Father to see you through your sadness. The love of God is a peacemaker when you become consumed with conflict. His love mediates and works out solutions for all willing parties. Conflict melts under the loving influence of God. Worry is consuming until it comes under the direct influence of God's love, for His love exudes peace. Thus, the peace of God and the worry of the world cannot co-exist. Fear can be all consuming, however, the love of God flushes out fear and replaces it with trust. Fleeting fear must be replaced by faith or it will return to occupy your heart and mind. The love of God floods your soul with faith. Fear vanquishes under the influence of faith. Moreover, His compassions never fail for God has a deep awareness and concern for your heartache. His compassions never fail for they give hope you can hang on to for future resolution. His compassions never fail for they provide companionship with your friend Jesus. His compassions never fail for they extend forgiveness to a contrite and hurting heart. His compassions solicit soul success.

Great is His faithfulness. His faithfulness is greater than the depths of the sea (six miles at its deepest point), and it is greater than the highest mountain (six miles at its highest point). The entire universe cannot contain the faithfulness of God, for it is far-reaching and deep. People will fail you, but God is still faithful. Work will fail you, but God is still faithful. Your health will fail you, but God is still faithful. Finances will fail you, but God is still faithful. Circumstances will fail you, but God is still faithful. You will fail, but God is still faithful. Great is his faithfulness!

Lastly, God does what He says He will do, so you do not ever have to second-guess the Lord. He is there for you, your family, your friends and your enemies. He is faithful. He cannot; not be faithful. For God to not be faithful would be like the sun not to rise, or the moon not to shine. This is not possible, just as it is impossible for God to be unfaithful. Therefore, wait on him for He is worth the wait. Use the opportunity of waiting to trust and obey Him, the Bible teaches, "I wait for your salvation, O LORD, and I follow your commands" (Psalm 119:166). He will be faithful to lead you to the right spouse, the right career, and the right friends. He can be trusted, so let go of your inhibitions and trust Him.

You can trust Him with your future, your health, and your eternity. You serve a great God full of love, compassion, and faithfulness!

A24 FAITHFULNESS REWARD

"To the faithful you show yourself faithful, to the blameless you show yourself blameless..." PSALM 18:25

Faithfulness is a relational two-way street. For example you have expectations for others to be faithful to their commitments and you want to model the same. If you tell someone you will meet them at 9 AM, then you need to be faithful and show up at 9 AM, even a little earlier. Time is precious and you do not want to disrespect another's time by spending it unwisely. The essence of faithfulness is doing what you said you would do. It is the integrity of following through with a commitment, even when it is costly. Commitments are not to be taken lightly, for instance see a verbal commitment as an unwritten contract. When you keep your word, you are true to yourself and others.

If you make a verbal commitment, it behooves you to make sure there is an understanding with all parties. If there are not clear expectations, there is good chance for miscommunication and a perception of unfaithfulness. The burden of responsibility is on the communicator. Moreover, margin-less living contributes to poor communication. If you are moving fast and are over-committed, your communication skills and follow through drop off. You may assume others understand you and know what is going on, but this is flawed thinking. People live busy lives as well, so they need you to slow down and show up with clear speech. Slow down, communicate more, and show up on time for appointments. Take a relational audit and create a "stop doing'"list so you are free for follow through. Follow the Lord's example as a promise keeper, "Let us hold unswervingly to the hope we profess, for he who promised is faithful" (Hebrews 10:23).

Fortunately, as a follower of Christ you have the Faithful One in your life to model the way. He has been faithful even in your unfaithfulness. He is faithful to forgive your sin and remember it no more (Jeremiah 31:34). He is faithful to flood your soul with peace, joy and contentment. He is faithful to give you friends and family who love you in spite of yourself. He was faithful to follow through with the Cross of Christ even through the cries of His only son, and the ultimate sacrifice of his life. God understands what it means to keep a commitment, even when it cost a great deal. He says in His Word to "let our yes be yes and our no be no" (Matthew 5:37). You do this because you want to be faithful to Him. Your faithfulness is rooted in God. Indeed, your faithfulness does not go unnoticed or unrewarded. One of the greatest rewards is the gift of trust. Faithfulness births and grows trust so that over time you earn the reputation of a trustworthy person.

Those who can be trusted with a little can be trusted with much (Matthew 25:21). Above all be faithful, because He is faithful for this is the reward of faithfulness!

> "They have taken some of their daughters as wives for themselves and their sons, and have mingled the holy race with the peoples around them. And the leaders and officials have led the way in this unfaithfulness." Ezra 9:2

Marriage is between a man and a woman and Christian marriage is between two Christians. This is God's plan, and attempts to circumvent His plan can lead to water-downed faith and embracing a lifestyle contrary to Christian behavior. This is the risk you take if you marry someone who is not a committed follower of Jesus Christ. Christian marriage has plenty of challenges on its own without confusing it with mixed belief systems and values. Two contrasting faiths are like blending oil and water. It doesn't work and it creates a mess. Opposites may attract, but a common faith is a must for a healthy marriage. This co-mingling of faiths as unwise and unclear, one example is the confusion of children. Whose faith do they follow? This creates insecurity in their impressionable hearts. People with differing faiths may be able to coexist, but they miss the intimacy of a mutual commitment to the same heavenly Father. It takes more than love for one another to have a happy, holy, and fulfilling marriage. A bountiful marriage is one in which both husband and wife are madly in love with Christ. He is the originator and sustainer of marriage. He models marriage with the church as His bride (Revelation 21:9).

One good question to ask a prospective life mate is, 'Do you love God more than you love me? If so, you will be in better hands as a husband or a wife. Without this level of faith in God, you lose the leverage of a loving Savior. Jesus Christ is the "plumb-line" in marriage. He is the baseline and the standard. His life, his death, his teachings, and his example set the stage for Christian marriage. There are boundaries and expectations that He defines for a successful marriage. Therefore, the wise husband and wife look to God and ask Him for direction, forgiveness, and ways to love each other. Your gratitude to God for His great love and forgiveness becomes the model of how you love and forgive your spouse.

The goal of Christian marriage is to be a reflection of our relationship with God. Marriage is a sacred relationship that God understands oh so well. He understands that your faith can become a wedge or a weld. He will galvanize your hearts together by faith. He will allow you to weather the storms together by faith. He will give you joy together by faith. He will allow you to experience life to its fullest, together by faith. He will give you wisdom to raise children together by faith. He will give you grace to live the Christian life together by faith. Most of all, He will allow you to enjoy Him and each other together by faith. Your common faith in Jesus Christ is the oil that lubricates your marriage machinery. It is the water that satisfies your thirsty soul. Let your marriage start with a common belief in the same God, the Father of your Lord Jesus Christ. Love Him and each other with abandonment and passion. This will pull your marriage together and drive you toward the same destination of hope and heaven.

A common faith commitment is a non-negotiable for the Christian marriage. Mold your marriage around your Master!

A26 SUFFERING SAVIOR

> "I offered my back to those who beat me, my cheeks to those who pulled out my beard;
> I did not hide my face from mocking and spitting." ISAIAH 50:6

The sufferings of Jesus cannot be totally comprehended. One thing is clear and that is Jesus experienced voluntary suffering. He offered himself as a sacrifice on behalf of the human race and it was a volitional act on His part. He willfully submitted to the will of His heavenly Father, which meant suffering. His heartache and mistreatment was the will of His heavenly Father (Mark 8:31-33). This principle is hard to process for those who want to profess problem free living. However, the way of the cross is not always smooth for it is littered with its own bumps and bruises. Jesus suffered for the sake of others and He calls His followers to be willing to do the same. The Bible says, "For it has been granted to you on behalf of Christ not only to believe on him, but also to suffer for him..."(Philippians 1:29). Suffering leads you to your Savior and Lord Jesus Christ. Jesus offered himself to His tormentors, as His adversaries plotted and schemed to bring Him down. They wanted to put Jesus on display as a mad man. If He was truly God, they reasoned, He would not allow this injustice to occur. However, the Creator allowed His creation to beat and bludgeon His only son. The back of Christ was bruised and beaten for your sake. His ribs were whipped with sharp bits of rock that dug into His flesh indiscriminately. These mob-motivated men racked inhumane lashes across His body, and facial hair was torn from His flesh. He did not hide His face or scour back. Rather, with a gaze up to heaven as if to say, "Father this is for Your glory," He displayed a grim face of grace. This face of forgiveness was baptized in the sick spit of sinful man. They desecrated His friendly face with determined drool. The frenzy of the crowd took over with verbal lashes. These ungrateful sinners beat Him down emotionally and mentally, as well as physically. It was a horrid site. It was one man's concentration camp. But Jesus submitted to this suffering only because He first submitted to God. And ironically the ones committing these hideous crimes are the very ones who could benefit from its results. They could embrace his death for sin, and receive His resurrected life.

Jesus carried this burden on your behalf and the rest of mankind. It was not an exercise in how much pain could be endured by one person. It was love, as Jesus loved you all the way to the cross. "Greater love has no one than this, that he lay down his life for his friends" (John 15:13). Without the love of God, the cross would not have happened. It would have culminated in the death of just another good man. Death would have been the end, but Jesus conquered death, sin, and Satan so you could do the same. His pain was your gain. He bore the cross so you could bear your cross. The way of the cross is an exercise in redemption. He bought you from the servitude of sin. No longer are you bound up in yourself and others, for He has set you free. You are exonerated by faith because He endured the cross, despised its shame, and is now interceding on your behalf at the right hand of His heavenly Father (Hebrews 12:2). This is cause for celebration. God does use all things for His good on behalf of those who love Him (Romans 8:28). Therefore, allow gratitude to well up and burst forth from your heart. You can because of the great love of God exhibited in the sufferings of Christ Jesus. He suffered for you. Can you do any less?

You serve a suffering Savior. You worship a suffering Savior that rose from the dead, so He could save you to the uttermost!

DIVISION'S DOWNFALL

> "Jesus knew their thoughts and said to them, 'Every kingdom divided against itself will be ruined, and every city or household divided against itself will not stand.' "
> MATTHEW 12:25

Division weakens, cripples, and eventually causes a downfall. Division is internal erosion that cannot stand up to conflicting turmoil from within. The greatest threat to a nation, an organization, a home, or an individual comes from the inside out. An implosion of unbelief threatens to bring down a religious person. He or she wants God, but the intellectual conflict cannot be resolved. Indeed, outside of faith in Christ this paradox will never be resolved. The same can be said for a church. The church can become its own worst enemy. If there is a watering down of the basic tenets of the Christian faith, then there is nothing substantial left to believe. If Christ's deity, miracles, and resurrection are in question, then the church is set up for division and ultimately death. A church split is normally the result of pride and/or heresy.

Moreover, a business is no less susceptible to internal strife and feuding factions. A business that sells its soul to the almighty dollar will do whatever it takes to bolster the bottom line. Conflicting values begin to divide. What started out as a business built on integrity, devolves into one of worldly avarice. Short-term compromise may prop up earnings, but long-term effectiveness will be like a sheep led to the slaughter. A culture without a true north is like a ship without a sail. Whoever is the most persuasive, persistent, and the loudest gets his way. This is a prescription for disaster. Indeed a nation, organization, or individual that fights itself will lose. Yes, there will be disagreements, but when all is said and done, there has to be unity of purpose. Think of two siblings who tussle against one another, but then unite their efforts to defeat the bully. Avoid a civil war from within, and fight the devil and his minions that are without.

Principles and values based on God's truth will stand, and whoever embraces them and lives for them will stand together. Your goal as a follower of Jesus Christ is to unite around faith in Him. He is your reason for living and dying. Jesus is the way, the truth, and the life (John 14:16). Therefore, unite forces around Him and His Word. Do not be distracted or divided by peripheral preferences. The color of the church carpet, the number of pipes in the organ, and church politics are not what you live and die for. It is the battle for the souls of men and women that unite believers. It is the proclamation of the Word of God in teaching and living that compel you to follow the example of Jesus and the great saints of the ages. The rallying cry for serious followers of Christ is, "Seek first the Kingdom of God and His righteousness" (Matthew 6:33). Your life echoes the exhortation to "love God and to love people." You are to take up your cross and follow Him. You are to serve unselfishly as Jesus served. You are to give sacrificially as Jesus gave. You are to love unconditionally as Jesus loved. You are to forgive abundantly as Jesus forgave. You are to be holy as He is holy. You can unify around this call to Christ-likeness. Yes, truth will divide the wheat from the chaff, but it also unifies believers. Truth flushes out the counterfeit and affirms the authentic. Jesus is the truth; therefore lift up the Lord. He says, "But I, when I am lifted up from the earth, will draw all men to myself" (John 12:32).

An exalted Jesus draws a diversity of people to Himself. You can unite around the holiness and truthfulness of Jesus!

A28 DEATH AND LIFE

"For if, when we were God's enemies, we were reconciled to him through the death of his Son, how much more, having been reconciled, shall we be saved through his life!
ROMANS 5:10

The death of Jesus leads to the life of Jesus. This is God's pattern for the follower of Jesus. Death leads to life. The Cross of Christ reconciled us to God by faith. The Resurrection of Christ empowered us for God by faith. The cross leads to the resurrection and the resurrection points back to the cross. You can't have one without the other. If the cross were the finality of Christ's work, then you would have no power to live the Christian life. If the resurrection had no cross, then you would still be condemned in your sin. The Christian who celebrates the cross, but does embrace the resurrection, will live a life of defeat. The cross without the resurrection is a defeat.

However, you do not have to live defeated because Christ did rise from His grave. He arose to validate the significance of the cross and prove His claims of Deity. But He did not stop with reconciliation to God. He also arose from the dead to give you His life. His resurrected life oversubscribes for you the power needed to follow, obey, and enjoy Him. His life in you emboldens you to witness for Him. His life in you sanctifies you during suffering. His life in you allows you to persevere. His life in you builds your character. His life in you gives you hope. It is the life of Christ that energizes you to live for Christ. Like Paul you can declare, "I have been crucified with Christ and I no longer live, but Christ lives in me. The life I live in the body, I live by faith in the Son of God, who loved me and gave himself for me" (Galatians 2:20).

This is living the resurrected life. "It is Christ in you, the hope of glory" (Colossians 1:27). You cannot live properly and purely without your resurrected Lord Jesus reigning over you and living through you. Without the life of Christ your faith is anemic, but with the life of Christ it comes alive. His life saves you from yourself to Himself. He saves you from reckless relationships to robust relationships. He saves you from financial servitude to financial faithfulness. He saves you from selfish whims to unselfish service. He saves you from irresponsible decisions to wise choices. He saves from a life of drifting to one of determination to follow God. Indeed, you are reconciled to God for the purpose of unleashing His life through you by faith. Die daily so you can allow His life to live through you. Do not capitulate to casual Christianity, for the tomb is empty of Jesus so your heart can be full of Jesus. His grave is lifeless, so can have life. The cross is about dying. The resurrection is about living. His life in you is the life you longed for; so let Him live by faith. Death leads to life and life points back to death.

He lives in you to live through you. Above all else, the death of Jesus leads to the life of Jesus in you!

SOUND DOCTRINE

"He must hold firmly to the trustworthy message as it has been taught,
so that he can encourage others by sound doctrine and refute those who oppose it."
TITUS 1:9

Doctrine is a belief system that is accepted as authoritative, for followers of Jesus Christ the Bible contains Christian doctrine that is believed, understood, and lived. Doctrine is critical because what you believe can be the difference between heaven and hell, and it is critical because it determines your behavior. Lastly, doctrine is valuable because it provides structure around faith, and thus bolsters and encourages you to a lifetime of growing and learning. Doctrine is not to be feared, but accepted as a support for abundant living. Doctrine helps you understand what you believe in a logical fashion, so you in turn can explain it to others inside and outside of the faith. Yes, doctrine can be abused and used as a club to knock others into line. But doctrine is not designed to discourage, only to encourage. Doctrine is not meant to be an intimidator; rather it is designed to lovingly lead disciples toward the ways of God. Your motive for understanding and learning doctrine is so you can know God more deeply and intimately. Doctrine is not an end in itself, so if your desire is just more knowledge, then doctrine will work against your Christian maturity. Sound teaching helps you discern false teachers, the Bible says, "Then we will no longer be infants, tossed back and forth by the waves, and blown here and there by every wind of teaching and by the cunning and craftiness of men in their deceitful scheming" (Ephesians 4:14). Certainly indoctrinate your children at an early age with God's belief system, so they can begin life-long learning. What better way than to mold their tender and teachable hearts with the doctrines of the Christian faith.

Some of the doctrines of the Christian faith are the Deity of Christ, his death and resurrection for man's redemption, and the indwelling of the Holy Spirit in the life of believers. God is your loving heavenly Father who judges fairly. Traditional tenets of the faith are the inerrancy of the Bible, the second coming of Christ, salvation by grace through faith in Christ, and the reality of heaven and hell. Other compelling truths are eternal rewards, God's ownership of everything, and the power of prayer. Allow these doctrines and others to marinate in your mind and heart. Let them become the foundation of your beliefs and behavior. Read about them, learn about them, and let them give you confidence that God has laid out a logical and inviting explanation for living and dying. This applies to His followers and for those who still need Christ. Make sure doctrine has been distilled into a life change for you. This is evidence of authentic disciples, Jesus said, "If you hold to my teaching, you are really my disciples" (John 8:31). The major teachings of the Christian faith are clear, so camp out there and do not be confused over other distracting issues. Make sure your doctrine leads you to evangelism and discipleship, because it is for your encouragement and defense of the faith.

Above all, keep it from feeding your pride and boring others. Use it wisely and do not abuse it!

A30 ABUNDANT FORGIVENESS

"Then Peter came to Jesus and ask, 'Lord how many times shall I forgive my brother
when he sins against me? Up to seventy times?' Jesus answered, 'I tell you,
not seven times but seventy-seven times.'" MATTHEW 18:21-22

Sin's offense hurts. There is no doubt about it. It wounds indiscriminately and it is no respecter of persons. Sin builds walls, as it separates and ravishes relationships. Just the sound of the word solicits negative emotion. It is deceptive, carnal, Christ-less, unfair, sad, and sometimes sadistic. Sin follows a process of desire, conception, birth, maturity, and death. James describes its diabolical development. "Then, after desire has conceived, it gives birth to sin; and sin, when it is full-grown, gives birth to death" (James 1:15). So sin is not to be taken lightly. Certainly its infliction of pain cannot be ignored for long.

Sin invites a response from the one it offends. One option is to fight sin with sin. This is messy and can be long and drawn out. No one (except Satan) really wins when sin battles sin. Thus sin is rampant and no one is immune from its consequences. It divides, belittles and it is relational suicide. Nonetheless, when you are sinned against, you are to forgive. When someone's sin assaults your attitude, you are to forgive them. When someone's sin berates your work, you are to forgive him. When someone's sin violates your trust, you are to forgive him. When someone's sin steals your joy, you are to forgive him. When someone's sin crushes your dreams, you are to forgive him. When someone's sin steals from you, you are to forgive him. This level of forgiveness is counter-intuitive and counter-cultural, but it is the way of Christ. Forgiveness is God's game plan. You will lose if you don't forgive, for unforgiveness is tortuous to the soul. It is unhealthy to the body and emotions. Unforgiveness fills prescriptions and leaves hollow lives in its wake. However, forgiveness is able to let go and let God be the judge.

Forgiveness cuts through the varying degrees of guilt and erases the entire debt. True forgiveness comes from the heart of the one offended (Matthew 18:35b). Forgiveness is not a flippant acknowledgement. It is a sincere removal of anything that is owed. When the offended one forgives, he wipes out the expectation for an apology, pay back, or change. It is forgiveness clear and simple. Forgiveness is letting go. It is letting go of the hurt, anger, and shame. When you forgive, you are free. You are free from the shackles of sin. When you forgive, you trust. You trust God to judge others in His time. His judgment is fair and just. God can be trusted with the consequences of sin's offense.

Lastly, you continue to forgive others because your heavenly Father continues to forgive you. The Scripture teaches, "Be kind and compassionate to one another, forgiving each other, just as in Christ God forgave you" (Ephesians 4:32). Without Christ's forgiveness, you are lost and undone. Jesus does not deal in forgiveness quotas. The forgiveness of the Cross was swift, full, final, and forever. Unlock your relational restraints with the key of forgiveness. Write a letter with tear-soaked ink that outlines your forgiveness. Call or e-mail someone today and let them know because you are forgiven, you forgive them. Set free others with forgiveness and you will be free. There is freedom in Christ.

Forgive fast. Forgive often. The forgiveness of Christ is forever!

CARE BY CARRYING

> "Then you saw how the Lord your God carried you, as a father carries his son, all the way you went until you reached this place." DEUTERONOMY 1:31

Thank God there are times He carries you in His arms. You walk with Him on the sandy beach of life, and for a time there are two sets of footprints. But there are those special and comforting times that you look down only to discover one set of footprints. Your footprints have vanished because your heavenly Father is carrying you as a father carries his son. There is a parental passion around God's heart for you. It is a persistent and patient passion that is relentless in its care. So, not only does He walk with you through life (which is enough in itself), He goes a step further. When you are at your lowest of lows and fear has frozen your faith, or when your passion for God is paralyzed and has jumped the track, He is there to carry you. He lifts you out of this state of confusion and carries you in His loving and secure arms. You do not have to wander around in self-pity and despair, turn to the One who truly cares. When others let you down, He is still by your side. Now is the time to humble yourself and allow him to lift you up and carry you for now. He may need to carry you during this rocky time in your marriage. He may need to carry you during this down cycle at work. He may need to carry you through this crisis of faith brought on by extreme disappointment. Do not be ashamed of the need for Christ to carry you, because He cares for you.

Therefore let go of your anger, embrace Christ and let Him carry you. Let go of your fears, embrace Christ and let Him carry you. Let go of your hurt, embrace Christ and let Him carry you. Let go of your depression, embrace Christ and let Him carry you. It is not shameful to allow Christ to carry you, but it is the wise thing to do. It may mean some of your goals need to be extended until you can regroup with Jesus. Plans may need to be put on hold and your vision realigned. This is okay; it is better to be in the arms of your heavenly Father than wandering around in bewilderment without Him.

Just as the wind lifts the wings of an elegant eagle, the Holy Spirit lifts you to soar with your Savior. To be carried by God is to need God. To be carried by God is to experience God. To be carried by God is to be loved by God. To be carried by God is to be intimate with God. This is your time to go to a level of relational depth with your heavenly Father that has been unknown until now. This is a season of your faith walk that will facilitate the maturing of your faith. Like a sensitive shepherd with a trapped sheep, He is bent over to untangle you from the snares of life and to carry you on His shoulders. Jesus said, "When found [a stray sheep], you can be sure you would put it across your shoulders, rejoicing, and when you got home call in your friends and neighbors, saying, 'Celebrate with me! I've found my lost sheep!' " (Luke 15:5-6). You see close and up front the caring face of Christ when you are carried, so peer deeply into His compassionate eyes and enjoy Him.

You can carry on, because He carries you and He will carry you to His divine destination. This is total abandonment and surrender to your Savior Jesus!

M2 WISE LEADERSHIP

"Choose some wise, understanding, and respected men from each of your tribes, and I will set them over you." DEUTERONOMY 1:13

The selection process of wise leadership can make or break an organization. You are constantly faced with this in our families, church, work, schools, civic groups, and professional associations. Yet, wise leadership does not come about as a result of pride's persuasion. It is not found in the 'tit for tat' of petty politics. Wise leadership is not discovered within a popularity contest, or a sterile assessment. Indeed, if someone is clamoring to fill a position of leadership, this is normally a flag. A wise leader would rather be drafted by others than to promote them self into a position.

So where do you look for wise leaders? A good place to begin is within the ranks of those who already exhibit wise leadership. You see it in the open and authentic environment they create in their work and home, and by their own honesty around personal weaknesses and strengths. Indeed, wise leaders are excellent listeners. They listen with the intent to understand. Wisdom desires understanding of what you are thinking and what you are feeling. You observe their wisdom in one-on-one conversation, as they know what questions to ask. They challenge you to think and offer counsel as is appropriate. Wise leaders are not gurus or know-it-alls. Instead, they are smart enough to understand the vastness of what they don't know. Moreover, those who know them the best especially respect wise leaders. If those in someone's inner circle lack respect for the person in leadership, so will those outside their immediate circle of influence. Indeed, respect comes over time by showing respect. It is the result of doing what you say and integrity in living out what you say you believe. Consistent Christ-like behavior invites raving reviews of respect. Wisdom and respect go hand-in-hand.

Lastly, wise leadership points you to God. Any infatuation with a leader as an individual is redirected to their heavenly Father. Wisdom will only remain in a humble heart. It is within the incubator of humility that wisdom germinates and flourishes. The Bible says, "He guides the humble in what is right and teaches them his way" (Psalm 25:9). Therefore, aptly so, a wise leader exhibits humility with his heart for God. God can entrust wisdom to the humble of heart, but He is stingy in giving wisdom to the proud for they cannot be trusted. It is the application of wisdom that matures relationships, facilitates faith, and grows business and ministry. Hear from the wise before you charge forward with a new opportunity. Ask your parents' advice about this new relationship. Pray to God for wisdom about your next steps. Wise leaders do not always tell you what you want to hear, but listen anyway. Their words are sometimes hard, and can seem at the time to be intolerant and insensitive for wisdom makes foolishness uncomfortable. It is wise leadership that leads you beyond selfish satisfaction. Wise leaders lead you to grow in your relationship with Christ.

So, follow wise leaders and be a wise leader, as opportunity arises prayerfully select and appoint wise leaders. Wise leadership promotes God's agenda, and His agenda is wisdom!

EARNEST EXPLANATION

> "Far be it from us to rebel against the Lord and turn away from him today by building an altar for burnt offerings, grain offerings and sacrifices, other than the altar of the Lord our God that stands before his tabernacle." JOSHUA 22:29

Be willing to give an explanation for your actions, because good people may have interpreted your right behavior in a wrong light. There has been a misunderstanding of motive and you need to take the initiative to clear up the confusion. Now is the time to over communicate, so where you have been wrong, make it right and where you have been right, make it clear. There is no need to degrade your defense into a war of words. Just state the facts and trust God with the results. Maybe your accusers are inaccurately associating your situation with an experience in their past. The emotions are similar, but your circumstances are totally different. Help your critics understand the context of your condition, and explain that you are present to assist not obstruct. You may have to prove yourself before you are trusted. There will always be people who misunderstand, or who are threatened by your good deeds. You may find yourself serving without the accolades of people to bolster your efforts. This will reveal your true motives. Are you serving for the pleasure of the Lord, or are you serving to please people? God is there to encourage you when you feel estranged from everyone. The Bible says, "The LORD upholds all those who fall and lifts up all who are bowed down" (Psalm 145:14).

However, once you have explained your actions and motives to another, you must trust God with the results. He is in control, and He will right any wrongs in His time. Trust that He will heal any harm inflicted onto your reputation. He can and He will restore your good standing in the community. The fiery darts of unfair criticism do sting severely and they solicit your rage, but allow the Holy Spirit to check your flesh and hold you back from being the greater fool. Foolish is the man or woman who flails back at their accusers with the harsh venom of vindication. Instead be patient and allow Jesus to be your advocate for He will drive home your point with divine determination. The truth will prevail. It is your calm reaction that contributes to a positive perception. It is through humility of heart and keeping a cool head that calamity ceases. The Psalmist declared, "You save the humble but bring low those whose eyes are haughty (Psalm 18:27).

You are in a position to reach out with an olive branch, so do everything you can to shore up the relational breech. Seek to understand why your friend's feelings are flooding his words and clouding his thinking. Do not focus on winning the debate; stress instead the sovereignty of God and His goodness. He is in control and He does want to give good things to His children. He can be trusted with this, so do the best you can and then watch Him work. Allow prevailing prayer to puncture any building pressure for Christ can defuse an explosive environment. Walk with Him in relentless surrender, be earnest in your explanation to others, and then patiently trust God.

Christ is your life and He is your defense, "This is what your Sovereign LORD says, your God who defends his people..." (Isaiah 51:22). Earnestly explain and then trust your Divine Defender!

M4 LESS IS MORE

"But the Lord said to Gideon, 'There are still too many men. Take them down to the water, and I will sift them for you there. If I say, 'This one shall go with you, he shall go; but if I say, 'this one shall not go with you,' he shall not go.'" JUDGES 7:4

Less of some things can mean opportunity to trust in God with more things. This is why the sifting by your Savior need not be discouraging. His goal is not to harm you, but to strip you from any dependence on yourself or others, and to rely solely on Him. Your financial limitations are an occasion to watch Him provide in ways that give Him the glory for your life. Less money means you have the occasion to trust Him with His creative provision. Indeed, the falling away of some of your friends stings, but your best friend Jesus still remains. You can become intoxicated with numerous relationships and miss engaging in intimacy with your heavenly Father. Fewer true friends will lead to richer relationships and more time with God. If your life is driven by one new relationship after another, you will dizzy in the servitude of shallow living. Having fewer earthly relationships means you have more time for your Heavenly One. Less is more.

Take the time to shed the weights of worry and watch God work. A surrendered life can be highly leveraged. However, a life independent from God is severely limited in its influence. He is positioning you for unprecedented leadership and influence. Now is the time to quit mourning your loses and move on. You have a new lease on life with the Lord, so follow His lead. Watch Him take your five loaves of bread and two fish (Matthew 14:17-19) and multiply them way beyond your efforts and enthusiasm. What God breaks, He rebuilds dependent on Him and more influential. This rebuilding process has simplified your life, so not revert back to complicated living. Less is truly more.

If "more is more" is your motto, you can easily become mean-spirited and hard to live with. A more is more mantra eventually becomes meaningless. You achieve and receive more to what end? There is no fulfillment outside of Kingdom-minded motives. If it is all about you, you will become miserable. If, on the other hand it is less of you and more of Him, everyone is happy. This is how God works, "He has brought down rulers from their thrones but has lifted up the humble" (Luke 1:52).

Therefore, lower the volume of activity and wait in quietness. It may be time to talk less and listen more. The calming presence of Christ is priceless, so tap into His reservoir of renewal. Less of worldly thinking and more of heavenly thinking leads to discerning the will of God. Do not just stand in awe at His robust accomplishments through your meager efforts. Now is the time to use this momentum generated by your Master. God is on a roll and you have the privilege of joining Him. By faith, stop doing two things before you add one. Slow down so God can speed up. Focus on quality and watch Him multiply the quantity. God wants to do more with less, so He gets the glory.

Decrease, so He can increase (John 3:30, KJV). Less is more, less of you and more of Him!

POURED OUT

"Not so, my lord," Hannah replied, "I am a woman who is deeply troubled.
I have not been drinking wine or beer; I was pouring out my soul to the Lord."
I SAMUEL 1:15

Sometimes your soul pours out in passionate prayer. The hurt is so deep, the loss is so great, and the burden is so heavy that your soul exceeds earnest prayer. Your emotions increase in intensity to the point your prayers become speechless. Somewhere between the bottom of your soul and the tip of your lips the words evaporate. Sometimes your extra heavy heart feels constricted and emits groans that only the Holy Spirit can discern, "In the same way, the Spirit helps us in our weakness. We do not know what we ought to pray for, but the Spirit intercedes for us with groans that words cannot express" (Romans 8:29). Indeed it is not only okay to go there, but it is necessary. This level of soul-searching prayer is what brings peace to a painted with pain. After your soul has been delivered onto God's platter of prayer, you are able to rest in His peaceful presence. It is during this non-trivial travail in prayer that your soul finds solace.

Like a woman in childbirth, your pain progresses until it is released by God's act of grace and gravity! Your burden is birthed and becomes a blessing. Your hurt has been gestating for months even years, so release it from your receding soul. It has lodged itself deep within and overtime has whittled down your joy. You have become hard to live with and you struggle to love yourself. Latch onto your Lord and not let go for He is there for you. He is listening even when you don't speak, or when your communication is a malaise of moans. Continue to seek the face of your heavenly Father for He is there a present hope, but if deferred your soul stays sick (Proverbs 13:12). It may seem silly to pour out your soul to One you cannot see, yet faith serves as the eyes that gaze upon your heavenly Father. Soul care is His passion for what you pour out in grief and resentment, He replaces with comfort and forgiveness.

Once you pour out your soul to your Lord, you can leave it with Him and move forward in the power and the peace of the Holy Spirit. Fill your now emptied soul with your Savior and let Christ cover you with confidence, serenity, and security. If you leave your soul empty of the eternal Satan will fill you with lingering lies like guilt and worry (Jesus explains this principle in Luke 11:24-26). A poured out soul gives the Lord more to work with. His love will lift you higher and higher, to heights of affection which angels are envious. What is poured out, He fills. What is broken, He mends. What is hungry, He feeds. What is thirsty, He quenches. What is hurt, He nurses. Allow Jesus to be the keeper of your soul. His nurture and care are unparalleled. A soul made whole is what generates gratitude and generosity. A soul poured out flushes out faithlessness and fear, which in turn can be filled with faithfulness and trust. People in denial may think you are strange or weak to pour out your soul to God. However, you know better because this is the avenue to intimacy. When you pour out your soul to the Lord, He fills you up with Himself.

A life full of Jesus is the best place to live. You can trust Him with this level of transparency. Don't doubt... just pour out!

M6 DIVINE DETOURS

"Saul said… 'Come, let's go back, or my father will stop thinking about the donkeys and start worrying about us.' But the servant replied, 'Look, in this town there is a man of God; he is highly respected, and everything he says comes true. Let's go there now. Perhaps he will tell us what way to take.' "   I SAMUEL 9:5B - 6

God's will for your life contains detours that are part of the process of building trust in Him and maturity in you. Your detour may seem dumb and a waste of time, but in reality it is part of God's great adventure. Detours are very valuable and pregnant with life lessons that cannot be learned on a well-beaten and familiar path. Your ability to endure this sidebar experience is a test humility. Your willingness to walk with God on what seems a tangential assignment has fruitful outcomes. Do not despise this detour for it is the time to learn things about yourself that have haunted you in the past. Take this time of testing to really understand your motivations, "Remember how the LORD your God led you all the way in the desert these forty years, to humble you and to test you in order to know what was in your heart, whether or not you would keep his commands" (Deuteronomy 8:2). Divine detours are meant to grow your dependence on Him.

The more accurately your self-awareness, the better you can comprehend your companions. The more comfortable you become with yourself, the better you can love yourself. The better you can love yourself, the more deeply and unconditionally you can love others, so become better, rather than bitter. Indeed, use this time and learn how to laugh at yourself for it is freeing to laugh with others about your idiosyncrasies. Your weaknesses are no big secret. Most everyone can relate to your impetuousness or your impatience because they struggle with the same. It is at your points of weakness that God wants to reveal Himself the most. This detour is designed for you to go deeper with Him, and with the significant others in your life. Be careful not to rush through this time and miss the blessing of becoming much better as a leader, friend, follower, lover, parent, and child of your heavenly Father. Divine detours are designed to make you better.

It is during God's detours that you begin to see life from a different perspective. You value and respect people more authentically and aggressively. Therefore, your relationships become more robust. You meet new friends and experience new things. The newness is a little daunting, because you have never been here before. But the familiarity of your heavenly Father is still there. He is your one constant and He is with you along this detour toward His best. Moreover, listen to the wise new friends He is sending your way. Honor them by prayerfully considering their advice, and then follow it when appropriate. Without this detour you would have missed the rich wisdom from these fellow pilgrims of the faith. New perspectives challenge old ones. Lastly, like a well-chiseled marble statue, the roughness of your life takes shape by the caring hand of your Creator. It is a gift of preparation, organization, and understanding, so listen to God through His word and trusted advisors.

Detours traveled alone will consume you with fear of danger and failure, but with companions they mature, excite, and humble you. Therefore, look for your Savior's signposts of wisdom for they lead you toward His best!

LOYAL FOLLOWER

> " 'Do all that you have in mind,' his armor-bearer said. 'Go ahead;
> I am with you heart and soul.' "   I Samuel 14:7

Loyal followers are hard to find, but once they are discovered wise is the leader who values them. They are rare and productive constantly looking for ways to make the leader successful in his or her God-given mission. They unselfishly serve behind the scenes, tirelessly and tediously. Because of a loyal follower's sixth sense to anticipate needs, they know how to excellence. They learn to prod the leader with thorough questioning, so the leader's intuition can be clarified and verified. The loyal follower is an encourager and an implementer. They know how to get things done by converting the leader's vision into reality. Without the skill and support of these dream enhancers, the visionary leader would only drown in their dreams.

Leaders devoid of loyal followers are not effective over the long term. You can beg, bribe, and berate followers into results for a season, but eventually this type of leadership will drive away loyal followers and leave only the weak ones. Indeed, the leader may start something, but it is the loyal follower who sustains the new initiative. They are comfortable not getting credit, though the wise leader gives it gladly and gratefully. It is no secret that the loyal follower is the engine that keeps the enterprise running smoothly. Therefore, reward loyalty with loyalty and appreciation for loyal follower who is taken for granted will remain loyal no more. Paul modeled help for loyal servants of the Lord, "Yes, and I ask you, loyal yokefellow, help these women who have contended at my side in the cause of the gospel..." (Philippians 4:3).

A wise leader learns to love loyal followers lavishly and unconditionally. Reward regularly those who embody the values of the organization. Thank them with bonuses and unexpected time off for you are better off when they take time off. Moreover, loyalty for followers is not meant to be an end in itself. They feel called to carry out the God-given mission of the ministry or business. Their loyalty is the fruit of their calling and the results of their respect. They respect because they are respected. When you honor and value your team or family, you invite loyalty. You value them when you sincerely consider their ideas and opinions. You respect them when you start and end meetings and conversations on time. You honor them when you do what you say and you respect them when you apologize for letting them down. You show respect when you listen and exhibit honor when you serve. You make them feel important, because they are important. This type of environment of love and respect will cause loyalty to run rampant. You will be unable to control or contain its energizing effect. Loyalty given lasts, while loyalty demanded dies. Look for the dispensing of loyalty first in the mirror at home and then watch it come back through the window at work. Jesus was loyal to the point of death on the cross, so be loyal to your Lord first and then loyalty to others flows naturally. Loyalty to the Lord means you worship Him in His holiness and you obey Him humbly and quickly.

You love Him with passion and purity and you follow Him by faith. Therefore, stay loyal to your loyal Lord and to your loyal followers for loyalty extends in all directions!

M8 TRAINED AND SKILLED

"Along with their relatives—all of them trained and skilled in music for the Lord…"
1 CHRONICLES 25:7

Skill needs training and training needs skill. You can be very gifted, but without the proper development of your gift, you are just scratching the surface of your potential. Things may have come easily for you up to this point, but in order for you to excel in the future, you require additional training. This is not designed to slow you down, but to build you up. Your skill level has served you well up to now, however God's next assignment is not to be taken lightly. He moving you toward this new opportunity so you will have an occasion to trust Him even more. In some respects, this is virgin territory for your experience and your abilities. Therefore, it is imperative you take the time to shore up your skills. Training means you are teachable and you care about developing your God given abilities. You want to do the job well and with excellence. By taking the time to train, you will have a much higher probability of success. But, be very honest with yourself and others. Make sure God has given you the aptitude for these new responsibilities. Can you eventually be excellent at this work? Book training, seminar training and on the job training are necessary for a full-orbed experience. Do not short change your training, for you will regret it in the future. The more narrow your role, the more specific skills are required. So, seek out well-defined training that is suited especially for you. Above all else, "…train yourself to be godly" (1 Timothy 4:7).

If you are chasing this role for status alone, you will struggle. However, if you relish this responsibility and would do it regardless of the pay, then you are on a productive path. God wants you in this role for service, not status. Your training and skill development is for the Lord. He is the one who got you here, and He is the one who will sustain you. Do not forget God. Your career development is not an end in itself. It is a means to the end of furthering His kingdom. Therefore, continue to dedicate your skills to Christ and allow Him to align your heart daily through prayer. He is the originator of your abilities. It is for the Lord's pleasure that you have been trained.

Make sure people know you are His and your gifts come from Him. If not, others will heap praise on you that can deflate your humility. Honor that is not redirected to God and others can go to your head. Your excellent skills, honed by rigorous training will invite accolades. So, be prepared to say thank you and then lay the kind affirmations at the feet of Jesus. He deserves all praise, honor, and glory. Your skill may give you an audience with Kings (Proverbs 22:29), if so do not be shy about your Savior. Focus on developing your talents with proper training, and trust God to open doors.

Be a good steward of the skills God has given you, and He will give back to you. Skills without training are dull, but sharpened skills produce excellent results for His glory!

> "David also said to Solomon his son, 'Be strong and courageous, and do the work.
> Do not be afraid or discouraged, for the Lord God, my God, is with you. He will not fail
> you or forsake you until all the work for the service of the temple of the Lord is finished.' "
> 1 CHRONICLES 28:20

God is with you and He has called you to this endeavor, therefore He can be trusted. At times the task seems overwhelming, but your large responsibilities are supported by your large Lord. Do not let the vast scope of the situation get you down. He has the relationships and the resources in place to carry out His commands. The vision may have grown way beyond what you signed up for, but do not sell short what your Savior can accomplish. You would not say God is limited, so do not allow fear and fretting to get the best of you. Instead, you can be strong, courageous and confident in Christ. When you linger before the Lord in reflection and repentance, his confidence begins to well up within you in quietness and strength. Fear melts away in the face of Jesus for His presence is reassuring and restful. There is no need to lose sleep over the wall of work that is looming. The Lord is the author of your labor; therefore stay true to His original blueprint.

You may have brought the vision to this point, and now you have the privilege to hand off the responsibility of its completion to another. The goal is for God's will to be done and for Him to be glorified in the process. So who completes the project is not as important is the project being completed in a God-honoring way. This is all about God and no one else. He has used you as His vessel, so give it up for God. Do not be afraid to hand over the reins to one younger and less experienced. God's grace can overcome lack of experience. God is with you, because He is with you be careful to not take on more than He intends. Indeed, you are a warrior representing another world. But the battle is His not yours, so fight in His strength not yours (1 Samuel 17:47). Comrades around you may have fallen, so take time to care for them and learn from their mistakes. People and processes are in your life to make you better and more effective for God. Therefore, stay true to your humble dependence on God and others. He will not fail or forsake you.

Do not interpret His temporary silence as a sign that He is unsupportive. This is a faith builder and a faith tester. Improper motives are manifested under pressure. He will use this time of pressure for purification. Your character will trump tragedy, so do not falter into fear and discouragement, rather stay true to the truth. This is His calling on your life; there is nowhere else to go. No amount of money or fame can dislodge you from His destiny. He has placed this dream in your heart. Others may walk away, but not you. Be encouraged His comfort may come in the form of the fervent prayers of the faithful. Moreover, make much of His faithfulness and less of your fears. Fear drains, but faith fills. One day you will celebrate Christ's accomplishments through you. In the meantime stay true to the task.

God is with you. He is here, and there is nothing to fear!

M10 MADE RICH

"You will be made rich in every way so that you can be generous on every occasion, and through us your generosity will result in thanksgiving to God."
2 CORINTHIANS 9:11

God's grace makes you rich in His ways. You are rich in mercy, love, patience, compassion and wisdom. When Jesus Christ became the Lord and Savior of your life, you received access to an eternal portfolio of resources. You no longer have to complain about not having everything you need. In Christ you have just what you need, when you need it and there are no shortfalls with the Lord. No one can make a run on heaven's bank, in other words the resources of God are within your reach. You can tap into the Holy Spirit moment by moment, at any occasion. The wisdom of the Almighty is available for you in "real time" prayer. "What does God think?" and "What would Jesus do?" are two questions to ask before you act. And if you are not sure of the answers, then by all means wait, pray, and ask people you trust for their advice and godly counsel.

Indeed, you are rich with the resources of God. Like oil reserves under the surface of property you manage, you have an abundance of energy of which you can take advantage. As the character of Christ continues to consume you, you can't help but receive the richness of His grace. People will begin to clamor for your time, because they want to learn how to leverage love or apply patience. It is a remarkable truth that you have been made rich in the ways of God. Your eternal balance sheet is robust and real, so review what you already have in Christ, and then daily count your many blessings. Account for the acts of God that overflow from your life. Because you have been given so much, you are uniquely positioned to give. Grace can permeate your giving, because grace permeates your life. You receive Christ so you can give Christ. You receive God's mercy so you can give mercy. You receive God's love so you can give love. You receive God's patience so you can give patience. You receive God's compassion so you can give compassion. You receive God's wisdom so you can give wisdom. You are rich in the ways of God so you can give the resources of God. This is His circle of generosity. The reason God makes anyone rich is for the purpose of hilarious generosity.

Happy are the generous for thanksgiving and appreciation explode from the heart of a generous giver. God gives money and the capacity for serving others so they can be given away. A blessing that is not passed on can erode into a curse. Therefore, look on every occasion as an opportunity to give. Give spontaneously and give with structure, but with both give prayerfully. Give money. Give time. Give expertise. Give hospitality. Give opportunity. Give grace. Give forgiveness. Give resources. As Jesus says, "Give and it will be given to you" (Luke 6:38). The best way to give is out of love, gratitude, and obedience to God. And when you give, you will receive. Most importantly, you receive the peace and contentment of Jesus, knowing you modeled His motives and His generosity.

God has made you rich in His ways, for His sake and the sake of others. Therefore, allow generosity to govern your giving for the glory of God!

CHOOSE YOUR BATTLES

"You will not have to fight this battle. Take up your positions; stand firm and see the deliverance the Lord will give you, O Judah and Jerusalem. Do not be afraid; do not be discouraged. Go out to face them tomorrow, and the Lord be with you." 2 CHRONICLES 20:17

Choose your battles wisely and by all means allow God to run interference for you. Some battles are just the enemy's distraction and he wants to divert you from God's best. Do not succumb to this attempt to seduce your ego. His goal is to keep you busy battling insignificant fires so you miss God's best. Let others fight these battles, so these skirmishes do not keep you from following through with priorities that only you can accomplish. Wise is the leader that says no to fighting battles more than he says yes. One well-timed no is much more effective that a dozen affirmative responses. This battle is not meant for you to fight. Yes, if you fight you may win, but why exert your time and energy toward this minor issue?

Take the same amount of resources and focus on fewer initiatives that are most important. Pride may have already shot the first volley, but you can still confess your impulsiveness and regroup. Stop before you regret committing your thinking and doing to this issue or person. Indeed, it is wise to choose your battles in parenting, marriage, and/or work. There always seems to be an issue to fight over. Instead of sparring over every perceived injustice, forgive for it is relational lubricant. Keep forgiveness at the forefront of your battle lines and then enjoy the peace that ensues. Because you are a gifted debater, you could probably win most arguments you engage in. But why win the battle and then lose the relationship? This is not a battle worth fighting. Save your bullets for battles that really matter like pride, pretension, and prejudice.

Lastly, the Lord is your first line of defense for the enemy is not a match against the Lord's battle forces. God mows down pride with humility. He obliterates pretension with authenticity. He crushes prejudice with acceptance. You have the honor and privilege of receiving your marching orders from your commander Christ Jesus. Jesus has a way of winning battles without a shot of cynicism ever being fired. Sometimes others simply implode as a result of their unwise choices. He has warned them in His Word and with the wise words of others. But now is the time to wait and not force the issue. There is no need to plow ahead and make your point. Let the truth settle in and do its work at the right time. You will accomplish more by fighting from your knees, so kneel before Almighty God and ask Him to fight this battle. Prayer is your secret weapon of success. It is His aerial attack strategy, as prayer crosses over enemy lines and accomplishes the will of God. Your confused child may be exposed in warfare with the world, if so stay diligent in the habit of covering them with prayer. Pray God will fight for them, even though they are unaware. Prayer matters, especially the fervent and faithful prayer of a parent, friend, or family member. Nevertheless, choose your battles wisely. Choose to fight fewer battles and trust God to fight more.

Most battles are distraction, therefore stay focused on Christ. He is your eternal Commander in Chief, ever engaged in battle on your behalf!

M12 HAPPY MOTHER

"He settles the barren woman in her home as a happy woman of children. Praise the Lord." PSALM 113:9

What makes a mother of children happy? Is it just the child? If so, there would be a world of happiness? Children certainly contribute to a mother's joy. Jesus said, "A woman giving birth to a child has pain because her time has come; but when her baby is born she forgets the anguish because of her joy that a child is born into the world" (John 16:21). However, offspring cannot be the only reason for a mom's feelings of fulfillment. In fact, if a mother's happiness is contingent on her children she will quickly become discontent. There is a greater motivation, which resides in gratitude to God and His glory. You can rejoice because God opens the womb and invites intimacy with Him.

Furthermore, the Holy Spirit initiates the miracle of conception (Matthew 1:20). Pregnancy is a gift from Providence. The Bible says, "Sons are a heritage from the Lord, children a reward from him" (Psalm 127:3). Therefore, you can be extremely grateful for the gift of God's child. Your son or daughter is a stewardship from your Savior. This new life is not competition for your time and money, rather it is an opportunity for service, faith building, and becoming more like Jesus. Have you written your heavenly Father a thank-you note for the gift of your child? Happiness comes to mothers who experience hilarious appreciation for the Almighty's entrustment of children. Indeed, be eternally grateful for the Lord's unspeakable expression of love through the life of your little one.

Lastly, children will frustrate you and let you down, just like you have done to your parents and God. So learn to liberally apply love, grace, forgiveness, and discipline in the same way you administer ointment to their ailments. Teach them the truth of Scripture, model for them faith, and joyfully watch as they enter into a personal relationship with Jesus. The disciple John experienced this, "I have no greater joy than to hear that my children are walking in truth (3 John 4). Moreover, mothers experience happiness when they praise God for the privilege of being a parent. Your role as a mom is your glory to God. You smile, because you know as you serve your child you are serving Christ (Mark 9:36-37).

Therefore, be happy, because your heavenly Father has blessed you. He has given you the gift of His son for your barren soul, and the gift of a child for your joyful service!

VIRTUOUS WOMAN

"A wife of noble character who can find? She is worth far more than rubies."
PROVERBS 31:10

A woman of character is not easily found for she is rare and valuable. Her appealing attributes come as a gift from God. Thank Him often if you are blessed with this quality of woman in your life. She is rare because of her focus on others in a self-crazed culture. For the follower of Christ selflessness is expected, but for our society as a whole it is an anomaly. She refuses to demean herself to a standard of mediocrity, because her goal is excellence in living. Duplicity is far from her thinking as she serves with authenticity and industry. No skills or gifts remain dormant in her active life. She channels her energies into the welfare of her family and is resourceful with financial opportunities. A woman of character is an anchor for her family.

Your character provides stability when challenges creep into your home. You are determined to do the right thing, regardless of the difficulties required. Character is more important than compromise, therefore you model the way for your friends and family. You are a rock of hope and consistency because God's Word is that for you. However, be careful to not take the world on your shoulders. This is God's job so do not hold a standard of perfection over your head. Leave yourself some wiggle room for mistakes because you will make mistakes. Let mistakes be a reminder of what to do and not to do in the future. They are a reminder of your dependence on God. Your goal is not to live a mistake-free life, but a life that loves God and loves people. Let Him continue to develop your character and grow you into a mentor of other women. Don't waste your wonderful experiences. Share them with younger women so they can grow in their character.

Men, love your wife of character. Tell her often how proud you are of her and do not be intimidated by her level of spirituality. On the contrary, celebrate her passion for life and her spiritual maturity. Allow her life to challenge you and inspire you to the same level of character development. Your virtuous woman is a tremendous asset. Your best and most strategic business decision is when you married a woman of character. She is uncanny in seeing things you do not see, and in saving you a ton of money and time.

Her influences is ubiquitous in your work and home, so encourage her burgeoning influence and opportunities. Become her biggest cheerleader. If she wants to start a business, help her start a business. If she needs some help with the house and lawn, make that investment. Free her to do what she does best. It may be teaching, mentoring, being a mom, sewing, or serving in a variety of capacities. It may be to take care of her parents during this season of life. Allow her to reach her full potential by giving her the cash, confidence, and resources to reach for her dreams. Be grateful for a woman of character is not to be taken for granted. Make a big deal out of her accomplishments, because they are a big deal.

Help her to pace herself and protect her from the encroachment of those with warped motives. Her character is a valued asset so honor and cherish it well!

143

M14 MOTHER'S COMPASSION

"Can a mother forget the baby at her breast and have no compassion on the child she borne? Though she may forget, I will not forget you!" ISAIAH 49:15

The compassion of a mother cannot be compared for she is forever fixed on her baby. She brought her little ones into the world, and she will love them throughout this world and into the world to come. A mother's resilient compassion toward her children is like the Lord's compassion, full and forever. She is Christ in the flesh when she weeps over the wants of her little ones. She is like Jesus when she instructs her "baby" to shun the world's foolishness and be wise in the ways of God. Sometimes she comes across as overbearing or over-protective, but it is all done with a heart of compassion.

She never forgets the needs of her children. All the little details become the language of her love: how they dress, where they go, whom they chose as friends, and what they eat, watch and read. A mom's questions are a clue they care. What is God teaching them? Are they making wise choices? Who will they marry? These are all questions of compassion. They know how to discern their children's desires and dreams better than the children do sometimes. Therefore, do not resist your mother's maneuvers to love on you. Receive your mom's compassion with gratitude and respect. She wouldn't call if she didn't care. She wouldn't ask so many questions if she didn't have your best interests in mind. A mom who loves Jesus and you is one of the best things you have going for you. She never forgets her baby. She is always there for you, just like your Savior and friend Jesus.

Your heavenly Father birthed you into His forever family. Because you are His child, His compassions excel, "Because of the LORD'S great love we are not consumed, for his compassions never fail" (Lamentations 3:22). Your sin or unwise choices may have separated you from sweet fellowship with your Savior, but His compassion beckons you to believe and receive. Believe with all your heart that Christ is in control and that He can lead you through this lethargic life stage. His forgiveness is forever and His grace covers a multitude of sins. Receive His compassion and be healed. Receive His compassion so you, in turn, can extend it to others. The most effective givers of compassion are receivers of compassion. Indeed, you can extend compassion to the one who hurt you, because Christ in you provides compassion. Moreover, model what your mom has done for you for years and follow what your heavenly Father has done since the beginning of time. Compassion facilitates intimacy and forgiveness. It builds robust relationships that resonate with grace.

Never forget that God doesn't forget. His compassion is constantly ready to respond to your hurt and discouragement. Compassion is not free to forget those it loves, so be a receiver and giver of compassion!

"These days should be remembered and observed in every generation by every family, and in every providence and in every city. And these days of Purim should never cease to be celebrated by the Jews, nor should the memory of them die out among their descendants." ESTHER 9:28

God-devised memories are meant to be remembered and to be relived. This is one of His methods of encouragement and faith building. Otherwise we run through life at break neck speed and tend to forget God. One way we forget Him is by letting the stories of His faithfulness die out. Instead of being consumed with an attitude of "what has the Lord done for me lately," we can celebrate what great things He has done in the past. The Psalmist understood this, "I will remember the deeds of the LORD; yes, I will remember your miracles of long ago" (Psalm 77:11). Most significantly, He altered the course of your life and eternity with your soul's salvation, through faith in His son Jesus. This is worth remembering and celebrating.

Your spiritual birthday is extra special, because it brought significance into your life. This is a memory to be relived and retold. Let others know of this transition in your life, which has led to a lifetime of transformation. One excellent tradition is the retelling of your salvation experience. You may choose to do this on your physical birthday. It is appropriate and appealing to all who love you. You relive the memory of your need for a Savior. Sin had barricaded you in the back room of your soul. You were trapped unable to break out of its bondage. But, by the grace of God and faith in Christ you were set free. Your eternal emancipation is worth remembering and celebrating. It is a big deal to be 'born again'! When this memory dies out, your faith is in danger of following suit. Tell your salvation story often, in a fresh and meaningful way.

Another good memory to relive is answered prayers. God answers prayers more often than you may recall. Therefore, consider recording and chronicling Christ's compassionate answers to your pelting of heaven with passionate prayers. As a result of answered prayer, He has saved souls, strengthened marriages, reconciled relationships, dispensed wisdom, revived those at the point of death, ceased wars, built churches, mended broken hearts, made whole the unhealthy, provided jobs, protected children, and orchestrated opportunities. He has created peace in the middle of turmoil, hope in the middle of despair, strength in the middle of weakness, victory in the middle of defeat, and forgiveness in the middle of rejection. His answered prayers have prevailed into posterity. These are worth recording and remembering for Christ's sake. Before you become discouraged, or live on the brink of giving up, it would be worthwhile to recall His faithfulness to our daily supplications. Answered prayers compounded over a lifetime are staggering.

Memories with your Master were made to memorialize. Therefore, relive them often and watch them grow and multiply your faith!

M16 MAN ATTRACTION

"…Naomi her mother-in-law said to her… 'Wash and perfume yourself, and put on your best clothes'… Boaz replied… 'don't be afraid. I will do for you all you ask. All my fellow townsmen know that you are a woman of noble character.' " RUTH 3:1A, 3A, 11

A woman of character attracts a man of character. However, if your goal is to control, you will attract insecure men who are not fully confident in their own masculinity. These are the men to avoid for their maturity is stunted at adolescent and they are high maintenance. You really want a man who lovingly leads by serving. A woman of character is a billboard of attraction to a man serious about servant leadership. He looks for this type of woman because he knows she can be trusted. She is a woman of character and her purity propels him to love her sacrificially and unconditionally. A woman of purity is a prescription for a godly man, however the ungodly are turned off by purity. It smacks in the face of their pretense and it embroils their patience.

Conversely a pure woman is a patient woman. She can wait on God to send her a man in His timing. Moreover, a woman of character is grateful for the little things and trusts God with the big things. Food, clothing, a home, work, and health are just the beginning of her thankfulness. Her list goes on: salvation in Christ, a loving husband, caring children, faithful friends, and a community of believers round out her gratitude. She is grateful, because God is good. He is good even when times are bad. A grateful woman attracts a grateful man. Furthermore, if you want to attract the right kind of man, do not stop with the development of your inner beauty. Peter said it well, "And let not your adornment be merely external — braiding the hair, and wearing gold jewelry, or putting on dresses; but let it be the hidden person of the heart, with the imperishable quality of a gentle and quiet spirit, which is precious in the sight of God" (1 Peter 3:3-4).

A woman also attracts a man with her outward beauty. It does matter how you look. Men are visual animals, so your appearance is the pathway to your character. Your character engages his head and your looks his heart. This remains true after marriage for it is not a pass for messiness. Do not take your man for granted by looking unkempt and sloppy. Smell good, look good, and taste good for him. When you take care of yourself, he takes notice. Plus you feel better about yourself, both physically and emotionally. Age need not be your enemy. Make it your friend by growing old gracefully. Exercising and eating right tells your man that you respect yourself and you respect him. Lastly, love God with all your heart. A woman who loves God attracts a man who does the same. God may be the father who never hugged and affirmed you. Talk to Jesus about your fears and insecurities. He knows you inside and out. He knows what you need; better than you know what you need. Your heavenly Father loves you, so let Him. An unloved woman is a woman most miserable, so allow God love you and in turn you can love your man. A woman who receives love is a woman who can give love. This is attractive. This attracts the type of loving man you need and want.

By God's grace stay attractive. Your inner and outer beauty will attract and keep the right kind of man!

WEDDING CELEBRATION

"On the third day a wedding took place at Cana in Galilee. Jesus' mother was there, and Jesus and his disciples had also been invited to the wedding."
JOHN 2:1-2

A wedding is a celebration of two people committed to Christ and committed to each other. This is cause for raucous laughter and teary-eyed gratitude. The solemn vows of the bride and groom are accented by the smiling kisses of both. The parents celebrate God's goodness in all of its facets. It is good to see your child embrace a spouse who will cherish and respect your "baby." It is good to see your child happy and content. It is good to see your child make wise choices. It is good to see your child dance with joy. It is good to see your child obedient to his or her heavenly Father. Weddings where Jesus is invited are the best!

A wedding is a preamble to the constitution of marriage. It is a deceleration of independence from self interests. It is interdependence on each other and dependence on God. A wedding is costly, but not nearly as expensive as the marriage. A wedding mirrors a marriage's need for mentors, prayer support, and planning. A wedding done well is a template for marriage. You keep the fires of romance burning brightly. You plan together and communicate almost real time. You spend budgeted money. You involve your family, in ways that are appropriate and honoring. You keep God as the centerpiece of your life. A wedding is not a fleeting moment, but rather a memory to be relived over and over again. A wedding is a reminder of God doing a beautiful work of grace in a world of hurt. It reinvigorates stale marriages. It staves off the pending demise of others. It affirms those who, by God's grace, have grown deeper and deeper in love since their own special day.

Most importantly invite Jesus to your wedding. He is the ultimate wedding planner. He is interested in every detail of your public expression of faith in Him. Indeed, your public display of faith begins with your private devotion. Once you have developed a personal love relationship with Jesus you can humbly exalt Him before friends, family, and the world. Private dedication precedes public declaration. An engaged couple without the individual engagement of faith is not ready for a wedding. A wedding requires much more than a starry-eyed look of love. Its prerequisite is a deep and abiding faith in God. Otherwise, the wedding becomes a big expensive party lacking the teeth of commitment and follow through. A wedding without Jesus is like an orchestra without a conductor. There is a ton of potential represented by a lot of well-meaning individuals, but there is no defined direction. There is no overall harmony of the musical instruments of husband, wife, family, friends, and faith. Jesus integrates the lives of all these well-meaning players into a beautiful concert called marriage. The wedding is but a prelude of the marriage concert, but what a beautiful beginning it births. Jesus is a gracious guest always looking for ways to intercede on your behalf and on the behalf of the other guests. His role model of servanthood will mark your marriage for a lifetime. Your faith in Christ is a marriage analogy for He is the groom and you are the bride. Your wedding is a picture of the joy of your salvation.

Your marriage is a life-long consecration of that commitment. Keep inviting Jesus, as He is the initiator of your wedding and the sustainer of your marriage!

M18 FAMILY BUSINESS

"King Asa also deposed his grandmother Maacah from her position as queen mother, because she had made a repulsive Asherah pole. Asa cut the pole down, broke it up and burned it in the Kidron Valley." 2 CHRONICLES 15:16

Family businesses can be a blessing or a burden. Working with people you love and trust is a blessing. But when family conflicts with faith, it becomes a burden because it forces a choice to be made. Jesus said, "Anyone who loves his father or mother more than me is not worthy of me; anyone who loves his son or daughter more than me is not worthy of me..."(Matthew 10:37). The choice may come down to whether you will follow God's desires or man's expectations. The answer seems easy and clear, but when you are in the heat of debate and negotiating, things are more difficult. You may be a son who works for your father and he wants you to take over the business one day, but your dad's faith is compartmentalized more to Sunday, while your faith is integrated throughout your everyday life. You have a strong desire to share your faith in the workplace, while your father perceives that approach to be unprofessional. So what are you to do? There is the tension of honoring two fathers, your heavenly Father and your earthly father. Be respectful, no matter what. There may need to be a clean break, so that you both can better understand each other and really pray and think through the best plan of succession. This was the plan of Abraham and Lot, "So Abram said to Lot, 'Let's not have any quarreling between you and me, or between your herdsmen and mine, for we are brothers. Is not the whole land before you? Let's part company. If you go to the left, I'll go to the right; if you go to the right, I'll go to the left'" (Genesis 13:8-9).

Most family business conflicts can be resolved before they occur. You can preclude these squabbles with very clearly defined principles, values, and expectations. As a family, define and document a family business credo. Your motto may be to glorify God by serving people with excellence. Whoever you are needs to be clearly worded and communicated creatively. The best communication is through the behavior of the people in the company. One business principle may be honesty, even when it costs money. You may also value generosity, so include it as something that is non-negotiable. Everyone on the team agrees that the company should give back to the community. You may decide to give cash in the form of 10% of your gross revenues. This becomes a company-wide discipline and everyone enjoys giving to their favorite charity.

The point is to involve others in the process, especially family members. Give them ownership. Trust them to make the right decisions based upon the agreed upon expectations. You may need a retreat or a family conference to hammer out your mission, vision, and values. But once defined, these values and principles become everyone's accountability, especially family members. Family members must model the values of the family business or it will fail. Do what you expect others to do and say what you expect others to say. Lastly, be willing to let a non-family member take a key management role.

You may need to go outside the family to get the expertise you need for this stage of business growth. God's will is what is best for everyone!

ASK WITH ASSURANCE

"Ezra came up from Babylon. He was a teacher well versed in the Law of Moses, which the Lord, the God of Israel had given. The king had granted him everything he asked, for the hand of the Lord was on him." Ezra 7:6

You can ask with assurance when the Lord is with you. You can ask for prayer when the Lord is with you. You can ask for money when the Lord is with you. You can ask for protection when the Lord is with you. You can ask for a friend when the Lord is with you. You can ask for wisdom when the Lord is with you. You can ask for understanding when the Lord is with you. You can ask for forgiveness when the Lord is with you. You can ask others to consider Christ when the Lord is with you. You can ask for boldness, wisdom, humility, strength, kindness, and opportunity when the Lord is with you. Therefore, do not limit your request to your influence; unleash your request based on His influence. Fear does not lack reasons why you cannot ask. Pride will strangle the life out of your asking every time. The chance of rejection can lead you to postpone your asking for a more convenient time. However, the longer you wait, the harder it can become to simply ask. Asking is not easy, but it is necessary. If you don't propose, you may not marry. If you don't ask for directions, you may wander around in frustration. Asking is an everyday part of life. Indeed, do not underestimate the power of God in your life, family, and work. His hand is on you for a reason and He has given you favor for a season. "God said, "Ask for whatever you want me to give you" (1 Kings 3:5b).

Yes, it is wise to ask respectfully and responsibility. You are not a "bull in a china shop," rather a sheep in God's flock. So ask prayerfully and in a timely manner. Make sure your ask has been preceded by proper planning and prayer. You have a finite amount of relational and emotional capital to spend, so budget accordingly. Do not wear out your welcome. Make sure to punctuate your asking with thanksgiving. Moreover, the number one reason people do not give is because they have not been asked. Blessings are left on the table when an ask is absent, and after you do ask, follow up your asking with a progress report, which includes measurable milestones.

Above all else stay immersed in Scripture. A proper perspective provides for a potent petition. It is when we lose perspective that our asking becomes anemic and even non-existent. God's Word will flush out your fears and replace it with His calm confidence. Seek the Lord and He will show you how and when to ask. His word is clear, "You have not because you ask not" (James 4:2b). Ask for His wisdom to marinate in your mind. The wisdom of God will facilitate your freedom to ask. Ask for humility and God will use this to tie down the trepidations that hold you back. It is easier to ask God than people, so ask God so you can ask people. Asking is God's methodology to accomplish His mission and it is an expression of trust. Therefore by faith, ask and you may be amazed at what you discover about yourself and God.

Don't ask and you may never know what you missed. Do ask and see what mighty things God has in store for those on whom His hand rests!

M20 THOROUGHLY PREPARED

"So I went to the governors of Trans-Euphrates and gave them the king's letters. The king had also sent army officers and cavalry with me." NEHEMIAH 2:9

It is very hard to over-prepare. Indeed, most do not struggle with over-preparation. Your nemeses is neglecting the real need for thorough preparation. When you rush ahead of God, you expose yourself to the nagging details about which you could have intentionally prayed and thought through. Pride tends to shun preparation, as it assumes too much and prays too little. When you take the time to prod those areas about which you are unsure, you discover insights that are invaluable to success. If, on the other hand you go off half-cocked with a "Pollyanna-ish'"naïveté, you are an excellent candidate for disappointment, or worse, failure. Irresponsible assumptions are foreign to faith for it thoroughly prepares on one hand and humbly prays on the other.

Preparation also includes the involvement of others, because you will not accomplish big things for God by yourself. Jesus didn't. He called the twelve to join Him. He also has people in your life whose hearts have been strangely moved to join you in this God-created opportunity. Let them in and do not be intimidated because they possess skills and experiences that you don't. Instead of lamenting the different backgrounds, personalities, and skills that surround you celebrate them. A well-rounded variety of relationships and resources bring strength to the whole. A true team is diverse and a secure leader accepts diversity as a key ingredient to the recipe of success. So unfetter your team from the fear of failure, by giving them the freedom to try new things and to test long-held assumptions and methods. Help others prepare by removing obstacles, "Build up, build up, prepare the road! Remove the obstacles out of the way of my people" (Isaiah 57:14). A team thoroughly prepared produces. Moreover, prayer is your most potent preparation. You cannot pray too much about your methods and motives. Pray for God to be glorified and for His will to be done. Pray for His provision and resources. Pray for relationships you have yet to enter into that will become critical allies in your God-sized project. It is through prayer that you preserve in preparation.

Lastly, change occurs primarily in the person praying. Your faith expands and your patience expands. Your love elevates and your vision grows. In a word, your character receives an extreme makeover. Prayer is the crowning jewel of thorough preparation. Prayer gives you courage to speak boldly and the wisdom to know what to say and how to say it. Prayer holds you back when you need to wait in silence. Prayer is preparation, as it aligns you with the Almighty's agenda. Thorough preparation is your friend. God does not waste preparation, but He blesses it. Therefore, be thoroughly prepared, and then follow through with the plan in a spirit of abandonment and gusto.

Weave prayer throughout your preparation, like a finely-stitched quilt, and then watch God work. Thorough preparation positions you to be used by God!

"I put Shelemiah the priest, Zadok the scribe, and a Levite named Pedaiah in charge of the storerooms and made Hanan son of Zaccur, the son of Mattaniah, their assistant, because these men were considered trustworthy. They were made responsible for distributing the supplies to their brothers." NEHEMIAH 13:13

God's primary prerequisite in selection for service is trustworthiness. He is not looking for the most gifted, the most talented, the wealthiest, the most attractive, or the most popular. God is interested in bestowing His blessing on those who can be trusted. Trustworthiness is an attribute that invites God to participate. It is an invitation for His encouragement, His wisdom, and His responsibilities. Being in a position where God can trust you is a humbling place. His trust is both energizing and daunting. The God of the universe trusts you to implement His will for your life. Because of your good name and faithfulness, He trusts you to represent Him well. He trusts you with His reputation, His truth, His children, His wisdom, His church, His spirit, His work and His Kingdom.

You serve and love a trusting heavenly Father who enjoys extending Himself to those who can be trusted. Therefore, do not shrink back from God's trust. He has given you this opportunity because He trusts you. You are responsible because He has put you in this position of authority. Your role is to represent Him responsibly, so be quick to give Him the credit for the success you are experiencing. Remain trustworthy because He can withdraw His blessing as quickly as He gave His blessing. Continue to bathe each day with prayer and thanksgiving. Seek wisdom and counsel from those smarter and more experienced than you for trustworthy individual is teachable. You are a lifetime learner, who understands the need to grow with the organization. Education and experience are meant to be tools for developing and extending your trustworthiness. Daniel trusted God in the middle of his test, "The king was overjoyed and gave orders to lift Daniel out of the den. And when Daniel was lifted from the den, no wound was found on him, because he had trusted in his God" (Daniel 3:28).

Moreover, people trust others who are trusted by God. The character qualities that are attractive to God are the same traits that solicit the trust of family, friends, and work associates. Your 'good name' is your most valuable asset. Guard it with a God-fearing vigilance. People love and respect you. This is an honor much greater than fame or fortune. People follow those they trust. Their investment of time and money is in direct proportion to your level of trustworthiness. "This is a trustworthy saying. And I want you to stress these things, so that those who have trusted in God may be careful to devote themselves to doing what is good. These things are excellent and profitable for everyone" (Titus 3:8). So let your life and actions, not your words prove you are trustworthy. Do more than what is expected. Keep your word and follow through. Indeed, attention to the little things builds big blessings. But, above all else, focus on "being" rather than "doing." Be who you are in Christ and the proper "doing" will follow. In Christ you are loved, accepted, forgiven and trustworthy. Abide in Him and others will clamor for your attention and time. Are you considered trustworthy?

If so, your life is an invitation for God and people to join you. Trust Him and others, and you will be trusted by both!

M22   SHOW UP

"When he [the king] saw Queen Esther standing in the court, he was pleased with her and held out to her the gold scepter that was in his hand. So Esther approached and touched the tip of the scepter." ESTHER 5:2

Successful living is about showing up, which means you are there at the appointed time, ideally a little early. Your mode of operation is to say less and do more, as your actions speak for themselves. You show up for work as a diligent employee even when you don't feel like it. You show up for a first date in spite of all the unknowns. You show up on the behalf of another even though they may not expect your sincere concern. You show up to exercise when your body begs you otherwise. You show up for a funeral when you don't know what to say. You show up at a wedding to honor the bride and groom's public declaration of a lifetime commitment to each another. You show up for church even when you feel guilty and insecure. Make it a priority to show up and you may be surprised at the result. Eager athletes show up on the end of the bench next to the coach. Those who show up at the right place, at the right time are the ones who experience God's best. You may meet a new friend or become reacquainted with an old one, which may lead to an unexpected opportunity. So show up, shut up and listen up.

You especially need to show up for God. Be ruthless about not missing your God time. Show up for God when you are sleepy, lazy, or lonely. Your desire may be waning but after you show up, your "want to" will grow. Show up for God and watch Him show up. It takes time to show up for God, but it is time well worth the effort and expense. You can't afford to not show up for your Savior. Perish the thought that anyone would stand up Jesus. Our Lord is not one to be left waiting. How unwise to rush right past God on the way to orchestrate oblivion or rearrange obstacles. He is waiting patiently for you to show up and be loved on by Him. Slow down, show up and pour out your heart to Jesus.

It is time to level with the Lord for His wisdom is waiting. You cannot maintain a break-neck pace with relational wreckage piling up. People feel manipulated and misunderstood, so pull up before you go over the cliff of complexity. You may need to burn busyness at the stake. Let the hustle and bustle of extreme activity become a martyr for mediocrity. Take the time now to show up for private prayer and petition to the great high priest, Christ. Show up in the presence of King Jesus and He will invite you into His inner court of care and concern. Like the five virgins who showed up prepared. "At that time the kingdom of heaven will be like ten virgins who took their lamps and went out to meet the bridegroom. Five of them were foolish and five were wise. The foolish ones took their lamps but did not take any oil with them. The wise, however, took oil in jars along with their lamps" (Matthew 25:1-4).

It is prudent to prepare to meet the grace, love and holiness of God. So show up in humility and see Him. Just show up for Jesus' sake and you will be radically served by an encounter with your living Lord!

"But now trouble comes to you, and you are discouraged; it strikes you, and you are dismayed." JOB 4:4

Life can squeeze you like a cold and insensitive mechanical vice. Before you realize it, you spiral down into a dungeon of dismay and discouragement. It is not a desirable or good place to live. Yet sometimes you find yourself drowning in a cesspool of cynicism, unable to get out. The harder you try, the more difficult it gets. Problems loom larger than life and there seems to be no hope for now. People let you down; they do dumb things and seem to care less. Dismay and discouragement have pressed you into a careless corner. You have become alone and afraid. It all seems unfair, because you have done your best to please God and others. You have served with a sincere and diligent heart. On the surface it seems like you have done all the right things, but you can't get a break. Even the people you respect the most seem to be ignoring you. To them you have become high maintenance; therefore you are off limits to those who used to seek your counsel. If they do come around it is only to hurl insults and conclusions about what you need to do differently. This may be one of the hardest times of your life. You really don't know which way to turn. It seems like you have exhausted all your options.

However, you still have Christ and He has you. Together you can triumph over trouble for it is temporary. Christ is eternal. He is your hope when life seems hopeless. He is your security when chaotic circumstances seem to be in control. He is your peace when fear locks its fangs into your faith. He is the truth when lies assault your thinking. Jesus understands your discouragement. Indeed, the Christian life is mostly lived between the valley and the mountain top. Now may be your valley experience, but there is a mountain top that lies ahead. The path is not always easy or pretty, but you can count on Christ as your companion. No hurt is too deep that the depths of His forgiveness cannot heal. No rejection is so severe that the allurement of His acceptance cannot comfort. No trouble is so crippling that the whirlpool of His trust cannot rehabilitate. Fear may have ambushed you, but His hope is there to rescue and release you from its prison of pride.

It is during times of despair that you can unashamedly draw deep down into the well of His grace. His grace is sufficient. His grace is generous and good; so stay immersed in the grandeur of His grace. Trouble will drain your tank of grace but trust refills it. Don't try to run the engine of your life without a full tank of grace. Otherwise, you will sputter along and eventually break down and burn out. God's grace generates hope and trust. Cling to Christ and dismiss discouragement. Keep Job as your model, "In all this, Job did not sin by charging God with wrongdoing" (Job 1:22). Be not dismayed but be hopeful and overcome trouble with trust in God.

This trouble is temporary, so look to the eternal. Jesus is your friend that sticks closer than a brother!

M'24 FEW DAYS

"Man born of woman is of few days and full of trouble."
JOB 14:1

Life is short, because relatively speaking there are only a few days to do God's will. So how can one be a better steward of this brief time allotment? One idea is to budget time similar to your finances. It is a precious commodity that cannot be used twice. It is fleeting and needs to be used for God's purposes. There are just a few days to be with your children at home, and then they are gone. This means, you have a few days to date your daughter and then another man will. You have a few days to take your son on excursions and then he will be busy with his own family. Be careful not to wish away where you are today for a brighter tomorrow. Be present in the present, or discontentment will eat away at the quality of your life.

Indeed, you have only a few days to be mom and dad to the children who live under your roof. Take advantage of this time, as you have a captive audience. You can use this season of life to train and teach them in the ways of God. Do not allow your own life's distractions to keep you from your family. It may mean changing jobs so you are not consumed by corporate. It may require lowering your standard of living and paying off your debt. There are only a few days left to follow hard after God, so not wake up one day having flittered away your faith opportunities. Money lost can be made up in other ways, however lost time with the Lord makes an eternal difference. If you are not careful, He gets the leftovers of your time and money. Give Him the first fruits of you few days and watch Him multiply the results in a significant way. He is a God who desires intimacy and relationship. He has numbered your days and it could be tomorrow or the next that you go home to be with Him. So when all is said and done your hope is in Jesus Christ, in His blood and righteousness. He understands what it means to live a few days and then go home to His Father, but His brief three years of ministry still resonate today. The quantity of your work/life ministry is not as important as the quality. Who are you developing in these few days that can carry on the mission of God's Kingdom?

Moreover, the management and wise use of time is a stewardship issue. Your agenda is meant to be a prayer list that validates your activity. Intentionality of your investment in others will throw off dividends into eternity. You can use these few days that are left to be proactive in your prayer life. Spend these few days doing less and listening more to God. He will use the quality of your life to accomplish His quantity of results. It is not the extent of your activity that impresses the Almighty; rather it is the focus of your heart on Him. A flurry of activity may actually cause your faith to falter. Intentional living becomes intimacy in-tune with the Almighty. Take inventory of your time. Stop doing the trivial and the unnecessary and replace it with the eternal and the necessary. Focus on the inner circle of relationships that really matter like the Lord, your spouse, children and parents.

There are only a few days left, so choose to use them wisely in light of what really matters most. Make these last few days your best days!

MENIAL TASKS

"After that, he poured water into a basin and began to wash his disciples' feet, drying them with the towel that was wrapped around him." JOHN 13:5

Jesus was the master of menial tasks. He was not afraid to get His hands dirty, literally. There was nothing or no one that was below Him for He valued everyone. Jesus put Himself into the shoes of others, so He could relate to their world and so He could serve them well. Success did not ostracize Him from the ordinary. His heart was service and He knew that service around menial tasks unlocks opportunities to influence. Moreover, as a follower of Jesus He expects you to follow His example, "I have set you an example that you should do as I have done for you" (John 13:15). Pride or dignity may cause you to resist things like working in a soup kitchen, tutoring an underprivileged illiterate, vacuuming the house, unloading the dish washer, taking out the garbage, washing clothes, running errands, house maintenance (though better stewardship may be to hire someone!), making photo copies, or returning phone calls. Yet, the execution of these menial tasks reflects Christ. No level of authority exempts you from serving others.

In fact, it is through your service that you truly lead. Otherwise people are just intimidated to produce results out of fear of your hostile reprisals. How much healthier it is for family, friends and work associates to be motivated by your service than your threats. It may start out awkward because it may take time for people to get used to you helping out. But when you start managing by walking around instead of hiding behind your computer, people will be amazed. Encourage by engaging personally with people and not just sending impersonal e-mail. At first they may resist, wondering what has come over you. But your willingness to roll up your sleeves will win them over. Start with a handwritten thank you note to your direct reports. Value them as your most important 'customer'. Wash their feet by constantly caring for them first.

Menial tasks can become mundane over time. They can become boring and predictable, so stay fresh and challenged. Do not be satisfied with status quo. Challenge the system and execute in a more excellent way. If you take for granted your position or technical skills, you may become sloppy in your service and lazy in your work. Always become better at what you do. Anybody can do anything for a short period of time. But it takes stamina and character to continue mastering the menial over the long run. Take continuing education classes. Improve your speaking and writing skills by engaging a speech or writing coach. Use technology to enhance and accelerate the menial. Nothing however, will ever replace your need to give personal attention to important details. The devil is in the details, so give attention to them. This keeps him from taking you hostage. Yes delegate, but do not make the mistake and abdicate. People appreciate your thinking of the details that affect them. Your accountability to carry out the menial makes others want to do the same, so plan ahead. Serve others where they least expect you to get involved then it becomes infectious. Therefore, be a contagious carrier who reflects Christ.

There is no task too menial for your Master. Join Him where He serves!

M26 REMAIN TRUE

"When he [Barnabas] arrived and saw the evidence of the grace of God, he was glad and encouraged them to remain true to the Lord with all their hearts." ACTS 11:23

Remain true to the Lord for He has remained true to you. Remain true because the grace of God compels you to. Remain true for He knows what is best for you. Remain true because you know it is the right thing to do. Remain true while others encourage you. Remain true because your obedience encourages others. Remain true with all your hearts, so the Kingdom of God advances aggressively for His glory. It is easy to sign up as a Jesus follower but follow through requires faithfulness, so remain true to your commitment to Christ. It does matter that you follow through for Him. It matters to Him, to you, to your family and to your credibility. It matters to those you have encouraged, those you are encouraging and those you will encourage. It matters that you remain true.

Furthermore, Satan will try to suppress your commitment by his limited power of disease, discouragement, and discontent. He wants you to forget God's faithfulness and fall into his trap of temptation. He wants you to walk away from your family and follow your own selfish desires. He wants you to think you are an exception to the rule of law and accountability. He will feed your pride until it starves humility into non-existence. Jesus said, "I know where you live—where Satan has his throne. Yet you remain true to my name. You did not renounce your faith in me..." (Revelation 2:13a). Indeed, the hand of the Lord is on those who remain true with all their hearts. However, He moves on from those who drift into perfunctory behaviors of pretending one thing and doing another. Begin by exposing any unauthentic living and seek to reconnect with Christ and others.

Moreover, the grace of God creates an environment of encouragement. You can encourage others to remain true because of the grace of God that has been extended to you. Grace encourages faithfulness. Grace realizes there is room for mistakes, yet still offers opportunities to remain true. Failure and faith can coexist. Moreover, encouragers engage others on a heartfelt level. You have the opportunity to come alongside husbands and wives, friends and relatives, new and mature Christians. You can encourage them to remain true to the Lord and to each other.

Encouragement extends hope rooted in a relationship with Jesus Christ. Your eternally based encouragement is not sentimental or shallow. It is a heavenly hope, evidenced by answered prayer. You encourage others exponentially when you petition Christ on their behalf. Cry out to your heavenly Father and ask that He keep your teenagers true to Him. Pray for your friend's body to be healed by the hand of God. Pray for marriages to learn how to love and respect under the influence of the Holy Spirit. Pray for your Pastor to remain true to his calling and to the One who extended his call. Pray for opportunities to pray with those for whom you are encouraging. Prayer is without exhaustion in its encouragement. Above all else, receive encouragement from the Lord and others to remain true. Then simultaneously and spontaneously extend encouragement to others to remain true with all their hearts.

Remain true because there is no limit to what the Lord can do. Giving up is not for you!

CALL TO MISSIONS

"While they were worshipping the Lord and fasting, the Holy Spirit said, 'Set apart for me Barnabas and Saul for the work to which I have called them.' So after they had fasted and prayed, they placed their hands on them and sent them off." ACTS 13:2-3

A call to missions is spiritually motivated, because it is initiated by the Holy Spirit and validated by mature leaders within the church. It is through worship, prayer, and fasting that God speaks clearly around calling. This is not to be taken lightly or half-heartedly for a missionary's calling is a work of God. God longs for the crown jewel of His worldwide creation to come to Him, their creator. The nations are never very far from the loving arm of Almighty God. He was born in the east and after His death His message spread like wildfire to the west. He is Lord over all the continents and countries on earth. Furthermore, the first missionaries were compelled by Christ to tell His good news of the cross and resurrection. Their commitment to spread the Word of God was not deterred by stoning or shipwrecks. If anything, their imprisonment and hardships galvanized their calling to carry forth the transforming truth of faith in Christ.

It was so clear to these cross-cultural Christians that the birth, life, and death of Christ fulfilled many Old Testament prophecies. His miraculous signs and the miracles of the early church were further evidence that their heavenly Father had His hand on Jesus and His church. Peter proclaimed, "Jesus of Nazareth was a man accredited by God to you by miracles, wonders and signs, which God did among you through him, as you yourselves know. This man was handed over to you by God's set purpose and foreknowledge; and you, with the help of wicked men, put him to death by nailing him to the cross. But God raised him from the dead, freeing him from the agony of death..." (Acts 2:22-24). He was the Messiah they had longed to see and hear, but the most riveting part of their missionary message was the resurrection. Jesus was the resurrected Lord and Savior of the Jews and the Gentiles. It was the grace of the Lord Jesus Christ that offered salvation to all cultures and civilizations. God was no respecter of persons and invited all languages on the planet to believe in Jesus. This is the message of the missionary called by God, set apart by the Holy Spirit and sent out by the church.

Moreover, a call to missions is a call to a multicultural mindset. A missions calling includes sensitivity to the valued customs and lifestyle of the nationals. There is not a sophisticated smugness, but a respect and willingness to adapt in humility and teachability to the locals who live on foreign soil. It is a spirit of service that our Savior blesses. The goal is to lead them to Jesus, within the context of their own culture. Missionaries teach national leaders to teach other nationals. The goal is to equip the saints within their own country and language to do the work of ministry. Missionaries are conduits for Christ. A sustaining work emerges around missionaries who hand off leadership from the very beginning. Furthermore, every follower of Christ can at least serve on a short-term mission trip. It is life changing and necessary to keep a proper perspective of God's heart. Missions are a microscope into the needs of the world. Pray for missionaries and be a missionary.

This calling is not confined to the super-spiritual, but to all who love God and people. So, prayerfully consider Christ's call to missions!

M28 CITIZENSHIP STEWARDSHIP

"But Paul said to the officers: 'They beat us publicly without a trial, even though we are Roman citizens, and threw us into prison. And now they want to get rid of us quietly? No! Let them come themselves and let us out." ACTS 16:37

Citizenship in a free country is a gift from God and it is not to be taken for granted. It is a stewardship with privileges and responsibilities. Millions of men and women gave their lives generations to come could live as citizens of a democracy and a republic united around principles founded in the Word of God. Citizenship gives you freedom for good or evil; therefore remind the culture of wise thinking and value-based living. This is the purpose of the regular election of government officials for your vote is their performance review. Voting is a responsibility of citizens to provide feedback to the God-ordained institution of government. This authority is used by God to carry out His purposes. The Bible says, "Everyone must submit himself to the governing authorities, for there is no authority except that which God has established. The authorities that exist have been established by God. Consequently, he who rebels against the authority is rebelling against what God has instituted, and those who do so will bring judgment on themselves" (Romans 13:1-2). Therefore, elect men and woman of principal who as statesmen will risk losing their House or Senate seat, because they govern by unwavering values founded in the Scriptures. They value life especially those who are unable to defend themselves.

The unborn and the elderly are top on their list to protect. They value marriage, one man and one woman engaged in holy matrimony. They reject a redefinition of marriage from those driven by money and immorality. They value national security, because freedom is not free. It requires sophisticated vigilance from terrorism and nuclear threat. Mostly, they value God and His Word. There is a humble submission and respect to the authority of Almighty God. So, your vote matters because your citizenship matters. Newly initiated citizens are fresh to freedom, so their determination, participation and appreciation make them grateful citizens. Therefore, see yourself as one of the worlds privileged few. Stay abreast of the issues and the position of the politician that represents you. Do they reflect your values? Are they consistent? Do they follow through with their commitments? If not, be a good steward and remove them from office. Replace them with someone hungry to do what's right in the right way.

Moreover, public service is a private trust. Pray for trustworthy men and women motivated by principal. Daniel was a government official of integrity, "At this, the administrators and the satraps tried to find grounds for charges against Daniel in his conduct of government affairs, but they were unable to do so. They could find no corruption in him, because he was trustworthy and neither corrupt nor negligent." (Daniel 6:4). Hold accountable cowards that hide behind compromise or enrich themselves with personal inurnment. God is in control, but He expects participation from people of the state. Look for leaders who will return prayer and the fear of God back into the public arena. Expect the language of the Lord to pepper their speeches.

We are citizens of a greater kingdom, who have a temporary assignment to engage in our earthly kingdom. Therefore, steward well your citizenship while you can. God expects engaged citizens!

> "Phillip the evangelist, one of the Seven… had four unmarried daughters who prophesied." ACTS 21:8B-9

Unmarried daughters need their dad. They need their mom, but they really need their dad. There is a transition that takes place during their teenage years that requires the wisdom, love and affection of dad. If his tender loving care is lacking they look for it in all the wrong places. Their emotions can become hostage to another male who does not have an objective agenda. The best interest of your young lady can hang in the balance of her hormonal hijacking. If her confidence is not secure in her Savior and in her dad, she will embrace a false security that is contingent on physical affection or an immature acceptance. They are fragile young ladies at the entrance of womanhood. The nurture, love and encouragement of their earthly father go a long way in enhancing their relationship with their heavenly Father. Unmarried daughters need and want their dad's attention. They may not overtly solicit your recognition, but you can bet on the inside they are craving for your care and encouragement. They want you to look them in the eye and say everything is going to be okay. They need to hear you say, "You will make it through college because you are someone who completes what you start. Quitting has never been an option for you." She desperately needs you to affirm your belief in her. So value her by complimenting her intelligence, beauty and brains. Praise her for her initiative and intuition. Hug her hard and often. Above all else, your unmarried daughter needs your unconditional love and acceptance.

Dads be aware of and avoid the trap of ignoring your daughter in the name of letting her grow up. This can just be an excuse for you to disengage and do your own thing during a time when she needs you the most. If she trusts that you are not there to smoother her, but support her then you can continue your incredibly wise influence. It is probably easier to solve a work issue than to sit across from your teenage daughter over dinner. Engaging a teenager is uncomfortable, but parenting is not for your comfort rather it is for her confidence. She needs to know that you pray for her and care for her. Be there to ask her suitor for his plan to stay pure with your daughter for a prayerfully co-created plan increases the probability for purity. Then hold them accountable to the plan.

One day your unmarried daughter will be married. Because you modeled for her the right kind of man, she will prayerfully pursue a like-minded husband. Do not down play your valuable role as a dad. Let other things like travel and meetings wait, so you can stay involved with her. You are releasing her to learn how to walk in the adult world. Just like you taught her how to ride a bike, you were there when she wobbled and fell. She trusts you to teach her the right way to ride. Don't be a dumb dad and miss her window into womanhood. Say no to other ministry opportunities so you can minister to this one whom you have for such a very short time. The applause of her dad will lead her into excellence and obedience. Your relational investment earns you influence. Praise her often for her wise choices and aptly remind her of authentic accountability.

Pray for and be with your unmarried daughter. When she is married she will want more of the same. Your baby will be married one day, so be a model of the man she needs!

M30 SHAMEFUL LUST

"Because of this, God gave them over to shameful lusts. Even their women exchanged natural relationships for unnatural ones. In the same way the men also abandoned natural relations with women and were inflamed with lust for one another. Men committed indecent acts with other men, and received in themselves the due penalty for their perversion." ROMANS 1:26-27

Lust by itself breaks the heart of God for it is disrespectful and degrading. It is a hybrid of coveting and sexual immorality. Lust to the Lord is adultery in the heart. Jesus said, "But I say unto you, That whosoever looketh on a woman to lust after her hath committed adultery with her already in his heart" (Matthew 5:28, KJV). It is virtual sex and it is not to be taken lightly. It is a sin against God and others. But there is something darker than lust, and that is shameful lust. Shameful lust is extreme, as it suppresses the truth and tries to justify itself with Scripture, psychology, and physiology. It lobbies for laws that will make its illegitimate lifestyle legitimate. It is crafty in its pursuit of corporate benefits that validate its behavior. Shameful lust is well-funded, well-scripted, intelligent, and engaging. It is a Christ-less conspiracy set on redefining the natural with the unnatural.

Shameful lust is shameless in its pursuit of acceptance. There is an eerie confidence that continues to advance its cause. It is scary because it seduces and intimidates some politicians and a few pastors into embracing its tenets. Shameless lust claims to be true when it is a lie. One of its goals is to invade every part of our life with legitimacy. Church, arts, film, education, military, government, and business are all targets for conversion to its cause. We don't know whether to laugh or to cry, but this is no laughing matter. It is the moral barometer of civilizations, past and present. The higher the tolerance and acceptance of shameful lusts, the lower the moral standards of society descend. The collapse of culture comes from within, so moral disregard and the redefining of marriage will bring a nation to its knees. The greatest enemy is not terrorism, but it is not staying true to God's truth. Moral decay rots society's security and is a slippery slope to irrational behavior and apathy toward God.

So what is the role of authentic followers of Jesus? Pray for Christians to repent from acceptance of shameful lust as normal. Pray for our Churches to come clean with God over its own lust, pride, materialism and unforgiveness. Pray for a revival of holiness. Pray for a return to the commands, principles, and values of Holy Scripture. Pray for the elevation of marriage as a picture of a believer's relationship with Christ. It is a covenant between a man and woman for life. It is a relationship of fidelity, commitment, forgiveness, love and respect. Exalt marriage and dethrone the debauchery of shameful lust. Pray for and in love confront church leaders who pervert Scripture to support perversion. God has not and will not bless shameful lust. Nor does God bless a country that condones behavior that suppresses the truth. Silence is acceptance. Ignoring is irresponsible. Ignorance is bad behavior. Get upset over your unconcern. Pray for those seduced into shameful lust to be authentically loved by their Savior Jesus. Pray those who know the truth will speak it in love.

The love of God and Christ-followers replaces shameful lust with legitimate love. Be like Jesus and love them to the Lord!

> "Godly sorrow brings repentance that leads to salvation and leaves no regret, but worldly sorrow brings death." 2 CORINTHIANS 7:10

"I am sorry" are three freeing words. I was wrong. You were right. I apologize. Please forgive me. All of these phrases communicate culpability. Sincere sorrow means you take responsibility. You initiate peace because your desire is to repair the relationship. Disharmony and disconnection are not acceptable options. Yes, someone may take advantage of your goodwill, but this is in God's hands. Have faith in the fact that God expects behavior that brings reconciliation. You put the relationship at risk if you resist humbling yourself and apologizing. Someone has to start by saying, "I am sorry." It is smart to extend your apology as soon as possible. A more powerful apology occurs when you admit your error, transgression or sin before you are found out. You take the first step to ask forgiveness because you know it is the right thing to do.

Godly sorrow sends a message of change for you want to change for Christ's sake. You have sinned against your Savior and those you love. The pain inflicted is not worth continuing in the same bad habits. No one ever regretted repenting of sin. Godly sorrow leads to repentance, which results in transformation. Change occurs around a humble and honest heart. So, where do you start? Family is a logical place to extend your apologies. You hurt your parents by breaking off communication and care. You have intentionally gone out of your way to not go there. There is a widening rift in the relationship. Now is the time to reach out and recover your relationship with your mom and/or dad. Take the time during the holiday season to pay a surprise visit or place a long overdue phone call. Start the conversation by saying, "I am sorry." Sincere sorrow is a relational magnet and trust reoccurs around repentance. When others sense you have really changed they extend trust. However, they may withhold trust until you prove yourself trustworthy. People who have been burned in the past by shallow and insincere sorrow will not automatically engage. They need time to see that your apology is authentic. Sorrow, which does not lead to change results in relational death. Indeed sincere sorrow hurts your heart for you weep visible or invisible tears of remorse. It makes you sick to think you let down the one who loves you the most.

On the flip side, be patient with those who ask your forgiveness. Forgive them and give them a chance to change while releasing your anger and the broken promises to Jesus. Give them over to the Lord and pray for their repentance. God can do more with a person heart in a minute, than a lifetime of nagging could ever accomplish. Do not hold them in contempt, rather entrust them to Christ. Give time for repentance to root out bad habits and destructive behaviors. Lies can be extracted by the everlasting love of God and replaced with His transforming truth. Accept apologies at face value and hope for the best. Pray for the work of the Holy Spirit to have His way in a humble heart. Be quick to forgive and just as quick to ask forgiveness. Replace fear with faith. Your sorrowful confession connects with Christ and with others. Therefore, take the first step and apologize.

Ask for forgiveness, surrender to your Savior. Become broken, for brokenness leads to freedom. Say, "I am sorry" and see how your Savior blesses your apology!

DARK DECEPTION

"The eye of the adulterer watches for dusk; he thinks, 'No eye will see me,' and he keeps his face concealed. In the dark, men break into houses, and by day they shut themselves in, but they want nothing to do with the light."   JOB 24:15-16

Everyone has a dark side that flirts with their feelings and tries to lead them astray. It is ironic that your dark side engenders fear and at the same time, a false and hollow hope. However, there is nothing about your dark side that is good. It is always attempting to seduce you into your old way of thinking and doing. It wants to pull a dark cloud over your soul and rain down discontentment and confusion. The dark side is filled with demons of discouragement seeking to seduce you into poor and even foolish decision making. It knows that one devastating decision can mark you for a lifetime. Indeed, the dark side offers the illusion that adultery is harmless and recreational. It reasons with you that in the cloak of darkness, no one will ever find out. You are led to believe that enough lies can cover up your dark deeds. This of course is fiction that some romance novels dismiss: "...you may be sure that your sin will find you out" (Numbers 32:23b). The light will eventually pierce the darkness and like scattering roaches you will be exposed. But, there is nowhere you can go that God is not present. He is light, so in darkness the light of His love exposes you. Why crouch in a dark corner of carnality, when you can be free in the light of Christ? Darkness promises freedom, but delivers bondage. The promise of God is grace, which results in faith's freedom. Christ is light in the darkness and His word is your flashlight of faith. In Him darkness recoils.

Your dark side will hound you until you get to heaven. So, in the meantime it is imperative to live in the light. Live in the light of God's love for it is here that you are accepted and kept secure. Live in the light of accountability for it is here that you have boundaries from the edge of darkness. Live in the light of Christian community for it is here that others can pray for you and with you. Live in the light of God's word for it is here that you gain His wisdom and perspective. Simply live in the light of Christ and He will repel the relentless rampage of your dark side, "But if we walk in the light, as he is in the light, we have fellowship with one another, and the blood of Jesus, his Son, purifies us from all sin" (1 John 1:7). Therefore, do not tamper alone with the temptations of your dark side or you may suffer the consequences of sins scars.

You can only gain authentic energy and excitement in the light. This far exceeds the artificial tantalizing that comes from submission to the dark side's temptations. No sin can be hidden from God, no matter how concealed it may seem in the deepest corner of darkness. Wise ones submit to the light rather than to the deceptive dark side. The dark side is full of unpleasant surprises, while the route of the Holy Spirit offers pleasant ones. Walk away from the dangers of the dark side. Nothing there is worth the energy and the horrific hurt that accompanies its mission. Tell someone today your deepest and darkest secrets. Exposure is the enemy of your dark side. Freedom in Christ comes from accountability with other Christ followers. You walk in the light together as overcomers with God and people.

Alone you backslide into our dark side. Therefore, surround yourself with lovers of the light. In the light you get it right!

CONTENTMENT'S CONCERN

"My heart is not proud O Lord, my eyes are not haughty; I do not concern myself with great matters or things too wonderful for me. But I have stilled and quieted my soul. Like a weaned child with its mother, like a weaned child is my soul within me. O Israel, put your hope in the Lord both now and forevermore." PSALM 131:1-3

Contentment is not concerned with matters out of its control. Anytime you try to manage circumstances out of your purview you grow discontent. Discontentment is a dangerous place to live because it may lead you to make a hasty and/or unwise decision. Decisions made under the duress of discontentment are not always the best. Contentment on the other hand is patient and prayerful in decision-making. Most things do not have to be decided right away. You can wait and watch God unfold His will. It may be time to make a bold move, but execute your transition smoothly and not in a jagged fashion. Contentment does not try to change people. This is God's job. Contentment accepts the fact that some people are best left to themselves. God will deal with them in His way and in His timing.

Contented people do not have to be in the know about everything around them. Too much information can get you into trouble for you are responsible for what you know. It may be that you are not ready for that level of authority. Be content and trust God with those issues that exceed your experience to understand or your capacity to implement. There will come a day when you are prepared for that role of confidant, but for now be content where you are. Do the best in your current position and let opportunities come your way. Contentment is a great place to live in peace and quiet.

Contentment is found by placing your hope in God. Hope in the Lord can never be taken from you. All hell can break loose but He is there, hope in God is a perk for today. If you can trust Him with your soul for eternity, you can trust Him during this incredibly brief time on earth. Hope feeds contentment like an appetizing meal feeds a hungry body. It is when you lose hope that you grow discontent. Hope can be found in Jesus Christ, so don't make it hard. He is not illusive or hiding. He is available for you. Contentment's hope is in God. If you place your hope in anything other than God, you set yourself up for major disappointment. Everything else in life is capable of letting you down, but not your heavenly Father. He is there for you and His desire is contentment. He desires contentment because He knows that pure joy and happiness are nurtured and able to grow there. Sad are the discontent; glad are the content. Driven are the discontent; called are the content. Restless are the discontent; peaceful are the content. Addicted are the discontent; satisfied are the content. Pessimistic are the discontent; hopeful are the content.

Be content and enjoy its outcomes. Contentment's concerns are few!

WISDOM AND UNDERSTANDING  JUN 3

"And he said to man, 'The fear of the Lord—that is wisdom,
and to shun evil is understanding.' " JOB 28:28

Wisdom is to fear the Lord, so a wise person fears God. You have no wisdom apart from the fear of God. This is why you can be smart and not be wise. You can be rich and not be wise. You can be educated and not be wise. You can be popular and not be wise. Very smart people have been known to make very unwise decisions. Intelligence does not guarantee wisdom. In fact the higher your IQ, the more susceptible you are to missing the humble access to wisdom. If you are left to your own limited perspective, without God's global view you become misguided. The more it looks like you don't need God the more you need Him. It is His wisdom that navigates you through complex and not-so-complex decision making. The wisdom of God is your warning not to fall to the flirtations of the world. It is your ability to draw on your moral fortitude with confidence and grace.

Wisdom is your greatest asset next to your relationship with the Almighty. The two are intertwined. But to fear the Lord is to relate to Him on His terms not yours. When you fear Him you know Him, but there is more to it than just knowing. When you fear Him you not only know Him, you follow Him and you obey Him. Yes, it is a relationship of love but it is also a relationship of obedience. When you fear God you never get over the fact that He is God and you are not. There is awe and an extreme reverence toward your supreme and superior Savior. Fear of God pushes you and prods you to remain prostrate before Him. It is a humble attitude that saturates your heart and mind. Pride and arrogance melt in the presence of a fearful follower of Christ. When you fear the Lord, you do not want to knowingly sin. You choose not to sin when you fear God.

The fear of the Lord liberates wisdom to run rampant within your understanding. Wisdom naturally leads to understanding, as it is an application of wisdom. Wisdom is what God thinks and understanding is how to incorporate His thinking into your every day life. Moreover, God does not dish out commands that are incomprehensible. His ways are the right ways and His wisdom leads you to understand this. Wisdom says, "A wise man fears the LORD and shuns evil..." (Proverbs 14:16). It means to escape from the appearance, the influence and the control of evil. Messing with evil is like messing with fire, you will get burned. Just a little bit of internet pornography is ammunition for adultery. Just a thimble full of flirting is fodder for unfaithfulness. Wisdom and understanding says you cannot handle evil's allure. When you get too close it is like getting sucked into the backside of a giant fan. You can reach a point of no return and get cut to pieces. Therefore, be wise and develop a storehouse of wisdom. Harvest understanding during this reflective season of life and reap wisdom from your relationships that fear God. Wisdom will come as you experience God and learn of Him from His word.

Wisdom and understanding are the gold and silver of emotional and spiritual wealth. Therefore, gain them and steward them well. Above all, the fear of the Lord facilitates wisdom and understanding!

JUN4 TEST WORDS

"For the ear tests words as the tongue tastes food. Let us discern for ourselves what is right; let us learn together what is good." JOB 34:3-4

Words are meant to be filtered and your ears are the first filter. If words travel unfiltered through your ears they can clutter and confuse your mind. Mixed messages to the mind are confusing and disconcerting. This is why words must be tested, like the tongue tastes food. Some words are bad for your mental health, while others invigorate and energize your thinking. This is why discernment is required with your verbal intake. If you process and apply everything you hear you will become a confused at best and experience calamity at worst. Your ears are meant to be a check point for truth. If lies attempt to enter by the orifice of your ears you need to arrest them with your good sense and send them on their way. The 'wheat and the weeds' (Matthew 13:29-30) do need to be separated once they are harvested by your ears. Wise ears exhibit keen insight and judgment, because ears without discernment are like eating a smorgasbord of all foods, the fried and the fresh. Eventually the unhealthy takes its toll and the intake of unsanitary words produces an ill-fit mind. Your mind is a product of what comes through your ears and eyes. Ears need as much coaching and accountability as eyes. Train your ears to value the eternal over the temporal. Educate your ears to reject lies and invite truth. If you have been told you are 'no good' or you are 'washed up,' then you have been assaulted by a bearer of bad counsel. In Christ you are good, and in Him there is always hope and potential. Indeed, discern these dangerous words and avoid them. Do not allow them into your thinking, lest you become mentally estranged from the eternal.

God made your two ears for testing, therefore digest His words often through the ears of your heart. Let God speak to you through prayer and reflection. His words are an effective filter for the words of others. Someone may tell you to trade your reputation for a short-term gain, but you have already heard God and wise people warn you to flee from this façade of fame. There is no need to ponder on pretentious phrases. Discerning ears automatically drop kick diseased words away from entering the playing field of their mind. Do not nurse or coddle sick words for they will only infect you with their adverse affects. Vile and wicked words are normally packaged by hurt and delivered with anger, so mostly dismiss the words of the angry. They are unproductive and hurtful, because words spewed in anger are quickly regretted and doggedly damaging.

Moreover, watch for the subtle words that suggest submission to something or someone other than God. These are the words that tend to look good on the surface, but come back to bite you with their hidden agenda. Take the time to test these attractive words. If someone says he wants to help you it is prudent to wait and get to know his or her intentions. Indeed, the words of the wise can be received promptly and embraced wholeheartedly. However, the words of fools need not make it past your ear lobes. If their foolish pronouncements slip in one ear, send them out the other one just as fast. Post the two sentinels of good sense and discernment at the entrance of your ears. Receive into your mind the best and the brightest in wise thinking. Reject the rest.

It is incredibly wise to test every wooing word with the wisdom of God. Let the intake of your words feed right thinking. Listen only to words that pass God's grade 'A' standards!

PROSPERITY RETURNS

"After Job prayed for his friends, the Lord made him prosperous again and gave him twice as much as he had before." JOB 42:10

Sometimes you have to lose everything in order to find God. It takes becoming broke before you can experience brokenness. Losing everything is difficult, embarrassing, and life-altering. Yet, when you have nothing but Christ to cling to you have what matters the most. Other possessions and even people can substitute as your savior, but He does not compete with anything or anyone. He alone desires 100% of your devotion and commitment, so be extremely careful and wise that affluence does not contest with Christ. Its allure and attention can be intoxicating. Money and work will come back to bite you if they are not kept in proper perspective. Therefore stay immersed in the scriptures, "Do not let this Book of the Law depart from your mouth; meditate on it day and night, so that you may be careful to do everything written in it. Then you will be prosperous and success-ful" (Joshua 1:8). The Bible is your behavioral baseline.

Moreover, robust relationships are fulfilling and necessary. However, a governor must be installed on your relational engine, for relationships are not meant to rival God. People may be rav-aging your time and energy, while leaving nothing for Him. Your heavenly Father deserves and desires the first fruits of your time and money, not what's left over. Perhaps you find yourself want-ing, because what you have worked for all your life is gone or on the verge of disintegration. Your spouse is threatening to leave and your children are confused and insecure. You are an emotion-al basket case and your health is waning. Nevertheless, when you are at the bottom there is no place to look but up. Now is not the time to give up on God but to look up to God. Look up to the Lord and pray.

Pray for honesty about your own pride and use this time of purging to prepare you for God's goodness. For the first time in your life you may be poised and in the best position ever to receive His blessings. He can make you prosperous again. There is no guarantee, but anything is achievable with the Almighty. It is when you repent of presumption, pretense and pride that God releases His everlasting power. God's forgiveness flows freely in a repentant heart, in contrast to a heart hardened like a dried up river bed. Engage in prayer for your friends and for your enemies. Pray for them to know, follow and fear God. Pray for them to flourish in their faith and forgiveness. Prosperity is meant to point you and others to God. Use this next round of wealth and success as a Kingdom platform. Learn from your past mistakes, so you can avoid future failure and become a facilitator of faithfulness to God. Your life is a now a resume of faithfulness to your heavenly Father. Failure has flushed out false living and filled you with holiness and Holy Spirit control. God may or may not bring you prosperity again, but if He does never forget where it came from and never forget where you came from. Use prosperity for good, before it uses you for bad!

JUN 6 SEASONAL FRUIT

"He is like a tree planted by streams of water, which yields its fruit in season and whose leaf does not wither." PSALM 1:3

So much of life is seasonal. Relationships are for a season. You experience good and bad for a season. You work a job for a season. You volunteer for a season. You attend a particular church for a season. You live somewhere for a season. You attend school for a season. You live life for a season. Life is one big season made up of multiple and varying seasons. Therefore, it is advantageous for you to adjust with each season, as you do with the four seasons throughout the year. When it is hot, you turn on the air conditioner. During the fall you enjoy the changing of the foliage. In the winter you wear a coat, drink hot chocolate, snow ski and give December gifts in honor of Jesus. The spring is all about new life and the incremental rise of warm temperatures and you celebrate the resurrection of Christ. All four of these annual transitions are for the most part invited and enjoyed. Each one is looked upon with anticipation and its arrival brings joy. This is God's desire for you as you approach life. Anticipate rather than dread, life change. Seasonal assignments in life are as much a part of God's design, as the four annual seasons we calendar. This season of your marriage and parenting will probably not thrive with last season's methods. Your young adult children expect to be treated as adults now not like immature adolescents. This new season in your career requires training and learning, so become a student of innovation and thrive. Your spouse's expectations are different now the children are gone; therefore adjust to their dreams.

Moreover, your greatest asset during seasonal transition is to stay rooted in God and His Word. Your stability is in the unchanging Almighty. Everything around you may be seasonal and changing, but He is your anchor of dependability. Now is the time to extend the roots of your trust deep into the soil of Scripture. Your level of readiness for the next season is contingent upon your current spiritual preparation. Be sensitive to the things of God now and your seasonal transition will be more seamless and natural. God is growing you into a mighty oak of influence that bears fruit seasonally. Your attention to life pruning, developing a healthy root system of dependency on God and avoiding sin's dreadful disease all position you for seasonal fruit bearing, "And let us not be weary in well doing: for in due season we shall reap, if we faint not" (Galatians 6:9, KJV).

Your fruit bearing takes on a different look and feel in each season. This is God's spice for your life. Before, your children may have been your primary ministry; now in this new season it may be mentoring other young men or women. Before you were so busy making money; now you have the experience and the capacity to wisely give it away. Before you were a giver; now you are a receiver. Before you served many relationships; now you focus on a few. Before you read more than you wrote; now you write more than you read. But, the compelling characteristic is how God is bearing beautiful fruit through you. The fruit is seasonal, but it is sensational because it originates in your Savior and Creator.

Therefore invite, prepare and look forward to life's seasonal opportunities. Then by God's grace, bear bountiful fruit in each season of life He brings your way. Go with the seasonal fruitful flow of your heavenly Father!

FOOLISH DENIAL

"The fool says in his heart, 'There is no God.' They are corrupt, their deeds are vile; there is no one who does good." PSALM 14:1

Denial can be death to God-awareness, and it is death to self-awareness. Denial can seem like a friend, but its friendship is short-lived and self-serving. It is deceptive with its promises of strange and unrealistic expectations. Denial causes you to believe lies about yourself and God. You may think you are good in a certain role, when in reality you are average at best. You may want to continue where you are, but for you to grow and for the organization to flourish you need to transition into another responsibility. You may have a passion to pitch in the major leagues, however if you cannot throw a baseball at least 80 miles an hour, you never will. Denial is cruel in positioning you for certain expectations and then failing to deliver.

Indeed, denial of God's existence is the worst kind of denial. It is like refusing to accept a sincere gift from an unconditional lover. Because you deny the lover's existence does not negate their gift. God is not too good to be true. He is good because He is true. When you accept the existence of God you accept the reality of His influence over you and His influence over the world. Denial of Deity is like saying the sun is not brilliant in its illumination by day and the moon by night. Moreover, it is foolish to deny a grand designer behind the human body. Common sense craves for an acceptance of God as creator. A fool has to work very hard to deny God's existence. However, denial's greatest driver may be the desire to behave badly. A fool denies God because he is morally challenged. The thought of God or anyone else telling him how to act is foreign to his foolish heart. Yet, everyday we all have to follow the instruction of some authority. A fool can attempt to remove all authority from his life with denial, but he will fail.

So be open to the evidence that points to the Almighty and intellectually honest about the historic reality of Christ's death and resurrection. Above all else, be honest about your motives for denying God. Is it expedient for your own lifestyle, or is it an honest appraisal of the facts? Honesty is the first step in overcoming denial.

God invites all to know and understand Him. Ultimately He cannot be denied. He may be denied for a season, but sooner or later His presence will press for a personal acknowledgement. Denial of God's existence is spiritual death, but physical death shatters denials claims. One second after death the reality of eternity will ring true. Post death there is no turning back. A fool's bed has been forever made by faithless living. Now is the time to 'wake up' and embrace Christ's existence. The Bible says, "But everything exposed by the light becomes visible, for it is light that makes everything visible. This is why it is said: "Wake up, O sleeper, rise from the dead, and Christ will shine on you." Be very careful, then, how you live—not as unwise but as wise..." (Ephesians 5:13-16). He cannot be denied and a fool will deny this to his detriment.

Denial is death, but acceptance is life. The wise choose life over death!

JUN 8 INTIMACY THROUGH BROKENNESS

"The Lord is close to the brokenhearted and saves those who are crushed in spirit."
PSALM 34:18

Intimacy with God and your brokenness go hand-in-hand. Your desire for intimacy with your heavenly Father will be accompanied by brokenness, as it escorts you into intimacy with eternal God. It is your date with destiny. A broken and contrite heart delivers intimacy with the Almighty. Do not despise your broken condition; rather delight in its opportunity for intimacy. You long to know Jesus in the power of His resurrection and the fellowship of His suffering (Philippians 3:10). These prayers were not in vain. Your brokenness is answered prayer. The answer may not look exactly like you expected. You may have anticipated a smoother route, a paved road without any bumps or pot holes. But the path of personal and intimate relationship with Christ is not always easy.

Most of the time intimacy requires difficulty. It is at this point of pressure and discomfort that some people disembark the train of intimacy. It is much easier to talk about an intimate relationship with Christ than it is to arrive at this point through brokenness. It is only when you surrender in total desperation and total dependency on God that you experience authentic intimacy. However this is an exercise in convenience. It is like placing a "Do not disturb" sign on the door of our life, in place of the "Clean up my room" invitation. Brokenness is inviting God to come in and cleanse your life. He does stand at the door of our heart and knock (Revelation 3:20). When you invite Christ into your broken lives, He comes in. Intimacy is then unleashed on His terms, not yours.

Intimacy through brokenness is not unlike relationships with people. Hardships and brokenness are meant to grow you closer to other people. Crisis will either drive you further away from someone or closer together. God's best is to make you relationally stronger with one another during a season of brokenness. But brokenness is not a one-time phenomenon. It is an ongoing part of the committed Christian's life. It is not like you swallow this hard pill one time and then are set for a lifetime of intimacy with God. Indeed, you are much the better when you experience a defining moment of brokenness. Once God has marked you with brokenness, then you are positioned for Him to build on this firm foundation. He will still use mini brokenness throughout your life. These regular occurrences are bricks of brokenness connected together by the cement of his grace. Over time, a life of brokenness becomes a stalwart structure of sanctification designed by God. Your brokenness is meant for your betterment. It deserves your embrace, rather than your rejection. If you fight brokenness, you delay God's best. You circumvent intimacy with Christ if you bypass brokenness. Focus your energies on changing you and not your circumstances. Christ will handle the circumstances, while you adjust your attitude. A life of brokenness is an invitation to intimacy. His closeness and salvation are worth this time of brokenness.

Don't buck brokenness. Instead, rely on Him, and get to know Him at this deeper level of intimacy. Brokenness leads to betterment for you are much better broken!

START YOUNG

"For you have been my hope, O Sovereign Lord, my confidence since my youth. Since my youth, O God, you have taught me, and to this day I declare your marvelous deeds." PSALM 71:5, 17

Start young learning the ways of the Lord. This is your wisest and best investment. Youthful learning is leverage for the Lord. You start young, so you do not have to wade through the muck and the mire of disobedient living. There is no need to stray and go your own way for you may end up back at the point where you originally drifted from God. Stay the course of Christ while you are young, and this will catapult you into an obedient adult. Youthful dependence on God results in an adult who depends on God. Do not kid yourself and think you can change your ways quickly, once you have entrenched unhealthy habits into your life. Nevertheless, young hearts need to be molded by their master, Jesus. God does a masterful job of making the young at heart into the image of His son, Jesus. He infuses youth with His spirit, so they become His image bearer.

There is tremendous energy and passion around youthful hearts engaged with the eternal. Do not despise your youth or let others do the same. Paul exhorted his protégé Timothy, "Let no man despise thy youth; but be thou an example of the believers, in word, in conversation, in charity, in spirit, in faith, in purity" (1 Timothy 4:12, KJV). Instead take God at His word. Depend on Him for your confidence, wisdom and security. God uses youth to accomplish His purposes. Even as those older in the faith falter in fear, your heavenly Father frees youthful hearts to attempt big things for Him. Courage and conviction fertilize well in a young and hungry heart for God. The Holy Spirit is calling forth faithful young people to further His Kingdom. Listen to the heart of your heavenly Father and do what He says. People are dying of distress and are neglected in their nutrition-less living. Yahweh is calling His youth to something much bigger than themselves. Indeed you can facilitate their faith with prayer, financing, and training.

Help the youth start early in their engagement with God. Teach them, train them, model for them, and then send them out to serve on the Lord's behalf. Youth do not need to be overly protected, but set free to think big for God. The larger the vision the larger their God, therefore present to them a God-sized challenge. Expect great things from young people who have a heart to follow hard after God. Do not underestimate their ability to be a catalyst for Christ. Release them to exceed your accomplishments in half the time. Pray for God to scatter young people across the connected planet. Now is the time to send them out in the power of the Holy Spirit. Use today's resources to prepare for tomorrow's results. Youth need not be coddled with the status quo, rather challenged to break out of boxes of belief that restrain. Invest and equip young people to roll up their sleeves and serve the poor. Children of the poor need your children to show them Jesus, by loving on them at their point of need. They can far exceed our efforts with your significant support, and persistent and powerful prayers.

Support the young, for a youthful person called by God and full of the Holy Spirit can change the world!

"A father to the fatherless, a defender of widows, is God in his holy dwelling."
PSALM 68:5

God helps those who can't help themselves. He is a defender of the poor and needy, for the disadvantaged are on the heart of Deity. Jesus came for those who recognized their need for God and appropriated His forgiveness and grace. Those who are poor in spirit are candidates for Christ's true riches. It is only when you recognize your spiritual bankruptcy outside of a Savior that you can receive the right kind of help. But the Holy Spirit is hovering back and forth over the whole earth. He is looking for those who need and desire Him. Every day millions of people go to bed hungry and die from diseases. Thousands of people each year are being murdered for their faith and their race. Their need is for preemptive measures of food, medicine, justice, and Jesus.

There is also the need to minister to those who have been ravished by raw racism and poverty. They are waiting for someone to care. A little bit of health care, a little bit of money, and a little bit of time can provide for the poor in ways most of us take for granted. A few hundred dollars can build an indoor bathroom and kitchen in the slums. It can be seed money to start a micro enterprise. A wooden cart can be purchased to transport fruits and vegetables to market. God's heart is to help the helpless. Therefore, pray for the poor and ask God to give you someone who could use your help. Grace is drawn to the needy, love edifies and kindness cares. Faith flushes out fear and humility hunts down the hurting and hangs out with them. Compassion shows up with resources that resonate where people live, so help the helpless in the name of Jesus.

Or, you may find yourself on the helpless half of the equation. We are all helpless to some extent. You may feel helpless in your current situation at work, with a family member or your physical condition. Your helpless position is God's helpful position. Engage your heavenly Father in your helpless circumstance. Lean on His love and request His wisdom. You cannot make it alone. There was a day that you may have thought you could make it without the help of Go or other people. But rejection of help is not how God works. Refusing help is refusing God's provision. Indeed, you receive the help of heaven so you can help others get to heaven. Help is a gift that keeps on giving. Because someone believed in you and helped you, you desire to do the same for another. So gain fresh perspective by looking to heaven for help. The Bible says beautifully, "I lift up my eyes to the hills — where does my help come from? My help comes from the LORD, the Maker of heaven and earth" (Psalm 121:1-2). Plead with Him to provide in ways you haven't thought of, but then ask others to help. When others are engaged in eternity's agenda they are happy and content. Blessed are those who become helpers in the purposes of God.

Be a giver and a receiver of help. Above all else, be helpful by giving help to the helpless. Help those who can't help themselves!

NO STRUGGLES

"They have no struggles; their bodies are healthy and strong. They are free from the burdens common to man; they are not plagued by human ills." PSALM 73:4-5

Having no struggles at all will never happen in this lifetime. Non-existent struggles are not possible, until you graduate to heaven's struggle-less environment with your Savior. The nice and the naughty alike struggle, though outwardly they may seem void of vexation. The righteous and the wicked both struggle to varying degrees. No one is exempt from struggles. Yes, there may be seasons of minimal conflict; however struggles are on the way. You are either struggling, about to struggle or have just finished struggling. Indeed, everyone from monks to the mafia struggle. Therefore, don't spend your life trying to insulate yourself from struggles. The Bible teaches, "For our struggle is not against flesh and blood, but against the rulers, against the authorities, against the powers of this dark world and against the spiritual forces of evil in the heavenly realms" (Ephesians 6:12).

You will stress out more from trying to avoid struggles, than you will from accepting their reality. This is not to say God would have us solicit struggles into our life. But He does understand that struggles are meant to send us to Him. Struggles look for a Savior, and Jesus is our friend in our fight against struggles. Moreover, envy can erode your eternal perspective by giving you a false impression of others who seem to live life without struggles. This is inaccurate and ill-conceived. No amount of money or power can completely drive struggles from someone's life. In fact, it may compound struggles because of the complexity of choices that are created. Someone's large amount of discretionary time may on the surface seem like they are without struggles, but they are not. There are still the internal struggles of sin and self against God's best. And there are the external struggles created by other people's choices and circumstances that are out of your control. You can join in another's struggle through prayer, Paul requested this "I urge you, brothers, by our Lord Jesus Christ and by the love of the Spirit, to join me in my struggle by praying to God for me" (Romans 15:30). Therefore, it is imperative to expose others to the light of God's love and to the care of Christ-centered followers.

Struggles are meant to grow you in Him and not drive you away from Him. Use struggles to your advantage, rather to your disadvantage. Struggles do not mean you are less spiritual. It may be just the opposite is true. Because of your sensitivity to obey God, you may struggle. You may struggle over the misunderstanding others have over your love for Christ. You may struggle because of the mistreatment from those convicted by your lifestyle. You may struggle to forgive because of the unforgiveness that is extended back to you. Struggles come in all shapes and sizes. Some things you can control, like what you eat and some you can't control, like your height. So go quickly to your Savior Jesus with your struggles. Use them as an asset rather than a liability in your relationship with God. Lean on prayer to persevere through this time of struggle, because struggles are about survival of the faithful. You are not alone in your struggle against sin, self and Satan. Therefore, stay true to the task of disciplined devotion to Christ and be with those who survived their struggles by the grace of God. His grace is sufficient no matter what the struggle.

Don't seek to be struggle-free. Accept struggles in stride with His greater purpose in mind. God uses your struggles for His glory!

Jun 12 SHEPHERD AND LEAD

"And David shepherded them with integrity of heart; with skillful hands he led them."
PSALM 78:72

Leadership requires the gentle touch of a shepherd and the persistent persuasion of a leader. Both traits are needed to lead effectively and efficiently. The wise leader pays attention on how and when to apply doses of each. When the troops are weary and worrisome there is a need to slow down and love them through this time of challenge. However, as they are licking their personal and/or professional wounds, keep them focused on the mission and ultimately keep them connected with their heavenly Father. A person freed up and accountable to God has more potential for productivity. Shepherding moves people beyond their own needs to their ability to serve others. This is their best therapy. Help people discover a need and then encourage them to engage in its fulfillment. Moreover, good shepherding requires awareness. You are aware of people's limitations of capacity and capabilities. Be careful not to overload and burn out your best people. You are aware of the training required to get people up to speed in their performance and productivity. You are aware of what motivates certain individuals, but not others. You are aware of how to best communicate with, and hold accountable people according to their style and expectations. You are aware if people around you are happy, sad, discontent or grateful. You are aware when they hurt and when they cry. You are aware because you care. Shepherding is caring, so take the time to shepherd and you will increase your probabilities of retaining your people. If you drive them instead of shepherd them you will eventually drive them away, so skillfully shepherd and lead the team.

An effective leader must also lead. Leadership is not afraid to mark a course and then embark the team toward the goal. Yes you collaborate and define a process, but then you move forward prayerfully and productively. Leadership is anticipating the next step and adapting as needed. It understands the big picture, and then communicates this grander vision in a compelling and consistent fashion. Leading implies progress toward a destination. It requires right results. Leaders feel a mandate and a calling from God to lead. They are good leaders, because they are good followers of Christ.

Leaders also give attention to detail and understand its value. However, detail does not derail them from reaching the goal. The analysis of data is necessary to make the wisest decisions possible. But, leaders avoid paralysis from analysis and move forward, testing the waters as they go. Leaders lead, whether they are liked or not. Their motivation is to execute the plan, not to appease the people. Leaders may be branded as insensitive because of their untiring focus on progress, excellence, and execution. But this is the role of the leader. There is no need for leaders to apologize for leading. Leaders shepherd and lead.

If you shepherd with a heart of integrity, and lead with your God-given skills then you are a leader worth following. Aspire to this level of leadership. This is the leadership style of David and Jesus!

FRESH FRUIT

> "They will still bear fruit in old age, they will stay fresh and green…"
> P<small>SALM</small> 92:14

Old age is an excuse to stay fresh. This is one of the secrets of staying relevant to your children and grandchildren. A fresh heart and mind feeds a healthy attitude. Therefore stay fresh in your learning, spiritual growth and maturity. Learning places you in a position to be fresh and attractive, but when you stop learning you stop growing. When you stop growing you become stale and unattractive. No one wants to be around someone who is disengaged from an inspiring word from God, or a fresh and interesting idea. Fresh people like fresh fruit are appealing, delicious, satisfying and good for you. You are attracted to people who have a fresh insight from Scripture, or have learned to better channel their energy into productive, rather than destructive habits. These wise men and women have aged well. Like a dust-covered bottle of wine they are highly valued. The outward signs of age are only evidence of a fresh heart dripping in an appetizing attitude. Focus on those who have fruit that remains (John 15:16, KJV).

Therefore, take the time to engage with the aged. Maybe calendar a day with a sage who has a proven track record of faithfulness to freshness. Take notes from their thoughts and then prayerfully apply them to your stage of life. A fresh mind is fed by a mind that devours books, sermons, CD's and small group interaction. You stay fresh when you give yourself the freedom to think outside the box. God stays sacred, but even certain beliefs about Him change for the better around fresh thinking. Fresh thinking does not necessary mean new information. It is however, the ability to understand and apply truth in a way that was foreign to you in the past. Like a traveler to a new land, freshness allows you to see things for the first time. This discovery of truth in a fresh way energizes and compels you to become better. You appreciate new thinking because it is really old thinking that is appreciated, understood, and appropriated.

Your age is your advantage, so leverage your years for Yahweh. Invite people into your life of learning. Allow them to sit on the luscious lawn of your life and learn what works and doesn't work for you. Old age is designed by God to be your crowning act of achievement and influence. Therefore take care of your body, so you can be in a healthy state of mind and heart. Physical fitness is an important part of staying fresh and green for God. You are all much better positioned to invest in others when you are not preoccupied with our own health issues. However, even in your weakness of body you can have a fruitful and appetizing life. Do not let your illness cause you to retreat from people. They may come to bless you, but this is your opportunity to bless them.

Let them see the love of God exhibited through your frail but fruitful life. Your body may be fading, but your faith is accelerating. So, stay fruitful and fresh until you see Him!

"Give thanks to the Lord, call on his name; make known among the nations what he has done." PSALM 105:1

God deserves and desires worldwide recognition for He is an international icon. The Lord is larger than the land of the free and the home of the brave, America. His Holy Spirit ignites the revivals of South America, He reigns as the Almighty of Australia, and His influence reaches Christians in communist China. His worship weaves in and out, and ultimately extends into the 1,200 dialects of India. He is Lord over Europe, Russia, the Middle East, the Arctic and Antarctica. There is no corner of the globe that is not a candidate for the glory of God. His great works are without boundaries and bring glory to His name. Indeed, His wondrous works include physical healing of cancer, tuberculosis, heart disease and leprosy. He delivers addicts from drugs and alcohol, and He still makes the lame to walk and the blind to see.

His fingerprints are all over creation. He is the creator of craters, sunsets, sunrises and hurricanes. He makes a sedated and silent volcano erupt with orange hot lava. He creates parrots, monkeys, lions, tigers, elephants, rhinos, and camels. Moreover, He gives a businessman the brains for innovation and creation. He blesses some families with wealth and others with poverty. He brings a smile to a face, and forges forgiveness in a heart. He answers prayer. His works are wonderful and worldwide. A slum child in New Delhi can read the same stories about Jesus as a privileged child in New York City. God is a doer. He is not stuck in some theological vacuum waiting for things to happen. He makes things happen in accordance with His will. Nations come and go in their level of vitality and vibrancy for God, but He remains the same ever working for His glory.

Therefore, seek to be intentional with the influence of God internationally. Time, energy and entrepreneurship need to extend way beyond the borders of home. Religion, churches, humanitarian help, hospitals and schools need to sever language barriers, and launch themselves into the hinterlands exuding hope. The world is waiting for a reminder of God. He has put it their hearts and He has painted it on the canvas of creation (Romans 1:19-20). He has also combed the conscience of man with His morals and sense of right and wrong. Your role as a follower of Jesus is to be Jesus to the nations. As an excerpt from the Doxology goes, "Bless the Lord, O my soul and all that is within me bless His holy name. He has done great things, He has done great things, He has done great things: bless His holy name." The great works of God need an encore with everlasting consequences. You need not sit in your seat of domestic doldrums any longer. You can rise even if alone, with a worldwide ovation of praise and thanksgiving to God Almighty. His truth transcends the vilest of hearts and the remotest of villages. Now is the time to use your discretionary time and money for large doses of global discipleship and evangelism. Leave a legacy for your Lord that engages for generations and with cultures of character.

Pray for the nations, go to the nations, serve the nations, teach and train the nations. And, say to the nations that God has done great things and will do great things!

MAN OF PRAYER

"In return for my friendship they accuse me, but I am a man of prayer."
PSALM 109:4

A man of prayer prays. It is his first line of defense and his most effective offensive strategy. Prayer is not an afterthought for a man of prayer; it is not a last ditch engagement with the eternal, but is top of mind. Prayer is not just being disciplined and determined, but is a desperate dependence on God. It is conversing with Christ and is not just asking God for goodies and/or guarantees. The man of prayer enters into intimacy with the Almighty. It is a realization that God is in control, and His wisdom is needed for life and work. Furthermore, prayer precludes pain by providing patience. It forecasts disaster by giving warning. It discerns clumsy and destructive decisions by cultivating understanding and discernment. A man of prayer avoids self-inflicted problems, because he prays first. He is medicine for the sick and refreshment for the soul. Prayer may be the best gift you can give someone. You may not have silver and gold to give, but you can give prayer (Acts 3:6). A man of prayer does not talk about praying, with a sentimental, "I'll pray for you." On the contrary with a seriousness of purpose and responsibility, he stops what he is doing and lifts to heaven the concerns of the one requesting prayer. As you hear him pray, a peace and calm overcome you. It is encouragement from on high. His is not a stale prayer but fresh, because the man of prayer has been in prayer. A man of prayer prays for his spouse and for the spouses of his children. He leads his wife in prayer. He keeps his logical mind in check, by checking in with Christ.

Start by getting on your knees for five minutes each morning. Prayerful posture is important to a man of prayer. His stature is humble and dependent. Therefore, humble yourself daily before your heavenly Father. Lay face down on the floor if necessary. Then get up and consider making a prayer list. However, do not sell yourself short by not feeling qualified to be a man of prayer. This role is not relegated to the super righteous. It is for adulterers, liars and murderers like David (Psalm 51). A man of prayer is still a man in recovery from sin. Sin does not cease to hound the man who prays, but it drives him to pray, and then sin's influence is stunted in the face of the man of prayer. It is hard to sin while you pray. There is accountability to God that encounters the man of prayer.

Indeed, there is a direct correlation between prayer and purposeful living. Being a man of prayer is not a badge to wear. Instead, it is a discreet lifestyle of continual prayer (1 Thessalonians 5:17). It becomes a habit of life, like eating and sleeping. Prayer for a man of prayer is not an elective. It is a required course. It is core curriculum. Moreover, the man of prayer cannot be pigeon-holed with his behavior and speech. He comes in all shapes and sizes, depending on his God given temperament. He is humorous and humble. He is loud and he is quiet. He is spontaneous and he is methodical. He is creative and he is concrete. He is eloquent and simple. However, there is one thing he is not. He is not proud and arrogant. People are his pleasure. Heaven is his home, where he checks in often. Jesus is his "go-to" man.

Worship, thanksgiving, praise and adoration all permeate the prayers of a man of prayer. A man of prayer prays!

JUN 16 WIFE SUPPORT

"Surely all the wealth that God took away from our father belongs to us and our children. So do whatever God has told you." GENESIS 31:16

Husbands need the support of their wives. Of course, it works both ways, as the wife needs to feel the support of her husband, but this is huge for a man. A God-fearing husband knows the Lord has placed him in a position of leadership. It is overwhelming sometimes because he can feel squeezed from the pressures of life. The last thing a husband needs to feel is distance or distrust from his wife. Your encouragement may be the only thing that is preventing him from giving up, so not underestimate the sustainability of your support. Your affirmation is valuable and powerful for the ongoing success of your husband. Men are not as self-sufficient as they might seem. On the outside he may seem invincible, but on the inside he is needy and desperate for recognition and validation. A man needs to know his wife trusts his decision making and his ability to provide for his family. Her confidence in him propels his self-confidence to higher levels. Your belief in your husband builds him up to believe in himself. It is difficult for a man to rise any higher than the opinion of his helpmate. Men long to be built up by their brides, so brag on him in public and affirm him in private. Look to your husband as the leader God has placed in your life. Pray for him to lead lovingly and wisely. Be patient not-to usurp his authority when things are not getting done. Trust him with God for He can handle him. Give him over to God and trust in the accountability of the Almighty. Sometimes a man needs to fail before he can be successful.

As a husband it is imperative in God's sight that you lovingly lead your wife and children. You may feel your wife is more qualified, smarter and more spiritual. These all may be very true. However, God's plan is for you to take the position of leadership in the home. She is looking for you to do whatever God has told you. Prayer is a mantle of responsibility that you bear. See prayer as a privilege to enjoy and not an obligation to tolerate. She will trust you more and more as you remain trustworthy. It takes time to overcome a track record of distrust. Remain in the process of listening to God, following His commands and then leading your family to do the same. There are days you don't feel like leading or even listening to the Lord. Life can be overwhelming. It can get you down to the point of walking away from all your responsibilities. But by grace you carry on in your commitment to Christ, your wife and your children.

It is foolish to flee from your responsibilities as a husband and father. Fools give up, but God has you in this position so you can learn about Him and His plan for you and your family. Do what He says with passion and abandonment. It may mean moving to another country. It may mean downsizing for a season. It may be organizing a family vacation. It may mean planning the calendar and budget for the upcoming year. Lastly, love leads. Love follows God and leads his family. Give your wife the assurance that you listen to and follow God. She will respect you and trust you for this.

Wives, support your husbands. Support him in ways he feels supported. Your support is life support!

HEART TURNER

"He will turn the hearts of the fathers to their children, and the hearts of the children to their fathers; or else I will come and strike the land with a curse."   MALACHI 4:6

God is a heart turner. His influence transcends any hard-hearted person. He can turn the hearts of kings. He can turn the hearts of parents. He can turn the hearts of children. God is a spiritual cardiologist. He can unclog the poisonous cholesterol of the hard hearted. His caring ablations can slow down the rebellious heart. He can even perform a heart transplant and replace the old heart with a brand new heart. This radical surgery is, of course, your conversion to Christ. Someone has a good heart if it is turned by God. The heart unaffected by God's recent touch is spiritually weak and unable to withstand the world's pressures. The heart is a spiritual muscle in need of exercise in faith and a diet of God's Word. This is God conditioning and is necessary to stay in spiritual shape. Your heart is in the hand of God. This is the ideal place for it to rest. He guards it. He cleanses it. He turns it. A heart in the hand of God is a defeat for the devil. He has to pry back the fingers of your heavenly Father to get to your heart. This is heaven's heart monitor. Give Him your heart and watch Him turn it toward Himself and to His will. God's work of heart is beautiful and breathtaking. Whether a young innocent heart or a seasoned guilt-ridden heart, He makes it into a healthy heart. Give your heart to God and trust him to turn it into what is best for you.

You risk rejection when you give your heart, but God can be trusted. He is a heart specialist and He has never failed in spiritual heart surgery. Trust Him with your heart for He already knows its intentions. He understands it better than you, so allow Him to diagnose your motives and then prescribe His character. Your heart is stronger in Him. Once he turns your heart toward Him then you are in a position of trust. You can trust Him to turn the hearts of others. A person cannot turn another person's heart, but God can. Pray to God and trust Him to turn the heart of your child back to Him and back to you. The same can be said of your dad or mom. Trust God to turn their hearts to Him and then watch their hearts long to be with you and your children.

Moreover, He can heal your wounded heart and turn the heart of your spouse back to God and back to you. He can change the heart of your friend on a dime. This time it is for real, because God did the turning. Your friend has truly shifted his addiction to affection for Christ. God has changed his heart. The heart of your work associate can soften. Pray for him or her. Model for them a heart turned heavenward and watch God work. Let them know you had a change of heart by God's grace. Lastly, trust God to turn the hearts of those who may be miles away. Your relationship may be slim to none. But these are the hearts that God turns for His glory. Like a raging river in His creation, He can turn a heart for His purposes in spite of its twists and turns. Leave your heart with Him.

Trust Him with the hearts of others. His heart is huge. He is a heart turner!

JUN 18 FAITHFUL FATHER

"A father to the fatherless, a defender of widows, is God in his holy dwelling."
PSALM 68:5

Most people long for a faithful father, who will feed them when they are hungry, love them when they are lonely, and care for them when they are crying. They long for a dad, who will listen to them when they wonder, encourage them when they are discouraged and discipline them when they do wrong. They are eager for a father, who takes time for the trivial, extends wisdom in the middle of worry and prays for understanding of God's will. God placed within you a desire to be loved by your father. Some fathers do well at being a faithful father and others do not. Some are extremely successful and others fail miserably. Fortunately, God is your model of a faithful father. Your heavenly Father fills the gaps of your earthly father. He is your faithful father.

Your heavenly Father deserves your respect and commands your love. He says to pray, "Our Father in heaven, hallowed be your name..." (Matthew 6:9). He is a father who is totally trustworthy. You never have to doubt God's word. What He says He means, and what He means He does. Your Father in heaven will not let you down on earth. Now sometimes it doesn't feel like He is faithful. There are times you do not have answers for the questions that gnaw at your heart and confuse your mind. It may be He is speaking, but you are not listening. It may be He is silent because He wants to grow your trust in Him. He will tell you what to do, in time, so while you wait, become better.

Your faithful Father in heaven is the Father of Truth. Jesus is truth (John 14:6). Satan is the father of lies (John 8:44). He acts like he is interested in your life, so he can destroy your life. He uses you for his interests. Therefore reject the lies of the devil and embrace the truth of the Lord. When you left the dark side of unbelief, you renounced your father the devil and embraced your heavenly Father through Christ. Lastly, be a lifetime learner as a faithful father. Each season of fathering is different. What worked in the last stage of your child's life needs to be adapted for the next stage. By faith, be flexible. As infants they need your gentle touch. As children they need your patient instruction. As teenagers they need you to be an example of love and forgiveness (someone has to be the mature one, I Corinthians 13:11). As adults they need your wisdom and friendship. In all seasons they need your time and trust. Above all else, look to your heavenly Father as your baseline for behavior. Being a faithful father does not mean perfection, but it does mean you depend on the Perfect One. You lean on the Lord for His loving care, so you can extend the same.

You can be a faithful earthly father, because of your faithful heavenly Father. Invite Him to love on you, and lead you into faithfulness!

PUSH BACK

*"I was pushed back and about to fall, but the Lord helped me.
The Lord is my strength and my song; he has become my salvation."* PSALM 118:13

Life can be a sequence of push backs. People push back. Projects push back. Progress pushes back. Circumstances push back. Sometimes it seems that everything and everyone is pushing back. How you respond to push backs will be the difference between living in peace or turmoil. It is very wise to walk lock step with the Lord during a push back period. Let Him be your help and strength. You will drive yourself crazy trying to determine all the reasons around the push back. Instead, let God handle this person who is pushing back. They have their reasons, noble or ignoble. God will judge a person's motive, not you. God is still working during this push back period, so use this time for more information gathering and for you to get to know and understand all the people involved. Push backs buy you time to develop a better relationship, and to craft a more accurate plan. A push back is not a failure, rather a time to regroup and do better. More often than not, a push back should not be taken personally. You don't know everything that is going on personally or professionally with all those involved. This push back may be for your protection. It is what is needed to guarantee God's best for you. He works His will in spite of, and because of a push back. It is disheartening and sometimes frustrating when someone close to you pushes back on a promise. They were sincere in the moment, but now have cold feet because they truly understand the commitment. You may need to push back on them, ask them to reconsider.

Indeed, you need to prayerfully push back when necessary. This is part of the maturing process. Say no if your heart is not in this opportunity. Many people have wonderful life experiences to offer you. Some contribute to God's best, and some are just expedient for them. Push back on those people who are too pushy. Help them understand your true feelings and aspirations. Your push back may be what it takes to persuade others to do the same. Push backs prayerfully orchestrated are powerful ways to progress in God's will. Your 'no' may be very well what's needed to transition to your 'yes'. This is the wisdom of pushing back. It disciplines you to wait on God. Why redo things in the future when you can push back now, and start off on the right foot?

Relationships void of push backs are fragile and unpredictable. However, relationships peppered with push backs are resilient and authentic. This is how you get to know each other. This is how justice is able to bubble to the top. Nonetheless, receive push backs from the Lord. A gentle push back from the Holy Spirit in the beginning is much better than a shove by the Spirit later down the road. Therefore, be prayerful and discern whether God is pushing back or pulling forward. In either case, Christ can be trusted.

Receive and give push backs as part of God's process. He is your help and strength. Above all else, do not push back Providence!

"Let a righteous man strike me—it is a kindness; let him rebuke me—it is oil on my head. My head will not refuse it. Yet my prayer is ever against the deeds of evildoers..."
PSALM 141:5

Invited accountability is the most effective accountability for uninvited accountability is temporary at best. Only as you actively solicit accountability will it produce the necessary results. Accountability is like prayer, many talk about it but few practice it. You know you are accountable when you have submitted to someone about a particular issue. It is normally better to submit to two or three people, so you gain the benefit of diverse perspectives and temperaments. You need some accountability partners who are honest about their own temptations. Then they are not talking in theory, but out of the passion of practical living. It is hard to avoid the accountability of someone who has been there. They will sniff out pretense and pride a mile away. You need people to hold you accountable who are completely and painfully honest. Playing with sin crushes your commitment to Christ. Therefore, allow your accountability team to get in your face and question you about the facts of the situation. Give them the whole truth and nothing but the truth, and do not receive their rebukes as a reason to harm you. See their loving accountability as an investment in your life. They are taking the time to walk with you, so you can change destructive habits and/or avoid making harmful decisions in the future. Pray for accountability from smart people with impeccable character and who are discerning. Above all else, remain teachable and do what they say.

Indeed, there are two forms of accountability: preemptive accountability and deliverance accountability. You may need some of both. Preemptive accountability is protection against pride. It is building an arsenal of actions aimed at avoiding adultery. It understands how to nip anger in the bud, before it raises its destructive head. It is developing good financial habits, before you are blessed with abundance. Financial accountability keeps you honest with a little, so you can be trusted with much. If you don't tithe while making a small amount, odds are you won't with a large amount. Preemptive accountability is looking ahead at trouble brewing on the horizon and adjusting before it makes land fall, "A prudent man sees danger and takes refuge, but the simple keep going and suffer for it" (Proverbs 22:3). It is proactive in prayer and courageous in wise behavior that adjusts away from approaching disasters.

Deliverance accountability, on the other hand is specific in moving you out of a current crisis. You wake up every morning knowing one more bad decision will cause everything to blow up in your face. It is a weekly phone report to your accountability group about your AA meeting and the results from your drug test, or a report from your internet surfing. It is your accountability group regularly asking your spouse how you are really doing. Deliverance accountability is immediate and in your face. It is action-oriented. It is an intervention of tough love. This level of accountability is more than likely your last chance for change. So, wise is the man or woman who invites loving accountability early into their life. Make it a normal part of your life early on and you will avoid crisis management later. Better is your accountable to the Almighty when you are accountable to those He trusts.

Therefore, send out your accountability invitations today. Some will RSVP and some will not, however, go with those God sends you!

INTELLIGENT DESIGN

"He determines the number of the stars and calls them each by name. Great is our Lord
and mighty in power; his understanding has no limit."
PSALM 147:4-5

God is the intelligence behind the design of all creation. The creation of space is His design. Every galaxy, universe, star, planet, meteor, and asteroid is a result of His intricate design. The craters on the moon He designed, so we could compare it to cheese. The rings around Saturn He designed, so we could marvel at its majestic beauty. The trajectory of the earth's axis He designed, so it would sustain life but not spin out of control. He positioned the sun at just the right distant from earth, so it would warm but not destroy. He knew all the planets' gravitational pull toward the sun would be needed to orchestrate one big simultaneous swirl. Every flickering light in the sky, big and little dipper and the North Star are all embedded in the intelligence of His design.

Common sense craves intelligent design. Logic longs for intelligent design. Faith frolics with intelligent design. Indeed, your conscience invites intelligent design, as a strong case for conviction. It is intelligent to include intelligent design in the repertoire of your rational thinking. The Lord's intelligence is astounding and all-encompassing. It cannot be measured or completely understood, but it can be adored and praised. His intelligent design is a facilitator of faith in Him. Intelligent design is an act of the Almighty and it is more proof of His profound power and might. The pure snow capped peaks of the highest mountains point in praise toward their divine designer in heaven. Their rugged stone faces are a reminder of the rock solid dependability of your Lord and Savior Jesus Christ. Anyone who has ever scaled an Everest-like mountain knows the intimacy and exhilaration of caressing the caring and rugged face of God.

When you engage with the intelligence behind the design of creation, you begin to dance with its Creator for intelligent design is not meant to be an end in itself. It is not just a lot of impressive scientific facts and statistics, but it is His coming out party that compliments His visit to earth in the person of His son Jesus Christ. Indeed, Jesus was enamored with the intelligence of His father's design. He spoke of the birds of the air, the lilies of the valley, and the stature of man. He described the Holy Spirit as a calm and unseeing wind. The new birth was contrasted with physical birth. Above all else, Jesus was the "Word" in the beginning with God, installing intelligent design throughout all creation (John 1:1-3). Therefore, intelligent design is God's fingerprint of faith. Anyone serious about his religion and equally serious about intellectual honesty will troll the depths of God's design. The sincere seeking of truth will most likely lead them to be caught by Christ. Sincere seekers of a Savior through science will not be disappointed, only amazed into engaging with the Creator Himself. Use intelligent design to galvanize your faith and validate your evangelism.

The truly intelligent invite Jesus Christ in as the interior designer of their soul. His outward and iinward design is matchless and magnificent!

"A fool finds no pleasure in understanding but delights in airing his own opinions."
P<small>ROVERBS</small> 18:2

Fools are fast to offer a cure before they understand the illness and this can be a deadly combination. Offering medicine to someone who may an allergic reaction could prove fatal. In the same way good advice is appropriate for the person and the situation. Anyone can offer an opinion and fools love airing his or her opinions. It is entertainment for they delight in talking about anything, as long as there is opportunity to talk. However, a babbling fool can get you into trouble; so do not be impressed by his words. Instead, measure his words by making sure he understands you and the topic of your concern. Look for principles, like avoid disciplining your child in anger. The last thing you need is foolish advice based on an individual opinion. Look for wisdom from someone who looks you in the eyes with empathy, and be patient to validate their ideas from a variety of respected sources. Invite influence from those who draw their wisdom from the word of God and avoid people who talk too much. It is impossible to understand without listening for an unsure heart does not need a quick fix, but a listening ear. Those seeking wisdom need someone who listens with understanding.

So, be very cautious what you say and how you communicate your care. Ask questions like, "Why do you want to do this," "What does your spouse think?," "Is this what you really want to do?," or "What do you think God is telling you?" Moreover, you can't go wrong by offering prayer support. The most appropriate counsel for you to offer may be to pray with the person seeking wisdom. Ask God to give them His divine counsel and directive. The wisdom of God obtained in prayer is the most valuable and accurate advice. You can't go wrong praying with and for others. They will thank you for your wisdom, when in reality you listened with understanding and prayed with them for their discernment. Your advice may not be as eloquent as a fool's self-appointed soliloquy, but it is much more soothing for the soul.

Lastly, do not seek to impress others with your wise words. Instead gain their trust and respect by truly seeking to understand their hopes and dreams. Learn what makes them afraid and what gives them peace. Find out where happiness and contentment resides for them. This level of intimate understanding gives you a microscope of understanding that focuses in on the DNA of their personality, temperament and past experiences that determine present behavior. Do not be afraid to wait on offering opinions until you thoroughly understand the person or situation. Wisdom comes to those who seek to understand first. Therefore, pray to see others as God does. Look for the good and don't be naïve about the bad.

But when all is said and done, ask first what God thinks. Listen to Him for the Lord's insight is 'understanding' at its best!

AVOID THE ANGRY

"Do not make friends with a hot-tempered man, do not associate with one easily angered, or you may learn his ways and get yourself ensnared."   PROVERBS 22:24-25

Avoid the angry and do not make friends with those easily angered. They are undependable and hard to get along with. You cannot predict what an angry person will do next. They may lie, lash out, sulk, blame or even kill if their rage is left unchecked. The source of their anger may be as simple as not getting their way, or it may be a string of broken expectations all the way back to a wounded childhood. Your role is not to fix them or to be their therapist. However, the times you do have to associate with them can be an opportunity for you to model peace and calm. But be very careful not to cross the line of becoming like the angry. Their impatient ways become your impatient ways. Their rude tendencies become your rude tendencies. Their sarcasm becomes your sarcasm. Their blowups become your blowups. Yes, the angry can change, but real change will only occur as God heals their heart. Unless forgiveness penetrates an angry heart, it is destined to remain the same. Hard and stubborn is a heart driven by anger. Unless anger is unwound by grace and love, it will unleash its furor suddenly and will constantly simmer just beneath the surface. You may be the object of someone's anger, only because you happen to be around them when they snap. They are a product of stuffed emotions.

Some angry people are hard to avoid because you live with them. What now? You certainly pray for and with them. Pray earnestly for the angry person you live with to allow themselves to be loved by God. The heavenly Father can squeeze out the venom of vengeance with His holy hugs. The love and acceptance of God can flush out foul language and faithless living. To be loved by God is to not remain angry for the Lord's love and anger cannot coexist. Unconditional love that is received melts the heart of anger. Furthermore in business be very careful not to partner with the chronically angry. You will regret it, and you will be angry with yourself for aligning with the angry. Even engaging with employees, vendors and customers who are engrossed in their anger is not healthy. God will provide more pleasant clients or staff. Cut loose those who linger, stew, and obsess over little things. It is not worth it. They will never be satisfied with your service or your sincere encouragement.

Anger-driven people are never content. There is nothing you can do that will make them happy. Their anger may subside momentarily, but you will remain on pins and needles, waiting for them to erupt at any moment. Moreover, angry children need to learn how to bring their hurts to their heavenly Father in prayer. Unprocessed hurt feelings will fester into anger. Help them to talk about why they have feelings of anger. What makes them mad at themselves? Unresolved anger is a time bomb waiting to explode. A safe environment to talk through your heated emotions is a great place to start. Channel your anger into proper passions that are sanctified by your Savior. Be angry at sin, while forgiving yourself and others. Avoid the angry and release your anger within to your heavenly Father above.

Friendship with the angry creates angst with God. Friendship with the forgiven (healed) promotes peace with God. Go with peace!

JUN 24 AVOID STRIFE

"It is to a man's honor to avoid strife; but every fool is quick to quarrel."
PROVERBS 20:3

Avoid strife for it creates a lot of sideways energy and is emotionally draining. Strife can be the result of someone who did not get their way, or did not feel heard or understood. It may be rooted in old fashion selfishness, but strife is more than an occasional disagreement. It is a bitter conflict and it can become a heated and violent dissention. Strife results in a struggle, fight, or quarrel. It is the opposite of living in peace. A fool looks for opportunities to disagree and engage in conflict. This is one way a fool feels important. He is able to get the attention of another by being a nuisance. A nuisance is in need of recognition. His or her insecurity finds security in strife. Strife is sport to the foolish. Any fool can find an excuse to engage in an argument.

Avoidance of strife does not mean you should not confront when there are disagreements and concerns. Being honest is important to healthy relational development. Talking through misunderstandings is not strife, but smart. Strife on the other hand, produces chronic chaos and confusion. There is always a swirl of strife around a fool. A person who creates strife is someone who strives. There are no moments of peace for the carrier of strife. Life seems to go from one crisis to the next. A foolish striver positions themselves against the world, because they do not know how to trust God and others. Their understanding of reality is skewed and jaded. Therefore, remove those who inflict the pain of strife, and then peace and calm will reign in their place. It is honorable to avoid strife. This is especially true for a man. Strife free living is a badge of honor that most men enjoy wearing. For a man, avoiding strife is the honorable thing to do. Strife strikes at his manhood and respect. He feels disrespected by the fool who is always discontent, disagreeing and in disarray. It is all about honor. You can have mature discussions that address disagreements in an honorable and respectful way.

But there is no need to foolishly feed on a frenzy of uncontrollable emotions. Fools jump to conclusions without understanding the context of the discussion. This is dishonoring to those who desire not to flail away in a cycle of strife. Strife can be avoided with patience and prayer. Truly seek to serve and understand the other person first and foremost. Put others' needs above your hurt feelings or your need to be right. Strife will cease with a humble response, but it compounds in the face of pride. Peace is the fruit of humility, while pride displays strife.

Put strife to rest with radical forgiveness and unconditional love. Start by honoring the one stuck in strife, for honor reduces ruckus!

MIDLIFE CRISIS

"Meaningless! Meaningless!" says the Teacher. "Utterly meaningless!
Everything is meaningless." ECCLESIASTES 1:2

Midlife is a natural time to do a life audit. This is the season to do a performance review of your passion and your life's productivity. You measure how well you have amassed money and acquired assets. You grade the success of your life on your position in the work place, your educational advancement, your character development and the quality of your relationships, especially family. Midlife is a time for reflection, regrouping and recalibrating big goals. If by God's grace, you have implemented His plan up until now, you look forward to what He has for you during the second half of life. But, a midlife crisis comes from meaningless living. You may have drifted from what God intended for you from your youth. You scoffed at His plan and purpose and replaced it with yours. Indeed, go back to your original God-given purpose, and misdirect the missile of a midlife crisis from crashing into your home. Revisit your God-given purpose for living. A proper purpose precludes meaningless living. Yet everyday men and some women meander into a midlife crisis. They think it is a release from responsibility, but midlife is meant to be a terrific transition, not terrible torture. It is created for celebration, not regret. Midlife is meaningful if rooted in the purpose of God and a future hope in Him, "For I know the plans I have for you," declares the LORD, "plans to prosper you and not to harm you, plans to give you hope and a future" (Jeremiah 29:11).

Maybe you did live the first half of your life off purpose, but you were successful by the world's standards. You may have more wealth than you ever dreamed, but your spouse and children do not really know you. You are relationally poor. Or, maybe you have been a good Christian, but bad things always seem to encounter you. Christianity feels like a farce. It is not what was promised to you when you started out in gleeful obedience. The hardness and insensitivity of some Christians is confusing. You are ready to toss it all out the window and start over with convenient obedience and lukewarm faith. But now is not the time to nose dive on Divine Providence. Yes, you may be tired and even sick, but stick with your Savior.

Life will be meaningful if you travel with your Master. He may seem hard at times and distant, but He is not without meaning. Your real midlife meaning needs to come from Him, so surrender and you will see success as God defines success. If adventure is what you crave, then pray and if the Holy Spirit gives you the green light then take your spouse overseas and serve the poor. Now that's adventure. Meaning comes from selfless living. A midlife crisis comes from selfish living. So run toward God and your family, not away from them. Make midlife your best season of life yet. Live it well driven by your God-given purpose and your future hope.

Allow your midlife crisis to draw you close to Christ. Moreover, enthusiastically embrace eternity and enjoy a midlife celebration. Meaningful! Meaningful! Life with the Lord is meaningful!

"What shall we say, then? Shall we go on sinning so that grace may increase? By no means! We died to sin; how can we live in it any longer?" Romans 6:1-2

Grace is a gift from God that requires responsible and wise stewardship. It is not a license to sin, but permission to live. Grace is all about living for God and walking with Him. It engages with eternity by approaching God's throne of grace with gratitude, awe and boldness. God's grace is a guarantee of eternal life. It is absolutely amazing because it is collateralized by Christ. There has never been a shortage of your Savior's grace. No group or individual has ever made a run on heaven's grace account. You can go to the bank with God's grace. It is as everlasting as the Lord. However though unlimited in supply, it may be the most under used resource available. People miss grace when they thrash around and stumble about in their own strength. They apply bad theology. They believe in salvation by grace through faith, but then drift into living in their own strength. Demons must chuckle when they observe Christians applying dead works. Working to earn God's favor after salvation is as futile as it was before salvation. Do not fall into the trap of graceless living for grace is God's remedy for the self-indulgent. Grace values community with people and communing with Christ. There is a spirit of acceptance and peace with those who often receive and apply God's grace.

Furthermore, learn to use grace responsibly. Grace is not a safety net for your fall off the cliff of sin for it still has its consequences. Grace is not an excuse to sin and is not your pass for disobedience. Grace is more than anything an honorable motivation for your attitude and actions. For example, harsh judgment and extremes are natural outcomes for graceless Christians. Without grace you gravitate toward being proud of not sinning. Yes, grace is a governor of your behavior, but it does not promote pride.

Grace means you have a stewardship of wise choices to manage for the Lord. It gives you permission to be free in Christ, but your freedom is for Him. His kingdom agenda is what drives grace. Grace integrates all of life around faith. Christ does not compartmentalize the sacred from the secular. Grace includes instead of excludes. It discloses rather than hides. Sin is subservient to your Savior's grace. Grace gives you the perspective and power for forgiveness and honesty. It is the delivery channel of truth. Grace is your excuse for extending forgiveness and continual chances to culprits. Use grace to remove sin's stain from any fibers of your faith. Indeed, as you extend grace you are more likely to receive grace. Be responsible with grace and you will be trusted with more.

Grace saved you from sin; so don't go back to your pre-grace condition. Because of grace you are free from sin, not free to sin. Therefore, be a responsible and gracious follower of Christ!

CHRISTIAN CELEBRITIES

"...there are quarrels among you. What I mean is this: One of you says, 'I follow Paul;
another, 'I follow Apollos; another, 'I follow Cephas; still another, 'I follow Christ.'
Is Christ divided? Was Paul crucified for you? Were you baptized into the name of Paul?'
I CORINTHIANS 1:11B-13

Christian celebrities sometimes create quarreling factions. But followers of Christ are not on theological teams competing to win. There is no competition in the Kingdom of God, yet human nature yearns for a hero. People want someone they can see that stands for excellence in eternal matters. This admiration for those who are extremely gifted in teaching, speaking, writing and leadership is not bad in itself. But factions occur when people proudly perceive their leader to be superior to all other servants of the Lord. They get caught up in the man or woman, and look down on others who are not as successful. Immaturity exhibits this when it promotes a person instead of the Lord.

There is an ugly co-dependence that is created by celebrity worship. The lines between leader and Lord become blurred when followers default to deifying a gifted man or woman. It becomes cult worship when Christian celebrities are not challenged or questioned. This is a warning for mega churches. Make sure the man does not become the center of attention over Christ. The pastor is called to equip the saints and exalt the Savior, while awe is reserved for Almighty God. You help your pastor by not putting him on a pedestal. Pedestals produce pride and position a pastor with a perspective that looks down. Honor him yes, worship him no. Leaders who compete with Christ are in danger of losing God's blessing. The accolades of man are a cheap substitute for God's eternal rewards.

However, there is an effective approach to diffusing a determination to create Christian celebrities. Gifted pastor/leaders can reject a rock star status by addressing in his teachings the dangers of an increasing admiration of a man, coupled with a decreasing love of the Lord. Parishioners who worship and fear God are to first walk away from Sunday sermons in awe of God, not enamored or entertained by man. If the end game becomes engagement with a person's personality to the exclusion of eternal accountability, a destructive and dysfunctional environment is brewing. Teaching and leadership are meant to be catalysts for Christ-centric living. Wise leaders become launching pads for truth as they point people to Jesus. Therefore, do not crave becoming a Christian celebrity. Maturity means you decrease and He increases (John 3:30). Deflect any attention that is reserved for the Almighty. Authentic leaders, teachers, and pastors pour out themselves for Christ's sake. They use subtle acts of service like feeding the poor to keep them humble.

Your Master is the main attraction, so celebrate Christ through worship, prayer, Bible study, and service. He is your Christian celebrity!

JUN 28 SELF DECEPTION

> "If we claim to be without sin, we deceive ourselves and the truth is not in us.
> If we confess our sins, he is faithful and just and will forgive us our sins and purify
> us from all unrighteousness."   I JOHN 1:8-9

Self-deception is scary and subtle for it can lead people to live a lie. It feeds pride and strokes ego with a sense of superiority. You become convinced you can outsmart others and even God because you are more successful, more educated, more experienced, or more winsome and attractive. Self-deception acts like it listens to the advice of others, but in reality it has already predetermined a course of action. It only listens to what it wants to hear, so it deceives and is deceived. Ironically it does its best work with sincerity and a smile, and there is no remorse, repentance or any hint of confessing wrong. Self-deception can justify its ways with the best of them. It is always the fault of someone else. Self-deception looks for the "speck of sawdust in the eyes of others," while ignoring the "plank" in its own eye (Matthew 7:3). It does not take responsibility for its actions and attitudes. It is motivated by control of those in charge. It gets real nervous when someone gets close to the leader for fear of losing its influence. Self-deception is a sick condition. It chokes the soul. It quenches the Spirit. It strangles love. It sucks the life from relationships. Self-deception is destined to stay in control unless there is a reckoning with sin. When you face reality of sin in your life, you take the first step in slaying self-deception.

Confession of sin creates an exit strategy for self-deception. Ask God to escort self-deception out the door of your mind and heart. Invite the Holy Spirit to reveal anything unclean in your attitude and actions. Confess pride, fear, self-centeredness or self-righteousness. Start by being honest with yourself. There is a common thread in all of your relational conflicts, so start by looking in the mirror. This is hard and humbling, but it is necessary to expose the enemy of self-deception. When you move away from the darkness of self-deception, you move into the light of God's revelation and love. He shows you step by step how to die to self and live for your Savior Jesus. Self is not to be negotiated with or pampered, but is to be slain by the power of the Spirit living in you. When you die to self, self-deception no longer lives. It is deceased.

By faith, have a funeral to self and come alive for Christ. Say a prayerful eulogy over the corpse of self that buries deception, pride, lust, greed and fear. This is what takes place when you confess your sins to God. You agree with Him about the severity of sin's influence in your life and He casts your confessed sins into the depths of the sea (Micah 7:19 KJV). So, set yourself free from the bondage of sin's self-deception. Confess and repent of your sin to your Lord and Savior Jesus. Make your confession complete by asking a small community of believers whom you trust to hold you accountable.

Confession allows you to see clearly and your perception is pure. Best of all you are free indeed, because He has set you free from sin and self!

LIVE IN THE MOMENT

"...for the Mighty One has done great things for me—holy is his name."
LUKE 1:49

Master living in the moment, by God's grace it can be done. Mary did. She could have missed the Mighty One working in her presence in the present, but she didn't. She took the time to trust God with an impossible outcome. Birthing a baby conceived by the Holy Spirit challenged her categories. It forced her to ponder in the present. She chose to be with her heavenly Father in the here and now. Nothing would keep her from living with the Lord and for the Lord in this faithful moment.

She could have lived in the past, worried over the rampant rumors of her perceived unfaithfulness. She was pregnant out of wedlock. People did not understand a pregnancy performed by God without a man. She could have lived in the future paralyzed in fear over what the human father of her child might do. He might desert her. He might divorce her. He might deny her. But when all was said and done she refrained from living in the past or present, she chose to live in the moment. Mary lived in the moment because she trusted her Lord with issues out of her control. She could not control what other people thought, or what other people might do. Therefore, she drank in the present like a tall glass of homemade lemonade on a hot summer day. Living in the moment fed her faith and satisfied her soul. Her son Jesus would save the people from their sins, and He would save her. She captured His significance and Christ captured her. Indeed He is with you in the moment, so you can live in the moment.

Living in the moment is what the Lord longs for you. This is where He does His best work. He knows that living in the moment engages you with His will, as it is lived out in the present. So if you are with your children, be with them. Laugh with them, cry with them, listen to them, play with them and pray for them. Lock eyes with your little ones and be with them. Turn off your mind and heart from running ahead to other issues, problems and people. These distractions will still be standing in line for your attention when you get back to work. Value living in the moment and you will live in the moment for you do what we think is important. Indeed, technology was made for man, not man for technology. For example turn off your phone, shut down the computer, and most importantly discipline your mind to be present. Bend your mind to listen well and honor others with your purposeful presence. Your undivided attention in the moment says you love and care. Trust God with all the impossible outcomes that await you. You have this one moment and then it is gone forever. So be engaged today and be with the ones you love. Live in the moment and other things will take care of themselves. Do this one thing and you will live the life God intended for you.

Master living in the moment with the discipline and love of your Master. Seize the moment for your Savior, people and self!

J<small>UN</small>30 PART COMPANY

"Is not the whole land before you? Let's part company. If you go to the left, I'll go to the right; if you go to the right, I'll go to the left." GENESIS 13:9

Do not be afraid to part company. It may be sweet sorrow in the short term, but in the long term it's God's opportunity to mature and grow your leadership and faith. Indeed, you can be proud of your accomplishments up until now. Ninety percent of your achievements have taken place in this place, and now it is time to move on to God's new assignment. You have developed your role at work into a mature position. Now is the time for a new person to come in and build on your documented processes and procedures. Your service is for a season. Furthermore, there are not enough resources or relationships to support your God-given vision going forward. He is stirring your soul toward succession, so develop someone who can surpass you. Look for your best leader and train that person to take the mantle of management.

This is especially difficult in a family related business relationship. There are personal emotions that accompany your professional commitments. It is more complicated, as you don't want to let down family. The family members can be blood relatives, or a family of believers. So be responsible. Do not leave them high and dry. Do not burn your bridges. Leave on good terms. You will need each other one day. You want to be able to look each other in the eyes and smile at social events. Moreover, a healthy organization is unified behind one leader. The reason for possible tension and conflict is that only one leadership style can dominate. You are destined for disagreements and confusion when two people are trying to lead an enterprise with two totally different philosophies of leadership. One leadership style is autocratic; the other is collaborative. One is process driven, the other is progress driven. One has a scarcity mentality; the other has an abundance mentality. One is risk-averse; the other is a risk taker. These differing styles can compliment each other in a positive way, but only one can be in charge. Only one person can ultimately make the decisions, or there will be quarrelling and hostile conflict. Arguments will erupt among the leaders and their factions. Therefore, be prepared to prayerfully part company.

Lastly, transition requires trust. Consider making change your friend, not your enemy. Invite in the unknown as God's will to make Himself known to you in a fresh and compelling way. You will get to know Him in ways you have yet to experience. Stay unselfish by giving more than is expected. Your attitude of honor will not go unnoticed. Indeed, make sure the Lord is clearly calling you to something and you are not just running away from something or someone. Do your homework. Let this new career opportunity pull you in more, rather than you pushing to make it happen. Be patient. Prayer and patience are your greatest assets during changing times. Part company and watch Christ work. Part company and everyone wins. Part company in a process that lets God get the glory.

Part company with the relationship intact. Above all else, part company prayerfully, absent of pride and ego. E-G-O edges God out!

APPOINTMENTS FOR LOVE

"Let us go early to the vineyards to see if the vines have budded, if their blossoms have opened, and if the pomegranates are in bloom—there I will give you my love."
SONG OF SOLOMON 7:12

Many things compete with your marriage. Work, children, parents, money, hobbies, friends, volunteerism, selfish desires and life in general can masquerade as marriage competitors. So, how can you transform these competitors to your marriage, into compliments to your marriage? First, when you make marriage a priority, the other important things that clamor for your attention become secondary and supportive. This is wisdom, because marriage is not meant to get the leftovers of your life for its vitality will melt in the face of neglect. Yet, if you are intentional in your marriage appointments it will flourish with freshness. Moreover, something in your life becomes a priority when it is acknowledged and embraced by your calendar. A marriage void of calendared appointments is a candidate for indifference with intimacy. Husbands and wives need focused quantity time with each other, because quality time flows out of quantity time. Quality time is a consequence of an environment with the least distractions. Cell phones are silenced and there is a cease-fire from interruptions. Fast from e-mail, so there can be a focus on friendship. Co-existing does not create intimacy in marriage, but intentionality to get to know one another deeply does. Romance is the result of regular real time together in communication, care and understanding. Furthermore, physical intimacy between husband and wife is part of God's game plan (I Corinthians 7:3-5).

Therefore, make routine appointments to love your spouse. Pull out your calendars and create a time just for the two of you. The best gift you give to your children, next to faith in God is a healthy marriage. So, make appointments for emotional love and physical love. Emotional love may be unfiltered listening and learning about the fears and fantasies of the other. Make your spouse feel secure by being trustworthy and respectful, and listen intently to their struggles and disappointments. Secondly, fatigue and busyness are twin tyrants looming over physical love. However, you can dethrone these detractors with focused time for a husband's release and a wife's fulfillment. Romance one another with a date night, by dressing up and smelling good, as if it were a grand occasion. Woo each other with the fire and excitement of youth. Adultery is not even an after thought in an enthusiastic love life. Yes, physical intimacy needs to be planned and prepared for and let any spontaneous rendezvous be a bonus. Make sure to calendar time where you have an occasional overnight together, or a week of vacation for just the two of you. Use the calendar to create emotional and physical intimacy. The Bible teaches there is a time for everything, even a time to love (Ecclesiastes 3:8).

Lastly, be a best friend to your spouse. Together you can enjoy a hobby, read a book, or watch a movie together. Love on him or her relationally with written correspondence and acts of service, or demonstrate you love by working on a project around the house or planning the finances. Make regular relational deposits in your marriage and your bank account of intimacy will increase. Above all else, make an appointment to love God and be loved by God.

Your spouse will love you better, if he or she loves Jesus more than you. Indeed, make appointments for love and you will love!

JUL 2 REBELLIOUS CHILDREN

"Hear, O heavens! Listen, O earth! For the Lord has spoken: 'I reared children and brought them up, but they have rebelled against me.'" ISAIAH 1:2

Rebellious children can drive you to your knees for they don't seem to care or concern themselves with their parents or the things of God. It is all about them, period. Prodigal young people can keep you up at night in worry and fear. These are the same children who used to be sweet and without any negative consequence. Their compliance was stellar for the most part, and their heart was honest and open. Now everything seems closed. All communication is shut down and relegated to rare grunts. If they need something, they will break the silence momentarily, only to retreat back into their shell of secrecy. Their friends influence them more than their parents who gave them birth and brought them up in the instructions of the Lord. Why? Their friends offer them 100% acceptance, understanding and love. Pride keeps the relational gap wide, whiled humility builds bridges. Now is not the time to 'write off' your rebellious child.

Give them up to God, and pray the Lord will use Satan and sin to show them the emptiness of self-centered living, but do not shut the door on the relationship. Do whatever it takes to initiate contact and communication. Build the relationship; do not tear it down. Get to know their friends, by inviting them into your home. Go as a family to a Christ-centered counselor. Pray for a mentor to influence your young person in wisdom and respect. Do not fall into the trap of fighting rebellion with rebellion. Hardening your heart is rebellion. Not backing down is rebellion. Rejection is rebellion. Any behavior that dismisses the character and attitude of God is rebellion against God. Work with God during this rebellious season of our child, not against Him. Grow in our dependency on God and avoid blaming Him and others. Do not let your child's rebellion get the best of you, or you may become bitter and hopeless. Instead, use this time of turmoil to search your own heart. Remain a model of compliance to Christ and to the authorities in your life. Rebellion is defeated in the face of love and acceptance.

Your child will wear down from the world's antics. He or she will want to come back to a home of safety, security and acceptance. Write them when they do not write back. Call them when they do not call back. Pray for them when they are hell bent on their own. Pray for God to bring them back to Himself, no matter what it takes. This rebellious spirit is probably for a season. Pray for them to come to the end of themselves and turn to Him. Pray for them to be influenced by other God-fearing followers of Jesus. In rebellion, they are bound up. In Christ, they are set free. Rebels make great leaders for the Lord. Be patient. Pray. Accept them where they are and watch God work. His timing may take longer, but His work is thorough and worth the wait. Don't beat yourself up over your children's behavior. Allow God to love on you, so you can love on them.

Let go of your anger and accept your heavenly Father's embrace. Acceptance squashes rebellion!

BE DECISIVE

"Give us counsel, render a decision."
ISAIAH 16:3A

Decisions can be illusive, like your shadow they can haunt you from behind or they can lead you from the front. Decisions are not designed to be delayed forever, unless of course they are related to an evil or wicked act. Decisions are meant to drive you toward God's purpose and plan for your life. He allows you to make decisions that determine His future for you. He gives you the counsel and the wisdom, but you make the decision. No one else can make the decision for you, not even God. This is your responsibility and opportunity. Fear may be delaying your decision. Pride may be prolonging your decision. Lack of trust may be troubling your mind with indecision. You may be cautious because a similar experience in the past did not work out so well. But, if you delay much longer you may very well miss this window of opportunity. Indeed, you have prayed about this and there is peace. You have sought wise counsel and there is affirmation. You have exceeded the normal amount of due diligence to make an informed decision. Now is the time to decide.

Say yes or no, but do not procrastinate any longer. It is not fair to those who depend on you, nor is it fair to those who believe in you. The bottom line probably relates to trust. Can God be trusted to lead you through the implications of this decision? Can He handle the 'what ifs'? The answer, of course is yes. God will not lead you into a decision that is detrimental to His plan for your life. There will surely be bumps along the way. The bottom may fall out, but He is still faithful. It is better to be in a storm with Jesus, than on the calm shore without Him, and 'no decision' is still a decision. If you continue to be indecisive, you have decided not to move forward, but you do not have to stand still. You can take this first step and then trust God with steps two and three. Do not become overwhelmed with what might happen tomorrow. Just remain faithful today. Do your best now and trust the Lord with later.

The same holds true for others stuck in indecision. They have strung you along, way beyond what is reasonable. It is responsible for you to give them a deadline. It is bad stewardship for you to linger too long around a dead end deal. It may be time to move on and "knock the dust from your sandals" (Mark 6:11, KJV). God may very well be shutting the door because of another's inability to decide. Do not see them as the enemy because of their indecision. This may be God's protection, so be grateful for this divine delay. But now move on with Christ in quiet confidence and bold creativity. Use another's indecisiveness to propel you forward without them. God has decided what is best. Decide to believe this and trust Him with the results. A life marred in no decision is messy and going nowhere. A life mixed with wise decisions is moving forward with their heavenly Father's help. Be a bold decision maker, because you can. Align your decisions with His wisdom for He has it all figured out.

Get the facts. Review the truth. Get counsel. Pray. Then decide to decide. By faith and by the grace of God, decide. This is the best decision!

JUL 4   BLESSED NATION

"Blessed is the nation whose God is the Lord, the people he chose for his inheritance…"
PSALM 32:1

God blesses a nation because of its prayers, not its power. He blesses a nation because of its character, not its commerce. He blesses a nation because of its trust in Him, not its advanced technology. God blesses a nation because of its fear of the Lord and not its fear of man. God blesses a nation who loves God and expresses that love in caring for the impoverished and diseased. God blesses a nation because of His church and not the size of its economy. Prosperity may be the result of a God-fearing nation, but it is not the cause. People believe in God when they get enough of themselves and realize there has to be more to this life than meeting their every need. God blesses a nation when individuals gather corporately in vibrant Christian worship, and the church is God's means to awaken a nation. Nations who try to control the church lose God's blessing. God's blessing cannot be governed. Every time government intercedes to manage faith, the faithful become more marginalized. Countries that restrict church competition and rely on a state church monopoly miss the mark. The church is meant to be released to restore the ravished character of culture. Christians are 'salt and light' (Matthew 5:13-14) in the middle of thirsty and dark nations. When believers gather together in a bond of love, they create a thirst for righteousness and shed light on the ways of the Lord.

Nations are wise who encourage competition among churches. Freedom of religion feeds faithfulness to God. God expects His church to grow and engage with the culture. This is how He changes a nation. When countries have church choices, they can compare what is best for their families. A church that drifts into irrelevance and isolation is of little concern to Satan. He wants religion to come across as ambiguous and antiquated. However, churches who are alive and well serve a mighty and compassionate Christ. These types of trusting institutions make a difference in their communities. A church that is growing and alive becomes a catalyst for good things. Indeed, God blesses nations where the church is allowed to compete. Stewardship trumps entitlement. Sick churches are not kept alive by outside funding. They either change or close. God blesses nations when His bride's worship is alive, engaging and relevant.

Therefore, avoid churches where membership is just a status symbol. Attend church where God is loved and feared, and worship where you see the Lord high and lifted up. Soak up the teachings of the Bible that transform your life. Band together with a group of believers who are disciples and who disciple others in the faith. Choose a body of believers where the character lessons you teach your children at home converge with their small group lessons on Sunday. If church is not working for you, then prayerfully find one that works best in this season of life.

God blesses nations who humbly seek Him, "…if my people, who are called by my name, will humble themselves and pray and seek my face and turn from their wicked ways, then will I hear from heaven and will forgive their sin and will heal their land" (2 Chronicles 7:14)!

SENSELESS ADVICE

"The officials of Zoan are nothing but fools; the wise counselors of Pharaoh give senseless advice. How can you say to Pharaoh, 'I am one of the wise men, a disciple of the ancient kings?' " ISAIAH 19:11

Be careful where you look for advice by avoiding senseless sources. If you want good advice about marriage, then seek out couples with a track record of love and respect for one another. Senseless suggestions, like living together prior to marriage need to be rejected and dismissed. If you want smart advice about business, then seek out a man or woman who builds a business with integrity. Stay away from business people who rely on senseless shortcuts to get short-term results. If your goal is wise stewardship of finances, then engage with those who are experts in earthly and eternal investments. Fend off financial charlatans, whose promise of get rich quick is senseless salesmanship.

Moreover, make sure you surround yourself with people who will tell you what you need to hear, not necessarily what you want to hear. Furthermore, people will feed your ego if you let them, so give the strokes to your Savior, before you start thinking you are something special apart from Him. You are not God's gift to the world. Jesus is. If you look long and hard enough you may eventually find those who side with your point of view, but agreement does not guarantee wisdom. Instead, invite unbiased, objective, and Bible-based advice. Follow leaders who follow wise advice. Flee from leaders who follow foolish and senseless advice. If your pastor, ministry leader, government official, or company president is heeding senseless advice, then there is a problem. It may be simmering under the surface, but there are issues ready to unravel. Don't be naïve and think things are all right. Things are not okay, and they will not get better until senseless advisors are replaced with wise and courageous ones. Leaders are a product of those with whom they are surrounded. So look at the character and competence of those who accompany the authorities in your life, for they are a mirror image of their advisors.

Things will not change until the board changes, the cabinet changes, the executive coach changes, or the management team changes. The principle of "you are who you listen to" is timeless and true. Therefore, pray for your leaders to surround themselves with men and women full of truth and wisdom. Trust the Lord for bold counselors who are not afraid to respectfully speak with courage and conviction. Ask God for advisors who are willing to give up their positions for the sake of principled behavior and beliefs. Someone who always agrees with you is a dispenser of senseless advice. Instead, gather around you those who ask the hard questions, and then listen with a teachable heart. Be willing to change your mind as you glean more accurate information. Wisdom is the ability to understand differing perspectives and then incorporate them into the best option and solution. This of course is all assimilated through prayer and being still before God. His advice is all-encompassing and eternally motivated.

The Holy Spirit is your highest and best counselor. Go to Him often for validation, revelation, and eternal advice!

JUL 6   A BEAUTIFUL MIND

"You will keep in perfect peace him whose mind is steadfast, because he trusts in you."
ISAIAH 26:3

A beautiful mind believes God for there is fidelity of faith that flows from a mind focused on the Lord. It is steadfast on its Savior because it trusts in Him. Contrary is an ugly mind conflicted and unsure. Its focus fluctuates between fear and faith. In an ugly mind there is a battle that fatigues faithfulness to the point of giving up. The mind's eye can become trapped in the temporal and lose its ability to trust God. This is tragic and terrifying for those who become mind numbing to the things of God. Depart from this double-mindedness (James 1:8), or you will lose heart and fracture your faith.

The mind is a beautiful thing if it is focused properly, but it can be disturbing and destructive when it loses perspective. The mind can play tricks on you, because Satan has his mind games. He tries to draw you in with his allure, but his thoughts are a farce and lead to faithless living. Therefore, ground your intellectual stamina in God so you can reject Satan's lies. Reject his temptation to remain restless for you can rest in peace because the 'Prince of Peace' reigns over your life. Reject Satan's leading into lust because you are loved by the everlasting love of your heavenly Father. Moreover, fill your mind with good thoughts... "Finally, brothers, whatever is true, whatever is noble, whatever is right, whatever is pure, whatever is lovely, whatever is admirable—if anything is excellent or praiseworthy—think about such things." (Philippians 4:8)

Good thoughts facilitate faith and God thoughts bring about a beautiful mind. A mind needs to be stretched like a heart needs to be exercised. An unused mind is a waste that atrophies and becomes ugly. It is a waste of time to have an unengaged mind. Mindless activity will get you into trouble. Therefore, think. Be a thinker and not just a doer. Engage your mind with large thoughts about the Lord. Reflect on His righteousness and the grandeur of His glory. Get beyond trivial thoughts to thoughts that trust in God. The quality of your life follows the quality of your thoughts. Classical books provide fertile soil for great thinking, the Bible not withstanding. Great thinkers help you develop disciplined thinking. Make it a goal to read, dialogue and debate with wise thinkers. This will help you think well. It is a beautiful thing to behold a mature mind. A messy mind never matures beyond just getting by. Therefore, discipline your mind. Stretch your mind. But keep trust in the Lord 'top of mind.' Trust in God is your lightening rod for wise thinking. Legalism leads to non-thinking and little faith. Your mind becomes fertile for deception without trust in the Lord. Therefore allow trust to become the scope in which your mind's eye gazes, and it will see perfect peace. The filter of faith massages your mind with God's fingers of love, joy and hope.

The mind of Christ is a lifetime of study that beautifies your thinking. A beautiful mind trusts and rests in the Lord!

UNWISE ARGUMENT

"Woe to him who quarrels with his Maker, to him who is but a potsherd among the potsherds on the ground. Does the clay say to the potter, 'What are you making?' Does your work say, 'He has no hands?' " ISAIAH 45:9

Do not argue with the Almighty, for it is unwise and unproductive. Debating Deity is a vain and proud proposition. How could you know better than God what's best? People possess a fraction of all knowledge; He owns all knowledge. Your perspective is limited at best; His view is all encompassing. You are the created; He is the Creator. You are worshippers; He is worshipped. You pray; He answers prayer. You receive grace; He gives grace. You sin; He forgives. You are human; He is God. Indeed, God does not mind sincere dialogue that seeks to understand. Questions regarding clarity of purpose and obedience are okay with Him. However, He rejects exerting energy around arguing with obvious obedience to His commands.

The best way to relate to God is with agreement instead of argument. Agree with Him about who you are, as He has made and gifted you uniquely. You do not need to be anyone else other than you. You will stay frustrated trying to fashion your life after someone else's. Let others inspire you to become better, but do not be overwhelmed by abilities. God may have given them a larger capacity for activities and relationships. Be who God wants you to be and do not argue with Him about not having the opportunities afforded to others. He knows what is best for you. Wouldn't you rather have time to enjoy your family than to make 30% more income? Or even double your salary? An increase in pay or a move to another city is not worth neglecting your family.

You may argue with God and even get your way, but there is a price to pay. Guilt, broken relationships, hurt, and anger are not worth the trouble. Maneuvering around your Maker to get something may come back to haunt you. Many times, arguing means you are not getting your way. Therefore, call a time-out. Take a prayerful pause and align your way with His. Arguments can be resolved with alignment of purpose. Stay true to His call on your life, take responsibility, and do not argue with God or blame others. You have an opportunity to deepen your faith during this time of uncertainty. Cling to your Savior for affirmation and direction. Accept the truth instead of resisting reality. God is in control and He can be trusted. He will send you the relationships and resources needed to accomplish His will. The enemy tempts, so debate the devil with God's word, while aligning with the Almighty's purpose for your life. Choose acceptance of God's will over argument. Acceptance allows you to channel your energy toward eternal matters.

Argue less and accept more. This is wise and acceptable to the Almighty. No need to argue!

HEAVEN'S HANDPRINTS

"See, I have engraved you on the palms of my hands, your walls are ever before me."
Isaiah 49:16

You are marked by God's handprints; from head to toe He has identified you with Himself. His hands molded you and made you into who you are. His hands are so enormous that He has engraved everyone into His palm. Like a life-sized dye cast, He has shaped your soul. This is why you desperately need His tender touch. You need the hand of God to reshape you daily into His original design and purpose. The hand of God never changes, but you do. You lose the shape of our Savior and forget who you are; a child of the King, forgiven, guiltless and grace-filled. You are free to forgive and set loose to serve others. He has engraved your name into His hand, never to be removed or soiled. Indeed, His hand is your protector.

Satan and his schemes must past through the hand of your heavenly Father to get to you. It doesn't mean you are always shielded from Satan, but it does mean you still rest in the Lord's care even in the middle of chaos. Jesus said, "I give them eternal life, and they shall never perish; no one can snatch them out of my hand. My Father, who has given them to me, is greater than all; no one can snatch them out of my Father's hand. I and the Father are one" (John 10:28-30). Therefore, allow your heavenly Father to hold you with His caressing hands of compassion. There is nothing more reassuring than the loving embrace of the Lord. His hands will not crush you, but will comfort you in your time of struggle. The hand of the Lord is an extension of His everlasting love. Peace and security are the residuals, which stay with you after you have been handled by God. His hands handle you, so you can handle others.

Everyday you meet people who are recipients of your handprints. You can extend open hands of acceptance or closed hands of rejection. You can embrace others with hands of understanding, or distance yourself with hands of shallow assumption. You can offer a helping hand of service, or expect other hands to serve you. Just as the hands of your heavenly Father mark you, so you mark others. Your spouse and children are covered in your handprints. They can be healthy handprints or handprints of emotional baggage and spiritual confusion. Hold them up close and help them feel your love and acceptance. Be vulnerable and truthful. Become open-handed about your dreams and your fears. A closed-fisted life is insecure, distrusting and distant. An open-handed life is secure, trusting and intimate. Handle others as your heavenly Father handles you, because you are a product of His grace.

See the scars from the unjust nails in your Savior's hands. See your undeserving self in your Savior's hand. His hands are your salvation!

> "This is what the Lord says: 'Maintain justice and do what is right, for my salvation is close at hand and my righteousness will soon be revealed.' " ISAIAH 56:1

Do the right thing, because you can't go wrong by doing what's right. The right choice may not be the easiest choice, but it will result in what's best. It is tempting to bypass what's right for what's convenient or expedient. However, convenience and expedience can get you into trouble if they become an excuse for not doing the right thing. The right thing may ruffle some feathers and cause you short-term suffering. Some people may reject you for doing what's right. Some people may avoid you, because your right choices are a reminder of their wrong ones. When you choose to do the right thing, you eliminate other unseemly options. This protects you from a series of unwise relationships. If you choose to hang out with those who have no spiritual aspirations, then you will find yourself indifferent to the things of God.

If your most influential relationship is bored with God, then boredom will seduce you over time as well. Investing in unhealthy relationships is not the right thing to do. Your parents and your friends have warned you not to go down this road of relational recklessness. You can still do the right thing by breaking off the relationship and seeking God for His best. His best is 100 times better than settling for someone who makes you feel alive without a firm foundation of faith. Be careful with whom you entrust your emotions. Your affections are not to be given away indiscriminately. The right thing is to first set your affections above, where Christ sits at the right hand of God (Colossians 3:1-2, KJV). Then trust Him as you dispense your desires to those worthy and who have your best interests in mind.

Doing the right thing is a matter of trust. Can God be trusted with the results of your right decisions? Yes, however you are on your own when you dismiss the wise counsel of those who really care. If you choose to settle for something less than best, then your outcomes will erode. To choose what's good over what's best is not the right thing. Indeed, God can be trusted with what happens when you break off a less than best relationship. He has someone better who will lift you up spiritually and not drag you down. So do the right thing and trust God with the results. It may very well cost you time and money, but what value can you place on living with no regrets? If it is a financial obligation, then take the high road and do what is more expensive though not expedient. Others may pressure you not to do the right thing, because their definition of right and wrong is diluted. So seek His God's definition of what's right. Do not be intimidated by others who are uncomfortable with your right choices. Choose right and trust God. Moreover, keep your attitude free from arrogance. Your right choices do not make you spiritually superior.

So do the right thing because it is the right thing to do with and attitude of humility, grace and patience. You can't go wrong doing what's right!

J<small>UL</small>10 DIVINE DIRECTION

"I know, O Lord, that a man's life is not his own; it is not for man to direct his steps."
JEREMIAH 10:23

Your life is not you own for you have been bought with a price. Your freedom was purchased by Jesus' sacrificial blood. He saved you from hell, sin and death. A great exchange took place when you believed in Jesus. What's yours became His and what's His became yours. The life of Christ became your life, "For you died, and your life is now hidden with Christ in God. When Christ, who is your life, appears, then you also will appear with him in glory" (Colossians 3:3-4). It is not your life to define, but His. God's ownership is the place to start defining your true self. Indeed, self-ownership can be reckless and unpredictable but God's ownership is dependable and predicated on His promises. The Bible is a treasure trove of how to define yourself. Scripture gives you a family tree of faith so you can trace back your religious roots. You are God's accepted child, though you suffer rejection from others you can cherish and enjoy daily acceptance from Jesus. He takes care of His own and He does not discard the disobedient to the trash heap of rejection. Your mistakes create an opportunity for Him to affirm His acceptance. There are still consequences to your sin, but He is always available to receive you back.

Moreover, He directs His own. His desire is for you to understand and follow His plan for your life. Praise God it is a step-by-step process and He directs your steps. Some days you may feel like you take three steps forward and two steps back, but do not be discouraged or dismayed. God is still directing your steps. Though tedious and laborious at times, the Lord leads you in lock step with Him. Walking in His steps is the wise way to walk. Do not run ahead thinking you have to set a record for speed or quickness. In fact, fast steps may cause you to back track and have to learn all over again what God was trying to teach you before you sped ahead. Walk patiently with Him and watch Him work. The Holy Spirit is your guide for instruction in His word and exercise in faith. Learn how to let the Lord direct your steps. Prayerfully listen to the quiet prompting from His spirit. Stop when you need to stop, speed up when you need to speed up and slow down when you need to slow down.

God directs the steps of a submitted and surrendered man or woman. Stubbornness is hard to direct and pride resists direction. Independence attempts to self-direct, so listen to your spouse or close friend. He may speak His next steps through them. Self-direction is like traveling alone to a new destination without a map or an orientation of your surroundings. It is futile and frustrating and leads to a fatalistic future. On the contrary, God-directed steps are a paragon for peace. You can rest in His far-reaching perspective and other worldly wisdom. He gives divine directions that determine His will for your life. Step by step He leads you. You can trust that His way, as the best way. Watch Him work in spite of adversity and lack of resources. Stay in step with your Savior and allow your Maker to define your moves.

Walking with the Lord is the wisest way to walk. Resist directing your own steps and rest in your walk with Him!

WORTHY WORDS

"Therefore this is what the Lord says: 'If you repent, I will restore you that you may serve me; if you utter worthy, not worthless, words, you will be my spokesman. Let this people turn to you, but you must not turn to them.' " JEREMIAH 15:19

Persuasive people can pour on the word. Like an avalanche of ice and snow, they bury you with spectacular speech. So be careful with persuasive people. They can talk themselves and others into just about anything. However, their words become worthless when their behavior does not back up their promises. Certainly everyone struggles with promising more than can be delivered, but a pattern of broken promises is suspect and needs accountability. Words become worthless when they are not backed up by noble character. Worthy words may be few, but that's ok if they get results.

It is much better to engage with someone who promises little, but delivers much. This person is wise to manage expectations well. However, avoid people who talk a lot and do little. Surround yourself with those whose words may be few, but whose actions far exceed your expectations. You do not have to impress people with persuasive speech that is void of substance. Serve them instead and let your words become a bonus. Make it your goal to value others more than they value you. Worthy words extend sincere and meaningful compliments for the inspiration of the individual. Worthless words praise others with the goal of getting them to act a certain way. Worthless words ring hollow and do more harm than good. Therefore, be a person who dispenses worthy words of wisdom. If you have a persuasive personality, be careful to place others before yourself. You will be tempted to manipulate others for your own needs instead of serving them at their point of need. Be very cautious how you use Christ's name to validate your decisions. Indiscreetly tossing around phrases like, "The Lord said," or "The Lord told me" is treading on the turf of worthless words. Make sure your motive doesn't degrade into using God-speech to get your way. These are the worst kind of worthless words.

Moreover, check your speech often. Do an audit of the tone and timing of your truth telling. Words can become worthless, even when they represent truth. People will not receive your words if they cannot overcome the way you give your words. Be patient, particularly if you are a discerning person. You have the ability to quickly size up people and situations. But, just because you immediately see it, does not mean it is the right time to say it. Indeed, be wise to communicate your insights with a gracious tone at a time of high receptivity. Anger is not the best environment to extend new insights. "I told you so" is not an attitude that builds rapport and invites your instruction. Look for teachable and tension free moments to share truth. Be prayerful with your words. Repent of judgmental gestures and ungracious goads.

Let Jesus lead you in what to say and how to say it. These are worthy words. These are words the Lord will use to carry out His will. God persuades people through prayerfully placed words!

"A shoot will come up from the stump of Jesse: from his roots a Branch will bear fruit. The Spirit of the Lord will rest on him—the Spirit of wisdom and understanding, the Spirit of counsel and of power, the Spirit of knowledge and of the fear of the Lord—and he will delight in the fear of the Lord." I<small>SAIAH</small> 11:1-3<small>A</small>

God provides spiritual resources for his children. The same spirit of the Lord that rested on Jesus is the one who indwells His followers, "You, however, are controlled not by the sinful nature but by the Spirit, if the Spirit of God lives in you. And if anyone does not have the Spirit of Christ, he does not belong to Christ" (Romans 8:9). The Holy Spirit provides you with all the spiritual resources needed to carry out His will. You need wisdom; He provides it. You need understanding; He provides it. You need counsel; He provides it. You need power; He provides it. You need knowledge; He provides it. You need grace; He provides it. However, resources without reception result in nothing. A parent can offer their daughter shopping, but if she chooses to attend a movie with her friend instead, she will miss her mom or dad buying her some cute clothes. God offers you His resources in a moment in time; so don't be so wrapped up in your plan that you miss His provision.

Everyday the resources you need are a prayer away. Wisdom is there for the asking. Understanding is there for the asking. Counsel is there for the asking. The same Spirit of God that empowered Jesus (Luke 4:18) does the same for you. The Spirit of the living God is at your beckoned call to give you good gifts. When Jesus left the Holy Spirit, He left you a comforter. Jesus is your friend and Savior. God is your father and Lord. The Holy Spirit is your guide and convincer. He will guide you in truth and righteousness. You cannot see the Spirit of God, but you can experience His effects (John 3:8). The Spirit is what puts a check in your spirit; so do not relegate Him to some obscure corner of your life just because you do not totally understand Him. The Spirit is what releases your spirit, so invite the Holy Spirit to congeal with your spirit.

The fruit of the Spirit will flow from your life, as He is unleashed. Love, joy, peace, patience, kindness, goodness, faithfulness, gentleness and self-control are the fruit-bearing consequences of the Holy Spirit's control. Your relationship with your heavenly Father is not complete without your filling of the Holy Spirit, "Don't drink too much wine. That cheapens your life. Drink the Spirit of God, huge draughts of him" (Ephesians 5:18, The Message). This is where your unremarkable religion can become a rejuvenated relationship. If your relationship with God is in a rut, then let the Holy Spirit fall fresh on your life. Fear God and allow the fruit of the Spirit to mold your character. Be accountable to fruit inspectors in your life. Let the Lord, and more mature friends help you purge back fruitless attitudes and actions (John 15:2).

As the fruit of the Spirit makes its way through your character allow His gifts to develop and come to full fruition. If you are gifted to teach, teach. If you are gifted to write, write. If you are gifted to lead, lead. If you are gifted to give, give. The Spirit of the Lord that rested on Jesus resources you!

"The apostles gathered around Jesus and reported to him all they had done and taught. Then, because so many people were coming and going that they did not even have a chance to eat, he said to them, 'Come with me by yourselves to a quiet place and get some rest.' So they went away by themselves in a boat to a solitary place." MARK 6:30-32

Wise leaders lead their team (and/or family) into a time of rest. They find a quiet place and rest together. Rest is required after extreme busyness, because your spirit begins to rebel against the hustle and bustle. The joy of service for God starts to fade and people become a drain rather than a blessing. It is time to break away to a solitary place for you cannot continue at a break-neck pace. It is unrealistic and borders on tempting God, even Jesus took a break. If you continually push yourself and others, you will eventually lose all energy and perspective. A driven heart becomes a judgmental heart. You begin to look down on people because they are not pulling their weight. Your joy is replaced with jaded criticism. You feel you are the only one who is really committed. Your peers have become slackers in your mind. Be careful; you may be serving out of your own strength and not the Spirit's. It is the Holy Spirit that sustains you over the long haul. Wise leaders understand the danger of an unsustainable schedule. You begin to sacrifice relationships in order to reach unrealistic goals.

Indeed, God gives goals as a guide and motivation, but do not be driven by the goal. Rather, be lead by the Holy Spirit so the goal does not become your God. Unchecked goal setting can lead you down the path of disappointment and disillusionment, so take time to develop the team and watch God work through them way beyond your capacity. Some of your team development, however, comes in quiet places. Find a quiet spot and calendar a time today for you and your team. They desperately need this enrichment both personally and professionally, without a retreat they will be unable to advance. Some may be on the verge of burnout or quitting because of discouragement. Solitary places allow you and your team to recalibrate with the vision, values and mission of the organization. Quiet times together build camaraderie and trust. A retreat is an investment; by taking time to pause you are able to continue with more effectiveness and efficiency. A quiet place is an opportunity to get on the same page with God, as your soul is refreshed and replenished. The wise words of Scripture leap from the pages and lodge in the crevices of your heart and mind.

A retreat into a place of solitude is an exercise of faith. You trust that routine matters will be taken care of in your absence. You believe the financial investment will return exponentially in lower employee turnover and increased productivity. A quiet place is ideal for relational vigor to erupt. Smooth relationships go a long way toward avoiding future issues and solving current problems. So retreat regularly for your sake and sanity, and retreat for the morale of the team. You hear more clearly when it is quiet. Your comprehension expands. Your body rests and your soul is renewed. A solitary place provides strength and stamina to finish well.

Sometimes the most spiritual thing you can do is rest in a quiet place!

JUL 14 REST FROM WORK

"There remains, then, a Sabbath-rest for the people of God; for anyone who enters God's rest also rests from his own work, just as God did from his. Let us, therefore, make every effort to enter that rest, so that no one will fall by following their example of disobedience."
HEBREWS 4:9-11

It is hard for some people to rest from their work. They love their work, enjoy their work and may even worship their work. Hard, smart and productive work is good, but worshiping work is bad. It is reckless and leads to ruin. It may be relational ruin, physical ruin or even financial ruin. But work that is worshipped gets out of hand quickly. There is only one that deserves worship and that is God. It is good to be proud of your work with pure motivation and to produce quality, but do not allow work to become an end in itself. Your true identity does not come from work, if so you are positioned for a roller coaster ride of emotion. One day you will feel secure and another day you will be swept away by insecurity.

As a follower of Christ, your identity is found in Him. This is one reason why rest from work is vital. When you work all the time, you tend to drift from your moorings of faith in Christ to faith in yourself. It becomes a trust issue, 'Can God be trusted for me to rest from my work?' Of course He can handle the work that remains, as He divinely redeems the time of your limited work, and produces more lasting results. Results that will last longer than if you worked all the time. After all, you are His workmanship in Christ Jesus. When you take the time to cease working, it allows God to accelerate His work on you. Some of God's best work takes place when you don't work. He works better when you don't. His work is a work of grace and it is a beautiful site to behold, so enjoy your Sabbath rest as He works on your heart. Allow Him to draw you to Himself, so when you go back to work you are refreshed and revitalized!

There is a trap to avoid as you take a break from work and enter into God's Sabbath rest. You can physically be away from work and still be at work mentally, so free your mind from this unfair activity. Do not make your mind jealous over your body's freedom from work. Rest your thoughts from work and you will discover your thinking is more robust and innovative when you reengage in your work. During your Sabbath rest, shift your thinking to the bigger thoughts of God and His plan. Superimpose simple faith in Him to the complex issues that are assaulting your rest. Your mind, body, and emotions are all part of your Sabbath rest. If your Sabbath rest from work involves people, then relate to them with relevance and relationship. Let them see the sincerity of your involved presence. Do not act like you wish you were somewhere else. Your rest is a time for you to relate the ways of God to others. Your life is a testament to God's faithfulness. Let others read it up close and personal. Your Sabbath rest can be a catalyst for others to reengage with God. Set the example and watch others follow. Your Sabbath rest gives others permission to do the same. It is worth it to enter into God's rest. It is not always easy to get there, but once you arrive it is well worth the effort.

His rest ignites your obedience and trust. So, rest from work and rest in Him. Then watch your work become better!

SABBATH OBSERVED

"Observe the Sabbath, because it is holy to you. Anyone who desecrates it must be put to death; whoever does any work on that day must be cut off from his people. For six days, work is to be done, but the seventh day is a Sabbath of rest, holy to the Lord. Whoever does any work on the Sabbath day must be put to death." E<small>XODUS</small> 31:14-15

Observation of a Sabbath is required for the follower of Christ. This rest and reflection on God is recognized as Sunday, the first day of the week. It is down time from work time. God requires it, because He knows your need for Him and your need to take a break from labor and earning money. Obsession with work and making money leaves no time for God and meaningful relationships. If you want to guarantee frustration, then spend all of your time working. You will become frustrated, and so will those around you. Or, if you spend all your time in leisure you will miss God's best. Work gives you the perspective to appreciate leisure. Leisure without work is like food without taste. Either of these extremes will lead you to a meaningless life.

Only when you are engaged with God in regular Sabbath times can you truly understand your life role. God is serious about being the focus of His Sabbath. This is not an option for Christians. Neglect of the Sabbath may at first seem like a little indiscretion. But over time if you are not intentional in your Sabbath experience it erodes into endless activity or mindless monotony. Indeed, beware of an outward observance, but an inward neglect of the Sabbath. If your mind is preoccupied with work that needs to get done, then you are defeating the Sabbath purpose. Do not use this pause in your week to create more work or worry about current work.

It comes down to trust in God. Can God take care of my work in six days if I chose to aggressively observe His Sabbath? This of course is a rhetorical question. The answer is yes. The reality is that He will accomplish much more in six days and a Sabbath than your efforts could ever attain outside of His game plan. God can be trusted because He made up the system. So, use your Sabbath time to disengage with the good and the bad. Focus on God, fear Him, love Him, worship Him and adore Him. Use this time to know Him, learn about Him and enjoy Him. Sabbath is holy to the Lord. Societies who ignore the Sabbath cease to have moral authority. There is no lasting appeal to a culture that slaves night and day for money. A life that works all the time is unattractive. Ironically, work is overrated and Jesus is underrated. Reverse their priority. Place Christ at the forefront of your Sabbath experience. Rest in Him, and rest with those who love Him. Sabbath observance is an eternal investment that keeps on giving way beyond your lifetime. Unrestricted busyness is a curse. It should be pitied, not admired. Break the chains of the bondage of busyness, and replace them with the freedom of resting in Christ.

It is holy to you and it is holy to Him. Therefore, rest with Him and reflect on His faithfulness!

J<small>UL</small>16 RESPONSIVE HEART

"Because your heart was responsive and you humbled yourself before the Lord when you heard what I have spoken against this place and its people, that they would become accursed and laid waste, and because you tore your robes and wept in my presence, I have heard you, declares the Lord."   2 KINGS 22:19

God responds well to a responsive and humble heart. It is guaranteed an audience with the Almighty. His heart is drawn to humility and commitment to obedience. He knows a heart responsive can be trusted with His truth. So when He finds someone responsive to righteousness, He has found someone who can be entrusted with His blessing. A responsive heart is teachable, tender to truth, and quick to obey. It is opposite of a hard heart. A hard heart stews in the juices of sin, while a responsive heart flees from sin's appearance. A responsive heart is action-oriented and chooses to change for good. You may have an attitude of distrust or anger, but the Lord's conviction penetrates your spirit. Instead of making excuses for this unacceptable behavior, a responsive heart seeks to become trusting and forgiving.

God and godly influences are constantly suggesting, teaching, convicting and prodding you to conform to the character of Christ. His Word speaks to your heart, and then your life responds back to Him with appropriate attitudes and actions. Therefore, living for Jesus is an act of worship. Your responsiveness to truth is a testimony of the living God. As you obey God, others are drawn to you and Him. This is a wise habit to model for your children. If you can impart to them a tender and responsive heart to God at an early age you have done them a great favor. Start young while the things of God are bigger than life. A youthful and responsive heart toward God has a better chance of becoming a responsive heart toward God during adulthood.

Lastly respond and remove any other affections that compete with Christ. If money drives your behavior, then put it in its proper place through generosity. If work is your worship, then calendar time for rest and find your security in your Savior. If television or the internet is your obsession, then unplug them for a season. Fast from e-mail, voicemail and meetings for a period of time and fill the void with quiet reflection around a responsive heart toward the Lord. Activity and noise can numb your sensitivity to the Holy Spirit's leadership. Therefore, seek to do less and trust God and others with what still needs attention. Others can take care of these issues, but you are the only one who can manage your heart. An unresponsive heart will suffer from spiritual blockage and eventually shut down. Exercise it well by responding to the things of God. He is looking for humble hearts to invigorate with His wisdom and discernment. Stay responsive to your heavenly Father, and watch in awe as He quietly, boldly and lovingly responds back to you.

A responsive heart to God is quick to obey Him and slow to sin!

RESTING PLACE

"God will speak to this people, to whom he said, 'This is the resting place, let the weary rest; and, 'This is the place of repose'—but they would not listen." ISAIAH 28:11B-12

Everyone needs a place to rest, rejuvenate, and restore their soul. A soul without rest is vulnerable to doubt, disease, and dread. Without soul care, you risk being ineffective for the long term. So, allow your soul to catch up with your activity through rest. A restless soul loses hope and perspective. So stop right now and take an audit of your soul. Is it strung out and anxious? If so, rearrange your schedule for rest before it rearranges you. A non-restful pace is unsustainable, and a restful place is necessary to persevere. Do not fall for the false feeling that activity somehow equals progress or success. Without rest you are going nowhere fast. If you intensify the pace, you are going nowhere faster.

Rest allows you to recalibrate your priorities and replenish your cistern of creativity. Your work rhythms may require a day with no scheduled appointments. Indeed, each resting places look different depending on your need. For example your resting place may be on the quiet screened porch, with a cup of coffee and a good book in hand. For someone else a resting place may be on a comfortable couch, napping while a steady rain pelts the rooftop in a seductive sequence. It can be in the park walking with your best friend, taking a secluded drive in the countryside or adventuring through an exploration of the great Northwest. Whether it is, the beach, the mountains or watching a good movie, make time to engage with your resting place. God speaks to you in your place of rest. This is one of His favorite spots to shape your soul.

Furthermore your resting place allows you to resist temptation. Fatigue causes you to stumble and fall along through life; if you are working through exhaustion you may be missing God. A lethargic life struggles to listen to the Lord and a heart worn down from weariness has a hard time hearing His voice. A depleted spirit is not the right condition for discernment and decision-making during duress can be dreadful. Therefore, go away to a resting place. Find God and find yourself under the canopy of His creation. A resting place is your protection from yourself, from evil influences and from losing perspective. Above all else, your resting place reveals God in refreshing way. His program takes on priority in His place of rest. Your confidence is resurrected. Your trust takes on a new level of intensity. Your patience gains a deeper understanding in what it means to 'wait on the Lord'. A resting place is for your sake and His. It is necessary to experience God's very best for you and your family. Discover your resting place in prayer and go there often. Repentance follows rest and robust relationships result from rest.

Your best and most creative ideas emerge from idle meditation on your Master. Wisdom resides in rest!

JUL 18 CLEAR MINDED

"You will keep him in perfect peace, Whose mind is stayed on You,
Because he trusts in You."   ISAIAH 26:3 (NKJV)

A clear mind promotes creativity, but cluttered mind clings to status quo. The mind is like the 'inbox' a computer. It can fill up really fast with annoying spam in the form of the worries of this world, or it can paralyze you with people whose requests exceed your capacity to respond. An unfiltered mind will stress out under the bombardment of information and invitations for action. There has to be a process to off load lingering 'action items' or you will be crushed under the influence of hyperactivity. If your mind remains flooded with a foray of items crying for attention, then your brain may default into a fetal position. Your 'hard drive' of sound thinking may crash. Pace yourself and allow most things to freely flow from your head to the 'trash bin' of trust.

Trust that God will take care of those things you do not have the time or the energy to tackle. You cannot be everywhere, do everything or please everybody. Indeed, a tired mind is set up for temptation. Fatigued thinking is irrational and unprepared. It limps along trying to catch up, while losing ground all the while. This is unfair to the stewardship of your relationships and dangerous to your well-being. Moreover, the ability to think clearly is a pipeline for the Holy Spirit to connect with your head and heart. God's spirit roams freely in an uncluttered and clean mind. It is here that innovation is born and the genesis of new ideas is birthed. So, be intentional about doing a faith flush on your thinking. Drive away the demons that play 'mind games' of fear and over commitment, and rely more on the wisdom of God and less on the cleverness of man.

Indeed, a person thinking clearly is a strong candidate for peace of mind. A person who gets quiet before the Lord will clear his mind in holy harmony with its Maker. There is a transaction and transformation that takes place in prayer. There is a transaction of trust that takes the pressure off the one offering the prayers. And the transformation of the Holy Spirit deletes worry and sin from the heavy-hearted and the high-minded. Prayer transforms a racing mind to one of reflection and recalibration with what really matters. Prayer reboots your life operating system to align with His and positions you for a cleansed mind. It is in the presence of Christ that priorities come into focus. You are 'kept' by the object of your affection. The Lord will keep you in perfect peace, because you trust in Him. He will give you the peace of mind to carry on. He will give you the patience to 'mind your own business.' He will give you the courage and the right spirit to 'speak your mind.' Therefore, keep 'top of mind' trust in your Savior and Lord. Allow

His creativity to flood your unfettered mind. A mind submitted to its Master will serve Him well. A mind created, crafted and kept by Christ is free and clear!

COVENANT EYES

"I made a covenant with my eyes not to look lustfully at a girl."
JOB 31:1

Pure eyes are a priority for a disciple of Jesus Christ. Eyes are highly regarded because they can be an evangelist for good or bad. When locked onto lust they are relentless in their pursuit of sin. Like a heat-seeking missile, they will accelerate their course until they reach its destructive destination. Eyes are like a missile, which need guidance from God, instead of a hot heart. Misguided eyes can easily choose the path of pornography become married to their emotional impulses. Misguided eyes can lead a person to be so preoccupied with destructive behavior that he or she becomes an embarrassment to themselves and a disgrace to others.

God takes seriously the stewardship of sight, but like any of His great blessings, eyes are meant for good. It is good to gaze at God's creation in all of its splendor and glory. How beautiful is the rush of a crystal clear waterfall; the intensity of it tumbling over moss-covered rocks into a quiet reflection pool at the bottom of its crashing course. This is a magnificent expression of our eyesight. Eyes are meant to enjoy beauty and not exploit it. If you have an eye for art and interior design, you are blessed indeed. God has given you perspective and creativity that most lack. Moreover, do not expose your eyes to everything. Of course, they cannot be sheltered from all sin. Eyes are not designed to be a recluse from the world. However, eyes are meant to be respectful of their Creator. Eyes are avenues for good or bad, Jesus said, "The eye is the lamp of the body. If your eyes are good, your whole body will be full of light" (Matthew 6:22).

When you covenant with your eyes, you covenant with your Creator. Your Creator God longs to guide your eyes, so trust as you follow God with your eyes. He is a guide who leads with caution and adventure. He will guide you toward love instead of lust. He will guide you into contentment instead of discontentment. When you see the stuff of others, you will thank God on their behalf and not covet with your eyes. He will guide you into generosity instead of greed. The more you have, the more you will give. When you see the needs of others you will respond generously, whether you have God-blessed abundance or modest means. Indeed, you are sometimes totally blind to bad choices that lurk ahead. But, because you have made a covenant with your eyes, your Creator will see you through vulnerable times. Moreover, He takes your contractual agreement with your eyes to heart. Your responsibility in this binding contract is making wise choices. For example, avoid exposing your eyes to enticing and erotic images. Your covenant requires you to inform others of your propensities for temptation. Do not traffic alone in your vulnerable places. God's covenants have restrictions and requirements, but all for your good. Having a covenant with your eyes liberates you from lust and any other addictive eye candy. Make a contract with your eyes, and then trust God to guide you away from gullibility into goodness, so you are not blind to the ways of the Lord. Therefore, understand and apply the terms of your eyes' covenant. God's terms provide boundaries with radical freedom.

Keep eye contact with God and you will be free indeed!

JUL 20 DRAW NEAR

"He said to me, 'The room facing the south is for the priests who have charge of the temple, and the room facing north is for the priests who have charge of the altar. These are the sons of Zadok, who are the only Levites who may draw near to the Lord to minister before him.'" EZEKIEL 40:45-46

Draw near to God, before you minister on behalf of God. This is the sequence for serving the Lord. Otherwise, you serve others in your own strength and limited abilities. Ministry without the Holy Spirit's empowerment leads to burnout and bewilderment. You are not meant to serve in the flesh for followers of Jesus have the privilege to draw near to Him, and be filled fresh daily with His Spirit and motivation. Draw near to Him and you naturally draw near to others. Indeed this is harder for driven people, as they are always on the go. Other pending activities persistently arrest their attention. It is hard for their minds to focus, because responsibilities flash into the forefront of their thinking. You cannot draw near to God because you fear failure and all its embarrassing ramifications, but this means fear has the upper hand. Hyperactivity is driving you because you fear everything depends on you. This is not a burden your heavenly Father desires for you to bear. No one can persevere in ministry or service under this kind of self-imposed pressure. It is up to the Lord whether you reach your goals or not. It may not be His will for so much to be accomplished so soon. Ministry that does not depend on drawing near to God does not last. A person attempting to serve Christ without drawing near to God will become overwhelmed and frustrated. Therefore, draw near and let the Lord whisper assurance and maybe some adjustments into your ear.

Make drawing near to the Lord a holy habit of your life. Change your thinking, so that no decision or activity will define your activities, until you have communed with Christ. Do not commit to do ministry until you have met with your Master. It is better to have one engaged in ministry who has first drawn near to God, than a dozen operating in their own strength. This is what gives Christian ministry a bad name. God is unimpressed with those flesh-driven fools who flash their good deeds like a badge of courage. He is even perturbed at this prideful display of service in His name.

So draw near to Him, and people become more dear and your needs become less. Draw near to Him in your heart, for this is where your affections lie. Draw near to the Lord and let Him touch your lips with life-giving words of hope, encouragement, and rebuke when necessary. Draw near to God and allow Him to unleash your giving, so you are freed in the Spirit to give with hilarious generosity. Draw near to your heavenly Father and experience His love and forgiveness, so you are aptly able to administer the same to your sometimes strained relationships. Draw near to God and rest in His grace and peace. Draw near and dismiss fear. Draw near and give Him your listening ear. His voice is soothing and secure.

Draw near to God and you will minister to others in His power. He is extremely accessible and close by, so draw near now. "Let us draw near to God with a sincere heart in full assurance of faith..."(Hebrews 10:22).

DECEIVED PRIDE

> "He [Nebuchadnezzar] said, 'Is not this great Babylon I have built as the royal residence, by my mighty power and for the glory of my majesty?'... "And those who walk in pride, He is able to humble."   DANIEL 4:30, 37B

Pride is deceived, as it walks in deception, believing things that are untrue. It thinks it is in control and is responsible for its accomplishments. Pride has an inflated belief in itself and a condescending attitude toward others. It is all wrapped up in its own agenda. Pride may even mouth the right words, but its behavior deceives its sincerity. Pride is a product of unaccountable living. Without checks and balances, pride develops a track record of deception that leads to defeat. Furthermore, the greatest deception of pride is to set itself up against God. You can go through the motions of religious activity without brokenness and obedience. This is the pinnacle of pride. The audacity to use God is the ultimate deception. God will not be used. He will not be mocked, nor will He allow pride to roam free. Pride tries to convince you that you are God's gift to the world, but that was Jesus. God gave us His son for the forgiveness of your sins. This reminder is meant to flush out pride and replace it with humility. Pride and humility cannot coexist. Humility understands and does not forget that God is the author of all good things. His Holy Spirit cuts through pride's deception and replaces it with humility's reality. The reality is, without the blessings of God people are paupers lost in pride.

Moreover, humility and brokenness break the bonds of pride. You know pride is losing its grip when you release control of your life. Humility lets go. You let go of recognition. You let go of hurt feelings. You let go of the past. You let go of judging. You let go of bad habits. You let go of your family. You let go of work. You let go of relationships. You let go of having to be right. You let go of having to have your way. You let it go and you leave it with God. This is what it means to trust God. Humility and trust go hand-in-hand, as much as pride and control. It is uncanny how humility and trust lead to more responsibility and power, while pride and control lose it. This is the great deception of pride. Pride thinks it is in control, but it is not.

Humility recognizes God's control and is trusted with more. When you humble yourself in your relationships, you will be given more peace and fulfillment. Stiffen up in pride and you will lose trust and joy. Therefore, give up on your way of doing things and submit to God's way. Do not force your agenda; rather acquiesce to the Almighty's. If you continue to demand control, you are deceived. Pride will cause you to lose what you desire most and receive what you most regret. However, humility exposes you to God's eternal benefits. He will bless you far beyond what you expect or deserve. The benefit of humility way outweighs the illusion of pride.

Humble yourself, before God does. The Bible says, "Humble yourselves, therefore, under God's mighty hand, that he may lift you up in due time" (1 Peter 5:6).

> "So I turned to the Lord God and pleaded with him in prayer and petition, in fasting, and in sackcloth and ashes." DANIEL 9:3

Prayer and petition is a privilege of Christ followers for solemn supplication to your superior authority and Savior, Jesus. When all is said and done, your hope for relief or answered prayer rests with your heavenly Father. It is focused faith on the Almighty above that absolves sin and melts fears. Indeed, fasting and prayer bring your privileged position of access to the Almighty into laser beam focus. He is great and awesome and worthy of worship. He has established a covenant of love with His children, which is engaging and eternal. He will judge the wicked and rebellious in His way and in His timing. He is high above us in heavenly holiness, but not so detached that He cannot hear the pleas of His people.

He is without sin, but He forgives sin. He judges, but He extends mercy. He is grieved over disobedience, but He rewards obedience. He is the God and Father of our Lord Jesus Christ. Scripture reveals Him in all His majesty and regal righteousness. No other 'gods' of this world come close to the God of creation. Idols are dumb and mute, unable to respond to prayer. On the other hand, prayer is precious to the Prince of Peace. This is His mode of communication and communing with His highest order in creation. Nature is unable to nudge God's heart in prayer, but you can. Animals have no comprehension of how to make an appeal to the Almighty, but you do. By faith, you are privileged people because you can petition and pray to your heavenly Father.

So go to the Lord in prayer and petition, often and boldly confess your sins and keep short accounts. Ask often for the peace of Christ to engulf your hearts and minds. Pray regularly for your enemies to be transformed by the love of God. Pray boldly for great and mighty things on His behalf; for healing from cancer or healing in relationships. Lift up to the Lord petitions for the salvation of friends and family members. Prayer is your first line of defense, not your last resort. Prayer means you care, and most will invite prayer, even unbelievers. Prayer to God is potent and able to penetrate the proudest of people. Prayer brings you to your knees in humble gratitude and the need for God and His wisdom.

Be an example of prayer and pray for others. The Bible says, "And pray in the Spirit on all occasions with all kinds of prayers and requests. With this in mind, be alert and always keep on praying for all the saints" (Ephesians 6:18).

SECRET TO SUCCESS

"He [Uzziah] sought God during the days of Zechariah, who instructed him in the fear of God. As long as he sought the Lord, God gave him success."   2 CHRONICLES 26:5

It should come as no surprise that success, as God defines it comes from seeking Him. For the follower of Jesus doing the will of God is the highest degree of success. As you follow God's will, you are successful. Success is not something waiting for you way out in the future. You have already achieved success if you are walking in step with your heavenly Father. Otherwise, you may have an outward shell of success, but inwardly and relationally you are a failure. Seeking God is a volitional and relational act. It is consciously and regularly seeking to understand your Creator. Seeking God is to know Him. Seeking God is to love Him. Seeking God is to praise Him. Seeking God is to worship Him. Seeking God is confessing and crying out to Him. It is enjoying the comfort of your heavenly Father. It is practicing the presence of Christ in you. You seek God at church, at home, at work, and with your friends. There is no place where He is off limits for seeking, other that hell itself. What a privilege and perk for Jesus people, anytime, anywhere, and for any reason, you can seek God. Therefore, seek Him just as aggressively during the calm as you do in the chaos. Jesus doesn't want to just be your crisis manager. He wants to be your Lord who leads you into wise living. The Bible says, "...seek the LORD your God, you will find him if you look for him with all your heart and with all your soul" (Deuteronomy 4:29).

Moreover, seeking God involves instruction from godly and mature believers in Christ. You cannot seek God in isolation. This involves the counsel and advice of those much the wiser. Seeking God involves validation from wisdom. Dangerous is the man or woman who attempts to seek God without submitting to godly teaching, mentoring, and discipling from gifted leaders of the faith. You learn to fear God from those who fear God. You learn to love God from those who love God. You learn to forgive from those who forgive. You learn to pray from those who pray. You learn to serve from those who serve. Seeking God comes from seeking the godly. Yes, avoid hero worship; no except Christ deserves this level of admiration. A wise way to understand God is to understand the godly. Hang out with those you want to be like. This is why church and community is vital to seeking God. You cannot seek God and not seek out the right people. Scripture teaches, "The heart of the discerning acquires knowledge; the ears of the wise seek it out" (Proverbs 18:15).

Lastly, seek God in His Word. The Bible is God's anthology and it is the revelation of Jesus Christ. Scripture is the first and last word on God. It defines Him, so it can define you. Know His Word and you will know Him. Read it. Memorize it. Meditate on it. Learn it. Above all else, apply it. Seek God in the scripture and you are successful.

Success is a result of seeking God. Therefore, seek Him more often than not. "Seek the LORD while he may be found; call on him while he is near" (Isaiah 55:6).

JUL 24 RIGHT MOTIVES

"Ask all the people of the land and the priests, 'When you fasted and mourned in the fifth and seventh months for the past seventy years, was it really for me that you fasted? And when you were eating and drinking, were you not just feasting for yourselves?'" ZECHARIAH 7:5-6

Right motives can be illusive for one minute you can be pure in why you do what you do, and then subtly you can slip into suspect behavior. Therefore, be relentless and regular in reviewing your motives. Pride is always looking to pounce on your purposes, so ask the Lord to cleanse your motives and mark them with His purposes. You can make faith in Jesus a filter for right motives. 'Why would Jesus do this?' is a wise question that helps you get to the heart of the matter. The 'why' question reveals intent and encourages honesty. Regularly asking the 'why' question addresses your motives. You may want to give to someone, but why? You may want to serve someone, but why? You may want to sacrifice an opportunity, but why? You may want to perform a religious duty, but why? Where does your devotion reside? What drives you to do good things? If your reasons are self-serving, then you have missed managing your motives for eternal purposes. Your motive may be to use religion and the church to promote your profession, but God does not like to be used for anything other than His glory (John 2:14-16).

If you serve because it makes you feel better or to feed your ego, your motives are dysfunctional. If you are trying to make up for your shady past or you are driven by guilt, then you are a good candidate for burnout. As a consequence, your misguided motives will cause others discomfort for it has a ripple effect on relationships and organizational dynamics. Unhealthy motivations that seek attention and credit will compromise principles and values in an effort to reach its desired results. It is driven by whatever means it takes to justify worthy results, but lasting fruit results from the seeds of pure motives.

Jesus said, "You did not choose me, but I chose you and appointed you to go and bear fruit—fruit that will last. Then the Father will give you whatever you ask in my name" (John 15:16). Therefore, do an audit of authenticity and stop doing acts of righteousness that draw people to yourself instead of to your Savior. For example fast and pray with discretion and give anonymously (Matthew 6:5-6). Do all for the glory of God, so your love for the Lord and people lift your motives to a grace filled level.

Continually allow the Holy Spirit to scrub your motivations. Ask often, "Why would Jesus do this?" Model His motivations, for right motives reap God's rewards (1 Corinthians 3:10-15)!

LAUGHING JESUS

"He will fill your mouth with laughter and your lips with shouts of joy."
JOB 8:21

Laughter is from the Lord. It is His medicine for the mind and therapy for the soul. The Lord laughs because He is the dispenser of laughter. You cannot give what you do not have, and He has plenty to laugh about. Just as an engaging parent intently observes his children, so God sees antics and behaviors that are hilarious. The Lord must laugh when He sees one of His children smile and do something silly, harmless and lighthearted. Indeed, He knows laughter is one way to get us through life's intense moments. God is not so serious that he cannot smile and laugh. How could Jesus have been 100% human if He didn't experience an old-fashioned belly laugh? Just hanging out with impetuous Peter would be reason enough to giggle under your breath, or even burst out into raucous, roaring laughter. Indeed, God has a sense of humor. You don't have to look beyond the mirror to verify this fact. His joy and laughter are a refreshing combination, in a day when proud piety has given laughter a bad name, God still laughs. He laughs, because you laugh, and you were created in His image. It is no laughing matter to think that God does not laugh. A world without laughter would be like a joke without a punch line, so look to the Lord of laugher and smile; He does.

God has given you permission to laugh. In fact He has put joy in your heart and laughter on your lips for a purpose. When you laugh, you relax. When you laugh, the cares of this world shrink and the Lord looms larger. When you laugh, you learn to enjoy life and the Lord himself. When you laugh, you look like the Lord. Laugh loud and laugh often. Moreover, generosity will fuel your laughter. It is cheerful giving that brings joy to the soul (2 Corinthians 9:7). Generosity ignites joy and laughter. No wonder the greedy frown and fret, there is no freedom to let loose and laugh. Laughless living is for losers. They are bound up in boring behavior. If you are too serious to laugh, you are too serious.

Seriously, you can be too serious for your own good. You may be more serious than God. Instead, throw back your head and begin by laughing at yourself. Take yourself less seriously, and God more seriously. A good laugh lends itself to longer and better living. A scoured face seems to rush quicker to the grave. Lean on the Lord for your laughter and make His joy your strength. Laughter infuses your faith with mercy and hope. You are not a naïve laughing fool, rather a joyful follower of Christ. Take time each day to laugh at yourself and to laugh with others. Recognize laughter as the Lord's way of leveraging a balanced and healthy life. Life without laughter is dull and mundane. Therefore, choose to lift up yourself and others with a good laugh. There is a time to laugh, so do it often and do it well.

The Lord may be laughing right now. He certainly is smiling. The Bible says, "He will yet fill your mouth with laughter and your lips with shouts of joy" (Job 8:21).

JUL 26 ATTITUDE ADJUSTMENT

"For seven days they celebrated with joy the Feast of Unleavened Bread, because the Lord had filled them with joy by changing the attitude of the king of Assyria, so that he assisted them in the work on the house of God, the God of Israel." EZRA 6:22

Attitude is everything, it can get you up or it can bring you down. It is a barometer of your heart, if your heart is not right your attitude will suffer. Attitude is critical, because it influences your course of action. If your attitude is negative, then your words and your behavior will follow a life of negativity. There is a difference in being a realist about negative circumstances, and living with a chronic bad attitude. Naïve are those who ignore warning signs of trouble, and carry on obliviously to the storm clouds of sin. However, your attitude is rooted in who you are in Christ, so there is no need to be fearful, guilty or insecure. The attitude of Jesus exhibited humility and servant leadership. His attitude was submission to his heavenly Father, which resulted in service, generosity and love for people. Jesus was joyful and hopeful, because He rested in the will of God. Furthermore, do not allow the bad attitude of others to influence yours. Be the attitude influencer instead. Greet a frown with a smile, crush criticism with affirmation, and listen patiently until fury loses its steam. A positive attitude will eventually outlast and over power a negative one. Most of all pray for those who thrive on negativity. Pray for them to be set free from their hurt, anger, guilt and insecurity. God has you in their lives for the purpose of reflecting an attitude adjustment by the Almighty.

God is the genesis of a right attitude, and He is the right attitude sustainer. He desires for His attitude to be our attitude. This is why you need a daily attitude alignment from your heavenly Father. Each day your attitude gets knocked around and abused by life. If left unattended your attitude will drift into wrong thinking, harsh words and bad behavior. Self-pity and anger can begin to replace selflessness and forgiveness. With just a little bit of daily tweaking your attitude stays in line with His. It is subtle but sometimes attitude adjustments need to be moment by moment.

Lastly, slow down and pray when you feel your attitude eroding. A bad attitude is not the time to make important decisions. You will regret every one you make during a time of emotional upheaval. Be patient and wait until your anger has subsided, your heart is cleansed and your attitude is objective. Almighty God is into attitudes that trust Him and reach out to others with compassion and understanding. Open-minded and reasonable attitudes lead to rich and robust relationships. Anyone can be negative, so don't be anyone, be different. Allow God to shape your attitude on the anvil of His heart.

An attitude molded by God is infectious and transforming. Allow Him to change yours, and then trust Him to change another's. The Bible says, "Your attitude should be the same as that of Christ Jesus..." (Philippians 2:5).

DESERT EXPERIENCE

"At once the Spirit sent him out into the desert, and he was in the desert forty days, being tempted by Satan. He was with the wild animals, and angels attended him."
MARK 1:12-13

Sometimes the Holy Spirit sends you into a desert experience. The purpose of this hard time is not punishment, but purity. God wants to purify your faith and grow your dependence on Him. Indeed the enemy does not sit still when he senses someone has escaped eternity's cover. He misses the principle that God uses all things for His good, even your enemies. Times of trial are full of temptation from Satan for he appeals to your pride, your physical appetite and your spiritual vulnerability. He wants to bring you down when you are at your weakest. He sees you alone and ready for the kill. Satan smells blood, but the blood he smells is not your demise, it is your salvation. It is the blood of Jesus Christ that covers you during this crisis time, in your desert of life.

Your desert experience may be a child that is away from God and away from home. It may be that your health is failing quickly and you are on the fast track to heaven's gates. Your desert experience may encompass loneliness and a Lord that does not seem to answer prayer. Heaven may be silent during this time of stress and distress. Your marriage may be in the ditch and even on the way to divorce court, so careful not to make a dumb decision during your desert time. He will carry you through. His angels are not passive to your plight, but present to minister to your needs. Your heavenly Father is sending reinforcements for your faith, so stay immersed in the Word of God because His word is your anchor during this time of ambiguity. The promises of God rain down like manna during desolate desert times. Feed your soul with Scripture and you will have strength to make through this time of turmoil. Look to the Lord for He cares. He is willing to make you whole and walk with you through this desert of distress. Do not attempt to gut it out without God and people.

Lastly you will be stronger as a result of this faith-stretching situation. What was meant to drive you away from God will draw you closer. The Holy Spirit knows better than you what you need to become more like Jesus in your faith and deeds. This desert experience will pass, so don't waste this pain and discomfort but use it to go deep with the Divine. Turn the tables with trust for your faithfulness inspires others to remain faithful. The irrigation of God's love, grace and forgiveness will flood your desert with new life and will be beautiful to behold. Jesus creates a paradise of character where the deserts of temptation once existed.

The Bible says, "Then will the lame leap like a deer, and the mute tongue shout for joy. Water will gush forth in the wilderness and streams in the desert" (Isaiah 35:6).

J<small>UL</small>28 FEAR REPRESSES FAITH

"Yet at the same time many even among the leaders believed in him. But because of the Pharisees they would not confess their faith for fear they would be put out of the synagogue; for they loved praise from men more than praise from God." JOHN 12:42-43

Fear represses faith and restrains its recognition. It holds back its boldness to believe and is not a friend of faith. Fear mistakenly believes it can coddle cunning men and at the same time claim Christ. This is a contradiction that does not stand up under the scrutiny of your Savior. Jesus requires unconditional commitment and unwavering loyalty. It is not all Jesus on Sunday and Jesus when it is convenient the other six days of the week. Covert confession is not an option for a follower of Jesus Christ. Yes in some parts of the world you have to remain under the rule of atheistic authorities. Discretion is both wise and responsible, but there is no doubt where bold believers stand. Faith is not motivated by fear of man, but by love of God. Faith does not seek to integrate other belief systems into Christianity. It embraces Jesus and Jesus alone. Believers who confess their faith in Christ are set free from fear. Confession is freeing while repression is constraining. Currently you may be flailing away on the battlefield of fear. You fear how others may perceive you if they know you fear God. They may label you as weird, narrow-minded, or judgmental. Confession in Christ risks being misunderstood for the sake of the Lord. It values praise from God over praise from man. Moreover, public confession of your faith may cost you. Leaders especially have a lot to lose by laying their beliefs on the line. However, how can you be a quiet Christian? What is your motivation? If fear is your reason, then you are wrong to continue down this road of cultural conformity. Where are the leaders who will live by principle even when it may mean losing power? Furthermore, don't use your faith just to get a following, and don't compromise your convictions just to please a group who refuses to respect your values. Fear-based decision making has no place for disciples of Jesus Christ. Do the right thing even though it may cost you votes, a job, a raise, a promotion, praise or opportunities. In turn you gain the confidence of Christ.

When you give up something based on principle, you gain His praise. When fear becomes your fortress, you fight a losing battle for fear is indefensible. There is not enough you can do to defend its revolving flank that exposes. Therefore, fight fear with a consistent and compassionate confession of Christ. Trust God to use your public confession for His cause and glory. Confession gives confidence and calm. It agrees with and proclaims the ways of God and builds your faith.

Fear melts under the heat of confession. Public confession of Christ refreshes faith and overcomes fear. The Bible says, "Through Jesus, therefore, let us continually offer to God a sacrifice of praise—the fruit of lips that confess his name" (Hebrews 13:15).

CUT TO THE HEART

"When the people heard this, they were cut to the heart and said to Peter and the other apostles, 'Brothers what shall we do?' " ACTS 2:37

The Holy Spirit cuts to the heart, and with laser beam precision He penetrates, probes, and prescribes truth. He is not satisfied with a surface relationship, but is motivated to move beyond insensitive chatter to the sensitive conscience. He is interested in claiming your conscience for Christ. When your heart is convinced, you are convinced. Your heart is the seat of your emotions and it is here that the hounds of hell seek to have their way. However, the Holy Spirit is ahead of the enemy. He is quick to deliver truth with clarity and conviction. One can choose to accept His promptings or ignore them to their regret. When your heart is strangely warmed, listen for the Lord is speaking.

No one else deserves your devotion or affection but Christ. It is when you give your heart mixed signals that you obstruct obedience. A divided heart will not stand under the scrutiny of the Spirit of God; so keep your heart for Christ and Christ alone. Cut free any other competitors for Christ's affection. Money, homes, success, children, work, travel and hobbies are a means to the end of glorifying God. The heart is heaven's home, not hell's playground. Therefore, do not hesitate to expose your heart to eternal purposes. Lay your heart before the Lord and ask Him to mold it with His Almighty agenda. Listen and apply truth to your heart. Invite the Holy Spirit's awakening of your slumbering soul for He is...God's change agent. Once the Holy Spirit has sliced into your soul, He expects change. Heart felt conviction that does not lead to change hardens the heart. Emotional awareness is only an appetizer that leads to the entrée of willful obedience. Action accompanies a heart cut by Christ. There is a humility that cries out, "What am I to do?" A hungry heart responds with an appetite for the Almighty. Everything else pales in importance compared to obeying God. A heart engaged by the Holy Spirit longs to love the Lord by obeying the Lord. There is a direct correlation of obedience to a heart cut by the Spirit, compared to a disobedient heart seduced by self.

The Holy Spirit is committed to conforming you into the image of Christ. The fruit of His work transforms you into a faithful spouse, engaged parent, loyal friend, wise mentor, loving leader and caring colleague. His inner conviction leads to repentance of sin, faith in Christ and community with believers. This is His mode of operation. If you do not recognize and respond to the Holy Spirit's persistent promptings, He may go away. He does not dwell where He is not wanted. Never numb your conscience to not listen to Him. Therefore, seek Him out. Christ left you His Spirit for the specific purposes of convicting, comforting and counseling. Pray for His power to permeate your feelings, thinking and behavior. He cuts to the heart because He cares. Jesus said, "But I tell you the truth: It is for your good that I am going away. Unless I go away, the Counselor will not come to you; but if I go, I will send him to you. When He comes, He will convict the world of guilt in regard to sin and righteousness and judgment (John 16:7-8).

JUL 30 PERSEVERING PURPOSE

"Therefore, in the present case I advise you: Leave these men alone! Let them go! For if their purpose or activity is of human origin, it will fail. But if it is from God, you will not be able to stop these men; you will only find yourself fighting against God." ACTS 5:38-39

The purposes of God cannot be stopped. No king or catastrophe can conquer Christ's will or ways. He is specific in what He wants done, as the Almighty accomplishes what He desires. Man may get in the way momentarily, but overtime the Lord's lasting purpose prevails. Resistance sometimes comes from religious leaders because their control is threatened. They drift into bad theology that equates time bound methods with timeless truth. Religion, if not kept relevant can become its own worst enemy, limping as it maintains status quo.

Indeed, Christ came to shake up the religious establishment. The emerging church is not new, but as old as the early church. It appeals for alignment around the practical purposes of Almighty God. God's good news is Jesus Christ, period. He does not have to be enhanced or embellished. You do not have to apologize for who He is or what He stands for. Jesus just needs to be exposed and unleashed. The purpose of the Holy Spirit is to draw others to Jesus. When you lift up Jesus with your life and lips, others are drawn to Him. Causes and people who are not of God will fail. You do not have to plan out their demise, it will happen in the course of Christ's good timing. God's purposes are creative and innovative. They are not bound by cultural norms or society's mores. Deity delights in doing things differently. Each generation seeks to define itself through music, art, technology, sports, economics, leisure and yes, religion.

Nevertheless, the Lord is large enough to apply His purposes in all of these environments. Music is His universal language of praise and worship to Himself. He is more concerned with the outcomes of awe and obedience as He is with style and rhythm. Art is His expression of Himself in human beings, nature and architecture. Artistic creators of beautiful design and genius of expression point to a much greater Designer. Modern technological advancements have accelerated our ability to communicate the Gospel of Jesus Christ around the world. Sports are a testament to our Creator's intrinsic intellect behind the pinnacle of His creation, the human body. Indeed, the best economic systems in the world execute commerce on principles found in the Word of God. The church has persevered because it is the Bride of Christ; the hope of the world, and God will carry out His purposes through the Body of Christ. He is not bound by time or tradition. His purposes persevere because He perseveres. Your part is to align with His purpose, and trust Him with the right outcome.

The Bible teaches, "In him we were also chosen, having been predestined according to the plan of him who works out everything in conformity with the purpose of his will..."(Ephesians 1:11).

DRASTIC MEASURES

"We took such a violent battering from the storm that the next day they began to throw the cargo overboard. On the third day, they threw the ships tackle overboard with their own hands." ACTS 27:18-19

Some situations call for drastic measures, and you cannot continue as usual or you will miss an opportunity to make major adjustments. Figuratively speaking your boat needs to be lightened for you to stay afloat. This may apply to finances, because of your increase in debt and your decrease in income, your spending must curtail drastically. Your lifestyle cannot continue to elevate on the back of credit cards and equity lines. This straw house of credit will collapse one day under the weight of one small crisis. One misstep can cause everything to quickly tumble down.

God's best is not for you to live on the verge of financial frustration and failure. Start now and pay down debt while you can. Your next job may not be as financially friendly. Prepare today for tomorrow's turmoil. It is not a question of if things can go wrong, but when things will go wrong. Adversity has a way of revealing bad habits. Success can mask mistakes, but failures bring them up front and center. Don't risk your relational well-being for the sake of stuff. Simple equals freedom; but complex can be bondage. Maybe you need to lower your stress by lessening your commitments.

Each season of life calls for an evaluation of what's needed. The empty nest marriage needs are much different than when the children scurried all through the house. This is especially difficult for a wife who has drawn emotional strength and security from the love of the children. She feels insecure and less significant when the kids are no longer under the roof waiting to be mothered. Yes she needs the love of her heavenly Father, but she desperately needs the love of her earthly husband. It is during this season of major transition in motherhood that a wise husband loves more. It may mean taking drastic measures in how you love your wife. She needs your love in ways she defines love. It probably means more communication, sensitivity and service. Do not let her frustrations and anger make you defensive, or cause you to shut down. She wants to connect. She is longing for love that only you can give.

You may need to give up a hobby or ministry role for a season. Margin may be the best medicine for your marriage right now. Don't ignore this need for major adjustments in how you love and respect your spouse. Take initiative so you don't become another divorce statistic, or just apathetically exist..

If you don't listen and understand her fears and insecurities, someone else will. Be willing to sacrifice career success for the sake of your spouse. Say no to the promotion, or to added responsibilities. Take her away, just the two of you for a long weekend. She needs to know that she matters the most to you. Brag on her beauty. Value her ideas and opinions. Take drastic measures if that is what's needed, because status quo will kill your marriage. You can do much more than maintain your marriage, and take drastic measures if necessary.

The Bible teaches, "Do not deprive each other except by mutual consent and for a time, so that you may devote yourselves to prayer. Then come together again so that Satan will not tempt you because of your lack of self-control" (1 Corinthians 7:5).

GOD'S TIMING

"There is a time for everything, and a season for every activity under heaven…"
ECCLESIASTES 3:1

God's timing can be frustrating, but it eventually leads to freedom. Perhaps you strongly desire something or someone. It is right at your fingertips, but you can't have it now and that frustrates you. The timing is not right for whatever reason. It may not be right for you and/or it may not be right for the other person. However, you can allow this frustration to lead you to freedom. Let it lead you to the freedom of knowing God may be protecting you from failure, because you are not ready for the grueling responsibility that lies ahead. There are still valuable lessons to learn where you are. It is like your last semester of school. You are way past ready for graduation, but there were still final exams to study for and pass. You need to do your best where you are, before you move on to God's next assignment.

Timing is everything. Your son really needs you right now during this challenging stage of his life. The insecurities of his teenage years are eating him alive. He needs extra attention and time from you to navigate through this uncertainty. This is a season, a season that will not be repeated. Your career can wait, children can't. Yes, children are resilient and may not even say anything during difficult times, but you can rest assured that they will never forget your being there for them. The security and confidence you sow into your children will stay with them for a lifetime. The reciprocal is true as well. Fearful and insecure adults were once fearful and insecure children. So, allow this season of life to build bridges rather than barriers between you and your children. It is just for a moment in time. In a blink of an eye, they will be gone.

Learn to celebrate various seasons of life. Do not resist them; rather, embrace them. Join the wonder of their realities. The marriage of your adult child is imminent, so celebrate the occasion. Do not let the stress of the details and the outlays of cash rob you of the joy connected to this momentous occasion. You can rest in the fact that He has brought these two together. This is what you have prayed for concerning your child. You have prayed for a marriage into a God-fearing and Christ-honoring family. You have prepared them the best way you know how. Ultimately it is in God's hands. As the father and the mother of the bride and groom, learn how to let go and allow them to become one flesh. Your relationship will look different going forward. This is a new stage of life. So do not try to control them, rather let go of them and leave them in God's hands. Your ability to adapt and adjust to new seasons of life has a direct correlation to your joy and happiness. Jesus understood this when He declared, "Dear woman, why do you involve me?" Jesus replied, "My time has not yet come" (John 2:4).

A2 BOLD GOING

"Then I heard the voice of the Lord saying, 'Whom shall I send? And who will go for us?' And I said, 'Here I am send me!'" ISAIAH 6:8

Bold going responds to God's invitation to join Him in going to unlikely places. These are places that need the love of Christ, where people smell differently, look differently, talk differently and act differently. But all these places have the same need for a Savior. Their hearts are hungry for God and they are waiting for someone to tell them the truth about Jesus. These cross-cultural encounters are not always romantic or noble. Sometimes they are hard and grueling. They become difficult when your body rejects the local food and water. Your body begins to groan for relief as their souls groan for a Savior. Your little bit of discomfort is well worth the salvation of souls. The joy of seeing others come to faith in Christ and grow in their faith cause you to forget any temporary ailments you may be suffering. The satisfaction of exposing Jesus to a Christ-less culture is compelling to your call.

The beauty is they become like Christ in the context of their world. You are not there to make them like you. You have the great privilege of leading them to be like Jesus. However, not everyone listens and believes. This process of loving them to Jesus over time can be taxing to your patience, some will resent you for 'trying to convert them' to your God. So, let your love and service of other national believers become an authentic example that keeps bringing the unbelievers back. Then they are drawn to Christians because of the love you have for one another. So stay available to the world on behalf of God. With 95% of the world's population outside the borders of America, how can Christians stay put for very long? Jesus instructs His followers to make disciples globally. You may be called to a short-term or long-term mission trip overseas. Either way, engage with God in this great adventure, but do not remain neutral and idle. Yes give money to missions, but don't stop there.

Move way beyond your money and show up on the ground with the Holy Spirit in your heart and the Word of God on your breath. Find those who are teachable and teach them the Word of God. Find those who want to lead and train them to be servant leaders. Seek out the evangelists and help them to evangelize. Build buildings, create jobs, birth businesses, start ministries, feed the hungry, clothe the orphans and widows. Do whatever it takes in the name of Christ to bridge the cultural gap with God. Do not feel like you have to have all the answers. Do not be afraid of the unknown or of illness. This is God's opportunity to grow your faith and perspective to another level. Your investment in going will make you a much better husband, wife, employer, employee, and Christian. Your theology becomes more balanced and robust. You discover that some of your beliefs have become westernized and unbiblical. You have inadvertently limited God, because of your own cultural restraints. God wants you to partner with Him to unleash your faith and the faith of others.

Do not be shy, but be bold in the power of the Holy Spirit. The Bible says, "But you will receive power when the Holy Spirit comes on you; and you will be my witnesses ... to the ends of the earth" (Acts 1:8).

TOTAL TRUST

> "Surely God is my salvation; I will trust and not be afraid. The Lord, the Lord,
> is my strength and my song; he has become my salvation. With joy you will draw
> water from the wells of salvation." ISAIAH 12:2-3

Total trust in God is available to every blood-bought follower of Jesus Christ. It means you give up total control and the Lord's assurance replaces your fear with peace. You cannot figure it all out, but you do have the capacity to trust Him totally. It is a trust issue and if He is who He claims to be, He can be trusted. If you can trust Him with the eternal salvation of your soul, you can trust Him with the temporal control of your life. If you can trust Him with the big things, you can trust Him with the small things. If He led you to the right spouse, He will give you the opportunities to provide. If He led you to a new career, He will give you the wisdom, finances and relationships to be successful. If He led you to be a missionary, He will build bridges across the cultural barriers that allow you to engage with the people. If He led you to have children, He will provide for the needed resources to be successful parents.

Wherever God leads He provides. What God initiates He completes. His part is provision and your part is trust. Don't fall into the trap of trusting Him with some things and not trusting Him with others. Distrust in God is distasteful and an insult to His integrity. How can God not be big enough to handle any situation? Health, war, teenagers, money, conflict, prosperity, relationships and people can all be placed into His hands. God can be trusted because He is trustworthy. The well of His salvation is infinitely deep. You have limited capacity to bear burdens, however His character and resources are unlimited. Without the support of a sympathetic Jesus you will be immobilized, even crushed under the weight of worry. Jesus understands and He is offended if you do not yoke up with His support.

No need to root around searching for answers when He already has it figured out. No need to sacrifice your health in worry and overwork when He offers peace and options you have yet to discover. No need to rush through life and then ask Him to bless your efforts after the fact. He can be trusted to lead you even before you put a prayerful plan into motion. Trust in God does not mean you act irresponsibly and seek forgiveness later. Trust in God means to patiently walk with Him in your decisions and choices. Slow down, look up, trust Him and watch Him reap extraordinary results. Partial trust leads to frustration and worry.

Total trust in Jesus leads to contentment, joy and peace. The Bible says, "Trust in the LORD with all your heart and lean not on your own understanding; in all your ways acknowledge him, and he will make your paths straight" (Proverbs 3:5-6).

A4 SHARPENED SKILLS

"If an ax is dull and its edge unsharpened, more strength is needed but skill will bring success." ECCLESIASTES 10:10

Life is not meant to be endless activity and busyness, without pause it loses its edge. A life worth living takes the time to sharpen its skills. Skill sharpening is an investment that will serve you the rest of your life. Do not settle for mediocrity; by God's grace seek to be the best in your life roles. Your commitment to sharpen yourself is much like a farmer. A wise farmer will use his seasonal down time to upgrade, replace and repair his equipment. He literally sharpens the tips of his plow, rebuilds the tractor engines, upgrades and cleans his equipment. A prepared farmer will not only survive but will thrive with this type of ever-improving motivation. In the same spirit there is a time to execute, and a time to regroup and sharpen yourself for the next initiative. Sharpened skills are an effective tool in the hand of God. He wants to use you to your full potential. Your part is to continually improve. Your activities and work will produce more lasting results when you take the time to hone heaven's gifts.

God wants to use your life to cut through life issues, like a sharp knife slices through a juicy ripe tomato. A skilled concert pianist practices the piano. A skilled writer searches out new words and becomes engrossed in sentence structures. A skilled speaker learns how to understand his audience and communicate one point in a variety of ways. A skilled mom quizzes other moms on how to become a better mother. A skilled golfer continues to hit balls way after the tournaments end. He smashes the little white objects into the night. So, seek out new ways to keep your mind sharp and engaged in new ideas.

Read about and learn from wise leaders of the faith whose writings have stood the test of time. Books are tremendous skill sharpeners. Join a book club to ramp up your commitment and accountability. You can attend seminars or pursue a graduate degree. Use a variety of tools to stay sharp. Sparks fly when steel is sharpened, which means there will be some discomfort and growing pains. You are either moving forward or shrinking backward there is no standing still.

As you sharpen your skills, you are moving forward. You are stewarding God's talents and gifts to their fullest. Swinging at issues with a dull life will lead you to the brink of giving up. For example sharpen your mind with the Word of God; nothing infuses a sharp mind like wisdom from above. His principles are like a whit rock on a battered blade, He smoothes the jagged edges of your roughed up life. Like an axe that has become chipped and blunted over time, He refurbishes it to a radiant and shinny silver edge. Discover your skills through assessments and the counsel of others. A hint: when you operate within your skill set, it is almost effortless to execute the plan.

Stay sharp and your skills may swing open impressive doors. Wisdom says, "Do you see a man skilled in his work? He will serve before kings; he will not serve before obscure men" (Proverbs 22:29).

RADICAL ROMANCE

"Let him kiss me with the kisses of his mouth—for your love is more delightful than wine."
SONG OF SOLOMON 1:2

Romance is not relegated to the young; indeed it can become more robust with age. This is one of God's ways to keep your heart youthful. The excitement of wooing your wife or husband is an important part of God's plan for marriage. There is nothing more boring than a marriage that has gone stale. Like an old and moldy piece of bread, the relationship becomes crusty and distasteful without the freshness of romance. There is nothing more exciting than a husband and wife who never get over pursuing one another. Sparks fly because passion is aflame for each other, and you avoid taking each other for granted when romance is robust.

Romance is a combination of physical, emotional, and spiritual dynamics. All three of these ingredients contribute to a romantic rendezvous. The spiritual element keeps God in the forefront. He keeps your motives pure. The motive to serve each other and speak each other's love language is top of mind. You want to please God more than anything else, even more than you want to please your spouse.

This love triangulation is healthy, as you worship God, and not your wife or husband. Love the Lord first, and you will love your spouse the best. Secondly, romance involves your emotions. Your best friend is your wife or husband. This is where you make your primary emotional investment. Share the depths of your heart, your fears, your failures, and your dreams. Romance thrives on friendship, because transparency is a bridge to laughter, crying, and comfort. Friends do not have to fix things, but they are there for support and encouragement. Friends forgive freely, and often. Friendship fuels the flames of romance.

Lastly, romance is physical. Make sure you are easy on the eyes for your spouse. Remember how you gussied-up for each other when you were dating? Some things need never to change, ;never stop dating. If you do, you risk losing your marriage or, at the very least, a mediocre one.

Once you 'catch' your life-mate you have to keep them. Your pre-marriage strategy of smelling good, looking good, and tasting good is all still good. So take the time to clean up, dress up, make up, and hook up. In addition, communication is critical for romantic results. Engagement of hearts in conversation leads to engagement of bodies in intimacy. Physical intimacy goes a long way in preventing unfaithfulness. Children are blessings from God, but do not let children stand in the way of a romantic marriage. Work is necessary, but not at the expense of romancing your spouse. Let your calendar and checkbook budget time and money for romance. Plan a weekly date night or an occasional overnight away. Communicate during the day with phone calls and/or e-mails. Take her shopping for a new outfit; surprise him with a romantic dinner. Mow the grass for her; hike with him. Romance is planned and very practical.

The Bible teaches, "The husband should fulfill his marital duty to his wife, and likewise the wife to her husband" (1 Corinthians 7:3).

A6 SORROW REMOVED

> "… he will swallow up death forever. The Sovereign Lord will wipe away the tears from all faces: he will remove the disgrace of the people from all the earth. The Lord has spoken."
>
> ISAIAH 25:8

Sorrow is the fruit of sin in a fallen world. Therefore sorrow has liberty to inflict pain. No one is immune from sorrow. Sorrow is created by sin, death, divorce, selfishness, poverty, rejection, loss and fear. Sorrow is all around and it circles its prey like vultures around a dead carcass, ready to pick away at the meat of your soul. Sorrow does not discriminate between races, gender, social class or stage of life. It is there to facilitate a weepy heart and a weary mind. It never goes away in this lifetime. Your sorrow may be overwhelming to the point of anguish and despair. You cannot take anymore. The hurt is about to drive you crazy. You cannot handle it. You have lost perspective and God seems a million miles away. Things have gone from bad to worse and you have nowhere to turn. You have hit a brick wall and life seems to be crumbling in around you. Sorrow is like a ball and chain around your joy, and you live in the regret of the past rather than the hope of the future. Your current circumstances have simply crushed you, and you are claustrophobic in your worries. However, you do not have to stay in this perpetual sadness. There is a way out, and there is hope. There is a balm for your cankered soul. You can be rescued from drowning in your sorrows.

Jesus is the Savior of your sorrows. He was a man acquainted with grief. Sorrow is not foreign to Him. He was a man of many sorrows. He was inflicted with not just one, but multiple sorrows. He is a sympathetic Savior waiting to soothe your pain. He wants to gently wipe away the tears, so ask Him to dive in and rescue you from your thrashing about in the deep waters of your sorrows. He at the very least will be with you. He wants to walk with you during this dark night of your soul. He does not want you to battle sorrow alone. Others may not understand, but He does. You may not know how to put your sorrow into words, but He still comprehends. Nothing is beyond the omniscience of your Sovereign Lord. His resources are limitless and always just what you need. Tap into a miniscule fraction of His grace and you can find peace and forgiveness. He comforts and caresses your heart, and He can break the chains of sorrow that grip your soul.

So, take the medication of His grace. Administer larger doses in the beginning to stop the spread of sorrow's infection. He wants you to experience His abundant life in Christ. He wipes away your tears in heaven and on earth. Sorrow's removal is His specialty. Let God remove your points of sorrow one by one. Like downed trees from horrific winds, He will lift them individually from the objects they have crushed. He will replace hurt with something healing. Sorrow is temporary with God. He fires the temp workers of sorrow and replaces them with the full-time workers of joy. Let Him remove your sorrow, and you will not be sad you did. You will be glad, and so will the many others who love you and pray for you. He is the Savior of your sorrows. The Scripture is majestic, "…and the ransomed of the LORD will return. They will enter Zion with singing; everlasting joy will crown their heads.

Gladness and joy will overtake them, and sorrow and sighing will flee away" (Isaiah 35:10).

"But Abram said, 'O Sovereign Lord, how can I know that I will gain possession of it?' "
GENESIS 15:8

You know by first knowing God. He does not leave you in the dark to grope around in unbelief. His goal is for you to go to Him for discernment and understanding. If assurance of knowing what God was saying came easy, you would be tempted to take the credit for your accomplishments with the Almighty. He wants you to know what to do, but on His terms. Many times knowing what to do follows belief and obedience. Take God at His word today and be faithful to His instructions. It may mean extending kindness to a nemesis at work, or praying more for your teenage child and saying less. Indeed, how to know follows how to be. Be patient and allow God to work in spite of your self-imposed deadlines. Trust Him as you wait on Him.

Furthermore, do not let your drive for possessions paralyze your trust and obedience. When you are ready, God will allow you to understand how to know you can have something. He trusts those who are trustworthy. Indeed, be faithful with your finances as it protects you from bypassing God's best. Personal debt can be a short cut to seeing God work, so rely on Christ not credit. It can easily take the place of God's provision. So take a financial reality check and start by paying off the credit card with the lowest balance. Money can draw you closer to your Master or drive you further away. You can know you are positioned to buy something if you have the cash for the purchase. Cash collaborates with the future, but debt presumes on the future. Paying as you go helps you to know the Lord's leading. So follow the Lord by faith. You know all you need to know, as you get to know Him. Knowing Him is your passage to knowing what to do. The Lord loves you too much to leave you in the lurch. He constantly communicates to His children through Holy Scripture. He may speak to you in a dream. He may be shouting at you through friends and foes. Circumstances may be squeezing you toward specific outcomes. Be aware of all that is converging around you for Christ does not work in a vacuum.

God is working all around you. Engage with Him in your crisis of belief. He will let you know what to do next. Trust God with this one thing, and ask Him for discernment on the next steps. Validate your idea with those who know you best and who hold you accountable. Be faithful with these small steps, and He will position and promote you to experience larger roles and responsibilities in His timing. Resist the temptation to rush to the next big thing. There are a lot of little miracles yet to be encountered. The lion's share of your vision may happen after you are gone. The continued execution of how to know may follow you into eternity. So set the table now for those to feast on your faith after your exit.

You know by knowing Him. The Bible says, "I keep asking that the God of our Lord Jesus Christ, the glorious Father, may give you the Spirit of wisdom and revelation, so that you may know him better" (Ephesians 1:17).

A8 GOD'S SENSE OF HUMOR

Sarah said, "God has brought me laughter, and everyone who hears
about this will laugh with me." GENESIS 21:6

God makes you laugh because of the incredible way He provides and answers prayer. You laugh out loud when you have a child, especially when the little one is unexpected. You laugh when you land a job or deal that was totally unexpected. You laugh when the Lord loves you beyond your wildest dreams; because of His extraordinary provision your joy and thanksgiving literally overflow into laughter. It is a respectful and grateful laughter to the Lord. Smiles are the refreshing fruit of laughter. He makes you laugh because He has a sense of humor. Heaven is not humorless for it is full of joy and laughing out loud. The Lord laughs with you and at you. He gives you laughter to remind you of His sense of humor. He gives you laughter to unleash joy and enable you to relax in Him. God is in control and you have His permission to laugh. It is tragic when there is failure to receive heaven's humor. It is a false belief that a smile is not spiritual, because piety likes to produce joy. God's sense of humor smiles, and to walk with the Lord means to laugh with the Lord. Think about the last time Jesus surprised you by joy. Reminisce on those answered prayers that seemed unlikely and almost irresponsible, but He smiled and said yes. Did you take the time to laugh out loud with the Lord? Awe and laughter are not mutually exclusive; they go together.

Moreover, celebrate God's sense of humor with others. Do not hold back your laughter with those you love and respect. Laughter is relational lubricant. It is an elixir for evangelism and discipleship. It is a marinade for mentoring. No one wants to be around laugh-less company. Don't wait to laugh only at special occasions like weddings and birthdays. Laugh in between those times. Laugh daily with others. Laugh out loud. It may be a child's performance at school or a church play. Laugh with them at their risk of being vulnerable and expressive. Laugh when things don't go just as planned at work and home. Laughter links to the Lord and each other. Laughter keeps you from taking life and yourself too seriously.

Certainly there are issues that are no laughing matter. Be sensitive to not laugh at someone's pain, but do not discount your ability to make others laugh. Your laugh gives others permission to laugh. Laugh at yourself. Laugh at your quirks. Laugh at your accent. Laugh at your life. Laughter is contagious. Laughter with another is love. You love on someone when you laugh together. Christ gives laughter as solace for your soul. You miss experiencing an important part of Christ's character when you choose not to laugh. Let go and laugh. Let go of anger and laugh. Let go of hurt and laugh. Let go of disappointment and laugh. Let go of false humility and laugh. Let go of pride and laugh for He has done great things.

The Bible says, "Our mouths were filled with laughter, our tongues with songs of joy. Then it was said among the nations, "The LORD has done great things for them" (Psalm 126:2)

SELF ANGER

"And now, do not be distressed and do not be angry with yourselves for selling me here, because it was to save lives that God sent me ahead of you."   Genesis 45:5

Self-anger is self-destructive, self-imposed and ruinous. It happens when we get mad at ourselves and do not forgive ourselves. We get hot headed over missed opportunities. We boil over into anger when we over commit and are unable to follow through with excellence. We 'kick ourselves' when we are not kind to others, and we regret after the fact that we lost our temper. We 'beat up on ourselves' for dumb decisions that penalize our family with financial stress. We quickly snap at others because of unmet expectations, and we can't even meet the unrealistic standard we hold over ourselves. Self- anger is a symptom of insecurity, unrealistic expectations and unforgiveness. It soars when there is no context for Christ-centered living. Without God as the governor of your plan you obsess unnecessarily. You worry about your adult children who make mistakes that could have been avoided. You blame yourself and become angry because you could have done a better job of teaching and training them in the wise ways of God. Self-anger gets the upper hand at work when you can't get others to carry out your agenda. You feel like you have failed as a leader, and forget this is how you grow as a leader. Therefore, take self-anger to your Savior before you self-destruct.

Jesus wants to work with you. Take a deep breath of trust in Him and exhale a prayer of gratitude and thanksgiving. Come under the yoke of Jesus and allow Him to bear your burden of pain. Do not second-guess yourself for the past is past. God can use the sins of your past to carry out His plan in the present. You cannot undo a divorce, but you can apologize, make restitution and be forgiven. You can forgive yourself and you can ask forgiveness from those whom you severely mistreated. You forgive yourself when you see yourself as God does. He sees you as a needy soul incapable of forgiving yourself without first receiving His forgiveness. Forgiveness first comes from your heavenly Father. It is a chain reaction of grace.

God forgives you so you can forgive yourself and others. This is how far-reaching the forgiveness of the Lord extends. His forgiveness is fluid. His forgiveness flows to the most significant and insignificant of hurts. Your self-anger will subside in the face of forgiveness, so let go of your resentment and embrace forgiveness. Jesus has already paid the price for your misdeeds and sins. You do not have to stay simmering in your anger over guilt. You are set free from self-anger because of our Savior Jesus. Replace resentment with repentance, pride with peace, and self-anger with your Savior's unconditional love and forgiveness. Give yourself permission to weep for tears heal a torn heart. Warm weeping dissolves self-anger like hot water over ice. Forgive and be forgiven. Love and be loved.

Replace self-anger with self-acceptance. Because the Almighty accepts you just as you are, so can you. The Bible says, "Accept one another, then, just as Christ accepted you, in order to bring praise to God" (Romans 15:7).

A10 GRANDPARENT'S BLESSING

"They are the sons God has given me here," Joseph said to his father. Then Israel said,
'Bring them to me so I may bless them.'   GENESIS 48:9

God's gift to grandchildren is to be blessed by their grandparents. It is significant for grandsons and granddaughters to receive this grand blessing. Grandchildren are certainly a blessing; who can argue this? Their smile blesses. Their laugh blesses. Their creative and passionate conversation blesses. Their infant coos and twinkle of an eye bless. Their honesty and love bless. Their trust and imagination bless. Grandchildren are a blessing without a whole lot of effort. The minute they showed up, they blessed. Grandchildren are a grand gift from God, but there is more to the grand blessing of grandchildren. They are created by God to be blessed by their grandparents, so not only are they a blessing to their grandparents; they are to be blessed by their grandparents.

This context of blessing is critical to the spiritual, emotional and physical well being of children. There is a greater family purpose beyond their immediate relationship with mom and dad. Indeed, this is more easily understood in an agrarian society where the family is close and connected. They are close in proximity and have aligned passions around work, play, home and church. Grandparents are there to bless with a kind word and an understanding ear. They teach grandchildren how to whittle a rough stick of wood into a smooth work of art. They modeled how to manage money and teach eating peanuts from a soft drink bottle. They bless you without you knowing you are blessed. Therefore position your family to interact and engage with their grandparents. Visit them often. Invite them over at holidays and on the spur of the moment. Create environments for your children to be blessed by their grandparents. They are not competition, but agents of Almighty God. Do not deny them the opportunity to be blessed and to bless.

The blessing of confidence, courage and candor come from being around grandparents who care. The few grandparents who could care less may very well come around, because God created them to care. Don't give up on them, but keep praying for their care to awake from its selfish slumber. Give them a chance for Christ created grandkids to be an object of their grandparents' affection and blessing. Encourage your children to visit the home of your parents, and trust God to unleash His blessing through your parents. Their unconditional love makes your child a better son or daughter, and you a better parent. Lastly, grandparents bless your grandchildren with a legacy of someone who loves God and people. Do not become the center of attention; instead lead them to fall in love with Jesus. God will live in your grandbabies beyond your life. Bless them with Bible reading and prayer. Bless them with worship at church. Bless them with stories and adventure. Bless them with generosity. Bless them with obedience to God. Bless them with a life worth emulating.

Grandchildren are not complete without the blessing of their grandparents. You invest in eternity when you bless your grandchildren. The Bible says, "The glory of young men is their strength, gray hair the splendor of the old" (Proverbs 20:29).

AUDACIOUS ASK

"The Israelites did as Moses instructed and asked the Egyptians for articles of silver and gold and for clothing. The Lord made the Egyptians favorably disposed toward the people, and they gave them what they ask for…" EXODUS 12:35-36

Once God paves the way, it is time to ask. You may have ask many times, but do not give up on the generosity of others. Giving is a God-thing. Asking is many times the Almighty's method of provision. He is pro-vision. Vision is His vehicle for mighty works. It may not make sense for people to get on board now, but God has been at work in ways we don't understand. He is the one who instills His fear and faith. We limit the Lord when we fail to ask others to participate in His almighty acts. Our procrastination may prevent others from experiencing God. It is not about our limited abilities. It is about Him and His works. It is freeing to ask on behalf of God and His great work. If the world can be audacious in their request for temporal needs, how much more can we be for eternal investments? Pride tends to paralyze bold requests. We don't want to look foolish or irresponsible. We place ourselves instead of God at the center of the request. Asking is all about the acts of Almighty God, not our lowly limitations. If God says so, then it is so. Reject excuses to slither out of your responsibility to show up on behalf of Him and present your case for Christ. Yes, pray before you ask on behalf of Almighty God, but there is no need to be shy for you to represent your Savior. Humble yes, but not shy. Shy is for the unsure. If He has led you to this point, then propose His plan, and ask.

Prepared people are expecting an "ask." God has prepared their heart. They are favorably disposed to you, and your God-given vision. And do not limit the Lord's provision. It may come from the most unlikely places. People you have never met before may want to purchase heaven's stock for the sake of His cause. Do not be overwhelmed by the number of zeros needed on their check. Money is not an issue to your Master. Your obedience to audaciously ask may be the only limiting factor. You are God's broker, therefore do not hold back; ask audaciously. Trust Him to touch the heart of those to whom you propose His plan.

Indeed, asking is not always easy; but it is most beneficial. The number one reason people do not give is because they are not asked. You may need to solicit donations for your ministry. If so, proceed with determined dignity and quiet confidence. You may need to ask for investment dollars in your business. Do it with an open hand, and trust God with the wisdom of your investors. Your ministry and your business are His. He wants His work to be more successful than you. You may need ten times the cash and resources you have needed in the past. Do not allow the largeness of the vision to scare you away. It is an attraction not a deterrent. Big vision attracts big people. It's all about Him. His provision is your Passover from a small vision and an exodus into the Promised Land He has prepared just for you.

It is time to move out of the bondage of visionless and limited living, and ask audaciously for the Almighty. Paul understood the principle of asking, "Confident of your obedience, I write to you, knowing that you will do even more than I ask" (Philemon 21).

A12 SIN'S REMEDY

"Moses said to the people, 'Do not be afraid, God has come to test you,
so that the fear of God will be with you to keep you from sinning.'" EXODUS 20:20

Sin has a feared enemy and it is the fear of God. The fear of God is not the only remedy for sin, but it is a potent vaccine. The fear of God and sin cannot coexist for long. It is a flame that consumes sin's combustible character. The fear of God repels sin and keeps it at bay. This is why the devil attempts to devalue the fear of God. He knows if we do not take seriously the fear factor of our heavenly Father, then we are exposed to sin's influence. Without the fear of God we are set up for serious sin problems. Cultures crumble without a moral fabric flush with the fear of God. Families fall into severe dysfunction when the fear of God is not lived out or understood. Individual lives lose their meaning and purpose when the fear of God is placed of the shelf. The fear of God is a force to be reckoned with by all who come in contact with their Creator. We can dismiss it as an old-fashioned doctrine (though it has been around since Adam and Eve), or we can embrace it as necessary for successful living. When we fear God, we find God. When we fear God, we love God and are loved by God. When we fear God, we understand that some things are off limits and we do not go there. When we fear God, we trust God. When we fear God, we run toward God in worship and away from sin in disgust. The fear of God is our friend, and it enhances our friendship with our heavenly Father.

Therefore, take the commands of God seriously. The Ten Commandments are a glossary of how to express our fear of God. An adulterer sins because somewhere along the way the fear of God did not matter anymore. The idols of materialism can consume us when we forget to fear God and instead worship at the altar of financial gain. The fear of God is what feeds children to honor their parents and it positions parents to lovingly raise their children. Indeed the fear of God is our fortress against the devil's devices. It is our motivation to put on the full armor of God, knowing we are no match in our own strength to defeat the devil. The fear of God is not a mindless and cold obedience; on the contrary it is thoughtful, prayerful and full of joy. It sees the opportunity to obey God as an honor.

Moreover, the trials and tribulations you may be facing are not meant to create an unhealthy fear that cringes before Christ, but rather a healthy fear that trusts Him in spite of this test in your faith. Do not allow the sorrow of loss, or the success of gain to keep you from fearing God. When you focus on our heavenly Father in worship and prayer, you can't help but fear Him. His character invites the fear of His followers. Fear Him and you will be set free from sin and self. Ego exits when entertained by godly fear. Pride is not present with the fear of God. Listen to the Lord and you will fear Him by faith. The secret to a sin-starved life is to fear God. Invite Almighty God to inoculate you from sin with the vaccine of His fear.

The fear of God is not friends with sin. Therefore do not be afraid to fear, wisdom says, "To fear the LORD is to hate evil; I hate pride and arrogance, evil behavior and perverse speech" (Proverbs 8:13).

GOD JOURNAL

"When Moses went and told the people all the Lord's words and laws,
they responded with one voice, 'Everything the Lord has said we will do.'
Moses then wrote down everything the Lord had said." EXODUS 24:3-4A

It is wise to journal for Jesus, for it captures the thinking of an ever-communicative Christ. When you document what God is saying, you understand more clearly and you remember more robustly. A dull pencil is much better than a sharp mind. Writing out words and wrestling with how to define what you feel crystallizes your thinking. A God journal allows you to chronicle what Christ is doing in and through you. It is an immediate reminder of His faithfulness. It is a time to unleash your anger to an absorptive white page and to celebrate answered prayer. It will one day bless those who may wade into your writings. A diary deals primarily with horizontal relationships, in contrast to a God-journal that engages with eternity. The world makes more sense when you see it from God's perspective, and His words are more penetrating and meaningful when you filter them through your heart and mind onto words on paper.

When you take the time to write out what God is saying, you see His fingerprints all over your life. It is reassuring to see Christ's copyright on your actions and attitudes. Journaling for God reminds you that He owns everything, including you. You are His representatives to a lost and dying world. Like an aware secretary, you are to listen intently to dictation from Deity. God speaks through Holy Scripture. He speaks through your body, soul, mind, and spirit. He speaks through people, both friend and foe. He speaks through money, or the lack thereof. He speaks through circumstances and in quiet prayer.

So, slow down, listen and pen the heart of God. His words do not wander far away when you write them down. You are reminded of "right" when you choose to write.

Therefore, find a quiet corner with a hot cup of coffee, tea or hot chocolate. Open the best-selling book of all time, and meditate on His timeless truth. Ask Him to apply His wisdom to your mind and heart.

With pen and paper (or keyboard) in hand, write-out what the Lord is saying to you. Write your letter from God and your letter to God. It may be one sentence, a paragraph or a page. The length doesn't matter. What matters is capturing your meditative moments, so you can decode Christ's heart for you. You can release your struggles and anxieties to your loving heavenly Father, and think through His will and plan for your life. Your God journal is evidence of His love and faithfulness. It builds a foolproof faith. It is not the style or flow that matters to your Father in heaven. Your words may be misspelled and your sentences fragmented. This is okay. God can take broken phrases and heal a fractured faith. Write about what's important to you. Your goal is not journalistic excellence. Your goal is to align your heart with His. A God-journal facilitates this outstanding outcome by faith.

Journaling is therapy and trust. Writing helps you and others remember God's faithfulness. The Bible says, "Then the LORD said to Moses, 'Write this on a scroll as something to be remembered and make sure that Joshua hears it...' "(Exodus 17:14).

A14 GOD CHOSEN

"Then the Lord said to Moses, 'See I have chosen Bezalel son of Uri, the son of Hur, of the tribe of Judah, and I have filled him with the Spirit of God, with skill, ability and knowledge in all kinds of crafts…'" EXODUS 31:1-3

God uses whom He chooses, and He equips whom He calls. When there is a vision to be cast, a mission to be accomplished or a task to be completed, Christ's call is to specific people for a specific purpose. The call of Christ is humbling, but His call is real nonetheless. It is a call to obedience first and foremost. Will you say 'yes' to Yahweh's call? He has chosen you primarily for your teachability and availability. He will grow you into the leader you need to be, but the Holy Spirit directs an obedient follower, not one stuck in the inertia of safety. You can be sure that your faithfulness in managing His giftedness mattered. God chooses those who have been faithful with what may seem like small gifts, so He can bring on bigger abilities. Your Lord is not slack in anointing and equipping you for the task. There is no vision that overwhelms your Father in heaven. He fills with His Spirit those who surrender to Him and His calling on their life. When you submit as His chosen one, His Spirit indwells and empowers you for His assignment.

Therefore let the Lord drive your spiritual development. You stay submitted, surrendered and obedient, and He will fill, anoint and baptize you in His spirit. This is not some mystical maneuvering; rather it is God's way of emboldening your faith and consecrating your character. Moreover, watch in wonder as He hones your skills. His desire for your next season of service is to elevate your knowledge and abilities to a whole new level. This may mean more formal education, or informal mentoring from more experienced men and women. It may require self-education and on-the-job training. Or, it may require a combination of all these initiatives and more. Submit your parenting skills, your leadership skills and your spiritual know-how to Him. Above all else, stay in Christ's school of prayer. The lessons learned in your prayer closet will instruct you way beyond what you can ask or think.

Lastly, prayer is an exchange of the natural with the supernatural. Prayer takes your finite understanding and empowers it with eternity's infinite knowledge, wisdom and discernment. Having the highest 'Intelligence Quotient' is not what determines whether you are chosen by God. It is a heart hungry for His wisdom that He chooses. It is a 'want of wisdom' that opens up the windows of heaven's resources, so desire deity. Prayer prepares your heart and mind to receive and apply the wisdom of God. Equipping and training develops your skills and abilities for the assignment at hand, and experience will lift your leadership to a new place of total trust in the Lord. There are no insignificant assignments from the Almighty, so tackle your new role with abandonment and passion. He has prepared you for this season; so don't look back. Only look forward to the Lord by faith. Be humbled. Be grateful. Be obedient. Be trusting.

Accept this fact: You are His choice. Jesus summed it up the best, "You did not choose me, but I chose you and appointed you to go and bear fruit—fruit that will last. Then the Father will give you whatever you ask in my name" (John 15:16).

IMPATIENT ACTIONS

> "When the people saw that Moses was so long in coming down from the mountain, they gathered around Aaron and said, 'Come make us gods who will go before us. As for this fellow Moses who brought us up out of Egypt, we don't know what has happened to him.' " EXODUS 32:1

We become impatient when things don't go our way, or when uncertainty looms over our life like a dark cloud. We become impatient when time seems to be running out, or when people don't act like we think they should act. We even become impatient waiting on God. We all wrestle with impatience from time to time. Hopefully you are not chronically impatient, if so there is a good chance you are discontent and even miserable. Impatience can be good if your house is on fire, but in the normal course of life it is not the best choice. Impatience can cause you to do things totally uncharacteristic of your normal behavior. You are prone to deviance if others prod you on for impatience does not like to be alone. Its emotions are fueled by the discontent of a group. Somehow the voice of reason suffocates in a crowded room full of discontent. Its words become garbled around intense grumbling, even level heads become dull when intoxicated by impatience.

The timing of impatience can be uncanny. God could have just performed a beautiful act like childbirth, and then suddenly we become impatient with meeting the needs of the totally dependent baby. We forget the joy of birth and revert back to the burden of bringing up a child, and complain about the inconvenience of infants. We become impatience with their cries that started out as cute, but helping anything to grow takes time. It takes a tremendous amount of patience. We can't shirk our responsibilities as parents, wives, husbands or friends. Indeed, be disciplined and patient to build. You can build healthy good things before they become broken bad things; build your life, your business, your family and whatever worth building, build to last. What you do while you wait determines whether you are patient or impatient.

Therefore, use this time of waiting to ratchet up your service to others. Service to others on behalf of Christ keeps you from being impatient around your own expectations. It diverts idle minds from believing Satan's lies; you avoid playing foolish mind games when you are engaged in unselfish acts of service. Secondly, seek the Lord in worship and thanksgiving, as they facilitate patience and contentment. You can't contemplate the goodness and greatness of your heavenly Father and not be infected with patience. Worship feeds trust, and trust is the parent of patience. The appetite you feed becomes who you are. Worship recalibrates your reasoning to reflect on the character of Christ. Lastly, pray for those who have not met your expectations. They may be spiritual leaders who seem to be ignoring you. It may be a spouse that is in a season of self-absorption. Your boss may be demanding and unreasonable. Your children are uncommunicative and uncooperative.

You can battle impatience with Christ's unlimited patience. The Bible teaches, "But for that very reason I was shown mercy so that in me, the worst of sinners, Christ Jesus might display his unlimited patience as an example for those who would believe on him and receive eternal life" (1 Timothy 1:16).

A16 CARELESSLY COMMIT

"Or if a person thoughtlessly takes an oath to do anything, whether good or evil—
in any matter one might carelessly swear about it—even though he is unaware of it,
in any case when he learns of it he will be guilty." LEVITICUS 5:4

Be careful with your commitments, because kept commitments are your creditability, and without creditability you are a shell of sincerity. Unfulfilled commitments come from complex living, but simplicity facilitates follow through. Simple living creates margin, which is a master at fulfilling commitments. It calculates them prayerfully and practically. Does the Lord want me to be part of this initiative, organization or relationship? A pause to pray protects you from overcommitting. Commitments need to be entered into prayerfully and also practically. Does this commitment align with your purpose, calendar and budget? If it crowds out a priority on your calendar or blows up the budget, it is not necessary. Furthermore, do not become overly influenced by the capacity of others. They may be overcommitted as well, or their season of life may offer them additional margin for added opportunities.

Moreover, what becomes the most frustrating are commitments you forget about. Forgetfulness may be a reason, but it is not an excuse. These commitments may be the worst kind, because if you don't even know you have let someone down there is no opportunity for restitution. Foolish is a man or woman who continues to commit with a debt of unexecuted obligations mounting on their credit card of commitment. Therefore, stop the crazy cycle of commitments before your word becomes bankrupt. Go to those who are still waiting in confused silence, and ask them for more time or ask them to let you out of the commitment. Ignoring them is not an option.

Above all else make sure you keep your commitments to Christ. He does not take commitments cavalierly. A commitment to Christ is bound by heaven, so it is never to be entered into carelessly. All other commitments flow out of your submission to your Savior. Your 'yes' to Jesus is not sentimental, but sincere and even sacrificial. His Spirit leads your conscience to commit. It may mean a big thing like salvation for at conversion you committed to believe in Jesus as your Lord and Savior, but your commitment to Christ goes way beyond conversion to our growth and maturity. As followers of Jesus you commit to follow Him in trust and obedience. You stay true to this commitment to follow Him even when it is not convenient, or when it may cost you something. For example you commit to church, because it is the Bride of Christ. We commit where Christ commits.. Are you engaged in His best? Or, have your commitments become a snare to Kingdom productivity? Do not commit for any more than you have time, money and character. Make Christ-centered commitments your filter of choice.

The Bible says, "So then, those who suffer according to God's will should commit themselves to their faithful Creator and continue to do good" (1 Peter 4:15).

SUCCESSION PLANNING

> "The priest who is anointed and ordained to succeed his father as high priest is to make atonement. He is to put on the sacred linen garments and make atonement..."
> LEVITICUS 16:32

Succession planning is about stewardship. You want to make sure that what you have been blessed to build is managed well after you leave. By God's grace you built a good reputation, and your enterprise is one people trust. They trust your management of finances. They trust your program, product or service to be one of excellence. They trust your character and that you do the right thing, no matter the cost. Smooth succession requires you to define and document what you do. Your job description is up to date and clearly defined. Codify the processes, policies and procedures that sustain the work. Make sure the systems run are defined, decentralized and do not depend on you.

Succession planning is a natural time to get the spotlight off you and onto the team. This needs to happen sooner rather than later. Wise leaders build a team that carries on the work long after they are gone. In a lot of cases the successor takes the effectiveness of the organization to the next level, because the founder is not there to hold him back. The gifts, skills and passions of a founder are much different from a leader/manager whose leadership style is designed for long-term steady growth. Succession planning is a sober time to look in the mirror and take an honest assessment of who needs to change. Leaders who plan for a successor succeed, but leaders who hang on past their prime hold back the enterprise. No succession planning can mean a slow death for the leader, his team and the organization. Therefore, pray for your replacement, for someone with a passion and calling for the mission of your business or ministry. Successors are not to be considered lightly. If they are not called and energized over the culture you have created, they are not a right fit. In fact, beware of forcing a family member into a wrong slot. Don't just look for those who are convenient, but trust God for someone who believes he is led by the Lord to engage with the vision.

Succession planning involves an objective and mature team who can come alongside the leader for accountability and validation. Hand-picked successors who are not validated by wise and discerning counselors are at risk. The succession planning process provides protection for all involved. So begin to think and pray about what type of person needs to eventually replace you and when this needs to occur. What is God's perfect timing and what is your role as the leader to execute its fulfillment? Talk with your board, investors or trusted advisors regarding your intentions. Ask them to begin to think and pray about the process. Everyone is replaceable in time and your service is for a season. Trust God with His business or ministry for He wants it to succeed more than anyone. Almighty God is the owner, so look to His Spirit to lead the succession process. Be prayerful, intentional and trust Him with the person.

The Bible says, "By the grace God has given me, I laid a foundation as an expert builder, and someone else is building on it. But each one should be careful how he builds. For no one can lay any foundation other than the one already laid, which is Jesus Christ" (1 Corinthians 3:10-11).

A18 FOLLOW UP

"Moses inspected the work and saw that they had done it just as the Lord had commanded. So Moses blessed them."   EXODUS 39:43

Follow up is necessary for effective leaders. It is necessary in your work and family. It is necessary as you manage and hold others responsible. Follow up means you care about the person who is performing the task and you care about the work being done. You follow up with your children because you care for them too much not to stay involved in their lives. They may seem distant and disinterested, but you still follow up. Relationships retreat for lack of follow up. Ego and pride resist follow up and expect others to initiate, however people forget. People do not place as high a priority on your activities as you do. They may even commit to a certain time, but because of busyness fail to follow through. Extremely active people need more follow up than is normally necessary. The temptation is to feel rejected because of a person's perception of disinterest. This may be the case however, you are responsible to provide gentle reminders and reengage them at a more robust level. Effective follow up is as much an art as a science. Yes, have a systematic style to your communications, but do not badger people by bombarding them with too much too often.

Furthermore, people do better when you 'inspect what we expect'; so take the time to inspect. Create margin for inspection and accountability. Follow up is an appropriate time to revisit expectations. The longer disconnected expectations are left unaddressed, the higher the probability for misunderstanding and failure. Frequent inspection leads to clarification and correction. Small adjustments along the way diffuse frustrations and any subtle surprises down the road. Do not assume that someone understands the first time. Don't assume you understand the first time. Make sure everyone is 'on the same page' and there is a coalition of efforts and resources. Also be willing to adjust, as thinking and engaged people will discover a better way of doing things. Encourage and reward their wise and resourceful innovation. Follow up frees people to give much needed feedback. Above all else, make sure the project and the process revolve around God's principles of work and relationships. It is imperative that everyone is aligned around the Almighty's agenda. His way is the best way; so do not compromise the non-negotiables that define the values and mission of the enterprise.

Follow up keeps a focus on the purpose of glorifying God. Follow up is for the purpose of wise stewardship, excellent communication and affirming accountability. Use your frequent follow up as a way to bless the other person. Make the follow up of the transaction or task a small percentage of the conversation. Use this excuse for relational engagement to find out about the person. Listen for their fears, their frustrations and their dreams. People want to know they are cared for, before they care to listen. Follow up leads to follow through, all for a greater purpose than any one individual.

Use your faithful follow up as an opportunity to bless others on behalf of God. For example, Paul wrote out expectations and then followed up in person, "Although I hope to come to you soon, I am writing you these instructions so that, if I am delayed, you will know how people ought to conduct themselves in God's household, which is the church of the living God, the pillar and foundation of the truth" (1 Timothy 3:14-15).

SIN OF SILENCE

"If a person sins because he does not speak up when he hears a public charge to testify regarding something he has seen or learned about, he will be held responsible." LEVITICUS 5:1

Responsible people speak up when necessary. Sometimes it is easier to remain silent, but God has not called us to a path of least resistance. We can stay silent, but eventually it will come out. It may come out in angry passive aggressive reactions related to our uncommunicative observations, of it may express itself in built up resentment or bitterness that eats away at our good nature and steals our joy. Suffering in silence is not God's design. His desire is for us to speak up under the influence of His Spirit, even if the words are hard and direct, God's Spirit can deliver them in a loving manner. When you speak up it means you care. We love the person too much to allow them to hurt themselves and others with self-inflicted attitudes and inappropriate actions. This is especially hard for men. Pride and ego keep us from being vulnerable to rejection or relational controversy, but we owe it to ourselves, to others and to God to speak the truth in love (Ephesians 4:15). Love compels you to take a relational risk and say something. You be faithful to speak the words and trust God with the results.

Furthermore, make sure to speak up and defend those who are defenseless. Rise to the defense of widows, orphans and the poor who are crushed under the weight of the world's injustice. You may not have to look very far. There may be family members who need your attention. Second, third and fourth chances are called for to model Christ's attitude of acceptance. Your reputation may become soiled because you choose to speak up on behalf of a seedy soul, but trust God. We can relate best to sinners because we suffer from the same temptations and sorrows. Christians are sinners saved by the grace of God, and no one is beyond God's reach.

Lastly, speak up for and serve the poor. The poor need a person they can trust. The poor need us to give them a voice against the greedy souls who seek to take advantage of them. They need financial training. They need medical supplies and education. They need nutrition. They need jobs. They need indoor plumbing. They need shoes on their feet and clothes on their backs. Mostly they need a growing relationship with Jesus Christ. The poor are drawn to Jesus when they see God's people stand up for them. They are attracted to those who care enough to sit in their homes and drink coffee, create jobs, and speak up on their behalf. It may be building Christian schools, so the poor can receive a quality education in a loving environment. It is time some of us break out of our bubble of affluence and expose ourselves to the sufferings of the poor.

You sin if you remain silent over those who are defenseless. The Bible says, "Religion that God our Father accepts as pure and faultless is this: to look after orphans and widows in their distress and to keep oneself from being polluted by the world" (James 1:27).

A20 STUBBORN PRIDE

"I will break down your stubborn pride and make the sky above you like iron and the ground beneath you like bronze."   LEVITICUS 26:19

Stubborn pride creates hardened hearts. It is shortsighted and insecure in its aggressive attempts to control. Stubborn pride acts like it has everything together and doesn't need the help of anyone, even God. Its stiff attitude is frustrating when attempting to work out conflicting issues. The demands of stubborn pride are unreasonable and its perspective is skewed toward itself. Stubborn pride resists change and misses out on improvement for the sake of the project, the team or its family. Everyone has to be careful of stubborn pride sneaking into his or her beliefs and behaviors.

Furthermore, stubborn pride rejects relational engagement that requires confession of wrong and forgiveness. There is an aversion to authenticity because this means admission of mistakes and failures. Stubborn pride will dig itself into a deeper hole of distant living before it takes a risk of being found out. However, in reality discerning people already understand the charade and the manipulation of a man or a woman who is unable to admit faults. Humility can help someone sucked into the seduction of stubborn pride; it melts under the heat of humility. God has a way of wrestling control away from stubborn pride. He will not stand by and allow stubborn pride to suffocate His servants. His passion is to break the spell of stubborn pride and bring it into relational reality. Humility means you fight fair together. You truly listen to the perspective of your spouse or coworker, without reacting defensively or judging too quickly. You are willing to change for the greater good and for the sake of pleasing your Savior.

The Lord loves us too much to stand by while we struggle under the influence of stubborn pride. Like a wild stallion with lots of will power and energy, we need brokenness and training. Almighty God is our master and trainer. He uses whatever means necessary to get our attention. His Holy Spirit is assigned to break our will and align our spirit with His. God is the one trying to get our attention. We may be mad at others, but our case is against Christ. His conviction is what causes us to cringe and shrink back from stubborn pride's relational poison. His brokenness leads us to let go of control and trust Him. He breaks us from the power of ourselves. He breaks us to be bold for Him. He breaks us and molds us into reasonable people who honor the views of others. Do not negotiate with stubborn pride, but break it under the hammer of humility, and replace it with love, respect and forgiveness.

God's brokenness brings down pride. The Bible says, "The eyes of the arrogant man will be humbled and the pride of men brought low; the LORD alone will be exalted in that day" (Isaiah 2:11).

"Priests… must be holy to their God and must not profane the name of their God. Because they present the offerings made to the Lord by fire, the food of their God, they are to be holy." LEVITICUS 21:6

Ministers of the Gospel submit to a higher standard and answer to a holy authority. There is something special and fearful about being a vocational servant of Jesus Christ. This is not a role to be undertaken lightly, or to be chosen casually like some do secular career paths. God places eternal expectations on priests, pastors and ministry leaders. Leaders in the church have the Lord as their baseline for behavior. Deviant behavior is an occupational hazard for those who lead on behalf of the Lord. The leader's character is his greatest asset. Someone cannot determine acceptable behavior based on what he wants, when the Bible and Church history have already defined the standard. How hypocritical and foolish to think leaders can flaunt immoral behavior when church members are disciplined for the same. Double standards may be for the uninformed and the unaccountable, but not for faithful and educated followers of Christ. How surreal to have to declare that character in the Church matters. A Church or ministry leader cannot practice immoral living and still lead the Bride of Christ. They cannot practice homosexuality, adultery, stealing or lying. They cannot practice unfaithfulness in any of its destructive forms.

There is a holy obligation for leaders to model and teach holy living as defined in God's Word. Holiness is not a creation of culture, but defined by God. Leaders of the God's church and ministry are to be holy as He is holy. Therefore, you can't say you are a leader on behalf of Jesus Christ if you embrace and endorse the very sin He died for on the Cross. It is the epitome of hypocrisy to follow this line of twisted reasoning. If someone is bent on breaking 2,000 years of church tradition and 4,000 years of Biblical teaching, then he should do it in the name of another religion, but not on behalf of Christianity. Do not use the Bible to defend your lame living in the name of the Lord, or the Church as a crutch for crude behavior. Wake up to the fact that you have a heavenly Father to whom we you will one day answer. Yes, He loves. Yes, He forgives. But above all else, He is holy. If anyone is hell-bent on hellish living, the Church cannot condone it.

Where does the Church draw the line for unholy living? The closer the line moves toward compromise, the closer the Church absorbs into the culture. We lose our saltiness and dim our light. We become good for nothing and trampled under the feet of fools. It must be laughable to the Lord that deviant behavior in church members, much less church leaders is even up for debate. However, holy leaders do make people thirsty for God. They shine their light of holy living on the Lord. Indeed, embrace His higher standard and expect this of your Church and ministry leaders. Elect men and women of the cloth who behave Biblically, whose character aligns with Christ's, and who model faithfulness not perfection. They are not conformed to this world but transformed by God's truth.

The Bible is clear, "Be shepherds of God's flock that is under your care, serving as overseers— not because you must, but because you are willing, as God wants you to be; not greedy for money, but eager to serve; not lording it over those entrusted to you, but being examples to the flock" (1 Peter 5:2-3).

A22 NON-VICTIM MINDSET

"No, in all these things we are more than conquerors through him who loved us."
ROMANS 8:37

Followers of Jesus are not victims, they are victorious and more than conquerors. You have overcome because Christ has overcome. There is no need to give in to the temptation of victimized thinking. A woe is me attitude places the focus on you instead of your Savior. Victims seek out sympathy from unsuspecting souls. Their desired outcome is an invitation for you to feel sorry for them. Ironically, their goal is to make you feel guilty for their sorry state of mind. They want someone else to fix their circumstances. Meanwhile, the victim remains immobile while stuck in a fear-based stalemate. Victims refuse to take responsibility, but when you take responsibility for your choices and your circumstances, you cease to be a victim. People who languish in a victim mindset do not last very long. Their life's inertia gets them nowhere and they finally experience the self-fulfilling prophecy of failure.

On the contrary, Christ frees you from the viscous cycle of victimized living. Christ is your confidence and the object of your faith. He gives you the security and strength to carry on even when you feel misunderstood, marginalized or rejected. Victimless living gets on with life. They shed feeling sorry for themselves and begin to serve others. They lift their discussions from the depths of despair to the heights of hope. Non-victims need God and people for the sole purpose of obeying Christ's commands. This is a healthy dependency that leads to overcoming the obstacles of fear, failure and faithless living. Therefore, do not allow your circumstances to define you. Christ has already defined you as more than a conqueror through Him. You are victorious in Him.

Moreover, help those seduced by and stuck in a victim mindset. Be patient while they process what possesses their thinking. Help them break what may be a family trait of defeatist living. Their parents may have been victims. Their grandparents may have been victims. For generations back, their legacy may have been marred by a victim mindset. Through Christ, lead them to break the chain of this corrosive thinking. Help them discover they need people to pray for them, not to feel sorry for them. They need the power of God to prevail in their life, instead of manipulation from man. They can rise out of the mire of a victim mindset by placing their family, faith and friends in the care of Christ. Jesus has overcome pain, suffering, and death. He transforms His children from victims to victorious followers. Therefore, be authentic in your adversity and honest about your fears and frustrations, but offer solutions not complaints. Pray for the power of God to fall fresh on you, for by faith victims vanquish.

Because Jesus has overcome, you have overcome. The Bible says, "...the Lamb will overcome them because he is Lord of lords and King of kings—and with him will be his called, chosen and faithful followers" (Revelation 17:14b).

ANGRY OBEDIENCE

A23

"...Moses said to them, 'Listen you rebels, must we bring you water out of this rock?'
Then Moses raised his arm and struck the rock twice with his staff. Water gushed out,
and the community and their livestock drank. But the Lord said to Moses and Aaron,
'Because you did not trust in me enough to honor me as holy in the sight of the Israelites,
you will not bring this community into the land I give them.'" NUMBERS 20:10B-12

Angry obedience is better than no obedience, but it is not the best obedience. It has its positive results and it has its negative consequences. It does get results but at the expense of dishonoring God and people. It's like a frustrated husband who lashes out at his wife, and says that he loves her because he provides her food, a home, a car and clothes. The fact of provision is true, but there is something ominous about the omission of love and respect in the tone of his defense. In this angry reaction, God is not glorified and self becomes the center of attention. Anger drives this type of response. It may be anger from the grumbling of ungrateful people. It may be anger at others whose capacity for work and activity does not meet your expectations. It may be anger for always having to be responsible for irresponsible people. It may be anger at oneself for not preparing others to do their own planning and implementation. Obeying God is more than going through the right motions. It is going through the right motions with an attitude that acknowledges Him as the source of provision and trust. Anger puts the Holy Spirit's self-control into hibernation. We are tempted to get angry with others for their ingratitude, when our own lack of trust in God betrays His grace. We get angry when we place too much on others and ourselves; anger limits us.

However, appropriation of God's grace infuses graciousness. His grace enables you to trust in the Almighty's agenda. You can trust Him and rest in His provision instead of rushing into angry reactions. You can get right results without being driven by anger. Ask God to replace your anger with His understanding. Submit to the control of the Holy Spirit. Your submission to your Savior positions you to walk in humility and not in pride. Pride is easily offended by those who do not live up to its expectations. Humility however, is patient and self-controlled. Humility is as much concerned about the means as the end. Ironically, at any given moment anger can push out humility and replace it with pride. It is a Christ-less coup of the heart. You become too driven when you run over relationships. Praise God there is a remedy to anger-driven living.

The remedy is to live at a pace governed by grace. Living without margin pushes out grace and incubates anger. Therefore, create more time for people and prayer. Grace-filled living is more relational and less transactional. Relationally motivated people ask caring questions instead of engaging in angry accusations. Their obedience to God is motivated by their fear of God. This honors Him, which in turn extends love and respect to others. Once you leave your place of prayer, you are still to pray. You pray without ceasing, and you ask the Holy Spirit to douse any flittering fires of anger that pride tries to ignite. Stop and discern the Spirit's prompting to pause in prayer.

Replace anger with peace and patience. The promised land of more opportunity awaits those whose complete trust in God is their motivation to obey Him. Pray as the Psalmist, "Give me understanding, and I will keep your law and obey it with all my heart" (Psalm 119:34).

247

A24 PRIDE FORGETS

"... then your heart will become proud and you will forget the Lord your God, who brought you out of Egypt, out of the land of slavery." DEUTERONOMY 8:14

Pride forgets where it came from. Humble beginnings and dependence on others seem to get erased from the memory of someone influenced by pride. Pride may get promoted, but it forgets those who contributed to the process of success. It is forgetful either intentionally or unintentionally. Pride loses its focus on who was really responsible in furthering its career. There is too much credit given to self and too little credit given to others. Pride forgets its family. Sometimes it gets so busy in work or play that it fails to involve the ones who provide the platform for its performance. Pride takes family for granted and ignores their needs. It is selfishly wrapped up in itself. Pride forgets the feelings of others, as it is insensitive and obnoxious. Pride is not afraid to crush someone's spirit on the way to success. Pride forgets others while humility includes others. Pride takes all the credit while humility shares the credit. Pride discourages while humility encourages. Pride pontificates while humility prays. Pride talks too much while humility listens liberally. Pride blames while humility takes responsibility. Pride is oblivious to good manners and courteous conduct. It is all about itself, with little or no regard for the needs of others.

Above all else, pride forgets God. It may talk about God but only as needed to rubber stamp its plans. Pride subtly uses God to carry out its agenda and it forgets to see God for who He is. Almighty God is high and lifted up. He is holy and His expectations are love, fear and obedience. Pride forgets that God governs the universe and all its inhabitants. God is engaged with you up to the smallest of details, and He knows where you are and where you need to go. He wants you to remember His pristine track record of faithfulness. His past provision is a predictor of His future provision. Pride forgets this, as it has amnesia to the things of the Almighty. Pride may say it believes in God, but its actions communicate agnosticism. It is too busy to create margin for its Master.

Therefore, it is imperative you allow Christ to keep your pride in its place. It can only be conquered with humble dependence on God, and obedience to His commands. Humility displaces pride and hunkers down before Divinity in prayer. Humility remembers God's faithful deliverance from darkness into light. It remembers God's salvation from sin and self to grace and service. Humility remembers to love God and people first, and subjugates its needs second. It has tremendous recall for good because it is led by God. Humility remembers how generous God is, and is generous in return. It understands and remembers what's important to the Lord, and then invests its energies toward His initiatives. Humility remembers to thank others and to pray for them. It is extremely grateful, and appeals to heaven on behalf of people.

Humility remembers because it cares. The Bible says, "Seek the LORD, all you humble of the land, you who do what he commands. Seek righteousness, seek humility..." (Zephaniah 2:3a).

"For I can testify about them that are zealous for God,
but their zeal is not based on knowledge." ROMANS 10:2

Activity without reality leads to futility, and this is frustrating and demoralizing place to live. Finances can be like this, as you can sincerely spend yourself into false affluence. Reality is that you have to pay for the assets that have been obtained by debt. Credit may cause you to check out of reality, but its consequences will roar back in real bills. Reality is that you cannot continue spending more than you make, for the math to work income must exceed expenses. Debt may suspend reality for a time, but it will eventually come crashing down from the overwhelming weight of credit's pressure. Finances are a reality check for they are an indicator of God's will. God speaks through money, or the lack thereof. Do not be afraid to wait and save before you spend. For example, take a low cost vacation you can afford instead of an extravagant one you can't.

Furthermore, be careful to not allow busyness to extract you from reality. Make sure you are engaged in the right activity, and are not just busy for busyness' sake. Verify information before you take a person or circumstance at face value. Before you hire someone call their references. Sincere commitment without collaborative understanding leads to dysfunction and anemic outcomes. This could not be truer than with religion. A religious zeal without engagement in reality becomes extreme, even fanatical.

So go with God's definition of reality, as He defines reality in His Word and validates it with His will. Therefore, the most effective way to remain in reality is to stay connected with Christ. Alignment with the Almighty assures reality. He is a reality check, along with wise counselors. This is why a humble and teachable spirit is a prerequisite to understanding reality. Do not allow your experience, success and intelligence to blind you from reality. Ask questions and really listen for a reality check of where you are and where you need to go. People vote with their time and money, so don't blame them if they are not responding, but ask them why. Most importantly, make sure your Church activity is grounded in the reality of a relationship with God. Religious activity does not equal relationship. Spirituality without faith in Christ skirts the reality of the need for repentance and redemption. Sincere spirituality based on wrong assumptions will get you into trouble. No amount of good deeds can substitute your need for a Savior.

Confession of your sin and receiving Christ into your life is the reality of how to begin a relationship with Him. Relationship with God by faith in Christ is foundational to understanding the world's realities. His perspective positions you to engage in reality with an eternal mindset. Prayer is your prognosis of reality, so go to God often for His reality check. Let Him define for you your need for change and maturity. Ask Him to use the realities of your situation to make you more like Jesus. Instead of denying or rejecting reality, embrace it. Reality is God's reason for dependence on Him and others. Accept by faith the Lord's reality check and rely on His grace. Activity grounded in reality is rewarding, so thank Him for keeping you in a place of blessing.

Jesus stated this reality, "I have told you these things, so that in me you may have peace. In this world you will have trouble. But take heart! I have overcome the world" (John 16:33).

A26 DISCIPLINE INVITES RESPECT

"Moreover, we have all had human fathers who disciplined us and we respect them for it. How much more should we submit to the Father of our spirits and live!" HEBREWS 12:9

Discipline invites respect from your children and your coworkers. Discipline is an application of accountability, and it is a consequence for unwise actions. If you are tuned in and discerning, you will apply discipline soon after the offense. Delayed discipline dilutes the dangers of bad decisions. If someone thinks they are getting away with something, they will drift further toward destructive habits. This is why it is wise to discipline our children sooner rather than later. They may not like it, but they will respect you for taking the time to correct their behavior. Furthermore, wise discipline means you define clear expectations and reasonable rules.

For example, your son or daughter needs to know in no uncertain terms that they will be disciplined for a disrespectful attitude, disobedient actions or dishonest speech. Write it down, have them repeat it back to you and then enforce it consistently. If they suspect they can slip by with undisciplined living, they will; most importantly discipline with loving patience. Discipline is not a club of correction, rather a laser of love. Wise discipline includes instruction. You show and tell why and how to live better by God's grace. You are leading your children to be responsible adults. Discipline done well creates discipline in the recipient. They learn discipline by being disciplined. One day they will respect you for your discipline. Better to engage in conflict today than to watch them destroy themselves for lack of discipline tomorrow.

Above all else, receive the discipline of your heavenly Father. Respect for God follows discipline from God. He disciplines because He loves. Because God cares, He disciplines. He is relentless in His loving discipline. You cannot hide from the long loving arm of the Lord. He will expose deeds done in secret. You cannot ignore God's principles and not suffer the ramifications of His discipline. He disciplines for your own good, as it is protection from further harm. His discipline stokes the fires of fearing Him.

Indeed the Almighty uses different avenues to deliver His discipline. His discipline may come through finances, relationships or health. Don't despise His discipline, or be surprised by His discipline. How you handle God's discipline can weaken or strengthen your faith for the fruit of God's discipline is intimacy. Closeness to Christ and others comes as a result of discipline. Furthermore, divine discipline is training in peace. His peace transcends the heart of those who receive well the discipline of their heavenly Father. There is no greater peaceful, easy feeling than knowing your Lord loves you. He loves with discipline, which leads to blessing. The Bible says, "Blessed is the man whom God corrects; so do not despise the discipline of the Almighty" (Job 5:17).

"I have much to write to you, but I do not want to use paper and ink. Instead, I hope to visit you and talk with you face to face, so that our joy may be complete."   2 JOHN 12

Some things are best communicated face-to-face. A proposal for marriage, a job interview, a mentor relationship, family time, explaining an issue or showing appreciation all thrive in an one-on-one relational environment. Fear tends to force us away from direct engagement with people. We sometimes avoid human contact because of overwhelming insecurity, fear of rejection or busyness. The season of face time with family evaporates unwittingly. They are off with friends, attending college and then married. Just as the song says, 'The cat's in the cradle and the silver spoon. Little boy blue and the man in the moon. When you coming home dad? I don't know when, but we will get together soon. You know we'll have a good time then.' Therefore calendar time daily, weekly, monthly and yearly with those you love. Invest time and money in face time with your son, your daughter, your spouse, your parents and your friends. Face time is when you see the fear in their eyes and extend the courage to continue. Face time allows your smile to shed a shadow of hope across a discouraged heart. Face time is your opportunity to discuss those hard issues and be sure the sincerity of your love is not missed. So, show up and love on them in person. However, most of all you need face time with your heavenly Father.

By faith, the eyes of our soul need to gaze at God. If we chronically miss coming alongside Christ, we burn out in our own strength. We desperately need face time by faith with Jesus. We need His affirmation and love. We need His instruction and correction. We need His warm embrace, face-to-face. We need His discernment and wisdom. He can give us all of these, at any time. Our Savior is spontaneous for our sake. Christ is on call for His children, but we still need structured time with Him. It is imperative that we instill the discipline of daily face time in prayer and engrafting God's Word into our mind and heart. Regular face time with God in Scripture is what transforms our thinking with truth, and keeps us from being conformed by the lies of lazy living.

You can tell when someone has been with Jesus. They have peace that brings calm. They have patience that extends a second chance. They have boldness based on wisdom. They have love that forgives. They have service that is relentless. They have faith that is strong. They have a hope that perseveres. People who have regular face time with Jesus are unique and pleasant. Therefore, linger with the Lord face-to-face. Invest time in your relationship with the Almighty. Keep an eye on eternity. Furthermore, create face time with family, friends, and those you lead and serve. Trust and intimacy comes from looking into each other's eyes. Take the time to discuss hard issues in person. Provide constructive and courageous feedback, and forging face time means you care.

Faithfulness in face time leads to robust relationships. Therefore, enjoy the joy of being with Jesus and friends. Moses experienced this, "The LORD would speak to Moses face to face, as a man speaks with his friend" (Exodus 33:11).

A28 A GOOD IMITATION

"Dear friend, do not imitate what is evil but what is good. Anyone who does what is good is from God. Anyone who does what is evil has not seen God." 3 John: 11

Imitation of good is good, but imitation of evil is bad. So, look for the good in others and compliment them with imitation. When you copy another's character, you extend an affirmation of who they are. You validate them when you follow their example. They are encouraged and you are equipped to live a better life. Everyone is happy when imitation of good is applied. But be discerning in your imitation of others. A smile does not assure that someone is good. People may be friendly only for their own sake. A religious person does not guarantee good. Probe their motives for being good and beware of self-righteousness and performance-driven living. However, when you discover a good person, you have a gift. Honor them with respect and recognition, and give God the glory for their goodness. If you want to grow as a giver, pray for generous givers whom you can follow. Pray for people from whom you can learn and emulate their goodness in giving. If you want to grow in your marriage, be around married people who put God first and their spouse second. You are wise to imitate the healthy habits of good people, because you can't be good alone. You need good examples to educate you. Goodness is relative, so make sure their goodness is from God.

Authentic goodness is from God. The Holy Spirit creates godly goodness in the heart of Christ followers. It is a goodness orchestrated and motivated by Almighty God. Goodness without God is sentimental, shallow and has no eternal consequences. It is only when your goodness promotes God that you are genuinely good. The God factor is what gives goodness depth and breadth. His goodness travels from one generation to the next. The goodness of God penetrates the hardness of hearts and the most evil of circumstances. It transcends cultures and language. When you imitate goodness given by God, you embrace a life with eternal consequences. This quality of goodness goes a long way in living, governing, leading and relating well.

So above all else, imitate the goodness of God. Look at the life of Christ and by God's grace seek to imitate Him. Jesus is your model for goodness. Taste the Lord and see that He is good (Psalm 34:8). The goodness of God satisfies your hungry heart. Moreover, be cautious not to do good deeds without first receiving the goodness of God in Christ. Your benevolent behavior promotes eternal good only when Christ has conditioned you. Godly goodness flows from the inside out. It is an internal imitation with eternal outcomes. Therefore imitate good, so when others imitate you they imitate a good thing.

Imitation of good begins by receiving Christ into your heart by faith. The Bible says, "So then, just as you received Christ Jesus as Lord, continue to live in him, rooted and built up in him, strengthened in the faith as you were taught, and overflowing with thankfulness" (Colossians 2:6-7).

ETERNAL GIFT

"And this is the testimony: God has given us eternal life, and this life is in his Son. He who has the Son has life; he who does not have the Son of God does not have life." I JOHN 5:11-12

The most significant gift we can give or receive is the gift of eternal life in Jesus Christ. This gift cannot be bought with money, and is given and received by faith. His birth, His life, His death, and His resurrection were all gifts. God's greatest gift to the human race is His son Jesus Christ. Eternity is a gift that keeps on giving forever and ever. Your eternal gift to someone could be represented in the form of a Bible, a book, a sermon or a conversation explaining the gospel of Jesus Christ, even pray about giving yourself as the Lord leads. If you are a believer in Jesus, He lives within you. When you give yourself you are giving Jesus. You can give yourself in service on behalf of Jesus. You can give money on behalf of Jesus. You can give a listening ear on behalf of Jesus. But when all is said and done, people around you do wonder about this gift. Deep down they desire God's gift. He has created us all to want His eternal gift. Give it away with grace, and trust God that others will receive it by faith. Believers bear the beautiful gift of Christ. Present His gift of eternal life wrapped with a red bow of belief.

Moreover, the gift of eternal life takes affect when received. An unopened gift communicates rejection to the giver. Your heavenly Father patiently offers His son Jesus as your gift of eternal life. You can receive it by faith, or you can reject it as unimportant or irrelevant. The best thing you can do for yourself and others is to accept God's gift of eternal life in Jesus. Without Christ becoming real and personal, you are destined for a life lacking proper purpose and a death with dreadful eternal consequences, but eternal life with Him is His expression of love and forgiveness.

God gave His son because He loved you. Christ was born for you. He lived for you. He died for you. He rose for you. His wish is to live within you. He wants to be your life. What an extraordinary gift God's grace has bestowed upon you. His part is to give; your part is to receive. Furthermore, receiving God's gift of eternal life has its benefits. Christ exchanges your old life for His new life. He lives within you and through you. His character compels you to live life to its fullest. He forgives you of past, present and future sins. He leads you, guides you and directs you. He comforts you when you hurt. He affirms you when you are right. He convicts you when you are wrong. He brings a smile to your face and a bounce to your step. He replaces greed with generosity, anger with forgiveness, pride with humility and gloom with gladness. There is no receiver's remorse after opening God's eternal gift, only joy unspeakable.

Jesus says, "Now this is eternal life: that they may know you, the only true God, and Jesus Christ, whom you have sent" (John 17:3).

A30 SERVANT LEADERSHIP

> "… whoever wants to become great among you must be your servant, and whoever wants to be first must be your slave—just as the Son of Man did not come to be served, but to serve, and to give his life a ransom for many." MATTHEW 20:26B-28

Servant leadership is service. It is not jockeying for position, nor is it politicking for power. Instead it is posturing for the opportunity to serve. This does not bode well for the insecure soul in need of abundant attention. Servant leaders avoid the limelight, and serve in ways that many times go unnoticed. The little things make a servant leader. It may be taking out the trash at home, or making the coffee at work. No task is too menial to the servant leader, but there is something bigger than behavior that distinguishes a servant leader. It is an attitude of how to make others successful. He or she knows if those around them are successful, then there is a good chance they will experience success. Self-service, on the other hand, builds a culture of mediocrity. It is all about taking care of my little world, and not giving any thought to the needs of other team members. The unspoken rule is survival of the fittest. This self-service contributes to a scarcity mentality. If I serve you then you may look better than me. You may get all the credit. This fear factor facilitates competition instead of cooperation.

Servant leadership is not caught up with getting the credit, for the servant leader has put to death the need for recognition. The attention and credit can easily flow to others, which is where it belongs. Egos cannot handle the attention for they toast in the limelight like a lily-white body in a tanning booth. Instead, the servant leader may give away opportunities that come his or her way. Creating value for others becomes the goal. Titles will come in God's timing, so seek to serve and let status find you. Jesus was the servant leader of all servant leaders. He boldly confronted the sins displayed by the religious hypocrites while washing the feet of His disciples. He ran out those who commercialized the temple, but had time to allow children to sit in His lap. He questioned the motives of threatened leaders of the day, while taking the time to feed and teach thousands of people. Jesus did not cower to the power brokers on the left or the right.

Instead, He challenged their theology and questioned their character. Jesus served quietly on most occasions and boldly as needed. No sincere seeker was neglected, and His motive was to serve for the glory of God. His ultimate service was laying down His life for the human race. Consequently, as a follower of Christ, you can become a better servant leader because Jesus seeks to serve through you. You can't, but He can. Submit to Him and watch Him use you to serve. Die to getting attention and credit while celebrating the success of others. Quietly volunteer for the next lowly task. Set up others to succeed. Give away your life and you will find it. This is the example of Christ. This is the model to serve and lead in the way of the Holy Spirit.

The Bible says, "But now, by dying to what once bound us, we have been released from the law so that we serve in the new way of the Spirit, and not in the old way of the written code" (Romans 7:6).

"If your brother sins against you, go and show him his fault, just between the two of you. If he listens to you, you have won your brother over." MATTHEW 18:15

Christians tend to be too nice,, and skirt conflict. However, Jesus teaches that healthy conflict is necessary for relational and spiritual growth. It is required to keep clean accounts with others and stay focused on Kingdom priorities. Conflict resolution may be uncomfortable, but if an issue or offense is ignored it can become ugly, and even explosive. Conflict resolution requires cooperation from at least two parties. There are two roles in the beginning stages of conflict resolution. One role is the confronter; the other role is the receiver. If you are the confronter, it is critical to communicate the facts of the situation. If you are loose with the truth and cavalier in your confrontation, the situation will worsen. You probably need to have the details documented and verified. The second critical aspect of the confronter is the spirit of the conversation. Do not inflict an accusatory tone in your voice. You are there in a spirit of reconciliation and healing. Avoid a condescending attitude, as you are a candidate for the same concerns you are bringing to your friend. Confront in a spirit of humility and grace with the truth in love.

The receiver, on the other hand, needs to beware of defensiveness, denial, and defiance. When confronted, the receiver needs to listen carefully and not interrupt with petty excuses. After hearing the accuser, the receiver can correct any misconceptions and inaccuracies. His spirit of correction is mature and level-headed. Moreover, in most cases the receiver needs to apologize. Nine out of ten times a sincere apology from the one receiving the rebuke remedies the situation. On the other hand, a combative environment will just escalate the debate into a stalemate. Then nobody wins. So, treat each other as God does and everyone wins. If there is not a private resolution, then there is the option of mediation. Mediation can involve one or two additional people. If two more are invited it is effective for each party to select one person, both who are respected by all. Everyone one should agree that the resolution of the mediator(s) is the final word. Whatever is decided will be accepted and implemented by both individuals. Lastly is church discipline. This publicly expels from the fellowship someone who is obstinate to remain in severe sin, while still claiming to be a committed follower of Christ.

Indeed, one of Satan's most effective plans is to lull us into ignoring conflict until it blows up into misguided confrontation. He keeps us busy, hoping the issue or person will go away. However remaining uninvolved plays right into the hand of the enemy. To engage with another is to care. To ignore and even gossip about another is betrayal. The mature follower of Christ seeks to lovingly warn others of the consequences of unwise decisions. When you take the time to confront another, you could save them from embarrassment and humiliation. They may listen, so give them a chance. Don't wait until they crash and burn, because they deserve a chance. An opportunity to change is grace. Praise God for those who have done the same for you.

We need each other. The Bible says, "Brothers, if someone is caught in a sin, you who are spiritual should restore him gently. But watch yourself, or you also may be tempted. Carry each other's burdens, and in this way you will fulfill the law of Christ" (Galatians 6:1-2).

SWORN FRIENDSHIP

"Jonathan said to David, 'Go in peace, for we have sworn friendship
with each other in the name of the Lord...'" 1 SAMUEL 20:42

Sworn friendship in the name of the Lord is serious and based on faith. When Jesus Christ is the central figure in a friendship, there is fidelity. Loyalty based on the Lord is an extremely strong bond for friends. There is not a wavering of commitment when Christ is central to the friendship. A friendship based on the Lord takes on the Lord's attitude toward friendship. He sticks closer than a brother. He never leaves or forsakes His friends. Jesus personified friendship as He served His friends, forgave His friends, loved His friends, taught His friends, rebuked His friends, prayed for His friends and gave to His friends.

Indeed, sworn friendship is committed especially during dire circumstances. There is a commitment to always be there for the other person. It seeks out the very best for a friend during hard times. This is when friendships require an exorbitant amount of time, money, and effort. They become high maintenance when they become caught in a crisis. It may be a situation of the friend's own doing, or a result of forces outside of his control. Your friend may be on the brink of bankruptcy because of poor financial decisions. You serve him even though he suffers from self-inflicted wounds. Your friend's health may be going downhill fast; if so be there to listen.

Sworn friendship in the name of the Lord defends you to the point of risking a right standing with other respected relationships. Faithful friends will stand up for you even when it costs them. It may cost them their job. It may cost them misunderstanding. It may cost them a promotion. It may cost them financially. But, because they are invested in you unconditionally, it is honorable to defend you, especially in your absence. They ask questions of your virtual critics like, "Have you talked to them about this?" or "I am surprised by what you say." Friends stick up for each other in the face of caustic critics. Love is not silent for it speaks up.

Lastly, sworn friendship in the name of the Lord lasts. It is not a fair weather friendship, but one that lasts through the ups and the downs. Acquaintances fade away over time, but faithful friendships based on God last for a lifetime. Therefore, take an inventory of your friendships. Define the ones built on God's principles, and give these godly relationships greater credence. Be intentional in your investment of time with sworn friendships in the name of the Lord. Do not take these special friendships for granted, by aggressively praying for them. Above all else, cultivate your friendship with Christ. His model of friendship will raise the quality of your friendships. His friendship is forever. His friendship is immediately accessible. His friendship is honest and loving. His friendship is faithful. Jesus spoke eloquently about friends, "Greater love has no one than this, that he lay down his life for his friends. You are my friends if you do what I command.

I no longer call you servants, because a servant does not know his master's business. Instead, I have called you friends, for everything that I learned from my Father I have made known to you" (John 15:13-15).

"So David inquired of the Lord, and he answered, 'Do not go straight up, but circle around behind them and attack them in front of the balsam trees.' " 2 SAMUEL 5:23

God's will is not always a straight line, and many times it requires deviation in direction. It may feel like three steps forward and two steps back. Following Jesus may seem like you tracked down a path that was not a part of His plan.

However, His plan is an adventure that cannot be confined to 'point A to point B' thinking. God is so much more creative than a predictability we can control. His 'will' keeps us trusting and praying. It keeps us looking to the Lord for direction and discernment. This is why we get confused at times. We strike out in one direction, and then feel led to move in a different direction. Sometimes He leads us down an entirely different path than where we started. The adventurous part of us likes this, while our cautious and security-seeking part grows fearful. Depending on your temperament, you can become unfocused because you thrive on adventure, or you can become afraid because you like things in their place.

So what is God up to? How do we harness the Spirit of the Almighty to lead us into His great adventure? It is imperative that we listen intently to the Lord. We are compelled to follow Christ, thus we desperately need His marching orders.

But the noise of life can easily drown out the Lord's tender call. His voice will not compete with cluttered living that does not listen. His voice is pure and plain, and He longs for our undivided attention. He wants us to turn down the racket of modern day conveniences, and come to Him. Like the distraction of boisterous rush-hour traffic billowing with horns, we can't hear our Lord because we are caught in a jam. But Jesus is in our jam, and invites us to listen.

He knows you can't handle His entire plan at once, so go with what He gives you. He doesn't bless a perfect plan, but obedience and trust. Go with what you know today, and trust Him with what you don't know about tomorrow. God's work is 'in the now'. Reality is where you ruthlessly pursue Him. So don't be shy to go where God says go, even when it doesn't make sense. He is positioning you for success.

Lastly, do not be afraid to engage the enemy along the way of following Christ, but confront him in prayer. Fight the unseen forces of evil by faith. The devil will try to distract you from following God's will. He will tempt you with the allure of wealth, women (or men) and wine. Do not become sidetracked by Satan. Put on the full armor of God. Lean into the Lord, and listen to His trusting voice. Dismiss the sultry voice of self-deception. The enemy is the great imposter. He disguises his voice to sound like God's. Indeed, be so in tune with the voice of Jesus that a counterfeit sounds like a shrill fire alarm you want to avoid.

Above all else, follow the Almighty even when it seems like you are going in a big circle. Jesus says, "My sheep listen to my voice; I know them, and they follow me" (John 10:27).

VISION COMPLETER

"He is the one who will build a house for my Name, and I will establish the throne of his Kingdom forever." 2 SAMUEL 7:13

God may have someone else in mind to complete your vision. If this is the case, you can trust Christ with this unexpected discovery. It may be hard to understand why you can't be the one to see the culmination of a lifetime of work. But in reality, His vision is always a work-in-process. If implemented properly, others should be able to build upon where you have labored. However, your work has not gone unnoticed. God has used you way beyond what you could have ever imagined. He has given you extraordinary opportunities, and you have been a good steward of them. So don't be greedy with the vision God has given you, be willing to share its fruits with other faithful followers of Christ. A vision is meant to be built upon and expanded by younger bold visionaries.

Indeed, Christ may have someone else complete your latest vision for God, but don't be any less abandoned to the Almighty's agenda. Attack your God-given goals with gusto. Support the one He has chosen to complete your work. You may have a business that you birthed, but now it is time for someone skilled differently to take over. This process of entrusting the vision to a leader God has chosen is exciting. You can prepare for the transition by bringing to bear the resources and relationships needed to increase his chances for success.

Wise visionaries properly prepare others to complete the original vision. They are then positioned to watch God reveal the next big vision. Leverage your influence for the success of your successor. Trust God, and He will lead you to someone who can complete the compelling work you started.

Pray about how you can serve the next generation in a way that increases their probability of successfully executing God's vision. It may be your son or daughter who needs your training and instruction in leadership and money management. The lessons you have learned, and are still learning, are invaluable. Slow down long enough to mentor. These skills are necessary for your progeny to see God pull off this bigger-than-life vision. Your faith in God will be a foundation for them to build upon. Teach them how to pray to God and trust His truth. Be a model of extravagant generosity, and show them selfless service.

Your 'vision completer' needs your confidence and support. Do not smother him or her with your well-meaning micro-management. Instead, let him craft the vision around his personality and preferences. His methods will probably be a modification of yours, if not entirely different. It is when your vision becomes another's that you know God is at work. Let go of your vision and let someone else run with it. This person will complete it better than you, because this is his calling. God has it under control, and what He starts He completes.

The Bible says, Moses commissioned Joshua as his vision completer, "So the LORD said to Moses, "Take Joshua son of Nun, a man in whom is the spirit, and lay your hand on him. Have him stand before Eleazar the priest and the entire assembly and commission him in their presence" (Numbers 27:18-19).

S4   EDIFICATION'S EDICT

"Therefore encourage one another and build each other up, just as in fact you are doing."
1 Thessalonians 5:11

People die a thousand deaths of discouragement, because daily life extracts courage from the human heart. Discouragement needs courage first from the resurrect life of Christ. He is our hope. He is our Savior. He is our Lord. He is our life. Because of Christ in you, you may be just the dose of courage needed for a friend to make it through another day.

Do not underestimate your ability to dispense courage. Your kind word is encouraging. Your warm smile is encouraging. Your generous gratuity is encouraging. Your presence is encouraging. Your listening ear is encouraging. Your investment of time is encouraging. Your wisdom is encouraging. Your encouragement builds up others.

What Satan tears down you build up. He tears down people, but you build them up. His goal is the demolition of faith, hope and love. Your God-given mandate is the building up of faith, hope, and love. Where Satan discourages, you encourage. Like a chess-match he is trying to deceive others into thinking they are trapped with no way out. He plays for a checkmate of discouragement, but you have courage and hope in King Jesus. He already has the devil checked and there not even a possibility for a stalemate. Therefore, deliver others from the devil's delusions with eternal encouragement. Take courage from God, so you can give courage to others. Lead others to this same fountain of eternal encouragement, so they can drink when no encouragers are around. Courage to the soul is what food is to the body. It is filling at the time but exhausts itself quickly, so dine at the table of God's encouragement regularly. His word is sumptuous, satisfying, and encouraging. Dispense His word to others in doses of daily encouragement. Human words are hollow compared to the meaty words of Scripture. The Bible is a reality check, as it is the Lord's large instruction book. His word is a baptistery of bold encouragement; for when you are immersed in the Holy Scriptures, you covered with encouragement.

It is not possible to consistently feed on the Bible and not be encouraged. Believe His word and you will be encouraged. His promises are true: He has forgiven you, He has accepted you, He loves you, He walks with you, and He desires you. This is encouraging! Be encouraged so you can encourage others. It is encouraging to encourage. You see a person breathe a sigh of relief and you are encouraged. You see them do the wise thing and you are encouraged. You train a child in the way that he should go. Then he lives for God and you are eternally encouraged. Give courage and you will receive courage. Choose the high road of encouragement over the low road of discouragement. Anyone can discourage, so don't be just another anyone. Be a Barnabas and God will be encouraged, you will be encouraged and so will many others.

The Bible says, "Rise up; this matter is in your hands. We will support you, so take courage and do it" (Ezra 10:4).

SUCCESS & FAILURE

"I, even I, have spoken; yes, I have called him. I will bring him, and he will succeed in his mission.... Isaiah 48:15 "If one falls down, his friend can help him up. But pity the man who falls and has no one to help him up!" Ecclesiastes 4:10

If the team is successful, the leader is successful; so it is imperative the team succeeds or the leader won't. Your role as the leader is to provide coaching, resources, relationships, teaching and training to the team. Help them craft their strategic plan and then let them execute the plan with excellence. Yes, there needs to be periodic assessment and feedback around the mission and objectives. But use this time of accountability for alignment and encouragement. The team wants to succeed, but they need to be assured that they are succeeding at the right things. Indeed, the team is where the leader has led them. If the team is unfocused and ineffective start by looking in the mirror. The leader sets the pace for focused, diligent, creative, systematic and wise work. Your affirmation and the ability to help others adjust contributes catalytically to team success. Therefore, don't hold back team members, but free around their passions, skills and gifts. You want the team to surpass any results you could accomplish alone. So allow the team to succeed by coaching, but not micro-managing. Provide feedback, resources, and training by investing in their personal development. Lastly, promote team members by giving them the opportunity to replace or surpass you.

Failure is an option for the wise leader for God fosters faith out of failure. Some of your best lessons are learned through failure. Nothing ventured is certainly nothing lost. It is imperative for the leader to give team members permission to fail, or even encourage them to fail. Team members who never fail are team members who need to fail. No failure means no innovation and no creativity. Small failures lead to big successes for this is the process for improvement.

The secure leader knows how to manage risk, when team members do fail the leader is there to infuse courage and perseverance. The road to success is paved with potholes of failure. Therefore, give the team permission to fail by encouraging them toward their goals and aspirations. This gives them the respect and responsibility needed for a willingness to fail. Allow them to craft their own plans. This ensures their ownership with passion around execution. Affirm them when they do fail. This invites them to continue taking risk. Our heavenly Father knows we will fail and He is there to pick us up and encourage us to move forward by faith. Carry on with Christ through the ups and the downs. He celebrates with us on the mountain tops. He comforts us in the valleys. We lose not when we fail, but when we give up.

So persevere, as you are a success in the eyes of your Savior. Wisdom says, "...for though a righteous man falls seven times, he rises again..."(Proverbs 24:16).

S6 CHALLENGE THE PROCESS

"Some men came down from Judea to Antioch and were teaching the brothers:
"Unless you are circumcised, according to the custom taught by Moses,
you cannot be saved." ACTS 15:1

Everything has a process, good or bad. A good process provides wise checks and balances and makes for a best decision, a quality product or service and excellent execution. A bad process rushes through an inferior design or a half-baked decision, and impedes progress. So a wise leader allows all processes to be up for debate. No process is immune to questioning, but the discussion is to be done with dignity and respect. Keep the conversation focused on process and not personalities. This is why everyone holds process with an open hand. If you become a rigid proponent of your pet process, then there is a good chance you will take any criticism of your process personally. Process, by design is what's best for the entire organization, not just a convenience created to accommodate someone's preference.

Therefore, do not overprotect process with smothering ownership. Furthermore, challenge the process with professional courtesy. You challenge the process with respect when you speak factually and do not react emotionally. This creates calm and communicates care.

You respect others when you listen to their ideas without becoming defensive. This allows for the best process to be discovered and supported by all. Lastly, respect keeps the best interests of the organization in mind. This facilitates teachability, teamwork and responsible stewardship. Anyone can complain, so challenge the process with thoughtful solutions not mindless meandering. Healthy organizations require everyone to think. No one's ideas are unimportant, from the mailroom to the boardroom everyone can come up with better ways to do his or her job. Think of creative processes that save time and money, utilize technology and then document your processes. Within a growing enterprise, the processes that worked last year will probably be lacking this year. If a process does not propel progress, then it needs to be replaced with a results-driven model. Processes serve the mission of the enterprise. Therefore, align your processes to accomplish the objectives of the organization.

Moreover, challenge the process with better ideas by researching other groups who have proven processes, because this invites innovation. Pilot new processes before implementation, because this enhances quality. Lastly, plan a process to challenge the process, because this reminds the team to think. God is into process. This is why He is symmetrical and systematic in His creation and design. His will is process-driven. Thankfully He is ultimately in control of the process. Therefore, challenge mediocre processes and create superior ones. And above all else, trust God in the process and with the process. God has a lot of passion around precision and process, The Bible says, "So make yourself an ark of cypress wood; make rooms in it and coat it with pitch inside and out. This is how you are to build it: The ark is to be 450 feet long, 75 feet wide and 45 feet high."

"Make a roof for it and finish the ark to within 18 inches of the top. Put a door in the side of the ark and make lower, middle and upper decks" (Genesis 6:14-16).

BE HONEST

"I know, my God, that you test the heart and are pleased with integrity. All these things have I given willingly and with honest intent. And now I have seen with joy how willingly your people who are here have given to you."   1 CHRONICLES 29:17

Be honest with yourself and be truthful about your strengths, your weaknesses, your limitations, your personality, and your character. Be who you are and who you can become with God's transforming power, but do not become a caricature of someone else. So be ever vigilant in your self-awareness. Take a variety of self-assessments and compare their results, become comfortable with one and make its language common place in your speech and practice. Submit yourself to a regular review from your supervisor and other team members, an open yourself up to scrutiny and feedback from your family and friends. Self-honesty comes from a teachable heart that listens to and learns how to improve from the perspective of its peers. Honesty means you confess what you don't know. You don't pretend to have all the answers, but you humbly seek to define the right questions.

Validate with others who know well what you do best. Is it analyzing data, writing, leading, strategic thinking, networking, communicating, recruiting, managing, nurturing relationships, supporting, planning or implementation to name a few? Discover what you do best and where you have the most passion, and then focus your time and attention there. It takes honesty to refrain from doing those things you like when your results are only average in their outcomes. Putting your courage and trust in others to carry out these interesting tasks will bring about the best results for everyone. Lastly, focus on what you do best. This leverages your time and promotes the best stewardship of your skills, gifts, talents and abilities. So be honest with yourself and be honest with others. Honesty with others admits and exposes what they already feel and know. It is a natural application of integrity, and is one of the top reasons people stay around for any length of time. It creates an environment of trust, which a safe place to work and live. Honesty puts rumors to rest and is as quick to communicate the negative, as it is to promote the positive. Honesty is secure enough to apologize to the team and come clean with a bad decision, or an awful attitude. Honesty is the best policy because everyone is free to be truthful.

However cover-ups and blame kill the spirit of a caring culture, but honesty breathes life, loyalty and professionalism. Be honest with others by caring enough to confront, for this keeps accounts short and cultivates trust. Be honest by confessing your mistakes, for this frees others to do the same and builds respect. Lastly, be honest by communicating the good and the bad, for this keeps everyone engaged in reality. Christ's mode of operation is honesty, and He expects us to strike from our vocabulary the dishonest habit of saying, "I'll be honest with you." Authentic honesty does not require a disclaimer. It is the natural response of someone who is honest with God, themselves and others.

Therefore be honest and watch God bless with joy, peace, love and respect. The Bible says, "An honest answer is like a kiss on the lips" (Proverbs 24:26).

S8 STAY FOCUSED

"I have brought you glory on earth by completing the work you gave me to do."
JOHN 17:4

Focus is the fuel to productivity and is free to stay on task. Focus facilitates God's will, and it has the ability to bring intensity to a situation, problem, or opportunity. There is a sense of urgency that pushes out distraction and brings clarity back to the matter at hand. Focused individuals understand that some things naturally drift out of focus, so they intentionally refocus. Mission drift ensues when the leader becomes distracted and unfocused, as well-meaning activities can distract the team or the individual from the original purpose.

The opposite of focus is to ignore or disregard. We lose focus when we lose interest, or assess a lower value to a person or opportunity. We lose focus when something else more attractive draws us into its influence, like a moth toward a candle we can get burned if we are not careful. We are forever fighting to stay focused because of bad distractions and good attractions. But we don't have to remain unfocused or focused on the wrong things.

When we stay laser-beam focused on the Lord important things become priority, and Christ becomes centric to our mind. We focus all the time. We may not focus on our most important options, but we focus. We focus on sports. We focus on having fun. We focus on finances. We focus on fitness. We focus on frustrations. Indeed, your mind and your heart tend to follow your focus. Your life aligns around where you focus, so by God's grace stay focused on Him and His will for your life. Focused faith goes a long way in experiencing God's very best. Focused intensity on the Almighty's agenda leverages His plan for your life. Focus brings freedom to do His will without reservations, so stay focused on the one thing He has called you to do and you will be amazed at the results. Become an expert in your field.

Above all else become an intensely focused person of faith and character. Your character determines your creditability with people. Your influence grows as your character grows; so stay focused on becoming more like Jesus. Laugh more and complain less. Relax more and worry less. Pray more and talk less. Give more and control less. One idea is to focus on your family. Focus more intently on your family than you do your work or hobbies. Put a puzzle together, take scuba diving lessons, plan a family reunion, organize a trip, or take care of a pet. Intentionally focus on your family now, while you have the opportunity and while they are interested. Your children deserve your intense focus. They will be gone soon, so zero in on them. Lastly, focus on God in prayer. Prayer brings into focus what matters most.

Prayer dismisses distractions and invites priorities. Jesus says, "But seek first his kingdom and his righteousness, and all these things will be given to you as well" (Matthew 6:33).

CONFRONT WITH TRUTH

"Instead, speaking the truth in love, we will in all things grow up in him who is the Head, that is, Christ." EPHESIANS 4:15

You confront because you care about the circumstance, the person and/or the organization. Non-confronters are driven by fear not care. They are fearful of rejection, of hurting someone's feelings, of losing their position, even their job. Fear drives out care and replaces it with delayed dysfunction. A non-confronting culture is filled with fear, gossip and resentment. A confronting culture on the other hand is safe, secure and rewarding. You are praised for speaking your mind. Authenticity is encouraged, and you speak up because you believe strongly in the values of the organization. You are compelled not to compromise excellence over expedience, or results over relationships. So you take the time to speak your mind with respect. You say what you mean and you mean what you say. Your clarity in communication means you want to resolve any relational rubs with a better process or program. You confront because you care, so confront often. This keeps any wrongs from turning into resentments. Confront caringly, for this shows respect that you want what's best for everyone. Lastly, confront calmly, and attack the issue not the individual; this invites dialogue. The spirit of confrontation defines its effectiveness.

It is also important to get the facts before you confront. Take the time to understand the situation and the people involved. Clarification around the truth avoids misunderstandings, and many times precludes major blow-ups. Without confrontation we assume inaccuracies that come back to bite us. Phrases like, "I didn't know you meant that" or, "I didn't understand, so I assumed..." Fact finding keeps us from wrongly accusing or, at the very least, wrongly assuming. Furthermore truthful speech delivered in love is accepted by teachable hearts. So honor the person, as this increases their receptivity. Apologize for your insensitive or inappropriate actions, for his disarms the other person and promotes trust. In the same way receive those who confront you.

If someone takes a chance to speak the truth in love, you are wise to receive it in humility. Truth is your friend not your foe. The more you appreciate and comprehend truth, the more you value confrontation and its delivery of truth. Security in Christ invites confrontation embedded in truth. Truth keeps you out of trouble and discerns the best options. Therefore, receive the truth in humility. Create environments that encourage this by being an example. Your willingness to receive truth and change; changes others. Reward those who receive the truth, as this motivates authentic behavior. Surround yourself with those who speak the truth and those who receive the truth, for this increases the probability of wise decision-making.

Christ is the master of confronting with truth, so confront in the spirit and clarity of Jesus. "The third time he said to him, 'Simon son of John, do you love me?' Peter was hurt because Jesus asked him the third time, 'Do you love me?' He said, 'Lord, you know all things; you know that I love you.' Jesus said, 'Feed my sheep' " (John 21:17).

S10 STRENGTHS AND STRUGGLES

"We all have different gifts, according to the grace given us…" ROMANS 12:6

Know and understand your strengths, because it is best to behave how God created you. By God's grace He places within you giftedness to carry out His plan. This is called your core competency. You may be a gifted leader, so lead. You may be a gifted coach, so coach. You may be a gifted counselor, so counsel. You may be a gifted administrator, so administer. You may be a gifted networker, so network. You may be a gifted writer, so write. You may be a gifted teacher, so teach. You may be a gifted servant, so serve. You may be a gifted artist, so create. You may be a gifted communicator, so communicate. There is a long menu of gifts, and you probably resemble several of them. Study your gifts, and you will discover your strengths.

Moreover, become comfortable with and accept the one thing you do naturally. It is effortless because God has engineered you for this. He gave you the skills and abilities to innovate, - create and produce these desired outcomes. However, make sure you do not confuse passion with strength. If you have the passion to speak, it is imperative you at least have the raw skill for speaking. Indeed, much of the technicalities of communication can be learned, but don't try to make yourself become someone you're not. Synergy for life and work come as you align passions and strengths. Take the time to understand what you do best and where you have the most energy, and then position your responsibilities at home and work to mirror this ideal. Do not be afraid to change and try new things.

Therefore, ask others to validate what you do best. Ask those who know you well to affirm where they see your passion protrude. Then, prayerfully align around both. You can know and understand your strengths by taking a spiritual gifts test, as this helps you define your God-given disposition. Take a personality assessment, for this helps you understand your temperament. Lastly, consider taking a psychological test, because his reveals your emotional intelligence and your leadership style. Be who God has made you to be and you will be free.

Furthermore, embrace and celebrate your struggles. They keep you humble. Do not resist accepting your struggles; embrace them instead. Make your struggles your servant by allowing others to do what you can't do much better. It is okay not to like details, but value them and those who manage them well. Your struggles beg the need for a team. It is in your struggles that you depend more on God and others. So be honest with yourself about what you don't do well. Accept the fact that even though you want to do something, you don't need to if others can do it better. They can free you to do only what you can do. Release your areas of mediocre effectiveness, as this gives others opportunity for excellence. Laugh at yourself, for this frees you from the tension of unrealistic expectations and allows you to enjoy life.

You are a valued member in the Body of Christ, "The body is a unit, though it is made up of many parts; and though all its parts are many, they form one body. So it is with Christ. For we were all baptized by one Spirit into one body…"(1 Corinthians 12:12-13).

PLOTTING EVIL

S11

"The Lord said to me, 'Son of man, these are the men who are plotting evil and giving wicked advice to this city.'" EZEKIEL 11:2

The sun never sets on evil, and alarmingly there are people as intent on evil actions as there are those committed to good ones. Like roaches roaming under the cloak of darkness, evil schemes are continuously hatched by hideous human hearts. The worst kind of evil is disguised in the robe of religion. They blame their terrorist tirades on a god of their making. They worship an idol of violence at the altar of racism, anger, un-forgiveness and hatred. There is no reasoning with religiously driven people warped in their warring ways. The realities of our world are riddled with religiously motivated people bent on evil. These religious fanatics are, of course, deceived and delusional.

Satan is smiling at these acts of atrocity aimed at innocent people. What better strategy for hell, than for people to murder in the name of religion.? This plan sends people to hell for eternity, and causes others to experience hell on earth. It is a hellish nightmare that is nagging more and more of the modern world. It can become a negative to true religion and a positive to a terror-filled belief system. Unfortunately, engineers of evil are engaged everyday in the execution of evil acts. They spend time, money and energy like an aggressive investor in a business project of monumental proportions. Their return on investment is measured by the evil outcomes of fear, intimidation, violence, mayhem and murder. However, there is an even more decisive battle raging that is unseen. It is the battle for the souls of men and women.

A person who comes to Christ in confession and repentance does not condemn others unlike themselves. Condemnation is for cowards not for Christ followers. There is no condemnation in Christ Jesus (Romans 8). An individual in Christ has new weapons in their arsenal of faith. Hate has been replaced with love. Violence has been replaced with peace. Death has been replaced with life. Retaliation has been replaced with forgiveness. Prayer is the primary weapon in spiritual warfare. A tsunami of prayer will penetrate the pride of those stuck in the sick and seductive talons of terrorism. Heaven's call is for followers of Jesus Christ to rise up in a powerful proclamation of prayer. We are the Body of Christ. When one member of the body suffers, the entire body suffers. Faith is not isolated. It is committed to the community of faith. Our friends in the faith suffering under the tyranny of terrorism need our unprecedented prayer support.

Fervent prayer flies in the face of fascism, disguised in a fanatical but false faith. We can act like we are isolated from international crises, but we are not. We will also be affected as long as evil doers are plotting evil. Until evil is totally transformed by the grace of God, we have a giant opportunity to invest in eternity. We have the remedy for radical religious jihads driven by evil intent; faith in Christ. Humbly and persistently we can present Jesus in our behavior and in our beliefs. He is the answer for atrocities hatched in hell. Heaven trumps hell, when trust in Christ is preeminent. Pray everyday for trust in Christ to triumph over tactics of terrorism. Evil plotters are no match for persistent and pure prayers. Pray for His Kingdom to come, on earth as it is in heaven.

The Bible says, "But mark this: There will be terrible times in the last days. People will be lovers of themselves, lovers of money, boastful, proud, abusive, disobedient to their parents, ungrateful, unholy... having a form of godliness but denying its power. Have nothing to do with them" (2 Timothy 3:1-2, 5).

S12 SAVIOR SATISFACTION

"Simon Peter answered him, 'Lord, to whom shall we go? You have the words of eternal life. We believe and know that you are the Holy One of God.' "
JOHN 6:68-69

Jesus satisfies, and He is all we need for life, death, and in-between. However, there are competitors with Christ that try to get in the way of our contentment in Him. Fear, envy and regret attempt to wedge themselves between our Savior's satisfaction and us. We forget that we have all we need in Him.

He has the wisdom we need for smart decision-making. He has the grace we need for love and forgiveness in relationships. He has the discipline we need to manage money effectively. However, when we deviate from the divine, we become discontent. Indeed, contentment comes from Christ for in Him there are no regrets from the past, no fears of the future and no envy in the present. Regrets can come in many forms: disappointment from a vanished youth, embarrassment from a busted marriage, or guilt over obsession in career advancement. But in Christ's economy regrets are not meant to remain, if they do they will drive us insane. He wants our past regrets to transform our relationship with Him into one that is more robust, because His forgiveness has freed us from our worldly weights of the past.

Forget what you have or have not done in the past, instead focus on what He has done. He has paid the price for your sin, as your sin bearer. Contentment comes in your consecration to Christ. He forever removes past regret with present faith.

Furthermore, fear of the future can freeze off your faith, because worry is a wart of discontent. Anxiety causes it to grow and disfigure your faith. Fear is seedy and seductive, and it leads down the path of anxious living. Fear and contentment cannot co-exist; they are mutually exclusive, but Jesus is the Alpha and the Omega. He knows what lies ahead for you, and because He is your Creator, you can be content in Him. The future is His invitation to trust Him, and it is meant to inspire hope not fear. You will anticipate what the future holds if you are aligned with the Almighty. Your life is not an accident waiting to happen, but an orchestration of Almighty God's. Christ is your conductor, so look to Him by faith and your life will sound beautiful, as it harmonizes with heaven and engages on earth.

Lastly, contentment in Christ has no room for envy in the present. God blesses who he wants to bless at His discretion. People are not your plumb line. You look to the Lord for your needs and wants. All you have is a gift from Him: your health, your family, your freedom, your friends, your faith, your finances, your mind and your heart, are all gifts from above. Your Savior satisfies, and after Him there is nowhere else to go. He has the words of eternal life, and He is your life. Embrace Christ and you will become rich in contentment. Embrace the culture and you will live poorly, never satisfied and defeated by discontentment. He is your sole source for satisfaction. Envy flees in the light of eternity.

Therefore live in the moment for your Master, and go to Jesus for joy and peace. The Bible says, "May the God of hope fill you with all joy and peace as you trust in him, so that you may overflow with hope by the power of the Holy Spirit" (Romans 15:13).

"Then Esther sent this reply to Mordecai: 'Go, gather together all the Jews who are in Susa, and fast for me. Do not eat or drink for three days, night or day. I and my maids will fast as you do. When this is done, I will go to the king, even though it is against the law. And if I perish, I perish.' " ESTHER 4:15-16

Spiritual preparation is necessary for divine guidance, and the Lord leads those who take the time to listen. Common sense does not need to be the final answer, as engagement with eternity is essential for the best decision. Therefore, take the time to prepare before you take on any additional responsibility. It is unwise and a waste of time to tackle terrific problems in your own strength. Instead, pray and fast. Pray and ask others to pray before you challenge the system or call into question a long-standing tradition. First, put pride in its place, as people are open to listen when our pride is in check.

You have the resources of heaven at your disposal. On your knees you can thank God for the trials you are experiencing. You can thank Him that in your adversity you feel the need to be loved by your heavenly Father. He comforts like none other, and conflict causes you to cry out to Christ. It may be a child that is hurting. It may be a friend who is pained over his or her fractured family. It may be a spouse who is struggling over unresolved anger and depression. Prayer and fasting along with others aligns our hearts and minds with the Almighty's.

Humility is quick to ask others for prayer support. This is part of spiritual preparation. It is not only your own heart that needs cleansing and healing, but also the hearts of those who support you. We are the Body of Christ, and we anguish in each other's pain and celebrate in one another's gain. But if you remain silent in your hurt, no one knows how to pray for you. They may assume that everything is okay, when in reality you are dying on the inside. Therefore, take a chance and speak up. People are willing to give up food and pray for you, because they love you.

However, once you have solicited the prayers and support of people you trust, be bold to follow through by faith. God has prepared you for a purpose. Do not waste His preparation. Steward well your preparation and watch Him bless with bountiful results. Courage and confidence converge around a prayerful process.

You can be bold now because you are spiritually prepared. You are prayed up, because you shut up and listened to the Lord. You lifted up your own fears and frailties, and He has heard your humble plea. The prayers of people are like a tailwind of trust that empowers you to move forward, but don't be surprised when someone opposes your courageous efforts. Some will not like it when you get the attention instead of them. But stay true to your calling.

Stay humble, trustworthy and prayerful for God knows your heart. Spiritual preparation invites God's blessing and people's participation. The spiritual giant Paul said, "Finally, brothers, pray for us that the message of the Lord may spread rapidly and be honored, just as it was with you" (2 Thessalonians 3:1).

S14 HURTING SPOUSE

"If one part suffers, every part suffers with it; if one part is honored, every part rejoices
with it. Now you are the body of Christ, and each one of you is a part of it."
1 CORINTHIANS 12:26-27

Sometimes our spouses experience hurt, it may be for a moment, for months, or in some chronic situations they may hurt over years. Hurt can come from a variety of sources: busy parents who lacked love can lead to childhood hurt, disappointments deposit hurt, lack of control contributes to hurt, shattered dreams hurt, and health issues exasperate hurt. Hurt may hover just under the heart of your spouse, or it may have inflicted deep wounds into the soul that desperately need God's healing hand.

Sadly, the scars of hurt can disfigure his or her countenance. So be aware, because your insensitivity can compound the hurt, or your sensitivity can cure the hurt. Hurt hurts.

When your spouse hurts, you hurt. You may hurt because of the empathy you feel for her pain, or you may hurt because of the hurt he or she has knowingly or unknowingly imposed on you. Hurt cannot be ignored, as it will expose itself mildly in public and wildly in private. Hurt will not go away unless there is healing.

Your tender touch brings healing. Your extra patience eases the pain. Your kind words are an ointment that soothes anxiety. Your gracious attitude is a legion of love ready to recapture the heart of your spouse. Don't give up reaching out to your hurting husband or wife. Yes, this is a time of inconvenience, and your goals may be on hold for now. You are in survival mode. Do not grow weary in doing well for in due season you will reap God's blessings (Galatians 6:9).

If you are the one who is hurting, go to your heavenly Father for healing. Let Him love you through this. Lay down your burden before it crushes your spirit. You cannot bear this burden by yourself or fix this alone. Your loving Lord wants to lead you into forgiveness and freedom. Release your regrets and disappointments to Him, and let go of your need for control. Demands for control are the fruit of fear, but Jesus can be trusted during this time of turmoil.

Don't buy into a false feeling of freedom that comes from pushing back. Instead, open up and let the Lord and your lover into your heart. Healing is an outcome of applying the outrageous love and forgiveness of God. Indeed, you may be in a mid-life reflection. You are tempted to walk away from your family, friends and faith, but it is a long and lonely walk that only enflames the pain.

Take 'scripts' from your Savior, and experience His healing for you and your spouse. Jesus said, go to Him for rest in your weariness and wholeness for your heart, "Come to me, all you who are weary and burdened, and I will give you rest" (Matthew 11:28).

LIFE LOATHING

> "I loathe my very life; therefore I will give free rein to my complaint
> and speak out in the bitterness of my soul." JOB 10:1

Some people loathe life, as it is a chore just to exist on earth. It is a burden to get out of bed and face the day. The Lord seems unsympathetic, like He is a million miles away. Some have a chip on their shoulder that is not easily removed. There is an overwhelming feeling of dread and disappointment. Their jaded perspective says, "People are out to get me and they don't care about my despair." Their glass of hope is half empty as is their soul. They have an aversion to the Almighty, their spiritual vibrancy has long since passed, and they feel punished by pain. Loathing is exhausting, as it exudes more energy to intensely dislike than to forgive and accept. Loathing speaks from the bitterness of its soul.

There is no security in Christ; only confusion and complaints. Complaints from people who loathe life become contagious to others who will listen to their unfounded fears. They begin to poison the good will of unsuspecting victims. Loathing leans its ladder against a wall of worry. They embrace the worse case and they skew others' thinking to begin questioning with unreasonable requests. Loathing is a killer of creativity and compassion, and it sucks the life out of relationships.

Jesus, on the other hand, gives life. He offers an abundant life, built on trust in Him. The Lord loathes sin and all its destructive ways. It is okay to loathe those things that are disgusting to Him, but do not loathe what the Lord loves. He loves us. He loves us in spite of ourselves. He loves us in the middle of our messy circumstances. He loves us in our anger and apathy. He loves us in our fear and faithlessness. He loves us in our discouragement and dislikes. He loves us too much to let us loathe our lives.

The love of God overcomes loathing. Loathing and love cannot coexist for love conquers all, "No, in all these things we are more than conquerors through him who loved us" (Romans 8:37).

So allow Christ to convert your complaints into compassion. He can replace what you lost with something better. Quit loathing life for it is a poor reflection on the Lord. Instead, accept life with all it has to offer, and see the good and the bad as part of God's plan. If all you experienced was success you would build relational walls around your life, but in your failures you extend bridges out of your brokenness.

People can relate to you when you admit your struggles and suffering. It is in your pain that your faith becomes creditable to those who want to know Christ. When the weak in faith see you love the Lord and life in your adversity, they are drawn to Jesus. When you choose love over loathing, you vote for vitality in your relationships. Love soothes your soul, seeks to be a blessing to others, and is a testament to trust in Him.

Jesus said, "The thief cometh not, but for to steal, and to kill, and to destroy: I am come that they might have life, and that they might have it more abundantly" (John 10:10).

S16 SAFE ENVIRONMENTS

> " 'Your brother has come,' he replied, 'and your father has killed the fattened calf
> because he has him back safe and sound.' " JOHN 15:27

Our soul seeks out safe environments. We are attracted to people we can trust, who accept us for who we are instead of who we need be. Safe environments give us security and peace. We can bear our souls because we know we are in a place of confidentiality, and do not fear rejection. A business meeting with a rigid agenda, pretense and pride is not a safe place to be yourself.

However, safe environments seek first to understand and there is no rush to judgment, but there is a rash of love. Safe environments still love us, especially when we are unlovely. Parents have the privilege of providing a safe environment for their teenagers transitioning into young adulthood. This can be a trying time for everyone, as your children are not babies anymore, so they do not want to be babied and controlled.

By God's grace you have trained them for such a time as this. This is your teenager's time of transition into maturity, and he or she may have to make a bad relational decision in the process. This is how he or she grows and learns, therefore as parents it is imperative you keep the home environment safe and not combative. Still speak the truth in love, but graciously with great patience and after much prayer. If your teenager doesn't feel safe at home, they will find safety and acceptance somewhere else, so create attractive environments.

Safe environments are also necessary for Christ seekers. People on the lookout for authentic faith need someplace to ask questions without being rebuffed for their elementary inquires. More mature believers have the opportunity to be there for those on their faith journey, but judgment is a juggernaut for safe environments, as it crushes with condescending attitudes. So be careful not to superimpose your high standards on a person or situation, and in the process squelch the safe environment. Share your own failures and struggles, as this builds bridges to the heart. Safe environments are void of pedestals of pride. Consider a Bible discussion in your home followed by a fun activity. Make Christianity attractive and not boring. Safe environments draw people to Christ.

Above all else, seek out a safe environment with your Savior. Your Lord longs to linger with you. He deeply desires to listen to your dreams and fears. It is in your safe place with Jesus that you are loved completely. Your heavenly Father feels your pain. In your safe place with Him, you are positioned to receive His love and blessings. Your safe place with God may be early in the morning with a cup of coffee, Bible and journal. It may be late at night before your head hits the pillow and begins its silent reflections. It may be on your lunch break in the shadowy sanctuary of a tree. It may be a walk in the woods, a jog on a treadmill or a run across a maze of sidewalks. It may be a quiet occasion in the mountains or an engagement with eternity at the beach.

God gives you safe environments for your soul's refreshment. It is here you can cry, laugh, complain, thank, create, give, listen and ask. Christ celebrates when you go to Him, and receives you just as you are, needy for love and acceptance. Safe environments are necessary for communication and trust, therefore, create and enjoy safe places, and go there often for your sake and the sake of those you love. The Bible says, "You will be secure, because there is hope; you will look about you and take your rest in safety" (Job 11:18).

FIRST GO BACK

"Therefore, if you are offering your gift at the altar and there remember that your brother has something against you, leave your gift there in front of the altar. First go and be reconciled to your brother; then come and offer your gift." MATTHEW 5:23-24

First go back and make things right relationally. Go back before you move on, or you will drive a relational wedge. The flesh wants to forget without addressing the real issues that divide, but this is not the Jesus way.

Christ commands us to humble ourselves and go back to seek reconciliation with fractured relationships. Disappointment with your parents may have severed communication, or a child may need your mature and forgiving love. You may have harbored resentment toward a friend over feeling left out. A work associate may have distanced himself because of a misunderstanding; as a result it is hard to serve heaven with broken relationships on earth. In fact, your worship reminds you of where you need to restore relationships. You are not to move on in your generosity and service to God until you first go back to the point of offense and make amends.

It is not a good thing to offer a gift to God with grudges still in your gut. An unclear conscience is unable to authentically associate with the Almighty and others. When you go back to the point of offense, you better understand the reason for the hurt and here is where healing begins.

Therefore, spend your time and energy in relational wholeness and then you can move on, but when you go back make sure you are prayed up. A gentle and humble attitude goes a long way in avoiding an altercation. Take more than your share of the responsibility by apologizing and making restitution (compensation for loss), as it enhances reconciliation in relationships. Use the right words in the right way, as wrong words said the wrong way wreck relationships. Right words delivered without pride brings healing and wholeness to the ruptured relationship. You can't move on until you go back to the point of relational departure.

It is here that deposits of gentleness, humility, and unselfishness move the relationship in the right direction. It is important that you fight for oneness, because your natural self defaults to division.

The way of the cross is the cure, as Jesus is all about relational reconciliation. His mission on earth was to reconcile man to God. His goal was to dissolve the distance between His holy heavenly Father and sinful man. This was the purpose of His death on the cross, as He came to reconcile relationships. Moreover, your ministry from God is reconciliation (2 Corinthians 5:17-19). How can you be reconciled to God in heaven and not to people on earth? God's expectation for His children is to come clean with those with whom there is division. This is the normal Christian life and is consistent living for the Lord. However, you cannot accomplish this counter-cultural commission by yourselves. The power of the Holy Spirit humbles your heart and heals, so first go and hunt for relational healing. Forgiveness forgets and moves on only after reconciliation. Move on after you mend the relationship, as wholeness with your siblings in the faith validates your life and ministry. The Bible says, "If anyone says, 'I love God,' yet hates his brother, he is a liar. For anyone who does not love his brother, whom he has seen, cannot love God, whom he has not seen. And he has given us this command: Whoever loves God must also love his brother..."(1 John 4:20-21).

S18 SMALL THINGS

"Do not despise these small beginnings, for the LORD rejoices to see the work begin, to see the plumb line in Zerubbabel's hand." ZECHARIAH 4:10 (NLT)

Small things are big to God, so they are not to be discounted or despised, as our Savior is in the small things. Our pride wants to get on to the larger and more important opportunities. It dismisses the mundane or the monotonous, but success and significance are also found in the small things.

A quiet smile to a restaurant server is small, but significant. A little gift to an unsuspecting sanitation worker is small, but significant. Learning the children's names of a blue collar worker in your company and occasionally joining them for lunch is small, but significant. Attention to small things makes people big, for example celebrate an office employee's birthday over breakfast or an important personal milestone over lunch or dinner. When we give attention to small things, we say we care. Private acts of love foster public loyalty and long-term commitment. It is the attention to small things that build great people and grow great companies.

This is also true with our children. If we want influence with them when they face big issues as teenagers and adults, it is imperative we show interest in the small things of their childhood. Parental investment in ballgames, recitals, school plays, scouts, church camps, outdoors, homework, shared hobbies and church all add up to an invitation to big things. Little things like tucking them in at night will one day give them the trust to invite us into the dark night of their soul. Investment in the small things invites influence with the big things.

Therefore, do not despise this season of small things. They are like seeds that eventually grow into grand and glorious opportunities of influence. There is a definite sequence of seed planting, watering, fertilizing and cultivating. The process can become boring and seem unproductive, but this illustrates how God works. Your Savior is into stringing together a sequence of small activities that lead to larger outcomes. So stay with the small things, for in due season you will reap.

God may allow you to harvest far beyond what you could have imagined in the beginning. How much is it worth for your spouse to become your best friend? It won't happen overnight, but faithfulness to the small things will facilitate the reality of your hopes and dreams.

Furthermore, when you experience a string of small things with Jesus, your faith becomes large. So be aware of the need for a little prayer to the Lord. Stay dependent on God along life's path of small steps. When He sees you being faithful with His small opportunities, He can then trust you with the larger ones.

The small things you do honor God: bowing a head before a meal, showing up early for an appointment, memorizing a brief Bible verse, or giving a small anonymous gift. Any small expression with the Lord in mind goes a long way. The Almighty values small things because everything is small to Him. He is large and in charge, but His small tests lead to His best opportunities. Don't miss this or you may miss Him. Big things many times are disguised as small things, so treat them with respect.

You never know when you might be serving Jesus or entertaining angels. Therefore treasure small things. They are big and they matter, and they may matter most. The Bible says, "Do not forget to entertain strangers, for by so doing some people have entertained angels without knowing it" (Hebrews 13:2).

TESTING PURIFIES

"But he knows the way that I take; when he has tested me, I will come forth as gold."
JOB 23:10

Testing purifies, as it brings out our worst and preserves our best. It is not always easy or enjoyable, but it is necessary to stay solid in our faith. Tests come in the form of people we may not understand or have yet to totally appreciate. They may rub us the wrong way, however this friction is what scrapes away the sin from our soul. God uses people everyday to purify our hearts from pride. Tests also come in taking on more responsibility at work. We have never done what we are doing and we feel inadequate and desperate to learn. This new assignment has us crying out to God for wisdom and discernment. We fail the test if we give up; but if we persevere we will make progress and eventually reach the goal. Tests are not meant to be torture, but a time that we can claim the promises of God. His word is truth and we are to value it more than our daily bread. Truth is designed as our survival kit during times of testing.

Truth is terrific because it reminds us of the bigger picture of God's faithfulness and plan. He allows us to experience difficulty to build our dependence on Him. If we lived in a highly controlled environment without crime or crisis, we would still have to live with ourselves. Our envy, lust and pride are ever looming to snatch away our joy.

Therefore, it is imperative that we drink daily from the fountain of God's Word. The Bible is our baseline for belief and behavior. Indeed, testing brings truth front and center. It turns our focus away from our pain to our hope and provision in the Lord. Understanding and applying truth make testing a blessing. We long for and receive God's love in the heat of our testing. We are purified that so we can see Him. He is holy God and a humble servant. We see Him clearly in our crisis of faith, as testing turns us toward truth and into the arms of Jesus.

It some sense your life is one big test, but its intensity is temporary. Sometimes you feel trapped by tests, as they can be smothering and discouraging. Your career transition is a test of whether your security is in prestige or in Christ. You struggle with, "What will people think?" and "Will they believe any less in me, because I took a lesser role?" But the truth is, God's will is always a step up, and this may be a test of your motives. Why do you do what you do? If it is all about you and climbing the ladder of success and financial freedom, then testing is necessary to purify your motives. Adversity brings out what is in your hearts and that is not always pretty.

God may be asking you to give up something, so He can give you something better. This test is meant to prepare you for God's very best.

Lastly, tests come down to trust. Can God still be trusted during this severe trial? You believe in your head that He can, but your heart needs to commit without reservation. How can you trust Him when circumstances seem to be swirling out of control?

You trust Him one day at a time, and you trust Him with the authorities in your life that still have questions and concerns. Testing purifies your faith to a higher level of trust in the Lord. By faith value this time of testing, and embrace it as an opportunity to be loved by your heavenly Father for tests turn you to Him. The Bible says, "Do not be afraid. God has come to test you, so that the fear of God will be with you to keep you from sinning" (Exodus 20:20).

S20 VISION REGAINED

> "I answered them by saying, 'The God of heaven will give us success.
> We his servants will start rebuilding…'" NEHEMIAH 2:20A

Sometimes we lose the compelling nature of our vision, as its cutting edge intensity becomes dulled. We become attracted to other good opportunities, but in the meantime the original vision loses its luster. A dull vision demands we regain a resurgence of energy and fire in the belly. Maybe you became bored because you met your goals and there were no next steps to a greater vision.

Your opportunity to trust God has been severely limited, and a monstrous and magnetic vision needs to be regained. You need a new vision that challenges your dependency on God and stirs your emotions. So pray for a vision that gets you out of bed in the morning, one that easily engages your mind and your heart. Maybe you need to start by going back to the original vision. What elements of the vision drew you in and upward to God?

Was it the size? Was it the results? Did it align around your passions? Was it bold and unpredictable? Compelling vision feels alive, and brings new energy to the vision bearer. We pulsate with life because we have to lean on the Lord. Indeed, we regain our vision when we unleash it from the confinement of our control. Spreadsheets are only an indicator, not an initiator. Numbers and plans are only a guide, and metrics only measure the vision. No one person can control the course of a regained vision. It may go toward destinations never dreamed about in the original vision. So pray big, and lead boldly like a leader with regained vision.

Convene your leadership team and/or your family to pray. Pray for a revitalization of God's vision for your life, enterprise, and family. Do not limit God for anything less than the grandeur of how His vision may unfold. Take some crayons and a sheet of paper, and ask each team member to privately and creatively illustrate the vision they sense God is giving. It's uncanny what Christ can do through such a simple, but profound process. Share the results with each other, and notice how He aligns your hearts as you prayerfully practice community under His accountability. Hold the tired vision with an open hand and watch God inject it with new enthusiasm and extreme possibilities.

So, recast the vision with Christ's calling, not something that can be controlled by man. Regain the vision by going to God and by approaching those who have yet engage enthusiastically.

There are new people waiting to join in with the regained vision. They may be notable leaders who are waiting for your invitation. Do not be intimidated by greatness, as this quality of person is what you need for the vision to go to from good to great. You also need a new crew of faithful leaders who will show up and do their part. Go after extremely ordinary people, who because of their focused passion get extraordinary results. Don't waste time with flashy talkers, move past their pretentious noise and invest in the quiet, faithful ones who get the job done. Regardless, the team must expand for the vision to expand.

The God of heaven will give you success; so regain His vision for His glory. The Bible says, "After this, the word of the LORD came to Abram in a vision: 'Do not be afraid, Abram. I am your shield, your very great reward'" (Genesis 15:1).

"Be still, and know that I am God; I will be exalted among the nations,
I will be exalted in the earth."   PSALM 46:10

God created us as human beings not human doers. Yet everything from our culture to our career, defaults to doing. We are taught by western society that if we are not busy, we must be lazy. There is a contemporary guilt that keeps us on the go. We are driven to do by some unseen capitalistic force. We are so intent on getting things done that we forget why we engaged in the process to begin with. It's all about progress and seeing it through to the end. It's all about the results, making the grade and exceeding the earnings estimates. After all, if you are really important, your cell phone will constantly vibrate and your e-mail will seduce you 24/7. This is the sad state of those of us who are trapped by doing, like an alcoholic in denial we are intoxicated by activity.

Our ego glosses over the need for God, as we justify driven behavior with bad theology. We act like the Almighty's hands are tied and it is up to us to make things happen, but God is not limited by our low view. He still governs the universe and our lives. Kings, presidents and dictators are still accountable to the Almighty's agenda. CEOs, entertainers and athletes still have a higher power in Jesus Christ to whom they have to answer.

Therefore, it is wise to get off our high horse of self-imposed importance, and be still before God. If we continue to race through life at a breakneck pace, we will break. Our health, finances and relationships are fragile, and eventually they will fracture under the pressure of habitual doing.

Indeed, we are humans in need, in need of being who God created us to be. Our God-given roles in life are a great place to cultivate our human being-ness.

For example, when we take the time to be a respectful child who honors our parents, we are being. Visit, call, or write regularly and you will be the child your parents need. You honor God when you honor them. Above all else be with God. There is a knowing and understanding of God that comes only from spending time with Him. Knowledge of God is not derived in depth from service only, but in sitting and reflecting on the Holy One being served. It is in your doing that you validate your being, and it is in your being that you purify your reasons for doing.

So, our life with the Lord begins by being with Him. It is in the stillness beside the waters of worship that you feel His presence (Psalm 23). God is not on the go and exhausted from His last intimate encounter with a needy saint. Therefore, make sure you make time for your soul's maintenance. Peace comes by aligning with the Almighty, and stillness with Him sharpens your body, soul and spirit. In stillness you see God. In stillness you feel God. In stillness you worship God. In stillness you receive from God. In stillness you are loved by God. In stillness you love God. In stillness you believe God. In stillness you see and know God. Allow your "doing" to flow from your "being", for stillness plus being equals dynamic "doing" for the glory of the Lord.

The Bible says, "The LORD will fight for you; you need only to be still" (Exodus 14:14).

> "… and free those who all their lives were held in slavery by their fear of death."
> HEBREWS 2:15

Jesus has conquered death; therefore followers of Jesus need not fear death. You may have a fear of dying, but not of death. For the believer in Christ, death is a pass through, as it is a transition from this life to the next. Death is not final for it is a doorway to eternity.

Indeed, it is the beginning of an eternity in the physical presence of Jesus. Everything we have experienced with Christ on earth is an appetizer of what is to come. Our faith can only digest a mere morsel of what God has in store for those who love Him. Do not let the prospects of death get you down, as it is a commencement to be celebrated. You have remained faithful in this school of life and now God has a glorious graduation in store for you. Yes there is some fear of the unknown, but there is a lot we do know that keeps fear in its place.

We know that death for the follower of Christ places them in an environment of sinless bliss. You can live and breathe without the fear of AIDS, murder, adultery, homosexuality, lying, cheating, pain, hunger, abortion or poverty. Life in heaven is not good; it is great. Death releases you from the pain of your current suffering. Your suffering has perfected your character and faith in Christ. Now you are ready to be received back home. Your suffering has drawn you into an incredible intimacy with your Savior. As a consequence, many others beyond your comprehension have been drawn close to your Lord. Nurses, doctors, friends and relatives stand in awe and fall on their knees in awe of your God.

Your death will not only set you permanently free, but it will do the same for the others who believe. Death is freedom, and it is not to be feared. So in the meantime, make every effort to prepare yourself and others for death. The fear of death creeps in where there has been no preparation. You can ignore its reality and you will still die. You can deny death, but not its consequences. You may have a chance to repent on your death bed, but why wait? Why take the chance of choosing hell over heaven? Death is not a lottery ticket, so not gamble with your soul. Go with God's sure thing, faith in Jesus Christ. He has died and risen from the dead, so He can be trusted. He has been there, dealt with death, and reigns overall in heaven.

Moreover, love on the dying. Everyone is dying; however, reach out to those closer to death's door. The depth of wisdom that comes from the dying reeks with the smell of heaven. That which is important falls from their lips, as priorities are aligned and lived. Being with the dying prepares you for dying, as it is preparation for the one receiving care and for the caregiver. Death is an absolute though dying may be sudden or a process, but either way God can be trusted. You have questions about the timing of death that may only be answered in heaven. Above all, God is good and God is great, thank him for every breath you take. Enjoy and celebrate death's release, because Jesus died and rose again you will do the same. Fear only God, and enjoy the benefit of death's freedom. The Bible teaches, "Death has been swallowed up in victory." "Where, O death, is your victory? Where, O death, is your sting?" The sting of death is sin, and the power of sin is the law. But thanks be to God! He gives us the victory through our Lord Jesus Christ" (1 Corinthians 15:54b-57).

Walk with the dying, for their edification...and for your own.

PATH OF LIFE

"You have made known to me the path of life; you will fill me with joy in your presence, with eternal pleasures at your right hand." PSALM 16:11

God set us on a path when we surrendered by faith to our Savior Jesus. His path is not without bumps, but it is by far the best path. It is an inviting path because we are accompanied by Christ.

Wherever Jesus walks, we want to walk. Where He goes, we want to follow. When He is out front, we have confidence in the direction He leads us. When we run ahead, we lose the advantage of Christ's compass. When we lag behind, we lose perspective and our focus of faith in Him. God's path is the most productive because this is where we walk with Jesus. Along the path with Christ, we hear His voice and He directs us in different directions. When we started out we were determined to go in one direction, but over time He has a way of revealing to us a better way.

Therefore, stay on the path with Jesus. Our direction determines our destination. We can be full of good intentions and still be on the wrong path. Good motives do not govern our outcomes and sincere dedication does not dictate our destination. The road we are on determines our route. We can pray about visiting Washington, D.C., and even plan a trip there, but if we strike out due west from Atlanta, GA., we will not arrive at our desired destination. The path you choose carries you toward or away from your goals. A loving and respectful spouse is on a path of understanding and accountability. An excellent employee is on a path of doing what he or she does best with diligence. A fulfilling friendship is on a path of service and unselfishness. Financial freedom is on a path of generosity, saving and wise spending. Paths have predetermined outcomes, so make sure to go down the God-honoring ones.

We can lose a season of our life by strolling down a wrong path. Therefore, do not be led astray down destructive paths. Addictions to work, drugs, alcohol and pornography lead us down the path of death. Leading an out-of -balance life is traveling down the wrong path toward a wreck. Get off, go back or start over; just don't be naïve and keep going.

Things can and will get worse unless you make a change of direction. Ask godly counselors to navigate your true north toward truth. God's truth will set you free from flailing around on an unproductive path. So, walk in the truth (3 John 1:3) and walk with Jesus, as He is the way, the truth and the life (John 14:6). Our spiritual, emotional, financial, relational and vocational directions need to converge into Christ's personal path designed just for us.

Therefore, it is imperative for God-fearers and Jesus-lovers to begin, continue and conclude on the path of faith in Christ. It is here that you enjoy His perpetual presence and full-on forgiveness. It is here that you are enlightened and secure. It is here that you are in a position to help others and be led by the Holy Spirit. It is here that you make your way to heaven, as the path of salvation starts by placing your total trust in Jesus Christ. The path of sanctification (maturity) is continual surrender, trust and obedience to Almighty God. The path of glorification in heaven is your ultimate destination.

Enjoy the path Jesus offers, one of joy in His presence and eternal pleasures in heaven. This is the most productive path of life. The Bible says, "And now I will show you the most excellent way" (1 Corinthians 12:31b).

S24 WARNING AND REWARD

"By them is your servant warned; in keeping them there is great reward." PSALM 19:11

The Word of God is our warning and our reward, as we travel through life. Like driving down a highway under construction, we may see signs warning us of a rough ride, closed lanes or a bridge that may be out. We do not ignore these signs because we value our life, time and automobile. So it is as our body, soul and spirit make their way through this life. We are warned by the Word of pending danger and by simple faith, we listen and become wise. Obedience to God's precepts is fundamental to successful living, and it is sin to know what to do and not do it. It can become stupid and foolish to ignore God's warnings. He may be trying to speak to you through your spouse, a friend or an enemy, so do not allow pride to deafen your heart. God's principles protrude from the foundation of your faith to barricade you from the exits of unwise decisions. Therefore, do not force down a door that does not freely swing open on the hinges of God's grace. The teachable grow wise, but the cavalier continue on foolishly.

The Bible is our mentor, our monitor, our reminder and the keeper of our conscience. Though the brilliant white from a freshly packed snowfall causes blindness to the skier, God's Word has the opposite effect on our soul. Its pure application to our lives lifts the natural blindness of our soul. The Bible burns away the fog of our confused mind and replaces it with focused and clear thinking. His truth makes our heart right and then gives it joy. When we heed the warnings of a risky financial commitment, we become rich in peace of mind. It is better to sleep peacefully in the night with our simple life than to awaken preoccupied by unnecessary complexity. He warns us because He loves us.

Do not reject the love of God that may be clothed in an outfit of warning. There are rewards to those who remain faithful and follow God's instructions. Rewards remind us of the goodness of God, and His grace is His grandest reward. He gives us grace to become His child. He extends us grace to be a faithful spouse, an engaged parent, a loyal friend and a loving leader. We receive grace everyday to forgive more and resent less. It may seem like you are losing, but this is but for a season. There is victory, even if it is a slender reward of a quiet conscience for your obedience.

Lastly, there are the rewards of God that transcend this life. He is all about eternal rewards. If heaven's outcomes are important to Christ, they are important to His followers. Christ will crown His children for cleaving to His service in the face of extreme success or depressing difficulties. Your faithfulness with His stuff determines your eternal rewards. What you do on earth with your time, talent and treasures defines the quality of our experience in heaven. Therefore, heed His warnings and send as much ahead as possible in saved souls and financial leverage for the Lord. Keep enough now to shine the brightest for Christ, but invest the rest in eternity.

This is His warning and His reward, so apply both and become the wiser. These are His true riches, Jesus says, "So if you have not been trustworthy in handling worldly wealth, who will trust you with true riches" (Luke 16:11)?

TAKE AND GIVE

"Take the talent from him and give it to the one who has ten talents."   MATTHEW 25:28

God has the prerogative to take and give. He can take what He has given you and give it to someone else. He can execute this transaction with or without your knowledge or understanding. Just because you enjoy His blessing today does not guarantee His blessing tomorrow. There is a direct correlation to your faithfulness and His blessing.

However, your relationship with Him does not always operate in a cause and effect process. For example, "in Christ" you are always accepted, and He gives His unmerited grace. So, your role is not to strive and strain to please Him. He wants you to wait on Him and to walk with Him. He invites you to rest in Him and to serve Hi' (albeit with gladness!). Obedience and faithfulness does determine your level of responsibility within God's Kingdom. Faithfulness allows you to enjoy God's blessings.

If you are not faithful with God's blessings, He may take them away and entrust them to some-one else. You have been blessed with resources, relationships, opportunities and skills. God has given you much, so this responsibility of managing His blessings is not to be taken lightly. What is not used for God's purposes could very well be lost for good. However, this is not a reason to live in fear for it may cause you to lose perspective of God's true nature.

God is not a cruel taskmaster waiting to crush one little misstep on your part. He does not superimpose unrealistic expectations on you to frustrate your progress. His will is doable, and His plan is discernable. He has given His children everything for life and godliness. Do not believe the lie that God is trying to catch you in a misdeed so He can bring swift and unfair judgment. On the contrary, His patience affords you many opportunities to get it right. He does however, expect continued faithfulness with what He has entrusted to you.

Time proves your ability to execute His will. Excuses are not acceptable, only Holy Spirit led risks are needed to explore options and test the waters of His will. After He gives you an assign-ment, look around you for the relationships and resources to accomplish the task. Look within you for the character to persevere and trust. Look to Him for wisdom, and look to others for validation and counsel. To do nothing when He has said to do something is not acceptable. If you remain in this state of denial and defiance, you may very well lose this opportunity. He can take what He has given to you and entrust it to another. If this happens to you, do not get mad at God, nor be resentful of the one who received God's blessing because of your unfaithfulness. Rather learn from this and become better not bitter. Let God restore you to a position of blessing. Losers need not linger in 'what ifs', so cut your losses. Leave behind your disappointments, and reinvigorate your faithfulness.

This is the time for God to restore the joy of His salvation. What He took He can give back. David cried out in brokenness, "Restore to me the joy of your salvation and grant me a willing spir-it, to sustain me" (Psalm 51:12).

S26 BEAUTIFUL MEMORIAL

"Aware of this Jesus said to them, 'Why are you bothering this woman? She has done a beautiful thing to me... I tell you the truth, wherever this gospel is preached throughout the world, what she has done will also be told, in memory of her.'" MATTHEW 26:10, 13

How do you want to be remembered, because the memory of your life will linger beyond your death? How will your obituary read? Your epitaph will define you; so how will it read? Will it point to God and people or to you? We will all have a memorial that reflects our life. It may be pigmy-sized because it is built around us, or it may be bigger than life because it is built around Christ. These are important and eternal questions that need clear definition. Your defining moments are building a memorial that will extend into the future. There are spectators watching you assemble a life memorial. Your family is watching, friends and acquaintances are watching, and the world is watching, but most importantly God is watching.

Some of your heavenly-minded cohorts will do more than watch. Their memories will intertwine with yours, creating a beautiful mosaic of God's faithfulness. Your memorial may be more a collaboration around community rather than individual accomplishments. Either way, stay in the process of keeping your life aligned with and for eternal purposes. Other well-meaning (and some not so well-meaning) pundits will try to dissuade you from a lifetime commitment to seek God's best. They may define God's will differently from you, for they have a wonderful plan for your life, but you have your own life to live. God's best for you may not be God's best for another, so take what God has given you and completely dedicate it to Him. Your commitment to Christ is compelling in itself. It provides the wet cement that forges together the bricks of your life experiences. As you construct your life memorial, consider a few things. Ponder the wisdom of making God your foundation. When He is your foundation, your memorial will stand for eternity. The memory of your lifelong acts of service for Christ and others may fade over time, but your God-based foundation will remain. Indeed, build eternal financial investments for Jesus into the architecture of your beautiful life memorial. Leverage your resources for God's Kingdom. Your memorial may be bricks and mortar that represent churches, schools, hospitals, businesses, community centers or homes. Whatever you build, build for the glory of God.

However, one word of caution is necessary. A Christ-centered charter governed by God-fearing leaders is required to keep an institution pure to its mission. Spend as much or more time and money on preserving the integrity of the vision, as on the construction of buildings. Otherwise, your memorial to Christ may very well be hijacked by heresy. Moreover, your memorial may consist of paying for the Christian education of your grandchildren. It may be funding initiatives and projects that leverage evangelism and discipleship in a country outside of yours. Your memorial building may involve serving Jesus in some obscure and remote part of the world without fanfare or appreciation. Whatever you do, do as unto the Lord. Resist the critics, embrace Christ, and be ever mindful of beautiful Kingdom memorial building.

The Bible says, "I will perpetuate your memory through all generations; therefore the nations will praise you forever and ever" (Psalm 45:17).

"When the teachers of the law who were Pharisees saw him eating with the 'sinners' and tax collectors, they asked the disciples: 'Why does he eat with the tax collectors and 'sinners?' On hearing this Jesus said to them, 'It is not the healthy who need a doctor, but the sick. I have not come to call the righteous, but sinners.' " MARK 2:16-17

Sick sinners need a Savior, and they are perishing all around us. Some are sick and don't realize their spiritually terminal state. Indeed, one of Satan's schemes is to keep the healthy saints from the sick sinners. Those dying in darkness do not know any different, and they are content to languish outside the light. However, we who are children of the light know better. If not for the grace of God penetrating our hard hearts, we would still be severely sick in our sins. Followers of Jesus have seen the light, and it has illumined our souls and healed our sick hearts. We have been saved from sin and from ourselves. Yes, there will be those who deny their sinful condition. They will avoid a spiritual doctor like the plague. Yet, we who are healthy cannot be deterred or discouraged, because our part is not to force our faith on others. This is an individual decision between them and God, but with grace, humility, and prayer we can pursue them and pray for them in their sick spiritual state. People fighting the onslaught of sin's disease, and their souls are emasculated by sin's torrid influence. Some physical illnesses cannot be cured, but sin's sickness can be cured in Christ. Perhaps you need to recalibrate your calendar to include time with sick sinners, because the sterile saints are consuming most of your time. Instead, take a risk and provide a sanatorium for sinners. They are dying by the droves and entering into eternity without Christ. Sick sinners need a Savior.

Care for them where you work and live. Convert your business into a platform of prayer for those who need Christ. Yes use discretion, respect and taste, but be bold. Time is short, and people need a Savior. They need a Savior for eternity and for now. They will become better citizens and better employees with Jesus in their lives. There is nothing quite as compelling as someone working as unto the Lord. In addition, use your home as a haven for sick sinners. You can become their heavenly hospice and watch God raise them up from their sin-sick bed. The harvest is white in need of labors. You may not feel qualified to practice spiritual medicine, but by God's grace you can be a soul caregiver.

An aspirin of John 3:16 provides relief and hope for a sick soul, so do not underestimate the potency of Scripture, especially elementary texts. Moreover, your story of righteous recovery provides hope to the sickly sinner, others gain courage that God can do the same for them. Your testimony may be the faith stretcher that carries them to Jesus. Your story and Scripture shared in a timely fashion are healing, so seek out sick sinners and love on them. Laugh and cry together. Some of the proud and insecure religious people will criticize you, but Jesus will smile. You have the cure, so live authentically and engagingly among sick sinners. The Bible says, "Since, then, we know what it is to fear the Lord, we try to persuade men. What we are is plain to God, and I hope it is also plain to your conscience" (2 Corinthians 5:11).

Once they see your human-side, they can appreciate your Christ-side.

S28 ACCOUNTABILITY'S CONSEQUENCES

"If your hand causes you to sin, cut it off. It is better for you to enter life maimed than with two hands to go into hell, where the fire never goes out." MARK 9:43

Accountability without consequences is powerless and ineffective. It is like a lion without teeth, or it performs like a car engine without oil. For accountability to work it has to cost you something, otherwise it is just a masquerade. You can say you are accountable and not be. You may be going through the motions and getting nowhere fast. You may have been accountable at one time, but do not kid yourself. Without consequences for your actions or inactions, there is only a façade of accountability.

When the smoke of activity clears, you still have not changed and may have even digressed in your behavior. This is a dreadful deception for the most dangerous person may be the one who thinks he is accountable and is not. He talks it, but does not walk it. There is a disconnection between his words and his actions. Is there a need for an accountability audit of your life? For example, the reason you are cautious not to drive over the speed limit is because of the potential consequence of a wreck and/or a speeding ticket. Do you have similar consequences in place for running too fast through life? Your body may be screaming for attention, as it may be writing you multiple warning tickets to exercise and eat right. Be careful not to mask or gloss over today's mild consequences for tomorrow's severe ones. Only the uninformed or foolish would drive a car without oil. The engine of course, would burn up. The same can be said for a life. A life lived without the oil of accountability will burn up or burn out!

Accountability starts with your time with God in prayer and Bible study. If this is currently difficult for you, then implement a meaningful consequence. If you are married, maybe you refrain from sex with your spouse for each day you miss your time with God. If you are single, missed time with God could limit or cease your internet time or social interaction. There are ways to make accountability meaningful.

Define for yourself a real consequence and stick with it. Drugs and/or alcohol may be your greatest temptation. The consequence of your mildest involvement with either could be checking into a clinic. You may be chronically late to appointments. There could be a financial consequence for every minute you are late. Indeed, if self-denial is a consequence of your accountability, then self-discipline will become more prominent.

You may need to write out a contract between yourself and God. Outline in this covenant agreement what you are committing to do in your relationships, finances and time management. State clearly the positive and negative consequences associated with each area of accountability. Ask accountability partners to sign the document as witnesses. There is something about defining the consequences of your accountability in writing. It is stated in black and white, and there is little room for interpretation. This may seem overkill, but few people are overly accountable. Start by submitting to God and His authorities in one area of your life. You will learn to trust them and then you can begin implementing consequences of accountability in all areas of your life.

The Bible says, "Therefore, it is necessary to submit to the authorities, not only because of possible punishment but also because of conscience" (Romans 13:5).

TEACHABLE HEART

" 'Well said, teacher,' the man replied. 'You are right in saying God is one and there is no other but him.' … When Jesus saw that he had answered wisely, he said to him, 'You are not far from the Kingdom of God…' " MARK 12:32, 34A

Jesus affirms a teachable heart for He knows it has potential to learn and understand the things of God. Thus a teachable heart is positioned to receive truth, and it is an attitude with more questions than answers.

However, a teachable heart does recognize truth when it comes knocking. It invites truth in to be examined, understood and applied. Truth invigorates the teachable heart, and there is a rush of spiritual adrenaline when it intersects with an open mind and heart. Pride plateaus it's learning, but a teachable heart continues to scale the mountain of truth. Thus, when God discovers someone who is teachable, He calls them wise. Wisdom comes from God; therefore a teachable heart learns the ways of God. Teachability is not offended by God, though there is a tension that arises when truth begins to facilitate changes in behavior and attitude. This change of heart seems somewhat innocuous from the outside looking in, but most of us do not like to be told what to do.

Change doesn't come easily, even as you understand that God has your best interests in mind, however the transformation is telling. Your character and behavior fall more in line with Jesus. Your spouse and children notice something different. Your patience, rather than your intimidation, becomes dominant. Your bad beliefs will be replaced with good ones, so let your teachable heart start first with God.

God is one. He is not many gods but one God. He is not a mini-god, but the great and glorious God of the galaxies.

God the Father, God the Son, and God the Holy Spirit are all one God. His oneness is to be worshipped and celebrated. Thus, your love relationship with the one and true God is not to be rivaled with any other gods. Any acceptance of other gods is unacceptable to God. He is jealous for you. Your love for anyone or anything will pale in relation to our love for Christ.

To love God is to make room for God in all aspects of your life. You love Him when you love others, when you give sacrificially, when you strive for excellence in your work, and when you pray and forgive others. Love is action, therefore love Him and allow Him to love you.

Let His expectations mold yours, because what God thinks trumps any other thinking. The Holy Spirit within you has the answers to the questions that consume your thinking. Follow His internal promptings, not the external clamor. What you believed yesterday will be dwarfed by what you learn tomorrow. Know God, love God, and learn of Him. He affirms a teachable heart as one who fears the Lord. The Bible teaches, "Assemble the people—men, women and children, and the aliens living in your towns—so they can listen and learn to fear the LORD your God and follow carefully all the words of this law" (Deuteronomy 31:12).

Stay teachable in your understanding of God.

S30 MONEY'S DISTRACTION

"Jesus looked at him and loved him. 'One thing you lack,' he said. 'Go, sell everything you have and give to the poor, and you will have treasure in heaven. Then come, follow me.' At this the man's face fell. He went away sad, because he had great wealth. Jesus looked around and said to his disciples, 'How hard it is for the rich to enter the Kingdom of God!' " MARK 10:21-23

It is easy for money to become a distraction, just the making and management of money takes effort and focus. Yet money becomes a subtle master if it is not held in check. We love what we think about, so if the majority of our waking moments are consumed by the thought of making more money, then we are distracted. Yes, we need to do our work with excellence as unto the Lord. However, if making money becomes the consuming focus, then our devotion to the dollar competes with our devotion to God. Billions of people wake up every day to make money, but are they making money for wise use, or is money using them? If a life is consumed by money, then very little is left over for a life well spent. Time and energy for others become scarce in the wake of compulsive money making. You may think that your current obsession with making-money is for the long-term purpose of autonomy.

This thinking is flawed because the follower of Jesus Christ is never really autonomous. A wealthy believer is still tethered to God's will, with an expectation for submission to community and Christ for accountability and service. Yes, finances afford you options, but only options that are under the prevue of God's will. A life of unshackled leisure and self-indulgence is not on God's radar. He may free you up to serve Him and others, but not to sit and soak. Too many options can be a distraction to God's best. So how can you avoid money's distraction?

The Lord will love you away from money's allurement for the here and now. He will love you into heavenly investments instead. Let Him love you away from the seduction of possessions. Then you will want to reciprocate love to your lover. If your love quotients are currently met by stuff, then your affections will gravitate in that direction. This is the nature of the mistress of moneymaking. When you allow money to love on you, you feel a debt to money, Then your emotions and energies feel obligated to love back. This is a subtle but effective tool in the enemy's arsenal.

An affair with money and possessions leaves nothing for the Lover of your soul. Without a love relationship with your Creator, you will become sad, even in the middle of more stuff than you ever dreamed. How ironic. A money lover's ultimate experience is emptiness.

So, there is a solution to money's distraction. By faith, regularly look into the loving eyes of Jesus. Let Him love you, and then you are compelled to love Him. Money's distraction is derailed by a love relationship with Jesus. When you love Him wholeheartedly, there is no room for money to distract. It is a love issue. When you love Him, your treasure is in heaven and not on earth. You cannot love God and money at the same time. This is double-mindedness. Receive His love, and love Him, not money. Give generously, especially to the poor. Then you can enjoy your citizenship in His kingdom with community, accountability and authentic love.

The Bible says, "Whoever loves money never has money enough; whoever loves wealth is never satisfied with his income. This too is meaningless" (Ecclesiastes 5:10).

DETEST DISHONESTY

01

"For the Lord your God detests anyone who does these things,
anyone who deals dishonestly." DEUTERONOMY 25:16

God detests dishonesty, and He desires honesty. Honesty is His policy, and it frees us to follow the Lord unencumbered and with a clear conscience. Honesty leads to peace of mind, and it allows us to keep short accounts and protects us from having to organize untruths. Honesty builds trust and raises relational integrity to a much higher level. Honesty is one of the top reasons people hang around for any length of time, as it creates an environment of trust. A trusting environment is a safe place to work and live, where are no surprises, and rumors are put to rest. Honesty is attractive as it assists authenticity. It is as quick to communicate the negative, as it is to promote the positive. It is secure enough to apologize to the team, and come clean with a bad decision or an awful attitude. Blame and cover-ups kill the spirit of a caring culture, however honesty breathes life, loyalty and professionalism.

Be honest with others by caring enough to confront, this keeps accounts short and cultivates trust. Be honest with others by confessing your mistakes, this frees others to do the same and builds respect. Be honest with others by communicating the good and the bad, this keeps everyone engaged in reality, and values the team. Lastly, be honest with yourself and God. Start by being honest with yourself. Be truthful about your strengths, your weaknesses, your limitations, your personality, and your character.

Be who you are, and who you can become with God's transforming power, but do not become a caricature of someone else. This is the tremendous value of self-awareness, so be ever vigilant in your understanding of yourself. Take a variety of self-assessments and compare their results. Become comfortable with one and make its language common place in your speech and practice. Submit yourself to a regular review from your supervisor and other team members. Open yourself up to scrutiny and feedback from your family and friends. Self-honesty comes from a teachable heart that listens from the perspective of its peers and learns how to improve.

Honesty means you confess what you don't know. You don't pretend to have all the answers, but you humbly seek to define the right questions. Validate with others who know well you and what you do best. Is it analyzing data, writing, leading, strategic thinking, networking, communicating, recruiting, managing, nurturing relationships, supporting, planning or implementation, just to name a few? Discover what you do well, and where you have the most passion, and then focus your time and attention there. It takes honesty to refrain from doing what you like, when your outcomes are only average. However, your courage and trust in others to carry out an interesting task without you will bring about the best results for everyone. Honesty with yourself promotes honesty with God. You can be honest with Him because He already knows. The process of coming clean with your Creator is more for your benefit. Honesty with heaven leads us to honesty on earth. Therefore, be honest with God and grow, as your honesty leads to His intimacy. Honesty opens a wide door to knowing your Lord and making Him known.

The Bible says, "And my honesty will testify for me in the future..." (Exodus 30:33a).

O2 TIME FOR TRANSITION

"Moses my servant is dead. Now then, you and all these people, get ready to cross the Jordan River into the land I am about to give to them—to the Israelites." JOSHUA 1:2

Death is a time for transition. It may be the death of a close friend, a parent, or a grandparent. Dead is hard, and it is a time for pause, but grief is a bridge to transition. You may be the leader now, as responsibility is knocking at your door. It is up to you to walk by faith through the Lord's open door into this new opportunity.

Do not let your lack of experience hold you back; your confidence is in Christ. Be very strong and courageous in Him, as He graduated your loved one or friend to heaven. He has left you behind on earth to carry out His mission. Divine destiny has deemed this inevitable transition to fine tune your faith. Furthermore, your struggle may be the death of a vision or a prayed over plan. You may have thought you were a 'lifer' in this particular career, but things change and people change. You grow in skills and abilities that may have been dormant ten years ago. Now God is tugging at your heart toward transition. His desire is transition based on truth, and the truth is, it is time for change. Your family needs a break from your break neck pace, so now is the time for you to go out at the 'top of your game'. Don't wait until you are asked to leave, but choose to leave so another leader can build on your good work with his new and much needed leadership style. Everything is for a season, as your winter of discontent is about to bloom into a spring of contentment.

Moreover, you may need to preside over a funeral of bad habits. Bury them deep into the soil of your Savior's love and forgiveness. Cremate your fears under the strong hand of the Lord, and make His confidence your confidence. Receive God's encouragement as your strength for life's journey. God is walking with you on this path of change; so do not fear because your heavenly Father is not far away. Your intimacy with Almighty God is your energy for living. Tap into His truth often, especially during transition, and trust Him with this life change.

His transformation of your character is a terrific transition. It requires a lifetime of surrender and obedience to Him.

Lastly, death is a time of transition to heaven. Life is preparation for death, and is one big transition toward your eternal transition. Because of this, it matters how you invest your time and money. Whom are you investing your wisdom and discernment? Who will model the principles for successful living that God has imparted to you as a wise steward? People are your greatest investment. One day you will transition to heaven, and part of the reward you receive from the Lord will be people you influenced for God. Therefore, use your ultimate eternal transition as your present motivation to pour into people. People need time and truth, so train them in the ways of God. Stay teachable yourself so you are fresh in your faith, and be mentored so you can mentor. Let your life of transition point to trust in God.

The Bible says, "Why, you do not even know what will happen tomorrow. What is your life? You are a mist that appears for a little while and then vanishes" (James 4:14).

DEVOTED THINGS

"But keep away from the devoted things, so that you will not bring about your own destruction by taking any of them. Otherwise you will make the camp of Israel liable to destruction and bring trouble on it." JOSHUA 6:18

Devoted things are sacred to our Savior Jesus. Things devoted to Him cannot be tampered with for our own selfish desires. We may have devoted money or relationships to Him. Our devotion to Him may be represented by a meaningful routine or a worshipful ritual. We need to respect as His those things in our lives we have devoted to Him. God is honored by our devotion. We hold Him in high esteem when we devote our marriage, our children and our friends to Him. He delights in devoted things, and is jealous over their ownership. We trust Him with devoted things because He can be trusted. Devoted things are not ours, but His. Think about things in your life that need to be devoted to the Lord. He desires devoted things, especially those things that bring Him the most glory. A good starting point is to devote your entire being to God. This does not mean you have to move to a foreign land and live in poverty, (though it might). This does not mean you have to quit everything you are doing and go to seminary, (though it might) This does not mean you have to talk in a religious gibber jabber, act strangely and draw attention to yourself, but it does mean you glorify God in your speech, attitude, and actions. Your devotion is a reflection of Him.

Indeed, devote your home to Christ. Use it for Him openly and freely. Create a home full of warmth and hospitality. See your living quarters as a sanctuary for seeking souls. People long to be in an environment that extinguishes loneliness. He has blessed you with a place that illustrates God's provision. Use it, so you don't lose it. A devoted home is a shelter from the storms of life, though it is not a conflict-free zone. There is still plenty that goes on in a home dedicated to God that needs His grace.

However, devote your home to the Lord, and watch Him work. He takes what is devoted to Him and uses it way beyond what you can imagine. Refrain from just using your home for you, and see it as a God-spot for weary wanderers. Encouragement explodes in a home dedicated to the Almighty.

Lastly, devote your family and work to your heavenly Father. There is so much you cannot control as it relates to family and work. Your best strategy is to lay them both at the feet of our Savior. Jesus takes your devotion of family, and sets you free from having to make them into something that you think is best. You can trust your spouse and children to Christ. They are His devoted possessions, so you can trust the Lord with your loved ones. Even in their struggles, you can trust them, because you trust Him. If you do not trust them, they have a hard time trusting you. It is easier to extend trust to those you have devoted to the Lord.

Moreover, devote your work and career to Christ. Give your job to Jesus. When you give over your occupation to Him in sweet surrender and devotion, you are freed from preoccupation with what ifs. What if I lose my job? How will I take care of my family? A career devoted to Christ knows the Almighty has the answers before we ask. Therefore, do not hold onto for yourselves what you devote to heaven. Your Savior secures devoted things. The Bible says, "Guard my life, for I am devoted to you. You are my God; save your servant who trusts in you" (Psalm 86:2).

O4 PROCESS DISAPPOINTMENT

"Cast your cares on the LORD and he will sustain you;
he will never let the righteous fall." PSALM 55:22

Process disappointment or you will remain in a disappointed cycle. Disappointment is meant to drive us to God and not away from Him. If disappointment is not processed, it harms our heart. It builds up like emotional plaque and blocks the flow of the Holy Spirit between us and Almighty God. The Spirit is quenched and we are left to function in our own strength, and this is a lonely place. Unprocessed disappointment leads to angry reactions. Whether it leaks out gradually or explodes unexpectedly, it is ugly. It causes others to ask, "Where did that come from?" and "Is he/she okay?"

Disappointed people become a dread to be around. They are unhappy with themselves and everyone who surrounds them. Disappointment is here to stay, but we can move beyond its influence. Daily we have opportunities to process disappointment. It may come in the form of a broken promise or an unmet expectation. You may find disappointment in your checkbook, your calendar, or when you step up on the scale. Sometimes disappointment is disguised in a remorseful purchase or commitment. Most likely, your disappointments revolve around people. They let you down, they don't act right, they don't give you the respect you deserve, or they don't seem to care.

So, since disappointment is a fact of life, how can we process it in a healthy manner? How can disappointment work for our advantage instead of our disadvantage? Processing disappointment properly begins with seeking God's perspective. We can begin to align with His view on the matter with questions like: "What does God want me to learn from this disappointing situation?, How do I need to change? How can I be a blessing to others in the middle of my extreme disappointment? How can I shift from my disappointment to His faithfulness?" These questions, and others like them, help us process disappointment in a way that makes us more dependent on God and less dependent on circumstances. He understands our disappointment and wants to meet us in the middle of our hurt. But He meets with us to move us beyond our disappointment into the satisfaction of our Savior.

Therefore, do not stay stuck in your disappointment. Move out of its ugly dilemma. You can transition from blame and lay claim to the Lord. Christ cares so much He overcame His own extreme disappointment when He cried out, 'My God, My God, why have you forsaken me?' (Mark 15:34) He cared by giving His life on the cross for you. Your Savior Jesus will sustain you in and through your disappointment. Indeed, make regular appointments with your heavenly Father to process your disappointment. Flood your soul with His grace and forgiveness. Pray for those who have let you down, and see them as God sees them, people who desperately need His care. How you process disappointment is a testament of your trust in Jesus. Therefore, cast your cares on Christ, and receive God's care so you can care for the disappointed. Process your disappointment by the grace of God for His hope overcomes disappointment.

The Bibles says, "And hope does not disappoint us, because God has poured out his love into our hearts by the Holy Spirit, whom he has given us" (Romans 5:5).

"…the Lord's love is with those who fear him…"   PSALM 103:17

Fear of God is access to the love of God. On the surface this doesn't feel right, but we discover this when we dive deep into God's character. His righteous attributes compel us to fear Him. We cannot contemplate for very long our awesome Almighty God and not be struck with awe. His goodness and holiness require our unrivaled worship and devotion. Fear of God flows from our innermost being, because He is the Holy One. He is mighty to save and worthy is His name. The degree to which we understand the character and nature of God is the degree to which we fear God. The larger the Lord is to you, the greater your fear of Him.

Indeed, this directly affects your capacity to receive God's love, as the Lord's love follows fear of Him. So when we choose to fear God, we choose to be loved by God. He loves intently those who fear Him. Our love is limited to our own devices when we strike out on our own without fearing Him, but when we fear our heavenly Father, we position ourselves to be loved by Him.

But it is important to understand that fear of God is more than respect, and it transcends awe. For instance when we are disobedient, we feel dreadful, and we are afraid of the Almighty discipline. Fear of God is very near to the love of God, as it helps us ascribe value to what God deems important. When you fear God, you are more able to discern wise choices. Because He trusts you, He gives you wisdom to understand His ways.

Indeed, the fear of God will lead you to understand His calling on your life. Therefore, fear Him and be loved and led by Him. Fear of God positions you to experience His very best. Yes, it is an attitude of dependence, but also one of tremendous freedom, because you can trust Him. Fear of God does not thrust you into a corner to quit. On the contrary, it compels you to persevere in doing right. It takes you on an adventure with the Almighty. Fear of God is freedom to do His will with abandonment, and it is fueled by His love. It is fruit from the fear of the Lord, so fear Him fully and then be unconditionally loved by Him.

Stubbornness and pride do not fear God, nor does unbelief fear God. Disobedience is fearless of God, and in these places void of fear, love is lacking. Sincere and lasting love is embedded in the fear of God. Love is shallow and conditional when motivated by sources other than God. He is love, He is holy, and He is to be feared. Fear of God will bring back your sense of shame in not doing nice things, or honest activities. Fear of God will bring dignity to all human beings, especially those who have no voice. Fear of God will remind you of what's important: purity, peace, hope, forgiveness, faith, honesty, holiness, generosity, and above all else love. He is waiting for God-fearing people to take Him at His word. His ways are not your ways, but His ways are the best ways. Therefore, follow Him in fear and receive an abundance of His love. God's love is looking to partner with God-fearing followers, so fear Him and be loved by Him.

The Bible says, "Let those who fear the LORD say: "His love endures forever" (Psalm 118:4).

06 OBEY HIM

"Although he was a son, he learned obedience from what he suffered and, once made perfect, he became the source of eternal salvation for all who obey him…"
HEBREWS 5:8-9

Obedience to God is the heartbeat of Jesus. He learned obedience, He modeled obedience, and suffering was His incubator to be educated in obedience. The best lessons we learn seem to come out of suffering. Anyone can obey when it is easy, however in the fire of adversity and pain, our obedience is put to the test. Will we obey even when it hurts, even when it costs us dearly, even when we don't want to, even when we are uncertain of the outcome? Obedience's tests unmask our motives, and untested obedience may just be the result of convenience.

So, be prepared to obey just because you know it is the right thing to do, when no one else but God will ever know. He is watching to see if we will obey Him when no one else knows, and others are caviler. Jesus knows from first-hand experience that obedience is what makes us more like Him. We experience Him in our acts of obedience. He assures us in our obedience. He loves us in our obedience. He empowers us in our obedience. God shows up in the middle of our obedience. It is so important to Him that He makes it a priority to bless our obedience. His blessing may not be recognized immediately. It may take months or years before we enjoy the fruit of our obedience to pray.

This is especially true when things are going well. It seems like we don't need God when we are fine. We unwisely drop our prayer guard and are exposed to a punch in the face by our adversary, Satan. The reality is that success and prosperity need to propel us to pray more. Progress demands prayer. How can we maintain this level of achievement, or move forward to conqueror new horizons without obedience in prayer? Success reveals a different type of suffering. We suffer from isolation, greed and pride. Without obediently seeking Him, we fail where it matters most. God smiled on our efforts and brought success. He is the author of progress by His providence. Therefore, we obey Him with our prayers. We obediently point our prayers toward heaven often and aggressively.

Lastly, when you passed from death to life, from darkness to light, you became a new creation in Christ. Your name changed from self to selfless, from control to trust, from disobedient to obedient. As Jesus followers, you represent heaven on earth, as you are the face of your heavenly Father. You obey Him because there is a higher purpose in life. You are ambassadors for Almighty God, hosts for heaven, and greeters for God. Therefore, even in hypocrisy you obey, so you obey your way to obedience. You obey because we are His, and you learn obedience from what you suffer. Obedience is God's ointment for living. The Bible says, "See, I am setting before you today a blessing and a curse— the blessing if you obey the commands of the LORD your God that I am giving you today; the curse if you disobey the commands of the LORD your God and turn from the way that I command you today by following other gods, which you have not known" (Deuteronomy 11:26-28).

You obey Him because you are His.

"But the Lord said to Samuel, 'Do not consider his appearance or his height, for I have rejected him. The Lord does not look at the things man looks at. Man looks at the outward appearance, but the Lord looks at the heart.'"   1 SAMUEL 16:7

Sometimes we limit ourselves, because we use a wrong measure of what is meaningful to God. What has the most meaning for our Master is what's in our heart. Our heart is His measurement for potential. A heart after God has unlimited upside potential. Heaven hunts down a heart hungry for God to accomplish its purposes. We can wait for the right opportunity because He is in control, or we can spend an inordinate amount of energy arranging our lives when ultimately God is the one who opens or shuts doors. God chooses who He wants to carry out His causes, and He first looks inward for a pure heart.

Therefore, a pure heart is our first step in doing God's will for the heart is where our motivations reside. 'Why' we do 'what' we do, incubates within our heart. This is why it is imperative that the Holy Spirit rubs our heart with the oil of authenticity. He massages out toxic motives, and keeps us honest. He is the best at calling our commitment into question. Am I serving Him for what I can get or for what I can give? He calls us to place the welfare of others above our own needs.

The heart is where goodness grows, as it is nurtured in a heart with Holy ambition for knowing the Almighty. Goodness is a natural outcome of a heart following hard after heaven.

Sometimes we attempt to compliment someone by saying he or she has a good heart. However, in some cases our comments carry a tinge of condescension. We add a "but." He has a good heart, but he gives no attention to details. She has a good heart, but she is not good with follow up. He has a good heart, but he cannot think strategically. He has a good heart, but he is not an effective leader. She has a good heart, but she is not very smart. So what do we really mean when we say someone has a good heart? A good heart does not guarantee success in a certain skill set, but it does position us for success. Indeed, both character and competence are necessary for success. A superb salesman without a good heart should be shunned. A dependable manager without a good heart will bring you grief. A leader who gets results without a good heart will run off good people. Make sure to align goodness of heart with goodness in skill, otherwise this disconnect will erode your work or family culture. Require goodness of heart with giftedness.

Goodness of heart comes from God. It is His gift not to be taken for granted. Learn to diagnose the heart. Outward trappings can trap you into recruiting or relying on the wrong person. Get to the heart of the matter, and observe how they relate to their spouse. Is there love? Is there respect? Marriage interactions bring out the heart. Look beyond a resume to results based on courage. Did she take risks for the sake of the team? The heart is the best long-term indicator of dependability. Skill can be taught, but character is conformed by a heart enamored with Christ. Like a skilled surgeon, allow the Spirit to keep your heart healthy for Him, and qualify others based on God's qualifications. Good hearts attract and keep good-hearted people. They attract God and retain His blessings.

The Bible says, "Now that you have purified yourselves by obeying the truth so that you have sincere love for your brothers, love one another deeply, from the heart" (1 Peter 1:22).

O8 ONE IN SPIRIT

"After David had finished talking with Saul, Jonathan became one in spirit with David, and he loved him as himself." 1 SAMUEL 18:1

Being one in spirit means you have reached a level of relational intimacy that few obtain. The loyalty, generosity, love, service, and depth of communication reach levels that are rare in relationships. For intimacy to grow, it is imperative that we get beyond the surface of self-indulgence and move toward selfless acts of service. People become one in spirit when there is no score keeping. There is no scorecard charting the rights and wrongs that have been committed. You know you are accepted by the other and they love you as they love themselves. One in spirit means you are comfortable with one another's company. There is a peace that penetrates your presence. Distractions diminish in importance when you experience oneness in spirit. There is an unspoken loyalty that leavens the relationship of those who are one in spirit. When one or the other is caught in the crossfire of life events, each knows his friend is close by to help.

Oneness in spirit means you hurt when your friend hurts. When he feels the barbs of rejection, you feel rejected. When she is the brunt of another's anger, you are taken back by the anger. When he is jarred by jealousy, you feel the pain of jealousy. When she is ravished by disease, you are available real time. There is an energized empathy that engulfs the relationships of those who are one in spirit. It is not a sentimental sensitivity, but one that is based on the sensitivity of our Savior.

The oneness of spirit around the Spirit of God is the most meaningful. Jesus is the best facilitator for real relationships. He is the glue that brings hearts together in oneness over what's best for God's Kingdom. Christ is the catalyst for unity around what's really important. His heart is for us to pray for unity around His will. Jesus has an intimate affect on friends who fear and love Him. Oneness around our one and only Lord and Savior Jesus Christ brings us close together. His Spirit binds the spirits of believers together in a bond the world does not understand. As we grow closer to Christ, we grow closer to Christ's followers. We are able to have oneness in relationships with those who are one with Christ. So, seek to go deep with those who are deep in the Lord.

Moreover, stay one with your Savior so you are positioned to be one in spirit with others who love Jesus. Oneness with the Lord means we are prayed up, confessed up, and cleaned up. We have abandoned ourselves to the Almighty in anticipation of His wants and desires for our life. There is an oneness with Christ because we sincerely seek to serve Him out of love and gratitude.

Oneness with Jesus leads to oneness with one another. Unity with the Unifier compels us into oneness of spirit with others who are unified in Christ. Therefore, pray for those God brings your way. Pray for them to experience oneness with the Lord and, as He leads, oneness in spirit with you. Get beyond the surface with your spouse, family, and friends. Go after God and each other in oneness of spirit.

Jesus prayed, "Holy Father, protect them by the power of your name—the name you gave me—so that they may be one as we are one" (John 17:11b).

HIGHLY MOTIVATED

"When the attendants told David these things, he was pleased to become the king's son-in-law…" 1 SAMUEL 18:26

Hold out until you are highly motivated, because there is no need to attack an opportunity if you lack motivation to persevere. If you get in because it looks good, but you lack motivation, you will struggle. However, motivated men and women are persistent to produce radical results. With them, there is no lack of confidence or determination. They are on a mission and they will not be denied. By God's grace they will get to the goal because they are motivated by a greater call. Moreover, just because someone invites you into a role does not mean God has called you to that position. Pray about it and make sure you are motivated for the right reasons to engage in this new endeavor. Discover what motivates you and then position your life and work to be motivated by these desires and outcomes. Money, results, and accomplishing excellent work may motivate you. Working with a team, a loving leader, the approval of others, winning, and your family may be a compelling motivation in your life. Good health, exercise, sports, travel, or a number of other good things may get you up in the morning. However, be wise and make sure your motivations align with Almighty God's.

God-given motivations are for the good of His kingdom. As followers of Jesus, we have been called to His greater purpose. This is why our motivation is not just to get rich. Most of us will live in frustration and disappointment if becoming wealthy is our primary motivation. Money-motivated living is meaningless. However, if the true riches of experiencing God are our motivation, then there is an excellent chance we will enjoy the wealth of God's grace. Its supply is endless and its applications are abundant. The motivation of knowing and following God is monumental. It provides momentum for living and dying. This is the level of motivation that allows us to live a focused life by faith. Motivations matter most when they are initiated by our Master. He is the master motivator, so look to Jesus for motivation, as His very presence motivates.

Therefore, above all else be motivated by engaging in God's will. Do not hold back for He has you here on behalf of heaven. You can be proud that you are His representative, because the Lord is your motivator, you do not lack motivation. Be who you are for Him, and do what you do for Him. Execute His game plan with excellence, and live like a man or woman on fire for God.

He is your motivation, because you work unto the Lord not men. People come and go, but Christ remains. You will never lack motivation if the Lord's will is your motive. Be patient, align your motives with His, and obey His commands. Jesus said, "I will not speak with you much longer, for the prince of this world is coming. He has no hold on me, but the world must learn that I love the Father and that I do exactly what my Father has commanded me" (John 14:30-31).

010 PROCESS ANGER

"Saul tried to pin him to the wall with his spear, but David eluded him as Saul drove the spear into the wall. That night David made good his escape." 1 SAMUEL 19:10

Process anger or it will preoccupy your attitude and your actions. Anger is a self-fulfilling prophecy of destruction, as it destroys peace and quiet, and ravishes relationships. Anger is acidic for it eats away your credibility, your health, and eventually your ability to function successfully in life. Anger is an ugly emotion, as it easily embarrasses itself, and humiliates others for sport. It has a way of expressing itself at the most inopportune times.

For example, one outburst of anger can turn a pleasant family drive to church into one full of fear and intimidation. Work environments build walls of distrust because of seething, and unresolved anger. Relationships never get beyond the surface because of the fear of anger's rejection. No one wants to be around an angry person, the Bible even says, "Anger is cruel and fury overwhelming, but who can stand before jealousy" (Proverbs 27:4).

Where does anger come from? There are probably a variety of sources. One is the result of not being loved and/or not loving. When a heart is perpetually unloved, it has a void that is first influenced by, and then filled with anger. On the contrary, a heart full of love has no room for anger. Love melts anger like the sun beating down on a milk chocolate bar at the beach. Cold anger is no match for the warm flames of love.

Love responds with understanding, instead of seeking to argue or defend itself. Love learns to forgive instead of holding resentment over the head of someone who has been deeply disappointed. Love moves on instead of seething in the stew of what should have happened. Love matures over mistakes made, while anger whines in immaturity. Furthermore, anger incubates in a hurting heart. A heart raw with emotion is a candidate for anger. Suffering may be hurting your heart, and you can't take it anymore. Your heart is crushed and wrung out by pain. You are extremely vulnerable to the influence of anger, so let the compassion of Christ heal your heart. Invite the Lord to love on you, and process your pain in prayer. Listen intently to the Lord for He does care. He does love you right in the middle of your mess. Invite the love of Jesus to do surgery on your soul. After the Almighty has loved on you, let others love on you. Love is salve for your soul, as you need the love and prayers of people to help you process your anger.

Moreover, you may be the brunt of another's angry outbursts, but do not take their anger personally. See that person as Jesus does, and extend forgiveness. Anger may be the defense mechanism another uses to keep you at bay, instead kill him or her with kindness. Initiate forgiveness seven times seventy, and pray for this person to be loved by God and by you. Anger is an ugly mask, so unveil with acceptance. Anger is your excuse to love and accept, not fight and flee.

The Bible says, "A fool gives full vent to his anger, but a wise man keeps himself under control" (Proverbs 29:11).

PRODUCTIVITY FOLLOWS PREPARATION 011

"Finish your outdoor work and get your fields ready; after that, build your house."
PROVERBS 24:7

God blesses a process of preparation, as His Spirit is more productive when it has preparation to work with on behalf of God's will. Our activities need to be more than just going through the motions without any meaningful results. God blesses prayerful preparation, and uses it to accomplish His purposes. Farmers understand how this principle of preparation leads to productivity. They show up, prepare the soil, and God's sun and rain does the rest. However, there is a massive amount of pre-work and ongoing care that contributes to the end results. So it is as we prepare our heart, our home, and our work.

Our heart houses our dreams, desires, and motivations. A clean heart has high leverage in the hands of the Lord. Therefore, it is imperative that we daily desire for Christ to create a clean heart within us (Psalm 51:10), as a cleansed heart gets righteous results. Our daily spiritual preparation is to come daily to God and offer our life as a living sacrifice to Him (Romans 12:1-2). The preparation of our character is foundational to furthering His will. If we rush past forging a deep faith, our productivity will at best leave behind temporal results, so it positions you now and for eternity.

Secondly, prepare your home and you will have a higher probability of watching your family flourish. It is in your home where faith is your first line of defense. A home built on the solid rock of your Savior will stand when the winds of adversity reach gale force (Matthew 7:24). So, make sure to invest relational and emotional capital in your family first. Do not wait and give them the leftovers of your life. Prepare your family by giving them the very best of your time and attention. A prepared home will result in a harvest of healthy relationships. Prepare your spouse and children by leading them in the ways of the Lord.

Your model of love and obedience to God will give them the motivation and courage to do the same. Teach them how to know God and why it is wise to obey Him. A prepared family is productive by giving creditability to Christianity. It gives moral authority to a man who wants to influence others for God.

Lastly, once you have prepared your heart and home, you are positioned to have maximum productivity at work. Take the time to listen to, understand, and plan with those whom you serve. Steward your time, resources, and relationships around robust planning, process, and accountability. Make meetings meaningful by engaging the participants in planning the agenda beforehand. Ask for ongoing feedback on how to improve processes and future projects. Wise work preparation results in accomplishing what's best for the organization.

Moreover, be prepared financially by not presuming on the best-case scenario. Hope for the best, but plan for the worst at work. Create a realistic financial model, as prayerful preparation follows a strategic sequence.

Productivity follows preparation, as the Bible says, "Stand firm then... with your feet fitted with the readiness that comes from the gospel of peace" (Ephesians 6:14a-15).

012 STRENGTH IN GOD

"And Saul's son Jonathan went to David at Horesh and helped him find strength in God."
1 SAMUEL 23:16

Strength in God is significant, as it is our stronghold when we are in serious trouble. It is our source of encouragement and our motivation to persevere. Strength in God is easily accessible and always available. His strength is an unlimited reservoir of resolve, for example it may see us through the dying, and death of a loved one. It lubricates the grinding grief of our heart and keeps us from total despair. The Lord's strength is what gives us hope when our financial fortunes are tentative at best, or have been swept away altogether, but His strength will see us through a malaise of money mishaps.

The sovereign strength of God is strong, unbending and unyielding. Our confidence may be crumbling, our health may be hemorrhaging, or our relationships may be a complexity of confusion. Perhaps you discovered someone is not who he claimed to represent. He lives two lives and now the truth is unfolding, and it is not pretty. In fact, he is coming after you because you are a threat to his being found out. So lean on the Lord, and draw your strength from your Savior. Prayer to the Almighty positions you to receive His power, so punctuate the power of God in your life with faith-filled prayer.

Moreover, God's instruments for infusion of His strength are His people. Invite in the encouragement of the Lord's angelic agents. They are His ambassadors of goodwill and their righteous residue reflects His strength. These are special friends who remain true when challenging things happen to you. Stick with the ones who stick with you, and do not be embarrassed to lean on others during these lean times. Like a transfusion of blood, you may need a transfusion of faith. Your prayer platelets have fallen below what's normal to a level of dangerous discouragement. Ask for prayer to be strengthened by God, and to keep you focused in the middle of your own gnawing needs. Ask for prayer to be an encouragement to those who have encouraged you.

Do not deny others the opportunity to strengthen you with their presence and prayers.

Lastly, be quick to strengthen others in the name of the Lord. Write a note of encouragement to a friend, or leave an encouraging prayer on a coworker's voicemail. In some creative way, let those who are struggling know you are thinking of them. Prayer retains employees, and engages friends. They will never forget those who reached out to them in their time of need. Each day seek someone you can strengthen in your Savior's name. In a sense, you are strength coaches for those you come in contact with on behalf of Christ. Your goal is to get them to God, and His strength will stretch their faith way beyond your initial encouragement. Strengthen your family in the Lord and you will be strong. Strengthen your peers in the Lord and you will find eternal energy. Unselfishly strengthen others in the Lord and you will find strength for your soul.

The Bible says, "Wealth and honor come from you; you are the ruler of all things. In your hands are strength and power to exalt and give strength to all" (1 Chronicles 29:12).

"David had just said, 'It's been useless—all my watching over this fellow's property in the desert so that nothing of his was missing. He has paid me evil for good.' " 1 SAMUEL 25:21

Sometimes we receive the opposite of what we expect, as our good deeds can encounter an evil response. Some of those we have served seem to have forgotten our faithfulness, and gratitude has faded from their memory. They forgot the fantastic fruit from our labors, and it has become all about what might inconvenience them. You were there for them at their point of need, but now in your need, they reject your request. It seems like a cruel joke. How could they forget your loyalty, and the investment of some of the best days of your life? Yet this export of evil is just what you are experiencing. There is a relational trade imbalance, as you are the brunt of an evil inequity. So what do you do when you are repaid evil for good? What is your response? Our flesh screams foul, and our anger wants to attack. How could someone show their appreciation for our good will with apathy and disassociation? We want to instantly repay their ingratitude by inflicting some type of loss or pain. How you respond in this moment of deep disappointment will reveal your true character. Anyone can act like a Christian as long as everything is going his way. It is easy to be nice when everyone else is nice. However, when supposedly mature leaders let us down, and even respond to our requests with hostility, what we do next defines our true self. This is a test in dependence on God.

When evil intent is injected into a relationship, we must resist firing back with equally evil actions. We cannot lower ourselves to this kind of school yard revenge. The question is not, "What is the right thing for them to do?" The question is, "What is the right thing for me to do?" You can reverse the tone of the verbal jabs by returning good for evil. When you choose not to fight false accusations by accosting your accusers you repay good for evil. You trust the truth will come out at the right time, in the right way. When you choose to forgive the malicious actions of insecure and mean men, you repay good for evil. When you pray for ungrateful souls to see God, you repay good for evil..

Above all else, anchor your hope for justice to be done in Almighty God. The Lord can take care of the business of dealing with evil people and their actions. Wait on the Lord to settle matters as He sees fit, especially if you have the power to crush someone. Trust Christ to take them down in His timing. Your window of reprieve is their opportunity to repent, so be patient. You would want this same grace extended to you. Evil doers may never change, but they might. It is a heart issue between them and God. In the meantime, when you encounter evil, repay it with good and then trust God. The goodness of God trumps evil, as it is no match for good.

The Bible says, "If a man pays back evil for good, evil will never leave his house" (Proverbs 17:13).

O14 TOO EXHAUSTED

"Then David came to the two hundred men who had been too exhausted to follow him and who were left behind at the Besor Ravine. They came out to meet David and the people with him. As David and his men approached, he greeted them." 1 SAMUEL 30:21

Sometimes you are too exhausted to take one more step forward, as your faith is fatigued and your energy is sapped. It is not because you are not spiritual, but you are spent. It is time for a rest; otherwise you are a prime candidate for burn out. Exhaustion is overwhelming unless you pace yourself. It is God's warning to slow down, and His appeal for you to adjust. You can choose to slow down, or your Savior will help you slow down, sometimes with sickness. Do not think you have to keep up with others who have a greater capacity, as God has a place for you to perform within your passion, skills and giftedness.

Following God does not mean you cannot vary your responsibilities. Variety is the spice of serving Christ, so be willing to humble yourself, and do something different. You may be surprised to see new enthusiasm erupt like a brilliant Roman candle on the fourth of July. Change in environments can keep you from coming apart from exhaustion. Maybe this means you pray for the project and the people, as it is the Lord's lever to move past persistent problems. Prayer brings peace, calm, and clarity.

Some will not embrace your exhaustion excuse, and they may even criticize you as weak or unspiritual. They might talk behind your back in resentment, but you cannot control the reactions of those you thought wanted what's best for you. They are probably feeling the effects of exhaustion themselves. Fatigue makes everyone feel a little fearful. They are venting their frustrated feelings rising from weakness, and you happen to be the most convenient target for their complaints. So pray they will have the courage and trust to rest in Him at the right time, for the right reasons.

In the meantime, take the time to recover from your exhaustion. Trust God with the results of your work, and trust that you will receive what's fair from the authorities over your life. You may need an extended sabbatical, or a vacation to properly extinguish your exhaustion. Use emptiness to enhance your relationship with the Lord.

Slow down, and be with your Savior, for His mercy extends you the opportunity to enjoy the fruits of your labor that led to your wearisome condition. By God's grace you will overcome exhaustion, but it takes time and faith. Trust Him and trust others with delegation to get the job done. The work will be there when you get back, so be patient. This is time for your healing, as He will make your relationships whole again. His grace and forgiveness cannot be exhausted. Therefore, overcome your exhaustion with His inexhaustible grace.

The Bible says, "He gives strength to the weary and increases the power of the weak. Even youths grow tired and weary, and young men stumble and fall; but those who hope in the LORD will renew their strength..." (Isaiah 40:29-31a).

TEARS OF GRIEF

"So David and his men wept aloud until they had no strength left to weep."
1 SAMUEL 30:4

Tears of grief transcend our normal emotions for they come from deep within our heart, and can erupt in uncontrollable crying. Tears of grief are given to us by God to express our larger than life losses. In the Lord's mercy, He allows us to weep. Tears of grief can flush out our fears, and foster our faith, as they represent a cleansing process. Tears flood our face and eyes, but we see Christ when they subside. We see Him as our comfort and caregiver. We may have been a care-giver, but now we need a caregiver. In our loss we need the Lord. We need the comfort of Christ to wipe away our tears and replace them with His hope. God shows up in our tears of grief in sympathy and soul care. Our tears of grief solicit our Savior's tender touch. What you have lost you may not get back soon. It is gone and its destiny is in God's hands, so do not lose hope because heaven wants to help. God is not passively dispassionate over your despair for He cares.

Your loss may be a loved one who voluntarily disassociated herself from your family. She grew tired of your influence and authority, and wanted to see the world for herself. Her departure may have been sudden and unexpected. You weep because you wonder if she will ever come back the same, but pray Christ will change her on her journey to find herself. Pray she finds Him, and embraces the good values you have instilled in her character. God will use your tears to keep her heart tender for Him. Present your tears of grief as a humble offering to Him.

Your loss may be material. The perceived value of these personal treasures is contingent on your capacity to remember. Your photos may still be framed in your mind's eye, though now absent from their frames. Thank God you still have the ability to remember, as memories are His gifts to be cherished and celebrated. Do not allow the physical loss to rob you of their emotional significance. Moreover, do not focus on fleeting financial losses. Money-motivated living makes for a roller coaster ride of uncertainty. Your grief will never subside if it depends on dollars. Lastly, let the Lord and others love on you through your tears of grief. God grieves with you, since He gave His son; He understands loss. Jesus weeps when you weep, as you are not alone in your pain and suffering. Tears are a liquid bridge to the Lord; they are a float of faith down the river of God's will. Grief is meant to lead you to the Lord. Therefore, receive the warm embrace of your heavenly Father, and invite His children to pray and care for you. When your tears subside, stay at the side of your Savior Jesus. Your weeping has washed your soul for service, and now you can tenderly engage with others in their tears.

"Use grief to leverage your life for the Lord," the Bible says, "...we can comfort those in any trouble with the comfort we ourselves have received from God..." (2 Corinthians 1:4b).

016 SHOW GOD'S KINDNESS

> "The king asked, 'Is there no one still left of the house of Saul to whom
> I can show God's kindness?' "   2 SAMUEL 9:3

God's kindness is unconventional, as it extends to the unexpecting and to the undeserving. God's kindness is king because it has no bounds, and it is not limited by past disagreements or conflict. His kindness does not cower in a corner for fear of being taken advantage. The kindness of God gets over grudges and reaches out to the unreachable. It transcends times of confusion and misunderstanding, and its design is to be distributed indiscriminately. Kings of kindness search out those who need it the most, and they don't have to look very far to find those who need a tender touch.

Who are candidates for God's kindness? Everyone with whom we come in contact on a daily basis is a kindness candidate. The cashier at the retail store needs a kind smile. The server at the restaurant needs a kind commendation, and a generous gratuity. An angry child needs kindness and love, and a discouraged spouse needs kind words of understanding, and not a speech on what to do next. Employees need kind instruction, and employers need kind feedback. Friends need kind accountability, and extended family needs your kind presence. The poor need kindness and care, as the afflicted, suffering, and rejected need a boatload of kindness. We can be kind because the Lord has been kind to us.

His kindness is our unlimited reservoir of kindness. Without our Savior shedding His kindness on us we have little capacity for kindness. It is because we have been blessed by the kindness of King Jesus that we are able to extend His eternal kindness to others. We don't deserve it, but He allows us to feast with Him by faith. His blessing is bountiful to the lovers of His father.

For the sake of Christ, God extends His kindness to Christ's friends. Our affiliation with Jesus opens wide the door of our heavenly Father's kindness, as it flows to those who follow His son. Devotion to Jesus is a magnet for our Master's kindness. Love Jesus and the kindness of the Lord will flood your life, and overflow into the dry, parched souls of those thirsty for kindness.

So, unleash the kindness of God on others. God's kindness brings out the best in everyone. They may suspect your actions and question your motives, because it is unusual to experience kindness that comes out of expecting nothing in return. Some hurting and cynical people will have to get used to God's kindness through you. It takes time to validate your vision for kindness in their life.

Therefore, do not grow weary in being kind to the one who suspects kindness. The kindness of God leads to a change of mind about motives. It kills critical spirits, and overcomes uncaring attitudes. Indeed, the kindness of God treats others as it wants to be treated, so don't be surprised that in the long run your kindness generates kindness. God's kindness is designed to be deployed once it is received. In a culture of kindness, families, and teams that fear God are forged.

The Bible says, "And God raised us up with Christ ... in order that in the coming ages he might show the incomparable riches of his grace, expressed in his kindness to us in Christ Jesus" (Ephesians 2:6a-7)

"One evening David got up from his bed and walked around on the roof of the palace. From the roof he saw a woman bathing. The woman was very beautiful…" 2 SAMUEL 11:2

The allure of temptation relates to proximity. If we position ourselves to be tempted, there is a high probability we will drift toward its deception. It is unwise to be out of position, and enjoy the cheap thrill of temptation. This is why we do not position our eyes in ways that lead to wayward behavior. Our eyes can be sentinels for our Savior, or they can be seducers of Satan. We have the choice, but God has given us His Holy Spirit to check our wrong positioning. Beautiful people are easy on the eyes, but they are not meant to mesmerize us into wrong thinking, and eventually bad behavior. Temptations immediate gratification seems harmless, but once it has us in a vulnerable position, it pushes for more ground until it captures our heart. If we discover ourselves in the wrong place at the wrong time, we are at high risk for temptation.

However, wise Christians position themselves to faithfully follow Christ. Following the Lord does not free us from temptation, but He empowers us to flee when we encounter its pull. Following God is not always fun, but it is fruitful, as He keeps us from caving into our covetous cravings. Indeed, we properly position ourselves toward God and away from temptation by prayer. It purges out pride and our tendency to take temptation lightly.

Moreover, it is wise to position ourselves under the accountability of people. We cannot stand up to the seduction of temptation, if we are secluded. Left to ourselves, we flirt with the fun temptation offers at the outset, but then it bites with its indiscriminate humiliation and hurt. We have all discovered that we do better when those around us remind us of the obvious. Temptation loves for us to ignore warnings, and become obsessed with the foolishness of our own isolated thinking. Positioning ourselves away from authenticity with others is a recipe for disaster. We all do much better when others are watching us.

Therefore, you position yourself wisely when you use power for people, instead of using people for power. Persons are meant to be blessed, not abused by power. So, use your influence for the sole benefit of others while trusting God that your own needs will be met by Him.

Otherwise, you are tempted to leverage others for yourself. You run through relationships, and discard them like an old t-shirt. People become expedient for your own selfish desires, and your temptation to live for the moment becomes master. Therefore, stay positioned to serve others and fear God. Selfless love positions you away from the grasp of temptation's talons. Above all else, do not depend on yourself alone. Discipline deteriorates without the forging fires of the Holy Spirit. With His wisdom and by His grace, avoid temptation's invitation.

The Bible says, "There hath no temptation taken you but such as is common to man: but God is faithful, who will not suffer you to be tempted above that ye are able; but will with the temptation also make a way to escape, that ye may be able to bear it" (1 Corinthians 10:13, KJV).

018 KINGDOM CITIZENSHIP

"But out citizenship is in heaven. And we eagerly await a Savior from there,
the Lord Jesus Christ..." PHILIPPIANS 3:20

Followers of Jesus Christ are not citizens of this world. This life is a pass through, as we are on temporary assignment as agents of God. We serve on foreign soil, for heaven is our home. Kingdom citizenship is easy to forget, as we sometimes begin to act like this is as good as it gets. But the best this world has to offer is of no consequence compared to even the least of what heaven has to offer. A sumptuous meal here is much better there. Wonderful worship here is no comparison to the chorus of angels there. Raving relationships here cannot hold a candle to the absence of sin and sorrow there. The beauty of God's creation here foreshadows the incomprehensible glory He has prepared there.

The struggle of sickness here releases to 100% wholeness there. The enjoyment of stuff here is laughable in comparison to the value of His heavenly rewards, and the comfort of the Holy Spirit here is but an appetizer to feasting on the countenance of Jesus. Things are much, much better back home in heaven. This is where our hope lies, ultimately and fully. Do not become enamored, taken in, or too comfortable with this world. It is passing by and we are passing through. The land of our origins is full of God and free in Christ. We can hold our head high because our King Jesus rules in majesty, holiness and grace. We are privileged to serve under the flag of His kingdom, and we represent the King of Kings and the Lord of Lords.

Yes, you are an ambassador for Christ, so it is necessary for you to remain on earth for now, for the sake of the gospel. You represent your Lord for others; so do not take your ambassadorship lightly or flippantly. Keep top of mind your responsibility to be a good citizen in the Kingdom of God. You can constantly be aware of opportunities to represent God's concerns, and draw others into His kingdom.

People are attracted to God, because they see Christ manifested in your life. They want to apply for citizenship in the Kingdom of God. Their Visas from this world are torn, tattered, and limited to the temporal in need of constant renewal. This is not the case when you immigrate to the shores of heaven. Your papers are good for eternity because you are now a citizen of an everlasting kingdom. Kingdoms of this world come and go, but The Kingdom of God is now and for evermore.

The Kingdom of Heaven is not without battles, so fight the good fight for the glory of God, and for the souls of men and women, boys and girls, and the unborn. The war is already won; so let others know they do not have to remain prisoners of sin. They too can become kingdom citizens right now. While you remain on earth, invite as many others as possible to submission under the Almighty's reign. Be humble, proud, and joyful of the fact that your citizenship is in heaven.

The Bible says, "But you have come to Mount Zion, to the heavenly Jerusalem, the city of the Living God. You have come to thousands upon thousands of angels in joyful assembly..."(Hebrews 12:22).

RELATIONAL STALEMATE

"And the spirit of the King longed to go to Absalom, for he was consoled concerning Amnon's death." 2 SAMUEL 13:38

A relational stalemate is when you are separated from someone with whom you have enjoyed good times in the past. You have loved each other with a rare level of relational understanding. You both have a lot invested, yet there is no communication from either of you. Misunderstanding may have led to disappointment, and disappointment may have led to anger, and anger to total rejection. In whatever circumstance you find yourself, it is not worth maintaining relational separation. The distance needs to be dissolved, as you owe it to each other, your family, the Christian community, and you owe it to God. There is a debt of love that is begging to be paid.

So where do you start? A good place to start is for the one in authority to make a genuine gesture toward reconciliation. You may want to invite your estranged friend, or relative into your home for a meal and conversation. Reach out to this person without any expectations other than to accept and love them at their point of need. Leave any behavior and attitude change to work of the Holy Spirit. Your first step of acceptance will at least breach the door of communication. It may take multiple lobs of love before there is any reciprocation, so be persistent and trust God with the results. It takes time for relational stalemates to become solvent, so don't stop initiating. Increase your overtures of acceptance.

Moreover, be open to a mediator. God can use a third party as a catalyst to break the chains of relational resistance. Wise and discerning friends, or even strangers can be a facilitator of rational thinking. Prayerfully chose someone both parties respect and will respond to willingly. This unbiased individual can be an instrument of healing sent by heaven. God can use a mediator to send forth His truth, so pray for someone with a spirit of gentle boldness who can keep you focused on facts and on the character of Christ. This godly bridge builder may be just what's needed to break the relational logjam.

After all, how much is it worth to be relationally whole again? How much is it costing you to remain stuck in this relational stalemate? Your Savior Jesus wants you to move beyond this relational rut. He knows that your relationship with Him will be impeded until you can come clean with your parent, your child, your employee, your employer, your husband, your wife, or your friend. Relational blockage with people contributes to blockage of intimacy with the Almighty. There is something bigger at stake than just an estrangement on earth, as there is eternal estrangement brewing. Your love for the Lord cannot be leveraged if you are not levering your love for others. Indeed, relational stalemates cannot be ignored. They are not going away, and will only grow in silent intensity. Ask God to give you grace so you can extend it often to the estranged, and be quick to apologize, and even quicker to love. Your reconciliation to your heavenly Father invites reconciliation to others. Therefore, receive His forgiveness and extend it to the other. Trust God to begin breaking the relational stalemate, and pray for healing.

The Bible says, "When a man's ways are pleasing to the LORD, he makes even his enemies live at peace with him" (Proverbs 16:7).

020 PROFITABLE PATIENCE

"Wait for the Lord; be strong and take heart and wait for the Lord."   PSALM 27:14

Life is normally lived waiting. We wait in lines. A teenager waits for his or her next birthday. We wait for job promotions. We wait for news from the doctor. We wait for the next meal. We wait for our future spouse. We wait for a lawsuit to settle. We wait for a meeting to conclude. We wait for those who have yet to keep their commitment. Every time we turn around we have an opportunity to wait. Why wait, because most of the time it what's best, and most beneficial. A vegetable gardener is a prisoner to waiting, but this an asset not a liability. A tomato is much tastier when it is red, large and juicy, rather than green, small and hard. The smart gardener will wait for the vegetables to ripen, though he will nurture the soil along the way and keep out the weeds.

There is a waiting cycle that must be completed before there is worthwhile fruit. If you did not have to wait, you may have been satisfied with how things have always been done. Now you have the opportunity to think differently. Maybe there are other people, or resources that can contribute to your project or plan? So when things do not go as planned, see it as an opportunity to improve the plan. Conversely, the very thing may be to provide help to another, as waiting is a lesson in loving others in spite of themselves, and even providing valued assistance during this parenthesis in your own life.

Most importantly, however, is to learn how to wait for the Lord. What a valuable asset to wait upon. The Lord God Almighty is worth the wait.

It is worth waiting for His joy, because it comes to uplift you, and bring a smile to your face. It is worth waiting for His peace that calms your soul, and allows you to sleep at night. It is worth waiting for His wisdom that provides discernment in the middle of conflicting options. It is worth waiting for His strength that propels you through adversity, and gives you confidence and perseverance for life's journey. It is worth waiting for His hope that uplifts you out of your despair and depression.

People camp out to wait and see a rock star, or pay big bucks to wait and meet the President; so waiting on God should be a cinch. Waiting is fundamentally patience with God, as He is running the universe. He knows what is going on, and He knows what is best for you. He knows. He knows. He knows. You can trust Him in your waiting. Use this sabbatical-like time to get to know your heavenly Father more intimately. Use this time to love on your family, and others like no other time in your life. Allow Him to mold your character, so that others will comment to themselves that you are somehow different. You are different because you have been with Jesus. Waiting is not just a passage to God's blessing. It is God's blessing. Wait for the Lord, because He is worth the wait.

The Bible says, "I wait for you, O LORD; you will answer, O Lord my God" (Psalm 38:15).

INFLATED VIEWS

"When Ahithophel saw that his advice had not been followed, he saddled his donkey and set out for his house in his hometown. He put his house in order and then hanged himself. So he died and was buried in his father's tomb." 2 SAMUEL 17:23

It is tempting to have an inflated view of our views, as we come to believe that our opinions are extra special. We evolve into elevated thinking that expects everyone to believe what we think is most important, or even preferred. What started out as humble recommendations for others to consider grow into mandates from our point of view. Unfortunately, this type of conditional counsel, and authoritative advice is driven by pride. The gift of discernment and wisdom is a great stewardship that requires a spirit of humility and graciousness.

Otherwise, no one will be able to hear our insights over the muffle of our arrogance. God does not need more self-appointed gurus, but He does desire humble servants who will submit to Him as vessels of truth.

Furthermore, we set ourselves up for rejection and unreasonable expectations, if we rely on the affirmation of others for our validation. If we are not careful, we tie our value to the degree to which our views are accepted. Acceptance becomes a barometer for our self-worth. This is dangerous because our views, of course are flawed. We are ever growing in our understanding, and learning of God's expansive truths.

Moreover, if we are teachable and maturing, our views from the past will become more accurate in the present. For example, we will probably be less judgmental, and more motivated by mercy. We will most likely take ourselves less seriously, and God more seriously, and as we grow in grace, our words will build up more than tear down less. Patience will become preeminent, and our inflated views deflate, as we depend more on God.

Healthy perspectives are born out of dependence on God. Your belief about God determines the way you approach life. If you get this right, everything else comes into alignment. Openness of mind is meant to be a trap for truth, not a license for liberalism. When you are convinced of a principle, clamp down on it with conviction. It is wise to be close-minded around your convictions, just make sure it is a conviction from God, and not just a personal preference. One thing for sure is God's engagement in every day life. The Almighty is not absent, but is alive and well.

Therefore, seek to lead others into a grander view of God. Keep Christ the centerpiece of your counsel. Make the Lord the beginning and the end of your advice. If you lead people to be accountable to God, you are wise. If they ignore this insight, they miss their Master's best. His view is the most valuable, so admonish them toward the Almighty's perspective.

The Bible says, "The way of a fool seems right to him, but a wise man listens to advice" (Proverbs 12:15).

"Now go out and encourage your men. I swear by the Lord that if you don't go out, not a man will be left with you by nightfall. This will be worse for you than all the calamities that have come upon you from your youth until now."   2 SAMUEL 19:7

Encourage your best people, and be careful not to take them for granted. It is tempting to give all of your attention to problems, and leave nothing for those who have stood by your side. Just because a person requires little leadership does not mean they are not needy. Someone who seems okay may be suffering in silence; they may not want to be a burden so they keep quiet. They know you are busy with bigger matters, and they don't want to be a bother, but this lack of attention can only last for a short season. Everyone needs personal care, and encouragement. Low maintenance leaders still need love and positive feedback.

Therefore, make it a priority to praise those who have been with you the longest. Love them or you may lose them. We all know our most fulfilling relationships are the ones that have stood the test of time. Something special happens relationally when you endure hardships together. There is a bond built that is hard to break, but even this quality of relationship needs nurturing. Old relationships become cold relationships, if they are not given attention. So take the time today and thank God for your most loyal friends and work associates. Pray specifically for their personal and professional needs.

Moreover, manage by walking around. Step into their offices and listen to them with no agenda other than understanding what they need to be successful. Be as engaged with their interests as you expect them to be with yours.

This line of thinking and encouragement especially applies to your family. Go out of your way to be with your spouse and children. Love and respect your spouse in a large way, as a child's love and respect for mom or dad will not rise any higher than the level they observe between their parents. Furthermore, make sure not to neglect your less needy child in preference to your needy one. Your compliant child still needs encouragement, and her obedient heart needs reassurance. She needs to know she is doing well.

Otherwise she will gradually grow discontent, and tire of being the good kid. Good kids sometimes think more attention will be given to them if they behave badly. Indeed, resentment can build into rage if encouragement is chronically withheld. Take the time to encourage all of your children; just like they need food and rest, encouragement is energy for their souls.

Lastly, retain relationships by encouraging others in their faith. People's greatest encouragement comes from Christ. Jesus will be there for them when you are not. Eternal encouragement is the most meaningful and long lasting. Without their anchor of encouragement being in the Almighty, they will lack contentment. He is the greatest encourager. He understands when you don't. He loves when you lack love. He listens when you are preoccupied with your problems. Encourage others in the Lord and they will be on board. Take the time to sincerely give much needed encouragement, so others can continue. Make sure to love those who love you, as encouragement is a two-way street. Dispense it liberally, and it will be hard for others to leave.

The Bible says, "But encourage one another daily, as long as it is called Today, so that none of you may be hardened by sin's deceitfulness" (Hebrews 3:13).

BATTLE FATIGUE

023

"Once again there was a battle between the Philistines and Israel. David went down
with his men to fight against the Philistines, and he became exhausted."
2 SAMUEL 21:15

Exhaustion means we are excellent candidates for encouragement. We cannot continue alone in our exhaustion. Our body and soul cry out for care. If we ignore exhaustion's warning signals, we will probably fail. Our health may fail. Our judgment may fail. Our faculties may fail. Our faith may fail. Exhaustion increases our probability for failure. It is imperative that in our exhaustion we recognize, and receive help from others. We have to trust that they will keep our best interests in mind. We are unwise if we think we can do everything. This overwhelming state compromises the quality of our work. Things slip through the cracks that would otherwise be taken care of. It is in our exhaustion that excellence exits our work and life.

Moreover, our character becomes fragile under the weight of exhaustion's pressure. Like a garlic press, the sweet juices of God's grace are squeezed out and we are left dry. Our patience becomes thin, and we lash out at undeserving souls. What would never bother us during times of rest soon become stressful, and an exhibition in embarrassment. Meaningless arguments begin to fill our minds, so there is no room left for pleasant thoughts. Exhaustion pushes us to the edge of unwise engagements, as we listen to sympathetic words from flirtatious lips. Exhaustion is prone to engage with any understanding warm body. There is a propensity to relax one's conservative convictions, so make sure you confide in your spouse and not someone else's. Intimacy is meant for marriage, so leverage exhaustion for a deeper relationship with your husband or wife.

Exhaustion is also God's way of getting your attention. You cannot continue to run hard in life, and leave out the Lord. He wants much more than surface acknowledgement on Sunday. Exhaustion is meant to engage you with the eternal. You are reminded in your weak state that He is your rock. He is your fortress, your deliverer, your shield, your stronghold, and your salvation. Because God is your refuge, you can rest in Him. We do not have to strive in your own strength. You can be infused with the Almighty's eternal energy, and everlasting love. It is in your exhaustion that your heavenly Father wants to love you wholeheartedly and unconditionally.

So let go and let Him. Let go of your unrealistic expectations that wear you down. Let go of your way of doing things. Let go of your timetable. Let go of the relationship that is wearing you out. Engage in activities and relationships that energize you. Yes, you need to be available, but rest in Him. Rest in Him, and leave the rest to Him.

Your gracious heavenly Father is the answer to your battle fatigue. Invite the Holy Spirit to fill you up by faith, allow God's grace to flush out your fears. The Bible says, "Find rest, O my soul, in God alone; my hope comes from him" (Psalm 62:5).

O24 JEALOUSY DESTROYS

"And from that time on Saul kept a jealous eye on David."
1 SAMUEL 18:9

Jealousy is destructive. It can destroy your reputation, your relationships, your health, and your favor from God. Jealousy is insidious, as it gradually creeps into your life over time. Slowly and surely it enflames your anger and paralyzes your joy. Instead of celebrating the success of another, jealousy resents not being the center of attention. A relationship that started out as supportive and encouraging can turn 180 degrees to one of criticism and betrayal. Jealousy creates relational dysfunction that begins with sympathy toward the one who is infected, but quickly regresses to dismay from those who are affected by jealousy's tantrums. Insecurity feeds jealousy, for there is a sense of not experiencing God's blessing in the same way another is experiencing God's blessing. 'Therefore I must be inferior' is the lie that is tolerated; if you believe this deception long enough it becomes a self-fulfilling prophecy, because jealousy feeds inferiority.

Jealousy is truly a green-eyed monster seeking to destroy everyone in its path. It does not discriminate, rather it indoctrinates at every level of society. Jealousy drives the poor to bad mouth the rich, because of their wealth and opportunities. The wealthy can become jealous of the less successful, because of their simple and carefree lives. Women are jealous of women, and men are jealous of men. You can become jealous of another's spouse, children or career.

You can even be jealous of one's relationship with God, because He is not blessing you with the same intensity that He is blessing someone else. Jealousy is a game that no one wins, and it makes Satan smile. So how do you deal with jealousy? If jealousy is directed toward you, seek to disarm it with confrontation and grace. Instead of talking about the jealous offender to others, confront the person in their disillusionment, and help them understand this destructive path. Like a skilled surgeon, jealousy needs to be extracted from the heart, and ultimately only God can complete the procedure. But you can be God's conduit to surface the issue and urge the offender to come clean. The person may not respond immediately, but at least you have planted the seed. Then others who have been silent will be inspired by your boldness, and they may speak candid to the jealous one.

Lastly, if you are the object of another's jealousy, do not make room for jealousy's accusations. If you are 'suffering' from success, quickly and often give God and others the credit for your good fortune. Leave no question for doubt that you recognize the contribution of the team, and you are just one of the facilitators of the process. Deflect attention from yourself to others and God.

Don't have a false humility, but an authentic humility that communicates grace and truth. Lastly, if jealousy haunts you and you are enamored with its seduction, admit it and confess it as sin. Do not be deceived any longer. Learn to celebrate the successes of others and let gratitude be the driving force of your life. Be content with what you have and trust God with what you don't have. Disciples of Jesus are to rise above immature and worldly ways. The Bible says, "You are still worldly. For since there is jealousy and quarreling among you, are you not worldly? Are you not acting like mere men? (I Corinthians 3:3). Be yourself and thank God that He has made you the way you are.

CHRIST CONFIDENT

"With your help I can advance against a troop, with my God I can scale a wall."
2 SAMUEL 22:30

In Christ we are confident, and He is our confidence. We do not have to waver in fear or regret if Jesus is with us. Obstacles can seem overwhelming, our faith may stumble, and fear may lead our flesh to falter in its commitment. This is when we lean into the Lord in prayer, and renew our confidence in Christ. It places our trust back on our unshakeable Savior, because so much of our confidence is based on perspective. Perspective reminds us of the right questions to ask. Has God called me to this current circumstance? Is He with those who have answered His call? Can I be confident in Christ and continue? Yes, you can advance in your adversity because the Almighty is not against you, but for you. You can scale your wall of worry by faith.

Moreover, our confidence can be crushed under the weight of cruel people. You may know people right now who are intimidated by your life. Instead of praising your good deeds, they are repulsed by righteous acts. Your life reminds them of how they once were or how they need to be. Your character makes them uncomfortable. They want you to change and relieve their pain of conviction. They want you to worship with them at the altar of mediocrity. People comfortable in their sin do not want to be reminded of their selfish motives. They instinctively attack anyone who is confident in their Christian walk. They want you to go back to your pre-Christ behavior so they will feel comfortable around you, so how does Christ want you to respond? He loves us through our bad behavior and malicious motives. He does not expect us to compromise our character or convictions, but He expects us to express our differences with grace and mercy.

Therefore, in our confidence we need not be combative with characterless characters. They are lost, hurt, and feel guilty and alone. What they need is the love of God to extend abroad in their heart and soul, so stay confident that you are Christ's conduit for His love. Respond to rejection with acceptance, and extend compliments to criticism. Reach out and love those who love to hurt, because they hurt.

Our confidence in Christ cannot be shaken because He is alive and well, so stand firm by faith. Move forward on your knees in prayer and dependence on God. Confidence in Christ is bold but humble. It is engaging but calm. It is quick to ask questions, but slow to answer in judgment. So, in your home be confident that Christ is growing the faith of your family. In your work be confident that Christ is developing your team's character and competence. In your own life you can be confident that Christ is in control. Above all else, your confidence is not based on your bank account, your clothes, or your looks. It is not contingent on where you live or what you drive. It is based on Christ alone.

The Bible says, "...being confident of this, that he who began a good work in you will carry it on to completion until the day of Christ Jesus" (Philippians 1:6).

026 BEST EFFORT

> "She did what she could. She poured perfume on my body beforehand
> to prepare for my burial." MARK 14:8

God expects your best, nothing more nothing less. Your best plus God's best is a productive combination, but be careful to not fall into the false belief that God will take care of everything without your efforts. Or, you can take the stress of everything on your shoulders without inviting the God component. Neither is healthy, nor right. He simply expects your best, and He understands your limitations. Your stage of life, giftedness, experience, availability, and wisdom all determine your capacity. The capacities of others will be more or less than yours, so do not make them your measure of how much. Instead, steward extremely well what God has given you.

There will always be opportunities, but consider each activity alongside your ability to give it your best. Do not commit under duress knowing that your ability to deliver is sorely limited. Instead, have confidence in God to say "no" now in preparation for a "yes" later. Your best will dwarf some other's best, and it will look like a pygmy in the shadow of another's. One scenario of superiority leads to pride, and the other of perceived underachievement leads to discouragement. Self-flagellation will not gain you points with God or people. They will replace respect for you with pity. On the other hand, do not become puffed up over your best. There is always another person who has done or will do better. Rest in the fact that you have glorified God and brought others into His intoxicating influence.

Your best mixed with God's best is dynamic. Yes, you have limitations, and you can only do what you can do, but with God all things are possible. He can arrange circumstances, relationships, and resources that intersect with your best.

Suddenly, your best, plus God's best, plus the best of others leverages outcomes you never dreamed could happen. Your $1,000 given to teach abstinence to teens in Africa will yield one result, but that same gift combined with $100,000 will far exceed a one hundred fold result.

Your decision to do less may accomplish a lot more, because your creation of best practices will multiple exponentially. Why settle for the wilderness of simple addition when you can celebrate the promised land of complex multiplication? Your best is a valuable resource, so use it for others, and to serve God's Kingdom. The more you exercise your best, the better you become. Your best may become the best; by God's grace you can be a genius in your niche. You can become an expert at what you do, so do what you can, and devote your best to the Lord. The Bible says, "The soldiers took sheep and cattle from the plunder, the best of what was devoted to God, in order to sacrifice them to the LORD your God at Gilgal" (1 Samuel 15:21).

DUE DILIGENCE

"Therefore, since I myself have carefully investigated everything from the beginning, it seemed good also to me to write an orderly account for you, most excellent Theophilus, so that you may know the certainty of the things you have been taught." LUKE 1:3-4

Simply put, due diligence is a process of gathering the facts. It is designed to validate assumptions and expose wrong thinking. Due diligence is necessary for wise decision making. You go through due diligence when you buy a house. Comparable home prices in the neighborhood are explored to affirm or deny the asking price of the house for sale. A home inspector is probably hired to check out the nooks and crannies. He is an objective third party that looks for roof leaks, foundation damage, electrical hazards, safe plumbing, and the overall sound structure of the home. His or her harvesting of information is vital to the final decision of the home purchaser. In some ways you apply due diligence to a prospective husband or wife. You observe his attitude toward his parents. You look for love and respect. The same can be said for their reverence of God. Are they submitted to Christ and in love with Him? First impressions may be positive, but more is required to be a wise decision maker. Due diligence can take time depending on the complexity of the issue or the deal. When hiring someone, you look at past career success and the opinions of references. A credit check reveals a lot about the responsible, or irresponsible handling of money. Purchasing a business is a long process of pouring over financial audits, researching market trends, interviewing employees and customers, and defining the criteria needed to value the enterprise. Due diligence is required on all levels of life to be a wise steward. So what has been the extent of your due diligence on God?

God deserves a thorough investigation, and your intellectual integrity requires a due diligence on God. Then you can have peace of mind knowing you objectively examined all the facts that relate to God. You may read books written by former atheists like C.S. Lewis that document their struggles with truth and lies surrounding God. Their life experiences become a road map for your own search, but mostly read and research the Bible. Let the Scriptures stand alone. Do not depend on the conjecture and assumptions of others who may or may not be objective in their evaluation of Holy Scripture.

Read the Bible with an open mind, and ask God to speak to your heart through His word. Yes, use sound rules of interpretation like the context and cultural implications. It is necessary to understand the immediate audience for whom the Bible was intended, but consider the Scripture's timelessness. What many times applied yesterday, applies today. The commands and principles of the Bible transcend civilizations and centuries.

In your due diligence of the Bible, explore the prophecies of the Old Testament. Consider the predictions that occurred hundreds of years before Christ and were fulfilled with mind-boggling accuracy. His place of birth, His method of death, and His provision of salvation are all embedded in the text. Study closely the life of Christ, and begin your due diligence in the book of John. He claimed to be God and the only way to God. If that is true, then it holds life-altering implications. Do not let the bias of another lead you down the path of least resistance. Your due diligence may very well lead you into a divine encounter. The Bible says, "For day after day they seek me out; they seem eager to know my ways... (Isaiah 58:2a)".

028 WELL SPOKEN

"Woe to you when all men speak well of you, for this is how their fathers treated the false prophets." LUKE 6:26

A result of following Jesus is that not everyone will speak well of you. This comes with the territory of commitment to Christ. It should not alarm us. This is how people treated Jesus. The crowds would praise Jesus for His authoritative teaching, but there always seemed to be a jealous group lurking. There were those in need of anger management who despised Christ's good works. His authentic living condemned their hypocrisy. His clear teaching made the teaching of the religious leaders look complex and controlling. Part of the cup we have to drink to be a disciple of Christ is not well spoken of, if we try to please everyone, we will end up letting down more people.

People intimidated into pleasing people become anxious, fearful and exhausted. You cannot do enough to satisfy some people, because there will always be something else that needs attention. Others are wounded, and hard to help. Their hurt has caused them to lose perspective, and unfortunately, you may receive the brunt of their frustration.

But by God's grace you can love them through this unsettling time. You can give them what they have denied you, as patience and forgiveness will go a long way to loving them to Jesus. Your life during times of duress validates your words. There is one you do want to speak well of you at all times, your heavenly Father. It does matter what God thinks about you. Of course, your acceptance is a done, because He loves and accepts you in Christ.

However, your ongoing maturity in the faith is a concern of His. He does expect you to trust Him more, and fear man less. He desires for you a love relationship with Him that is seamless, spontaneous and sure. You want to hear from Him the tender words, "This is my son in whom I am well pleased" (Matthew 3:17). His affection is your affirmation, so it does matter what God thinks about you.

When God affirms your place in life, then you can rest assured. Do not waver when the conflicting opinions of others seek to urge you their way. Your stability is in God. He is your rock and refuge. His validation matters most, so rest in Him and do not react to the unrealistic expectations of others. Only you, led by the Holy Spirit, can define God's expectations. There is a good chance someone will not understand your faith walk, and maybe even give you a hard time.

Doing the right thing may cost you a relationship or financial remuneration. Indeed, be concerned if no one is speaking well of you. Your obedience to Christ may draw out the firestorm of criticism from some, or it may be subtle rejection that stings. Either way, pray for and love them regardless of their unfounded words. God knows and that's all that really matters. The Bible says, "May integrity and uprightness protect me, because my hope is in you" (Psalm 25:21).

LOVE MUCH

"Therefore I tell you, her many sins have been forgiven—for she loved much.
But he who has been forgiven little loves little." LUKE 7:47

The breadth of your forgiveness reflects the depth of your love, and a person who is forgiven much loves much. Outside of God's good grace, we all have the same wall of sin between us and Christ. We are separated from God by our sins, but the cross of Christ tore down sin's barrier. By faith we are forgiven of your sin and adopted by God as His child. By receiving the grace of God, we transition from the rags of this world to the riches of heaven.

Forgiveness is cause for gratitude and thanksgiving. For some forgiveness was more pronounced, because sin was more prevalent. Upon further reflection our sin debt could have been more serious than we realized, or were willing to admit. The lust in our hearts was addictive and anger in our attitude was caustic, but God forgave us, and He still forgives us. This is another reason for love to resonate in our heart. Not only has Christ forgiven us of past sins, but also His grace cancels out present and future debts of sin. The massive coverage of His forgiveness is pervasive. There is no place you can go where the love of God cannot find you. You can run but you cannot hide from the love and grace of God. If you are depressed, He loves and forgives you. If you are frustrated, He loves and forgives you. If you are confused, He loves and forgives you. If you are lost, He loves and forgives you. If you are afraid, He loves and forgives you. If you failed, He loves and forgives you. If you are unfaithful, He loves and forgives you. Nothing can separate you from the love and forgiveness of God.

Therefore, you can love much because you have been forgiven much. Gratitude explodes from your heart when you ponder the depth of His forgiveness. The all-inclusiveness of past, present and future sins are wiped clean. The guilt is gone. The shame is erased. Your conscience is clear. You are freed up from sin to love. Your gratitude toward God compels you to love Him and people. Sin has been replaced with your Savior Jesus. He loves through you. Love is your primary language because you have been changed. You are a new creation in Christ. It takes a little getting used to because of the bad habits attached in sin to your past life, but you are a new person.

Christianity was not added to your life like an appendage. Instead, Christ became your life. Now you live from the inside out. Your heart is full of love and forgiveness because of what God has done for you. You love continually and passionately because He has loved you with an everlasting love. Meditate on and measure the extent of your forgiveness from God. Can you fathom where you would be without the grace and forgiveness of God? Celebrate His forgiveness with love. Thank Him often for His forgiveness. Show your appreciation to God for His forgiveness by loving others unconditionally. Love the undeserving. He did. He does. He will. The forgiveness of God is matchless. The forgiveness of God is boundless. The forgiveness of God is freeing. The forgiveness of God facilitates love. The forgiveness of God produces love. Let this truth consume and compel you. To be forgiven is to love. You can love much because you have been forgiven much. The Bible says, "We love because he first loved us" (I John 4:19). The forgiveness of God is limitless.

O30 ATTENTION TO DETAIL

"Are not five sparrows sold for two pennies? Yet not one of them is forgotten by God. Indeed, the very hairs of your head are numbered. Don't be afraid; you are worth more than many sparrows." LUKE 12:6-7

Attention to detail means you care. When you show intimate interest in something or someone, you value them. This is the nature of your heavenly Father. No concern misses His interest. Every bird is known by God. Each cardinal, sparrow, black bird, vulture, robin, eagle, condor, bluebird, hummingbird, wren, dove, and quail is cared for by God.

Yet, the cost of a bird compared to the cost of you is incomparable. It is like comparing the value of a glass sliver to a radiant diamond. It is analogous of a bicycle to a Mercedes. It is like setting a nest and a mansion side by side. It is laughable to surmise any kind of similarity in value. Yet God values you like the jewelry, the automobile and the home. Your worth outstrips all of His creation. You are the pinnacle of His portfolio.

You are His most valued asset, as He knows and understands the details of your life. He of course is more intimately involved with you than you are with you. This is reassuring. You may be right in the middle of a maze of uncertainty. Life could not be more confusing. Your marriage is in chaos. Your career has hit a dead-end. Your finances are at a new low. Your motivation to move forward is like walking in a malaise of molasses. Life is not fun right now, but the one with an eye on the sparrow has His heart on you. His care is beyond your comprehension. He is relentless and reassuring in His compassion. Let Him into the details of your life. He already knows, and He has your best interest in mind. Your heavenly Father does know what is best for you. No need to fear, God is as near as prayer. His attention to detail invites you to trust and lean on Him.

If details are important to God, then they should be important to us, but details are not always easy to manage. They can become cumbersome and cranky. Like a angry albatross, they hang from our neck of responsibility asking for attention. This is why you surround yourself with people passionate about areas in which you are not. People's passion points flush out important details. It may be time for you to trust others with these critical details screaming for your attention. They will probably do a better job than you in managing them anyway. You are still accountable for the details, but delegate the responsibility. This will free you up to give overall vision and leadership. You cannot cover all the details only God has that capacity. You will go to an early grave if you stay on this obsessive trajectory. A supportive assistant is invaluable, so start here. Be aware of the overall details and give close attention to the ones only you can manage.

Otherwise, you will be average at best in your execution. Most of all trust God and others with the shepherding of details, but as you trust provide friendly follow up. You can do for others what God is does for you for He gives affectionate attention to the details surrounding your life, so replace fear with faith and hope in Him.

The Bible says, "We wait in hope for the LORD; he is our help and our shield. In him our hearts rejoice, for we trust in his holy name" (Psalm 33:20-21).

"I will not speak to you much longer, for the prince of this world is coming. He has no hold on me, but the world must learn that I love the Father and I do exactly what my Father has commanded me."   JOHN 14:30-31

The prince of this world is alive and well. His methods are fear, intimidation, and deception. He flaunts his pretentious power over a decaying world. He maneuvers around in a spiritual disguise. He wants you to have just enough of Jesus to disappoint you, but not too much that you depend on Him. His desire is for partial obedience to the commands of Christ so that your love for Him is sentimental and shallow. Then when pain and suffering grow in intensity, you will lose confidence in the Lord. He wants your love for the Lord to be conditional on everything being okay, and not unconditional regardless of the outcomes. Adversity is the adversary's most intense weapon of distrust. Satan desires to sift your faith with the sands of suffering. He tries to extract your joy in Jesus with jealously over the good fortune of others, and a jaded belief that God is distant and disinterested. He demands you to believe that death is the end and no good can come out of your grief and loss. But, followers of Jesus do not have to believe his half-truths. You are free to instantly, willingly, and completely obey God's commands. This is the evidence of your love for the Lord. Love is where joy gestates. Hate is where anger incubates. Obedience to God makes you an overcomer. There is nothing the devil can demand of you without first going through God. He tries to make you think you are eternally exposed, but you are elaborately entangled by eternal security. Christ is in His Father, you are in Christ, and Christ is in you (John 14:20). The prince of this world is powerless to pry you from the Prince of Peace.

The Prince of Peace is large and in charge. He has taken the temptations of the tempter and turned them into His purposes. Jesus uses allurement for power and converts it into servant leadership. Christ stands greed on its head and transforms it into generosity. The Lord arrests lust and rehabilitates it into unconditional love. The Holy Spirit harbors discernment and direction during the dregs of distractions and distrust. The temptation for resentment and bitterness is trumped by everlasting forgiveness. Jesus is all about calm in the middle of confusion. He is light in the middle of darkness. He is peace in the middle of war. He is joy in the middle of sadness. He is acceptance in the middle of rejection. He is love in the middle of hate.

The Prince of Peace has formed an army of the faithful. Hear His voice, learn of Him and obey His commands. The enemy is no match for the Master. The enemy tries in vain to recruit those gone AWOL, or who have drifted behind enemy lines. Nevertheless, fight the good fight. Rescue the perishing, and care for the dying. The battle is not yours, but the Lord's. You cannot sustain yourself in your own strength; instead rely on your Savior's. Do not fall for the tempter's tactics for his tricks are no treat. Faithful followers of Jesus trust wholeheartedly, love unconditionally, and obey instantly. Surrender is what we signed up for. The enemy shudders when you surrender to your Savior and not to him. The unseen war was fought and finished at the cross. The Prince of Peace rules eternally. He is the winner for now and for evermore. The Bible says, "He seized the dragon, that ancient serpent, who is the devil, or Satan, and bound him for a thousand years" (Revelation 20:2).

GODLY GOAL SETTING

"He replied, 'Go tell that fox, I will drive out demons and heal people today and tomorrow, and on the third day I will reach my goal.' " Luke 13:32

Goal setting was a part of Christ's thinking. First and foremost His goal was to do the will of His heavenly Father. This is the goal that got Him out of bed in the morning. It was a joint mission with the Holy Spirit. His goal was also to serve the people. He cast out demons, healed, and taught. Jesus was a focused individual with specific goals in mind.

His example is a model for goal setting, so keep God and people the priority. If you do not set goals, you will reach them every time. If you do set goals, you will reach some, modify others, and miss a few. For the extremely thorough and cautious temperament, it is hard to plan toward something, and then not see it accomplished. However, this is part of trusting God to help you meet the necessary goals and wait on the others.

On the other hand, there are some personalities that set too many goals that are unrealistic. Yes, all things are possible with God, but not to the point of irresponsible planning. Too many goals can overwhelm you and water down your effectiveness in reaching the right ones. This is where prayer is critical in goal setting.

Ask God what his best is for your life. Ask Him how to pace yourself over the long term, so your family develops robustly and your health is enhanced in the process. Goals are a guide to be adjusted daily, weekly, monthly and annually depending on their nature and the timing of their necessity and implementation. There is a logical flow in goal setting. Make sure your goals flow out of your God-given purpose. If your purpose is to glorify God by being a faithful husband, an available father, a loyal friend and a loving leader, then start there. Let your purpose statement be a filter for your goal setting. If a goal does not pass muster with your purpose, then omit it out and move on. Goals are not meant to be barnacles that slow down your life ship. Goals are meant to free you up to focus on God's will. Goals are like billowing white sails powered by the winds of the Holy Spirit. The Spirit's empowerment moves you forward by faith.

Daily time with God is a good goal. A regular marriage conference and marriage teaching with your spouse is a good goal. Give 10% and save 10% is a good goal. Using your work as a platform for ministry is a good goal. Exercising three times a week and eating a balanced diet are good goals. You may even have a God-given goal to travel around the world. Go for it! Write down what God is putting in your heart. Set a time table that is not so rigid that it cannot be adjusted. God works through goals, so be a prayerful goal setter and watch Him work. You may be surprised what He can accomplish through you. Simply writing down your goals may give you just the needed inspiration and accountability to attempt great things for God. Prayerfully set goals and watch Him work.

The Bible says, "In his heart a man plans his course, but the LORD determines his steps" (Proverbs 16:9).

N2 FINISH WELL

"Suppose one of you wants to build a tower. Will he not first sit down and estimate the cost to see if he has enough money to complete it? For if he lays the foundation and is not able to finish it, everyone who sees it will ridicule him, saying, 'This fellow began to build and was not able to finish.'" LUKE 14:28-30

To finish well is to plan well, and to plan well is to understand the cost of commitment. The commitment to follow Christ is not an added luxury, but standard equipment for the Christian. To plan to finish well is to plan to follow Christ daily in humility and sacrifice. To finish well tomorrow means you finish well today. Finishing well does not imply a perfect life, but it does require a submitted life. This is a life that is under the authority of Jesus Christ, so finishing well is all about the life of a committed disciple of Christ. You can start the Christian life ablaze with the fire of your salvation, fresh and contagious for Christ.

However, if the fuel of understanding and applying God's Word is not added to your initial enthusiasm, you will burn out. You will not finish well. People may even observe, 'I thought you were a Christian. 'Didn't you used to attend church?' Finishing well is about joining with God to accomplish His will. Thus finishing well is a building process. It is daily discerning God's best and then following Him wholeheartedly. Finishing well is a process that over time begins to take shape. Your faithfulness gives you credibility to invest in others what you have learned. You share with them out of brokenness, what works and what doesn't work. You are more likely to finish well when you are pouring yourself into others, as it provides accountability.

Now you may have sons-in-law who are looking to you for leadership. You are one of their role models. Don't take this lightly. Your children and grandchildren will greatly benefit from your finishing well. It is imperative to pace yourself by God's grace, so stay in the race until you make it to heaven. Spectators are not needed for this life, only for the life to come. Finish well by becoming wiser today than you were yesterday. Love and forgive more today than you have in the past. This is the essence of finishing well. It is becoming more like Jesus in your attitude and actions. This race of righteousness sweats out our sinful acts. Unrighteous anger is replaced by patience. Fear is replaced by trust. Pride is replaced by humility, and addictions are replaced by love. Be encouraged. If you are growing in Christ and building a life of obedience, you are finishing well.

Lastly, you can finish well in spite of a soiled track record. God loves to take your false starts or your backsliding ways, and place you on the road to finishing well. Stop today, turn from yourself, and turn to Christ. It is never too late to finish well. The wreckage from your past may still haunt you at times. But forget what is behind and press forward for the higher calling in Christ. He is your new reason for living. He is your life. He propels you forward to finish well. For His sake you will finish well, for your family's sake you will finish well, for the sake of others you will finish well. By God's grace, plan to finish well and you will.

The Bible says, "After Job had prayed for his friends, the LORD made him prosperous again and gave him twice as much as he had before" (Job 42:10).

"To some who were confident of their own righteousness and looked down on everybody else, Jesus told this parable..." Luke 18:9

Self-righteousness is ugly. It is ugly to God, and it is ugly to those around them. Self-righteousness is a blind spot of the worst kind, as it invites avoidance. Everyone is offended by it except the one exuding its offensive odor. There is an air of rejection waiting to be injected into its victim. Their goal is to afflict the comfortable. They look for those comfortable in 'sin' as defined by their self-righteous standards. They strain to apply their petty preferences to everyone else. It is really sad in a sense, if it were not so pathetic, yet many of us have been down this harsh and critical road. Much to our embarrassment we have been the culprit of caustic and unfair judgment toward others.

Conversations inevitably degrade to a tone of us verses them. It is a slippery and seductive slope that sucks one into a nauseous cycle of one up-man-ship. It becomes a competition of who is the most spiritual. It may be measured by tone of voice. The rationale is that the most spiritual sounding voice must be the most righteous. What is even more "spiritual" is to accent their spiritual tone of voice with churchy words and phrases that only the insiders can interpret. Religious activities become a parade of people hungering and thirsting for the accolades of others. Passion for God is replaced by pleasing and sucking up to people. It is a sad state of affairs when the self-righteous become the influencers.

Sincere Christians become confused and non-Christians are repelled. The heart of Jesus is riled by the self-righteous. It is not acceptable to Him nor should it be to us. Pride is the driver behind self-righteousness. It hijacks a good discipline like prayer and turns it into a sideshow of sorts. Ironically, what God meant for good is twisted into evil. A self-righteous person who prays draws attention to himself rather than God. God must shudder when He witnesses the feeble attempt of a self-righteous prayer. It leaves the lips of the self-righteous and falls to the ground never making it toward Christ's consideration. Pride pulls prayer back down to earth. Prideful praying is ineffective and unacceptable to God.

Can pride really engulf a praying person? Unfortunately, this is absolutely true. This is why it is imperative for God to root out pride in our lives on a regular basis. Pride never goes away. Pride lusts after God's job. Pride is not content in the role of a humble, submitted, and obedient follower of Christ. Pride puts others down to build up its own ego. Humility, in contrast, is quick to build others up and bridge them to God. The humble are quick to confess their sins and shortcomings. There is a self-awareness and understanding of their blind spots, so avoid self-righteousness like the plague. Root out sin in your own life and watch the righteousness of Christ shine through you. Humility is the remedy for self-righteousness. Humility launches prayers to heaven and attracts the ear of God, so talk to the Lord on behalf of people, not about people. He pours out His grace on the humble. His grace purges out self-righteousness, so prayers are heard and answered for Christ sake.

The Bible says, "If my people, who are called by my name, will humble themselves and pray and seek my face and turn from their wicked ways, then will I hear from heaven and will forgive their sin and will heal their land" (2 Chronicles 7:14).

"He who speaks on his own does so to gain honor for himself, but he who works for the honor of the one who sent him is a man of truth; there is nothing false about him."

JOHN 7:18

God is easy to honor, because He is the most honorable. We honor and esteem God because he is God. His position is without comparison. His role of King of Kings and Lord of Lords is matchless. Nothing can compare with the God and father of our Lord Jesus Christ. He is high and lifted up, never to sin and always to forgive. He is not always understood, but He can be trusted exclusively. Honor and glory goes to the One who can be thoroughly trusted. His word is His bond; it is never to be broken. This is trust at the highest level.

Therefore He solicits honor by His very nature. He is the most deserving of honor. His character calls for it and His holiness demands it. Foolish and unwise are we when we honor ourselves. Self-honoring is as about as awkward as the physical act of patting yourself on the back. It looks strange for one thing, and secondly, it draws attention to the wrong person. Honor is to be given, not taken. It is to be bestowed, not withheld. The act of honoring God facilitates authenticity. Honor means you are about truth and you flee from what is false. There is a divine dignity in your behavior and speech. It is easy to honor God because he is honorable. It is a privilege to honor God because He has honored us with His presence. Do not substitute God's place of honor with anyone or anything, especially yourself.

Honoring God starts with attitude. Honor by definition means you revere, respect and fear God. You speak His name with hallowedness and humility. There is God and there is none other beside Him. Your words are a reflection of your attitude, therefore they are honorable, and you esteem Him by the way you live. You do certain things, like honor others, because you honor God. You do not do certain things, like abuse your body, because you honor God. You recognize your body as the temple of His Spirit; therefore you honor Him with clean living. Your speech is free of obscenities, because you honor God. You love your wife because you honor God. You respect your husband because you honor God. You honor your parents because you honor God. The bottom line is you honor what God honors, and you dishonor what He dishonors. This is why you embrace righteousness and abhor sin. Honor is what God desires and what He deserves. Honor Him first and it becomes natural to honor others. If you reverse the order, it is impossible to honor Him with a whole heart. Your true life in Christ flows out of honor for God.

A life of honoring God and others means you graduate to heaven with honors. Honor Him with your time, treasures and talents.

MUCH FRUIT

"I am the vine; you are the branches. If a man remains in me and I in him, he will bear much fruit; apart from me you can do nothing." JOHN 15:5

Much fruit that remains is the goal of a disciple of Christ. This glorifies God and accomplishes His purposes. Fruit-bearing glorifies God because He is the source of life for the fruit. No fruit can be produced without God. The branch is intrinsically dependent on the vine.

Therefore, we as followers of Christ cannot take credit for the fruit because the fruit comes from Jesus. He is the manufacturer of fruit and we are the distributors. The fruit remains luscious as the Father prunes back the unproductive branches. We do not always invite pruning, as it is painful and disfiguring in the beginning, but over time submission to painful pruning produces beautiful and long-lasting fruit. Trust your heavenly Father with the pruning process, and you will be much better off.

So, what is the nature of this fruit He is creating and nurturing through us? It is the fruit of character and souls. As we abide in Christ, we become more like Christ. This is a natural result of remaining in Him. We become like the ones we hang out with the most. We start to love more unconditionally, because God is love. We experience a fullness of joy, because the joy of the Lord becomes our strength. A holy contentment flushes our countenance, because the peace of Christ reigns over our hearts. An unselfish servant spirit fills our heart, because Jesus set the ultimate example of servanthood.

Fruit-bearing is character-driven on behalf of souls for the glory of God. Character is a conduit for the Holy Spirit to draw others to himself. You are saved for more than goodness. You are saved to bridge others to God. Much fruit that remains is the result of God working through a humble, obedient, and submitted life for His glory.

Therefore, it is imperative you remain in Christ for maximum fruit bearing. This is the position from which God leverages His greatest works. It is from here that much fruit is produced, and where the results remain with eternal consequences. You remain in Christ by faith. It all comes back to trust in Him. You take Him at His word. You believe His word. You obey His word. Remaining in Christ is not an onerous task. It will be painful at times, but not burdensome. Early on, allow God to sever the small green twigs of sin that bud on the branch of your life. This is much better that waiting for His massive pruning. Bad branches distract and hold back fruit bearing. You also remain in Him as you live in community with other believers. They become God's encouragers and pruning shears as well. Men need to get real with men, and women need to be transparent with women. Relational honesty and unity is one of God's ways of remaining in Christ. Learning, growing and applying God's truth automatically default to remaining in Him. Seek out truth religiously and relentlessly. Be a model of remaining so others will be inspired to do the same. Branches do not thrive in isolation, but in the orchards of evangelism and discipleship we remain in Christ.

Then the fruits of character and souls are harvested on an eternal scale, all for the glory of the great gardener, God!

"Now, brothers, I know that you acted in ignorance, as did your leaders. But this
is how God fulfilled what he foretold through all the prophets, saying that his
Christ would suffer. Repent then and turn to God…" ACTS 3:17-19A

Ignorant acts can hurt deeply, as they unwittingly harm others who are innocent recipients. These sins of ignorance are blind culprits. If those who have sinned in this way were aware of the suffering they caused, they would be men and women most miserable, who quietly rage within. They rage because there are costly consequences to acts of ignorance. Ignorance is certainly no excuse, and it has no power to erase its results. In most cases ignorance exacerbates the situation. It makes it worse because there is not an understanding of the hurt that has been inflicted. Loved ones may be suffering in silence because you wounded them unknowingly.

Nonetheless, they are still wounded, and the wound has festered over the years. It has gotten worse to the point the anger lashes back unexpectedly. Wounded people wound. The truth that is known in their head somehow bypasses changing their heart. There is a dearth of discernment. It becomes a chore to give and receive love. The ignorant act may have injured them as a child. Is this your story? You never felt like you measured up to your dad's expectations. The more you excelled the higher he raised the bar. Your father followed the wrong example of his father. There were no parenting seminars; just do the best you can. Your mom may have smothered you with her well-meaning nurturing, but to the point of building resentment in your independent heart. The culmination of these ignorant acts has caused you to become overly sensitive and under confident, so repent from your resentment and let God heal your heart.

Jesus was the brunt of ignorant acts. The mob's hysteria was facilitated by the anger of their leaders. It was an ugly scene. Jesus suffered immensely because people acted ignorantly. This is why His parting words included forgiveness for their ignorant sin. "Father, forgive them for they do not know what they are doing" (Luke 23:34). They did not understand they were bruising and beating up on a good man. They did not realize they were bringing on great hurt and suffering to the son of God. They had not thought through the consequences of their guilty postmortem. Yet Jesus forgave, and on an even greater scale God used the sin of mankind to forgive mankind. This is the wonderful work of God's grace. He takes mixed up motives and bizarre actions, and brings us back to Jesus. This is why your wound is not the final act in your life's drama.

He is drawing you to Jesus in humility and forgiveness. He has already died for your sin and the sins of your ignorant inflictors. You can let go and let God refresh you and them. They may never change, but you can. When you accept and forgive them, you will experience and feel the acceptance and forgiveness of your heavenly Father. Write out how God loves you and watch Him heal your wound. Your confession and repentance applies doses of healing to your heart.

The consequences of ignorant acts need not be forever, so cease the perpetual hurt and suffering. Today's forgiveness brings tomorrow's healing!

INFLUENCE INFLUENCERS

"He had been quarreling with the people of Tyre and Sidon; they now joined together and sought an audience with him. Having secured the support of Blastus, a trusted personal servant of the king, they asked for peace, because they depended on the king's country for their food supply." ACTS 12:20

You may not have access to the person at the top of the organization, but you may be able to build a relationship with someone who does. Do not get discouraged over the aloofness of the leader. Seek rather to influence those who influence him or her. You can remain stuck in your critical cycle, or you can get to work at getting to know an influencer. This is the realism good leaders recognize. It may take time but over the course of months and years you can build trust and credibility with those who have the same.

This is the process of influencing. Your leadership will only extend as far as your influence, and those you are able to influence. Take heart, you are probably three relationships away from the most powerful person in the world. Yes, the President of the United States is surrounded by influencers that one day may be recipients of your influence. Of course it is an influence of degrees, but that is in God's hands.

Instead of staying discouraged in your present predicament, seek to influence your way forward. Start by serving others because you influence through serving. Others value you when you sincerely value them. This is the crux of service. I value you and what you stand for and because I value you, I want to serve you unselfishly for God's glory. Over time, those you serve will be attracted to your character and solicit your opinion. People trust sincere and serving hearts. Before you know it, your servant leadership has opened doors of influence you never dreamed. CEO's of very successful companies ask for your opinion and accountability. Influential leaders begin to seek out your wisdom and advice. But it all starts by first effectively influencing those in your immediate circle of relationships. You have the potential to influence influencers when you influence first those who know you the best.

There is one more prerequisite to influencing influencers, and this is foundational. Your influence will extend the furthest when you are perpetually and passionately influenced by God. Being influenced by God means you are qualified to properly influence others. When you come under the influence of the Holy Spirit, you become a viable candidate for influencing influencers. You can boldly influence because you have been humbly influenced. You have submitted to the influence of God, godly mentors and a discerning spouse. You are as steward of influence, so do not waste it or take it for granted. It is a gift of God that can literally affect nations for Christ. As you influence, seek God's best for the other, not what you can gain.

Do not sell short godly influence. It gets behind enemy lines. It moves the hearts of kings, queens, moms, dads, pastors and business leaders. God is grooming your heart to influence influencers. Stay humble, teachable and truthful. By God's grace your shadow of influence could linger longer and more fully than you can imagine.

Stay influential through radical influence by God and His leaders. Then you are qualified to influence influencers for God's glory!

N8   GOD'S LAW

> "Therefore no one will be declared righteous in his sight by observing the law; rather through the law we become conscious of sin." ROMANS 3:20

The law of God matters. It matters a lot, because it is a definition of God's standards. Idolatry, coveting, stealing, murder, lying, dishonoring parents, adultery, worship of other gods, the misuse of God's name, and forsaking the Sabbath all break the law of God. And when we break the law of God we break the heart of God. Law breaking is a serious offense, so observation of the law of God need not be understated or overemphasized. It becomes understated when it is ignored, and it becomes overemphasized when it is exploited.

The law of God is not to be ignored or exploited. The purpose of God's law is to reveal our sinfulness and our desperate need for a Savior. It unveils our portrait of pride. It is our wicked pride of self-sufficiency that sends us to hell, without Christ rescuing us by faith in His death and resurrection.

Yes, it is mission critical to understand and observe the law of God, but it is foolish to depend on your keeping the law as justification for your sin. God's law is not an end in itself, but a means to an end. The law of God exposes, but does not save. His law is like a lighthouse perched on the cliffs overlooking a raging sea. The bright-collated beam of blinding rays cuts through the darkness and peril to warn of the jagged rocks below. The Lord's warning with light also invites you to a safe cleft that is embedded in the rocks above. To just observe the light is peril, but to allow it to lead you to its source is salvation. In the same way the law of God exposes your sin that leads to death and separation from God.

Beware moralists. Your strict compliance with the law is not your ticket into God's good graces and His Heaven. If this becomes your motivation, you will never feel good enough. Your judgment of others becomes part of your justification with God, after all your righteousness far exceeds many others, perhaps the majority. But what started out as seeking justification before God can become justification before man. God, not man, is the standard.

There is no way to measure how good is good enough. This is why you can never earn or deserve God's grace. The danger to the other extreme is to use your liberty in Christ irresponsibly. Salvation in Christ by faith is not a pass for moral compromise; on the contrary grace-based living is fueled by the truth of God. The more you understand and apply the grace of God, the more you fear and obey Him. These complimentary characteristics of God are synergistic in their effect, not polarizing.

Grace and truth bring balance. Law points to the need for faith. Love for God is expressed in obedience and fear of God. Good works are an expression of gratitude to God. Allow the law of God to liberate you from trying to earn your way back to God, or to heaven. You can rest in the fact that faith in Christ has already paid your sin debt. Also, let the high standard of God's law facilitate fear of God. He is holy and righteous. We have all broken His law and are in need of an advocate. The Lord Jesus Christ is your mediator with God.

The Bible says, "For this reason Christ is the mediator of a new covenant..."(Hebrews 9:15).

RACIAL RECONCILIATION

"Then the Lord said to me, 'Go I will send you away to the Gentiles.' "
Acts 22:21

Race divides. It inherently needs reconciliation. As followers of Jesus Christ, we are expected to be on the forefront of racial reconciliation. Christ is color blind. There is no preference between Jew and Gentile, black or white, yellow or brown. They are all precious in his sight. Yet, every day millions are disenfranchised or killed because of their cultural heritage and color of skin. Where pride and ego drove the human race into different geographical and racial directions, Christ reunites us. He is the racial reconciler.

The feet of Jesus are level for all races. Sin is the only explanation for one race's sense of superiority over another. It breaks the heart of God. Jesus went way out of his way to love a racial outcast in the Samaritan woman (John 4). He was compelled by the Holy Spirit to reach out across class, cultural and racial barriers. In the same way and spirit, God is leading you to reach out to others different from yourself. He is calling on His disciples to be intentional in healing past hurts, and serving current needs. Some will receive your sincere service, and others will question your motive. But when all is said and done, your part is to go and be a blessing, and God's part is to facilitate trust and healing. You probably do not consider yourself a racist. That is, you do not feel or act better than another human being just because of your race.

However, to be silent or to not intentionally reach out to another culture is passive racism. It is subtle, but the same ill-effects occur. The offended or disillusioned ones are still stuck in their inferior state of mind, economics, and education. It is not the role of government to figure this out. Rather, it is the mandate of the church, because Christians know better. We can model the way of racial reconciliation like Jesus and the early disciples.

Consider a weekly one-on-one study for a year with someone of a different race. Learn about their culture, history, and hurts. Indeed, racial reconciliation happens one person at a time and it happens relationally. Do not wait on someone else to come to you. You go to them. Yes, it is a little uncomfortable, and yes there will be misunderstanding. But Jesus is the standard bearer and the relational mediator. He represents all races, and He created the different races.

Let the Bible be your foundational source of racial reconciliation. Start today on a cross-cultural mission. It may be someone at work or in your neighborhood. Invite their family into your home for a meal. Serve them every time you get a chance and watch God work. Then the world will see in Technicolor that you are truly disciples of Christ, because you love one another races will be reconciled and God will be glorified. Jesus said, "By this all men will know that you are my disciples, if you love one another" (John 13:35).

"Therefore, if you have disputes about such matters, appoint as judges even men of little account in the church!"   I Corinthians 6:4

A lawsuit is not an option for two believers in Christ; otherwise there is no difference between followers of Jesus and non-believers, which means there is no distinction in values, standards, beliefs and morals. So, Christian mediation has a much greater effect for two individuals who are locked in a relational crisis. There is a much greater purpose at work, which is to be a good example to the church and to those outside the church. Your obedience with this opportunity for mediation matters.

Your family is watching. Your friends are watching. Your foes are watching. God is watching. In the middle of conflict and disagreement, it is of great consequence that you remain true to the process of mediation. Do not be discouraged or downtrodden. God can be trusted to work it out. Yes, it takes time, and yes it is painful at times, but this may be the result of not dealing with issues in a timely fashion. Early on, if you are mad or disagree with a decision or behavior, talk it through. If you wait for the misunderstanding to fester, the foundation of trust begins to crack. Your communication ceases and lies begin to creep into your thinking. Before long there becomes a stand off and both parties feel hurt and disrespected. Bad news needs to travel fast so it can be processed and corrected. Your current situation calls for Christian mediation because a severe disagreement has occurred, as hurt hovers over the relationship.

It is extremely critical at this point to check your anger at the door, before you enter the room of mediation. Make it your goal to restore the relationship, rather than getting what you feel you deserve, because the relationship is what's most important. What you think you deserve may be inflated compared to what you really deserve. This is why a trusted, fair, and wise mediator is invaluable. Whatever the mediator decides is to be accepted by both parties. The mediator will define the facts and listen objectively to both sides. After verifying the facts and processing the information, the mediator will offer a solution that is beneficial and fair to both parties. At this point you can chose to forgive, trust and move forward, or you can chose to stew in your self-pity.

Everyone wins when everyone chooses to grow through this process. If you listen intently with a heart to learn, you will come away a better person in Christ. It is through conflict that pride and arrogance either flame up or fizzle out. The goal is the latter. Do not see this disagreement as an affront to you, or an opportunity to get even. See this process of Christian mediation as purging away your own sin. You will learn from this, as you will not assume certain things in the future. Make sure you value the relationship over riches. Money can be made up, but an offended brother may be lost forever. It is not worth it to live in relational disrepair. People are more important that getting what you want. Focus on the spirit of the original agreement. You have the opportunity to serve them instead of demanding from them, so take the high road.

Die to your expectations and watch God work for His mediation is masterful!

"Love is patient..." I Corinthians 13:4

Love by nature is patient. This is why those couples who are in love in the beginning exhibit an inordinate amount of patience. What is said, what is done or not done have a patient pass embedded in the relationship. Lover's believe, "I will let you down. You will let me down. I will act immaturely. You will act immaturely. I will struggle with fear. You will struggle with fear." You both need patience for love is patient. If there is no evidence of patience in a relationship, then there is a love deficiency. Love expresses itself in patience, for example you serve your children because you love them. They are sometimes silly and are prone to foolishness, but you still love them, because you love them you are patient with them.

This may become more of a challenge when you relate this thinking to relationships outside of your family. A work associate or a stranger, especially someone outside the faith, is harder to love. You barely know them, therefore how can you love them? Or, the most difficult to love is someone who has offended you. We tend to lose our patience with those who are offensive. So here is an important distinction to make. You love someone, not because they necessarily deserve it, but because they are created in the image of God. Jesus loved them so much He died for them. You can still disapprove of their behavior and love them. Your willingness to tolerate delay may keep the relationship intact. This is love. This is patience. Your calmness and self-control may be the very thing needed to stabilize the situation. Wake up loving, go to bed loving and love in between. This environment of love will nurture and produce patience, lots of it.

God understands this because He is love. Therefore, He is the epitome of patience. If anyone has the right to lose his patience, it is God. Everyday He deals with billions of sinners, many of whom are demanding their way. Some are oblivious to God. Some are harsh and angry toward God. But, because of His great love for mankind, His longsuffering endures rejection and apathy. He feels compassion, not defiance, toward someone flailing away in criticism toward Christ, yet lost in their sins. His love expands, rather than contracts in the face of your failures. His capacity to love is greater than ours, and his propensity for patience is also greater, but followers of Jesus have the Holy Spirit dwelling within them to love through them. The state of an unredeemed sinner is a limited love. The condition of a saved sinner is Christ's capacity to love.

Thus, you have the potential to a higher degree of patience. Allow Christ to love through you and watch your patience grow and expand. Do not fall into the trap of an angry rebuttal. People and situations tend to cool off tomorrow. You still confront, but in the right timing and in the right way. Invest in patience and the pay off is exponential. Express patience and everyone is in a better state of mind to discuss the facts. Love the unlovable. Love the undeserving. Love the impatient. Love keeps your motive pure. Love feeds a healthy perspective.

By your love you can be patient, because love is patient. Jesus patiently loved the unlovely, the Bible says, "Jesus looked at him and loved him..." (Mark 10:21).

"Praise be to the God and Father of our Lord Jesus Christ, the Father of compassion and the God of all comfort, who comforts us in all our troubles, so that we can comfort those in any trouble with the comfort we ourselves have received from God."
2 CORINTHIANS 1:3-4

Comfort is not a once, but recurring and compounding. It is a gift that keeps on giving, as it can cut through any calamity and bring healing and peace. It can transcend circumstances because it is the very nature of God. He is the God of all comfort, and no one is immune from His comfort. There is no trouble looming that can out pace God's comfort. If you slow down and listen, His comfort will catch up and cover you. He is relentless in His comforting pursuit. He comforts the comfortless. Life may currently have you in a very uncomfortable place. You are a little embarrassed and a lot unsure of yourself, but one thing you can be sure of is the comfort of God.

Your situation is not unique for He has been there before with His battalion of comfort comrades. Let Him in, and do not continue to wrestle alone in your discomfort. You were made to be comforted. It is not a sign of weakness to be comforted by God. On the contrary, it is strength and wisdom. He is your celestial comforter. His blanket of comfort is always available to bring rest and deep sleep. Do not toss and turn in your troubles.

No matter how terrible your circumstances, His comfort has you covered. His comforter of compassion and love overcompensates for adversity. It is a warm, soft, and soothing comforter that is tailor-made for your bed of life. Do not toss off its warm embrace, as it is for your benefit and not your harm. Yes, it probably means slowing down so you can receive his calming comfort. So trust him. Rest and relax in the arms of your heavenly Father.

Lastly, He comforts you, so you in turn can comfort others. You can express your comfort without even saying you have been there. Handling yourself with grace and concern speaks to the comfortless friend to whom you are extending a helpful hand. The small things inject comfort. Take care of a stressed-out mom's child so they can relish in a much-needed break. Pay someone more than they deserve so they can feel some financial comfort. Leave a pertinent prayer on a friend's voicemail, so they can hear your comforting intercession on their behalf. Write an encouraging note of concern and love to bolster a comfortless heart. God created your comfort for you to pass on to someone else. Comfort compounds because this is the purpose of its creation.

You are a facilitator of God's comfort. You are not responsible for the recipient's response. Their anger may blunt their gratitude. Their hurt may hinder their faith. But keep in mind that your motive for extending comfort is your own gratitude to God for His comfort in your life. Give comfort not to receive from the comfortless, but because God has comforted you. His comforter covers all of life's bed of troubles.

The Bible says, "I will fear no evil, for you are with me; your rod and your staff, they comfort me" (Psalm 23:4b).

"He must not be a recent convert, or he may become conceited
and fall under the same judgment as the devil."   I TIMOTHY 3:6

Leadership in the world does not automatically guarantee leadership in the church or ministry. In fact, if you are a new believer you need not sign up for highly visible leadership in a spiritual environment. Your character more than likely needs sanitizing from the stains of sin. You do not want to bring into a leadership role any baggage that may burden you. Take your time and get to know the current leadership. Serve them and allow them to get to know you. It is tempting to jump right in soon after becoming a Christian. After all, you are so grateful and energized to do good works. Your business experience seems fitting for service on the board of a church or ministry. But this may the worst thing for you. There is the very real chance that your premature elevation to spiritual leadership leads to pride and conceit. Why put yourself in a position to fail?

Be patient and let leadership opportunities come to you. Serve in the nursery and love on little babies and children. Park cars, write a check, volunteer in the kitchen, greet people or help stuff envelopes. The point is to crawl before you walk. Develop a reservoir of humility that can douse any flames of conceit. A new believer is not fit for significant leadership in the Christian community. It is not fair to the person, nor to the people he is attempting to lead. Leadership in the church and ministry requires much more than passion and availability. It requires a seasoned walk with Christ that leads with grace, truth and wise judgment. This only comes through experience and maturation vetted by the application of knowledge. So there is a warning to those who are responsible for recruiting and placing leaders in roles of responsibility. Do not do a disservice to someone by assigning responsibilities to them when they are not ready. There is always room for growth and learning, but in situations requiring mature faith and character, be very prayerful and patient. It is better to have an empty leadership position, than to have the wrong person filling a slot. Pray for God-called leaders to lead. Pray for leaders who understand the grace of God and the judgment of God. Pray for leaders who lead by example. Pray for leaders that lead by serving. Pray for leaders who point people to Jesus and not themselves. Pray for leaders who will not superimpose slick sales techniques, but instead challenge people to look to the Holy Spirit for their direction and confirmation.

The temptation is to rush in and lay hands on someone too quickly. The needs are overwhelming and it makes sense to draft a person who is highly successful in the marketplace. But why jeopardize the current wise and humble culture of leadership that has evolved over the years? There will always be another potential leader. Hold the qualification bar high for leadership in the church and ministry. Do not settle for anything less than someone who is managing his own home well. God will raise up mature leaders in His timing. Quality is attracted to quality. Therefore trust God for quality leaders who are full of the Holy Spirit. Keep developing and apprenticing those with potential, but let God grow them. A good rule is to know someone at least a year before you entrust them with significant leadership. Mature leaders are patient. Wait on God to send them your way. Mature leaders are worth the wait. Mature leaders wait for mature leaders!

N14 GODLY TRAINING

"...train yourself to be godly. For physical training is of some value, but godliness has value for all things, holding promise for both the present life and the life to come."
I TIMOTHY 4:7B-8

Godly training is profitable now and for eternity. It does not mean you are some super spiritual person who cannot relate to others. On the contrary, godly means you have the character and sensitivity of Jesus. Thus you understand and relate to people very effectively. It is not all about you, but about others and their needs. You encourage when there needs to be encouragement. You rebuke when you need to rebuke. You teach when there needs to be teaching. The godly know how to laugh, cry, pray, hope, work hard and trust in God. Godliness comes in all forms. Every temperament can express godliness. If you are an extrovert your godly expression may come in the form of humor or encouragement. Your ability to make people laugh (not at the expense of someone else) is godly. Your passion to encourage and build up others is godly. Godliness is certainly expressed through your character. Your honesty is godly. Your diligence is godly. Your pure motive is godly. Your generosity is godly. Your compassion is godly. Your boldness is godly. Your leadership is godly. All of these behaviors that reflect the way Christ would behave are godly. Godliness is behaving as Jesus would behave. It is not a certain voice inflection or body language, because those can be pretentious and ungodly. It is having a heart and mind that expresses as Christ would.

True godliness points others to God. It provides value for all things: body, mind, soul and spirit. Godliness, however, does not happen accidentally. There is intentionality to godliness. Just as the body benefits from physical training so the mind, soul, and spirit benefit from training in godliness. The most effective training comes with consistency and repetition. It is not a complicated process, but it is exercising faith. The muscles of faith expand and contract when engaged in everyday life. Training involves prayer instead of worry. Praying works on your heart. It is your spiritual cardio workout. Worry works like plaque and cholesterol clogging the flow of God's faithfulness to you. He is faithful always, but you must receive his faithfulness by faith. Prayer facilities this and provides a free flow of faith. In addition fasting keeps your focus on the Lord.

Training in godliness means the word of God becomes your spiritual diet. If you replace the word with the world you will settle for spiritual junk food rather than Jesus. Snubbing God's word is like substituting chips for chicken. This cheap imitation of spiritual nutrition eventually disables your godly maturity. Lastly, training in godliness requires service to others. You work out your faith in good deeds. You serve others for the glory of God. This is training in godliness. This has tremendous value now and forevermore.

Therefore, train well and you will be transformed. Over time, look into the mirror of your soul and you will see Jesus. There are benefits to training in godliness, The Bible says, "Know that the LORD has set apart the godly for himself; the LORD will hear when I call to him" (Psalm 4:3).

WOMEN TRAIN WOMEN

"Likewise, teach the older women to be reverent in the way they live, not to be slanderers or addicted to much wine, but to teach what is good. Then they can train the younger women to love their husbands and children, to be self-controlled and pure, to be busy at home, to be kind, and to be subject to their husbands, so that no one will malign the word of God."   TITUS 2:3-5

Women have an obligation and opportunity to train other women. This is necessary for the development of mature disciples of Christ. Training goes beyond teaching. Teaching tells you why and what you need to do. Training shows you how to do what needs to be done. Training takes time and patience. It is moving two steps forward and taking one step back. A trainer does not give up on the trainee when they fail. Instead, they hang in there and help them through the bumps in the road. Women need to communicate the need for training, before training can take its full effect. Someone who is hungry for training will seek out a trainer in the ways of God. So, you may be approached because the fruit of your husband, children, and home are rich and luscious. Do not dismiss the interest of another woman to learn from you.

Your potential trainee is not looking for perfection. She is looking for someone who is honest with her mistakes, who can transfer her wisdom to an eager learner. Your posture as a trainer of other women is one of a fellow learner. The trainer learns as much or more as the trainee. You do not have to look very far to find trainee candidates. Start with your family and friends. Daughters and nieces are a good place to begin. Show them how to handle money. Expose them to tools and resources that teach them how to spend, save, and give their money wisely. Walk them through ways to reign in impulsive spending and replace it with a spending plan (a budget!). Your financial training will be a life-long gift, which will help them preclude the pain of unwise debt and financial bondage. Train women in the priority of purity. Nothing does more to instill confidence and attractiveness than having a pure mind and body. Model for them a definition of beauty that is from the inside-out. Train them to be smart and wise in the ways of God. Unpack the Bible for them in an inviting way. Show them its relevance and its ability to provide truth and instruction for life. Train them in respect for their husband. Wise is the woman who disagrees with her husband respectfully. A man will receive a woman's concerns if delivered at the right time in the right way.

Train women first and foremost to love God and to embrace Him as their heavenly Father. A woman who allows her heavenly Father to love her can more effectively love her earthly father. He loves her body, soul and spirit. Train women in forgiveness. Forgiveness heals hurt. Hurt unchecked in a heart eats away at joy. Hurt that perpetually hangs out in the heart brings illness and emotional fatigue. Train them to let go before the hurt drives them to a life of shattered and unproductive relationships. Lastly, train women to train other women. They will become more accountable in their own actions as they train other women. Training is for a lifetime. It is a big part of God's plan in faith maturity and mentorship. Train well. One day you will receive an encouraging note of gratitude from one of your trainees. This makes it all very, very worthwhile.

Be trained and then train others. The Scripture teaches, "And the things you have heard me say in the presence of many witnesses entrust to reliable men [and women] who will also be qualified to teach others" (2 Timothy 2:2).

N16 EXCEED EXPECTATIONS

"Confident of your obedience, I write to you, knowing that you
will do even more than I ask." PHILEMON 21

Exceed expectations because God has done the same for you. He has done what He said and more. There is nothing halfway about God. He does things right and then throws in a little bit extra, and even overwhelms us with His grace. Therefore, when God or others ask something of you, go for it with gusto. Exceed expectations. Make it a goal to bring more value to a relationship than you receive. If someone asks for prayer, then pray right then and there. Make it a habit to pray regularly for those in need, especially those who request prayer. Exceed expectations in your prayer for others.

Exceed expectations in your work. You work to not just get by with the minimum requirements, but to give glory to God. What better way to make Christianity attractive than to work with excellence. When you exceed expectations, you open the door for others to inquire about your motivation, the Lord Jesus. Exceeded expectations may facilitate advancement in your career. People want to work with and for someone who goes the second mile. They want to reward and hang out with someone who exceeds expectations. When we exceed expectations, we know at the very least there will be satisfaction on behalf of the ultimate One we serve. Lastly, exceed expectations with your attitude. A positive and can do attitude goes a long way in making relational deposits. There are a lot of things we cannot control, but our attitude is one we can. Go over the top with an attitude of gratitude and generosity. Be exceedingly grateful!

Marriage is another environment for you to serve beyond what is expected. Make it a goal to out serve your spouse. Marriage is an opportunity to give respect. No one in marriage has ever complained of too much love and respect. It is not possible to over respect, or over love your spouse. Look for creative ways to love and respect them beyond their expectations. Exceeded expectations in the home make for harmony and contentment. The home is all about others, not you. Yes, there are times you feel the need to be spoiled, but first seek to spoil and serve others. You receive blessings and encouragement beyond measure when you serve in ways that exceed others' expectations. It is not a game of keeping score on who has done the most for the other lately. Rather, it is dying to your own expectations, so you can exceed the expectations of your spouse and children. You have the option to exceed what God expects of you. Model this for them. Why just get by with God? A prayer of salvation is the beginning of belief and a lifetime love affair with the Lord. He has a treasure trove of adventure waiting for those who will take him at His word, and dare to exceed his expectations. So, if God asks for 10% giving you want to exceed His minimum requirement. If He asks for one day of Sabbath, you want to give Him daily mini Sabbaths. If He asks for your heart, you want to give Him your life.

Go more than one mile for another, by giving others what they don't deserve. Exceed expectation for heavens sake!

FLAWED LEADERS

"…since he himself is subject to weakness. This is why he has to offer sacrifices for his own sins, as well as for the sins of the people."   HEBREWS 5:2B, 3

Even the best of leaders are flawed. Jesus Christ was the only flawless leader to ever live. The rest of us operate in the flawed category. The wise leader will acknowledge this, as his flaws loom over his life like a canopy of accountability. The smart leader uses his flaws to facilitate a closer walk with Christ. As the adversary accuses you of your flaws, agree with him. Use your flaws as an asset rather than a liability. The leader who fails to flush out his flaws into the open is pretentious and positioned for a fall. Flaws can only hurt you if they remain concealed. Exposed flaws wither in their influence under the heat of confession and repentance. This is when you go to your flawless heavenly Father and ask for his forgiveness and grace. Ask him to use your flaws to further his Kingdom.

Many times God works through us in spite of ourselves, so lay bare before Him your fears, insecurities, weaknesses, and flaws. Watch Him do a beautiful work of transformation. Your weaknesses become His strengths that carry out His purpose. Where you feel out of control, He is in control. He is the pilot and you are the co-pilot. Trust Him to guide you through the complex instrument panel of life. Your flaws do not surprise Him, because He knows they can keep you close to Christ. Your honest feedback to others about your flaws frees others to do the same. Pretension crumbles and honesty flourishes in a culture of self-awareness and openness to one another's flaws. Therefore, be patient with the flaws in others. We recognize the flaws in others, because they are flawed copies of ourselves. Normally what ticks you off the most are your flaws exhibited in the life of another. Cut them some slack and learn how to use their flaws to facilitate God's will. Allow flaws to promote relational intimacy rather than relational hostility. Flaws are a friend who can lead us closer to God and closer to each other. Flaws remind us all that we are a work in progress. Flaws begin as concealed imperfections. Just as flaws lead to the shattering of an imperfect crystal under pressure, they can lead to our brokenness. Flaws make us better, if they lead to our brokenness.

The world is made up of flawed people. Those who recognize and accept this use it to their advantage. Leaders have a unique opportunity to set the example in this area. Your ability to be honest about your own flaws sets the course for those you lead. Season your language with, "I am sorry that is a weakness of mine", or, "Please be patient with me; I am a work in progress. Details are not my strength." Or, "Help me not to over commit. I can say yes to too many things and fail to do any of them well." Or lastly, "I was wrong. Please forgive me." This honesty and transparency creates a safe environment for the authenticity of everyone. Flaws revealed lead to freedom, but flaws concealed lead to bondage. Do not project a flawless image, but one of learning, growing and many times struggling. Make confession and repentance a normal part of your vocabulary and behavior.

Focus on the flawless leader Jesus. He will never let you down. Your flaws are meant to facilitate faith in your heavenly Father!

N18 GOD'S PAYMENT PLAN

"For we know him who said, 'It is mine to avenge; I will repay,'" and again, "The Lord will judge his people." It is a dreadful thing to fall into the hands of the living God."
HEBREWS 10:30-31

Someone may be in debt to you. They may owe you money, a reputation, an apology, a job, or a childhood. But God is asking you to let go and let Him. Let Him handle this. He has a payment plan for those who are in debt to his children. It may mean He wipes their slate clean with minimal repercussions. It may mean their stiff neck forces God to bring them to the end of themselves through trials and tribulations. Or, it may mean what awaits them is an eternity of reaping in hell, what has been sown on earth. But God's position is one of judge and jury. You do not have to carry this burden or responsibility. Your role is to forgive and to trust God with the proper judgment and consequence.

Life gets complicated and draining when we take on the responsibility of making sure a person gets what he deserves. This is arrogant and unwise on our part. How can we know what others deserve for their injustices, neglect, and self-absorption? Our role is not to play God, but to serve God. Playing God is a never-ending disappointment. We were not made for that role. The Almighty can only fill these shoes. And He does have it under control. There is no indiscretion or blatant injustice that is off His radar screen of sensitivity. He picks up on every 'little' sin. So, rest in the assurance of knowing God will pay back in His good timing, and in His good way. Give this person or issue over to God. Do not bear the responsibility of executing pay back time. Your role is to forgive and let go. God's role is to establish a payment plan of justice and judgment. Yes, your parents may have blown it through their own selfish tirades. Their immature choices may have built up over time and led to divorce. Because of their indiscretions and unwise decisions you grew up in a less than favorable home environment. But look at their faces. The hurt and the consequences are etched in their countenance. The results of their wrongs have caught up with them. They need your grace and forgiveness. Be a good son or daughter, and by this you may facilitate healing for your parent's soul. Sin has its own harvest of heartache, not to mention breaking the heart of their heavenly Father. Trust God with your parents. Let Him worry with what they deserve.

You can bring reconciliation to the fractured family relationship by forgiving. Once you have forgiven, trust God to administer whatever punishment is deserved or undeserved. He may see a broken and contrite heart in your offender that leads to their salvation and freedom in Christ. Your forgiveness and unconditional love may be the very thing God uses to illustrate what they can experience up close and personal. Forgive and give. Forgive them of their hurt, insensitivity and selfishness, and then give them over to God. Trust Him with His repayment plan. He owns the pay back process. His vengeance may be swift, it may be delayed, or it may be dissolved. Regardless, you do the right thing, and trust God to do the same. Vengeance is His, not ours. Pay back time is up to God. We have enough in our own lives to consider. Pray for yourself and others to avoid falling into the hands of the living God for it is a dreadful thing!

"Therefore, since we are surrounded by such a great cloud of witnesses, let us throw off everything that hinders and the sin that so easily entangles, and let us run with perseverance the race marked out for us." HEBREWS 11:1

Dead heroes inspire you to live life to its fullest. Those who have endured hardship and were treated unfairly inspire us through our current tests and temporary trials. Most of us have not suffered to death because of our faith in Christ. But some have. Others have been down the road that denies earthly wealth, only to receive heaven's riches. Heroes of the faith knew a better way. Theirs was the way of faith in God and obedience to His expectations. No temptation of the world was strong enough to pull them away from the moorings of their walk with God. Even on some of their death beds, there was an uncharacteristic unselfishness and generosity.

Heavenly heroes do not languish without hope on the eve of their home going. Instead, they are busy bestowing blessings to those who will be left behind. These heroes of the faith have an eye on heaven in worship, while they quietly wind down for the conclusion of their earthly assignment. "Precious in the sight of the Lord is the death of His saints" (Psalm 116:15). Look for heavenly heroes who may have lingered across your lineage. You may be surprised to discover the faith of former generations was robust and alive. Or, you may need to adopt one of heaven's saints who can represent one of God's finest heroes. Let them motivate you to live a life worthy of God's calling. Let their past faithfulness propel you to do the same in the present. We all need heroes who have overcome adversity by faith in God, and who knew how to enjoy Him, during times of difficulty and during times of peace. Your heavenly hero may be a godly grandparent who walked faithfully with the Lord and is now peering down from heaven's portal. You watched your grandmother and/or grandfather persevere through adverse conditions. They kept a relationship with God that flourished and grew, up to the very end of their life on earth. Money was not an issue for them because they learned to be content with a home, food and clothing. Relationships are what mattered the most to them. They always seemed to have time for you. Phone conversations did not seemed rushed and their door was always open. In their presence there was a serenity and stability that had heaven as its origin. You experienced a little bit of heaven each time they graced your presence.

Now is the time to allow the death of your heaven-bound hero to have even more of an impact on your life. Let their going home galvanize your faith. They remained faithful to the end, even though they did not receive their full reward in this life. Their life of perseverance with God is a tremendous motivation for you to do the same. You still worship Christ, but let your heavenly hero facilitate a deeper walk with God. You hero is dead, but their influence is greater now than when they walked the earth. Ask God to engraft their passion for His word in your heart and mind. Listen to their words of encouragement, and become more secure and confident. They were bigger than life. Now in their death they have heaven's platform for even greater Kingdom leverage. Your greatest hero is Jesus, but be encouraged to remain true to the faith by these lesser ones who reside in heaven. Because one day, you may very well do the same for another!

N20 HONOR MARRIAGE

"Marriage should be honored by all, and the marriage bed kept pure, for God will judge the adulterer and all the sexual immoral." HEBREWS 13:4

Marriage is a sacred institution of God. It is not to be taken lightly, or treated lightly. It may be easier in most cases to get a marriage license than a driver's license, but this does not give you a license to live a reckless marriage. When you honor marriage, you understand the commitment and prepare for its success. Marriage requires much, much more than love. It is not a convenient way to guarantee sex, and then just divorce when you get tired of one another, or don't love one another. To honor marriage is to make a lifetime dedication to one another. Just as Jesus is committed and faithful for eternity to His bride the church, so should be your position toward marriage. It is honorable to stay with your husband or wife through difficulties and triumphs. It is honorable for money to serve and strengthen the marriage, but it is dishonorable for money to become the consuming focus of marriage. Do not marry for money. This prostitutes the purpose of an honorable marriage. A marriage can and will remain honorable with or without money. Honor is not a slave to money, but money can serve to honor a marriage. You honor God when you honor marriage. You honor marriage when you keep God's definition of a man and a woman exclusively devoted to, and in love with each other, submitted to the authority of Almighty God.

Furthermore, the marriage bed is to be kept pure. Do not chase after a fantasy of sexual perfection with someone other than your spouse. Sex outside of marriage is wrong and breaks the heart of God. Adultery crushes the heart of your spouse, as it is not a causal infraction. However, leave it to God on how and when to judge the adulterer. Hold back your rocks of verbal assault and forgive. Keep the marriage bed pure and honorable by falling deeper and deeper in love with the man or woman God has given you for this life-long marriage relationship, so commit to one another that divorce is not an option.

Create boundaries together. It is a wise rule to never be alone with someone of the opposite sex. You avoid placing yourself in a compromising position, and at the very least you do not project an appearance of evil. A marriage discipline of fidelity takes effort, definition and accountability. Yes, you trust your wife or husband, but do not be naïve to think that temptation, Satan and other lonely souls are not out to snare your spouse. Be on the offensive to plan purity by honoring your spouse with your words. Disappointing and dissatisfying words about your husband or wife, which are shared indiscreetly with the opposite sex, will fuel the fires of unfaithfulness. Unfaithfulness starts with words, is furthered by a disrespectful attitude, and is executed by actions facilitated over a meal or a walk with a 'friend'. Therefore, remain true to your marriage vows and to your marriage mate. Work with each other, by letting God define what is wise and unwise. Exercise patience and understanding. Create a robust love life between one another. A satisfying sex life at home is a strong preventative to adultery outside the home.

Above all else, honor your marriage by first honoring God!

"For if you possess these qualities in increasing measure, they will keep you from being ineffective and unproductive in your knowledge of our Lord Jesus Christ." 2 PETER 1:8

The Christian life is not designed for maintenance, or meant for maintaining. The Christian who is vibrant and alive is a maturing disciple, as a growing believer in Christ you are in the process of adding to and developing your character. Your faith is not static; rather it is dynamic and nimble. You are building a life of character that can stand the winds of adversity and the blessings of prosperity. As a conscientious character builder you are to possess these qualities of Christ in an ever-increasing measure. "For this very reason, make every effort to add to your faith, goodness, and to goodness, knowledge, and to knowledge, self-control; and to self-control, perseverance, and to perseverance, godliness, and to godliness, brotherly kindness, and to brotherly kindness, love." (2 Peter 1:5) So your process of character development is a conscious effort. It starts with faith and ends with love. These are the bookends of God's expectations for your character. He may start with faith because it is the doorway to Him. Faith is how you approach God and how you appropriate His virtue into your life. Faith allows you to find your heavenly Father and learn from Him. Faith gives you ears to hear and a heart for change. Love, on the other hand, deals with motive. Everything you do needs to be inspired by love for God and people. The greatest from the trilogy of faith, hope and love, is love!

So start by asking God to increase your faith. An expanded capacity for faith and trust opens the door to other opportunities for life transformation. Faith is first base so do not run past it. Faith taken for granted is not faith; so do not disguise shallow or flippant religious-speak as faith. Faith is focused on God, and there is a relentless resolve to understand Him and His word. The Bible is a treasure trove of understanding into the character of God; faith is bolstered through the Bible. Your faith is ignited by the Scripture. It becomes radically robust as you feast and learn of God through his Holy Writ. Do not underestimate the potential of increasing your measure of faith by knowing and applying God's word.

Lastly, use love as warm oil to massage truth into your life and into the life of others. Like a sore muscle life needs the soothing effect of love. Love understands honoring a relationship over being right. Love motivates faith and is motivated by faith. Your love gives you permission into the life of a person. If they know they are loved, then your influence is trusted. Let love lace your life like garlic immersed in a delicious Italian meal. You can smell its attractive aroma, preceding its appetizing taste. With an ever-increasing measure the aromatic effect of your love will precede your presence. People want what you have when they are unconditionally loved. So, make sure what you are offering them is authentic. Be a love doctor, who graciously administers the love of God. Do not settle for the maturation of your past character. Seek Him even more humbly and aggressively now to increase your measure of character.

Keep adding to your character, His character, as this is effective and productive. Keep your life book between the bookends of God's character. Your life then becomes an attractive read!

"But whoever hates his brother is in the darkness and walks around in the darkness; he does not know where he is going, because the darkness has blinded him." I JOHN 2:11

Hate confuses. It confuses the giver and it confuses the recipient. Hate corrupts our character and corrodes our faith. Left unchecked it will damage, or destroy everything in its path. This is why it is critical to address hate before it becomes all-consuming. Hate is deceptive in its origin, and insidious in its application. It is an argument waiting to happen. It is bred in the womb of unresolved anger. It lashes out unexpectedly and unfairly. Hate has a chip on its shoulder that carries the weight of the world. Nothing seems right to a person controlled by hatred. They disagree, just to disagree. Hate is always inviting others to join the company of its misery. It is a sad and shameful place to live. Deep down the person driven by anger is desperate, but the desperation has not yet driven them to God. Thus, the fruit of hate is confusion and blindness. There is no way out for the one who stays in the perpetual place of hate. Hate emits an intense dislike and animosity toward others. And, ironically this is the behavior from others that comes back to haunt the hater. Those dispensing hate become hated. Eventually the hostility and the animosity will kill. It kills relationally, emotionally, spiritually, and physically. Hate spins your life out of control. You end up hating life and everyone who comes in contact with you. Sadly, but true, a hate-motivated person hates himself. So, how can hate be combated and expelled from a person's life?

You fight hate with love. God is love. He is the lover of your soul. He can cut through a hardened heart that harbors hate. His love illuminates where hate keeps you in the darkness. Receive the love of God and you will be loved. You will be loved purely and unconditionally. You will be loved like you have never been loved. The warm glow of God's love melts away the fear that hides behind hate. When you are loved by God you can love yourself. When you can love yourself you can love others. Let God in on your heartache. Let God in on your hurt. Let God in on your hate. He can love you through this. He will meet you right where you are. Let Him love on you. It is the love of God that will see you through this malaise of malevolence. Let go of hate and grab hold of God. Hate kills, but love lives. Hate resents, but love forgives. Hate is harsh, but love is kind. Hate confuses, but love clarifies. Hate is darkness, but love is light. So, begin to walk in the light of Jesus Christ. By faith receive His love and forgiveness, and then do the same for others. Life is too short to miss God's best, so come clean in confession to God and those offended. Allow God and others to love you through this time of torment. Deep down you probably hate to hate.

Direct your hate toward evil and become a generous giver of love. Love God and hate sin!

STEWARD SUCCESS

"Watch out that you do not lose what you have worked for,
but that you may be rewarded fully."   2 JOHN 8

Success is wise stewardship; so do not take it for granted. God has blessed you for a purpose and success is part of His purpose for you. However, if you do not steward wisely and responsibly the blessing of His success, you may very well lose it. Success means you have the attention of your peers and others in your industry and community. Your success over the years may even have gained the respect of many you have never met. Your family respects you. Your church respects you. Your friends respect you. Your work associates respect you. But success is not designed to lull you into apathetic work and lazy living. Success is meant to drive you to your knees in gratitude to God. Success is an opportunity to seek God for His wisdom regarding a new set of problems and opportunities. Normally, current issues require different answers from those in the past. The process of solving them may be similar, but the solutions are different. You have faired well until now without a structured Board of Directors or Advisory Board, but because of your level of success, one or both of these may be necessary so you have expert advisors and wise counsel surrounding you. Accountability and wise counsel are a big part of stewarding success. Also, use fiscal restraint. It may take you five years instead of two years for you to reach certain financial milestones. It is better to extend your goals and avoid unnecessary leverage. Even if people want to throw debt at you, reject the flattery and just say no. This is wise stewardship of success.

Now that you have enjoyed some level of success you do not have to prove yourself. By God's grace you have earned the right to serve in the role of influencer. You can prayerfully set trends and experiment with new processes and products. But develop these new initiatives from the platform of prayer. Do not take unnecessary risks. Conserve your successful results and build your organization from a position of strength. Use success as a springboard for innovation and excellence. Do one thing well, and another thing well, and another thing well.

Success can cause you to run ahead of relationships and resources. You can avoid this trap of over-subscribing to activity by staying regimented with a process that leads to thorough execution. You have worked hard for the success you are experiencing. So, be even more accountable in your life and work. Make sure your character keeps up with your success. The foundation for maintaining success is for the depth of your character to support the breadth of your success. If you as the leader do not model this, you will lose. You will lose your best people, you will lose new opportunities, and you will lose your success. The stewardship of success is daunting without God's wisdom and the godly counsel of others. Slow down and be coachable. Look into the mirror; ask what needs to be changed, and then change.

Do not lose what you have worked for, and His reward is your greatest success, "His master replied, 'Well done, good and faithful servant! You have been faithful with a few things; I will put you in charge of many things. Come and share your master's happiness!" (Matthew 25:21).

"You will be made rich in every way so you can be generous on every occasion, and through us your generosity will result in thanksgiving to God... Thanks be to God for his indescribable gift!" 2 CORINTHIANS 9:11, 15

Gratitude to God is a natural overflow of generosity. For example, the gift of salvation in Christ is indescribable. He gave when we did not deserve. He still gives, even though we are undeserving. His gift of liberty is freeing. His gift of health is healing. His gift of relationships is rich. His gift of peace is calming. His gift of wisdom is confidence. His gift of the Holy Spirit is comforting. His gift of finances is security. His gift of himself is reassuring and humbling. Gratitude explodes from our hearts when we are reminded of his generous gifts. They are incomparable and incomprehensible. Thanksgiving to God is a tremendous opportunity to unleash joy. This is one of the fruits of gratitude. Joy, joy, joy, joy down in our hearts, because He came down to earth and into our heart. This is an occasion for a righteous, but raucous celebration.

Gratitude to God can be a moment-by-moment expression. Even in the middle of the worst of circumstances, your thanksgiving to God is appropriate and needed. Look beyond your current condition to your heavenly hope. He has prepared a place for you, and His preparations are not lacking. They are just what you need and desire. So, your thanksgiving is for what He has done in the past, His current provision and what He has prepared for you in the future. God's generosity is without competition. You can be very, very grateful for this. Let thanksgiving escape from your lips often. Use it to put out the fires of fear and worry before they spread too far. Thanks be to God, for you are made rich. Yes, in Christ you are made rich. You have everything needed for this life in Christ. As a consequence of your management of His riches you can be ridiculously generous. This is the natural result of thanksgiving, because of your deep gratitude to God, you are called and compelled to give. Gratitude invites you to generosity. You cannot experience authentic thanksgiving and not see it birth giving. It is a beautiful process, because God has given to you, you give to others. At the moment you receive the gift of God, generosity is conceived in your heart.

This is why your heart feels pregnant with thanksgiving. It will explode without the regular birthing of generosity to others. This expression of gratitude results in action. It is tangibly and regularly giving to people for whom Christ died. The poor need food, a job, and Jesus. Orphans need parents, a home, and Jesus. Divorcees need acceptance, healing, and Jesus. The angry ones need gentleness and Jesus. The confused need clarity and Jesus. The bankrupt need financial wholeness and Jesus. Opportunities abound that invite your generous expression of gratitude. Gratitude is one of God's prescriptions for discontentment. The two cannot comfortably coexist. Thanksgiving gives the credit for your accomplishments to God and others. Without either you would not be in your current position of influence and success.

Gratitude is generous. Gratitude is content. Thanks be to God for his indescribable gift. The Bible says, "Give thanks to the LORD, for he is good; his love endures forever" (1 Chronicles 16:34).

GREATER JOY

"I have no greater joy than to hear that my children are walking in the truth."
3 JOHN 4

Greater joy is the outcome of children who walk in the truth. Parents are joyful. Grandparents are joyful. Mentors are joyful. The children are joyful. So, children walking in truth are an excellent goal for parents. Walk in the truth yourself, while at the same time training your children to do the same. Truth walking is joyful living. So this begs the question, 'What is truth?' Truth is what God defines as truth. Hence, Jesus is truth. When we examine and learn about Jesus we begin to know and understand truth. Once Christ enters your life, you have an uncanny capability to embrace truth, because truth resides within you. You can point your children to Jesus. Your belief points them to Jesus. Your behavior points them to Jesus. Your words point them to Jesus. Your note of encouragement points them to Jesus. Your decisions point them to Jesus. Everyday you have the opportunity to point your children to Jesus. Walking in truth becomes as natural as breathing. Walking in truth is not always easy, as it requires the ability to stand-alone. Even when your closest friends choose to reject or ignore truth, you embrace it instead. Walking in truth is not a trouble-free life. It may, in fact, facilitate conflict, but you remain steadfast in your commitment to truth living, and truth telling. The truth is when you and your children walk in truth there is no greater joy.

So, it just makes sense that parents become truth-seekers, truth-livers and then transferors of truth to their children. This is a gift that keeps on giving. When you give your children the truth, you give them the way to live an abundant life. Your parental heart swells with pride when you see your children choose truth over a lie. The by-products are numerous. Not only is there great joy that comes as a result of truth living, there is freedom, peace, security, and productivity for the Kingdom of God. Therefore, do not be afraid of the truth. It is your friend. Truth is on your side. Truth can be trusted.

Be careful, however, to validate truth with God's Word. Make sure your feelings are not accepting a façade of truth. When you believe a lie on behalf of truth you will suffer relational friction and joyless living. Some masquerade truth because it benefits them. Expose those who peddle truth on behalf of deception. Look to the truth-giver Jesus Christ for the final word. The Bible is crystal clear in all matters related to living out truth. God's truth is clear. Its application may be hard or fuzzy, but His truth is transparent, timeless, and not trendy. As a parent make it a priority to teach your children truth. Make sure their education is based on the truth of Scripture, for there is no other truth. Lead them to Jesus, so they can fall in love with Jesus. Yes, challenge them to be intellectually honest with the premise that Jesus is truth, and that the Holy Spirit will guide them in all truth. Truth is not illusive. So, live it, seek it, and pass it on to your children and others.

Greater joy is awaiting all who hang out with truth. Invest in truth, and receive a return on investment of no greater joy!

"I wrote to the church, but Diotrephes, who loves to be first, will have nothing to do with us."   3 JOHN 9

There is a competition that is unhealthy. Normally it is good to strive for excellence in innovation and execution, but there is a dark side to competition. If being number one reduces you to a relational peon or an ego manic, then there is a problem. If your drive to excel beyond competitors causes you to become unethical or immoral you have crossed the line from competitiveness to compromise. A love for first at any expense is a lethal strategy. This myopic motivation to achieve unrealistic short-term results strangles teamwork and demoralizes the most loyal. There may be some victories in the beginning, but long-term superior service will not happen without competition that has a greater purpose. This is why it is important to periodically examine your drive to achieve. Is it for your kingdom or God's Kingdom? Is it for the praise of man or is it for the pleasure of God? Is it to crush the competition or is it to be an enterprise of excellence? Is it out of jealousy or is it to do your very best? Unchecked competitiveness will isolate you from the realities of developing yourself, your business, your ministry, and your family. Ego-driven leaders have nothing to do with those who question their methods and motives. There is this insatiable desire to be first, or to be your very best at any cost, but there is a more excellent way.

A Christ-centered motive goes a long way toward healthy competition. In some ways there is no competition in the Kingdom of God. On the other hand, there is in reality a good competitiveness. You can strive for excellence without cannibalizing your walk with Christ, and your care for people. Becoming the best is a result of right priorities, not the reason for right priorities. There is a healthy and productive competitiveness. It is one that constantly calls the organization and the individual to improvement in effectiveness, efficiency, and execution. In some ways you are competing with yourself. You are seeking, by God's grace, to better who you are and what He has called you to do. You are allowing Him to transform you from the inside out. Thus, you are becoming better, because of the Lord working in and through you. It is good to compete with yourself. Are you a more passionate follower of Christ today than you were yesterday? If not, you may be the victim of unhealthy competition.

Lastly, this calls for a stern warning. Do not compete with God, because you will lose every time. This is the essence of an ego-driven life. A pregnant ego challenges God. It seeks to suppress (consciously or unconsciously) the will of God. An out of control ego runs way ahead of God, and later asks Him to bless the mess. You cannot rival God, so do not ask Him to join your team, rather humbly enlist on His. Satan is the most vicious competitor, and he is your true rival. Everyday is he vying for your heart and mind. His competitive methods are fiendish and unfair. He contends utmost for your soul. The only way to crush this unholy competition is through Christ. You win when you die daily to self and live for Christ. This is your competitive strategy and eternal edge. Love yourself third, others second and God first. Then being first will take care of itself.

Therefore, be faithful, patient and trusting, and all will come in His way and in His timing!

FAITH FAKERS

"These men are blemishes at your love feasts, eating with you without the slightest qualm—shepherds who feed only themselves. They are clouds without rain, blown along by the wind; autumn trees, without fruit and uprooted—twice dead." JUDE 12

Faith fakers are active within the community of faith for themselves. Some have even enlisted in an evil espionage. They are not true members of the faith, if so they would be bearing fruit that remains, rather than plastic and unproductive fruit. Their misguided motives wreak havoc, like an unsuspecting stealth bomber. They speak the right words and are persuasive, but their behavior is inconsistent and untruthful. Faith fakers are tireless trouble makers. Be on the guard for those who wear their faith on their shirt sleeves. They talk a good game, but they play poorly. There is no follow through, and no give-and-take, but wise and discerning people will expose faith fakers. They have no patience for their shenanigans. Do not waste your time or money on those with unholy ulterior motives. What they claim is too good to be true. It is only expedient for the moment. It is all about making them look good. Do not be naïve for faith fakers will seek to infiltrate your church, your family, your ministry, and your business. Nothing is truly sacred for those who prostitute faith for their own purposes. If you are currently engaged with a faith faker, challenge his behavior. Deal with the facts only, because he is illusive and ambiguous with the truth. If your attempts to corral him or her have failed, take someone with you to help clarify the severity of the situation.

Faith fakers cannot be dealt with passively. They will not go away until they are exposed and held accountable. Hopefully they will change, but they may slither off into some other unsuspecting group. If you are a faith faker you can change. You do not have to live in this façade and fantasy of faith. You can experience the real thing. Faith comes by hearing and hearing from the word of God (Romans 10:17). Study the lives of Ananias and Sapphire (Acts 5:1-5), and Simon (Acts 8:18-24) and see the demise of those who either lied to the Holy Spirit, or a leader who attempted to use the Holy Spirit for unholy personal gain. Their fate was final. Their influenced ceased, because their faith faking caught up with them. We all are faith fakers to some extent. We struggle at times to be who we are. This is okay and normal. Without struggle there is no growth.

However, faith faking is an entirely different issue. It is using God and others for selfish and non-Kingdom outcomes. If you have become trapped in faith faking, you can stop playing the game. You can wave the white flag of submission to God. You do not have to be in control. Capitulate to Christ and exercise authentic faith in Him. Make your motive and goal to serve people, not use people. Live a value-add life, not a parasitic life. If your disruptions have been public, then seek public forgiveness and retribution. If they have been private, then seek out the offended parties and offer sincere confession and repentance. You cannot remain a faith faker forever. The energy required to maintain the lie is intolerable. Instead, rest in God. The depth of stamina He provides is inexhaustible.

Simply follow Christ with an unfeigned faith and love. The Bible says, "The goal of this command is love, which comes from a pure heart and a good conscience and a sincere faith" (I Timothy 1:5).

"These are the words of him who is holy and true, who holds the key of David. What he opens no one can shut, and what he shuts no one can open. See I have placed before you an open door that no one can shut..." REVELATION 3:7-8B

The doors God opens cannot be shut, and the doors God shuts cannot be opened. So, you approach a shut door or an open door the same way, by faith. It is by faith that you walk through an open door and it is by faith that you walk away from a shut door. Do not let a closed door discourage you. This just means God has something better in store for you and your family. If you get impatient and try to force open the door then you may spend the rest of your time in this new situation forcing things to happen. Instead, you want to be invited in, if you have to barge your way into a circumstance then you are asking for trouble. Many times a closed door can be the best thing for you.

If a relational door is not open, then grow deeper with God during this time of transition. A wrong relationship can lead you away from God rather than toward God. Trust He has someone just for you for He has your best interest in mind. And don't be afraid to revisit a closed door. What He closed today, He may open tomorrow. Or, maybe a door was open for a season and now it is closing. A career door has closed. It has been a great run. You have contributed mightily to the enterprise. The organization is much better off than when you first came. You can be proud of your accomplishments. God has used you for His glory. So, do not overstay your welcome. This is time for you to live life fully and not to languish in self-pity or self-denial. Use this transition to execute God's will and encourage others by your obedience.

However, there may be an open door that is inviting you, but an open door does not require you to pass through. It can be a passage into the adventure of following Christ, or it may be a test of patience. An open door does not guarantee God's will. On the other hand it may very well be God's best for you. You would much rather feel pulled into something, instead of pushed. If a brand new initiative is inviting you in with energy and enthusiasm, this is excellent. Take the open door seriously. Go off and pray about it. Seek godly counsel without positioning the facts in the favor of your feelings. Try to be dispassionate and unbiased, be willing to walk away from this attractive opportunity. There will be another deal. There will be other opportunities that are even better. After your prayer and due diligence, and the open door still stares at you with peace and affirmation, follow through by faith. It is better to be with Jesus in the middle of an uncertain place, than to be smothered in certainty without Him. He opens and shuts doors according to His will. His doors swing on the hinges of providence. He is a wise and kind doorman. See the door, walk through or walk away, but do both by faith. Always look for the doors of God for they represent His best. His are doors of destiny.

Ask for prayer, as Paul requested, "And pray for us, too, that God may open a door for our message, so that we may proclaim the mystery of Christ, for which I am in chains" (Colossians 4:3).

DIVINE DESIGN

> "They lay their crowns before the throne and say: 'You are worthy, our Lord and God, to receive glory and honor and power, for you created all things, and by your will they were created and have their being." REVELATION 4:10B-11

God is the intelligence behind the design of creation and life. He is the architect of the universe and the engineer of eternal life. Because He is the wisdom behind the world, He did it right. The soft, pinkish blue sunset, He did it right. The brilliant, bold and bright sunrise cascading over the tree-tops, He did it right. The pure snow-capped mountains projecting toward heaven in reverence, He did it right. The luscious green and gorgeous vegetation, He did it right. The deep blue seas and the baby blue sky, He did it right. The furry and sometimes ferocious predator-like animals, He did it right. The multicolored bugs and beetles, He did it right. The chirping sparrows, the clacking seag-ulls, and the hovering hummingbirds, He did it right. Fish, shrimp, whales, and penguins, He did it right. Mostly, the intricate design of water and flesh, called the human body, He did it right. He is the intelligent designer of earth and its inhabitants. It takes more arrogance than faith to believe otherwise.

He has given us intelligence to understand that He is the intelligent designer. If we cannot accept that God is behind intelligent design, then we are not being intellectually honest. The evidence is overwhelming. Its affirmation quietly rests within our hearts, its confirmation floods our minds, and its declaration explodes from out mouths. He cannot be ignored. Ironically, some who claim superior intelligence reject God as the Intelligent One. This is the pitfall of pride. Pride blinds to the simple truth that we are not the smartest. Intellectual snobs conjecture, contrive, complicate, and compromise Christ as God and creator. This is hard to accept because faith in Christ moves man from the center of the universe, to worshiper of the Creator of the universe.

So, because of God's vastness that is validated by His intelligent design, He deserves your utmost for His highest. He is worthy of your praise, adoration, and all glory. It is no accident that heaven is full of hilarious hallelujahs on behalf of God the Father, God the Son, and God the Holy Spirit. Heaven is a raucous revival of real live worship for Christ who was slain for your sins. In heaven there is no debate over who reigns over heaven and earth. It is a settled issue, for the object of our affection and all gratitude and praise will be for Jesus. Anything good than has been accomplished by God through you will be laid at the feet of Jesus. Your crown of rewards will not be proudly worn on your head; rather it will be placed before the lowest spot in front of Christ. Heaven is all about Him, just like Christmas is all about Christ. Your time on earth is preparation for Him and for heaven. Worship of Him on earth is but an appetizing morsel of what you will have to feast upon when you gaze upon His face in heaven. His design of you and me, and creation is not only intelligent; it is good. Therefore, worship Him now in preparation for worshiping Him later.

Praise, honor, and all power and glory go to God. He deserves it and He desires it, and we have the wonderful privilege to express it. This is His intelligent design!

"After this I looked and there before me was a great multitude that no one could count, from every nation, tribe, people and language, standing before the throne and in front of the Lamb. They were wearing white robes and were holding palm branches in their hands." REVELATION 7:9

Heaven is multicultural. Representatives from Africa, Asia, Europe, Australia, Antarctica, North America, and South America will populate heaven. The people are almost as diverse as the numbers are uncountable. There will be no apartheid, no racism, no castes, no poverty, no bad boundaries or social barriers. Heaven is made up of a variety of people worshiping one God. However, even though heaven is multicultural it still has its distinctions. Heaven is a distinct place (Christ's domain), populated by a distinct people (followers of Christ), who are worshiping a distinct God (the Father of our Lord Jesus Christ). It is diversity with definite distinctions. Heaven without diversity would be like a man-made club. It would only be a place to gather with others like you. Heaven is inclusive, not exclusive. It invites in anyone in the world who places their faith in Christ. It is exclusive worldwide of those who remain in their sin of unbelief in Jesus as God who became man. So with these destitutions of belief and diversities of culture, there is one focus and that is the worship Christ. He is the reason for the Christmas season and He is the reason for Heaven. The worship of Jesus, the praise of Jesus, the adoration of Jesus, the appreciation of Jesus, the service of Jesus, the comfort of Jesus, and the rest of Jesus. And we will experience this Christ-centric haven with brothers and sisters of all skin colors. Red, yellow, black, and white they are all precious in his sight!

The disunity man created at Babel was countered by the unity Christ created on the cross. We have a reinstitution of unity in heaven because of the shed blood of the Lamb... Jesus! But we do not have to wait until heaven for our reunification. As followers of Jesus we have each bowed our head, heart, and knees at the foot of the cross. The ground is level at the foot of the cross. Believers in Jesus are on the same playing field, with the same trajectory toward Heaven. Therefore, we can serve God and each other with no fear of prejudice or pride.

It is out of humility and gratitude we love God and each other. Our time on earth is but a prelude to heaven. So, you can travel overseas and sit in a slum for the first time, and laugh and cry together because Jesus is your life. He brings you together from 6,000 miles away to worship Him. Your net worth or lack thereof does not matter. All that matters is Jesus. He compels you to unify around Him with other believers. They will know we are Christians by the love we have for one another. Christianity is multicultural because heaven is multicultural. It is something to enjoy now, because we will enjoy it for eternity. This is the spice of life and the spirit of heaven. Multicultural Christianity has been, is now, and is forevermore. Escape from your sub-culture. Enjoy the full experience of Christ's multicultural family. It is preparation for Heaven.

The Bible says, "Clap your hands, all you nations; shout to God with cries of joy" (Psalm 47:1).

GOD'S MESSENGER

"David said to Abigail, 'Praise be to the Lord, the God of Israel, who has sent you today to meet me. May you be blessed for your good judgment...' "
I SAMUEL 25: 32-33A

God dispatches His messengers daily. You can expect a regular word from the Lord through others. They may represent His envoy of much-needed encouragement, or they may engage you with a regiment of rebuke. Whether He sends a positive or a negative word, it is critical that you concur with their instruction. Your emotions may be driving you in one direction, because you have been treated unfairly, even inflicted by a gross indiscretion. But God's messenger is imploring you to take the more reasonable road of understanding and forgiveness. Just because you have been wronged, does not mean you are to wrong. Anybody can do that. It takes strength of character to not retaliate.

God is in control, so leave them in His hand. Let the Lord deal with them in His timing. God's messenger may be telling you to wait. This opportunity staring you down does not deserve your acceptance. Your pride and ego have nominated you to the task, but you know in your heart it is not the wise thing to do. Listen to God's messenger and avoid a year of regret. Money and status are not worth jeopardizing your marriage and your health. There will be other opportunities, much better ones that will fit in your next season of life. It is easy to ignore, reject, or argue with God's messenger, but think twice before you debate with Deity's representative. They are ambassadors of heaven reaching out to you on earth. He has things under control, and desires His very best for your life.

Many times God's messenger is in the form of a friend who knows you all too well, and has seen some of your destructive patterns over the years. He has your best interests in mind. Their desire is for you to learn from your unwise decisions of the past, and flourish in the future. They are taking a risk with their friendship, because they care. If they were self-serving, they would shut up. So, listen to God speaking through your friend, especially when it is not what you want to hear. He also speaks, frequently through your spouse. They love you, and yes they may be fearful and insecure, but it is because they don't want you to miss God's very best.

Do not allow ego and pride to blind you to their warnings and concerns. They may not understand all of the 'ins and outs' of business, but they do understand the Holy Spirit's promptings. This is a level of discernment, which God has wisely given to them, as your gift. Make sure you receive it and use it well.

Lastly, reward God's messengers. This is behavior that deserves recognition and appreciation. You reward the behavior you want repeated, and you rebuke or ignore the behavior that you want to cease. Do more than say you agree. Instead, make a big deal over their determination to deliver the truth. Instead of blowing off the messenger of good will, invite them into your circle of influence. Promote those who persist in pitching the facts. God's messengers can be trusted, because they bear news from your heavenly Father. Therefore, take seriously their words, and act accordingly. Listen actively to God's messengers, and in turn become one.

The Bible says, "He who listens to a life-giving rebuke will be at home among the wise" (Proverbs 15:31).

D2 HE CARES

> "Cast all your anxiety on him because he cares for you."
> 1 PETER 5:7

God cares about you. He cares about your job. He cares about your fears. He cares about your spouse. He cares about your children. He cares about your parents. He cares about your worries. He cares about your finances. He cares about your car and your house. He also cares about your character. He cares about you caring about Him and caring for others. He is a caring God. You cannot out care God. His capacity to care is infinite, and his competence to care is matchless. You can care because He cares. There is no care of yours that God does not care about. If it is important to you, then God cares about it. Yes, you will experience misdirected cares, but God's desire is to come along side you and realign your cares with what He cares about the most. He cares enough to bear your anxieties and to replace them with His peace and assurance.

When you give God your worries you in turn receive His calming presence. God's system of care is counter-cultural. God transforms your cares into what He cares about; so cast your cares on Christ. Equally spiritual people may cast their cares on God in polar opposite ways. One may find release in a quiet written prayer, while another may feel cared for by God through ruckus worship. Let another's processing of anxiety be a guide and not a guilty comparison.

You know God cares immensely. So how do you cast your cares on Him? By faith, you let Him care. He cares and can be trusted, therefore allow Him to do what He does best. You allow Him care for you. This does take humility on your part. You are acknowledging a desperate need for God. Your declaration of dependence is two-fold. You admit you are anxious, and can't handle your worry alone. Secondly, you submit to the fact that only God can handle this level of concern. Hence, your submission to God allows His care to consume your anxieties. Your care giving to God is recurring. Over time He helps bring your feeble faith and misguided mind into focus on Him. What started out as a burden, He transforms into a blessing. Your pain becomes productive.

You become free to care for others, because you have been freely cared for by Him. Your perspective takes on a heavenly flavor. Do not wait until matters get worse before you off load on the Lord. Go to God first, because He cares the most. Let bad news travel fast, because He already knows. A carefree attitude is cultivated by an all-caring God. The more you allow Him to care about your worries, the less you have to care. Then you can focus your care on people and eternal issues. Let God be consumed with your cares, so you are not. Then you can lead others to your all-caring Christ. Care for them like Jesus. Your care will lead to His care. This is the beauty of the circle of care. You do it right and they will want your God. You care for others, and they will want the God that cares for you. Keep your caring Christ-centered. You care because He cares. You can care because you have let Him care for you. Keep the circle of care rotating.

Do not grow weary of caring; He doesn't. He cares for you. Therefore, give Him your cares and experience His care. Christ is your #1 caregiver. Jesus said it well, "...do not worry about your life..."(Matthew 6:35).

"Nehemiah said, 'Go and enjoy choice food and sweet drinks, and send some to those who have nothing prepared. This day is sacred to the Lord. Do not grieve for the joy of the Lord is your strength.' " Nehemiah 8:10

God's joy is free and available for all who will receive. The joy of the Lord is limitless. It is like a wellspring of living water that flows forever. You cannot pump it dry even if you wanted to. No thirsty soul who has ever tasted God's joy has been dissatisfied. The weak soul is rejuvenated under the influence of heavenly joy. An athletic victory is fleeting, to be enjoyed only so briefly, but the joy of the Lord penetrates into the depths of who you are. God's joy wells up to provide resilience during times of testing. This is the result of tapping into His divine resource. Natural resources deplete over time, but the joy of the Lord is infinite. The joy of the Lord also travels way beyond happiness. Happiness is based on your circumstances; joy is based on your faith in God. Your circumstances will change, and with every change comes the possibility of losing your happiness.

God never changes, therefore the chances of losing your joy are nil, if you are focused on the Joy-Giver. Just as you depend on the local power company to provide your home's electricity, so the wise follower of Christ looks to God for his provision of joy. God's joy is ready and waiting to be deployed into your heart. He is not stingy. Go to the eternal dispenser of joy and receive what the world cannot sustain and money cannot buy: the joy of the Lord is your strength. So how can His joy be retained?

The joy of the Lord comes through the channel of faith. This is the coupon you need in exchange for this wonderful prize. Your faith is bolstered and made alive through the word of God. This joyful energy does not come from a cursory reading of God's word, rather a reading for understanding, application, and transformation. Joy explodes from the pages of Scripture as we understand our utter dependence on God and His tender compassion and mercy. Your mind is washed from the sin-stained lies of the world and you begin to believe the truth that you have great significance in God's eyes. Your exposure to the repetition and teaching of the Bible garners understanding. Your understanding of whom God is and what He has done, and is doing for you will cause joy to explode in your heart.

Furthermore, His strength created by His joy will sustain you even in the most difficult of circumstances. Holy Spirit initiated life-change spews joy over you and every one around you. "I have no greater joy than to hear that my children are walking in the truth"(3 John 4). When a more mature Christian witnesses a young believer growing in the faith as a result of their discipleship time, it brings joy. When a spouse experiences unconditional love from their life mate as a result of a divine encounter, it brings joy. Application of God's word solicits joy.

Lastly, joy comes from celebration over God's faithfulness. Regularly recall the goodness of God. Once you were blind and now you see. Your family, your health, your friends, your career, your opportunities, your joy, and countless other blessings are all gifts from God. These precious memories are cause for celebration.

This is reason to be joyful. This is the joy of the Lord. This is the source of your strength. Be joyful in Jesus, so you can be strong in your Savior!

D4 WICKED PROSPERITY

"Why do the wicked live on growing old and increasing in power? ...
They spend their years in prosperity and go down to the grave in peace." JOB 21: 7, 13

You can live a life of prosperity without God. People die with "stuff" but without a Savior. As followers of Christ we know death is the great equalizer, but it bothers us at times to see the wicked get ahead during their life on earth. It seems that God's blessing does not discriminate between good and evil. A dedicated Christian can live in the most difficult circumstances while a vile person lives a life of ease and luxury. There are times that criminals prosper while law-abiding citizens suffer. This injustice rubs us the wrong way. We become angry when it appears that evil is better off than good. We are bewildered when things go wrong for a good person, while everything goes right for a bad person. It messes up our neatly organized categories and our fool-proof theology. This may be the reason you gave up on God. You could not accept this unfairness. God should not allow these inequities, but this is the fruit of freedom.

God's allowance of free will permits the wicked to get ahead. Someone may go through their entire life without God, make money, and enjoy the good life. God may not muzzle men who manipulate or strike down those who steal, but their demise awaits them. If people choose to live a Christ-less life now, then they have prepared themselves for a Christ-less life for eternity.

If this life is all we can expect then some of the wicked may win, but thankfully there is a much greater picture. This life is but an introduction to a greater documentary called God's story. This life is but an appetizer to an exquisite banquet called the marriage supper of the Lamb. This life is but a preamble to coming face-to-face with the One who is the Word. This life is but a blink of an eye compared to having our eyes wide open in worship for eternity. This life's pleasures are but a taste to the tip of the tongue compared to reveling in the glory of God, and the enjoying each other without sin. There is a bigger story, a larger life, and a plan much more elaborate than we could ever envision. There is an unseen world beyond this world. There is a much greater purpose than just living for oneself, creating a lot of wealth, and dying to the dirt.

Instead, God wants you engaged with Him and His activities. It may look like wickedness wins out but it doesn't. It is a dead-end street. It is a fast track to nowhere. Even in this life there are consequences to wrong choices. A wicked lifestyle may lead to premature death, rebellion, or bankruptcy. So what if some have made it to the top but crushed people along the way. There may be a few insecure 'yes men' who are impressed, but only because they fear losing their jobs or, in some cases, their lives.

Wickedness may appear to win, but it loses. It loses big time. In this life it loses life, sleep, relationships, honor, peace, forgiveness, grace, God, family, freedom, and respect to name a few. In the life to come, it loses eternity with God and His saints. Do not let the pseudo-success of the wicked disillusion you. Pray for them and become a magnet of grace to which they are drawn. If you encamp with the wicked, surrender to Jesus. Evil eventually loses the war, so come over to the winning side before it is too late.

The Bible says, "Therefore the wicked will not stand in the judgment, nor sinners in the assembly of the righteous" (Psalm 1:5).

"...they went immediately to the Jews in Jerusalem and compelled them by force to stop. Thus the work on the house of God in Jerusalem came to a standstill..." EZRA 4:23B-24A

Don't give up. You may be facing a temporary setback, but God's purposes will not be thwarted. It may seem like life is on hold and everything has come to a stand still. You have worked so hard to get to this point and it looks like the opportunity has vanished. Hold it with an open hand, as it may have disappeared. If so, God has something better.

It is not time to get mad, but glad. What God initiates, He accomplishes. He hasn't forgotten about you or your circumstances. He is on top of the situation. This is a temporary setback. This is a good time for you to catch your breath and reflect on the great things He has done so far. You have been running hard, so pause and prepare for the next stage of personal and professional growth. You do not need to venture into opportunities for which your character is not ready. The last thing you want is to move forward without the depth of wisdom, patience, relationships, and operational skills needed to complete the project. The motive of your adversaries is to crush your project, but God is taking what was meant for evil and using it for good.

The unfair criticism of others is a cheap way to distract you, so ignore their insults. Immature people act immaturely. Do not lower yourself to their level of behavior. Otherwise you may never get out. You may become stuck by spinning your wheels and becoming defensive. Focus on God, not your distracters. He is the one who has led you this far, and He is the one who will lead you through to completion. If everything was easy we might take God's blessings for granted, or we might forgo gratitude to God.

Lastly, the Lord knows what is best. He knows how to align everyone's hearts involved in the project. Sometimes there is even an ironic twist. He may eventually use the endorsement, resources, and relationships of your biggest critics. The ones who rolled a boulder onto the road may be the very ones who remove the obstacles and provide you fuel for the journey. Isn't it just like God to turn the tables?

Obstacles become opportunities. Adversaries become advocates. Critics become cheerleaders. Enemies become emissaries, and setbacks become a tremendous springboard for God's will. Take heart, and keep your head up. It is the darkest before the dawn. Hang in there with Jesus, and He will hold you up. Your Savior will sustain you. God's purposes will not be thwarted, so believe it and watch Him work.

The Bible says, "Now finish the work, so that your eager willingness to do it may be matched by your completion of it, according to your means"(2 Corinthians 8:11).

D6   MODEL THE WAY

"I have set you an example that you should do as I have done for you." JOHN 13:15

We start by modeling with our attitude. Attitude is everything. It is the difference between goodness and greatness. It separates the mature from the immature. Attitude is what causes - people to give up or persevere. Indeed, the leader has a responsibility to inspire hope with an optimistic attitude. Anyone can be negative and assign blame, but wise is the leader who is positive and takes responsibility. This is the attitude God blesses. He dispenses more opportunity to one whose attitude is aligned with His agenda. The attitude God honors is humble, unselfish and hopeful in Him.

Therefore, proper attitude alignment requires a prayerful attitude. This attitude depends on God and seeks out His wisdom. It is a positive attitude that always looks for the good in an individual or situation. It is also an appreciative attitude. Gratitude generates a right attitude because it rarely complains. So our attitude is infectious, but our actions also speak volumes.

It is also imperative that we model with attractive actions. Behavior validates our beliefs. If we say one thing and do another, we are dishonest with ourselves and others. Actions are a barometer of our character. Appropriate actions earn us the right to influence and lead. If we are inconsistent in our actions, we confuse the team. Consistent actions facilitate faithfulness in followers. Moreover, the manner in which we arrive at our definition of right actions is important. The greater context of work expectations is based on the principles found in God's Word.

The Bible is our baseline for behavior. For example, respectful behavior is illustrated with collaborative discussions over strategy and execution. Wise actions then become the pattern of an effective and efficient culture. Wise actions align around follow through. We do what we say and say what we do. Wise actions also solicit feedback from everyone. We rely on the wisdom of the team over one's own perspective. The Bible defines right actions, so everyone on the team may not believe in Jesus, but they all agree to act like Jesus.

Lastly, you model with your words. Words can build up or tear down. Your words can be pure and encouraging, or poisonous and discouraging. Moment by moment you have the opportunity to inject courage into our colleagues with truthful, kind and caring words. A good rule of thumb is to measure your words prayerfully and patiently before we speak. Do not allow anger and harshness to dominate your delivery. Use words as ointment rather than an irritant. Your words are a reflection of your heart. A healed heart produces healing words. Therefore, use words wisely by speaking as you would like to be spoken to, with a spirit of compassion. When you speak, build up rather than tear down. Speak the truth in love. Choose caring conflict over insensitive passive aggression. Words matter, so model your speech well.

Above all else, model the way by following Jesus' way, as He stated, "I am the way and the truth and the life"(John 14:6a).

THINK THE BEST

"Do to others as you would have them do to you." LUKE 6:31

Think the best of others, because this is what you expect them to think of you. Give them the same benefit of the doubt you desire. Believe that they have your best interests in mind. The temptation is to default to cynicism and be suspect of their motives, but leave this to God. We cannot judge a man or a woman's heart. One role of the Holy Spirit is to convict and lead others to a higher level of Christian maturity. Our role is to trust the good will of those God has placed in our lives. It is especially important to think the best of those closest to us. Husbands, think the best of your wives. Wives, think the best of your husbands. If they love God, they want His very best for your life. Their questions are not meant to be critical, but to bring clarity, connection and accountability. Pride resists this level of trust and maturity.

Pride does not want to think the best of others. Pride would rather gut it out on its own and not have to listen to the loving counsel of those who care. This is especially tempting to teenagers growing into young adults. They want to figure things out on their own and not be told what to do. But wise is the young person who will think the best of the authorities in their life. Their mom and dad who love Jesus are full of good will. They want God's very best for their own flesh and blood. Your parents do not want to control you, they want to support you. There is a huge difference. Support means they trust you and they entrust you to God. They think the best of you and believe you will make the wisest decision. Your parents pray for you and care for you. Their intentions are pure and without wrong intent. Listen to them. Your parents are one of God's means to His best.

Lastly, think the best of others because God does. When God looks at His children, He sees Christ. He doesn't look at them as sinners stuck on themselves. The Lord looks at His followers as full of potential for Him. They are still rough around the edges in sin and the world does roughen us up at times, but beyond the scares of sorrow are hearts that want to move forward with their heavenly Father. He reaches out to His children and offers opportunities. He thinks the best of us, because we are His. You can't get any thicker than the blood of Jesus Christ.

It is easy to get into the eternal family of God; you believe, and it is impossible to get out; you're secure. He does not disown us for our dumb mistakes. He forgives us, and thinks the best of us;, so you trust in God and others. Trusting others' intentions does not mean you are irresponsible. You still follow-up, verify facts and ask questions. You still hold them accountable, but your defining attitude is trust. This is harder as we get older, but let your Savior put your suspicions to rest. Choose to think the best of people and circumstances. It is much more than being positive. It is a deep-seeded trust in the core of your being, given to you by God.

Think the best of yourself, your spouse, your friends, and your work associates. You trust when you think the best. After all this is how you want others to treat you!

D8 OUT-SERVE

"Now that I, your Lord and Teacher, have washed your feet, you also should wash one another's feet. I have set you an example that you should do as I have done for you…"
JOHN 13:14-15

Out-serve your spouse. This is not natural to our selfish self, but out serve your spouse, and you will start to see positive differences in both of you. Service makes them feel cared for and makes you feel fulfilled. Service makes them feel loved and makes you feel rewarded. Service makes them feel respected and makes you feel significant. Of course unappreciated service can wear you down over time, but trust God. Allow Him to supply the strength for your service. If the Lord is not empowering your service, you will eventually burn out, and possibly become resentful. Bitter service does not last, but joyful service does.

Serve your spouse out of gratitude to God for giving them to you. Serve them in the routines of life and when they least expect it. Serve them where they want to be served, not just where you want to serve them. It may be unloading the dishwasher, taking out the garbage, mowing the lawn, house maintenance, or taking care of the cars. Their objects of service may include an organized family, dinner at home, being on time, keeping a calendar, or planning a trip. If you are unsure, ask them how they like to be served. Furthermore, carry this attitude of 'out serve' into your occupation. Be one who serves in the work place, especially if you are a leader or manager. Quietly and clandestinely clean up the break room, even wipe out the gooey microwave with its burst of flavors matted to the inside. Service from a sincere heart values and respects others.

Our Savior modeled service. He did not come to be served, but to serve and to give His very own life as the ultimate act of service. When we enlist in the service of God's Kingdom, we become full-time servants of His. Service for our Savior is a thread that runs through the life of everyone who is lead by the Lord. If Jesus is your model for leadership and living life, you serve. He served the least and the greatest. He served the sinners and the saints. He served the rich and the poor. He served singles and He served families. He served mad and He served glad. He served when He was tired and He served when He was rested. You could not out serve Jesus, because His service was motivated and fueled by His heavenly Father. Intimacy with the Almighty compels you to serve.

Ironically Jesus served others even at the point of His greatest need. When engulfed in His own personal crisis, He chose to serve others instead of being served. The night before facing imminent death, He served by washing feet. Use this same selfless strategy of service and watch the world run to Jesus. In the middle of your own 'Last Supper' experience, serve. When you are rejected, serve instead of retaliating. When you are forgotten, serve instead of feeling sorry for yourself. When you are hurt, serve instead allowing your heart to harden. Furthermore, serve for Jesus' sake and not your own. Make it a lifetime goal to 'out serve' all you come in contact with, especially those closest to you.

To "out serve" yields an outstanding outcome. An "out serve" attitude is other-centered and Christ-focused. You can't "out serve" Christ, but you can be a conduit of service on His behalf. Seek to 'out serve' others for your Savior!

> "Esteem her [wisdom], and she will exalt you; embrace her, and she will honor you.
> She will set a garland of grace on your head and present you with a crown of splendor."
> PROVERBS 4:8-9

Embrace and celebrate with the Lord. Discover where the Lord has passion and join Him. Learn what He likes and dislikes. His wisdom is supreme. Embracing God's wisdom and celebrating with obedient living gives Him glory and honor. You become a trophy of God's grace when you embrace and celebrate His character. It takes a lifetime of learning from the Lord; so don't be overwhelmed.

Embrace and celebrate His forgiveness and you will find yourself forgiving. Embrace and celebrate His peace and you will discover you are peaceful. Embrace and celebrate His patience and you will become patient. God is worth the energy to engage around His eternal agenda and wisdom. Moreover, make this a mantra in marriage, and relationships as well.

Embrace and celebrate your spouse's interests. If sports are one of his passions, then embrace and celebrate. Instead of quietly complaining because of competition from an afternoon of football, make some nachos and have a supreme pizza delivered. His passion for you increases when you embrace areas in which his energies engage. If shopping for a special occasion is one of her passions, then embrace and celebrate. Let it sink in that she wants to look nice, especially for you. Be patient while she picks out an outfit and then help her buy some shoes that match. When you finish shopping, go for coffee and talk.

You have just embraced and celebrated. You discovered where someone else's passions lie and joined them in celebration. Don't see someone's interests as competition. See their hobbies or activities of enjoyment as an opportunity to join them, honor them, and get to know them better. Wisdom embraces and celebrates.

Lastly, you may not understand the next steps for your life, but the Lord does. Latch on to His train of trust and ride with Him to your next destination. But make sure to celebrate along the way. Embrace your current situation as God's will; and do your very best to execute with excellence. Celebrate along the way so you can enjoy the fruit from your heavenly Father. God is working so take the time to celebrate His goodness, mercy, and grace. Lives are being transformed as people are meeting Jesus face-to-face for the first time. The salvation of souls is at an all-time high in heaven's stock market index. The opportunity for the globalization of the gospel is unprecedented, so slow down to celebrate. Embrace your uncertain future and celebrate the current outstanding outcomes. Embrace and celebrate, and your relationships will flourish instead of frustrate.

Above all else embrace God's eternal wisdom, and celebrate the honor and grace He gives back!

D10 CONFESSIONAL PRAYER

"The people came to Moses and said, 'We sinned when we spoke against the Lord and against you. Pray the Lord will take the snakes away from us.' So Moses prayed for the people." NUMBERS 21:7

Confessional prayer comes clean with God. There is sensitivity to the Spirit that abhors sin and its consequences. It knows it is in need of repentance and forgiveness. Ironically, our sin may come on the heels of a great act from the Almighty. God may have worked mightily in our mist, but we forget to thank Him for His recent past provisions, and we rush to judge whether He or others will see us through our uncertain future.

We grow impatient when God does not give us immediate results, though we have seen Him work things out beautifully before. Unless we catch ourselves, we spiral down into fearful living. We know in our head He is faithful, but our heart is drawn away in fear. So confessional prayer comes full-circle, and comes clean with Christ. We get honest about our own grumbling and complaining. We take responsibility for our own bad attitudes. We can't change the other person with whom we have conflict, but by God's grace we can change ourselves.

We may not be able to improve our circumstance for the better, but we can become better by acting like Almighty God is in control. We can throw ourselves on the need for His mercy and forgiveness. He listens to our contrite prayer of confession. Our sincere pleas to sovereign God solicit Him to forgive our sin, so confession matters. It moves the heart of heaven when He hears your cries. Your prayer of repentance engages God. Your teachable heart is how the Spirit is able to bring about life transformation. There is no need to stay on the treadmill of temptation and tentative obedience. Step off with the Spirit's help and run by faith. Lastly, use your confession of sin as an invitation for others to intercede on your behalf.

Your prayer of repentance is not reserved for God alone. Accountability grows when we ask for prayer over our awful attitudes. Yes it is humbling and sometimes humiliating, but the prayers of godly people are a lever for the Lord, and a surge of the Spirit's support. Sin loses its grip when you involve praying people over your process of repentance. We do much better when we ask a friend to pray that our lustful looks at an attractive person, become glances of admiration and respect. Our role as a faithful husband or a loving wife is reinforced by specific prayers for a marriage that models unselfishness. Ongoing prayer reinforces our confession. We succeed at resisting sin when we know others are praying for us. We have a much higher probability for change when we confess our sin to God, and to the saints that love us too much not to pray for us and hold us accountable.

Therefore, pulverize any preoccupation with sin by confessing your need for prayer and accountability. Sin slithers back into its dark corner when exposed by the light of confession and prayer. Reveal your secret sin to somebody you trust. Ask them to pray for you, as it facilitates freedom and healing.

The Bible says, "Therefore confess your sins to each other and pray for each other so that you may be healed. The prayer of a righteous man is powerful and effective"(James 5:16).

"For the Lord your God has chosen them [priests] and their descendants out of all your tribes to stand and minister in the Lord's name always." Deuteronomy 18:5

Our best ministry motive is for our Master Jesus. It is not for our need to be needed. It is not for our desire to be recognized for our unselfish service. It is not our past guilt that we are trying to make up for with good deeds. Unhealthy motives for ministry lead to burnout and regret. Your service for the Lord becomes laborious when you strive in your own strength. You lose the joy that jolted you into ministry for Jesus in the first place.

Ministry is not meant to be about your service, but about His worship. Make sure you are not subtly shifting the attention toward your accomplishments instead of the Almighty's. Proper ministry motives point to the object of our ministry, the Lord Jesus. You are a conductor for Christ. He orchestrates His work through us. You pay the price of training and equipping, but He pulls off His concert of grace. As Christ's conductor you point the baton away from yourself. You minister in the Lord's name on behalf of others, and help them discover their God-given talents and gifts. You lead them to bring their skills and abilities together in a beautiful sounding piece of ministry music on behalf of their Master. Your ministry motive is to convene gifted followers of Christ into a concerted effort of service for His glory, so seek to understand what others do best. Connect them with complimentary relationships and then watch God do the rest. If you fulfill your ministry role right, you may be forgotten, but He will be remembered.

So stand and minister in the Lord's name. Do not stand and minister in your name, or only in the name of an institution. Stand and minister in the name of your Savior Jesus. He is our motive for ministry. He called us to carry out His will and implement His plan. It all comes back to Christ. So in your family, minister to them on behalf of the Lord. Do not care for them so you can control them. Instead serve them unselfishly and trust the Lord with their future outcomes. At your work minister to others unconditionally, not for admiration and attention, but on behalf of God. Do not wear your religion on your sleeve, but roll up your sleeves for your Savior and serve.

Lastly, live as one chosen and called by Christ. Called people cannot help but embrace and recognize their Caller. Christ called, you answered and obeyed. You do what you do because of Him. He called you to this career. He called you to this city. He called you to minister on His behalf. Never forget who called you and what He called you to be and do. Focus first on the One who called you, and second on your calling. If you focus only on your calling you become confused, and your faith falters. You become the center of attention, not Him. Your calling is a means to the end of glorifying God. It is not the destination. He has chosen you for Himself. You are owned by Almighty God. You minister in the Lord's name, so make your ministry motive for your Master Jesus. Above all else, you decrease and He increases. Pure ministry motives promote Him. The early church leaders modeled this,

The Bible says, "Paul greeted them and reported in detail what God had done among the Gentiles through his ministry" (Acts 21:19).

D12 SERVE THE SERVANT

"Be careful not to neglect the Levites as long as you live in the land."
DEUTERONOMY 12:19

Servants of the Lord need to be served, because they constantly in serve. Those who serve the Lord on our behalf are special servants. They are special because God has called them out to a life totally abandoned to Him and to people. Vocationally they are His. Spiritually they are His. Emotionally they are His. Indeed everyone who follows Jesus is called to do the will of God, but His ministers, missionaries and ministry leaders have a mandate from their Master. They are called to a specific area of service for Him. It may be teaching, preaching, leading, singing, worshiping, administrating or equipping. This is their vocation and how they make a living. It can be terribly tiresome at times.

Servants of the Lord can be overworked and unappreciated. It is hard to serve a congregation when you feel like everyone is your boss. Serving the Lord as an employee of the church has the potential of seven days of work. A Pastor or staff member may have a family activity planned, but if a funeral or relational crisis arises within the fellowship they are called on to intervene. Service is second nature to servants of the Lord, but we don't need to neglect their needs. Their faith becomes fragile. Their emotions become frazzled. Their bodies fatigue. Their teenagers rebel. They feel financial pressures. They become tired of being good. Servants of the Lord need to be served, before they burn out or bail out. Their smile may mask their hurt, so come along side them and pray for them.

Vocational ministry leaders are not immune to sin. In some ways their temptations are more intense. They represent God, so Satan cannot stand for the Lord's servants to remain faithful. He takes advantage of their sensitive spirits and tries to lead them into immoral acts. If a church or ministry leader is not served in a proper way, he will be drawn to improper means of attention. So surround your vocational Christian workers and love on them. Do not take for granted that they feel loved and appreciated. On the contrary, they are probably struggling and tired. They need a revival of rest and relaxation.

Above all else, serve your servants of the Lord with prayer. Pray for them daily to be filled and led by the Spirit. Pray for them to be secure in their Savior Jesus. Pray for them to find their confidence in Christ. Pray for them to place their total trust in God. Pray for them to hope in heaven and provide hope on earth. Pray for them to worship God with a fresh faith and a pure heart. Pray for them to share their burdens and be accountable. Pray for them to pray. You serve your servants best by prayer. Prayer is an act of worship and love. Prayed for people pull through by faith. Prayed for people feel loved. Pray about how to best serve the precious servants of God in your life. Sincerely serve them, as this gives them staying power and praying power. Above all this honors the Lord's servant, and Almighty God.

The Bible says, "The elders who direct the affairs of the church well are worthy of double honor, especially those whose work is preaching and teaching...The worker deserves his wages" (1 Timothy 5:17, 18b).

TREASURED POSSESSION

D13

"For you are a people holy to the Lord your God. The Lord your God has chosen you out of all the peoples on the face of the earth to be his people, his treasured possession."
DEUTERONOMY 7:6

God followers are His chosen and treasured possession. If you are possessed by God, you are treasured by God. Of all the people on the face of the earth, you were set apart by Almighty God when you believed in Jesus. He looks at you differently since you were saved by His grace. Your value proposition increased dramatically once you trusted Christ as the propitiation for your sin. Your salvation was not a casual exchange in beliefs. It was your crucifixion and your resurrection. Your old way of living died, and the Holy Spirit brought you to life in Christ. It was a transformation of your character to His. When you surrendered to the Lord, you gave up all rights to be right. No longer do we lean on your own understanding, but you cling to Christ for His. You are eternally possessed and valued by God.

Do not underestimate God's valuation on your life. The world may scoff at your faith, and even call it foolish to worship your unseen God. Their valuations on faith are foreign currency to them. Unbelievers have no baseline for belief, so they devalue and ignore followers of Jesus as irrelevant and antiquated. Enemies of your Savior may seek to play down your commitment to discipleship as fanatical, and a phase you are "going through". But don't rate your religion based on how others value your faith. People with bankrupt beliefs have little regard for those who practice a robust religion. Your self-worth flows from faith in your heavenly Father. Look to Jesus for affirmation and validation. He is your source of strength and security.

Let Almighty God appraise your life and work. His appraisal of you is off the chart in eternal valuations. Your increased value to the Lord is not based on a 3% annual inflation rate. Your increased value to the Lord is based on how much He has of you. So, surrender everything to Him. Surrender your worries. Surrender your spouse. Surrender your work. Surrender your family. Surrender your fears. The more you give over to Him the more valuable you become. The value of your life's stock increases the more of you He possesses. You are His precious child and treasured possession. Like gold and silver is to this world, much more you are to God. He loves you. God is your owner.

Therefore it is imperative you refer often to His owner's manual, the Bible, on what to learn and how to live. Following Jesus is a lifetime of obedience and growth. You never arrive, but only graduate to new opportunities for faith. So give it all up for God. You are His and His alone. Value yourself as He does, more precious than all the wealth of this world. You can hold your head up because you are His. You are a child of the King. In Christ you experience true riches. See yourself as God does, as a reflection of His son Jesus. You are His valued possession, holy and His.

The Bible says, "For he chose us in him before the creation of the world to be holy and blameless in his sight. In love he predestined us to be adopted as his sons through Jesus Christ, in accordance with his pleasure and will"(Ephesians 1:4-5).

D14 ARROGANT DEFIANCE

"So I told you, but you would not listen. You rebelled against the Lord's command and in your arrogance you marched up into the hill country." DEUTERONOMY 1:43

Arrogant defiance destroys our fellowship with God. It destroys our relationships with people. It destroys our security. It destroys our peace. Arrogant defiance doesn't listen to reason because it already has everything figured out. It is a caricature of confidence, and acts like it has it all together, but in reality struggles in fear. Arrogant defiance laughs at warnings and ignores wise counsel. It strikes fear into anyone who gets in its way, and plows ahead without regard to the collateral damage it inflicts. Relational and financial wreckage is in its wake, before it finally awakens. Arrogant defiance may seem sincere, but sincerity betrays its hurling forward into foolish activities. It may finally wake up to reality only to find itself defeated and crushed under the weight of unwise decisions.

This is the dark side of driven leaders. You can become intoxicated with power, and think you are invincible because of past success. In fact, your pride can feed you the lie that your past - success guarantees your future success. Pride can blind you to the need for teachability. Pride breeds an arrogant attitude void of accountability. It is a deadly combination that leads to a devastating character flaw. Don't think you have it all together. None of us do. We all need the benefit of prayer and wise counsel. There is no need to plow ahead without prayer. A door may be open but it does not mean you need to walk through. A door may be closed. Be patient. Do not force it open with manipulation or man power. Take the time to pray and exercise due diligence. Let God lead you.

The Lord does not underestimate the enemy. He knows what it takes to defeat Satan, sin and self. He knows whether you are ready or not to move forward in faith. Just because He used a similar scenario in the past to propagate His will, does not mean He will use the same pattern going forward. He will provide the needed resources, relationships and wisdom. It may be the responsibility of being the spiritual leader of your home. He has a mentor in the wings for you to learn from, do not go at it alone. It may be the issue of fear that needs to be conquered in Christ by faith. It may be the fruit of humility you need in your heart. After all, humility may be the greatest weapon feared by the enemy. Humility positions you to receive God's grace.

Therefore lean heavily on the Lord before you lead others. Your leadership and influence affects more people than you realize. Their safety and security has been entrusted to you by Almighty God. Be courageous, but temper it with wisdom. Be a visionary, but lead in patient humility. A humble spirit defeats arrogant defiance. Surrender to your Savior and the enemy will see you're serious. Arrogant defiance will be conquered with the help of your heavenly Father. Stay if He says stay. Go if He says go.

Above all else, exercise grace, patience, courage, faith and humility. An individual conquered by Christ is able to conquer the enemy's strongholds. Submission to your Savior defies arrogance!

> "If a man has recently married, he must not be sent to war or have any other duty laid on him. For one year he is to be free to stay at home and bring happiness to the wife he has married." DEUTERONOMY 24:5

Newly married couples need to focus intently on each other. Your first year of marriage sets the stage for the following years. If you get off to a rocky start you will carry those wounds into subsequent years. Marriage is meant to be a marathon not a sprint, so do not short-change yourselves starting out. Be intentional in your intimacy and seeking to understand each other. At the outset of marriage there are fewer distractions that divert you from getting to know each other. Now is the time to learn how to love and serve one another, because marriage in the beginning begs for more time and attention. It is your opportunity to have an all out interest in each other. Marriage isn't meant to get leftovers of energy, communication and intimacy. An unattended marriage is like a garden without a gardener. As time passes neglect produces a crop of weeds that choke out the fruits and vegetables. A mismanaged garden lacks a meaningful harvest, so it is in marriage, without planting seeds of love, cultivating patience, and weeding out selfishness. Your first year of marriage is an opportunity to store up a barn full of good memories. Serve unselfishly and see God work, for your wedding was only the beginning of His good work.

Moreover, make the first year of marriage a focus on God. Use this time to study the Bible and its teachings of how to be a husband and how to be a wife. As the husband, take the lead as spiritual leader of your home. Grow in your confidence to be Christ's servant to your spouse. She needs you to lead on behalf of the Lord. For example, collaborate with her with meaningful conversation, and pray daily with her and for her. Go to church with her, take sermon notes, and engage in worship with praise and adoration of Almighty God. Do not allow work to overwhelm your marriage, if it does you may need a new job. As the wife, be patient with your husband's career for work can preoccupy a man unwittingly. He needs you to help him set boundaries around business.

Above all else, love each other unconditionally, forgive liberally, and serve unselfishly. Embrace and celebrate differences, think the best of the other's intentions and try to out serve each other. Apply these disciplines and you are off to a good start in your marriage. If you have been married for any length of time, do not despair if you are not there yet. You may have messed up that first year like many of us did. You can still stop bad habits and start new ones. It may be harder now that time has hardened your heart in some areas, so take a marriage inventory and ask the Lord to lead both of you to a new level of love. Go on a second honeymoon and spend significant time wooing one another.

Place your marriage above the children and work. Mandate quantity and quality time for your marriage with daily conversation and weekly dates. Abandon yourself to your marriage as if it were your first year. Live in anticipation and excitement to what Almighty God is up to for you. Minister to each other in your marriage, and your marriage will become a ministry to others. Stay focused on your marriage with the intensity of that first year. Ask God to move your marriage forward for Him. Marriage is meant to be a picture of our relationship with Jesus, so grow old together joyfully, always learning how to love better.

The Bible teaches, "Let him kiss me with the kisses of his mouth—for your love is more delightful than wine"(Song of Solomon 1:2).

D16 ADJUST PLANS

"David inquired of the Lord, and He answered, 'Do not go straight up, but circle around behind them and attack them in front of the balsam trees.' "
2 SAMUEL 5:23

Many time plans are made to be adjusted. The Lord is in the business of leading and guiding us through the planning process of discovery. It is imperative that we remain nimble and flexible to His leadership. What worked yesterday, may not work tomorrow. Prayerfully seeking the wisdom of God is the GPS (Global Positioning System) needed to define His process and locate His destination. Do not be afraid to scrap the old plan, and script a new one. God delights in leading you in through the informal back door, and not necessarily the formality of the front door. What your friend experienced may be just the opposite of your experience. This is why it is wise to follow Christ's critical path. The path of Jesus may seem perilous, but you can be guaranteed His presence is in the middle of your planned adjustments. If you remain bound by your plan, you may miss the freedom of His. Man sets the plan, but the Lord extracts it from his heart, though it may not seem logical at the moment. Yes, it is somewhat embarrassing to change course for the umpteenth time. However, better to make a midcourse correction and suffer a little shame, than to wait too long and be humiliated by stubbornness. God's best many times is not a direct linear path; He is most creative in leading us on a trail of trust.

The plan of God requires ongoing prayer that asks Him to purify your motives and clarify His plan. Ask Christ to confirm your coordinates with His direction. Whatever path you are blazing, He has been there before. It is typically harder to discern God's best when you are encountering someone or something for the very first time. There are many unknowns, and so many opportunities to pursue. So over-apply due diligence by not rushing into first-time experiences with blind optimism. If you do, you might regret it. Trying to rush God's will is frustrating, and will cause you to fret. God's will, reflected upon ,and clarified, is encouraging and will cause you to rest. It is okay to change today, if He has amended what He told you yesterday. Just make sure the Holy Spirit is guiding your steps.

Lastly, it is not unusual to discover His best over a process of time. If you make His minor adjustments daily, your recourse does not seem as radical. If you refuse to discern His plan daily, then one day you will wake up in need of a revolutionary reaction. So much so perhaps, that you scare people away. So, be wise to let God lead you down what may be the unconventional road of His will. Inform others along the way so they are not surprised by any sudden change. Humility is willing to allow the Lord to lead in a different direction. Wisdom is able to get it done, while leading others to do the same. Expect the plan to need adjustment, and trust God with the outcome. Adjustable plans are the best laid plans. Hold your plan with an open hand, which rests in the hand of the Lord.

The Bible teaches, "We humans keep brainstorming options and plans, but GOD'S purpose prevails"(Proverbs 19:21, The Message).

BRIDGE BUILDER

"Like water spilled on the ground, which cannot be recovered, so we must die. But God does not take away life; instead, He devises ways so that the banished person may not remain estranged from Him." 2 Samuel 14:14

Sometimes people do dumb, stupid, and even shameful things. Their unwise choices may have inflicted great harm, and even compounded into calamity and crisis. They are foolish because they chose to inflict pain, when they knew better. Sin has caused them to suspend their good sense and Biblical worldview for a season. It is a season of misery and messiness. They are confused, alone, and humiliated. However, they may not be at a point to admit their mistakes, but deep down in their soul there is a wondering of how much they have disappointed God, and those who love them the most. They feel banished and betrayed for sin does complicate matters, and now they are caught in a web of deceit that will not let them go. They have lost perspective and seem to be swirling down into a spiritual and a relational malaise. Not only are they estranged from their loved ones; they are estranged from their heavenly Father.

Separation from God is a lonely place. You can know for certain that your estranged loved one is conflicted, confused and bitter. It is the love of God and your love that will bring them back to their senses. Sin has confused them and they have lost their bearings, but you know the way. It may take a third party to counsel you and coach you through this process of reaching out, but do not underestimate the effectiveness of your ability to build a relational bridge.

Relational bridge-building is not easy, and it takes time. But it can become necessary to woo the wandering one back home. Yes, they have made their bed, and now they are sleeping between its twin sheets of fear and insecurity. However, the bridge you are building leads to a bed of acceptance and peace. This current war of words is in need of a cease fire. No one wins over a vicious and venomous volley of blame. Instead, a bridge-builder prays; he prays to first be changed. They accept blame, and replace perceived rejection with action-oriented acceptance. A bridge-builder calls, writes, and sends gifts of encouragement, and even takes the initiative to over-communicate. A bridge-builder seeks to understand, and then love the estranged one, at their point of need.

Maybe your child is living with an undesirable roommate. Reach out and get to know this person who is negatively influencing your son or daughter. By God's grace become the influencer of the influencer. Invite them into your home and love them to God. Let your home become a magnet of grace that draws them into a reminder of what's good and right. The bridge you build may not be used immediately. But just its presence speaks volumes to your availability, care, and compassion. One day circumstances will unravel for your estranged loved one. When it does, you want your bridge of love and acceptance starring them right in the face. Stay faithful as a relational bridge-builder, like the cross of Christ is God's bridge to you. The cross you bear is your bridge to broken people, so continue to pray and pursue this Christ-honoring outcome.

The Bible teaches, "All this is from God, who reconciled us to himself through Christ and gave us the ministry of reconciliation"(2 Corinthians 5:18).

D18 EXTEND KINDNESS

" 'Don't be afraid,' David said to him, 'for I will surely show you kindness for the sake of your father Jonathan. I will restore to you all the land that belonged to your grandfather Saul, and you will always eat at my table.' "   2 SAMUEL 9:7

Kindness is a killer application for the Christian. It is killer in the good sense of the word. Kindness kills fear and replaces it with hope. It kills insecurity and replaces it with security. It kills rejection and replaces it with acceptance. It kills pride and replaces it with humility. Kindness kills the bad, so the good can have room to grow. Like the effect of Roundup™ on unwanted weeds, kindness cuts to the root of sin, and infects it with grace and love. As a follower of Jesus, what compels you the most is the gargantuan kindness He has bestowed upon you. Undeserved, you were captured by the kindness of God. He captured your mind and, in the process, flooded it with kind thoughts toward others, even your adversaries. He captured your mouth, and filled it with kind words of affirmation and encouragement, extending them to those thirsting for verbal kindness. He captured your behavior, converted it with other-centeredness, so now you are guilty of random acts of kindness. Everything about you has the potential to exude kindness, because God is, and has been, kind to you. You can count on the kindness of God leading you and others to repentance. Kill others with kindness, and watch God bring them alive.

Gratitude to God for His kindness is a sterling reason to extend kindness to others. However, gratitude also results from our horizontal relationships. You feel compelled to be kind to a family member of a friend, because of the kindness they extended to your child or spouse. Kindness and gratitude are first cousins. When you are grateful, you search for people and ways to extend kindness. It may be a graduation gift, your presence at a wedding, or a hand-written 'thank you' note. You want to support those who support you, and those whom you love. Kindness has this powerful effect on people to care. It is the gift that keeps on giving. It seems you cannot pay forward enough with kindness. No one has ever complained of receiving too much kindness. You cannot overdose anyone on kindness. On the contrary it is healing and wholesome.

Kindness is a picture of Christ. It is not only godly, it is God-like. Therefore, diffuse the rumblings of harsh words and replace them with kind ones. Otherwise, you can say the right words in an unkind way, and defeat your purpose of being open and honest. People cannot hear what you say, if the manner in which you communicate is unkind. A kind delivery of hard words has a much higher probability of acceptance. Kindness comes from a grateful and prayerful heart that is focused on Christ. You cannot help but be kind when you are captured by divine kindness. Extend the quality of kindness that has been extended to you.

For Christ sake, we can be kind to one another. The Bible teaches, "Make sure that nobody pays back wrong for wrong, but always try to be kind to each other and to everyone else"(I Thessalonians 5:15).

> "During his lifetime Absalom had taken a pillar and erected it in the King's Valley
> as a monument to himself... Absalom's head got caught in the tree.
> He was left hanging in midair, while the mule he was riding kept on going."
> 2 SAMUEL 18:18A, 18:9B

Ego has the propensity to hang you out to dry. It snares your soul, as an enlarged ego tends to shrivel your heart. Ego entangles a man's motives around self-interest and self-credit. An ego has an insatiable desire for recognition and power. It is sad to watch. Its need for accolades is an adolescent attitude at its worst. An unchecked ego is your enemy that will lead you down pitiful paths of regret. Left to its own devices, your ego will talk you into things that feel good in the moment, but have humiliation as a final destination. An out-of-control ego exaggerates self-importance, and creates conceit.

Conceit and Christ-centered living are mutually exclusive. Either Jesus is calling the shots, or Jesus is just a front for an ego-infested life. Unless my Christian vocabulary and behavior is void of ego, I am just using God to get my way for my benefit and my glory. E-G-O stands for edging God out. It is all about me. Evangelism driven by ego is a cheap way to solicit converts to Christ. Teaching, motivated by ego, is shallow and sentimental, even if the words are accurate and deep. Leaders led by ego insist on having their way. Everyone recognizes ego's effect, except the one mastered by its deception. Diffuse ego's illusion with truth, before it implodes your life.

Humility, accompanied by confession of your need for God and people, will pin it to the ground so you can then walk unencumbered with Christ. The Holy Spirit takes a submitted ego and transforms it into effective eternal results. So, allow God to daily bend your ego toward Him. Eventually, His influence will develop habits in your life that channel the energies of your ego into Kingdom pursuits. Joy in living becomes service to others and intimacy with your heavenly Father. Money, power, recognition, and control all fade in importance. What becomes valuable is pointing people to Jesus. Your motivations become mercy, humility, and justice.

Ego says yes to self, humility says no. Ego says yes to power, ego says no. Ego says yes to fame, humility says no. Ego says yes to always being right, humility says no. Ego says look at me, humility defers to Jesus. Ego erects monuments to man, humility builds the Kingdom of God. Do not allow your ego to estrange you from eternity.

Die today to your ego, and live for Christ. Seek-out others to forgive, and others from whom you can ask forgiveness. You can make the first move in forgiveness, because you have nothing to lose and everything to gain. Pride feeds ego, and humility starves it. So, harness your ego to the hull of heaven's ship, as an eternal perspective edges out ego. Let Christ convert your ego from a liability that's loathed...to an asset that's admired.

The Bible says this about Moses; "He regarded disgrace for the sake of Christ as of greater value than the treasures of Egypt, because he was looking ahead to his reward" (Hebrews 11:26).

D20 EXHORT TO ENCOURAGE

"You love those who hate you and hate those who love you. You have made it clear today that the commanders and their men mean nothing to you. I see that you would be pleased if Absalom were alive today and all of us were dead. Now go and encourage your men…"

2 SAMUEL 19:6-7A

It is easy to obsess over your agenda and forget to encourage those closest to you. Your attention and energy gets so wrapped up in your needs that the needs of others vanish from your interest. It can become a love-hate relationship. You can love more what you don't have, to the neglect of what you do have. Those who know you best do not feel the love. In some cases they may interpret your absence of attention as hate. You have friends who love you, some who would even die for you. How valuable is that? Your family admires and respects you. They have been patient with you during times of distraction. Your health is robust and business is good, so refocus and reengage with reality.

A good place to start is by encouraging those who have remained loyal and committed during your time of disengagement. They have been true and faithful to you and to the Lord. Let them know, in no uncertain terms, how grateful you are for them. You can tell them with a barrage of verbal encouragement, or show them with acts of service. Take the time to make the coffee or dispose of the trash. Begin a systematic process of rewarding behavior that exemplifies the values of the enterprise. Whatever you do, do not be hesitant to shower with appreciation and affirmation. No one can be encouraged too much, but be ever mindful of not giving enough encouragement.

Family members and work associates slug away daily in the grind of the mundane. You are uniquely positioned as an influencer in their life. Use the influence of your smile to solicit a smile back. Spend your relational capital to ask others in your network to encourage your friend with an opportunity, gift or words of wisdom. What you have is for the benefit of others. If you do not take the time to encourage them, they will go to someone who will. Your teenage child needs your encouragement. They may act cool and self-sufficient, but they want you to pursue them with radical encouragement. Schedule a bi-weekly dinner just to listen to the heart of your child. Listening and understanding allows you to apply encouragement at their greatest point of need.

Lastly, encourage by asking questions. Proper questioning communicates care. People do not need more answers to irrelevant questions. People need to be encouraged to define the right questions, and then discover God's answers. This may be the most effective way to encourage someone. Always point them back to God and His game plan. God's vast reservoir of encouragement is virtually untapped. Human encouragement is finite; heaven's is infinite. Therefore, encourage others to engage with eternity. Your heavenly Father's encouragement is everlasting. Your encouragement is good, but His is great. So, be relentless in encouraging others to go from good to great. Be encouraged to encourage.

The Bible says, "But encourage one another daily, as long as it is called Today, so that none of you may be hardened by sin's deceitfulness" (Hebrews 3:13).

POSITIONED FOR BLESSING

"He is like a tree planted by streams of water, which yields its fruit in season and whose leaf does not wither. Whatever he does prospers." Psalm 1:3

Blessing looks for those who are in a position of dependency on Almighty God. This is wise positioning for a Jesus-follower. We are blessed when the roots of our faith draw from the waters of God's Word. It is when we take the time to plant our faith by the banks of God's living water that we come alive. This is where the fruits of humility, honesty, and humor grow. The water of God nurtures us like liquid vitamins. The cheap soda of self-dependence will only slow down our faith walk. It's the water of God that hydrates our souls, not man's generic substitutes. We may attempt to plant our lives next to a stream of self-sufficiency only to find ourselves thirsting. It is the water of God's Word that we are to drink day and night, because it creates abundant life. The effects of God's Word are not always immediately evident. It takes time for it to make its way into the root system of our beliefs.

But eventually, an eternal perspective begins to take shape, as we become saturated in the Word of God. Plant your life close to an understanding and an application of Scripture. The Bible is your baseline for belief and behavior. When God sees someone who is immersed in the principles of His word, He has found someone He can trust with His blessings. He extends His best to those who are planted next to the truth of His Word. He trusts those who trust Him. He bears fruit though those who depend on Him.

The fruit of a faithful life flourishes over time. Your influence compounds as you follow Christ. It may seem like you are in an insignificant season. This is not true. All seasons with your Savior are significant. You may live in a confusing season, but your confusion is Christ's opportunity to bring clarity. This is a significant time for your faith to bear fruit. Faithfulness brings clarity during uncertain times. Do not wish away this season, as it is a time for you to go deep with Him. It is on the anvil of adversity that appreciation and gratitude are forged. You may thrive in a season of prosperity, and it is tempting to walk away from God and continue on your own. But in doing so, you leave the spirit of humility, and dependency on God. He brought you this far. So stay faithful as your finances flourish, and more aggressive in your generous giving. Live for the Lord, not for yourself.

The blessing of God's fruit comes when you avoid the advice of the wicked, and cling to the counsel of Christ and His followers. The wicked try to define a better way. They want to lead you astray. But Jesus is the way. You cannot improve on Christ.

Faith in Him is not always flashy, but it bears the fruit that matters. It is the fruit of children who honor their parents. It is the fruit of fidelity between husbands and wives. It is the fruit of an unselfish friendship. It is the fruit of a caring culture at work, home, and church. It is the fruit of wise and generous giving. It is the fruit of fearing God and having a friend in Jesus. Therefore, by faith stay in a position to be blessed. Wise positioning invites God's blessing. Prosperity is looking for those who depend on the Lord.

The Bible says, "Blessed is the man who makes the LORD his trust..."(Psalm 40:4).

D22 INTIMACY TRUSTS

"Those who know your name will trust in you, for you, Lord, have never forsaken those who seek you." PSALM 9:10

Intimacy trusts. This is the outcome of knowing God. Knowledge is best when it exercises itself against the name of God. His name is above every name. It is at the name of Jesus that every knee will bow and confess Him as Lord. It is much better and much more desirable to know His name this side of eternity. No name is close to carrying the weight, reverence, respect, devotion and influence than the Lord Jesus Christ. By knowing His name, we begin to understand the attributes of the Almighty. Patience, peace, holiness, love, discipline, mercy, and grace all emanate from the name of Jehovah our one and only God of creation. Because we know Him, we trust Him. Because we trust Him, we want to know Him deeper and more fully.

Faith is an intelligent grace. There can be knowledge without faith, but there can be no faith without knowledge. Knowledge carries the torch before faith and illuminates its path. Paul defined his faith experience when he proclaimed, "For I know whom I have believed" (I Timothy 1:12). A blind faith is as bad as a dead faith. Our heavenly Father desires for us to have an informed faith. Devout ignorance confuses and makes wrong assumptions. It misses intimacy because it is based on a caricature of Christ. Know Him and you will trust Him. He is there for us to seek Him. By faith, you find Jehovah, Jireh, Elohim, Shaddai, Adonai and Yahweh. Intimacy trusts when it rests in Almighty God.

Intimacy trusts because there is a bond of belief that cannot be broken. When we wrap our thread of faith around the mooring of our Master, we are secure. No storm of life will cause us to stray because we are anchored in Him. We trust Him because He is utterly and thoroughly trustworthy. His name has never been soiled by sin. Jesus is not only a good name, it is a great name. His name is wonderful. His name is beautiful. His name is to be honored and cherished because He is our God. Feel free to drop His name often to those that need encouragement or rebuke. No need to hold back the name of Jesus. Yes, mention His name with grace, but not apologetically. His name is who we trust. We point people beyond ourselves to One who is much, much more capable. We name the name of Christ.

Lastly, intimacy with individuals is trusting. This is the nature of intimacy with God or man. You cannot get to know someone authentically, and not be positioned to trust them. If their genuine self overwhelms you with hypocrisy, you will lose respect and trust. But when you get close to genuine followers of Jesus, you see beyond their quirks. You appreciate their uniqueness and embrace their differences. You honor them for being who they are, and you better understand each other's world. You begin to honor and respect those you get to know. Not only do we love them, we respect them. You get beyond your biases, and you believe in them.

Intimacy trusts. The Bible says, "May the God of hope fill you with all joy and peace as you trust in him, so that you may overflow with hope by the power of the Holy Spirit" (Romans 15:13).

"You save the humble but bring low those whose eyes are haughty." Psalm 18:27

Humility is the doorway into God's salvation. It is an entrée into an exciting life with the Lord. God saves the humble, but brings low the haughty. He lifts up the humble in heart, and brings down the haughty. A haughty look may be masked for a while but, eventually, it comes out. The face is a direct reflection of the heart. Our countenance can be hard and uninviting, or it can be soft and accepting. The haughty find it hard to take responsibility for their ill will and anger. They blame others while becoming victims of their own pride. Haughty eyes have blurred vision of God, and shy away from serving people. It is all about 'what's in it for me?' It stiff-arms our Savior. The eyes of the haughty are cold, callous and distant. They are consumed with themselves with only a faint remembrance of Christ. They don't remember what they wish to forget. Haughtiness forgets humility. However, this comes back to haunt the haughty.

Humility, on the other hand, woos the blessings of God. It has bountiful benefits. God's presence permeates an environment of humility. It is an atmosphere of humility that engages the Almighty. The Lord looks out for the family or work associates that value humility. He saves them from unwise decision making and irresponsible living. He saves them from themselves. Humility also encourages honesty. It encourages honesty about our dreams and disappointments. It recognizes the tremendous need for God to consummate the vision, and, as we depend on God, we see Him work. Humility also learns how to process disappointments. There is an acknowledgement of anger, and the need for healing. God saves the humble from bitterness, and replaces it with brokenness.

Humility benefits relationships. It is a lubricant for love, and the fuel of forgiveness. A humble heart helps husbands and wives learn how to compliment each other's strengths and weaknesses. It cultivates appreciation of each other's differences, and spurns its irritation. It checks our conversations before we position ourselves for a win/lose dialogue. Humility first understands, and then seeks to be understood. Humility is a prerequisite for relational success. It diffuses pride and inflates patience. Humility is quick to honor and slow to blame. It keeps us in the good graces of God, and people.

Lastly, run from false humility formed out of fear, deception, and pride. Instead, cultivate authentic humility through prayer, honesty, and community. Surrender daily to your Savior with a sense of overwhelming dependence on Him. We are to submit on our knees so He doesn't have to bring us to our knees. Humility is conceived in an honest heart, one that understands its limitations. It is comfortable with its strengths and its weaknesses, and not afraid to speak up and not stifle its emotions.

Furthermore, humility is best harnessed among a Christ-centered community. Let people you respect into your life. Otherwise, "a companion of fools suffers harm" (Proverbs 13:20). Haughtiness is hurtful. Humility is beneficial, so sign up for its benefits.

The Bible says, "You save the humble, but your eyes are on the haughty to bring them low"(2 Samuel 22:28).

D24 FIRST CHRISTMAS

"Today in the town of David a Savior has been born to you; he is Christ the Lord.
This will be a sign to you: You will find a baby wrapped in cloths and lying in a manger."
LUKE 2:10-11

The focus of the first Christmas was Jesus. It was His day. There was no competition from commercialism seeking economic gain. The gifts were given to Him. God was the recipient of gratitude and generosity. He was glorified on this day of salvation for all who would come to believe in Jesus as God's only son. There was an anxious appreciation for the Almighty's descent into the decadence of humanity. There was no feuding from other faiths jockeying for position to be in the spotlight of the Savior. On the contrary, there was a religious respect and humble worship from those who traveled great distances from their diversified origins of belief. On this day Jesus unified sincere seekers of truth.

The first Christmas, however, was not without controversy. Politically, He was a lightening rod (some things never change). Government leaders felt threatened, as if a traitor had infiltrated their influence over the masses. Involuntary spies were sent to validate His presence. Once His birth had been verified, the powers-that-be went to work. Insecurity and fear drive people to commit irrational acts, and this was no exception. So what started as a celestial coronation for the Prince of Peace, ended with jealous leaders taking severe and deadly action. The Christ child was driven from their pitiful, but powerful presence. They destroyed other God-fearing people in the process. The community was cast into chaos when Christ was removed from their culture.

We can learn from the first Christmas to keep Christ central in worship and society. He is the wonder of our worship. He is the reason for our giving gifts. It is because we celebrate His birthday that we pause to pray, reflect, and plan to follow His will in a more robust and intentional manner. Our Master came to earth, and made Himself like man. He took on the form of a servant though He could have crowned Himself as King. He pointed us to the love and forgiveness of His heavenly Father. The Christ-child was born of a virgin. He was God who dwelt among us, but sometimes we forget Him, even on His birthday.

One reason we have failed to keep Christ in Christmas is we have failed to keep Him in some of our churches. Why should the culture embrace the Christ of Christmas, when some of our churches have marginalized their Master? Let's start by inviting the Almighty back into our churches with fresh and revitalized reverence in worship, evangelism and discipleship. Let's prayerfully and responsibly only 'lay hands' on leaders who fear God, hate sin, love people, and teach the Bible. Christmas is losing its luster for the Lord, because Christians have forgotten to fear God.

His birth is only significant if His death and resurrection are significant. The Christ of Christmas becomes compelling when we as followers flock to Him in faithfulness and obedience. Let all of us who name the name of Jesus revisit Him in the awe, and worship of that first Christmas. Let's exclaim with enthusiasm to a hurting world that He has come to heal broken hearts and revive sick souls. We unapologetically celebrate His birthday with passion because God is with us. He is transforming us into the likeness of His son. Let's make this Christmas like the first Christmas. Let's invite the Holy Spirit to fill our hearts with forgiveness, joy, hope, peace, and love while we worship our Lord together. The first Christmas fuels our faith and recalibrates us to Christ!

"Today in the town of David a Savior has been born to you; he is Christ the Lord… Suddenly a great company of the heavenly host appeared with the angel, praising God and saying, 'Glory to God in the highest, and on earth peace to men on whom his favor rests.'"
LUKE 2:11, 13-14

The birth of Jesus is meant to be a grand celebration. The angels in heaven accompanied by a celestial choir kicked off Christ's coming out party. It was something to behold. It was not a passive holiday greeting. It was instead a bold and jubilant MERRY CHRISTMAS! It was merry because there was a festive spirit in the air. Eternal God had come to meager man. Our Creator came face-to-face to correspond with us and care for us. The celebratory scene in heaven cascaded toward earth and crashed upon unsuspecting shepherds. God started his gleeful disclosure with those whose labor illustrated His heart. Shepherds knew shepherding. So, now the Great Shepherd Jesus had come. The flock of His fellow man could dance a merry jig, because Mary was with child. So, this is another rip-roaring righteous reason for followers of Christ to exclaim, MERRY CHRISTMAS!

Eventually, Mary was overtaken by gratitude to God for being chosen by God. But in the beginning of God's revelation to her, she experienced disbelief. She felt she did not deserve this type of recognition or honor. But, she later gave in to God. It was not about her. It was about her baby Jesus. He would save the world from their sin, and she would serve as the surrogate mother of God. Once she took all this in she suddenly exploded in praise and adoration to God. Mary's manifesto toward being chosen by God, still shouts, MERRY CHRISTMAS, 2,000 years later! How many more opportunities today do you and I have to exclaim gratitude to God? He has chosen us, therefore by faith Christ indwells us. This intimacy with the Almighty drives us to our knees in appreciation and awe. Because of this heart-felt joy, our life and lips cannot help but announce to a wandering world, MERRY CHRISTMAS, MERRY CHRISTMAS, and many more MERRY CHRISTMAS. Yes, you too, can experience a MERRY CHRISTMAS!

We can be merry because of Mary. Mary's submission and obedience has given mankind the opportunity to be merry. MERRY CHRISTMAS for the grateful follower of Christ is like breathing. It is as natural as saying hello or goodbye. It is the vernacular of the forgiven.

So, be valiant with your gracious greeting, MERRY CHRISTMAS. Indeed, trying to refrain a Christian (especially on the birthday of Jesus) from being merry, is like telling a child who just received a favorite toy to cease from joy and laughter. It is not possible. It is ludicrous to think one or many can stop Jesus followers from celebrating his birthday with a MERRY CHRISTMAS. We are merry Christians because it is a MERRY CHRISTMAS! We are jolly, joyous and jovial, because we are merry. We are cheerful and effervescent, because we are merry.

You cannot take Merry out of Christmas any more than you can take Thanks out of Giving. It is un-American. It is dishonoring for the one for whom it is intended. Therefore, be merry so indeed your MERRY CHRISTMAS is authentic and inviting. It is good to not take MERRY CHRISTMAS for granted, because it reminds us to not take God for granted. Be merry this Christmas. He is.

Merry Christmas to all, and to all a grace-filled life!

D26 HEART DESIRE

"May he give you the desire of your heart and make all your plans succeed."
PSALM 20:4

Desire determines focus. We desire food when hungry and then we romance a nice meal. We desire water when thirsty and then we guzzle cool liquid refreshment. We desire sex for pleasure and procreation, so we get married and grow in intimacy. We desire for people to like us, so we serve them at their point of need. We desire financial freedom, so we work hard and smart, and save money. We desire love and respect, so we give love and respect.

Desire can be good or bad. We can desire fame for ego's sake. This is a dangerous desire. We can desire a physical relationship outside of marriage or with someone other than our spouse. This destroys respect for ourselves, and the respect of others toward us. We become consumed with selfish desires, and then discover we are all alone. The best heart desires are those conceived by heaven then birthed from our heart into God's will.

Our heart desires need a Christ-centered context. Otherwise they drift toward selfishness and self-centeredness. Heart desires without a rudder of righteousness meander, and become meaningless to what matters most. Right heart desires submit to authorities. Above all else, they surrender to the authority of Almighty God. It is impossible for an untamed heart to totally trust God. An untamed heart still wants to call the shots and include God as needed. This is a recipe for unhealthy desires. If anyone had the potential to strike out on His own without God's input, it was Jesus. But even Jesus said, "Yet not as I will, but as you will" (Matthew 26:39). He eagerly desired to eat the Passover meal with His friends before He suffered (Luke 22:15). When God's desire is first and foremost, then our desires align with His desires.

How do we align our heart desires with His desires? It first lines up with God's individual purpose for your life. Start with the general purpose of bringing glory to Him. Do your speech, conduct, attitude and vocation bring glory to Jesus? Do you leverage your roles in life for the glory of God? Do you seek to be an employee who brings glory to God in your work so He will use that to evangelize your associates? Your character development will draw them to Christ. Your unconditional love for the lost will draw them to salvation.

Start with the great desire for God's glory. Then, within the context of Christ-centeredness, define your other desires. His vocational purpose for you may be to become an excellent lawyer, student, minister, homemaker, athlete, or technician. Wherever your labor, execute your employment for God's glory. After you have prayerfully planned out your desires, trust God for their success. He is the one that brings our plans to fruition. A farmer knows how to plow and plant, but it is God who causes the crop to grow. You create the best plan by faith, and then ask the Holy Spirit to ignite it into action.

Wake-up every morning and invite your Savior's desires into your heart, and by God's grace watch your plans succeed!

> "Even though I walk through the valley of the shadow of death, I will fear no evil,
> for you are with me; your rod and your staff, they comfort me."
> PSALM 23:4

Fear engages an ongoing assault on our heart and mind. If left unchecked, fear can whip up our imagination into a frenzy of anxiety. Though only an ounce of what we fear may come to pass, we tend to give it a ton of attention. It is madness when we are overcome by fear. It may be the fear of death that dilutes our faith. It may be the fear of failure that drives us to control. It may be the fear of rejection that keeps us from speaking up. It may be the fear of financial ruin that refrains us from risk-taking. It may be the fear of divorce that shatters our dreams of a fulfilling family. It may be the fear of losing a job that becomes a self-fulfilling prophecy. Whatever fears preoccupy our thinking, we are not alone.

Jesus walks with us through our valleys. He may not deliver us out of the valley, but He most certainly does not abandon us in the valley. He walks with us through the valley of doubt. He walks with us through the valley of shame. He walks with us through the valley of transition. He walks with us through the valley of disease. He walks with us through the valley of the shadow of death. Our fear many times is but a shadow of Satan's. It seems like reality, but it is not. It is but a reflection of the evil one. So we have no need to fear because our heavenly Father casts His long light of love. A shadow assumes a light.

Therefore, the light of Christ is there to guide us through the shadows of our soul. Death stands next to our path of life and attempts to cast a shadow, but the light of heaven guides our way. We trust Jesus and overcome fear. We trust the Lord with the known and the unknown. There may be consequences from relational baggage that we still unpack from our past. This is fruit from foolish choices for which we have to take responsibility and trust God. Good can still come out of unwise actions, but good is gained as we regain our trust in Christ. In our valleys, we can forget our faith and be consumed by our fears, or we can slow down and let the Lord love us through this time of loss.

No amount of pain can separate you from the love of God. Pain may be smothering your soul, but do not give up on God. Immerse yourself in the Psalms where David sometimes drowns in doubt. But by faith, wisely lifts an arm to the Lord. No one suffers well alone. It is with the Almighty and the prayers of others that we make it through. So go to Christ for comfort. His tools of trust invite us. He repairs our broken spirit with His rod and His staff. He comforts our crushed heart with His caring touch. At the very least, the Lord will bring clarity to your confusion. Saturate your soul with truth and you will flush out your fears. Trust Him as you face your fears, whether of death or life.

Trust in Christ is a bridge to His comfort. Above all else, trust in the Lord overcomes fear!

D28 PEACE FAKING

"Do not drag me away with the wicked, with those who do evil, who speak cordially with their neighbors but harbor malice in their hearts." PSALM 28:3

Peace faking is futile. It is futile because it becomes frustrating for everyone. It is like you shadow box with someone's intentions. You think you understand what they mean but their heart betrays their true beliefs. A peace faker is a professional at concealing their real feelings. For whatever reason, they hide behind a plastic smile while their anger simmers beneath the surface. Maybe they are afraid of rejection. Maybe they are intimidated by the opinions of others. Or maybe, on the base side, they withhold their true intentions for their future advantage. They intentionally conceal their agenda, saving it for the element of surprise. They have learned the manners of deceit, which do not 'rock the boat,' until they are ready to reveal their true selves. Peace-faking is painstakingly fatiguing. It drains its host, and eventually sucks the life from its relationships.

Peace -faking is prudent for the pretentious. It is driven by pride. It is a way to disengage with reality, and make a mockery of meaningful relationships. When you are around peace-fakers you never know where you stand. They may agree with their words, but then their behavior blows up in delayed disagreement.

This happens in marriage. A passive man, by nature, does not reveal his true feelings to his overly aggressive wife. Marital bliss conceals his concerns for a season and then he falls into a pattern of pretending he doesn't mind serving her every need. However, malice begins to bubble and hatred haunts his thinking. Eventually he wants out because his needs have not been met. He can't stand the sight of the one to whom he vowed a lifetime of commitment and love. Therefore, it is imperative that we are all real in our relationships. The worst type of dishonesty may be living a lie. The Lord does not linger with liars. Christ is very cool toward hypocritical living. Dishonesty dissolves trust with its deceit, and dissimulation is a deterrent to trusting relationships. Proverbs 10:18 states, "He who conceals his hatred has lying lips, and whoever spreads slander is a fool."

However, peace faking can be overcome by faith. Faith is a facilitator of honesty. There is no need for us to conceal our concerns or hide behind our fears. We can trust God to bless our honesty when we are hurt or misunderstood. Furthermore, speak-up and share your true self. Openness leads to authenticity. It is risky but rewarding, to be authentic.

The true peace that comes from expressing yourself is liberating. Those who have intimidated you in the past will take notice of your resolve to be real. They will respect you as one who has a prayerful opinion and expresses it with humility. Those with whom you engage in healthy conflict may disagree with your ideas, but they will respect your well thought-out response. Moreover, avoid peace-faking personally, and call the bluff of behaviors that cultivate peace-faking. Peace-faking is for fools and the immature. It is a waste of time, and has no place for followers of Jesus.

Faith flourishes in unfeigned living, so overcome peace-faking by faith!

BE STILL

"Be still, and know that I am God; I will be exalted among the nations,
I will be exalted in the earth."   PSALM 46:10

Be still with your Savior for it positions you to see and hear God. Stillness sets you free from busyness that can betray your trust in God. It is hard to be still in a society that values busyness and suspects stillness. We are made to feel guilty if we are not constantly on the go. Why else would we stay habitually connected to computers and caffeine? However, busyness is not a badge of honor, but a sad and seductive addiction. Overdone busyness is a lack of focus on God and trust in His provision. However to 'be still' is the standard for serious followers of Jesus.

Be still and rest. Be still and reflect. Be still and think. Be still and pray. Be still and write. Be still and enjoy your family. Be still with no agenda. Be still and see things more clearly. Be still and know He is God. Being still is an investment that pays into eternity. Practicing stillness regularly means you trust God with the big things like relationships, the future, finances, family, a job, and your health. Stillness also means you come to understand the small things and don't sweat them because you know your Savior is in control. Stillness aligns our hearts with Almighty God. It is in our expressive stillness that we muse His grace.

Yes, there are seasons of busyness that make stillness seem foreign. An infant requires intense attention. A move to another home involves significantly increased activity. Launching a business or a ministry is an all-consuming affair. Starting something new most likely means you are extremely busy. However, do not use your busyness as an excuse to ignore God. Push back from your fatigue that comes from forgetting to be still. In your busyness you can still carve out time with Christ to be still. Busyness is not meant to be a habit, but for a time. You are not designed to stay there. You move on, and don't allow busyness to backlog. You pass through busyness on the way to being still.

Lastly, fill your stillness with the significance of knowing God. This is a potent perspective that facilitates faith and trust in the Lord. It is here that you are humbled with a massive dose of dependency on divine guidance and wisdom. It is in your stillness that you see God for who He is, high and lifted up, deserving of your honor, praise, and adoration. The sovereignty of God screams in your stillness.

God grows bigger when you slow down and rest in the shadow of His stature. It is in your stillness that you see the unseen activity of the Almighty. The Holy Spirit is melting hard hearts. He is orchestrating authorities in your life to bend you and them toward God. He is drawing men and women to Himself in the middle of Christ-less cultures. Stillness shows you what your Savior is up to and gives us a lively hope that you can have. Stillness shows you the way. Stillness is God's way of working with you. Stillness saves time. Be still, and you will see Him exalted among the nations and in the earth.

Stillness knows God.

D30 GOD'S PURPOSE ACCOMPLISHED

"For God has put into their hearts to accomplish his purpose by agreeing to give the beast their power to rule, until God's words are fulfilled." REVELATION 17:17

God will accomplish His purpose. It may be with or without us, but He will execute His will. God does not back down, or hold back when it comes to the fulfillment of His wishes. He knows what is best, and is bent toward carrying out His good will. Nothing can stop God from accomplishing His purpose. War cannot stop His purpose, because He will draw people to Himself during the atrocities of war. Illness cannot stop His purpose because He will reveal His care, compassion, and sometimes healing, during the eventual breakdown of the body. Death cannot stop His purpose. God will graduate believers in Christ to heaven, and non-believers in Christ to hell.

Sin cannot stop His purpose because Christ forgave sin by His death on the cross. Sinners cannot stop His purpose because there are consequences for wrong, and ultimately judgment by God. Satan cannot stop God's purpose, because what the devil means for evil, God can use for good. God's purpose is a freight train that travels down the tracks of obedience and disobedience, saints and sinners. Its momentum on behalf of mankind cannot be stopped. He will not be denied. Even the delay of His ultimate purpose gives more lost souls the opportunity to get on board, by placing their faith in Jesus. He will ultimately reign on earth as King of Kings and Lord of Lords! In the meantime, there is still time for others to voluntarily bow to His kingship, instead of ultimately being forced to bend their knee to God. His purpose will happen, so it makes sense to work with God, and not against God to accomplish His purpose.

So what is the purpose of God? One purpose of God is to adopt everyone into his family that believes Jesus is His son. "For God so loved the world that he gave his only begotten son, that whosoever believes in him, shall not perish but have everlasting life" (John 3:16). Anyone who calls on the name of the Lord will be saved, and this accomplishes one of God's greater purposes.

Another purpose of God is completing the work He has given you to do. Jesus said it best, "I have brought you glory on earth by completing the work you gave me to do" (John 17:4). Your individual obedience to God accomplishes His purpose for you. This is a significant thing. Your obedience matters. You are contributing to the greater heavenly mosaic of God's glorification. Your fulfillment of God's purpose helps others do the same; so do not apologize for this. Stay laser-focused on executing God's purpose. Pray about it and seek the Scripture to better understand God's purpose for you. Equity in eternity never goes down, so buy a lot...and buy early.

His purpose will be accomplished. Find out where He is working, and join Him to fulfill His mission!

"Behold, I am coming soon! My reward is with me, and I will give to everyone according to what he has done."   REVELATION 22:12

Jesus is coming soon to wipe away all sin and sorrow. He is coming to eradicate sin, suffering and death. He is coming to cast the devil into the lake of fire for eternity. He is coming to reward everyone according to what he has done. He is coming to reign on earth as the King of King and the Lord of Lords. Jesus is coming back a second time. He came to earth the first time in a humble stable, as a precious baby, destined to be a simple servant of God.

He is coming a second time upon a bold cloud of glory, as a wise warrior of God. He will wield the word of God, leading a train of angels in worship of God and judgment. He came the first time to teach and preach that the Kingdom of God is at hand. He will come the second time to establish the Kingdom of God on earth. He gave his life on His first mission on earth; He will take life on His second mission to earth. His first coming justified our sin. His second coming will judge our sin. He submitted to kings His first time to earth. Kings will submit to Him at His second coming. What the disciples wanted and expected the first time will be accomplished at the second coming. They wanted to serve Jesus in his Kingship, but they missed a step. The Messiah had to ransom the sin of mankind first, before they could rule over mankind. For the faithful follower of Jesus Christ we invite Him to come. Soon and very soon we are going to see the King. We long to see our Lord. We can go to Him or He can come to us. Either way is okay. Whichever is best in His big scheme of things is what we most desire. The more time there is between his two comings, the more time we can be about his Kingdom business.

Therefore, the promise of His second coming compels His followers to loving obedience. We do not want to be loafing when He returns. We do not want to be lacking in loving people when He comes back. We do not want to be embarrassed at His majestic and mighty entrance back into earth's atmosphere. Instead, we want to be submissive to his Lordship in our individual lives. We want to model for a lost and dying world that we have a hope that is eternal with Him now and forever. We want to continue our fervent prayer of, 'Thy Kingdom come, on earth as it is in heaven.' We want to serve the Bride of Christ, His church, with unselfish love and dedication.

We are all part of the wedding party for Christ and His Church. The Holy Spirit is the wedding planner. God the Father is the officiator of the ceremony. Now is the rehearsal. Do you know your role? Are you dressed for the part? Are you ready for this grandiose processional to heaven? We will weep for the opportunity to be a part of this wondrous wedding in glory. We will weep with joy, thanksgiving and gratitude. We will weep with excitement. We will weep when we see loved ones and saints who have gone on before us. We will weep in His presence. We will sob uncontrollably when we see His face. Our emotion will run rampant.

Then Jesus will quietly, lovingly and most gently, compassionately wipe away our tears. Our tears of sorrow will be removed, never to be seen again. Our tears of joy will be kept, as part of our heavenly reward. Come Lord Jesus. Come in your way and in your timing. We bid you to come.

When He comes, we will be transformed and be like Him. Therefore, we can't wait. Come Lord, we are ready. Come quickly. We can't wait. COME LORD JESUS, COME!

ABOUT THE AUTHOR

Boyd Bailey is co-founder and Chief Executive Officer of **Ministry Ventures,** a non-profit enterprise that certifies small to medium size ministries in best practices. Founded in 2000, Ministry Ventures has helped 45 faith-based ministries raise over 15 million dollars and impact over 40,000 people. Prior to Ministry Ventures, Bailey was the National Director for **Crown Financial Ministries.** He was instrumental in the expansion of Crown into 30 major markets across the U.S. He was a key facilitator in the 25 million dollar merger between **Christian Financial Concepts** and Crown Ministries. Before Crown, he and **Andy Stanley** started First Baptist Atlanta's north campus; and as an Elder, Boyd assisted Andy in the start of **North Point Community Church.**

Boyd was born in Huntsville, Alabama, and received his Bachelor of Arts from Jacksonville State University and his Masters of Divinity from Southwestern Seminary in Fort Worth, Texas. He and his wife, Rita, have been married 29 years and have four daughters and two son-in-laws who love Jesus!

Boyd serves on the boards of **Ministry Ventures, Treasures, The Infocus Group,** and **Atlanta Christian Foundation.** He is engaged in a mentor program with six other younger ministry/business leaders, and he and Rita lead a couple's community group in their home. Bailey has co-authored a small group curriculum, written several articles and is presently working on his third book. He is founder and President of **Wisdom Hunters,** LLC. His hobbies and interests include history, reading and writing, investments, leisure travel, speaking, sports, movies, exercising, the outdoors and his greatest passion is hanging out with his family!

email: bbailey@ministryventures.org   *office:* 770-558-8172
www.ministryventures.org • www.wisdomhunters.com

GENESIS
1:1.................23
3:1.................24
13:9............192
15:8............231
21:6............232
25:21...........65
31:16.........178
41:49...........15
45:5............233
48:9............234

EXODUS
12:13..........117
12:35-36.....235
13:17-18........70
18:19a, 24....20
20:20..........236
24:3-4a........237
31:1-3..........238
31:14-15......207
32:1............239
39:43..........242

LEVITICUS
5:1.............243
5:4.............240
16:32..........241
26:19..........244
21:6............245

NUMBERS
20:10b-12....247
21:7............358

DEUTERONOMY
1:13.......18,132
1:31............131
1:43............362
7:6..............361
8:14............248
12:19..........360
18:5............359
24:5............363
25:16..........287

JOSHUA
1:2............288
6:18............289
22:29..........133

JUDGES
1:12-13..........66
7:4..............134

RUTH
3:1a,3a,11...146

1 SAMUEL
1:15............135
9:5b-6..........136
14:7............137
16:7............293
18:1............294
18:9............310
18:26..........295
19:10..........296
20:42..........257
23:16..........298
25:21..........299
25:32-33a.....349
30:4............301
30:21..........300

2 SAMUEL
5:23.........258,364
7:13............259
9:3.............302
9:7.............366
11:2............303
13:38..........305
14:14..........365
17:23..........307
18:9b,18a.......367
19:6-7a........368
19:7............308
21:15..........309
22:30..........311

1 KINGS
3:2-3...........115
3:12a............22
3:24-25.........21
10:24.............7

2 KINGS
22:19..........208

1 CHRONICLES
25:7............138
28:20..........139
29:17..........263

2 CHRONICLES
15:16..........148
20:17..........141
26:5............215
26:15b-16a....116

EZRA
4:23b-24a......353
6:22............218
7:6.............149
9:2b-3......114,125

NEHEMIAH
2:9.............150
2:20a..........276
8:10............351
13:13..........151

ESTHER
4:15-16........269
5:2.............152
9:28............145

JOB
4:4.............153
8:21............217
10:1............271
14:1............154
17:11............41
21:7,13.........352
23:10..........275
24:15-16........163
28:12-13a, 28...11
28:28..........165
31:1............211
34:3-4.........166
42:10..........167

PSALMS
1:3.........168,369
5:3..............45
6:3..............44
9:10............370
14:1............169
15:4............107
16:11..........279
18:25..........124
18:27..........371
19:11..........280
20:4............374
23:4............375
27:14..........306
28:3............376
31:23.......112,113
32:1............196
34:18..........170
42:1-2.........105
46:10.......277,377
49:20...........14
55:22..........290
56:3-4...........43
59:16............42
61:2............104
68:5.......172,180
71:5,17........171

73:4-5...........173
78:72..........174
92:14..........175
103:17..........291
105:1..........176
109:4..........177
113:9..........142
118:13..........181
131:1-3..........164
141:5..........182
147:4-5..........183

PROVERBS
1:7..............13
1:8-9...........17
4:8-9...........357
6:1a, 2a, 3....78
11:2............10
18:2............184
20:3............186
22:24-25......185
24:7............297
27:6............108
31:10..........143

ECCLESIASTES
1:2.............187
3:1.............225
4:10............261
7:18b..........103
10:10..........228

SONG OF SOLOMON
1:2.............229
7:12............193

ISAIAH
1:2.............194
6:8.............226
11:1-3a.........204
12:2-3.........227
16:3a...........195
19:11..........197
25:8............230
26:3.......198,210
28:11b-12......209
45:9............199
49:15..........144
49:16..........200
50:6............126
55:8.............8
56:1............201

SCRIPTURE INDEX

JEREMIAH
3:22-24...............123
10:23...........27,202
15:19...................203
20:9.......................28
22:13.....................29
26:24.....................30
29:6.......................67
33:3.......................31
LAMENTATIONS
1:11.......................39
5:15.......................40
EZEKIEL
11:2.....................267
40:45-46...........212
DANIEL
4:30,37b...........213
9:3.......................214
HOSEA
6:2.........................26
11:4.......................71
13:13.....................12
14:9.......................19
JOEL
2:23.......................72
2:25.......................25
AMOS
5:19.......................73
6:1.........................74
OBADIAH
1:1.........................75
JONAH
1:1-2.....................76
1:12.......................77
MICAH
3:11.......................79
7:7.........................80
HABAKKUK
2:4b.....................122
3:19a.....................81
ZEPHANIAH
3:17.......................82
3:18.......................83
ZECHARIAH
1:16.......................69
4:10.....................274
7:5-6...........85,216
9:9.........................86
10:2.......................87
MALACHI
1:6.........................88
4:6.......................179

MATTHEW
5:23-24...............273
7:21.......................32
11:28-30...............33
12:25...........34,127
13:58.....................35
18:15...................255
18:21-22.............130
20:11-12...............37
20:26b-28.........254
25:28...................281
26:10,13.............282
MARK
1:12-13...............219
2:16-17...............283
6:30-32...............205
9:43.....................284
10:9.......................89
10:21-23.............286
11:15-16...............90
12:32,34a.........285
14:8.....................312
LUKE
1:3-4...................313
1:42.......................91
1:49.....................191
2:10-11...............372
2:11,13-14.........373
6:22.......................92
6:26.....................314
6:31.....................355
7:9.......................110
7:47.....................315
8:37.......................93
10:28-29.............94
12:6-7.................316
13:32...................319
14:27...................102
14:28-30.........320
15:20.....................95
18:9.....................321
22:45.....................96
JOHN
2:1-2...................147
2:10.......................97
4:38.......................98
6:3.........................99
6:68-69.............268
7:18.....................322
12:23-24.............118
12:42-43.........220

13:5.....................155
13:14-15.............356
13:15...................354
14:30-31.............317
15:5.....................323
15:27...................272
17:4.....................264
ACTS
2:37.....................221
3:17-19a.............324
5:38-39.............222
11:23...................156
12:20...................325
13:2-3.................157
15:1.....................262
16:37...................158
21:8b-9...............159
22:21...................327
27:18-19.............223
ROMANS
1:26-27.............160
3:20.....................326
5:10.....................128
6:1-2...................188
8:37.....................246
10:2.....................249
12:6.....................266
12:3-4.................109
1 CORINTHIANS
1:11b-13.............189
6:4.......................328
12:26-27...........270
13:4.......46-50,329
13:5.............51-54
13:6.............55-56
13:7.............57-60
13:8.......................61
13:13.....................62
2 CORINTHIANS
1:3-4...................330
7:10.....................161
9:11...........36,140
9:11,15.............342
EPHESIANS
4:15.....................265
5:31.......................64
PHILIPPIANS
3:20.....................304
COLOSSIANS
2:13-15...............101
4:7-8...................106

1 THESSALONIANS
5:11.....................260
1 TIMOTHY
3:6.......................331
4:7b-8.................332
2 TIMOTHY
1:5.......................121
TITUS
1:9.......................129
2:3-5...................333
PHILEMON
21.........................334
HEBREWS
2:15.....................278
4:9-11.................206
5:2b-3.................335
5:8-9...................292
8:5.........................16
10:30-31.............336
11:1.....................337
12:9.....................250
13:4...............63,338
JAMES
1:2-3...................120
1 PETER
1:7.......................111
5:7.......................350
2 PETER
1:8.......................339
1 JOHN
1:8-9...................190
2:11.....................340
5:11-12...............253
2 JOHN
8.........................341
12.........................251
3 JOHN
4.........................343
9.........................344
11.........................252
JUDE
12.........................345
REVELATION
3:7-8b.................346
4:10b-11.............347
7:9.......................348
13:18a.....................9
14:12...................119
17:17...................378
22:12...................379

IN KENYA WITH 410 BRIDGE

My wife **Rita** and our youngest daughter **Anna** just returned from Kenya, where they were transformed by the grace of God, and the love of Christ followers. They went to serve at the **Havila orphanage** and **Ngammba school** outside of Nairobi, and instead were the ones who came away extremely blessed. We are passionate believers in what God is doing through 410 Bridge.

Would you prayerfully consider giving to these communities who are being developed in the name of Christ?

www.410bridge.org

Each one should use whatever gift he has received to serve others, faithfully administering God's grace in its various forms.

1 PETER 4:10